RETURN FROM THE NATIVES

RETURN FROM THE NATIVES

HOW MARGARET MEAD WON THE SECOND
WORLD WAR AND LOST THE COLD WAR

Peter Mandler

YALE UNIVERSITY PRESS
NEW HAVEN AND LONDON

For information about this and other Yale University Press publications, please contact:

U.S. office: sales.press@yale.edu   www.yalebooks.com
Europe Office: sales@yaleup.co.uk   www.yalebooks.co.uk

Set in Goudy by IDSUK (DataConnection) Ltd
Printed in Great Britain by TJ International Ltd, Padstow, Cornwall

Library of Congress Cataloging-in-publication Data

Mandler, Peter.
    Return from the natives: how Margaret Mead won the Second world War and lost the Cold War/Peter Mandler.
        pages cm.
    ISBN 978-0-300-18785-4 (cl: alk. paper)
1. Mead, Margaret, 1901–1978. 2. World War, 1939–1945—Influence. 3. Cold War—Influence. 4. Cultural relativism. 5. Anthropology—Government policy—United States. I.Title.
    GN21.M36M36 2013
    306—dc23
                                                                    2012051253

A catalogue record for this book is available from the British Library.

10 9 8 7 6 5 4 3 2 1

For Mel, and in memory of Audrey

Contents

List of Abbreviations   viii

Introduction: Return from the Natives   x

1   From the South Seas (to 1939)   1

2   Culture Cracking for War: I. Allies (1939–44)   45

3   Among the Natives of Great Britain (1942–5)   87

4   Culture Cracking for War: II. Enemies (1942–5)   123

5   Culture Cracking for Peace (1945–50)   177

6   Swaddling the Russians (1947–51)   223

7   Return to the Natives (1947–53)   255

Epilogue: To Vietnam, Iraq, Afghanistan   287

Notes   293

Bibliography   335

Acknowledgements   353

Index   356

Abbreviations

AAA	American Anthropological Association
AID	Agency for International Development
ARPA	Advanced Research Projects Agency
ASTP	Army Specialized Training Program
BIA	Bureau of Indian Affairs
CIMA	Coordinated Investigation of Micronesian Anthropology
CIO	Congress of Industrial Organizations
CIR	Council on Intercultural Relations
CNM	Committee for National Morale
COI	Office of the Coordinator of Information
CSPR	Conference on Science, Philosophy and Religion
EPTA	Expanded Program of Technical Assistance (of the United Nations)
FMAD	Foreign Morale Analysis Division (of OWI)
FSI	Foreign Service Institute
HRAF	Human Relations Area Files
HRRI	Human Resources Research Institute
IPA	Institute for Propaganda Analysis
IPR	Institute of Pacific Relations
LSRM	Laura Spelman Rockefeller Memorial
M-O	Mass-Observation
MO	Morale Operations
MOI	Ministry of Information
MSA	Mutual Security Agency
NSF	National Science Foundation
OB	Overseas Branch (of OWI)
ONR	Office of Naval Research
OSS	Office of Strategic Services
OWI	Office of War Information
PWD	Psychological Warfare Division (of SHAEF)
PWE	Political Warfare Executive
R&A	Research and Analysis Branch (of OSS)
RCC	Research in Contemporary Cultures
SAA	Society for Applied Anthropology
SCC	Studies in Contemporary Cultures
SEAC	South-East Asia Command
SHAEF	Supreme Headquarters Allied Expeditionary Force
SSC	Studies in Soviet Culture
TA	Technical Assistance
TCA	Technical Cooperation Administration

Abbreviations

UNESCO	United Nations Educational, Scientific and Cultural Organization
UNRRA	United Nations Relief and Rehabilitation Agency
WFMH	World Federation for Mental Health
WRA	War Relocation Authority

Introduction
Return from the Natives

The journey out is also a journey home. When, at the end of the nineteenth century, the first modern anthropological fieldworkers went out in search of 'primitive' peoples in the South Pacific and in the remoter parts of North America, they were not only looking for people different from themselves, they were looking for themselves as well. The common view then was the social-evolutionary one, that the varieties of humanity were arrayed along the rungs of a ladder of civilization, with 'primitive' peoples at the bottom and modern Western peoples at or near the top – but it was a ladder that peoples might travel along, some more slowly than others. The study of 'primitive' peoples could therefore be a study of one's own ancestors, and perhaps not so very distant ones, either.

Some of these early fieldworkers developed such a sympathy for the 'primitive' peoples among whom they lived that they began to doubt whether the ladder of civilization was really so long, or indeed whether it existed at all. And when the Great War dealt a series of stunning blows to the ideals of 'civilization' – those who witnessed mechanized slaughter in the fields of Flanders found it hard to feel superior to anyone, and the appeal of 'primitive' simplicity (always an undercurrent in Western culture anyway) was vastly enhanced – the anthropological enterprise changed dramatically. The ladder of civilization crashed down and appeared to come to rest on its side; the array of cultures now presented itself not vertically but horizontally. Peoples were still very different, but no longer stood in any obvious hierarchy. The idea of 'cultural relativism' blossomed. In this new relation, 'primitive' cultures in some ways seemed *more* different from so-called 'civilized' ones: they were no longer the ancestors, just people who did things differently. This relation also offered new ways to compare cultures. 'Civilization' was no longer the norm. If 'they' do things differently, how does that make us look? Or, more powerfully, if 'they' do things differently – and we are no longer so obviously superior to them, so obviously the future of the past – what might we learn from them?

These two impulses – to use the observation of so-called 'primitive' peoples, as the anthropologist Richard Handler has put it,[1] either for social satire or for social engineering (or both) – gripped the imagination of anthropologists in the middle decades of the twentieth century. The opportunities to learn something immediately useful from 'primitive' peoples seemed suddenly to give anthropologists (formerly the students of backwardness) a powerful relevance to a growing public that looked to the social sciences generally to help them steer a course through the turbulent rapids of modern life. Yet anthropologists were always tempered by a third impulse – the impulse that had sent them off on the journey out in the first place – to find peoples *unlike* themselves. For the journey out is never just a journey home. That sense of the value of cultural diversity in its own right never left the pioneering anthropologists, and gave them a third way to apply their learning to their own people: the role of cultural intermediary, teaching peoples how to get along together, to learn from one another, without blurring into or becoming one another. Cultural relativism sometimes *insisted* on cultural difference, even when it wasn't there.[2] Anthropologists could thus claim to be disinterested experts in intercultural – or indeed international – relations on a global scale.

This book is about the most famous anthropologist who ever lived – Margaret Mead – and her efforts to apply her tools, honed on 'primitive' (or, as she came to call them, 'simple, homogeneous') peoples in the South Pacific, to problems of international relations between what she called 'contemporary' peoples such as her own, the Americans, and her third husband's, the British. Between her return from Bali in 1939 and her return to New Guinea in 1953, Mead did no fieldwork among 'simple, homogeneous' cultures and devoted herself very largely to theorizing, writing and lobbying on issues relating to 'contemporary', mostly Western, cultures. This period uncoincidentally spans the years of international crisis leading to the Second World War, the war itself and the renewed crises of the early Cold War. It represents one of the peak periods of social scientists' involvement in public policy and a peak period, too, in their engagement with the popular imagination. Mead was determined that anthropologists should not lose this opportunity. The economists had 'won' the First World War: that is, after the war they had become government's most trusted academic advisers. Here was anthropology's chance to take a place alongside them. Between the late 1930s and the early 1950s, her steel-trap mind fastened on the problems of international relations that mattered most to policymakers and the general public – how to prevent a European war; once war had broken out, how to cement Anglo-American relations and how to defeat the Germans and the Japanese; then, after 1945, how to come to terms with the Russians and the Chinese; and, finally, how to create a new world order embracing all the peoples of the world.

Among those who know anything about Margaret Mead – and her reputation has suffered a vertiginous collapse since her death in 1978 – this phase of her career is the least well known. Most know her as the early publicist of cultural relativism during the 'flapper' era of the 1920s and early 1930s, when two books – *Coming of Age in Samoa* (1928) and *Growing Up in New Guinea* (1930) – made her an international celebrity, and an acknowledged expert on how 'other' people managed the difficult business of child-rearing and the storms of adolescence. In another, equally notorious, phase of her career, in the 1960s and 1970s, she almost dropped her persona as an anthropologist and became 'grandmother to the world',[3] an oracle on a range of gender, moral and social issues, from race relations to working mothers to the threat of nuclear war. In the years before the anti-authoritarianism of the late 1960s spread throughout Western culture, experts were still in hot demand to help ordinary people balance up the increasingly complex trade-offs of modern life. In this phase Mead was certainly one of the most famous women in the world.

Why has the intervening phase – between 1939 and 1953 – dropped almost completely out of even historians' memories? After all, Mead's visibility to contemporaries hardly dipped between the flapper and the grandmother phases. At the height of the war, in 1943, the *Washington Post* named her as one of the eight 'outstanding women of the modern world' alongside Eleanor Roosevelt, Madame Chiang Kai-shek and Eve Curie.[4] In the late 1940s a flurry of high-profile articles in popular and intellectual magazines spoke knowledgeably and often positively about Mead's 'return from the natives'[5] and the implications of her methods of cultural relativism for the future world order. Since then, rumours, insider stories and (more recently) dark insinuations have proliferated about Margaret Mead's secret war; but this book is the first to tell the full story of Mead's notorious and ill-understood 'national character' studies that formed anthropology's most important contribution to hot and cold war in the mid-twentieth century. Why has this episode, spanning more than a decade and engaged with all of the most important questions of world politics, been almost entirely forgotten?

The answers to this question will tell us a lot about the politics and culture of the period between the late 1930s and the early 1950s, and about how far we have travelled from them since the 1960s. For one thing, growing consciousness of globalization and the interconnectedness of the world has led to a widespread loss of belief in the distinctiveness of nations. During the Second World War – especially during the Second World War – nationalism was still seen as a central and inevitable part of human life, and the idea that nations not only had radically different cultures but also, as Mead insisted, radically different 'national characters' or personalities was not only credible, but was seen as absolutely crucial to matters of war and peace. Social scientists today rarely show interest in (or, where they do, rarely give much credit to) ideas of deep-rooted national difference. That has increasingly been the case since the 1950s, when the Cold War was being fought on a global rather than a national basis. Neither policymakers nor, in the US, the general public wished to believe that people in other nations were different; on the contrary, they wanted to see them as very much like themselves, just misguided or misled, or suffering under the yoke of tyranny. 'Cultural relativism' gave way to ideological universalism.

By the time cultural relativism revived in the late 1960s, international consciousness was so heightened that the idea of emphasizing the difference between *nations* now seemed absurd or even pernicious; attention had shifted to differences between men and women, between minority and majority ethnic groups, and especially between 'the West' and 'the Third World'. By that point Mead's role in analysing national difference in the 1940s appeared to be *part* of the Cold War, to be repudiated, rather than, as I will be arguing, itself a casualty of the Cold War. Her distinctive role had by that stage been subsumed in a wider indictment of the very idea that social scientists in universities should involve themselves in power politics. The post-Vietnam generation of academics drew a straight line from the involvement of Mead and her generation in the war against fascism, through their alleged implication in dirty tricks and skulduggery during the Cold War, directly to complicity with the Vietnam War.[6]

A study of Margaret Mead's role in the Second World War and the Cold War thus has implications for the bigger question of social science's embroilment with the US government and public policy, both in the middle decades of the twentieth century, when its power and funding and public appeal were at a peak, and today. The match between social scientists' commitments and ambitions, and the US government's policy goals, was never as neat as the post-Vietnam generation of scholars has alleged. Anthropology was a special case: as a new and at first rather 'exotic' discipline, it attracted more than its share of misfits and outsiders to the power elite – immigrants, Jews, radicals, women. Its first loyalties seemed always, even at the height of its romance with 'civilized' cultures, to lie with the 'primitive' peoples to whom its early fortunes were tied. This has not stopped the post-Vietnam generation from lumping anthropologists in, often indiscriminately, with more obvious targets such as the economists and political scientists who eagerly joined the US government's efforts to 'modernize' the developing world in its own image in the 1950s and 1960s, an effort that did culminate (and implode) in the

Vietnam War. One of the purposes of focusing on Margaret Mead is to show how even this most ambitious and power-seeking of anthropologists was thwarted by the nature of her fundamental moral and intellectual commitments to cultural relativism from securing the place at the table alongside the economists that she craved; thus her return to the natives in 1953. But the argument can be extended from anthropologists to others – psychiatrists, social psychologists, sociologists, probably even some economists – whose intellectual sympathies were not to begin with so closely aligned with the power elite and whose professional ambitions were never so easily seduced by grants from government agencies and like-minded foundations. The paths taken by these social scientists half a century and more ago can cast light on the current predicament of social scientists who are asked to collaborate in government interventions at home and abroad – in places like Iraq or Afghanistan – and who have to ask themselves where their sympathies ultimately lie, to whom their loyalties are ultimately owed.

Another reason to zero in on Mead is that her personal and 'inner' life are so amply documented that it is possible to trace her thought processes at the time when she was making the crucial choices of what to study and how, and with which collaborators, and to be funded by which agencies. Illuminating these thought processes allows us to recall that social scientists are not bloodless automata, responding in a Pavlovian way to the dictates of power elites or grant-funded bribes, as they have been frequently described by the post-Vietnam generation. They are, rather, like readers of this book, most often intelligent, self-aware and self-critical people – something that is especially true of the psychoanalytically steeped academics of Mead's generation, and is another reason why her archive is so full and revealing. Where they did go with the flow of power and wealth, they did so for reasons, and they (generally) explained those reasons to themselves and their peers with articulacy. And where they went against the flow – which they often did – they explained that too.

Mead's amply documented life has hitherto been mined most fruitfully for what it tells us about her relationships with the men and women with whom she was sexually, emotionally and intellectually involved. In addition to one fine journalist's biography and many slighter works of biography, there are now no fewer than five books devoted to Mead's mentor and lover Ruth Benedict.[7] My book is not a biography, and it is not primarily about Mead's relationships, but any book with Mead at its centre must be concerned with those relationships – both because of the kind of person Mead was (immensely, almost voraciously, gregarious) and because of the kind of cultural theory she employed, which was always about relationships, both between individuals and (an analogy she drew with alarming directness) between cultures. In the period of her 'return from the natives', relationships with three people in particular (and their relationships with each other) loomed largest: Ruth Benedict, Mead's teacher, early inspiration and leader of the the postwar 'national character' studies until her early death in 1948; Mead's third and last husband, Gregory Bateson, with whom she returned from Bali in 1939 and developed the wartime 'national character' studies in such an intimate association that it is very hard to tell their ideas apart; and the man to whom Mead turned after the break-up of her marriage to Bateson at the war's end, Geoffrey Gorer, who in some ways proved her Achilles heel. It matters very much that these four people (Mead included) comprised two men and two women, two Americans and two Britons. Sometimes they thought they learned as much about national difference from each other as they did from 'scientific' study – a dangerous temptation and one they couldn't resist. At times their story will sound like a mid-twentieth century joke that begins: There was an American, an Englishman, a homosexual and a scientist. . . . It did not, however, feel like a joke at the time.

Mead and Bateson in the field

CHAPTER 1

From the South Seas
(to 1939)

Margaret Mead was born in Philadelphia in December 1901. Her parents were both social scientists, her father a professor of economics at the Wharton School of the University of Pennsylvania, her mother a sociology graduate of the University of Chicago who started but never completed a PhD on the Italian immigrants of Hammonton, New Jersey. Mead liked to claim in later life that she was a third-generation feminist – her paternal grandmother, Martha Ramsey Mead, who lived with them, was a college graduate, a career schoolteacher and an advocate of progressive education. She was not always grateful for this supportive background and felt sometimes that her forebears had had the advantage in that they had to struggle to define themselves: 'most of them were first generation women who had gone to college . . . the first generation people worked awfully hard. . . . The women who elect to belong to that first generation are unusual almost always. They have to prove that they can do something that everybody said they couldn't, and this applies to women mathematicians or women welders.'[1] Still, she also saw benefits from her 'third generation' status. For one thing, she understood from her earliest childhood experience that mental qualities were not sex-linked – 'I had my father's mind, but he had his mother's mind'[2] – and, for another, she always felt valued, her adult potential recognized from an early age. Her 'serene untroubled development' that she owed to making common cause with parents and grandparents helped her grow up quickly, she thought. 'All the energy which most of my contemporaries had to put into reconciling affection for their elders with honest revolt against their teachings, I could conserve to use for my own development.'[3]

Mead's family was large, warm but not stifling, with three sisters and a brother as well as the resident grandmother and parents. As with her feminism, she was born into a stable, immediately recognizable, ethnic identity as a White Anglo-Saxon Protestant. Both her parents impressed upon her their distinctive variants of this American ethnicity: her father's rural, Methodist, common-sense version, steeped in the Bible and the English classics; her mother's urban, Unitarian, more avant-garde version, which gave her a useful critical sense but which she never quite took to heart like her father's.[4] That combination of love of the 'insider's position' with the critical eye of the outsider – not just living *in* a culture but conscious *of* it – again manifested itself at a very early age, as she lapped up the rituals of WASP family and community life, but with a playfulness and even a knowingness that could be disturbing in one so young. She teased her parents, for example, by insisting on baptism into the Episcopal Church at age ten, an affiliation that she stuck to her entire life and in later life pressed on her own daughter, as both a part of her ethnic tradition and as a useful and comforting discipline in its own right.[5]

With this background and degree of self-consciousness, the young Margaret Mead might have seemed fated to become a social scientist, but in fact her adult life began more conventionally. She had only just turned sixteen when she became engaged to a young candidate for the Episcopal ministry, Luther Cressman. She hoped to join him in New York (while he trained at the General Theological Seminary) but her father insisted that she begin her education at his alma mater, De Pauw University, in straitlaced central Indiana. After her year's probation at De Pauw, Professor Mead relented and allowed his daughter to transfer to Barnard, the women's college of Columbia University, close to Cressman in upper Manhattan as well as to the manifold excitements of New York City in the Jazz Age. It was at Barnard that she blossomed socially and intellectually. Progressive Barnard required its undergraduates to take courses in social science, and Mead was happy enough with her sociology and psychology classes, thinking about following in her mother's footsteps. After graduation in 1923, she took a Master's in psychology very much in her mother's line, assessing the performance of Italian immigrants on intelligence tests in her dissertation. At the back of her mind were still fairly conventional notions, of 'service' to the community, of her marriage to Cressman (finally celebrated at the end of the summer after graduation), possibly of life as a socially conscious vicar's wife as he took up his first parish in Brooklyn. But in her senior year at Barnard she had taken an anthropology course, and in the year of her Master's the ideas and contacts that course seeded wrought a change of discipline, of purpose, of life itself. To grasp why such a novel discipline as anthropology, redolent of distant lands and strange peoples, could exercise such a magnetic attraction over a young woman firmly rooted in America and with a strong social conscience requires first some understanding of the appeal of social science in general to her generation, and then the particular appeal of cultural anthropology.

The rising generation of social scientists trained and promoted in the interwar period has had a bad press. Characterized as 'nervous liberals', they have been portrayed as upwardly mobile petty bourgeois from small-town America rendered anxious by the social changes of the Jazz Age – immigration, race-mixing, Bolshevism, sexual deviancy and free-thinking of all kinds, which they encountered on going to college or graduate school in the big city – who saw in social science a chance to stake a professional claim for themselves in scientific expertise and other forms of 'objectivity' and at the same time to develop new means of 'control' over a fractious, fragmented American society.[6] That story undoubtedly fits the careers of a lot of the young people – especially the young men – who were fighting their way up the career ladder in the early decades of the twentieth century, and who as a result of their own upward mobility and the jaundiced eye they cast on the irrational exuber-ance of the masses might indeed have had fundamental doubts about democracy. In Mead's own analysis of her elders – tinged with a little nostalgia for the prewar years – those who grew up before the First World War were 'members of whole cultures' that had broken up since, and the experience of that transition could be traumatic – but it could be liberating too.[7]

Academics, arguably, were just as likely to experience it as liberating as traumatic – it made them excitable as much as 'nervous'. The vogue notion of the immediate postwar years – popularized in *Social Change* (1922) by the sociologist William Fielding Ogburn, whose course at Columbia Mead took that very year – was 'cultural lag'.[8] Ogburn's idea was that in periods of rapid social change the material conditions of life changed more quickly than values and attitudes: 'culture' lagged behind. This idea had an obvious appeal to young people moving out of small-town America and eager to leave behind the traditional values of old-time religion, the patriarchal family and narrow career horizons. After Ogburn's book, it got its widest circulation from *Middletown* (1929), Robert and Helen Lynd's classic study of small-town USA, which bore the hallmarks of an 'objective' study of 'representative' America but also implicitly bemoaned Middletown's 'cultural lag', evident in conservatism, smugness and insensitivity to social change; as Robert Lynd later wrote, one of their goals was to help Americans free themselves from their 'habituated past'.[9] At the time this past was so habituated that most Americans had not even considered that they had a 'culture', much less that it could, or might, or needed, to change. The idea that there was something immaterial that acts of moral and intellectual courage could alter could be galvanic for budding academics: 'culture' was their new frontier, the thinking person's alternative to industrial entrepreneurship or party politics.

While Ogburn's own response to 'cultural lag' might have been fatalism – that culture always would lag behind, and at best could only be helped

to catch up with the more powerful forces of social and economic change
– that was not the reaction of the young Margaret Mead taking his course
at Columbia in the early 1920s. For her as for so many others, the big
discovery was that 'culture' existed at all – that it existed even in the US,
though there were then no books about it or tools to analyse it.[10] Some
made the leap to the realization that it could (perhaps should) be changed,
using myriad tools, from the progressive educational methods Mead's
grandmother had employed to the studies and proposals that sociologists
like the Lynds were generating. But these ideas about cultural change
were still inchoate, and highly various, and by no means obviously about
a reassertion of 'control', still less 'an infinitely more subtle form of social
control' in the guise of social engineering.[11] Perhaps 'culture' didn't
have to follow behind social and economic change, but was something
you could choose, play with, be creative with? Perhaps many roads led
from Middletown?

Given the range of choices before her, why, if Mead was, like many of
her generation, so stimulated by the idea that America had a culture
susceptible to purposive change, did she almost immediately convert to
anthropology, and forsake the Italians of New Jersey or New York for
Samoa? To answer this question brings us to Franz Boas, and takes us back
to that pioneering generation before the First World War.

* * *

Trained in the German school of ethnography in the 1880s, Franz
Boas was never as entranced by the 'ladder of civilization' as his British-
trained rivals in the coming discipline of anthropology. German scholars
had a long tradition of acknowledging and respecting cultural diversity,
coming as they did from a historically fragmented nation without a
global empire. Boas's curiosity about the world's peoples took him from
the Royal Ethnological Museum in Berlin to long periods of pioneering
'participant-observation' among the 'Eskimo' (Inuit) and 'Indian' (Native
American) peoples of North America from the 1880s. Ultimately,
pressured by mounting anti-Semitism in the German universities and,
as Germany began to vie for Great Power status, a narrowing tolerance
for theories of cultural diversity, Boas transplanted himself permanently
to North America, ending up at Columbia University in 1896, where
he founded the first PhD programme in anthropology on that side of the
Atlantic.

In a European context, Boas's German school, emphasizing the
historical development of different cultures on their own paths, had
been pitched against the British school, with its unilinear ladder of
civilization.[12] In the US, Boas had to contend with advocates of the

British ladder of civilization but also with another, tougher opposition in the form of 'race science', which sought to demonstrate deep, ineradicable biological differences between peoples such as 'Negroes' and 'Caucasians' in American society itself. His school at Columbia thus became a magnet not only for those who took a profound personal pleasure in encounters with wide variations in the human world, including a lot of immigrants like himself, but also those who found in anthropology a political mission aimed against segregation and racial injustice closer to home.

Boas was more comfortable with the first of these missions. His personal experience of 'participant-observation' had had a profoundly transforming effect on his own psychological make-up. 'Participant-observation' has drawn a lot of criticism, not least from 'participant-observers' them-selves.[13] There is no doubt that it involves a good deal of what psycho-analysts call 'transference', whereby the patient projects conflicts and anxieties on to the analyst; the anthropologist similarly ventures out into the world seeking a change of scene, or solutions to personal problems, and ends up projecting these personal needs on to the people being observed. Yet Boas was not seeking a substitute 'home' among the Eskimo; he was to some extent trying to escape the confines of 'home' as tightly defined by Western civilization. It was the Eskimo's *difference* that impressed him most – the unexpected ways they found to be human, which ideas about biological fixity or about an evolutionary 'ladder of civilization' were too straitjacketed to encompass.[14]

For this reason Boas was wary about excessive politicization of the anthropologist's work, an imposition of the West's own agenda, however good the intentions. He emphasized to his students that their first respon-sibility was to 'their' culture: that is, their adopted culture of study, not their home culture. This gave students a sense of ownership in 'their' culture, which could lead to impositions of their own, a neopaternalism as it were, but it also impressed upon them that the ultimate task of the anthropologist was the recording and preserving of cultural diversity in the world. In these early years before the First World War, cultural diversity was coming under severe pressure from real Western imperialism, including from the United States, which was discovering its own imperial mission in places like Cuba, the Philippines, Samoa and China at just this time. Of course, the assertion of cultural diversity required a stern rejec-tion of theories of racial difference and superiority. Boasian cultural anthropologists fought a bitter internecine war with the older, more estab-lished tradition of physical anthropology which focused on biological differences between peoples. If anything, this struggle intensified after the First World War when the American government implemented immigra-tion controls, partly based on 'eugenic' arguments about the unfitness of immigrant stocks provided by physical anthropologists. But by the 1920s the Boasians had more or less won this struggle within the anthropological profession and provided a base for carrying the struggle out into the wider society. Boas was not entirely happy about this political struggle. He had taken courageous public stances against what he saw as the neo-imperial elements of the First World War and had suffered government investigation for his public statements and his membership of the American Socialist Party. But he discouraged his students from distracting themselves with politics and pressed them to return to their responsibilities to 'their' cultures. It was enough, he thought, that the demonstration of myriad diverse solutions to common human problems in the cultures of the world might make Americans ponder how necessary or fixed were their own cultural peculiarities.[15]

Boas's purism made many of his students restless. They loved him for his Old World civility and for his passion for the Eskimo and other forgotten or outcast peoples. But they found his insistence on the randomness, the historical accident of the way different cultures interacted – borrowed from and lent to each other, and went off their separate ways – limiting. They were not content with demolishing the pseudo-sciences of biological determinism or social evolution: they needed a creed of their own. They were keener to get into the hearts and minds of 'their' peoples, to see them in the round as more than a list of traits, to find out what made them tick.[16] As they dispersed around the country carrying with them the Boasian creed – Alfred Kroeber and Robert Lowie to Berkeley, Edward Sapir to Chicago and later to Yale – they developed the master's teaching, emphasizing more and more over time the ways in which cultures cohered, hung together, and the methods by which one might explain and anatomize that cohesion.[17] A parallel movement in Britain, 'functionalism', explained this coherence by seeing culture as a response to basic human needs and problems: every element of the culture had a 'function' that could be related back to those basic needs. Boasians found this too crude and too condescending to 'primitive' cultures; they craved nobler and more self-conscious processes of cultural development that were more consistent with Boas's sense of the high calling of the anthropologist.[18]

When the young Margaret Mead encountered Franz Boas at Barnard, taking his course in her senior year, she was captivated both by this sense of mission and also by the engaging personality of 'Papa Franz' himself. Boas was famously supportive of women. He chose to give courses at Barnard for that reason, and was almost single-handedly responsible for the feminizing of the anthropology profession in these foundational years. Of the fifty-one anthropology PhD students at Columbia before his death in 1940, twenty-nine were men and twenty-two women; in contrast, of the thirty PhDs in anthropology at Chicago, only two were women, and of the fifty-three at Harvard, not one was a woman.[19] 'Papa Kroeber' and 'Uncle Lowie' carried on Boas's tradition at Berkeley.[20] In general, Boas's civil welcome to all sorts and conditions of people, including a lot of Jewish immigrants like himself, was a striking feature in the highly establishmentarian atmosphere of the Ivy League. Then there were the compelling stories he wove of distant peoples waiting to be discovered, recorded and defended. Mead's own memory of what drew her to anthropology was the Boasian practice of 'collecting masses of vanishing materials from the members of dying American Indian cultures'; 'it was in terms of the urgency of this salvage task that I decided to become an anthropologist'.[21] However, at this early stage her contact with Boas was very heavily mediated through his teaching assistant, Ruth Benedict, and it was Benedict's reinterpretation of the Boasian mission – characteristic of the younger students' bias towards cohesion – that made that mission feel personal to Mead.

Benedict was half a generation older than Mead, but only a few years ahead of her academically. She had grown up before the war, mostly in upstate New York. Like Mead's mother, she had direct experience of America's new cultural diversity, working for a time in Buffalo as a 'friendly visitor' doing charitable work among the local Polish community; but she found this experience dispiriting, as both the language barrier and her own partial deafness made true communication impossible. After a liberal education at Vassar College, like Mead with Cressman, she entered too quickly into an ill-assorted marriage; finding herself childless and unhappy, she had then taken up anthropology as a student of Boas's to try to find her way out of this dead-end. At the time she met Mead she had not yet finished her own PhD on the Plains Indians. Mead always claimed to envy Benedict for having grown up before the war. Those Victorian origins meant that Benedict's awakening to 'culture consciousness' was a natural result of struggling against outdated mores, against 'cultural lag'. In contrast, Mead's happy early life had made her more accepting of the world in which she had grown up, so that her dawning appreciation of the 'culture' all around her was more of an intellectual and less of an emotional experience. Certainly Mead lacked the passions, the more deeply personal motivations, that drew Benedict to anthropology: her mounting sense of deviancy, as she proved unable to have children, grew dissatisfied with her marriage and ultimately found herself attracted sexually to other women; her disappointment with her own culture for providing too few opportunities for her to discover her 'true' self, her 'personality' (to use the vogue word of the time); her need to find a more fulfilling role as a woman than wifeliness, motherhood or even 'service'. Anthropology for Benedict provided more than a role: it suggested clues to her own unhappiness; it asked why a given culture proved more congenial to certain inborn temperaments than others, or why some cultures seemed better able than others to accommodate a wider range of temperaments. Whereas psycho-analysis – another fashionable new discipline at this particular juncture, for similar reasons – insisted that 'civilization' had almost irreparable defects to which the personality had to learn to conform, anthropology suggested instead that some cultures provided more scope for different personality types.

Like many of Boas's students, Benedict was also drawn to the image of wholeness, of coherence, that 'primitive' cultures seemed to offer. She was hardly nostalgic for the kind of 'wholeness' that her own culture was in the process of abandoning, those stifling small-town mores that her generation of feminists had struggled away from, but this did not stop her imagining a new kind of wholeness that might be built up again with more room for individual 'personality' and growth, yet also a shared sense of meaning and belonging.[22] In this quest she was helped along by another, slightly older, student of Boas's, Edward Sapir, who had worked at the Geological Survey of Canada until he moved to the University of Chicago in 1925. Sapir's marriage was equally unhappy and his restless searching for self had led to the same interest in the ways in which culture set the terms for individual expression of personality. At the time Benedict met Mead she was immersed in a life-changing correspondence with Sapir, explicitly about the poetry both were writing, implicitly about their lone-liness and their search through anthropology for the secrets that made 'personality' comfortable with 'culture'. In the process, they began to beat out a new field, 'culture and personality', that took Boasian cultural anthropology on to fresh psychological terrain.[23]

These were the personal and intellectual contexts into which Mead plunged when she encountered Boas and Benedict in her senior year at Barnard. No doubt Benedict's search for solutions to her failing marriage and need for a higher purpose appealed directly to Mead's unarticulated dread at her own immediate prospects. And Benedict had a personal allure too – a firm and quiet self-possession (something magnified by her partial deafness), a quality to which the noisy and rambunctious Mead was always attracted in others, as well as a sexual charge to which she found herself responding. But then Mead found herself responding to a lot at this exciting time in her life. It was not long before she met Sapir and started a sexual relationship with him as well. Poor Luther Cressman didn't stand a chance. The relationship with Sapir was short-lived:

Benedict persuaded her to end it, and Mead did so by posing to Sapir first as a neurotic and then as a nymphomaniac to make him feel that he had rejected her rather than vice versa. The irony is that Mead thus presented herself as the kind of lost soul that all three of them saw as a characteristic but problematic modern type – 'a symbol of everything I detest most in American culture', as Sapir later wrote to Benedict.[24] Later Mead would say that this was her first, most lasting lesson in the dangers of psychological manipulation. The idea of 'culture and personality', as Benedict and Mead would develop it, was to help people understand themselves better, not to give outsiders an unfair grip on them.[25] But the Sapir affair cemented Mead's life to Benedict's.

Despite the personal impulses that attracted them to it, neither Sapir, Benedict nor Mead felt at this stage that the 'culture and personality' idea was immediately applicable to 'modern' cultures such as the one they inhabited. As the US gradually overcame its cultural lag in the newly liberated 1920s, it appeared less and less coherent, more fragmented, looser and less prescriptive. The young Boasians had mixed feelings about this fragmentation. On the one hand, they mostly welcomed the greater freedom it gave the individual, and the consciousness it fostered of a greater diversity of legitimate ways of living. On the other hand, their direct experience with 'primitive' cultures caused them to mourn the loss of wholeness and mutual connection they found there. The tight cohesion of 'primitive' cultures also made it easier to study them and to show how they developed ways of living different from those available in 'modern civilization'. However, Benedict and Mead differed rather sharply from Sapir in their evaluation of modernity. As women exercising new freedoms, not very firmly attached to men, and indeed as women taking sustenance from each other, they were not nearly as alienated from the American brand of modernity as Sapir.[26] Unlike France or Russia, Sapir complained, American culture did not offer in exchange for greater fragmentation of individual functions the heightening of the spiritual life that he thought essential for a 'genuine' as opposed to a 'spurious' culture. 'Primitive' cultures had the dual advantage of making the individual feel both useful and creative in every aspect of their lives; American culture, so scornful of tradition but also of true individuality, offered only 'the flat and tedious sameness of spiritual outlook, the anaemic make-believe, the smug intolerance of the challenging, that so imprison our American souls'.[27] Benedict and Mead thought this too snug – and too smug – a correlation between simple, 'well-coordinated' cultures and 'genuineness', on the one hand, and modern, 'uncoordinated' ones and 'spuriousness', on the other. Their principal doubt about 'modern' cultures, at least in the 1920s, was simply that they appeared too uncoordinated to study with the anthropologist's methods. 'I don't feel sure about them,' Benedict wrote to Mead while they were discussing Sapir's writing.[28]

Furthermore – and here was another point of difference from Sapir – Benedict and Mead remained closer to Boas's urgency about the need to document and testify for the 'primitive' cultures. Sapir liked to mock Benedict and Mead's strong sense of mission: 'Must everybody contribute his share toward the saving of humanity?' There was a hint again here that 'the saving of humanity' was women's work, whereas only men could cultivate 'an inhuman absorption in a purely intellectual pursuit' that would yield the greater academic goods.[29] Undoubtedly Benedict and Mead did inherit from their mothers and grandmothers of the progressive era a strong do-gooding instinct. But Benedict's early realization of the limitations of 'friendly visiting' and her struggle to define for herself a professional identity had made her conscious of, and hostile to, the progressive idea that was used to keep women in their place, something Mead had learned from her: 'the notion of "Service" . . . you have made seem such a real bogey – such an effective moist cloth on hopeful activity,' the younger woman wrote.[30] If they retained an idea of 'service', it was the more intellectual and professional version offered by Boas in the specific political environment of the postwar world: the search for a 'lasting peace' between nations, including peoples emerging from colonialism, based on mutual respect and an awareness of the salience and righteousness of cultural difference. Here was a way of serving humanity without serving as a 'footstool'.[31]

* * *

As she turned in her Master's year to devising a PhD topic that would satisfy Boas, Mead looked for a field of action that would address the psychological interests that she and Benedict shared, that would lead her to 'designs for living' different from America's that could be used to illustrate the full range of human possibilities, and that would give her possession of 'her own' culture to nurture and champion. Fortunately Boas was waking up to the possibilities of psychological research. Disproving the Freudian idea that all human beings thought and felt alike would have the same value as challenging evolutionary theory's idea that all human beings climbed the ladder of civilization in the same way. Liberal Americans' embrace of Freud as one of their own was typical of their hubris: they liked to think that everyone in the world was just like them – obviously an assumption that still needed smashing.[32] And if his younger students found they could identify more closely with 'their' peoples by studying their cognitive and emotional processes, and not just anatomizing their language or listing their culture traits, then that would have more profound effects that Boas approved of mightily.

He thus began to give way to these tendencies. Ruth Bunzel – 'Bunny' – was encouraged to study creativity among the Zuni Indians.[33] To Mead, Boas suggested a study of adolescence. 'Adolescence' – a new concept – was then all the rage. The psychologist G. Stanley Hall had propounded the popular theory that the emotional storms and generational tensions of adolescence as experienced by American youths were a universal biological phenomenon, the kind of asssertion almost designed to attract Boas's scepticism – and Mead's, with her own relatively untroubled adolescence in mind. 'Were these difficulties due to being adolescent or to being adolescent in America?' Boas asked.[34] To answer this question, he proposed that Mead survey some of the American Indian tribes in which he and his students had specialized, but she was having none of that – she wanted 'her own' culture, and after some furious bargaining with a protective Boas (mischeviously egged on by Sapir), they settled on Samoa. For her part Mead was thrilled with both the topic and the setting. This was precisely the kind of study she and Benedict had mooted, 'the psychological attitude of the individual under the pressure of the general pattern of culture'. And she would have 'her own' culture in as remote a setting as Boas could be persuaded to allow her.[35]

Mead left for Samoa in the summer of 1925 and returned in spring 1926. She worked quickly and found what she had set out to find – that the physiological changes in adolescence universal to humanity were handled in quite different ways culturally in Samoa than in America. Samoan 'casualness' about the speed and nature of adolescent develop-ment reduced the 'pain', although with the drawback that such a 'shallow' level of affect was unlikely to produce adult personalities of great inten-sity.[36] (There was a shot at Sapir here: not all 'primitive' societies provided the full-blast existence he craved.) This famous piece of fieldwork has come under fierce attack from both Left and Right since Mead's death – her eagerness to vindicate Boas's principles is seen as projecting upon the Samoans her own agenda, an agenda variously interpreted as political correctness by the Right or American imperialism by the Left.[37] But in these still-early days of participant-observation, Mead's methods were no worse than average and probably, given her relative sensitivity to the values and feelings of others (including girls and women), better. She did have an agenda when she set out, but it was no more than the general Boasian aspiration to teach tolerance by illustrating the richness and variety of cultural diversity – 'more or less excluding our own because here we were too deeply involved for genuine objective understanding', as Boas taught. An agenda aimed more squarely at American culture did not really blossom until she returned from her fieldwork. Back in New York, she was encouraged by a fellow anthropologist, George Dorsey, who had had a popular hit with *Why We Behave Like Human Beings* in 1924, to go for a big audience with a trade publisher, an alluring title – 'Coming of Age in Samoa' was Dorsey's idea – and a more direct address to American interests. William Morrow, the publisher Dorsey found for her, specifically asked her to add two chapters on 'what all this means to Americans', and after some hesitation Mead complied.[38]

Even this unprecedented irruption of anthropological method honed on 'primitive' cultures into American modernity was severely limited by the Boasians' own uncertainty about internally diverse modern cultures. In venturing gingerly on to American territory, Mead confessed to a double reservation. First, Samoan prescriptions couldn't easily be prepared for American use because, unlike Samoans, Americans, living in 'a motley, diverse, hetereogeneous modern civilisation', have choice. Second, even the choices they faced were less homogeneous internally: 'Because our civilisation is woven of so many diverse strands, the ideas which any one group accepts will be found to contain numerous contradictions.' She did think that Americans of all varieties could learn lessons in lowered intensity from the Samoans, in order to relieve self-imposed pressures generated by the nuclear family and interfamilial competition – most notoriously, they could learn that 'Sex is a natural, pleasurable thing' – though she acknowledged that some of these pressures could also produce valuable forms of creativity and personality. But her most important point – it occupied the whole of the final chapter – was the Boasian one that learning about diversity was its own reward. What America needed most was 'education for choice', preparing its young ones to recognize and embrace the unprecedented variety of lifestyles available to them, 'the high point of individual choice and universal toleration which a heterogeneous culture and a heterogeneous culture alone can attain'. It was, in a way, the lesson of 'cultural lag' again, but in Boasian dress: get rid of the superannuated mores, but don't impose a new set. Only 'primitive' societies needed to observe a 'single standard'; a modern, heterogeneous culture could choose from among many.[39]

Coming of Age in Samoa was a sensation – not an overnight one, but it crept up on and conquered American hearts. It also divided opinion, but in a way that only sold more books. A lot of Americans read it as a straightforward utopia, encouraged in doing so by a long tradition of viewing Polynesian islanders as happy, uncomplicated, semi-naked sensualists, as well as by William Morrow's dustjacket depicting Polynesian lovers holding hands under a palm tree, and by Mead's unusually lyrical prose. Some anthropologists read it the same way, disapprovingly. E.E. Evans-Pritchard spoke dismissively of the new 'wind-rustling-in-the-palm-trees' school of anthropology. His older colleague A.C. Haddon grumbled at the substitution of the 'lady novelist' for the professional ethnographer.[40] More seriously, Alfred Kroeber recognized the break-through for Boasian cultural relativism that Mead had achieved: her 'pen-pictures . . . of quite extraordinary vividness and semblance to life' were able to demonstrate not only to the professional anthropologist but also to a wider audience that 'these Oceanic civilizations, in spite of damage and losses, remain essentially native in that their fabric of society is still sufficiently coherent to retain its vitality'. But he did not approve of Mead's ventures into modern American culture, which seemed 'meagerly unsatisfactory' in comparison, a betrayal of the anthropologist's commit-ment to seeing a culture whole: 'to the ingrained anthropologist, who all his life has been schooling himself to see his own culture really on one horizon with all others, the singled-out interest in the here and now per se must come as something of a shock.' Mead had nervously feared that it was just impossible to see her own native culture as clearly in the round as she felt she could see the 'primitive', and now Kroeber – an ally – was sadly confirming that her instinct had been correct.[41]

In any case, Mead would have agreed with Kroeber that the principal value of participant-observation in 'primitive' societies was not directly to shed light on ourselves but to show us all the different ways of being 'them', and thus only indirectly to reveal 'our potentialities and limitations'. If she had wanted to tinker with American culture, she would have done what later, suspicious historians have claimed most social scientists of this era did – experiment on them in a laboratory. As Mead herself said:

> We can carry out innumerable carefully controlled experiments with university students and still know nothing about the kind of thing studying peoples in different living cultures can teach us. But most people prefer to carry out the kinds of experiments that allow the scien-tist to feel that he is in full control of the situation rather than surren-dering himself to the situation, as one must in studying human beings as they actually live.[42]

And then there was Boas, niggling at her elbow, reminding her that time was short for some of these living cultures. So almost immediately, with *Coming of Age* still in press, she set off again, for the Admiralty Islands off the coast of New Guinea – and not alone this time. On the way back from Samoa, she had met and fallen in love with a New Zealand anthropologist, Reo Fortune, who helped her settle the Luther Cressman problem. Fortune also helped her settle a Boas problem, for his chaperonage would relieve Boas's paternal anxieties about letting his famous young protégée venture deeper into uncharted territory. In the fall of 1928, Mead rejoined Fortune in New Zealand, marrying him in October; in November they travelled as husband and wife to the Admiralty Islands.

In this field trip, which lasted until summer 1929, and in their next, which spanned a longer period, from 1931 to 1933, Mead essentially repeated the pattern and method, with similar motives, of her Samoan venture. *Growing Up in New Guinea* (1930), Mead's report on the Manus people of the Admiralty Islands, followed the model of *Coming of Age* so closely as to be taken in Kroeber's review as its 'second volume'. Once again the main thrust of the book was to show Americans[43] how differently other cultures handled basic human functions, in this case the education of the young. It helped that the Manus were so very different from the Samoans: adults lived a very disciplined and driven life, 'a kind of sterile caricature of those aspects of American life most disliked by the liberals, emphasis on property, on success, lack of interest in the arts, etc.', as she gleefully noted later.[44] In other respects, too, they shocked liberal American sensibilities: fathers, not mothers, were the dominant parents, and although children were in some ways left free to roam and frolic without direction, in others (arranged marriages, strict respect for property) they were subjected to the most rigorous preparation for adult life. What Mead liked about this latter contradiction was that it complicated the more simple-minded 'progressive' ideas about education prevalent in her own culture – neither 'freedom' nor 'discipline' alone would do. One thing that shocked her about the Manus, on the other hand, was the way in which boys in particular were given a lot of freedom in childhood and then a lot of responsibility in adulthood. This disjunction, requiring a sudden adaptation, left young men 'stripped . . . even of self respect', and forever after hard, sceptical and pragmatic.[45] Here Mead was beginning to probe the most basic processes of cultural reproduction – how children 'learn' their culture.

> Human nature was malleable, yes; children could be given years of freedom apparently emphasising other values from those which ruled the lives of their fathers and mothers, yes. But there were limits to this malleability. It was no use permitting children to develop values different from those of their society. The adult forms . . . always won. Human nature is flexible, but it is also elastic – it will tend to return to the form that was impressed upon it in earliest years. From this it follows

that 'Culture is very, very strong. You cannot alter a society by giving its children of school age new behaviour patterns to which the adult society gives no scope.'[46]

That warning about the limits to social engineering was a swipe at the Soviets, who had been experimenting with 'progressive' education themselves, but who were learning that '[t]he spectacular experiment in Russia had first to be stabilized among adults before it could be taught to children'; the consequence otherwise would be more 'cultural lag', not less.[47] But Mead also sent out her old warnings about simple-mindedly analogizing between 'primitive' and complex, modern societies. Trying to match up education with adult values would be fruitless in a society with so many incompatible adult values: children of the same parents 'may take such divergent courses that at the age of fifty their premises may be mutually unintelligible and antagonistic'.[48] To drive the point home, she added an appendix trouncing the methodology of the behavioural psychologists who were trying to identify American cultural norms and engineer them for social order: it just couldn't be done in a complex society where 'the cultural norm' hardly existed, still less in a laboratory where the environment was so controlled and artificial that only 'simple and undifferentiated' processes could be identified.[49] The 'lessons' she adduced were ironic ones: social reform was much harder than progressive educators imagined; children were not one thing or another but all kinds of things; it was easier to diagnose 'cultural lag' than to know how to rectify it. Still, she felt she was picking up all sorts of clues about how 'primitive' societies did hang together, how children learned to become adults and what kinds of learning made for a happier form of adulthood than others. These might be building blocks for an approach to social reform if she could ever work out how to get a purchase on the slippery diversity of her own, American culture.

For the time being, though, there were so many more 'primitive' cultures to sample, so many more variations of culture and personality to chart. After a dispiriting summer trying to be a good Boasian and sample an American Indian culture, the Omaha – too adulterated by Americanization to form a coherent body of study, and made miserable by it too – she and Fortune returned to the field in the autumn of 1931. This time their ambitious goal was to scoop up a sequence of distinct cultures on varying terrains in New Guinea. They had both been inspired in part by a course they had taken with A.R. Radcliffe-Brown, visiting Columbia from the University of Sydney that summer. Radcliffe-Brown was one of the principal inspirations of the British school of social anthropology, which looked at the social structure rather than the culture of 'primitive' societies. But like the Boasians he believed that study of 'the simplest forms' gave clarity about the forms of all societies, and encouraged his students to consider 'a large number of varieties of the same type' so as to grasp the full variety of possible organization.[50]

New Guinea, with its scattered peoples separated by barriers of terrain and as yet relatively 'unmissionized' by Western influences, offered ideal scope for such a venture. First Mead and her husband spent some time among a mountain people, the Arapesh, 'an exceedingly simple culture' in which both men and women seemed 'parental, cherishing and mildly sexed'; then they travelled up the Sepik River where at different landings a number of distinct (and more complex) cultures could be found, including the Mundugumor, quite different from the Arapesh – 'fiercely aggressive, highly sexed and noncherishing' – and ultimately the 'Tchambuli' (Chambri), where the women ran the show while the men, 'catty, exhibitionistic' and self-absorbed, devoted themselves to mind games, theatricals and decorative arts.[51] Initially Mead was again studying different forms of child-rearing, but her restless mind – and also her growing frictions with Fortune – caused her to turn increasingly to the ways these cultures defined what we would now call 'gender roles'. She was irritated by the manner in which she and Fortune had differed over the Arapesh, whom he thought soft and 'feminized'; but as the male Arapesh were 'feminized' too, she thought, why associate the culture with women? Then the Mundugumor were too hard and aggressive for her, while her husband liked them; but the female Mundugumor were as 'masculine' as the men, so why associate their culture with men?[52]

The not entirely fortuitous juxtaposition – not entirely since she was looking for this anyway – of two quite different cultures with little apparent sex differentiation, the Arapesh and the Mundugumor, and a third culture, the Tchambuli, with high sex differentiation but with poles reversed vis-à-vis Western norms, got Mead thinking about cultures as *patterns*.[53] What distinguished a culture was not just its unique combination of practices but the way it organized distinctively a set of common human variables, such as temperamental differences between individuals, or the dichotomization of male and female. Thinking about culture in this way provided a structure within which complexity could be better accommodated. You could describe a simple pattern based on one variable – say, temperament: did a culture favour a particular temperament or combination of temperaments? You could then superimpose a pattern based on another variable – say, sex roles: did a culture differentiate clearly between men and women (like the Tchambuli) or not (like the Arapesh and the Mundugumor)? You could then consider how the two patterns related: for instance, a culture that tolerated a diversity of personality types but differentiated strongly between sex roles might tend to interpret 'deviant' personality types in a sexualized way. Mead would hypothesize that the interaction of these two patterns might explain the difficulty homosexuals experienced in her own American culture, where deviant personalities were typed as sexual deviants and then subjected to punishing sex-role strictures.[54] Clearly, the more patterns you considered in this way the more devilishly complex the overall pattern got – the '*big problem*', she wrote to Benedict in July 1932, was 'how to systematize the different types of characterizations' – but the whole idea at least opened the door to more comparisons with 'modern, heterogeneous' societies such as that of the US.[55]

By the time Mead and Fortune got to the middle stretch of the Sepik River where the Tchambuli lived, at the beginning of 1933, two influences were precipitating the rapid development of her thought along these ambitious lines. The first was Ruth Benedict's, in the form of the manuscript of her *chef d'oeuvre*, *Patterns of Culture*. While Mead had been accumulating cultures in the field, Benedict had been doing similar work from her desk at Barnard. *Patterns* compares accounts of four cultures: her own study of the Plains Indians and (with Ruth Bunzel) of the Zuni, Fortune's of the Dobu and Boas's of the Kwakiutl. Making the standard Boasian move against biological determinism, Benedict presents these cultures as products not of race but of cultural creativity, from among the myriad possibilities that a plastic human nature affords. Making a culture is presented almost as a work of art, in which a people unconsciously select traits that suit their needs and conditions, and weave them into a coherent whole: a similar process to that described by the British anthropologists' functionalism, where local needs and conditions determine social structure, but are more holistic and creative. Benedict's own strong personal and professional preference for coherence is evident in her assertion that 'A culture, like an individual, is a more or less consistent pattern of thought and action', and in her suggestion that cultures that are less coherent tend to be discordant or shallow.[56] Her descriptions of the individual cultures spell out the distinctive 'patterns' or 'configurations' of each, which combine economic, social and psychological characteristics. The Zuni have economic abundance, a complex social structure and a rich ritual life; they are sober, realistic, collectivist. The Dobu live economically straitened lives; have a complex social structure that carefully organizes violence; and are passionate, competitive and suspicious. Economy, society and psychology are all intricately interlocked; it is impossible to say which was prior or causative, something that distinguishes Benedict's version of holism from the British school of functionalism or Abram Kardiner's later version of 'culture and personality', both of which privilege material conditions.[57]

Part of the mass appeal of *Patterns* – after publication in 1934, it went on to become a bestseller, with over a million copies in print – was that it provided snapshots of personality types that Americans, with their passion (Mead thought) for 'self-rating',[58] liked to use to compare themselves and their neighbours. Benedict encouraged this by using catchwords such as 'Apollonian' and 'Dionysian' – borrowed from the German thinkers Nietzsche and Spengler – to contrast the Zuni and the Plains Indians.[59] Though she feebly discouraged such a practice,[60] she was also playing into a long-standing tendency in Western societies to sum up their own and others' 'souls' or 'minds' or 'national characters' using a few handy stereotypes – a tendency at something of a peak at the time of *Patterns* as Westerners became more familiar with their neighbours (and others more distant) in the First World War and through the activities of international organizations such as the League of Nations. Nor did Benedict entirely rule out applying such epithets to complex, modern societies. Although she dutifully informed the reader that Spengler's own attempts to do so had failed because Western civilizations, with 'their historical diversity, their stratification into occupations and classes, their incomparable richness of detail', were 'not yet well enough understood to be summarized under a couple of catchwords', nevertheless she too had opened a door. 'Cultural configurations are as compelling and as significant in the highest and most complex of societies of which we have knowledge,' she insisted. It was only a matter of time before the material they presented was sorted and organized, such as by combinations of patterns – Benedict instanced class and personality, much as Mead would offer sex and temperament.[61] If anything, she proposed, fast-changing modern cultures needed *more* consciousness of their culture patterns in order to avoid 'cultural lag'. With a livelier sense of her own sexual 'deviance' than Mead, she not only warned against unnecessary stigmatization of 'deviants', but suggested that the latter might be useful in signalling new ways of being that might be fruitfully worked into the culture pattern.[62]

The other influence that pushed Mead towards a more capacious idea of 'culture pattern' was the presence of Gregory Bateson. The young British anthropologist, a student of Radcliffe-Brown's, was working at the time among the Iatmul people of the middle Sepik, and when he heard that Mead and Fortune were seeking to move on from the Mundugumor he welcomed them to his territory and steered them towards the nearby Tchambuli. Mead fell for him as soon as they met. He had that quiet self-containment that she had loved in Benedict, and a kindliness that she associated with the English gentleman, which contrasted sharply with Fortune's stereotypically masculine aggression. The threesome grappled intensely – famously, crammed into an eight-by-eight-foot mosquito hut (and both Fortune and Bateson were very tall men) – over their intellectual differences, which became their personal differences, and vice versa. Fortune's jealousy was magnified by the influence of Benedict, whose sexual relationship with Mead had already caused him much grief, and whose approach in *Patterns* seemed much more to Mead's and Bateson's taste than to his own. By his own account, he vented his feelings by flinging his copy of the manuscript of *Patterns* into the Sepik, only because he couldn't punch Benedict in the nose, thus confirming to Mead her judgement about their temperamental incompatibility, but he could not so easily dispose of Bateson.[63]

Meanwhile Bateson and Mead were clicking on all fronts. Bateson had been seeking a less mechanical and sociological model of culture than the one he had got from his functionalist mentors, one that would also take into account a culture's 'emotional tone or ethos'.[64] His background as a biologist – his father was a famous geneticist and his undergraduate training at Cambridge had been in Natural Sciences – caused him to demand a truly 'scientific' approach to culture but also one that captured the complexity of the human animal better than functionalism's emphasis on social structure as a response to basic human needs. He joined in enthusiastically with Mead's attempts to combine the biological factor of 'temperament' with the cultural factor of sex-roles. Together they hammered out a scheme for what they called the 'squares', which diagrammed all of the possible combinations of temperaments with sex-roles. In theory any individual could be placed at a particular location in a field defined by two axes – a 'north-south' axis, which charted sex-roles from 'male' to 'female' as conventionally defined in the West, and an 'east-west' axis, which charted a range of temperaments from rational and controlling to mystical and relational. For years thereafter they used 'the squares' as shorthand to describe acquaintances and, although Mead was uneasily aware that by doing so she was reducing cultures to just a few key patterns, to characterize cultures too.[65] Mead drew heavily on their joint work for the book that came out of this extended field-trip, *Sex and Temperament in Three Primitive Societies* (1935). For his part, Bateson got what he was looking for from Mead and Benedict: an understanding of psychology (both cognitive and affective) to interweave with social structure, an avowedly 'configurationist' analysis that he set out in the book that came out of his own fieldwork, *Naven* (1936).

Most of all, Bateson and Mead got what they both wanted – each other. By the time the trio separated in spring 1933, Mead and Fortune's marriage was all but over and Mead and Bateson's had been seeded. As

Mead required of all her most intimate relationships, the joint project that she and Bateson were embarking on was intellectual as much as it was sexual and emotional. The combination of Benedict's 'patterns' and their own work on interweaving multiple cultural distinctions into frameworks like the 'squares' had convinced them that they were on to a version of 'culture and personality' applicable to the most complex cultures, including their own. The fact that for once their experimental subjects were not 'primitives' but, inside that mosquito hut, an Englishman, an American and a New Zealander could only have reinforced that orientation. Mead went back to New York, and Bateson to Cambridge, thinking about Americans and Englishmen and how they related; Fortune wandered disconsolately off, first to London and then to Sydney, thinking very black thoughts indeed. But the Western world they all returned to in the spring of 1933 was a different place from the one they had left a few years before.

*   *   *

Much had happened between 1931 and 1933. The Great Depression had deepened to its lowest point in the United States and spread around the world. Franklin D. Roosevelt had been elected president and taken office, promising a 'New Deal' for Americans that involved much more than a spate of fresh government programmes – it brought with it a new spirit of democracy, in social and economic (and cultural) life as well as in politics. The Depression had also brought the Nazis to power in Germany and triggered an emigration of Jews and political dissidents whose number included many distinguished social scientists of democratic sentiments, many of whom ended up in the United States, where the lion's share of academic jobs was to be found.

These transformations had made the American scene peculiarly favourable to the 'culture consciousness' of Boasian anthropology. The coalition that Roosevelt represented was much more ethnically (and even to some extent racially) diverse than the Republican majorities that had dominated American politics in the 1920s. It organized rather than marginalized the ethnic communities of Italians, Irish, Jews and other Central and Eastern European and Balkan ethnic groups that now formed large proportions of the major cities. It sought to serve the social and economic interests of 'Negro' (African-American) communities both in those same cities and in the rural South, though, dependent on Southern Democratic votes, without making serious moves towards explicit racial equality. The New Deal was much franker about acknowledging not only the fact but the virtue of cultural diversity than had been those 'nervous liberals' after the First World War. Most tellingly for the anthropologists, the Bureau of Indian Affairs under its new director, John Collier, reversed a policy of forced assimilation and began restoring cultural integrity to the various American Indian groups, and in 1934 Collier set up an Applied Anthropology Unit to assist in this process, the first significant government initiative to employ professional anthropologists for public purposes.[66] The work that sociologists (including Mead's mother) and anthropologists had been doing on ethnic identity – in many cases against an official policy of assimilation – also now came into its own. Instead of bemoaning cultural fragmentation, New Dealers groped towards a new vision of America as a 'nation of nations': a microcosm of the world.[67] This enterprise would require a more self-aware approach to cultural difference – just the kind of culture consciousness that anthropology prescribed.

The New Deal did not, however, naturally turn to anthropologists (or other social scientists) to achieve these goals. Its byword was democracy. The New Deal coalition was itself built up of myriad jostling, conflicting interest groups, each with its own organization, some more democratic than others. Social science was not always well equipped to deal with the realities of democratic politics. But neither was it congenitally ill-disposed to democracy, as the 'nervous liberal' diagnosis supposes.[68] On the contrary, many social scientists (including, gingerly, many Boasians) had, as we have seen, been galvanized by rapid social changes since the First World War into thinking how a complex, modern society might act together to accommodate those changes culturally. In the 1930s especially, many – such as the sociologists Robert and Helen Lynd[69] (the celebrated authors of Middletown) and the social psychologists Gardner and Lois Murphy[70] – were inspired by the ideas of the philosopher John Dewey to argue for a more 'purposive' social science that would provide aid and comfort to democratically decided cultural change. It is often said that the provision of 'expertise' is itself intrinsically undemocratic, but that surely depends on the forms that expertise takes, the terms on which it is offered and the ends to which it is put. The 'expert' can be a social engineer, acting covertly and manipulatively, but also, more or less democratically, a critic, a teacher, a facilitator. 'Purposive' social scientists argued that at the very least their open espousal of democratic values was preferable to the alternative, a hiding behind 'objectivity' that meant social science was as, or more, likely to be deployed for frankly anti-democratic purposes. This argument gathered strength over the course of the 1930s, as the rise of dictatorships in Europe strengthened the powers arrayed against democracy, and as refugee scholars added their voices to the chorus for a purposive, democratic social science.[71]

Boasian anthropology was part of this movement, but not necessarily at its forefront. Boas himself had not wanted his students to obsess about their own culture, yet even he was influenced by the changing mood of the 1930s – how could he not be, as a humanist, a Jew, a refugee himself of a kind? – and, having recovered from a period of depression after the deaths of his daughter, son and wife, he had thrown himself into work on behalf of refugees, anti-Nazism and anti-racism. His acolytes were caught unawares. 'He has given up science for good works. Such a waste!' Benedict told Mead on her return from New Guinea. But Benedict, now with a permanent position of her own at Columbia, was edging in a similar direction herself – though not so much giving up science for good works as turning her science to more clearly political uses.[72]

Patterns of Culture, as we have seen, was her bravest statement yet that even a complex, modern society could use its culture consciousness to address 'cultural lag', but, following Dewey, she was decidedly not recommending social engineering in order to 'control' society, even overtly, much less covertly, by means of new cultural norms. 'No society has yet attempted a self-conscious direction of the process by which its new normalities are created in the next generation. Dewey has pointed out how possible and yet how drastic such social engineering would be.' Her awareness of the 'human suffering and frustration' that norms of any kind imposed on 'deviants' such as herself forbade any such 'categorical imperatives'. Instead, she recommended a much looser awareness of diversity itself as a conscious policy – a transferral of the Boasian recognition of 'cultural relativity' between peoples to the diversity of peoples within America, something we can see as congruent with the 'nation of nations'.[73]

'Cultural relativity' between cultures did not necessarily make Benedict an ethical relativist within her own culture. As many people have since pointed out, her recommendation for diversity in her own culture did not flow so directly from her anthropological science as her fancy footwork sought to imply; it was more a personal preference. Benedict wasn't shy of expressing her personal preferences about cultures – she was perfectly clear about how much more she liked the Zuni than the Dobu or the Kwakiutl. On the other hand, she didn't conclude from her preferences that she had any right to dictate to the Dobu or the Kwakiutl how they should live, any more than she had a right to dictate to the Americans how they should live; she did, however, as an American, have a right to seek to persuade, including by use of her 'expertise'. In this context, *Patterns of Culture* – published shortly after Mead's return from New Guinea – shows how the temper of the times was shifting even a determined Boasian opponent of 'good works' in that direction, and also how

Boasian caution about 'social engineering' imparted a democratic flavour to those 'good works'. As Judith Modell has suggested, Benedict's was more the 'teaching' than the 'engineering' style of social reform.[74] Furthermore, the advocacy of cultural anthropology for a 'culture-conscious' approach to domestic social science itself had a democratizing effect on other social sciences, as the attempt to match reform programmes to the culturally specific 'needs' of 1930s America pulled many sociologists and social psychologists away from their abstracted laboratory environments, tinkering with the behaviour of experimental subjects, to consider more closely the lived experiences of real American people.[75]

By the time of her return from New Guinea, Margaret Mead was already one step ahead of her mentors. She had been advocating a relaxation of norms to suit a rapidly changing society ever since *Coming of Age in Samoa*. Her reading of *Patterns of Culture*, reinforced by Bateson, was moving her beyond diversity to try to grasp what common frameworks did or could hold a diverse, modern culture together. She was delighted to find that, even before *Patterns of Culture* was published, other social scientists – and, significantly, sources of funding such as foundations – were more open to a wide-ranging 'culture-conscious' exploration of contemporary America and the possibilities for purposive social change. The key figure in her (and many others') explorations along these lines was Lawrence K. Frank, with whom she had corresponded briefly before she had left for New Guinea – introduced by Robert and Helen Lynd – but who now became a crucial enabling figure in her public life.[76]

Larry Frank is often cited as the classic case of the 'nervous liberal' who sought to contain and cure social disorders created by democracy between the world wars, and there is some truth to this characterization, but his career also shows how changeable and susceptible to the fresh winds of the New Deal such a figure could be.[77] Frank had come to prominence in the 1920s as an assistant to Beardsley Ruml at the Laura Spelman Rockefeller Memorial (LSRM). Ruml *was* a social engineer of the 'nervous liberal' variety and, in his time at the LSRM, Frank learned to speak Ruml's language. Ruml and Frank recognized the problem of 'cultural lag', but rather than presenting its solution as a subject for democratic deliberation – and contemplating as one resolution the facilitation of greater individual expression – they spoke confidently of the solutions of 'science' and the goal as 'learn[ing] the habits of *group* activity which the machine process demands'.[78] To his critics, Frank's view is summed up in the title of his 1948 book, *Society as the Patient*, with its message that 'our culture is sick, mentally disordered, and in need of treatment', the implicit suggestion being that people like him were the doctors who would prescribe 'new patterns or sanctions' in order to achieve a 'cultural reorganization' in the interests of social stability.[79]

But Frank was no intellectual – as Helen Lynd put it, he wasn't 'a well-educated person', he had no 'field'[80] – and his writings display no consistent argument or even much of a tendency. At times he shows what appear to us now to be the most unpleasant 'normalizing' tendencies, aimed at controlling ordinary people in aid of the status quo;[81] at other times he sounds like a starry-eyed utopian in advocating 'new ego-ideals that look toward non-pecuniary goals and avoid the exploitation of society', or like a hardened radical in urging the study of Marx and Freud to show how '[c]ulture coerces and dominates the individual', and exhorting democracy to choose its own fate rather than leave it to 'business and financial controllers'.[82] In other words, 'society as the patient' could imply anti-democratic social engineering, or democratic (even radical) social reform, or an accommodation between diverse individual needs and wants and overt social goals; or, as it did in Frank's work, all of these things at different times.[83] Frank's importance was less as the propagator of his own ideas and more as the impresario for others', and although at the LSRM he followed Ruml's line, as he subsequently moved around the foundation world he gained more responsibility and his patronage became more promiscuous. As Mead put it in 1938, 'Larry Frank is a strange, muddled minded person, who never the less is a sort of genius at coordinating ideas; he has a marvelous nose for people and for new and promising ideas . . . He is the most imaginative and intelligent Foundation secretary I know.'[84]

From his early days at the LSRM, Frank had shown an interest in anthropology and shown, too, that he appreciated its critical edge. Anthropology demonstrated that the solutions to 'cultural lag' were manifold.[85] While still working for Ruml, in 1930–1, Frank funded a pioneering seminar run by Edward Sapir and John Dollard at Yale that imported scholars from around the world in order to make a systematic comparison of the different personality configurations in different cultures. It was a failure – because, Frank himself later admitted, Sapir had no workable theoretical framework to explain these differences, and so all he got was anecdotal gossip, too much like the hoariest old stereotypes about 'national character'. But it was an interesting failure, which Mead and Benedict built on in their own much more ambitious programme after the war.[86]

By the time Frank and Mead resumed contact – they met face to face for the first time at a New Year's party in 1934 – Frank had moved to the Rockefeller-funded General Education Board, where his interest in 'culture and personality' was focused on facilitating educational reform.

He had been organizing with Robert Lynd a series of 'culture and personality' conferences in Hanover, New Hampshire (near his own holiday
home in Holderness) and, finding Mead immediately congenial, invited
her to the biggest conference of them all, a month-long sojourn at the
Hanover Inn in summer 1934. The nominal goal was to draw up a curriculum for schools and colleges on 'human relations', but in the event the
high-powered participants turned instead to a more theoretical consideration of the interactions of culture and personality, along Benedict's lines,
though now from a more interdisciplinary perspective, incorporating sociology, social psychology, psychoanalysis and education. 'Larry sat one one
side, a green shade over his eyes, and most of the time let us argue,' Mead
recalled. Therein lay the excitement – it was her first intimation that
people in other disciplines were asking the same questions.[87]

The most important influence to which Mead was exposed at Hanover
was what would come to be called neo-Freudianism. 'Neo-Freudianism' is
a loose term to describe a wide range of contemporary thinkers who
accepted Freud's basic account of the human psyche but not his relative
indifference to how the psyche functioned in different social and cultural
situations. By thus emphasizing the role of social and cultural forces rather
than universal 'drives' in the individual's achievement of mental integration, the neo-Freudians brought together psychoanalysis and cultural
relativism, most famously in Erich Fromm's attribution of neurotic symp-
toms prevalent in modern society to specific features of capitalism in
Escape from Freedom (1941). This recipe of social and political solutions
to individual problems had obvious attractions for social scientists who
aspired to be more than therapists for patients; it also nicely captured
the New Deal moment in which social determinants and individual
aspirations were equally valued, and in which a greater optimism about
the chances for individual and social reform was possible than in Freud's
orthodox view of 'civilization' as a fundamental barrier to human happiness.[88] Some neo-Freudians, such as Harry Stack Sullivan (who worked
closely with Edward Sapir), were psychiatrists most interested in a culturally specific diagnosis of individual maladies. Others, like John Dollard,
were sociologists interested in how individuals' psychological states
affected their reception of social and cultural norms. Others were
orthodox Freudians whose own social experiences caused them to doubt
their mentor's universalism: this was a common reaction among Jewish
émigré analysts (such as Karen Horney and Erik Erikson) who became
convinced that the very different cultures of Weimar Germany, Nazi
Germany and New Deal America created (and were created by) quite
different psychological problems. As another influential neo-Freudian,
Abram Kardiner, put it: 'even the most conservative and reactionary of

the psychoanalysts had to recognize that the changes in the external environment had something to do with how people felt, because this was the first time they had ever seen it, black on white' – a recognition catalysed both by the impact of Nazism and by 'the vicissitudes of America during the Depression'.[89]

While most of the neo-Freudians were driven by strong 'clinical' instincts to prescribe treatment to both individuals and society – as with other social scientists, with varying motives and politics – Mead's interest at this stage was largely driven by a more theoretical orientation to discover clues as to how culture patterns were created and maintained in individuals, in both 'simple' and 'complex' societies. With Bateson's scientific language still echoing in her head, she saw in neo-Freudianism an opportunity to move beyond Benedict's pretty but vague ideas about a culture 'choosing' its pattern. At the Hanover conference her chief inspiration was John Dollard, who updated her on the joint work he had done with Sapir and Sullivan – fortunately Sapir was not present – and who introduced her to the other most important neo-Freudians, Erikson, Fromm and Horney. From these various influences Mead derived both a new way to schematize cultures, and a set of exciting new ideas about how cultures got those schemas and how individuals within cultures internalized them. She became persuaded of the profound effects of child-rearing practices on the formation of the individual 'ego', and of the ways in which cultural values and mores were projected into the individual via the 'superego', the culture acting as a kind of parental conscience. As a result, she began to think of cultures as differentiated by the varying degrees of 'ego' strength and the different kinds of 'ego' ideals they generated in adults.[90]

After Hanover, Mead participated in further discussions and collaborative projects with her new friends, especially with the neo-Freudian educationalist Caroline Zachry, who was working on a school and university curriculum for 'human relations'. In part because it was funded by Larry Frank's Rockefeller money, this work in 'progressive education' has also been attributed to 'nervous liberals', motivated by anxiety about their weak-kneed fellow citizens and seeking to use schools and hospitals to stamp out deviancy and suppress revolutionary social change.[91] There were undoubtedly people who thought that way.[92] But such motivations can hardly be attributed to Mead and her closest associates. Most of her best friends were 'deviants', and insofar as she had offered any prescriptions for her own culture, they were aimed at making more, not less, space for deviance.[93] She was not, at this stage, very political, it is true; what with all the time she had spent in the field, she had not even voted since

1924 and had missed out on most of the excitements of the Depression and the New Deal.[94] If she had been more political, she would probably have attracted more, not less, blame from posterity, for not being revolutionary enough.[95] Unlike the émigrés – who might be allowed to have had good reason for being so – she was not worried about latent 'authoritarianism' in American culture and did not see any pressing need to channel her fellow citizens' 'aggression' or to impose 'self-discipline' on them.[96] Her work with Zachry was principally devoted to raising 'culture consciousness' among the young – 'education for choice', as she had put it in *Coming of Age in Samoa* – to equip them to understand and manage rapid change for themselves, not to prescribe norms, still less to 'adjust' individuals to an undemocratic culture. She persistently criticized the 'progressive' educators for their social engineering – for their 'teleological' approach based not on facilitating choice but on what they had already decided were society's 'needs' – and urged instead that education raise awareness of cultural diversity and biases rather than promote a spurious 'objectivity'.[97] Citing Larry Frank, she reminded the progressive educators that 'history is written as we go along and man's fate is not predetermined . . . knowledge of social laws gives us freedom to choose, not merely a guidebook to the shortest road on an already completed map of the future'.[98] All of the 'culture and personality' school, because it saw those entities as linked, believed that there had to be some degree of 'adjustment' between them. But this was not necessarily about covert 'social engineering'; it could be, rather, a frank acknowledgement that any social changes that affected the whole culture, whether arrived at democratically or not, would have – would require – corresponding psychological changes, and vice versa, something that neither progressive educators nor Soviet social engineers had properly acknowledged.[99]

In any case, Mead's fundamental interests and loyalties remained with the 'natives', a point that is lost if one considers her reflections on other cultures solely as a commentary on her own.[100] Since returning from Samoa, she had nominally had a full-time job as a curator at the American Museum of Natural History, from which she had taken leave to do her fieldwork, but where she retained responsibility for the representation of Pacific peoples. She wrote no more about American culture in this period than she had done in concluding her books about Samoa and New Guinea. Her principal contributions in this line were to continue arguing for 'the lessening of rigidity in the classification of the sexes', without eliminating sex distinction altogether, in order to accommodate the widest possible array of combinations of sex and temperament which it was the glory of a complex modern society to allow.[101] Although she saw disadvantages to this messiness – the mixed messages people got from a culture that was both diverse and rapidly changing could easily be a recipe for unhappiness or 'neurosis' – it remained a fundamental and irremediable characteristic of complex modern cultures, however inconvenient to the anthropologist's search for neatness.

Otherwise her turn to neo-Freudianism was woven into her existing analyses of the 'simple, homogeneous' societies among which anthropologists did fieldwork. There was still time, with Dollard's help, to build neo-Freudian perspectives into the comparison of the Arapesh, Mundugumor and Tchambuli that appeared as *Sex and Temperament in Three Primitive Societies* (1935).[102] In order to develop this application of psychoanalysis to fieldwork, she and Benedict arranged regular meetings with Fromm and Horney, where the anthropologists would describe 'primitive' cultures and the psychoanalysts would speculate about the kind of ego structure each entailed, and what methods the culture was using to inculcate it: for example, shame, guilt, trust or just a sense of humour.[103] Benedict used these clues to begin drawing up a handbook giving 'psychological leads' to future anthropological fieldworkers.[104] Mead then compiled by far her most systematic and thorough comparison of 'primitive' cultures, *Cooperation and Competition among Primitive Peoples* (1937), which collected no fewer than thirteen cultures, including 'her own' Samoans, Arapesh and Manus, other favourites such as the Zuni and the Kwakiutl, and some new cultures drawn from a team of graduate students and postdocs at Columbia. The comparisons combined considerations of economic and social structure with a sensitivity to the distinctive 'ego ideals' of a culture and its methods of inculcating them.[105] Mead was delighted to find that the results persuaded Benedict of the need to specify much more clearly the determinants and mechanisms of 'character formation' in 'primitive' societies, and to take more account of social as well as psychological factors, than her aesthetic approach in *Patterns* had allowed.[106] And she was not content to rest there. All the time Mead was plotting her next bout of fieldwork – in Bali – and how to arrange it so that she could do that fieldwork with Gregory Bateson.

* * *

The Britain to which Bateson had returned in 1933 had changed just as much as Mead's America. Domestic problems absorbed social scientists in the same ways; one product was the experiment in 'Mass-Observation' launched by the anthropologist Tom Harrisson, which used a variety of techniques to give a democratic voice to public opinion. But social science had made less of an impact on British universities, which in turn had made less of an impact on society; and there was nothing like the New Deal to rally intellectuals to the banner of social reform in 1930s

Britain, which was governed by an unadventurous 'National Government' on the principle of 'safety first'. Settling down in Cambridge to write up his own New Guinea research, Bateson found his strongest political feelings evoked by the deteriorating international situation, which was much closer to home for him than it was for Mead. In December 1934 he wrote a letter to *The Times* against the view that 'man is innately savage and born with a tendency to warfare'. Given a demonstrable variety of levels of aggressiveness in the 'primitive' cultures studied by anthropologists, there must be 'some cultural factor at work which effectively determines whether a community shall habitually fight', he wrote, but he was not yet willing to venture many clues as to what that factor was, still less to analyse its presence or absence in his own culture.[107]

Nevertheless, just as Mead's adoption of neo-Freudianism was aimed at part in complicating her understanding of culture pattern sufficiently to accommodate 'modern' societies such as her own, so Bateson found himself generating new theories of the determination of culture patterns from his work in New Guinea that resonated with the disturbed international situation around him. Following Mead and Benedict, he now thought of culture not just as an adaptation to economic and social circumstances as his functionalist teachers had taught him to do, but also as a psychological pattern, an 'ethos' (to use a word favoured by Benedict), producing a stylized or 'standardized' individual. It was easier, he felt, to compare the 'ethos' of a number of cultures than to compare their specific social and economic circumstances, because the number of psychological configurations was limited – here we can detect the influence of the 'squares' plotted out with Mead and Fortune on the middle Sepik – although a perfect description of a culture would have to take into account the interaction of the ethos with other factors such as social structure.[108]

Again building on the geometrical pattern of the 'squares', Bateson imagined a culture's ethos as comprising a complex grid of interlocking relationships. A 'functional' relationship in a couple – such as the one he formed with Mead – developed from a complementary set of interactions between two people, whose reactions to each other built up the relationship in a 'circular' process: what he and other pioneers of cybernetics would later come to define as a 'feedback loop'. Similarly, a 'functional' culture – and both functionalists and Boasians betrayed an anthropological bias towards assuming that on the whole cultures did function smoothly and coherently – must develop from a host of complementary interactions, which bonded individuals into groups, and groups into whole cultures; 'feedback' was evident in every part of the system and also between parts of the system.[109] The process by which individuals and groups differentiated themselves within the culture, yet still remained in a 'dynamic equilibrium' with others, Bateson dubbed rather awkwardly 'schismogenesis'. Schismogenesis between complementary pairs – men and women, masters and servants, parents and children – taught them how to be different but also how their complementary differences made them interdependent, parts of a larger unit. Although such a 'completely circular or reticulate' system of cause and effect had no single cause or driver, Bateson had absorbed enough of Mead's interest in child training and development to draw particular attention to the ways in which children and adolescents picked up the cues about the ethos of their culture and their place within it, which they would then apply systematically to all aspects of their adult life – the crucial process of 'learning how to learn'.[110]

In this period in Cambridge after his return from New Guinea, Bateson developed these theoretical insights in the context of writing up his research on the Iatmul, which he published as a heavyweight anthropological monograph, *Naven* (1936). The 'naven' in question was a ritual denoting the keystone relationship among the Iatmul, between the mother's brother and his nephew, which set the tone for the ethos of the whole culture.[111] Following Mead's example, Bateson interspersed his highly technical expositions of ethos and schismogenesis among the Iatmul with illustrations of how the same processes worked in his own culture. He used the example of 'a group of young intellectual English men or women . . . talking and joking together wittily and with a touch of light cynicism' to show how group interactions policed an ethos, 'a standardised system of emotional atittudes', by stigmatizing inappropriate remarks as 'blunders'. Every detail of life around him at St John's College, Cambridge now breathed of ethos: 'The Latin Grace, the arch of the college, the snuff after dinner on Sundays, the loving cup, the rose water, the feasts – all these cultural details constitute an intricate series of channels which express and guide the ethos.' Even the most complex culture could be imagined as a gorgeously geometrical web of interlocking ethoses:

> This intimate relationship between ethos and cultural structure is especially characteristic of small segregated groups where the ethos is uniform and the 'tradition' very much alive . . . when we come to consider not isolated groups but whole civilisations we must expect to find much more variety of ethos and more details of culture which have been separated from the ethological contexts in which they were appropriate and retained as discrepant elements in an otherwise harmonious culture. Nevertheless I believe that the concept of ethos may

valuably be applied even to such enormous and confused cultures as those of Western Europe. In such cases we must never lose sight of the variations of ethos in different sections of the community and the curious dovetailing of the ethoses of the different sections into an harmonious whole, whereby, for example, peasants with one ethos are enabled to live happily under feudal lords who have a different ethos.[112]

Here Bateson betrays a yearning, which he shared with Mead, to find some ultimate coherence even in his own 'enormous and confused' culture. What then explained not cohesion, but the reverse, fragmentation, such as he saw all around him in the international system? To answer this, Bateson considered what might make schismogenesis go wrong. For example, what might make complementarity lose its 'dynamic equilibrium' and run out of control, leading not to mutual recognition but mutual estrangement; or, hypothesizing a different kind of 'schismogenesis', not complementary but 'symmetrical' or competitive, what might drive healthy, emulative competition into hostility?[113] The international system of Europe, which had seemed in reasonable equilibrium for much of the nineteenth century, had broken down, he thought, because patterns of 'complementary' schismogenesis – principally, mutually beneficial trade – had been overborne by patterns of 'symmetrical' schismogenesis, or international rivalry. That in part had been a result of domestic efforts to build 'complementary' schismogenesis among classes and ideologies at home by bonding them against an external enemy – a rewording of a standard Marxist analysis of 'imperialist war'. Unlike the Marxists, however, Bateson saw these processes not as intrinsic qualities of the capitalist system, but as to some extent unconscious processes that could be altered simply by one becoming conscious of them. As he wrote in the anthropological journal Man in 1935: 'It is possible that those responsible for the policy of classes and nations might become conscious of the processes with which they are playing and cooperate in an attempt to solve the difficulties.' However: 'This . . . is not very likely to occur since anthropology and social psychology lack the prestige necessary to advise; and, without such advice, governments will continue to react to each other's reactions rather than pay attention to circumstances.' It was that old jealousy of the economists again.[114]

Despite this gloomy conclusion, Bateson was sufficiently well connected at Cambridge (and correspondingly self-confident) to make a stab at offering advice. His ideas about applying 'symmetrical schismogenesis' to the European situation arose from conversations he had had with Alan Barlow, a senior civil servant, married to one of William Bateson's students, Nora, herself something of a Cambridge aristocrat as the grand-daughter of Charles Darwin.[115] He cooked up an elaborate piece of psychological manipulation – a premonition of the 'black propaganda' to which he would succumb in the Second World War – 'to give [Mussolini] a nervous breakdown' by aggravating his schismogenic relationship both to his own advisers and to his enemies, and thus 'push him further into war so that his downfall is assured'. 'It's all very fiendish,' he admitted in a letter to Mead, 'but I really believe it is worth attempting.' Through a Fabian friend, Amber Blanco White, he tried to get an audience with Lloyd George; when that failed, he sought a hearing from the Foreign Office through an international banker he met at High Table at St John's.[116] One can imagine the reception this young anthropologist – without experience in foreign affairs and without even any formal psycho-logical training – would have received in 1935 for his proposed exercise in psychological warfare some years before a real war offered a proper warrant for it. Sadly, he concluded to Mead:

> We are just a little too late all along the line. I don't mean you and me – that will probably come out all right or so I still trust; I mean sociology and psychology. If we had the products of ten years work of a dozen first class people on the lines we now know, schismogenesis squares strict sociology and the rest, we could almost certainly even now clean up the mess – indeed if that knowledge were general the mess would be inconceivable. But we just haven't got it.[117]

There was only so far his connections and his privileged self-belief could take him. With Mead – 'you and me' – he was on safer ground. They had spent long periods together in the summers of 1934 and 1935 and plighted their troth. With the international situation so clouded – and impervious to their own interventions – the call of the 'natives' had again sounded. At the end of January 1936, Bateson boarded ship for the Dutch East Indies; the plan was to rendezvous with Mead in Singapore, where they were to be married, and then set off together for Bali.

*   *   *

A few weeks before she boarded her own ship, Mead had just met the man who would become the leading candidate to succeed Bateson as her fourth husband. Geoffrey Gorer was eerily like Bateson in some ways and crucially unlike him in others. He had been a contemporary of Bateson's both at Charterhouse and at Cambridge, where Gorer had read Classics and Modern Languages. Like Bateson, he had picked up some anthro-pology at Cambridge when it was still marginal and unfashionable.[118] But while in conventional respects an insider like Bateson, Gorer was also self-consciously more of an outsider – Jewish (the son of an antiques dealer who went down with the *Lusitania*, leaving Gorer independently wealthy), bisexual and more ideologically and aesthetically estranged from his own culture than Bateson.[119]

Like many young intellectuals coming to maturity in the slump, his keen personal and aesthetic sensitivities had been wounded by the misery and ugliness he perceived around him. The Puritan tradition, modern urban life and the grim homogeneity of the mass-produced society had, he felt, conspired to make England 'the most hag-ridden and almost the ugliest country (architecturally) in the world'.[120] Where some might have retreated from this horror into an aesthetic or literary redoubt, Gorer was moved to address it, either for selfish reasons – 'I cannot myself be happy when surrounded by unhappiness' was his self-diagnosis in 1935 – or out of guilt, as Mead thought. Whatever his motives, his reaction was common enough among privileged young Cambridge graduates in the early 1930s.[121]

Gorer had already developed a clear explanation for what ailed England (and 'Western civilization' more broadly) by the time his first book, on the ideas of the Marquis de Sade, was published in 1934. It was an explanation that would, essentially, frame his approach to the English throughout his life. His twin guides were, as for so many of his generation, Freud and Marx, and together they brought him roughly to the position of the neo-Freudians. From Freud he took the fundamental psychodynamic assumptions: that the driving forces in humans were sex and death, that these forces could not be denied but had to be expressed in some form, either constructively or destructively, and that modern civilization was predicated on the repression of these forces, leading to neurosis and occasional catastrophic outbreaks of destructiveness. But in the spirit of the 1930s he saw Freud as essentially a prewar figure with 'an unjustifiable pride in European civilization'.[122] From Marx, therefore, he took the critical view that modern civilization could be transformed – up until the late 1930s, he still believed, by a socialist revolution[123] – to provide constructive outlets for these pent-up psychic forces.

Gorer's idiosyncratic refinement of these ideas about human motivation sheds further light on his motives in approaching his own culture. Although he believed that the most natural and most constructive psychodynamic outlet was sex, Gorer's personal view was that sex, 'though pleasant', provided 'no such lasting ecstasy and final solution' as the likes of Freud and D.H. Lawrence would have us suppose. Another effective outlet was what he would come to see as 'mastery', which could be destructive (expressed as aggression) or could be guided into constructive channels, including mastery over objects and ideas. Gorer's compulsion to diagnose others' unhappiness could be seen as a constructive form of 'mastery-over' others by means of intellectual work, one that fits with his gentlemanly sense of *noblesse oblige*. Or, as Mead put it in a kinder moment, 'he is happy and he is a deviant, and so it is the 90% of the world who are different and unhappy and should have things fixed up for them'.[124]

Whatever his motives, the combination of a strong antipathy to the society in which he grew up and a personal mission to address its ills through close study presented a paradox: how to study his society without being contaminated by it. At first Gorer dallied in Paris, Berlin and Florence with a literary, political and largely homosexual crowd; tried and failed to become a man of letters, like so many others of his generation seeking to emulate his friend W.H. Auden; then, almost on a whim, he essayed quasi-ethnographic, quasi-touristic expeditions to West Africa and Southeast Asia. In Bali he glimpsed utopia for the first time: the Balinese, he felt, had found the near-perfect formula for eliminating 'fear, guilt and duty' (the three predominating neuroses of his own civilization) by channelling their energies into the constructive outlets of sex, art and 'creativeness of any sort'.[125]

Towards the end of 1935 he moved on to America in order to try an approach to something more like his own culture[126] (without being too much like it), and here his path crossed with that of Margaret Mead, who would turn out to be the perfect partner for his quest. Gorer had read her books, including *Sex and Temperament*, and had been attracted by their analytical, 'scientific' approach, and when he arrived in New York on an exploratory visit he put out feelers to see if he could arrange a meeting. Mead was about to sail for Bali and said she wasn't interested, but Benedict, who had read and enjoyed Gorer's account of his West African travels, *Africa Dances*, told her not to pass up the chance of a new recruit: 'if he wants to meet you it means he wants to be an anthropologist seriously, and you *must* see him, because he has a wonderful eye, and would do magnificent work.' So they had lunch, during which Mead tried to persuade him that anthropology offered methods 'better than the combination of journalism and fine writing which he had been using', assuming that it was a one-off chance to sell him her trade.[127] In the event she got more than she bargained for from the meeting. Bateson cabled her to put off her departure for a month until he was ready to join her, and as a result she spent several weeks very much in Gorer's company. She found him immediately compelling. He had that gentlemanly courtesy that she liked in Bateson, and as with Bateson it overlay the warm, sympathetic personality that they had concluded she and Bateson shared – in the language of the squares, they were 'Southerners', as opposed to Fortune's cold, controlling 'Northerner'. But Gorer was more expressive than Bateson and in that sense still more like Mead – an 'excitor', in their private language, though with a moralizing self-righteousness that Mead found alternately amusing and alarming, an outrage at 'things with capital letters such as Christianity and Race Prejudice and War' and an impulse to put them right.[128]

They talked endlessly, sharing their different obsessions – Mead serving up doses of anthropological method and psychoanalysis, teaching him the private language of the 'squares', Gorer hitting back with his views on art, religion and clairvoyance, and his Balinese experiences. It annoyed her that he was so patronizing about America, in that upper-class English way. He took her to a striptease show, with which he had developed a fascination, and against which she warned him: 'if one sits in New York and goes to burlesques, one's picture of the country is pretty odd.' But the rapid give-and-take of ideas – the 'very easy quick type of communication' into which they fell so naturally and which continued for the rest of their lives – was exhilarating; it is impossible to be sure, but the feeling was probably intensified by sex.[129] She always spoke of him as one of the smartest men she knew, and to her that meant one of the sexiest too. For his part he was also smitten, at least intellectually; Mead complained that he was not susceptible enough to sex, or even to 'falling in love'.[130] He had tired of his status as an amateur, roving restlessly around the globe, the poor little rich boy with a social conscience; anthropology – science – offered him a handle on the world, 'a discipline'[131] in both senses of the word, which the rest of the world might respect. As her postponed date of departure neared, they stood back to consider what had passed between them. 'I am not sure yet exactly what you have done for me or to me, but I know it's a great deal,' he wrote. 'My meeting you has been one of the really important things in my life.' 'You know that this encounter has meant as much to me as it has to you. God knew what He was about when He kept me from sailing in December,' she replied.[132] She left happy, knowing that Gorer had promised to stay behind in New York and undergo a course of instruction with Benedict. But she had neglected to tell him that she was planning to marry Bateson en route, and when he found out from Benedict two months later, it nearly spoiled for him what he had seen as their joint enterprise. Perhaps Gorer was not as unsusceptible as he pretended.[133]

*   *   *

Mead had missed a lot while she was in New Guinea in 1931–3; she missed more while she was in Bali in 1936–9, and she knew it. The debates of the early 1930s as to the purposes and values of social science continued and intensified. The idealism of the early New Deal wore off but as the threat of authoritarianism abroad mounted – from Mussolini, Hitler, Stalin – fewer social scientists hid behind 'objectivity' and there was more consensus about the value of democracy. Differences remained between 'nervous liberals', who still worried about the reliability of the American people and wanted to stiffen their backbone with propaganda and other means of social control, and the more idealistic 'purposive' social scientists, who saw themselves as contributing to the building of democracy. To some extent, however, the counterposing of 'totalitarianism' to democracy made it harder to argue for the use of the manipulative methods associated with the former even in defence of the latter.[134] On the other hand, the threat of 'totalitarianism' made it difficult even for arm's-length Boasians to keep their distance from domestic politics.

Ruth Benedict was no exception. After Boas's retirement in 1937, she took over much of his self-appointed role as the conscience of the discipline. She signed up to a variety of causes, including anti-fascist relief efforts in Spain and Austria, the defence of democracy in Latin America and the defence of academic freedom at home. Reluctantly, in large part because she knew Boas wanted her to, she agreed to write a popular book against racism.[135] In her own anthropological thinking she was becoming more 'purposive', now thinking about 'the social conditions and types of social sanctions that make possible a sense of freedom', both for the group and for the individual. What conditions best enable a culture to assess its own needs? What conditions best empower individuals to chart their own path within a culture? Without abandoning cultural relativism, she was playing up her ethical non-relativism as an expert participant in her own culture.[136] Yet she retained her suspicions of organized politics. 'A dozen different Leagues and Commissions for Democracy in one form or another want me to work with them,' she wrote to Mead in 1939, 'and it's mostly time wasted when I do; oftenest I don't.'[137] In these increasingly polarized times, it was hard to be anti-fascist without being at least implicitly pro-communist, and this Benedict and Mead were both determined not to be. 'It's true enough that there are a few more things – at least in the Russian ideal – with which one sympathises,' Mead wrote to Benedict at the same time, 'still I think there is less danger in repudiating those few bits than in giving any aid and comfort to the theory that one must be either a communist or a fascist – don't you?'[138]

When Boas retired, Benedict did not replace him at the head of the Columbia anthropology department. The Columbia administration were not yet ready for a woman in a position of leadership. Instead they imported Ralph Linton, who had been developing a rival school of 'culture and personality' at Wisconsin. Linton fitted awkwardly into Boas's department. He had initially intended to study with Boas, after his demobilization following the First World War, but had put the old man off by appearing for their first meeting in his military uniform. He was an aggressive womanizer: a 'man's man', in the language of his own culture, one of those domineering 'Northerners' in the language of the squares. Instead of working together, he and Benedict formed separate poles in the department. Linton ran a seminar with the neo-Freudian Abram Kardiner, similar in purpose to the informal group Mead and Benedict had created with Erich Fromm: ethnographers would file through, describing cultures, and a psychoanalyst (in this case Kardiner) would provide a Freudian 'diagnosis'.[139] Seen from the outside, there was not all that much to differentiate Linton and Kardiner's enterprise from Mead and Benedict's. Many contemporaries regarded them as part of the same movement.[140] And, indeed, Kardiner funded an anthropologist, Cora Du Bois, trained in the Boasian tradition at Barnard and Berkeley, to do fieldwork in the Dutch East Indies in support of his work.[141] But despite the evident similarities, Benedict and her students were horrified by this new manifestation of 'culture and personality', which seemed a step backwards from their own formulations. There was a strong gendered charge to this difference – a contrast between Benedict's idea of culture as a creative search for a 'design for living' (an idea coded as feminine in their own culture) and Linton and Kardiner's idea of culture as a psychological adaptation to 'basic needs' determined by the hard facts of the material environment (an idea similarly coded as male).[142] This gendering was intensified further by overt sexual conflicts – Linton and Kardiner were repelled by Benedict's love for women, Benedict by their hyper-masculinity – aggravated by Linton and Kardiner's more orthodox Freudianism, with its grim view of homosexuality.[143] (This put Cora Du Bois, a more-or-less undisguised lesbian, in some tricky situations.) It was also politicized – Linton didn't like even the limited extent to which Benedict committed herself to the Left. As Benedict wrote to Mead, he had informed the Social Science Research Council that 'we're a bunch of reds in the department, and he's told others that he has the names of the "communists" in the department. Well, there *are* some communists, and some who have been communists and now are out. Everything is dynamite these days.'[144]

Among Benedict's chief tasks while Mead was away was to take charge of Geoffrey Gorer, and to make sure that the febrile political atmosphere didn't carry *him* away, vulnerable as he was to political delusions of grandeur. Immediately after Mead's departure, Benedict set Gorer to work on the handbook on psychological leads for fieldworkers, both as a crash course in anthropological method and in hopes of getting him interested in doing some fieldwork of his own. Unfortunately at the same time Gorer fell into the hands of John Dollard. Since the Hanover conference Dollard had been moving away from 'culture and personality' towards a more psychiatric perspective. Sapir was in decline – he would die prematurely in 1939 – and this had robbed Dollard of a crucial relativist influence. More depressingly, he had done some important fieldwork of his own among blacks in the American South and become fatalistic about the opportunities for social and cultural change. Increasingly he turned to thinking about ways of reconciling individuals to the culture they found, reducing their 'frustration', which he felt led to nothing more constructive than 'aggression'.[145] Gorer found that these 'frustration-aggression' hypotheses chimed with his own gloomy diagnosis of the unhappiness of the English. He talked seriously about taking up a post at the Yale Institute of Human Relations, where Dollard worked, 'to do a fairly novel survey of American culture as manifested in adolescents – Growing up in New Haven, if you like'. Dollard was trying hard (for the time being, unsuccessfully) to get Gorer to undergo psycho-analysis with his Yale colleague Earl Zinn – something Mead and Benedict typically resisted, as too much like brainwashing.[146] Again, there was a sexual or temperamental dynamic at work here; Mead thought of Dollard as one of those bullying 'Northerners' she generally disliked and who saw aggression everywhere because he had so much stored up within himself. (It didn't help that Dollard was now working closely with Linton and Kardiner.) That was the problem with Freudianism: it was too obsessed with a certain Western type of aggressive male personality, leaving no room, for example, for people who just wanted to plough their own furrow.[147]

Less seriously – but even more to Mead's distress – Gorer worked up a little book on American culture based on his personal fascination with burlesque, published in 1937 as *Hot Strip Tease*. As Mead fumed to him, this was hardly advancing his claim to scientific credibility:

> I can't see how a serious student of 'Our culture' can think that the publication of a book with a title like that is congruent with future work in cooperation with institutions like the Institute of Human Relations at Yale. You already have to live down – from the narrow academic point of view – everything you have written, for assorted and dissimilar reasons of subject matter, treatment, political views and an acceptance of extra-sensory phenomena. Isn't that enough, plus the fact that your training has been unorthodox and that you have been – from the stand-point of the underpaid academic man – disgustingly successful, and have

had much too interesting a life, without adding to your handicaps a book called *Hot Strip Tease*.[148]

But she was thinking of herself as well. A partial use of her and Bateson's methods, applied casually to one bizarre fragment of American culture, would only do damage in the long run:

> you can't have applied the rigorous methods which make for scientific work. In Naven, after doing the whole culture, Gregory takes one small bit and analyzes it in the light of the whole. But in Hot Strip Tease, you take one small bit and analyze it – or so you describe it – trying to wring the implications of the whole from the bit. This is something which I think ultimately we should be able to do, and something that it is necessary to do, but we can only develop our methodology by being sure what the whole is, the first few times we try it . . . the whole thing is dangerous.[149]

Such gibes hit Gorer in a sensitive spot. He was contrite, and very much against his instincts he agreed to take on an exercise in real fieldwork, which involved a few gruelling months in the Himalayas studying the Lepcha people. He wrote candidly to Mead in Bali in February 1937:

> I am not, I think, an ethnologist pur sang; my preoccupations still are, as I told you[,] predominantly concerned with my own culture, and the remedy of our present discontents; but the revelation of the concept of culture and personality which I received through you and Ruth has seemed to me so important, that, for the last few months, I have been devoting nearly all my thoughts to it; and now I am putting myself into the 'ethnological situation', less perhaps to find out about the Lepchas than to try and find out what it is like to be an ethnologist . . . In short, I am trying to find out 'by being my own rabbit' what is the value of ethnology for extrapolating into our own culture.[150]

Gorer hated his time in the Himalayas. He claimed to have contracted both back problems from a fall and an intestinal disorder: what he called 'sprue', nowadays known as coeliac disease. In truth he had neither the physical nor the intellectual appetite for the hard work that ethnographic research involved.[151] Nevertheless, 'horrified by the way I had behaved' over *Hot Strip Tease*, he tried hard to keep his intuitions 'rigorously within bounds' and write a serious book, published in 1938 as *Himalayan Village*.[152]

This show of good faith went some way to mollifying Mead, but Gorer's analysis of the Lepcha still bore the marks of his simplistically Freudian understanding of 'civilization'. Much as he disliked the Himalayas, he was fond of the Lepcha: like the Balinese, they seemed to him a happy people, free of frustration and aggression. But they owed this to their primitiveness: due to their isolation and the terrible challenges of their mountainous kingdom, they had had to channel all of their psychic energies into 'wresting a livelihood from their environment'. While this struggle kept them uncompetitive and pacific, it left no energy for them to develop *out* of their primitiveness. It also meant that they had no lessons to teach a civilized culture, where in conditions of plenty an excess rather than a deficit of 'personal and national aggression' was the chief problem to be resolved.[153] Mead was irritated at this lingering influence – from Marx as much as from Freud – of old-fashioned social evolutionism. Gorer's obsession with the problems of 'civilization' meant that 'you are really asking all over again the old question, how did they get from *them* to *us*, only you have phrased it the other way around, *why didn't they get from them at least part way to us*. As you yourself point out, putting ourselves in the foreground is bound to vitiate scientific thought.' Gorer admitted that he did believe in 'unlinear development': 'I don't say that all societies must advance towards the European elaboration, but that, *if* they do advance (they may be static or declining) it will be in that direction.' As Mead feared, he had never quite swallowed the full dose of cultural relativism that the properly trained anthropologists had sucked up from Boas: he still believed that Western civilization was superior, or at least inevitable.[154]

And Gorer was back in Dollard's hands. Dollard liked *Himalayan Village*. Whereas Mead thought it too Freudian, Dollard thought it not Freudian enough – he simply didn't believe that any people, however primitive, could resolve sexual frustration so easily.[155] He was still working on Gorer to come to Yale and undergo psychoanalysis with Zinn, and Gorer was persuadable.[156] 'I'm really very excited about the stimulus-response aggression-frustration hypotheses; they seem to give answers to a great number of my present dilemmas and to open up the possibility of a psychology and sociology with [a] fairly strict and controllable scientific basis,' he wrote to Mead. Furthermore, he vastly preferred Dollard's clinical approach to taking life histories from individuals to the messy business of participant-observation. But he was still torn. He dallied again in London, contemplating fieldwork in Denmark ('the most successful European community I know'), but was frightened by the looming European conflict. Benedict worried that he was about to lapse back into his amateurish lifestyle.[157] 'I still wish you could see a primitive society' like New Guinea, wrote Mead wistfully in October 1938, from New

Guinea where, as it happened, she and Bateson had moved to conclude their long spell in the field.[158]

*   *   *

As all of this busy correspondence indicates, while in Bali in the late 1930s Mead was hardly insulated from the political and ideological turbulence of the West. Her first responsibilities were, of course, to the Balinese, and to the contribution Mead felt they could make to her theoretical understanding of culture and personality. In Bali she combined her interests in child-rearing with Bateson's ideas about the importance of relationships to the culture pattern by focusing very intently on capturing parent-child relations in minute detail, using the novel aids of still and motion photography. As Bali was itself a complex and diverse culture, it was possible to move around and to sample a lot of apparently different subcultures – 'creaming the culture', as she put it[159] – in the hope that something essential could be captured about parent-child relations, an abstraction but, it was hoped, not a simplification of complexity. 'I am still not perfectly clear in my mind about the problem of tackling these complex cultures and the legitimacy of different types of cross-sectioning,' Mead wrote to Boas, aware of his sensitivities. 'But we have tried to assemble as many types of cross-sectioning as possible.'[160] She was more than ever convinced of the need for fieldwork to study whole cultures, after which one could interpret individuals within their culture, rather than Dollard's 'life history' approach which looked for the culture through the individual and lost the sense of pattern, and with it an understanding of cultural difference.[161]

But, just at the time that she was chiding Gorer for patronizing the Lepcha, she was having the same problems with the Balinese. She didn't like them, and for similar reasons to Gorer's doubts about the Lepcha. They were 'lovely creatures . . . lovely the way wild deer or birds are', but they were 'fey'. 'There is no internal strain, no conscience, no guilt, no drive, of any sort to make them awkward or maladjust, or – human.'[162] This wasn't a function of 'primitiveness': it was precisely their highly developed social structure that made their low-temperature character possible, and their culture represented a deliberate *choice* of safety and equilibrium over risk and change. But it wasn't a choice that Mead herself, reared in a rapidly changing society, could muster much sympathy for, and she found herself strangely anticipating those biases she would reprove in Gorer:

> although at the moment they may be much less unhappy than most Europeans, I continue to think that European civilization may be going

somewhere, whereas Balinese distinctly is not and never has been. They demonstrate very prettily under what conditions a fey culture can survive, by means of [an] iron-clad social system, and I am interested in documenting that, but I don't think God meant feys as culture planners . . . I don't feel that this [is] something that I would call happiness.[163]

In betraying such preferences, Mead was also yearning for home – for the happiness of a complex and rapidly changing culture such as her own, and a role for herself as a 'culture planner', something she had seen as needed for as long as she had been aware of 'cultural lag'. To us today, this again may look like anti-democratic social engineering.[164] But, while her language of planning shows more faith in collective reason and order than we tend to have in our disenchanted present, there was nothing necessarily anti-democratic about it. It was still about 'education for choice', about engendering a culture consciousness so that really existing cultural situations and their alternatives would be clear to all (something that a static culture like Bali's didn't require). 'The man in the street . . . no longer takes his social forms for granted . . . The creaking and groaning of the social structure has made him socially conscious,' she wrote in July 1939, introducing a new edition of her popular works packaged together as *From the South Seas*. It was the job of the social scientist to lay out the choices. The point of studying simple, homogeneous cultures in this context was not to advocate 'a frightened retreat to some single standard', but rather to build confidence in the possibility of culture planning: to try to find 'a more ordered heterogeneity . . . a world of interrelated and integrated values which will replace both the homogeneity of the savage and the confused and frustrating heterogeneity of the twentieth century'.[165] Or, as Benedict put it, the point of fieldwork was always to ask: 'Are there mechanisms so that the group . . . *can* pursue a common goal and what kind of a goal – and what are the consequences? Then you go on from there.'[166] Mead was anxious to go on from there.

So was Bateson. He was following European events closely and again champing at the bit to offer his insights into intercultural relationships to the powers-that-be. Not having had the Boasian training, he saw no intrinsic virtue in presenting the 'full length portrait of a culture', and he had instead the scientific conviction that the purpose of science was 'to answer problems, to elucidate principles'.[167] He was jealous of those, such as Tom Harrisson of Mass-Observation, who had remained in the thick of things.[168] In early 1938, he and Mead had agreed to move on from Bali to go back to the middle Sepik, to gather pictures and film of the Iatmul that they could use for direct comparison with their Balinese results, and then to return to Britain, where Bateson would try to get a permanent job and Benedict might be able to join them on a sabbatical.[169]

It didn't quite work out that way. En route to Britain, Mead found – after long periods of infertility and several miscarriages – that she was pregnant. The couple stopped in New York. Mead found a nice young paediatrician with psychoanalytic training, named Benjamin Spock, with whom she could plot her own child-rearing strategies. They had a lovely summer holiday with Larry Frank and his new wife, Mary, in their New Hampshire holiday home, Cloverly. They were still planning to travel onwards to England to have the baby. But time had run out: it was September 1939. Whether they liked it or not, for the foreseeable future, Mead and Bateson had returned from the natives.

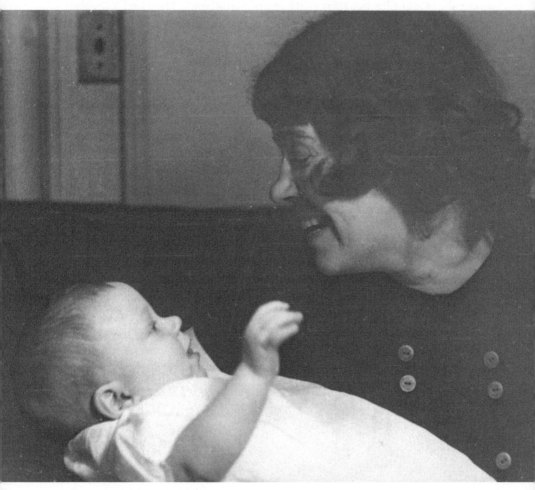

Mead and baby Cathy

CHAPTER 2

Culture Cracking for War
I. Allies (1939–44)

In the first phase of her career Margaret Mead was driven by many motives. Initially drawn to social science by her family background and by a conventional desire to 'do good', her loyalties were then broadened under the influence of the Boasian mission to explore and defend the integrity of 'primitive' peoples' cultures. In *Coming of Age in Samoa* and other popular books that followed, she used those understandings of 'primitive' cultures to comment on her own culture, increasingly convinced that a theoretically and methodologically rigorous anthropology ought to be able to shed light on cultures of any complexity. In fact, the complexity of her own culture seemed to require a greater 'culture consciousness' than was necessary for the inhabitants of 'simple, homogeneous' cultures. Rapid social change and growing social diversity had created unusual problems of 'cultural lag' – a gap between the old rules and new impulses – which only a much greater degree of self-consciousness and self-reflection could address. Awareness of the more organic choices that other cultures had made might facilitate the organizing of diversity at home, as well as raising consciousness about the great differences between one's own culture and others'. Cultural relativism did not require an ethical relativism in relation to one's own culture. But it did tend to foster in Mead and her circle an ethical commitment to a cultural framework that favoured change and diversity – 'ordered heterogeneity' – rather than a solution to 'cultural lag' that replaced an old set of norms with a new set. Such a solution was in any case congenial to her 'flapper' generation, and to Mead in particular, firmly determined as she was to preserve her personal freedom and to build her professional authority in a culture still in the grip of very narrow ideas about women's proper orientation to marriage, career and expertise.

War upset this careful balance between 'self' and 'others', and between various different selves, and it narrowed Mead's options. Most obviously it cut her off from fieldwork among 'primitive' peoples, thus threatening the basis of her authority. In order to play a more active role in the war effort – to capitalize on the enhanced prestige she had earned for anthropology in the 1930s by harnessing it to the supreme social mission of the

1940s – she would have to make sudden leaps and exaggerated claims about her expertise in 'contemporary' cultures without the reassuring dialectic that knowledgeable reference to the possibilities of 'primitive' cultures had provided. Furthermore, she could no longer work principally to her own agenda. War set its own agenda: it required patriotism, leadership, armed conflict, all firmly badged as 'masculine'. 'Choice' was no longer an option; unity was the new imperative; more order, less heterogeneity. Not all cultures could be uniformly respected – some were now enemies. Still more 'masculine', the military and government had a chain of command in a way that academia, public opinion or even the foundation world did not. Despite all these vicissitudes, Mead and other social scientists involved in the war effort had more freedom of action – and a more creative role in raising consciousness of their own culture and of others' – than is often recognized. Yet the parameters of action were fundamentally changed by war. The 'return from the natives' in wartime was a risky and controversial move, the riskiest and most controversial of Mead's entire career.

* * *

At first, though, the war was not Mead's, but Bateson's. The Germans invaded Poland on 1 September and Britain declared war two days later. This was a war that Bateson like many others had been expecting for years, and for years he had been storing up frustration at his inability to apply his expertise to avert it. Now he was determined to apply his expertise to win it. Encouraged by the British consul in New York to return home and volunteer for war work, with mixed feelings he left behind his pregnant wife and sailed almost immediately. On the voyage over, his heart sank somewhat, as Bateson reflected on his failures to dent the official mind in 1935, but on arrival he made a genuine effort to throw himself into the fray.[1] He could imagine a number of possible applications for his expertise. On the home front, he could use his ideas about schismogenesis – the tendency in any dynamic relationship to differentiate the parties – to try to reverse the tendency to differentiation and build unity instead – what he called 'zygogenesis'. This would require a close study of how communication between groups and individuals within British society actually worked in order to determine how to improve it. On the international front, the same techniques of zygogenesis might be used to reverse the tendencies of the 1930s to ever greater international tension and to build international unity, even a world federation of nations. The only problem there, Bateson hypothesized, was that while schismogenesis had a natural tendency to build up to a quasi-sexual 'release' – that is, open conflict or war – it was harder to imagine what build-up during zygogenesis might lead to. What 'total involvement' could world federation summon up? Was there sufficient satisfaction simply in tackling such a complicated activity as federalism? Getting overexcited by his sexual analogy, Bateson was connecting interpersonal relations to international relations in a way that would become paradigmatic for himself and Mead over the next decade. 'Ought we to aim at changing character structure so as to make orgasm in general unnecessary and trust to this being enough to make climax between nations unnecessary? Or would it be easier to alter the international behaviour (or the intranational) so as to provide the orgasms of total involvement? – but in some less harmful form.'[2] Here he put his finger on the key question that Gorer and Mead had wrestled with in discussing the Lepcha: was it better for the health of a society as well as its individuals to harness or dispel interpersonal tensions? With their heterodox neo-Freudian views, Mead and Bateson clearly thought the latter was possible; and now the stakes were higher – for resolving interpersonal tensions offered the prospect of resolving international tensions as well.

On the darker side, Bateson could also imagine using schismogenesis in propaganda to *increase* division where necessary, for example, in provoking tensions within German society or in rallying combatants to fight their enemies. This was where he initially tried to make his mark. Writing to E.A. Benians, the Master of his Cambridge college, St John's, shortly after his arrival, Bateson explained the application of schismogenesis to 'black' propaganda as 'a sort of emotional jiu jitsu, in which the *spontaneous* reactions of the opponent are played upon and increased to his undoing'. This would require both a study of the Germans' own propaganda, to capture their internal dynamics, and a study of the Germans' misinterpretations of British propaganda, to see how such misinterpretations might be deliberately played up to nefarious effect.[3]

But Bateson came up against a brick wall, in seeking to influence either 'black' propaganda against the Germans or 'white' propaganda to boost morale among the British. The British propaganda effort, then in the hands of a fledgling Ministry of Information (MOI), was in a very primitive state. It was partly a matter of disorganization. At the outbreak of war, MOI had scooped up hundreds of British intellectuals to manage its propaganda campaign, but had no idea what to do with them; by the time Bateson arrived people were already drifting away in disappointment. But it was also, as Bateson rightly complained, that the authorities were completely unsympathetic to anything like a 'psychological' approach. As he saw it, this was simply a matter of philistinism – an old-fashioned British preference for 'common sense' over more sophisticated techniques. He wrote splenetically to Mead at the end of September: 'The general attitude of the Foreign Office seems to have been on the lines – "That there Hitler – 'e's mad. It ain't no bloody use talkin' to 'im." Just about that – the degree of psychological sophistication that one expects in a public bar.'[4] But there was also involved, as Bateson refused to see, an old-fashioned British liberalism that was suspicious of government manipulation for any purpose, fair or foul. The MOI came under a hail of criticism in the early years of the war from a citizenry, and a free press, hostile to the very idea of a squad among them of 'snoopers'. This was an attitude that Bateson, with his strong sense of intellectual entitlement, would never fully understand, but those social scientists who stuck with the war effort in Britain learned to adjust to it, and found much greater success later in the war, by steering away from 'meddling in morale' and concentrating on instead 'explanation and publicity'.[5]

Having failed through his Cambridge connections to penetrate the MOI, Bateson turned to another, possibly more open, field of action offered by a non-governmental body, Mass-Observation (M-O). M-O was an operation that ought to have been sympathetic to Bateson. Launched a few years previously by the sociologist Charles Madge and the anthropologist Tom Harrisson, it was an early attempt to use new social-scientific techniques to give a voice to democratic public opinion that better captured its diversity and psychological complexity. Unfortunately, partly due to the more eclectic, almost aesthetic, orientation of its founders, and partly due to Harrisson's difficult personality, Bateson found working with M-O tantalizing but ultimately frustrating. Geoffrey Gorer had already clashed once or twice with Harrisson in a friendly way, criticizing the unscientific nature of his survey techniques – a case of the pot calling the kettle black, or perhaps of 'symmetrical schismogenesis', competition between similar rivals.[6] Almost immediately after arriving in England, Bateson had cabled to Mead: 'Tom Harrisson very bright unoriented welcomes theory.' By mid-October, he had begun to have doubts:

> I don't think I can really stand Mass Observation . . . Charles Madge is a charming and honest person and I like him very much – perhaps I can contrive somehow to see more of him and less of Tom. He (Tom) is of course a magnificent dynamo and gets things done, but his dynamism seems dependent on complete freedom from criticism . . . any voice that sounds like criticism, whether it arises from somebody else or from his own inside, just gets brushed aside – 'There's no time to go into that now', he says. And at the pace he goes, there *is* no time. And combined with all this, he has too much lust for success, fame, leadership and what not – and there you have the ideal culture medium for growth of Ballyhoo.

Bateson had an explanation for their personal frictions in the language of the 'squares', but as with Gorer it may not be necessary to look beyond a degree of competitiveness between two strong-minded male intellectuals who had quite similar tasks in mind:

> No – I don't think it will do, and I shall just have to go on the streets again and try to find some other niche in which to make myself useful. And it's a hellish business this looking for some sort of organisation. All the problems are so large and the amount of detail involved so enormous, that one can do nothing by oneself and so must be attached to some organised group. Mass-Observation promised almost to be the solution – and it isn't.[7]

His worst forebodings about the British lack of receptiveness seeming to have been realized, Bateson's thoughts began to turn back to America. On 7 December he applied for a permit to return, and on 8 December the best possible reason to return arrived in the form of Mary Catherine Bateson, named after her father's aunt and her mother's deceased sister but always known as Cathy.[8] While Bateson waited for a place on a ship, he continued his observation of wartime communications in Britain with a view to applying his ideas about schismo- and zygogenesis in an American context. 'And by god,' he wrote robustly to Mead in early January 1940, 'if the idea looks like working there, we will shoot it in hard over here later.'[9] He was back in the US with wife and daughter within weeks.

* * *

The story Geoffrey Gorer gave out was that when he returned from a holiday in Mexico with his mother, the day after Bateson boarded ship for England, the British authorities had already changed their minds and were advising people like him to stay in America, as he could be more useful there than at home. It nearly broke Mead's heart that Gorer stayed and Bateson didn't – 'why had you been in such a hurry,' she wrote to Bateson – but Gorer's version may have only been a half-truth. Gorer was very conscious that he was wealthy enough to dally where he chose, and his aversion to English life was hardly moderated by the threat of bombs or boring war work.[10] He had returned to America from London earlier in the year to do some research on Hollywood for John Marshall of the Rockefeller Foundation's Humanities Division – an extension of the provocative ideas about Americans' loneliness and sexual frustration and the outlets they found in popular entertainment that he had floated in *Hot Strip Tease*. In Hollywood he found a home-from-home with Mead's sister and brother-in-law, Priscilla and Leo Rosten. Back in New York he joined a study group that Marshall set up on wartime communications strategies very much along the lines that Bateson was pursuing in Britain.[11]

But that was only a part-time occupation. At a loose end, 'limp and low', as Mead told Bateson, 'sure that everything is going to turn out in the worst possible way', he decided to succumb to John Dollard's persistent efforts to get him to join the Institute of Human Relations at Yale.[12] Among other advantages, it offered him a domestic base to which he could transfer his mother from Blitz-threatened London. They settled into a household together in New Haven in September 1940. From this point on, Gorer's Freudianism, and especially his conviction of the centrality of infant training, certainly intensified. It was around this time too that he developed his interest in the work of the heterodox British Freudian Melanie Klein, which placed a heavy emphasis on the innate aggression of infants and the rage they exhibited in their interactions with their mothers, an emphasis congenial to Gorer's grim view of the vast bulk of humanity.[13] Finally he underwent his own analysis with Earl Zinn at Yale – something that Mead, Benedict, Du Bois and others of their circle with unconventional sexualities always resisted. Psychoanalysis did not, however, seem to make Gorer uncomfortable with his own sexuality, possibly because he always claimed not to care very much about sex.[14] Yet Gorer was still enjoying his freedom, and the louche life he could lead on visits to New York among the burlesque theatres and Greenwich Village bars that he had got to know on his previous visits. There is some evidence that he contracted a few intimate relationships with men, notably with a young classical scholar, Erl Olsen, who had joined the National Guard in the hope of fighting in an anti-fascist war. Olsen was killed in action in France in July 1944 and Gorer would later dedicate his book on the Americans to his memory.[15] In theory, Gorer was as morally committed to the war effort as Bateson, but in this period before America's entry into the war he was more committed to his own lack of commitment.[16]

* * *

When Mead and Bateson were reunited in January 1940, they joined a war effort that was rapidly building momentum among American intellectuals. This may seem an odd notion, given that America's entry into the war was nearly two years off, but it testifies both to their own personal sense of mission and to a wider consensus among social scientists at the time that war was coming and that social science had something vital to contribute to it. This consensus had been building, as we have seen, around the growing sense of an international threat to democracy from Nazism, a threat now realized with the advent of war and intensified after the Hitler-Stalin pact. 'Nervous liberals' and democratic social reformers drew closer together. Their convergence was a two-way street. 'Nervous liberals' came to trust their fellow citizens more; democratic social reformers felt less anxious about the dangers of 'social engineering'. There was more agreement on the need for 'values' to be taken into account in the application of social science to social problems: 'objectivity' alone was not enough. 'Nervous liberals' took on some of the Deweyan language of democracy as a tentative, experimental learning process, accepting the contrast in means as well as ends between democracy and authoritarianism. For their part, seeing the need for unity, democratic social reformers toned down their exhortations to conflict and change, preferring to see social change as something that could come naturally to Americans.[17]

As a result of this convergence, most social scientists – apart from Communists and some fellow travellers – at the end of the 1930s shared a sense of emergency that warranted a more interventionist stance. That did not mean that their differences melted away, or were not discussed; on the contrary, public debate about what *kinds* of social-scientific intervention were warranted intensified. For example, the Conference on Science, Philosophy and Religion in their Relation to the Democratic Way of Life (CSPR) was convened annually from 1939 precisely to hash out these differences; Mead and Bateson became fixtures of the conference and its annual volumes from 1940.[18] The Rockefeller Communications Seminar that Gorer attended in 1939–40 was another place where differences between instinctive social engineers and instinctive democrats were aired. The range of positions represented there gives some indication of the diversity of views still prevailing among social scientists: social engineers who took it for granted that they should back the nation's leadership 'to secure consent'; more neutral 'objectivists' (Lynd thought Gorer fell into this camp) who were 'largely content to describe what happens, with the implicit assumption that it will somehow be useful'; others with 'a more cautious appraisal of the value of science as an instrument of social reform and of scholars as intermediaries between the state and the public'; and still others like Robert Lynd who argued for an aggressively 'purposivist' espousal of democratic planning.[19] Its final report predictably took a middle-of-the-road stance that represented the consensus on the need for 'two-way communication' between people and government and for 'intelligent consent' in democracy.[20]

* * *

Among those palpably affected by the change of tone brought on by the European war was Ruth Benedict. As she had taken on more of Boas's responsibilities, she had become more closely engaged with contemporary American politics, but something had continued to hold her back: the relativism that demanded equal respect for all cultures, the relativism that she hoped would make room for more nonconformist personalities in her own culture, the fear that politics was intrinsically anti-diversity, intolerant, normative. But as the threat of Victorianism faded, and the threats to democracy mounted, she had begun to move 'beyond relativity'.[21] She found the outbreak of war deeply troubling, and personally disruptive; her plan for a sabbatical year with Mead and Bateson in England in 1939–40 had to be dropped at short notice. Instead she spent the year in Southern California, where her sister Margery lived, writing the popular book on racism that she felt she owed Boas. Over the course of that year she found a new peace, a new partner, Ruth Valentine, and a new agenda.[22]

The advent of war highlighted for Benedict the problem of aggression. As we have seen, a number of different positions were being taken around her on this question. The more orthodox Freudians saw aggression either as an innate feature of humanity or as a necessary product of civilization, generated, as Dollard argued, by the 'frustrations' that civilization necessarily imposed. Mead's critique of Dollard was that although, as a Quaker, he was nominally a pacifist, temperamentally he was a 'Northerner' and inclined to see aggression everywhere, a tendency stoked by his Freudianism. Gorer's variant on Dollard's position was that the psychic energy that manifested itself as aggression could as easily manifest itself in other ways: 'mastery' or creativity or sex. Mead had complained that Gorer overlooked the possibility that, depending on their cultural training, humans might just accept a low-energy state – although she conceded that this came at a cost to the diversity and excitement that marked her own culture. Under the pressure of class and race conflict and now of war, both Mead and Benedict were coming to see that their relativist dependence upon 'primitive' cultures with different character structures that didn't require aggression was of diminishing usefulness – and possibly even dangerous. Western culture *was* diverse and exciting, but also aggressive, and although its character structure *could* be changed slowly, its aggression was an imminent danger. So they turned to consideration of 'social inventions' – political interventions – that might minimize the dangers of aggression more immediately.[23]

During her time in California and in the following year, resuming her growing responsibilities at Columbia, Benedict laid out a programme of political interventions that might address both the international and the domestic problems of aggression, culminating in her Anna Howard Shaw lectures at Bryn Mawr College in 1941 – never published but meant to provide the spine of a new book that would go 'beyond relativity'.[24] In her

writings in this period she frankly avowed a preference for 'social cohesion' – an attribute, she noted, that was appreciated more in wartime than
in peace – and prescribed 'societies where nonaggression is conspicuous'
as models. To some extent shadowing Mead and Bateson's thinking about
the mutually reinforcing qualities of relationships within cultures, she
identified the crucial factor making for such societies as 'social orders in
which the individual by the same act and at the same time serves his own
advantage and that of the group': what she called high 'synergy'. This was
easy for primitive societies, made up of a small number of homologous
units, but it could be managed in complex, modern societies as well, so
long as units were made interdependent; it was 'a problem of making the
separate services compatible with self-interest'. In complex, modern societies this was, explicitly, a problem for the State: for democratic planning.
'The problem is one of social engineering,' she suggested, principally
towards securing greater equality. Although it was possible to imagine
complex, modern societies based on inequality (but mutual responsibility), in the present circumstances what Western societies needed in
order to address the problem of aggression was more equality on political,
economic and racial grounds in order to foster that crucial sense of interdependence. 'Synergy', in other words, was to achieve what Bateson had
sought through 'zygogenesis', an ethos of common cause. Like Bateson
too, Benedict connected 'synergy' at the domestic level with 'synergy' at
the international level – nations had to learn to approach each other with
a sense of interdependence just as individuals did. 'Small scale or large,
the fundamental condition of peace is federation for mutual advantage.'[25]

On one level, all of this is unexceptional. Many liberals and socialists in
America around 1940 were arguing for democratic planning, social equality
and world federation. But this was Ruth Benedict, who a decade earlier had
been fighting shy of politics, trying to keep people's options open, relying
on the infinite realms of possibility indicated by cultural diversity around
the world, and suggesting at most for America more pluralism and less
social engineering. 'Education for choice' had been Mead's slogan. Now
Benedict was saying explicitly that education for choice was not enough.
In her race book she wrote, in what was surely a rebuke to herself and to
Mead: 'The fatal flaw in most arguments which would leave to the schools
the elimination of race conflict is that they propose education *instead of*
social engineering.'[26] She still thought education for choice was crucial, to
ensure that people can 'genuinely actualize their own personal selves', but
she now thought that it was equally important to 'organize the social order
so that group interests do not conflict but mutually reinforce one another'.[27]

* * *

53

Thus Mead, Bateson and Benedict had all registered similar influences that inflected their thinking more or less subtly, yet they did not all act in quite the same way. Benedict remained in the background, thinking, writing, lecturing, still sticking principally to her 'science'. Mead and, especially, Bateson threw themselves more actively into the war effort. This was partly a matter of circumstance. Mead had her museum job to return to, but Bateson was unemployed, immensely frustrated by his British humiliations and burning to act. Mead saw an opportunity to cement her relationship to Bateson – which had undeniably been bruised by his absence during Cathy's first month – by working alongside him, and indeed these years before America's entry into the war formed their last close period of collaboration.[28]

Fortunately for Bateson, the growing consensus among liberal intellectuals behind a more interventionist stance provided him with multiple opportunities for action after his return from Britain in early 1940. Psychologists and sociologists, in particular, with their interest in the domestic scene, focused on the question of 'national morale'. The very phrase tells us something about the reorientation of intellectual opinion. Progressive social scientists had since the First World War been suspicious of 'propaganda'. A number of them had formed the Institute for Propaganda Analysis (IPA) in 1937 as a democratic counterbalance to what Robert Lynd called 'pressure agencies secretly grinding private axes'. In 1940 IPA began to fall apart. Too many of its members wished to drop its oppositional stance and begin preparing for a war against fascism. Some of these dissenters joined the psychological branch of a new organization, floated by the wealthy art historian Arthur Upham Pope in the summer of 1940, called the Committee for National Morale. At the same time, Mead and Frank set up their own Society for the Study of Personality and Culture – really just a mailing list of neo-Freudian social scientists eager in an 'emergency situation' to apply 'pure' science to '[t]he problem of how to preserve morale, yet retain balance and objectivity, how to keep up enthusiasm but prevent hysteria'. At Harvard the sociologists Talcott Parsons and Edward Hartshorne formed yet another morale committee under the umbrella of a Harvard faculty group grandiosely named American Defense.[29]

Mead and Bateson spent the summer of 1940 with the Franks at Cloverly in New Hampshire. They also had some new companions, the English teenagers Philomena and Claudia Guillebaud, the daughters of Bateson's economist friend Claude Guillebaud, who had been evacuated to the US for safety, as well as visits from their New Hampshire neighbours Robert and Helen Lynd and Gardner and Lois Murphy. Larry Frank put them in touch with Arthur Upham Pope and soon Bateson was working full time as secretary to the Committee for National Morale: 'fifteen hours a day,' Mead wrote to his mother, 'in the center of the planning . . . living on a thin frayed edge of excitement for he has had very little experience of big heavy pressure offices and lots of tiring conferences and deliberations.'[30]

What did this work involve? Like most of these organizations, the Committee for National Morale sprang out of a need to do something when there was nothing yet to be done. Interventionist intellectuals were highly frustrated at the apparent apathy of the isolationist American public, and infuriated by the stubborn resistance of their own Communist and fellow-travelling friends. The first task, then, was to engage the public's interest. Beyond this, the need was to find ways to focus public attention on the struggle against Hitler. Opinion, however, differed as to how necessary or difficult these tasks were. Talcott Parsons, for example, in this instance falling into the 'nervous liberal' camp, harped on the 'anomie' and 'disorganization' besetting the American public and the need for strong 'elite' or government action to offset them.[31] Bateson was not immune to such feelings himself. He had his pent-up frustrations to cope with, but beyond that, 'being English', as he said (or upper-crust English as he should have said), he knew that he had a greater tendency to authoritarianism than Mead and others reared in a democratic tradition. As he wrote to the pioneer American multiculturalist Horace Kallen at the height of his frustration in the spring of 1940:

Being English, perhaps I am less frightened of authoritarianism than you. Certainly, so far as authoritarianism in science is concerned, while I occasionally stub my toes against it and wish that there were less of it, I certainly would not abolish it even if I could. The most I would do would be to ensure so far as possible that authority should be entrusted only to first rate people. My objection is not to hierarchies as such, but only to hierarchies with stupid inferior people at their head . . . I therefore think that the desirable course for this country is towards more centralisation, more authoritarianism, and less internal conflict . . . I do think that as efficient and as civilised an autocracy as can be devised should be put there as soon as possible – and incidentally I am not optimistic about the likelihood of this.[32]

In practice, however, Mead persuaded him that his own understanding of culture required him to work with Americans like an American rather than like an Englishman. That is, as he had argued in his discussion of schismogenesis, a whole culture could only bond in ways compatible with the ways that individuals and families bonded in that culture. A type of hierarchy imposed from above or outside would be fruitless, indeed counterproductive.[33]

Bateson and Mead therefore picked up the threads that they had left dangling when they left for Bali in 1936 – the clues that schismogenesis and neo-Freudian understandings of infant training had provided as to how even the most complex, modern societies could be understood in terms of relationships – and tried hastily to tie them together and connect them to possible wartime applications. If much of this work proceeded on a fairly abstract plane, it must be remembered, first, that there were no immediate practical applications, and second, that Bateson knew almost nothing about America. He had not so much as set foot in the United States before 1939. His presence there was now involuntary. Besides, his intellectual tendencies were abstract and theoretical. He continued to seek a general theory of culture in terms of relationships, as well as ways to act upon the relationships characteristic of a specific culture in order to achieve maximum unity. Any individual relationship could be a clue to that general theory. Philomena Guillebaud remembered those early summer evenings of the war in Cloverly taken up with screenings of the cine film Mead and Bateson had brought back from Bali – she was proud to be allowed to set up the projector – as the assembled company of social scientists scrutinized the way mothers cradled and nursed their babies, the way children related to each other and to their parents.[34] The Guillebaud sisters were also themselves under scrutiny: Mead and Bateson watched them closely to see how these English girls interacted with their American peers and with adults as well as with each other. As Philomena recalled: 'There were many, many cases when I would catch Margaret and Gregory sort of cocking an eyebrow at each other because one of us had said something which was interesting.' In fact, Cloverly was a kind of living laboratory for the study of Anglo-American family relationships – in addition to the Guillebauds, there was the Mead-Bateson relationship itself, and their own relationship with baby Cathy and her British nanny.[35]

Over the course of 1940 and 1941 Bateson and Mead strove to find ways to 'explain' a culture in abstractions that were both theoretically satisfying to themselves and of potential use to the war effort. It was only now that they began to talk about 'national character'.[36] This usage represented a significant shift from the 'configuration' or 'pattern' or 'ethos' that had dominated their discourse in the 1930s, not only recognizing that in wartime conditions the cultures they were studying were in fact nations (Britain, America, Germany), but also more fully incorporating the neo-Freudian emphasis on 'ego' or 'character' formation in infancy and childhood. While this was a natural shift under the circumstances, it involved some dangerous confusions and oversimplifications that would store up trouble for the future. 'National character' had by 1940 already had a long, slippery history as a popular way to sum up a nation's 'soul' or 'mind'; in this guise it often purported not to be a simplification or an abstraction but an essence or even a totality. Benedict had warned against this slippage in *Patterns of Culture* but she had also made use of it to popularize her own idea of 'pattern'. However, while 'pattern' and 'ethos' were themselves abstractions, they were meant only to be frameworks into which other cultural components (for example, different temperaments) could be fitted, and on which other frameworks could be superimposed, as Bateson had done in *Naven* (showing how ethos interacted with cognitive and social structures) and Mead had done in *Cooperation and Competition* (showing how character structure interacted with social and economic structures). Now Bateson and Mead were reliant on the one abstraction – 'character' – to stand for the whole culture. Furthermore, they were assuming that this one abstraction could be treated as uniform to all intents and purposes across the whole of a complex, modern nation.

Even at this early stage, their most sympathetic fellow social scientists were concerned about these leaps. At the 1941 Conference on Science, Philosophy and Religion, in her first systematic presentation of their new ideas, Mead employed 'an integrating system of values' that took the character structure 'as almost an abstract synonym for the culture as a whole'. The Harvard anthropologist Clyde Kluckhohn – while commending the 'rigorous' and 'holistic' approaches 'which students of non-literate societies have perforce had to maintain' – nevertheless wondered whether they could be quite so easily carried over to the study of complex, modern societies with their 'class and regional sub-cultures': 'Can one properly speak of one "integrating system of values" for New England and the Southwest, for the members of the C.I.O. and the farmers of the Middle West?'[37] A few months later the social psychologist Gardner Murphy voiced similar doubts. Again querying the 'bizarre' degree of 'uniformity and stereotypy' assumed across the culture, he also doubted whether the character structure as inculcated in childhood was enough to explain behaviour: did not, for example, economic conditions experienced in adulthood also affect behaviour, sometimes decisively?[38] Bateson and Mead's response to these criticisms was to point to the emergency. Since they were narrowing their focus only to those aspects of personality and culture relevant to nation-level attitudes and institutions (the army, the political leadership, national allies and enemies, war aims), it was appropriate to think in terms of 'national character', a necessarily more 'thin and stripped' abstraction than some previous formulations but the one relevant to the current crisis. And if character structure could not cope with *all* aspects of behaviour – although Mead and Bateson did insist that all aspects of culture at least 'hung together', so character structure must be connected in some way to everything else – nevertheless it offered clues to some of the most important aspects of behaviour relevant to war which could be used in propaganda.[39]

'Instead of despairing in face of the fact that nations are highly differentiated, we shall take the dimensions of that differentiation as our clues to the national character' was Bateson's alternative approach.[40] By 'dimensions of that differentiation' he meant the characteristic relationships that members of a culture formed, especially in childhood, and then exhibited in manifold ways in later life, as he had hypothesized in describing schismogenesis, that style of relationship he took to be the 'highest common factor' of a nation's character. Relationships, he had argued previously, could be 'symmetrical' (that is, competitive) or 'complementary' (relations such as 'dominance-submission', 'exhibitionism-spectatorship' or 'succorance-dependence', all of which played a part in parent-child relations). Now drawing on his own understanding of British culture, Mead's of American culture, and the émigrés Kurt Lewin and Erik Erikson's of German culture, as well as a series of 'verbatim recorded interviews of individuals from different nationality background', he began to think about the different forms these relationships took in the different cultures. Both Britain and America had strong elements of symmetrical as well as complementary relationships. Morale-building required a channelling of these competitive elements outwards, suggesting, thought Bateson, that Allied propagandists shouldn't attempt to cover up wartime failures or reverses, but rather use them to stimulate renewed effort. Differences between Britain and America in their complementary relationships, however, required a modulation of this strategy between the two nations: 'A rather concentrated diet of "blood, sweat, and tears" may be good for the English; but Americans, while no less dependent upon symmetrical motivation, cannot feel their oats when fed on nothing but disaster.' In contrast, in Germany 'the community is chiefly organized on the basis of a complementary hierarchy in terms of dominance-submission', which was best fed with a diet of unrelenting triumphs, as evidenced in their characteristic propaganda about overwhelming victories.[41]

Plumbing the depths of human motivation in this way thus offered extraordinary new opportunities for social engineering, for good or ill. Drawing on the ideas of Erich Fromm, Mead thought that Western cultures were peculiarly susceptible to this kind of manipulation – and she saw this as a problem as much as an opportunity. In Western cultures, her argument ran, people's sense of self – their 'ego' – was substantially shaped in childhood by their 'introjection' of parental values in the form of a conscience or what Freud called the 'superego'. The internal struggle that this entailed for the growing individual – between their drives and interests and the parental conscience – made Western cultures more dynamic and unpredictable than those that relied upon other sanctions such as fear, or belief in the supernatural, or a more direct imposition of community norms, but it also left room for more manipulation of character from outside influences – for ill (as shown by the dictators) or, possibly, for good.[42] At the 1941 Conference on Science, Philosophy and Religion, Mead argued that a sense of 'moral responsibility' was a natural result of the functioning of the parental conscience in Western culture, and could be harnessed both to improve leadership and to preserve 'initiative' and 'spontaneity' in the citizenry. But Bateson was particularly – some might say unpleasantly – fascinated by the overwhelmingly formative process of 'learning how to learn', by which the very tendency to 'initiative' and 'spontaneity' could be implanted in children:

> We can either have the habit of automatically looking before we cross the street, or the habit of carefully remembering to look. Of the two I prefer the automatic, and I think that, if Dr Mead's recommendation implies an increase in rote automatism [she had not said this herself], we ought to accept it. Already, indeed, our schools are inculcating more and more automatism in such processes as reading, writing, arithmetic, and languages.[43]

There were a number of checks on this kind of manipulation which Mead, in particular, was determined to assert. First, it was important that morale-building only seek to work on those motivations that were already present in the character structure. Anything else would be counterproductive: it would lead to 'psychological conflict', would 'debase and confuse its victims'. That was the difference between morale-building and propaganda, 'those manipulative processes which act upon any and all latent attitudes regardless of whether the resonance evoked will conflict with the coherent and socially adaptive structure'. (In wartime this was figured as one of the differences between 'white' and 'black' propaganda.) What she didn't say was that this position was already a retreat from her prewar view that a healthy society might *not* align its social goals with individual character structure. Then, the tight social control of Bali had been a warning, and made her appreciate better 'the advantages of running a society at right angles to the individual life, instead of forever counting upon enlisting each citizen's major motivations to get the streets cleaned and the walls mended'. Now she was proposing – much as Benedict was with her notion of 'synergy' – to align the individual's 'major motivations' as closely as possible with social goals: an indication of how much the war emergency had changed things.[44]

But second, in her 1941 Conference statement, Mead enunciated a more complete programme for the social scientist seeking to promote social goals in a democracy. She reminded social scientists that they were *part* of their culture, not above it. They could participate as citizens in the determination of democratic goals, and then as social scientists they could propose means to those ends, but they should not – indeed, without working against the current of their own culture, they could not – impose 'blue prints' of their own. 'Direction' or 'orientation', not destination, was the furthest they could go. This was precisely the position she had taken with progressive educators in the late 1930s, when she had argued against their stipulation of society's 'needs' in favour of 'education for choice'. Bateson now endorsed this, in the very same passage where he recommended 'rote automatism', on the grounds that democratic cultures could not prescribe democratic ends by undemocratic means: 'in social manipulation our tools are people, and people learn, and they acquire habits which are more subtle and pervasive than the tricks which the blue-printer teaches them.' The blueprint would be undone by its own techniques. The Nazis, with their undemocratic goals, were freer to use whatever manipulative techniques they could devise.[45]

For all these provisos, Mead was undoubtedly moving closer to the 'nervous liberals' with whom she had openly disputed before the war. Bateson's imperious scientism was only one influence; her own sense of urgency about the war, and her fear that other, more overtly manipulative social scientists might get the jump on anthropology, were others. But she had decided to use her 'culture consciousness' to align fundamental motivations with the war effort, and in doing so she made some unlikely allies. In late 1940 she joined a group of industrial anthropologists and others interested in government work, led by Eliot Chapple, of whom she was otherwise suspicious, to found the Society for Applied Anthropology. In the 1930s Chapple and his friends had devoted themselves to helping industrialists 'adjust' their workers to achieve 'equilibrium' with the culture of the plant. Though their language was a democratic one of reciprocity, the definition of 'equilibrium' was firmly in the hands of the employers and there was no sense, as there had been in some of Larry Frank's writings, that the 'culture' needed to adjust to individuals as well as vice versa. Nevertheless, Frank had roped Chapple into the Committee for National Morale (CNM) at the same time that he had recruited Mead and Bateson. Chapple and his circle were not entirely to Mead's taste – she found them too keen to think 'in mechanical terms' that sounded 'fascistic' to non-Americans – but they were at least ready to consider wartime applications of anthropology, which the American Anthropological Association was not yet.[46] Furthermore, they seemed more savvy than Arthur Upham Pope – 'an ass,' thought Bateson – and possibly better at navigating the 'crazy business' of Washington lobbying. Mead, Bateson and Chapple had had some meetings with Washington higher-ups, though as yet to no avail.[47]

There was, in fact, a propaganda ministry in waiting from the summer of 1941, the Office of the Coordinator of Information (COI), under William 'Wild Bill' Donovan. It even had a Psychological Division including Edward Hartshorne from the Harvard morale group, with an orientation similar, and connected, to CNM. In fact, Robert Lynd had tried to persuade COI to get Bateson to run it, and some of Bateson's thinking with Erik Erikson on the psychology of Nazism was aimed at it.[48] But its early work was handicapped, as Hartshorne saw it, by 'the public feeling of hostility toward the term "propaganda"', as well as continuing doubt about the war itself, so it confined itself to collecting rather than 'out-giving' information. At this tentative stage it was never going to be very receptive to the more egregriously psychoanalytic analyses.[49] Both on practical and on principled grounds, Mead had already concluded, it might be easier to make headway on long-term planning for the postwar period than to try to penetrate the thick hide of a Washington bureaucracy only slowly gearing up for war.

* * *

Unlike Bateson and Gorer, Mead and Benedict always had Boas's injunctions to consider all of the world's peoples in mind. For that matter, they still had the old man himself in their lives, just about: he would die at the end of 1942, in the midst of a denunciation of racism at the Columbia University Faculty Club. The Arapesh and the Iatmul, the Kaingang and the Chukchee remained at the forefront of their thinking, even when they were writing about the Germans, Americans and British.[50] At a time when the Boasian instinct to 'social satire' was collapsing into 'social engineering' on the home front, cultural relativism *between* nations remained for them an imperative. This principle became highly problematic when applied to the enemy – Germany, Italy or Japan – but all other nations of the world, and the Axis powers themselves after the war, had to be considered principally as future allies. As Benedict had done in propounding her idea of 'synergy', so Mead took at least as much – and usually more – interest in improving communication between nations as within her own. Her adoption of the oversimplification of 'national character' for a particular culture such as that of the Americans was motivated both by her desire to apply anthropological thinking to problems of national morale and as a shorthand for enabling comparisons of – and analyses of interactions between – multiple cultures in transnational settings.[51]

Already while Bateson was still in England at the start of the war, Mead had been plotting with Larry Frank to secure Rockefeller funding for a research scheme to apply anthropological methods to the study of European nations for purposes 'which will be useful after the war'. This idea had not yet crystallized into a comparison of national characters (and ways of facilitating their interactions), but was rather a mishmash of approaches that might build anthropology into postwar planning: 'a study of European international culture, the ideas about international relations, the stereotyped roles of each country in each country's eyes, the standard conflict situations, the clichés "greatest threat to Europe since Ghenghis Khan", "Trouble in the Balkans", etc. which operate at least as much as economic forces in shaping statesmen's conclusions.'[52] This didn't work out – Frank had less clout with Rockefeller than before – and Bateson got pulled into the 'national morale' work instead. But Mead did not give up. At the end of 1940 she had drafted another plan for Frank's consideration. This now built on the 'national morale' work and asked the same sort of questions that Bateson was asking about nations in wartime – What was their response to failure? How dependent is the individual ego upon the existence of an enemy or on national prestige? – but posed instead about the European nations in peace, to manage their reconstruction. The pitch was again aimed at policymakers who might otherwise be tempted to consider reconstruction only as an economic question, whereas 'the national characters of the various peoples of Europe' would need to be taken into account to meet 'other needs of the peoples who are to live under the plan'.[53] This idea also went nowhere; there simply weren't clients for postwar reconstruction plans before the war had even started.

Yet Mead kept her eyes on the prize. She made another big push in October 1941. This time Larry Frank got the ball rolling and attracted the interest of Edwin Embree, an old Rockefeller buddy of his who now headed the Julius Rosenwald Fund, principally a race-relations body. Again Mead wrote the pitch, and again practical questions of postwar reconstruction were paramount. If peace were to be established on a permanent basis, it was imperative to get 'the psychiatrist, the psychologist, the sociologist and the anthropologist' to the peace table alongside the economist. Statesmen simply didn't appreciate 'the order of change' necessary to make a lasting peace: it would require changes not just in political and economic structures but also 'in the training of children, in authority relationships within the home, etc.' So far this sounded like a more ambitious version of social engineering for national morale, unimpeded by democratic scruples. 'Cultural relativism' did not apply to the enemy. But Mead's horizons were broader than the immediate problems of postwar reconstruction. The long-term goal, she said, was the incorporation of 'national character' into the future organization of world government – not to make other peoples more like Americans (probably impossible and definitely not desirable), but to get Americans and others to acknowledge their national differences in the great projects of international cooperation that awaited. What began as a question of relations between 'the leading victors and the leading vanquished nations' – i.e. Britain, Germany, Russia, China, Japan and the United States – would then broaden to tackle the reconstruction of the whole of Europe and finally begin to address relations between the whole of the world, including Asia, South America and Africa.[54]

Appealing to Embree's race-relations agenda, Mead called this 'the orchestration of cultural diversities'. This was a direct echo of her 1930s programmes for education in multicultural America: 'orchestration' of cultural differences now not on a national but on an international basis. As Larry Frank explained it in a widely circulated manifesto, what this meant was nothing less than a new world order with cultural relativism embedded at its heart: 'what kind of world order do we seek: the dominance of Western European peoples and culture, of our religions and our peculiar scheme of political and economic activities, our relatively parochial way of life, or a world in which different peoples can live according to their own values and traditions, their own assumptions and beliefs and their peculiar sensibilities[?]' In this postwar order any agreed universal standards would have to be 'accepted and put into practice within the framework of the diverse cultures just as we translate agreements into different languages and symbols'.[55] It was a grand scheme, and all Mead was asking for was a measly sum to maintain an office that Bateson could staff. Despite initial doubts about the 'too superficial or over-simplified' idea of national character being pushed at him, Embree bit.[56] Mead got the American Museum of Natural History to provide office space. The Council on Intercultural Relations[57] was born – just in time, for after Pearl Harbor in early December 1941 America entered the war and at last there were 'consumers' for anthropological understandings of the world.

*   *   *

It is often assumed that the war was a turning point in the 'nationalization' – even the 'militarization' or 'weaponization' – of social science, its recruitment to a narrow agenda in support of State interests, the persecution of its enemies abroad and the manipulation and control of the citizenry at home.[58] The portrayal of social scientists as 'nervous liberals' since the First World War serves as a supportive backdrop to that analysis.

But just as the professional and ideological commitments of interwar social science were far more diverse than the 'nervous liberal' diagnosis implies, so the impact of the Second World War differed greatly along lines of age, gender, temperament, expertise and ideology. Social scientists did not march into war in lockstep; they fanned out according to their life situations and their ideological commitments.

The budding social scientists who were of draft age often had no choice – they were drafted into menial, desk or combat jobs that rarely bore any relation to their career aspirations. This denial of choice frequently led to a revulsion after the war from the whole idea of government service. A young protégé of Gorer's, for example, David Schneider, had just started a PhD at Yale when he was drafted. He spent the war as a clerk in Washington, straining at the bit to get back to his thesis and out into the field, and as soon as possible after the war he was doing fieldwork in Micronesia. His wartime experiences had only aggravated his left-wing immigrant's mistrust of the military and its role in American imperialism.[59] Because of their youth and near-universal conscription, this cohort accounted for the majority of social scientists who had war-related employment.[60]

The minority beyond draft age had more choice. The most gung-ho gravitated to serious military and espionage work. If you were well connected and old enough, but not too old, you could slip into a top military rank and be rewarded with considerable operational responsibility. This sort of role appealed especially to the more conservative or conventionally patriotic types. Carleton Coon, the right-wing Harvard anthropologist, had used his field experience in North Africa to secure work for himself on behalf of military intelligence and the covert side of Donovan's COI even before the war broke out; by May 1942 he was in Tangier working for Donovan as a secret agent, preparing for the American landings.[61] G.P. Murdock, who had been largely responsible for reorienting Yale's department towards more conservative engineering goals after Sapir's death, was commissioned as a lieutenant-commander in the Navy and helped soften up the Pacific islands for naval occupation.[62]

For those unable or unwilling to go into uniform, there could be a very wide range of options indeed, but this depended on qualifications and inclinations. Sociologists had relatively few options, because their expertise was mostly domestic and – despite the hopes for the centrality of 'national morale' before Pearl Harbor – American public opinion proved hostile to any overt manipulation on the domestic front in wartime, much as had been the case in Britain. A close study by Abbott and Sparrow of sociologists' wartime employment found that fewer than 15 per cent worked in the government service, and those who did were concentrated in just a few agencies.[63] The largest group (there were fifty-two in all) worked in the Department of Agriculture, which before the war under the left-wing New Dealer Henry Wallace had made a big investment in 'survey' work meant to connect government and public opinion; Ruth Benedict had played a role in its prewar 'school for instruction in the administration of democratic principles'.[64] The next largest group, and often seen as the most important for the postwar development of sociology (though still a tiny group – including only twenty-one of 1,300 sociologists available), worked for the Research Branch of the War Department. There, under the conservative statistician Samuel Stouffer, the kind of individual and group manipulation most prized by 'nervous liberals' was not only possible but highly desirable – army morale could be manipulated in a way that civilian morale could not.[65]

Anthropologists were more in demand and had a wider range of choices, especially, of course, the women, of whom there were many more than in other disciplines. Although there is no survey as thorough as Abbott and Sparrow's, contemporaries estimated that a half of all anthropologists were employed in full-time war work. As early as December 1942 there were at least a hundred in Washington, enough to hold a business meeting that substituted for the annual meeting of the American Anthropological Association. In addition to the agencies for which sociologists worked – Agriculture, the War Relocation Authority (responsible for Japanese internment camps) – because of their rare linguistic and cultural skills, anthropologists were in heavy demand at agencies more directly involved with the world war itself. Along with missionaries and businessmen, they could provide basic information – about languages, local conditions, terrains – regarding parts of the world hitherto unknown to most Americans but vital for the war effort, such as the Pacific Islands, East Asia and North Africa. Uniquely, they could provide insights into the distinctive habits and ways of thinking of the people in these areas, vital for negotiating use of their resources, for recruiting them as allies and where necessary for occupying and controlling their territory. More broadly, they could devise propaganda engineered specifically for the unprecedented range of cultures mobilized by the Second World War. Whereas 'psychological warfare' had previously been administered haltingly and based on some simple universals (fear, anxiety, attachment) proposed by psychologists, now 'culture and personality' seemed tailor-made for subtler modes of communication aimed at specific cultures – something only anthropologists could supply.

Many of the newly recruited anthropologists concentrated in the two bodies into which Donovan's COI split in early 1942: the Office of War Information (OWI) for 'white' propaganda, and the Office of Strategic

Services (OSS), for 'black'.[66] By the end of the war Gorer and Benedict had worked for OWI, Bateson for OSS, and Gorer for their British equivalent, the Political Warfare Executive (PWE).[67] The role of social scientists in OSS is best known because of the glamour attaching to secret (mostly 'black' – manipulative) work. A vast army of social scientists was employed in Washington in OSS's Research and Analysis Branch (R&A), preparing background analysis of the people and places at which OSS propaganda and field operations were aimed; it incorporated among other bodies the Psychological Division of COI. But the Harvard historian William Langer who ran R&A cultivated a profoundly academic environment which earned it a reputation for cool detachment and professorial unreality – hence its nickname, the 'Chairborne Division'. This was not helped by Langer's fondness for humanists with a deep understanding of European culture but less interest in propaganda and morale than OSS might have liked. Two thousand R&A reports piled up in the vaults in Washington but, R&A's historian concludes, while they may well have provided a stream of useful empirical information about Europe, the high-flying cultural analyses of which the authors were so proud probably had more impact on postwar academia than on the conduct of the war. To some extent this detachment broke down in the later stages of the war, as R&A was reorganized along operational lines, with interdisciplinary divisions for Europe/Africa, the Far East, the Soviet Union and Latin America, as well as R&A outposts overseas and field units very close to the front. But as late as 1945 the head of the Europe/Africa Division, the Yale historian Sherman Kent, was complaining that 'for reasons I do not profess to understand . . . it appears easier to get out a 250-page epitome of what Europe will be like in 1986, to be delivered tomorrow morning at 8:30' than to get 'a 2-page summary of what you most want to know about the job you're doing'.[68]

OWI's story is less known, although its work was more public. Originally it was intended to be the domestic morale as well as the overseas white-propaganda agency, but public and political pressure progressively cut down its domestic operations; 'OB', the Overseas Branch, was where most of the action was. The boss of OB was the left-wing playwright Robert Sherwood, a strong believer in a 'people's war' and in OWI's 'strategy of truth'. He hired a freewheeling lot of like-minded publicists and propagandists who played a major role in shaping America's worldwide image – and in shaping America's image of the world. Among them was Mead's brother-in-law Leo Rosten, a restless, wisecracking Renaissance man who had lives as a sociologist (specializing in Hollywood, in which capacity he had been helpful to Gorer), humourist (author of the legendary *The Joys of Yiddish*), novelist, screenwriter, Anglophile dandy – and as deputy director of OWI, with responsibility for 'the official presentation of the Axis nations to the people of the United States'.[69] OWI was also under constant pressure during the war from both Left and Right – accused on the Left of slipping from 'honest information' into 'slick sales-manship', and on the Right of crypto-communism – which ultimately led to Sherwood's replacement in September 1944, the end, says OWI's histo-rian, of the 'hopeful, idealistic, and often independent efforts of the liberal propagandists in the OB'. Throughout the war, however, OWI's social scientists had more freedom of action and more direct input into the operational side of OWI, precisely because OWI was itself more distant from military operations; radio and print propaganda were not so clearly subject to military imperatives as black operations near, at, or behind the lines. Towards the end of the war, as American armies advanced, OWI came closer to military operations and also therefore came into conflict with OSS. It had its own overseas outposts, including a huge London office in advance of D-Day, and as propaganda efforts intensified the line between white and black blurred and the agencies fought furiously over control of radio output and airborne leaflet drops. The greatest chances for social scientists to have a direct impact on the course of the war would come in 1944 and 1945 as US troops – and their propagandists – closed in on Europe, Asia and the Pacific.[70]

Most social scientists – though probably fewer anthropologists – remained in their academic posts, running a skeleton crew for the higher education system. This did not necessarily remove them from war work. There would be a growing demand for war-related education, notably the training (in languages and cultures) of military personnel moving into enemy territory, and increasingly of 'civil affairs' officers, that is, military personnel needed to run occupation governments towards the end of, and after, the war. Schools of Civil Affairs were operating by 1943 at Virginia (for the Army) and Columbia (for the Navy); subsequently they spread to Harvard, Yale, Michigan, Chicago and Stanford, and there were smaller 'Foreign Area and Language' centres at dozens of campuses as part of the Army Specialized Training Program.[71] A steady flow of guides and hand-books to foreign cultures emanated from the Civil Affairs Division of OSS R&A. On the whole they were fairly superficial – as one OSS officer described the Civil Affairs Handbook on the USSR, 'largely political in content, with a touch of Emily Post and Dale Carnegie . . . a guide on how to get along with the Russians, how to avoid committing certain faux pas, and what to expect of persons trained under the Soviet system' – but in the hands of a 'culture and personality' specialist they could add a novel intercultural dimension too, offering tips on how Americans appeared psychologically to foreigners as well as vice versa.[72] Some of the civil-affairs schools also tried to teach intercultural relations, although they encountered resistance from the hard-headed soldiers and sailors they trained, who interpreted '[d]escriptions of the social context for individual behaviour' as 'providing alibis' for the enemy.[73] Even teaching about 'friendly' natives on the Pacific Islands was crippled by a 'strong racial bias' among the Navy personnel being trained.[74] The difficulty here was that the most unfamiliar peoples were being taught by the most culturally sensitive – that is, while historians, political scientists or literary specialists could teach about Europeans, it was left mostly to anthropologists to get across the particularities of the Burmese, the Thais, the Malays, the peoples of Micronesia and Melanesia, even the Japanese. Their task was correspondingly more difficult, but the potential to introduce a shocking new element of cultural relativism was also greater.

* * *

Margaret Mead chose none of these options. With a toddler at home and a job not on a university campus but at a museum, she could have sat out the war entirely, cultivating her garden. But that was the last thing she wanted to do. On the contrary, the choice she made was the one that gave her the maximum involvement with the minimum of constraints. Almost as soon as war broke out, as a result of her earlier connections with the Department of Agriculture, Benedict had been asked if she would accept war work running the Committee on Food Habits, nominally part of the National Research Council; she declined and recommended Mead instead.[75] Mead jumped at the chance. This minor appointment had many virtues. It would give her more exposure to the varieties of American culture – one of her principal themes would be the need to tailor nutritional education to the peculiarities of ethnic groups – and, more importantly, it gave her an entrée to the Washington lobbying world that had hitherto stymied her. Most importantly of all, it was a low-pressure job that gave her tremendous latitude. Merging her household with the Franks' on Perry Street in Greenwich Village, she left baby Cathy in Mary Frank's capable hands and began shuttling between New York and Washington, interspersed with road trips to the vast range of American communities. Bateson was left to staff the Council on Intercultural Relations in Mead's tower office at the museum, feeling sometimes like a glorified clerk and also – though he himself had encouraged Mead to go to Washington – abandoned.[76]

Mead saw her Washington job as 'a base from which I could coordinate various kinds of anthropological input into federal programs'. Although others in these programmes later jibbed at the implication that they were in any way her emissaries, nevertheless Mead's Washington operation did function as an informal clearing-house for anthropologists in government, in the way that Samuel Stouffer's Army Research Branch did for sociologists. Even Eliot Chapple considered Mead 'the Washington front for the things we were trying to do'.[77] She had her own staff at the Food Habits Committee, including the young anthropologists Rhoda Metraux and Natalie Joffe. She lobbied persistently and effectively for jobs for her friends and allies in a wide variety of agencies. Once this network was assembled, she ran 'a very intensive seminar discussion of the modern cultures we are working on', linking her closest friends across agencies – Gorer and Benedict (OWI), Bateson (until he was sent abroad by OSS), Rhoda Metraux (Food Habits and then OSS), the Russian specialist Philip Mosely (State Department), an old friend from her Balinese days, Claire Holt (OSS) and a few others – 'to exchange information that otherwise would have been stamped "top secret" and never made available' and experiment with new techniques and new modes of analysis. Much of this work was boiled down and circulated widely in position papers generated by the Council on Intercultural Relations (CIR) – one advantage of doing only 'white' and non-secret research – in order to propagandize for 'the systematic inclusion of culture at the highest levels of policymaking'.[78]

These were busy and happy years for Mead. They entailed more physical, intellectual – and ultimately, it proved, emotional – distance from Bateson, but there was compensation in the presence of Geoffrey Gorer in Washington for most of the war. Mead felt greatly needed and *important*. In contrast to the politically tense New Deal years, or the much tenser Cold War and Vietnam years, the Second World War was, she argued later,

> a curious and unique war in which liberals and conservatives, middle-of-the-roaders and extremists, all believed that the war had to be won. So we did not have the internal tensions that we had in other wars, and we had a fine group of consumers in the State Department, in the OSS, in the OWI, in the armed services.[79]

Nor was she regularly touched by the ethical challenges involved in the more manipulative kind of morale or black propaganda work. On the whole she kept to the white side where she felt more comfortable. Ever since her disturbingly successful manipulation of Sapir, she had registered the harm that could be done by 'playing into somebody's distorted imagination', and in the national morale work she had, as we have seen, been concerned to minimize the psychological damage that the wartime emergency might wreak. Although it was easier to set aside these reservations when in the thick of war work – and easier after the war to inveigh against 'the horrors of psychological warfare' – she remained conscious of these dangers throughout. As she wrote irritably to the overzealous Gorer in the summer of 1942: 'I am not really anxious to destroy this world in which we live but to build upon it . . . I do not want my ideas – at least with my blessing – put in a setting of destructiveness instead of a setting of a fundamental love combined with a desire for change.'[80] As a consequence, she devoted nearly all of her own war work to the two cultures she knew and loved best – the American and the British – and to cementing their alliance as a blueprint for how postwar relations between all cultures could work. There was also in this choice a deliberate element of keeping her hands clean, the better to empower her for the return to relativism after the war and 'the orchestration of cultural diversities' on a global scale. In any case, she felt completely in control of, and thus responsible for, her own actions. Unlike those wartime social scientists who 'worked through organizations' and thus had 'only a partial control over the action – broadcast, subversive newspaper, propaganda appeal to surrender – or alternatively the appeals to cooperation and help – which followed', she thought herself 'almost single handed the executant of my own insights'.[81] Her hands felt not only clean, but untied.

* * *

Geoffrey Gorer's choices went in quite a different direction. As he emerged from his New Haven cocoon after the US entered the war at the end of 1941, he was drawn to the more manipulative side of psychological warfare and specifically to the study of the enemy. In that letter of summer 1942 where she laid claim to 'a setting of a fundamental love', Mead was contrasting herself to Gorer: 'you do hate the Puritan Character and the Christian religion, you are guilty about being white, you are guilty about being happy – when you are, and your strictures therefore have a very different quality than mine, more acid, perhaps much more true.' Thus, she thought, his yen for 'a setting of destructiveness'.[82] On the other hand, this was a division of labour that she had helped to construct. In the summer of 1941 she had put Gorer in touch with a New York psychiatrist, Richard Brickner. Brickner had produced a draft of a book entitled *Is Germany Incurable?*, which offered a diagnosis not only of Hitler but of the entire German nation as clinically paranoid. Gorer's job was to tone down Brickner's own paranoid obsession and to render the book suitable for consumption by policymakers.[83] He dived with relish into the task that autumn, and started for the first time since the European war had begun 'the heartbreaking attempt to stir up some interest in my potential capacities among the People in Power'. As he wrote to his brother Peter in September:

> What I should like to do would be first of all to use all the available techniques for studying the Nazis as is and making hypotheses; and then do a number of controlled experiments of changing single variables – which would be possible under prison conditions, almost like a laboratory – to see what methods would be most promising for manipulating post-war German society.[84]

After Pearl Harbor, he switched almost instantaneously to work on the Japanese. Within a week of the American declaration of war he had been asked by the Psychological Division of COI to start pulling together a compendium of 'all that is known on Japanese psychology'. It is hard to believe that Mead didn't have a hand in that assignment, too. Although Gorer was officially displaced within weeks when COI hired John Embree – son of the Edwin Embree who was funding the Council on Intercultural Relations and one of the few anthropologists with field experience in Japan – nevertheless he threw himself into his own idiosyncratic analysis of Japanese character structure over the first months of 1942, initially under the auspices of CNM. By March he had already completed his first draft of 'Japanese Character Structure and Propaganda', a memorandum that became CIR's first general circular in April.[85]

Gorer's memorandum on Japanese character structure was really the first of the 'rapid diagnostic studies' of national characters for which Mead and her circle became famous, or notorious, during the war. Later Mead would root this series in Bateson's and Erikson's work on the Germans in 1940, and it is true that the eclectic palette of techniques that Mead's team perfected in their postwar studies can be traced back to Bateson's fertile period in 1940–1: the use of the ideas behind schismogenesis to reduce national cultures to abstractions based on the family drama; consideration of how to use relationships to build morale and to engineer propaganda; interviews with American ethnics and émigrés to gather material on foreign cultures 'at a distance'; and analysis of images in film such as Bateson and Erikson attempted with a Nazi propaganda film, *Hitlerjunge Quex*.[86] However, little of this work appeared in print and what did achieved a very limited circulation. In contrast, Gorer's Japanese memorandum – which rested heavily on one technique, the analysis of infant training in the formation of adult character structure – was very widely circulated and achieved an instant notoriety across the range of government agencies; its content and impact will be assessed in chapter 4.[87] Gorer also used it as bait to try to land himself a real job.[88] By September he had attracted an offer from OWI – '2-way propaganda analysis to and from the Far East with a voice on the policy board' – which was just what he wanted, except that it would have meant moving to San Francisco. A few months later, he landed the perfect job with OWI's Bureau of Overseas Intelligence in Washington, very likely thanks to Leo Rosten, Mead's brother-in-law who was a deputy director of OWI. Planning to despatch his mother back to England, he rented a grand apartment in the capital, filled it with 'well chosen paintings' and dug in for the duration of the war.[89]

Gorer enjoyed his new job hugely – not least for the opportunity it gave him to turn his restless mind to a quick succession of only loosely related tasks. 'Everybody agrees I'm an expert, but nobody is quite sure what I'm an expert in,' he wrote to his brother Peter, 'unless it's a question of economics I agree each time that that's my specialty.'[90] At first he worked for both Rosten and William Whitney, another deputy director, as a kind of freelance on the German question. With Mead and Rosten, he interviewed an American GI who in his younger days had been an early recruit to the Hitler Jugend, for clues to Nazi methods of indoctrination and how to unravel them.[91] He offered liberal advice to Rosten and Whitney on how broadcasts to Germany might be spun psychologically for maximum effect, and evidently liked dicing with black propaganda, though at OWI he got little exposure to that kind of thing, which was more the province of OSS.[92] It was all very 'interesting', he told Benedict, but he still found being so far from the action 'extremely frustrating'.[93]

In spring 1943 he was diverted away from German work in OWI, for which, in truth, he had little expertise, amid so many better-qualified personnel. In April he essayed with Mead a 'rapid diagnostic study' of the Greeks, commissioned from the Council on Intercultural Relations by the Children's Bureau to provide psychological advice on how to handle Greek refugees.[94] This was the sort of challenge they both relished. According to Mead:

> We had five days to do it. Geoffrey Gorer interviewed Renzo Sereno, who was an Italian with a Greek aunt and knew about Greeks. We took the information and built it into a set of hypotheses. Then he spent the weekend with Professor Dorothy Lee at Vassar, and she arranged interviews with some twenty-seven people. Then he and I met again and came back to Washington and sorted things out, and he dictated the memorandum Monday morning. Our basic finding was that there were just two parties in Greece: the people who are against the government and the people who are against the people who are against the government.[95]

Perhaps due to Mead's involvement, the Greek study offered a more balanced diet of historical and sociological as well as psychological explanation for what was diagnosed as the extreme individualism of the Greeks, 'the compulsive hostility to all symbols of superordinate authority'. But the most eye-catching part of the memorandum was, as in the Japanese memo, the character analysis. Some attention was paid to the 'warm and safe nest completely surrounded by love and indulgence' in which the Greek infant was reared, with generous feeding and late toilet training (though also the tight restraint of swaddling, which Gorer chose to ignore in this instance) cultivating an optimism and 'lack of foresight' in the adult. But 'the central thing', explaining resistance to authority, was 'that the base of Greek character is a fantastic fear of castration, based on punishment and threats, chiefly made by the mother, for infantile sexuality' (that is, forbidding masturbation): and this was held to explain not only attitudes to authority but also the sacred status of women ('castrated, and castrating') and the 'well-attested preference for anal intercourse' with prostitutes, virgins and other men.[96]

Gorer and Mead loved doing this kind of work together, the bundling together of psychological 'clues' about a national character from a variety of key sources and hypothesizing from them about the character structure: what they called 'culture cracking'.[97] The speed and urgency made them feel powerful, and it re-created for them the rapid and intuitive exchange of insights that had first bonded them in January 1936. They got a special kick out of using the still rarely heard language of child training and infantile sexuality. Not everyone felt the same way. Dorothy Lee asked for her name to be removed from the report when Bateson circulated it to the Council on Intercultural Relations list:

> I am opposed on principle to the quick, impressionistic, two-dimensional sketch; I accept it only from Margaret, because she has magic which no one else does. I am such a slow too-careful worker myself, that I just can't bear to have my name associated with this other sort of work that says to hell with the accuracy of the details. In addition I am anti-psychoanalytic . . . I must add that though I consider the memo excellent for its original purpose, and that those values which have to do with the child have been caught and well presented, I don't think it is good just in itself, just as giving an authoritative picture of Greece.[98]

Unfortunately, Katherine Bain of the Children's Bureau circulated the report across government agencies without 'tearing off the part called "A Psychoanalytic Intepretation"' – which, she apologized to Mead, she ought to have realized 'would make a lay person quite disturbed' – and when the Greek Embassy got a hold of it she had to promise the Greeks 'that the material will not be released and is not beng used'.[99]

But Gorer now had the bit between his teeth. Almost immediately he was offered the chance by OWI to do a similar national-character analysis of the Burmese in support of psychological warfare against the Japanese occupation and in anticipation of an offensive.[100] Without any native informants, he had to rely mostly on indirect evidence – a few scholarly accounts, interviews with military intelligence officers, notes supplied second-hand from intelligence officers in the field. Perhaps it was healthy for Gorer that he couldn't get exactly what he wanted: one interviewee, a Captain Christian, was too modest, 'somewhat disturbed by any question fringing sex'; notes from an OSS officer were 'far too generalized to make sense. They repeat with variations that the B. don't like the British, hate the Indians, want to be independent and admire the Americans on account of their missionary efforts' – disappointing in light of the fact that the OSS officer in question was an anthropologist, David Mandelbaum. Mead could not help but get drawn into these rather titillating specula-tions. Her own perusal of the notes, she wrote to Gorer, suggested that Burma was an 'impotence culture in which the woman is the guardian of masculinity (aggression), which she on occasion grants to the man', probably connected to an infant-training regime based on threats rather than rewards.[101]

Sure enough, this was close to the analysis that Gorer came up with in July. Like the Greeks, the Burmese enjoyed feeding on demand and casual toilet training, which bred 'optimism and cheerfulness' and 'a marked lack of compulsiveness'. As with the Greeks, there was a worm in this apple: an intense relationship between the (male) child and his mother of 'heavy supercharged emotional complexity', which alternated between loving, teasing and sharp reproof (including again a ban on masturbation), making him 'the woman's loving, unwilling slave'. Girls, in contrast, were trained to be the businesslike household manager. As a result, 'the fundamental Burmese character' was 'founded on the factual and psychological domina-tion of women'. There was, however, 'a final twist which makes Burmese character so paradoxical and Burmese behavior so unpredictable': at school, boys were trained in Buddhist principles of male spiritual perfec-tion, and this gave at last some outlet for 'masculine pride'. That final, superficial gloss encouraged men to act as though they were dominant when they were not, and women to feign subservience. The political consequences, Gorer thought, were gloomy. Burmese character – at least that of the men – manifested 'a curious type of moral irresponsibility' which made democratic government and a market economy nearly impossible. But the prospects for anti-Japanese propaganda were rosier. Every effort should be made to break the sense of kinship with the Japanese as fellow Asians. 'The Japanese should be presented as stupid, barbarous, heretical pagans, deeply involved with defeated Europeans, and never as romantic, law-breaking desperadoes.' More positively, Burmese women could be appealed to almost as rational beings – play up the Japanese contempt for women and the Allies' corresponding respect – but Burmese men should be tempted in the manner of gamblers betting on an Allied victory.[102]

As it happens, there was a real Burmese expert in government, J. Russell Andrus, who had taught economics in Rangoon before the war and was now in the Far Eastern Section of the Commerce Department. Andrus's view of Gorer's Burma memo was strikingly like Lee's of the Greek memo. He thought it deeply flawed in the key details – Gorer had depended a lot on what he took to be a low birth rate, but Andrus argued that small family size was actually a result of a high death rate – and he dismissed its child psychology as 'overdrawn' and oversimplified. He had a higher opinion of Burmese men and their capacity for self-government than Gorer. However, he tended to agree with a lot of the conclusions about propaganda, though he came to them by very different routes, preferring an analysis rooted in political economy.[103] In light of this and other critiques, OWI's official memorandum, 'Background for a Basic Plan for Burma', retained much of Gorer's analysis, watered down in its psychological language but presenting Burmese men and women much as Gorer had, and endorsing the propaganda point of which Andrus had most approved: 'taking advantage of Burmese love of gambling and narrating the events of the war as inter-group contests reported like sporting events.' The psychological language continued to be watered down further as the plan moved up the feeding chain to the Chiefs of Staff, from where the psychological warfare 'directive' became 'policy' but was necessarily very general.[104] Gorer's analysis and his propaganda points remained in circulation for more focused use in the field wherever they were deemed locally suitable. As we will see, by a fluke of history one of the key OSS operatives in the field in Burma when the Allied offensive finally kicked off in 1944 would be none other than Gregory Bateson.[105]

What was the use of Geoffrey Gorer? It is clear that his Freudian provocations were regarded in Washington (not to mention the field, when they got that far) as rather sensational – and also as rather ridiculous. As Mead would have been the first to observe, that was practically the function of the cavalier English gentleman at the heart of the American war machine. Gorer's American colleagues enjoyed laughing at him behind his back. Even before he set foot in the US reviewers had typecast him as 'one of those young Englishmen whose aplomb is as amazing as it is infuriating'; he had 'the egregious pedantry of conceited youth, in love with its own theories and ideas', yet those theories and ideas were still 'tremendously interesting'.[106] Once in America he could appear a figure of fun. Leo Rosten liked to tell the story of encountering Gorer outfitted for his safari to Hollywood for Rockefeller in 1939: 'wearing no stockings or socks, broad sandals, violent green trousers, orange shirt, planter's straw hat – he told me proudly he thought he was being a good anthropologist – he said to [the] salesman, "I'm about to make a trip to Hollywood and I don't want to stand out."' Rosten fairly doubled up with laughter. '*Nobody* dressed like that.' He could only conclude that the salesman had gleefully dumped on Gorer his 'worst schlock stuff'.[107]

On the other hand, there was something magnetic, almost priceless, about such a figure in wartime Washington. There was a certain glamour attaching to Gorer, who lived the high life in a fancy Washington apartment. Rumour had it that he was living there with a lover who was both a cab driver and a cousin of the poet Edith Sitwell – a rumour not completely incredible in all aspects, as Sitwell was a good friend of Gorer's mother.[108] His confidently expressed opinions were not easily ignored. Mead was surely not alone in loving 'that delicate upperclass British art of outrageous understatement', as her friend Philleo Nash commented.[109] An English gentleman with a potty mouth was perhaps best of all. Gorer's Freudian language sounds crude and condescending to our ears – sometimes racist, although it must be said that Gorer was an equal-opportunities snob, the ordinary English seeming to him quite as frightful as the ordinary Burmese. The condescension his American contemporaries expected – indeed, it was exactly in the exhibitionistic mode that Mead and Bateson attributed to all English authority figures. The crudity was more shocking, though from Gorer's cultivated lips it gained some cachet. Freudian language was gaining currency at the time, including among 'straight-talking' men. So long as Gorer didn't use it to impugn his American interlocutors' own masculinity – something Mead worried about – it could be seen as a useful handle on the weaknesses of others, just the kind of magic bullet propaganda analysts were seeking. If there were other ways of getting to the same conclusions – as Lee and Andrus felt – that didn't necessarily damage Gorer's credibility. His wartime memoranda circulated widely, in government circles and, thanks to Bateson's busy mimeograph machine at the CIR, well beyond. They were read avidly across a variety of agencies, used as background for propaganda and as cues to intercultural training in the civil affairs schools.[110] And when, after completing his Burmese report, he finally landed his dream job – 'enemy' propaganda (both Germany and Japan) for PWE, still based in Washington at the British Embassy – not only was it deemed vital to replace him at OWI in what was now called the Division of Cultural Analysis, otherwise known as the 'culture-cracking units',[111] but he even got to name his successor.

*   *   *

Ruth Benedict had spent the first year or so of the war strangely quietly at Columbia. Boas's death made her solely responsible for keeping up his legacy. Very much in Boas's line, she accepted a commission from the Public Affairs Committee to write a popular pamphlet against racism (*Races of Mankind*) with a left-wing student, Gene Weltfish, which attracted a lot of attention when a Kentucky Congressman tried to get it banned for asserting the intellectual equality of blacks and whites. It ended up selling almost a million copies and spawned an innovative animated film.[112] She did some war-related teaching and research on 'contemporary' cultures, attempting some modest 'culture cracking' on the Dutch and the Norwegians, and writing a report for the Children's Bureau on the Norwegians similar to Gorer's on the Greeks.[113] But it was not until Gorer's move to the British Embassy, and his suggestion that she replace him at OWI, that she was galvanized into considering full-time war work in Washington. No doubt Mead's blandishments made a difference – she was thrilled to add Benedict to her private seminar.[114]

One reason Benedict may have been keen now to take up the offer was that OWI was reorienting itself towards Europe and the problems of occupation and reconstruction that would ensue after D-Day. This was just the kind of internationalist work that Mead had been daydreaming about before Pearl Harbor. Although, as the Greek episode had demonstrated, there were dangers in applying a frank national-character analysis to friendly peoples, Mead wouldn't consider the enterprise worthwhile if the findings weren't as applicable to peace as to war: 'We could confine our initial operations to the enemy countries who would not have spokesmen to dispute the disconcerting clarity of the discussion. But if we did this we would be associating anthropological analysis with hostility which we are most unwilling to do.'[115] Now Leo Rosten had thrown his weight around and got a substantial budget for 'Personality and Culture studies of European countries' under the social psychologist Leonard Doob.[116] As Benedict explained the task to a psychiatrist she was trying to recruit:

> this is an opportunity for extending personality and culture research into Western Civilization . . . Results of this research will be pure gain for our knowledge of cultures even though there will be certain questions which we will not be able to answer from the data obtainable . . . Both the Army and the Lehman Commission [on postwar relief and rehabilitation] have already shown their interest in the cultural aspects

of international relations and I need not tell you how important this will be if it is followed through.[117]

Benedict saw her first task as balancing Gorer's impressionistic neo-Freudianism with a more rigorous and systematic approach to 'national character'. When the Council on Intercultural Relations had sought to inject a 'culture contact' dimension into the curriculum of the Army Specialized Training Program,[118] she had argued strongly against an over-emphasis on child training, on strategic grounds:

> Bitter controversy can be stirred up by suggestions that such teaching as is proposed depends upon granting that all cultural behavior is a matter of child rearing. We know how important this theme should be in such instruction, but to base the appeal upon it seems to me bad tactics and unnecessary. I think the basic appeal should be that this is a way to give instruction in cultures as wholes . . . the technique of instruction there-fore is to make the student apprehend culture as it is concretely appre-hended in terms of people's behavior. Such teaching involves interrelating law and economics and family organization and politics and seeing them all as expressed in individuals' actual behavior. This seems to me tacti-cally a better point to stress than resting the argument on child rearing's being the dynamics of culture . . . Such teachers can make the Army see these people *as people* with their own regularities of behavior. It will make them see the culture as a whole.[119]

She took a similarly balanced approach in her OWI work, allowing for the fact that her task was explicitly psychological. As she wrote in her own job description, for each national character that she was asked to analyse, her task was to survey all of the existing secondary literature in all disci-plines (including translations of those in foreign languages), to collect all relevant information from other government agencies (including cables, intercepts, news and intelligence, and specially tailored information from OWI's own outposts), interview first- and second-generation immigrants and refugees to get at 'the rearing of the child in the home', then to prepare a fifty-page memorandum covering the culture pattern, its rewards and sanctions, and attitudes relevant to the war (such as authority, violence, fate), and finally to sum up with 'suggestions for psychological warfare'.[120] This was that eclectic palette of techniques of which Mead boasted after the war – not Gorer's one-track Freudianism. Instead of a week, Benedict gave herself a few months for each culture.

Equally congenially, Benedict's culture cracking for OWI at first steered clear of 'the enemy' and anything smacking of black propaganda.

She did have to clean up after Gorer; one of her first tasks was to water down his Burma memorandum into the 'Background for a Basic Plan for Burma', This may explain why her biographer found this memo 'surprisingly' less sophisticated than the subsequent studies she did on her own – it was Gorer's work, not hers.[121] She also had to continue his interrupted work on the Asian theatre – 'cultural surveys of areas such as Thailand, Indo-China and Occupied China; pattern of reports similar to that on Burma' – by undertaking Thailand in summer 1943. But thereafter her work swung for more than a year decisively to Europe and to preparations for Allied occupation and reconstruction, splitting the relevant national cultures with another anthropologist on the Cultural Analysis staff, David Rodnick.[122] She did a full-scale memorandum on Romania in the autumn of 1943 and then, as preparations for D-Day mounted, she returned to Holland (with Doob) and Norway (with Rodnick), briefing all manner of personnel likely to follow the landings and winning special plaudits for her 'Background Material for U.S. Troops for a pamphlet for the Dutch'.[123] By early 1944 she was so much in demand that she was offered extra staff and even tried to lure Erik Erikson from his California psychoanalytic practice to help her with the family material:

> I am doing work here in Washington that I'm sure would interest you and on which I certainly need your help ... I'm trying to build up a backlog of knowledge on what different civilised nations want in life and how they go after it. It isn't ideal because I can't go and see them in their native homes. But a lot can be blocked out just the same, and someday the rest can be added. It is very striking to me how much good psychological material on the culture can be got from people now living in America.

Her hypotheses were phrased in much subtler terms than Gorer's. In the Dutch, she told Erikson, she detected 'some sense of being closed in in a limited sense, that is communicated early to the child ... the mother's role is to inspect constantly, and they get a sense of a watching eye that helps to make them the Puritans they are. It's a good problem: how are Puritans made anyway?' And then she added, significantly: 'Geoffrey thinks there's some castration threat.' She paused. 'Maybe. But I can't satisfy myself.'[124] Soon she would have the opportunity to recast Gorer's theses on the Japanese as well – fatefully, for the future reputation of the 'national character' studies.

*   *   *

While Mead oversaw her friends' and associates' dispersal into the government agencies to do culture cracking for overseas propaganda, she reserved for herself the biggest task on the biggest stage: culture-cracking the Americans for themselves. Over the first six months of the war she used her travels for the Food Habits Committee to gather material on Americans in their diversity and in their localities, and to pull together with Bateson the work they had done on 'national morale' since early 1940. Then in three weeks at the Franks' summer home Cloverly in July 1942 she wrote *And Keep Your Powder Dry*. Couched deliberately in an American vernacular meant both for easy accessibility and as an experiment in communication – 'making a statement about a culture acceptable to those it described'[125] – this short book made a great impact at the time, and also subsequently in starting a new tradition of psychological portraits of American culture. There was, of course, already a long tradition, from de Crèvecoeur in the eighteenth century and de Tocqueville in the nineteenth, of writings about what made Americans exceptional, but this was the first to take on board the newly intimate address to the unconscious recesses of the heart and soul, a venture Mead approached with greater care than Gorer.

She started out from a sociological point: that Americans were immigrants. This excluded Native Americans and African-Americans – who, she thought, had their own cultures – but it aimed to connect the WASP pioneers with the subsequent waves of European ethnic immigrants who populated modern cities like her native Philadelphia. Immigrant status meant that Americans were fundamentally different from stay-at-home Europeans. They were less rooted, more mobile (socially as well as geographically): no matter how old the family, 'we are all third generation' in our distance from tradition.[126] This was not quite the same thing as saying 'we are all middle class' – citing the sociological studies of Lloyd Warner, she was careful to point out the real existence of class in American society – but it did produce a *culture* without 'absolute class standards' and with a uniform ethos based on movement and success.[127]

So far, fairly familiar. But then she moved to the neo-Freudian themes of child training and family relationships – the nation-specific family drama that she was increasingly using as a shorthand for national character. A mobile population had fewer community sanctions to rely upon – fewer 'rules' – and was therefore more reliant, as Erich Fromm had suggested, on the internalized conscience (the 'superego') 'introjected' into the child's ego by the parents. Here was the famous Puritan conscience of the American pioneers, summed up in the English soldier and politician Oliver Cromwell's alleged admonition to his troops: 'Trust in God, my boys, and keep your powder dry.' Freud had since taught us to see that God was simply one form of the introjected parents. In modern American culture, 'parents' meant 'mother'. While the pioneer generations might have benefited from an active, participatory father, the modern urbanized family with the working father and the domestic mother placed unusual burdens and responsibility on the latter. Here Mead had to tread carefully – contemporaries were worried about 'mother domination' ('momism') – and she had already tangled with Dollard, whose anti-momism she thought anti-woman. She made a point, therefore, of introducing cross-cultural comparisons, showing that the responsibility needn't always be the woman's, and needn't always be onerous. The problems of the American family were specific to America and specific to today.[128]

Most importantly, the 'third generation' culture meant that children had a distinctive relationship to both of their parents that again distinguished them from Europeans. Drawing on Bateson's relational schema, Mead hypothesized that the cultural distance between American parents and their children – aggravated in periods of rapid change and 'cultural lag' – inculcated in the children an unusual attitude to authority. Whereas European parents were the 'exhibitionists', teaching the rules, and the children the 'spectators', soaking them up obediently, American children tended to be the 'exhibitionists', boasting of their superior knowledge of rapidly changing conditions – a form of rebellion against the superego climaxing in adolescence, but at the same time an attempt to secure their parents' love. Instead of measuring themselves against their parents' standards, they tended to refer instead to peer-group standards, something that could engender democracy, though also conformism. This emphasis on a longer-term process of cultural learning that extended beyond infancy through later stages of the life cycle – something she had worked on with Erik Erikson – helped protect Mead from the Freudian oversimplifications to which Gorer's analysis was prey. Its impact was enduring, as we will see in influential postwar developments by Erikson and David Riesman. It also allowed Mead to incorporate her earlier concerns about 'cultural lag', but writ large: it turned out that 'cultural lag' between the generations was not only a post-Victorian phenomenon, it was an *American* phenomenon across history.

What were the implications of this American character structure for questions of war and peace? Mead made no bones about the fact that one of the principal aims of *And Keep Your Powder Dry* was to gird the Americans for war: thus the rather obscure but appropriately military metaphor in the title. To suggest, however, that it was part of a deliberate, long-term campaign to 'militarize' the Americans – a 'paean to war' – is somewhat wilfully to misunderstand Mead's attitude to aggression.[129] As we have seen, this was a long-standing concern of hers and Benedict's. She certainly did not see aggression as an innate characteristic of humans or even as an inevitable product of civilization. She did connect it to certain valuable features of American culture, however, and she was certainly keen to harness what aggression there was to fighting the war against fascism. On the other hand, she was very concerned about the long-term effects that a channelling of aggression into war might have on subsequent generations, and even at the height of the war she kept her eye firmly on the broader prospects for building not only a peaceful America but also a peaceful world – in which she thought, rightly, America would play a significant role.

In an article in the *New York Times* the week before Pearl Harbor, she had written insistently that fighting is not an instinct, that humans can be trained not to fight as easily as to fight, but that if we must fight it would be better to fight for something positive – 'a valuation of peace', 'a positive affirmation of life'.[130] Her goal was to induce the Americans to fight against fascism – which in their isolationism they were then appearing to shirk – but only to do so in positive ways that would not distort their existing character structure. In *And Keep Your Powder Dry* she argued further that Americans were not a particularly aggressive people – thus their 'passivity' before Pearl Harbor. The 'third generation' type was wary – Americans live in 'a world which is too mixed and too unpredictable' – and had learned not to fight unless absolutely necessary. As Bateson had suggested to her about the Americans: 'Back to the wall positions are therefore not best for him. His best position is in a fight which somebody else started, for which he cannot blame himself and for which no one else can blame him, getting in good hard punches and surprising himself at how well he is doing.'[131] Mead summed this up as the 'chip on the shoulder' attitude: you put the chip on your shoulder and you don't fight until someone knocks it off, but if they do knock it off, you hit back hard and then you boast about it. Pearl Harbor was the chip on our shoulder, that made us feel we had to fight. She was very proud of this insight, which she saw as one of her greatest contributions to the analysis of American 'morale' and how it might be addressed in wartime propaganda.[132]

However, she explained, the purpose of this propaganda was not to make Americans more aggressive, but only to harness existing energies towards the necessary job of defeating the Axis powers. Once that job was done, their 'unreadiness to engage in violence' might again be made a virtue and, she hoped, the American drive for 'success' and 'movement' harnessed to worthier tasks. The Puritan conscience that had taken a hard knock in the Great Depression, when it felt punishment had been visited upon it for no good reason, might be revived by success in war, but it could as easily be turned to internationalist goals as to nationalist ones. In Mead's view: 'We want a world without war more than we want to be merely a strong nation.' But she knew there were other views – what some saw as Henry Luce's 'clean fascism', 'a new imperialism' speaking 'in the ruthless terms of American big business'. It was up to people like her to show Americans that their drive for 'success' and 'movement' could be directed to 'a world of plenty, of great expansion, of room for everybody to make a contribution and succeed . . . with a moral purpose'.[133]

All of this was said as plainly as possible: detailing the means as well as ends (it is surely the whitest of white propaganda that tells its subjects how it is supposed to work), making clear that the ends were various and a matter of democratic choice. Explicitly repudiating Bateson's call for 'centralization', Mead criticized the New Deal for its excessively pater-nalist methods and argued that war mobilization could only be achieved by restoring responsibility to the smallest possible units: the township, the block, the trade union branch, the ship. In a democratic culture, 'social engineering' from the top or by deception simply wouldn't work – it would backfire, cultivating expectations and behaviours in both the engineer and the engineered that were incompatible with the democratic ethos. Similarly, in a democratic culture, the social scientist could not stand outside the culture and manipulate it by blueprint, in 'a mere lifeless aping of the mannerisms of the natural sciences'; it could only stand *inside* the culture and raise awareness of its processes, pointing out how various goals might be achieved by harmonizing with those processes. Echoing Robert Lynd's call for a purposive social science, Mead was not abjuring her own personal goals for her society; but she *was* abjuring the dream, or the nightmare, of science, 'the element of absolute control'. In theory, 'social science can also give us the premises, the knowledge by which we could – if we would – fit men to a fixed mold, beat them and bend them until they were unable either to escape from it or to rear children other than themselves. Therein lies the terrible danger of fascism.' The demo-cratic social scientist had, fortunately, no choice but democracy. There was a loss in control and determinacy of outcome, but a gain in efficacy in that the social scientist and the people were working together, with the culture rather than against or on top of it.[134]

There was, of course, a circularity about much of this argument. It was easier for Mead to disclaim 'absolute control' when her analysis of the American character seemed to align so well with her desired outcomes. To be fair, she admitted frankly at the beginning of the book that it was written deliberately in familiar American language in order to make it sound like common sense. It was an odd thing for an anthropologist to be doing – explaining oneself to oneself – and she wouldn't be doing it if it weren't for the state of emergency. 'If we were not at war . . . I would be on a ship, bound for some South Sea island.'[135] After the war she would encourage anthropologists of other nationalities to do the job of describing the Americans. The close alignment of her analysis with her aspirations was also, as Marc Stears has argued, a product of a period when democratic radicals had come to believe that social change could grow naturally out of the 'American creed' without the need to resort to social engineering or utopianism.[136] Mead was not, however, always so optimistic. The American people didn't do what she wanted them to do either in the 1939–41 period, when they stood aloof from the war against fascism, or in the period after 1950, when they became obsessed with anti-communism. The war represented, therefore, a distinct window during which Mead felt that the American people and their 'character' were peculiarly receptive to her 'purposive' goals – and she was determined to make the most of this opportunity.

And Keep Your Powder Dry marked a new phase in Mead's career as a public figure. Her freedom of action in wartime, when many others were sorely preoccupied with full-time war work, allowed her to build a visibility and an authority to which she had long aspired. In her early career, her immensely popular books could be seen as exotica – exciting but not too serious – and her own authority was correspondingly diffuse. Her early attempts to break into the mass-circulation magazine market had been thwarted by this perception of her limited relevance. That changed in wartime, when she wrote for *Vogue, Mademoiselle, House and Garden, Woman's Day, Look, Harper's*, the *New York Times* and the *New York Herald Tribune*.[137] She began to mix with the truly powerful. Eleanor Roosevelt asked her for advice in dealing with popular racism. The Washington hostess Elsa Maxwell organized a dinner for leading politicians and columnists to hear her views on anthropology and international relations. Even the mogul Henry Luce, despite the crack about 'clean fascism', told his friends that *And Keep Your Powder Dry* was 'one of the most influential books he had read in ages'.[138] This was the point at which the *Washington Post* named her one of the 'eight outstanding women of the modern world'.[139] Much of this attention was evidently still constrained by notions of a 'woman's realm'. A full-page profile in the *New York Post* in May 1944 – tellingly headlined 'Anthropology Is Such Fun!' – shows the efforts mass-market journalism could make to restrict and pasteurize her authority. The piece is dominated by photographs captioned 'Dr Margaret Mead is 42 years old, but she doesn't look her age', and the text zeroes in on her upbringing and family life (mysteriously editing out one of her three husbands). Even her private seminars were rendered as 'intimate gatherings', albeit odd ones featuring a whiteboard and coloured crayons, as 'Most of the people we know want to make diagrams before the end of the evening'.[140]

Yet Mead was adept at turning the 'woman's realm' into the human realm. Most reviewers of *And Keep Your Powder Dry* saw that the heart of its argument was the way in which the American family drama formed the American character. This not only attributed considerable significance to mothers – without tipping over into 'momism' – but also attributed considerable significance to Mead's own sphere of expertise. No reviewers thought it inappropriate for Mead to comment on the war effort or postwar plans, even though they might doubt some of her explanations and conclusions. They tended to characterize her in the persona of a parent or educator, writing in a language 'any high school student could understand' and revealing 'what makes us tick'. Her optimism and confidence in the American people were seen as very much in the spirit of the times, and although this might make her analysis appear quite 'conventional', despite the social-scientific language, by the same token it made the social-scientific language seem a natural and credible way of approaching the national character.[141] It was, precisely as she intended, the 'public' language that a democratic social science needed to speak – not the 'private' language of black propaganda, which she tried to avoid, or even of Gorer's Freudianism, which she personally found stimulating but came to regard as practically useless because it put others off.[142]

Mead was not, however, satisfied with writing the occasional magazine article, or even a widely circulating book like *And Keep Your Powder Dry*, or speaking, as she now frequently did, on radio or lecturing to civic groups. Her greatest ambition was to embed the 'culture and personality' idea at the heart of intercultural relations, not only for wartime purposes of cementing national and Allied unity, but also in anticipation of the postwar task of 'orchestrating cultural diversities'. The purest applications of 'culture and personality', she felt, came not in fostering self-understanding among Americans – that involved the anthropologist in tricky questions of ethical non-relativism – but in fostering mutual understanding *between* cultures. For this reason, she always felt her greatest contribution to the war effort lay in showing the Americans how to communicate fruitfully with a foreign culture – albeit their closest ally, the British – and vice versa. It was, she often said, her classic case study in 'the application of anthropological methods to understanding between peoples': not just to understanding 'understanding', but actually to making it happen. And despite the existence of many more experts on Britain than on Greece or Burma, it was on the literal as well as figurative terrain of Britain that Mead's wartime influence reached its absolute apex.[143]

Bateson and toddler Cathy

CHAPTER 3

Among the Natives of Great Britain
(1942–5)

Before Pearl Harbor, Margaret Mead had already identified the Anglo-American relationship as one of the key targets for the application of 'culture and personality insights' to intercultural relations. In setting out the principal goals of the proposed Council on Intercultural Relations (CIR) in 1941, she prioritized, first, understanding the Germans, second, understanding the Americans and, third, understanding the British, 'especially as it affects mutual understanding and ability to cooperate'. With her eye firmly planted on the postwar 'orchestration of cultural diversities', she saw the Anglo-American relationship as a natural starting point, 'because cooperation between the United States and Great Britain will be vitally important and the quality of that cooperation may make or wreck any peace plans'. If successfully orchestrated, that relationship might then serve as a model of how one world of many cultures might work.[1]

Of course, this was not an innocent calculation. The American and the English cultures were the two cultures she knew best, and with which she felt truly comfortable. (Just as she tended to base her cultural idea of America on a core of WASPs and ethnic immigrants – excluding those such as African-Americans who had a different character structure – so she tended to base her cultural idea of Britain on a core of 'Englishmen', and, as we will see, a very particular type of Englishman at that.) The development with Bateson of the new idea of 'national character' had been beaten out on the terrain of their understandings of their own national cultures. Ever since those momentous days in the mosquito hut in New Guinea, too, their ideas of how individuals communicated and formed relationships – an interaction between temperaments and between cultures – had been formed on Anglo-American ground. The appearance of new case studies in Anglo-American relations – Mead-Gorer, Benedict-Gorer, the unique experiment of Cathy Bateson, her British nanny and the Guillebaud sisters – provided a steady supply of grist to the mill. Mead's study of the American national character in *And Keep Your Powder*

Dry owed a lot to the *misunderstandings* of America she observed in Gorer and Bateson. Although the book was in fact dedicated to her grand-mother and her daughter, she joked that she ought to have dedicated it to Gorer, 'whose brilliant misunderstanding of points in American culture has made me examine those points more sharply'.[2] There was a methodo-logical benefit to be gained from studying the Anglo-American relation-ship as well: because the Americans and the English shared so much in terms of language, history and tradition, it was more difficult for them to see the fundamental differences between them, which only a national-character analysis could bring out. As she put it after the war: 'Essentially, on matters of character structure for instance, English and American culture differ as greatly as Balinese and American character structure, but the historically related content of the two cultures, obscures this fact very thoroughly.'[3] This assumes both that English and American culture do differ 'essentially' and that 'character structure' is a good instance of that essential difference, regardless of the 'content' of the two cultures – the string of assumptions for which Mead was to come under heated criticism. But it also highlights how important those assumptions were to the claims she was staking for expertise in intercultural relations.

Mead's selection of the Anglo-American relationship as her own personal mission highlights another crucial aspect of her wartime policy: to avoid associating anthropological analysis with 'hostility' and manipu-lation, in order to use wartime to prepare a programme for peace. There was no demand for black propaganda in the name of Anglo-American relations. OSS and its British counterparts in PWE had little or no interest in the subject. There was no call for secrecy and only a little anxious surveillance of her work by the white propaganda agencies, OWI and MOI. This degree of freedom provided for Mead her favoured status as 'almost single handed the executant of my own insights' – not only preparing the ground for the postwar in wartime, but actually starting to build it.[4] If *And Keep Your Powder Dry* was an experiment in 'making a statement about a culture acceptable to those it described', Mead's work on Anglo-American relations represented the next step, an experiment in making statements about a culture acceptable both to itself and to another culture. As such, it represented a further step towards the 'orchestration of cultural diversities' that would be necessary in a postwar world of infi-nitely multiplying intercultural communications. Until the end of her life she used it as a glimpse of the world that might have been, 'the future dream of an ordered world society of peoples, in which each may stand in his own appointed place and find it good'.[5]

*   *   *

Always conscious of her WASP heritage, Mead considered that she had as intimate an acquaintance with the 'contents' of English culture as anyone:

> In childhood, I was read English and American books by parents who had not begun to discriminate between them in the sense that one set were treated as more foreign and less a part of my tradition than the other. I . . . learned a rhythmical version of the Kings of England at the same time as I learnt the alphabet. I was taught that I had had Tory as well as revolutionary ancestors, and therefore had no lineal obligation to a perpetual feud with the British crown. Years of participation in the services of the Episcopal Church, gave me a familiarity with the Book of Common Prayer. The English novel was of course such a commonplace that I once passed an examination in English History, which I had never studied formally, simply on the accumulated bits of historical novels. My father quoted Chesterfield and Macaulay, Motley and Burke almost as often as Veblen and Schopenhauer. British and American anthropology have always remained in close touch with each other, and as students we studied Tylor and Rivers as part of our own scientific tradition. A continuing interest in literature and poetry had meant that I had followed T.S. Eliot across the Atlantic and W.H. Auden on his opposite voyage. During my years in British mandated territory I had learned to see the point of most of the jokes in Punch, a task about as difficult as it is for an Englishman to learn to tell advertisements from reading matter in the New Yorker.[6]

Despite this substantial overlap in 'content', however, she also claimed that even before she began to apply 'culture and personality' insights to complex, modern cultures she was 'prepared to believe that English culture was "another culture", not simply an ancestral form, or a modern pure form of my own'.[7] Certainly, when she and Bateson began to think about the structural (rather than substantive) differences between complex, modern cultures in the mid-1930s, the difference between British and American character structure was very often their first case in point. That had been part of the game in developing the 'squares', thinking about the ways in which culture patterns accommodated similar temperaments differently, and the ways in which a man and a woman from different cultures came together in a couple. It had arisen casually in *Naven* when Bateson detected 'a standardised system of emotional attitudes' in 'a group of young intellectual English men or women . . . talking and joking together wittily and with a touch of light cynicism', or noted the approved behaviours and customs 'emphasising and stabilising the ethos of the group' in 'an army mess or [at] a college high table'.[8] It had become a playful part of the Mead-Bateson relationship during their long separations in the mid-1930s, when Mead spoke about internalizing English cultural norms as a way of getting into Bateson's head, almost cohabiting his consciousness. Just as any behavioural detail about a culture could be a clue to its pattern, so the solo performance of any quotidian task could be a performance of their relationship if done in the right frame of mind. 'I really am getting the point of view of an authentic British subject,' Mead had written to Bateson delightedly in November 1935.

> Yesterday I ordered new glasses frames and the question came up, filled gold which will break in three years or solid gold which can be soldered forever. If I had been thinking as an American I would have taken the filled. Thinking or trying to think in your long time terms, I got the others with a note that that point would now be off the family budget for good.[9]

A more systematic effort to 'crack' English culture and the ways it might differ from and interact with American culture only began with Bateson's return from Britain in early 1940. As we have seen, Cathy, her English nanny and the Guillebaud sisters offered cultural clues – 'points', in their private language – by the minute. Mead and Bateson took particular delight in observing the Guillebauds' interactions with other girls of their age in the New Hampshire neighbourhood of Cloverly, their summer retreat with the Franks: 'the constant rubbing of cultural and national differences', Bateson observed in a June 1940 letter to his mother, was both pregnant with significance for their own theories and also a good lesson in intercultural relations for the girls themselves.[10] With America's entry into the war, Mead turned in earnest to Anglo-American differences. Over the winter of 1941–2 she talked intensively to both Bateson and Gorer about these differences and, as we have seen, when she sat down to write *And Keep Your Powder Dry* in the summer of 1942 she was always thinking in terms of how Americans differed from Europeans – with the English usually standing in (implicitly if not explicitly) for Europeans. By the spring of 1943, as the American authorities began to focus on Britain as the springboard for the reconquest of Europe, she was amply stocked with 'points', both on the essence of the English 'national character' and on how it worked in interaction with the American.[11]

Mead and Bateson's early 'hypotheses' about the English national character were heavily dependent on Bateson's thinking about schismogenesis and how it played out in the typical English family drama. The first hypothesis was that many 'complementary' relationships, such as the all-important parent-child relationship through which so much 'learning to learn' went on, worked in diametrically opposite ways in Britain and America. (This was the kind of thing that made Mead say that the English and the Americans were as different from each other as they were from the Balinese.) In the US, the rapidly changing 'new' country, children were equipped by their parents only with a rough set of survival tactics, and in practice the children had to teach the details of the culture to their parents; this set up a fundamental complementary relationship in which the child was the 'exhibitionist' and the parent the 'spectator'. In contrast, in Britain, the archetypal 'old' country, children could be taught the details of their culture by the parents as a fixed set of rules or 'code', and the fundamental complementary relationship was one in which the parent was the 'exhibitionist' and the child the 'spectator'.

Lest anyone worry that this might make the English seem too 'submissive', like the Germans, Mead and Bateson explained that the English parent taught the child independence by sending him away to school – or, at least, the upper classes sent their male children away. 'I don't know what happens in lower classes,' Bateson granted candidly, and girls tended to disappear from this schema, much like the Scots and the Welsh. Nevertheless, the initial parent-child relationship stuck (indeed, became acceptable, because it *didn't* require true submission), and was reproduced in all other authority relationships encountered in adulthood: 'the parent at breakfast, the newspaper editor, the political spokesman, the lecturer, or what not.' As a result public behaviour in Britain was 'styled on a paternal model, gentle but firm' while American behaviour was 'styled on a filial model, in which the child, unsure of his ground, overstates in order to get and keep parental interest'. Such differences accounted, Mead and Bateson thought, for a lot of intercultural miscommunication: 'To an American eye, the English too often appear "arrogant", whereas to an English eye the American appears to be "boastful". If we could show precisely how much of truth and how much of distortion is present in these impressions, it might be a real contribution to interallied co-operation.'[12] The trick was to come up with a relationship *between* the two cultures that satisfied the learned needs of both. One idea Mead had was that Americans looked upon the British the way a younger brother might look upon an older sister, so that in mediating communication between them you needed to know not only about parent-child but also about sibling relationships in the two cultures. With the help of her Food Habits assistant Rhoda Metraux, she devised a questionnaire on sibling relationships to be administered to Vassar undergraduates. Not much came of it; it was too complicated – bad enough that Americans and

English had such different public behaviours based on parent-child relationships, but to try to accommodate their sibling relationships too . . .[13]

A second hypothesis, which modified and clarified some of the gaps in the first, was that whereas the key relationship in America was the binary parent-child relationship, in Britain there was a tendency to form in addition 'ternary' relationships, where the job of the middle party was to educate the junior in the ways of the senior party. For example, the nurse teaches the child how to relate to the parent, the government minister teaches the people how to relate to the monarch, the NCO teaches the private how to relate to the officer, the prefect teaches the boy how to relate to the schoolmaster – or, as at Bateson and Gorer's school, Charterhouse, 'the head of long room' teaches the 'fags' how to relate to the 'monitors'.

This refinement had the advantage of explaining what went on at boarding school, obviously a crucial stage in child training according to the first hypothesis, and it also underscored some key differences between Britain, America and Germany. While reinforcing the Old World/New World divide – Britain and Germany were rule-bound cultures, while America was more freewheeling and competitive – the ternary relationship allowed Mead and Bateson to portray the English authority structure in a gentler light. Rules were not imposed, but taught as part of an 'abstract code'. That explained to Mead why the upper and lower classes could appear to have more in common with each other than with the middle classes: they were both taught, by someone, how to behave to someone else (the upper-class child was taught by its nurse how to behave to its mother, the working-class child was taught by its parents how to behave to higher classes), a structure that was lacking in the 'nurseless' middle-class household. It also allowed her to draw another line between the Germans and the English. Admittedly, the rule-bound English and German families lacked the personal touch of the close mother-child bond in America. Yet the 'nurseless' middle-class household in England was groping towards a middle way, in which the exhibitionistic mother 'gives much more time to the disciplining of the children, and teaches them how to behave towards *herself*'; thus the rules of good behaviour were not an impersonal but a 'personal code', and the 'English fidelity to a code' approaches closer to the 'personalization and particularity of American ethics' as opposed to 'the impersonal, abstract sense of duty of the Germans' as depicted in Kurt Lewin's studies. This hypothesis was not perhaps so useful in devising novel means of intercultural communication between the English and the Americans, but it did have real ideological benefits in keeping one's Old World enemies distinct from one's Old World friends.[14]

The third hypothesis extended the distinctive complementary pattern of the English family to take in symmetrical relationships too, for, despite the 'learning how to learn' that took place in a complementary (family) relationship, most adult relationships in England as in America were symmetrical, that is, based on similarity (and competition) rather than difference. Still, the difference in complementary relationships affected symmetrical relationships too. As Mead argued in *And Keep Your Powder Dry*, the English boy could be taught the rules of how to fight with his peers – this prepared him to fight with all-comers – while the American boy was taught to be wary, to think for himself and to fight when *he* deemed it necessary. The English boy went into the fray confident of his business and of the sufficiency of his aggression; setbacks didn't faze him and he fought best with his back to the wall: 'The back to the wall position depends on the English basic assurance that they have more aggression than they need. When your back is against the wall, then, by the rules of the game, every ounce of aggression that is in you must come out. And, if you keep the rules and hit hard, you always win. That is the English conviction.' The American, as we've seen, was in a more ambiguous position. He doesn't fight until he has to. When he has to, he fights hard and surprises himself by how well he does it (and gets in a little exhibitionistic boasting while he's at it, 'a sort of whistling in the dark . . . as he tries to live up to an unknown demand upon his unknown strength'). But he may be easily discouraged and doesn't respond well to early setbacks.

Nevertheless, both the English and the Americans were taught – either by a 'code' or by mother-child nurturance – how to develop these healthy symmetrical relationships, in what was known in the Anglo-Saxon world as 'fair play'. In Germany, by contrast, the whole culture was dominated by complementary relationships of dominance and submission, and Germans therefore were not stimulated to endeavour by meeting strength with strength, only by meeting strength with weakness: the bully-coward relationship. Bateson admitted that there was a superficial implausibility about this latter thesis – could 'a pure dominance-submission hierarchy . . . ever exist as a stable system'? – but that did not stop him and Mead from indulging in the cliché that 'fair play' was a distinctively Anglo-American ethic. Once again, the hypothesis aimed to provide hints for propaganda by distinguishing clearly between the English and the Americans, while at the same time classing them together in distinction to the Germans – not always an easy formula to satisfy.[15]

* * *

Though lacking the most provocative Freudian elements of Gorer's infant-training hypotheses, Mead and Bateson's diagnosis of Anglo-American difference was not uncontroversial in its own moment, and many of its elements may appear suspicious or even risible to us today. As an account of the English alone – without Scots or Welsh or Irish – the schema relied to a ridiculous degree on observation of a thin stratum of public school- and Oxbridge-educated families; if Bateson knew little about the 'lower classes', that is, 80 per cent of the population, Mead knew less. Much later criticism of these and similar anthropological theses on the 'English national character' focused on empirical studies of 'lower-class' family life which showed it to operate on quite different models – to which Gorer sometimes retorted that these 'lower-class' families weren't really English at all, but Irish slum-dwellers.[16] Furthermore, Gorer's and Bateson's understandings of English family life were in the 1940s already considerably out of date: their own childhoods had been played out before the First World War, and Bateson had as little experience of the upheavals of 1930s Britain as Mead had had of 1930s America. It was a signal disadvantage of the psychological as opposed to the sociological or political understanding of national character that it was not so sensitive to periods of rapid social and political change; it made the 'national character' seem more static, tenacious, in a way uncomfortably like the biological understanding it sought to displace. Then there were the questionable assumptions about the significance of the family drama for the rest of national life, which relied not only on some controversial neo-Freudian precepts but also on a 'configurationist' belief that a culture, like an individual, was 'a single *organized* entity, such that all its "parts" or "aspects" are mutually modifiable and mutually interacting,'[17] not in its 'contents' but in its principles of organization. This substitution of psychological and anthropological insights for the usual tools of analysis of national life – history, arts and literature, economics, politics – offended established interests, and sometimes seemed alarmingly counter-intuitive. Were the English and the Americans really as different from each other as they were from the Balinese, in any *crucial* respect?

On the other hand, Mead had the same arguments on her side as she had had in diagnosing the American national character, plus some additional ones. This was an emergency, and a novel type of emergency. Propaganda required a different kind of analysis and a different mode of address from the 'traditional' Anglo-American circuits of diplomacy, connoisseurship and English literature. To address millions, you needed to get down to their psychic core. Furthermore, as we have seen even with Gorer's national-character studies, the 'scientific' diagnosis of the English national character might usefully build upon, and improve upon, older national stereotypes. England was an old country, rule- and tradition-bound, with a paternal ruling class and an honourable code of 'fair play' and government by consent; its people were docile but sturdy, able to defend themselves when their backs were against the wall, as, conveniently, they had just shown at Dunkirk. As England had gradually become more democratic, its own commentators had tried to develop ideas of an English national character that genuinely reflected the feelings and experiences of all classes – not an easy task given the size and diversity of the nation. Gorer's friend George Orwell expressed just this concern in his famous essay *The Lion and the Unicorn*, at precisely the moment Mead and Bateson were puzzling over their hypotheses:

> Are there really such things as nations? Are we not forty-six million individuals, all different? And the diversity of it, the chaos! The clatter of clogs in the Lancashire mill towns, the to-and-fro of the lorries on the Great North Road, the queues outside the Labour Exchanges, the rattle of pin-tables in the Soho pubs, the old maids biking to Holy Communion through the mists of the autumn morning – all these are not only fragments, but *characteristic* fragments, of the English scene. How can one make a pattern out of this muddle?[18]

Orwell did make a pattern out of this muddle, for some of the same reasons as Mead – to raise national morale, to define war aims against the Germans – and using some of the same tools. Orwell was not averse to considering the influence of 'upbringing and so forth' but he employed a much more promiscuous array of data, not all seen as mutually reinforcing, including some of the 'contents' of the culture such as literature, which he saw as constitutive and not only as providing clues to something else.[19] Though Mead's psychological analysis was less immediately popular in Britain than in America, it served the same ends as those at which Orwell and many other British intellectuals were aiming. It did seem to provide an added dimension of psychological penetration into the character of the whole of the people, which was crucial to the war effort and which also appeared to be both more 'democratic' and more 'scientific', if in an American way. What she also needed to do, she knew, was to find a way to 'phrase' it that was equally acceptable to the English and to the Americans.

And although the novelty of the method provoked queasiness, it did also attract 'clients', especially in 1943 as the war began to shift in the Allies' favour and a huge influx of Americans into Britain seemed in the offing. At the beginning of 1943, Mead, Bateson and Gorer put their heads together to develop practical ways of adding their anthropological perspective on Anglo-American relations to the mix. Their first initiative was to propose to *Time* magazine, the bestselling news weekly, a feature on 'Anglo-American communication' for both the English and American editions, with English and American co-authors, playing up the difference between 'English self-confidence and assurance and indifference to the rest of the world, and the American's fundamental lack of that confidence and interest in the opinion of the rest of the world'.[20]

In February 1943 this work was diverted into a radio programme for the CBS School of the Air of the Americas, 'Science at Work: It's Human Nature', which Mead was asked to take on as a piece of anti-racist propaganda, 'to emphasize that cultural not racial differences were crucial'. Mead seized this opportunity to do a full-blown pilot in intercultural communications – one of her wartime contributions of which she was most proud. The complexities seemed daunting: how to address multiple audiences at once in a language aimed at the character structure of each but acceptable to all? Then she had a brilliant idea. Since the brief for the programme was to demonstrate cultural differences, why not *perform* them in the family setting where Mead had most vividly imagined them? Thus arose the 'breakfast table' broadcast. Mead's idea, based on a casual comment in *And Keep Your Powder Dry*, was to portray a series of typical families from different cultures at the breakfast table – a literal representation of the family drama in comparative perspective. In the end, five were chosen: Chinese and Chinese-American, to make the initial point that it is not race but culture that determines character, and then, predictably, German, American and English. The broadcast, written with Murray Dyer (a US-based British scriptwriter and a psychological warfare expert with OWI), went out first on 8 March 1943, deftly enacting Mead and Bateson's ideas about the differences in complementary family relations.

At the German breakfast table, the father splutters orders and bemoans the decline of manners since his own father's day; the mother nurtures the children and placates the father; father and son exult over the massive superiority of the local football team. (Mead later admitted that this depiction was overdrawn, but she blamed it on her informants – émigrés – and their 'ambivalence about their native land'!) At the English breakfast table, the father issues his commands in more measured and abstract terms (though he also bemoans decline) and the children get away with a little more mischief; both father and mother direct in terms of the rule-book ('Sugar first, John, before you pour your milk on your porridge'); father expresses quiet confidence in England's victory over the Australians in Test cricket; he proposes to take his son to his tailor to be measured for a suit. Then the Americans: father is slightly hapless, bemused; the children run rings around their parents and banter aggressively with each other; mother tries desperately to keep order; and the *son* asks his father, rather than vice versa, to accompany him to the high-school hockey game. The scenarios are interspersed with commentary from Mead herself, in the persona of 'an authority in this matter', running 'a series of experiments' 'illumined' by her analysis, which rams home the message about the different attitudes to authority. That message is polished off with a final pair of scenarios – comparing an English to an American lecturer – showing how the breakfast table reproduces itself in wider social life: the understated voice of authority on the one hand, the boastful, cocksure show-off on the other. The broadcast ends with a hopeful message; that because human differences arise not from race or climate but from upbringing, 'it *is* possible to change human nature'.[21]

Encouraged by the success of this exercise, Mead, Bateson and Gorer sat down to hammer out a proposal for further broadcasts on 'Anglo-American similarities and differences' which could embed more of the complexities of intercultural communication. The ambitious plan was for a series of programmes, co-scripted by an Englishman and an American, set alternately in Britain and America, and depicting varied scenes of daily life at home, at work, at play and at war. The thorny problems that had been thrashed out for the *Time* proposal, of portraying the different characters in mutually acceptable ways while at the same time conveying a message of common cause, were carefully addressed. An English family would have to be chosen that came closer to an American family than the usual stereotypes: 'an English middle class urban family (the sort of family who would send their son to a good grammar school) belonging to a non-conformist church preferably Methodist. The usual stereotypes, dukes, butlers, cockneys, and rural people speaking dialects must be rigorously excluded. This middle class thread is the strongest thread between English and American middle west culture.' Mead added: 'the family in [the film] "In Which We Serve" of the chief petty officer, played by John Mills, is about right.' Though 'such a family as this is not so popular with either producers or audience in England', it would play better in America. To compensate, for the English audience, the American family could be handled more broadly, as 'genuinely different, exotic, fascinating, and still a systematic culture in its own right'. The scriptwriters were encouraged to remain alert to the crucial attitudinal differences. The Americans need to be persuaded that their 'big sister' is serious and moralistic like them, not suave and clever-clever, getting away with murder; the English need to be persuaded that their brash and irresponsible nephews were in their own way as serious and moralistic as them, not just boastful purveyors of a casual 'line'. Americans need to be reassured by victory; the English can 'take it'. Americans believe in independence (for colonies as for children); the English want slow steps. Americans praise; the English criticize.

The goal was to emphasize the growing commonalities. Each broadcast was to be split not only between American and English scenes but also between 'as we were' (prewar) and 'as we are'. The ultimate message was the same for both sides – 'these are the kind of people we can work with on the same job' – but it had to be phrased in two ways, so that the Americans could conclude, 'Why, they are just like us', and the English, 'They have their own way of going about things, but it seems to work out all right.'[22]

After long negotiations between CBS and the BBC, the series proposal was turned down. Coordinating studio work on both sides of the Atlantic at the height of the war was too complicated logistically; the radio bosses might also have felt that it was too complicated conceptually. But the one substantive criticism that was offered by Davidson Taylor of CBS – like Dyer, a psychological-warfare expert himself – raised a warning signal about the acceptability of national-character analysis for wartime propaganda generally:

> We were afraid that the comparisons would inevitably prove invidious to one nation or the other, and whereas in peace time this would not be a serious matter (in fact it would be a good thing in the long run), we did feel that in war time we might be damaging the friendship of the two countries by underlining issues which might cause an increase of current friction.[23]

No matter how carefully handled, in other words, there were limits to how far propagandists were willing to use the idea of difference in the name of unity.

*   *   *

By this point, the spring of 1943, Anglo-American relations had become the frontline of the propaganda war. 'There is now an intense curiosity about America all over the British Isles,' wrote a military attaché in the London Embassy to Robert Sherwood, the head of OWI's overseas operations. 'It will either be fed creatively and wisely by us, resulting in an understanding of the real America, or it will be fed haphazardly, resulting in misunderstanding and frustration.' OWI's London Outpost, run by Victor Weybright, was 'the front for one of the most important psychological battles in the world'. Over the course of 1943 it ramped up its operations enormously, increasing a small staff of forty-four to 1,600 by D-Day in 1944. It was put under an OWI British Division with a former Congressman at its head and vastly expanded its range of activities. Among the new initiatives was a 'famous program of American speakers', organized in conjunction with MOI, acting as ambassadors and publicists, both 'rather big literary or national names' and recognized specialists 'who would concentrate on a small but influential group of English people in disseminating information regarding American life, character and institutions'. Among the big-name speakers, the one who made the biggest splash – and who stayed the longest – was Margaret Mead.[24]

Mead was a logical choice for this programme, for a number of reasons. She was a member of the editorial committee of the Writers' War Board, a private organization subsidized by OWI, partly as a way of evading Congressional bans on domestic propaganda. It focused on mobilizing writers to influence public opinion both against the Germans and in favour of the Allies, and also, pleasingly to Mead, of international cooperation in the postwar world. As with the rest of the war effort, the board increasingly bore down on Anglo-American relations in 1943 and among other projects sponsored a glossy monthly magazine, *Transatlantic*, instigated by the US ambassador in Britain, J.G. Winant, and published by Penguin Books, which sold out its entire run in print-starved Britain.[25] Following the success of *And Keep Your Powder Dry*, the board adopted 'an anthropological trend', planning a regular column entitled 'Things Are Different Here' and inviting Mead to attend a meeting in New York in April to discuss it. Alas, as was often the case, Mead was away in Washington, so they got Bateson instead. 'He was, in a shy, over-sized way, extremely genial; but he seemed to find us a very strange group and gave me the impression that he would have felt more at ease on Bali,' wrote the editorial committee chair to the *Transatlantic* editor, but Bateson nonetheless promised that Mead would contribute.[26] Mead was unusual in being not only an expert on, and an ambassador for, America, one who could speak to and for women as well as men, but also now an expert on Anglo-American relations in particular, so it was hardly surprising that she topped the list of proposed speakers for OWI/MOI tours of Britain. In all, ten speakers were organized, for two-month tours, but Mead's stretched ultimately from July to November.[27]

She seemed remarkably eager to take on this long and onerous responsibility. Cathy could be left happily in the care of Mary Frank. Bateson, however, was still stewing. Despite making strenuous efforts, he had failed to come up with any serious war work for himself. He had worked independently with Erik Erikson on German character structure, pulled together some of the Balinese materials, played a sporadic role in Mead's Washington seminar and staffed the CIR office. An attempt to find a more permanent niche putting together intercultural materials for the Army's specialized training programme was dragging on without results. He was feeling useless and miserable. Still, he claimed he very much wanted her to go.[28] And she certainly wanted to go. She saw the trip as killing several birds with one stone – a mixture of motives that would cause her some difficulties with the authorities. On the one hand, there was her official responsibility to fulfil speaking engagements all over the country lined up by MOI. In between engagements, MOI wanted to show her off as a distinguished visitor to civic dignitaries. While accepting – or tolerating – all that, Mead was more interested in meeting 'people with diffusion value', the '"thinking pulse" of a community': journalists, teachers, social scientists, social workers, health officers. Such activities could be justified by reference to her special role as a welfare expert (thanks to her Food Habits work) and as an anthropologist (whose high-level advice was most likely to benefit other social scientists), and also on the grounds that she needed to understand the English in order to interpret the Americans to them. But they overlapped with, and to some extent camouflaged, another motive about which she was less candid – the desire to do fieldwork.[29]

Aware of the limitations of 'study at a distance', evident in Gorer's work on Japan, Greece and Burma, Mead was desperate to observe the natives of Great Britain much as she had observed the natives of New Guinea and Bali. During her trip she took field notes much as she had done in the South Seas. When her executor Rhoda Metraux deposited these notes in the Mead Papers in 1980, she attached an explanatory note: 'MM Fieldwork in England 1943 ... The remarkable thing is that MM collected – and kept – material exactly as she would have in any other field – except that, because of wartime conditions, there is no private data at all (possibly in notebooks?), only what openly relevant to OWI, etc.'[30] Thus it was not only dignitaries and 'high-level people' in welfare and social science, but also a good range of 'ordinary' people at work and especially at home, and most especially adults with children, that she wished to see. This intention is perfectly clear in Mead's instructions to MOI 'on the sort of things which I should like to see' given shortly after her arrival in early July.

> I should like to see the way in which all the wartime adjustments in regard to food and women and children work, and I am especially interested in seeing these at the operational level. I am more interested in talking with the woman who runs one British restaurant [the nationalized canteens] than with the one who has supervision over fifty, I am more interested in seeing nursery schools at work than in talking to supervisors. I should like to see something of the way in which conscripted women are placed. I'd like to sit in on some staff conferences in social agencies, schools, juvenile courts, etc. I should like to go

to committee meetings where actual local procedures are decided upon. I should like to see not only the specific wartime adjustments to bombing, such as different types of shelters, but also such things [as] trade union meetings where matters of social welfare were under discussion. I want to see schools, playgrounds, settings in which I can watch adults and children together. I should like to have just long enough interviews with the people at the top to ensure an entree lower down the scale.[31]

Touring the country for the next three months, she had to engage in some hand-to-hand combat with her MOI handler, Margaret Owen, as the demands of a speaker tour warred with the demands of a social scientist and the even more exigent demands of a participant-observer.[32]

*   *   *

Mead arrived in London on 2 July. Her previous experiences of Britain had been brief and conventionally touristic; this was her first attempt to apply her 'culture consciousness', and she found the results disorienting. The familiar 'contents' of the culture kept obscuring her view of the crucial character differences she was seeking. 'It's a frightfully difficult job, Gregory, the most difficult I've undertaken,' she wrote to Bateson after a few weeks; 'so much of the time everybody seems very familiar and just people, and I like them, and individual differences seem so much more obvious than cultural regularities.'[33] She was lonely and missing her husband badly – or so at least she reassured him constantly – and feeling frustrated by the first few weeks of endless orientation interviews with women, family and welfare experts lined up by MOI. Perhaps, too, she could feel Bateson slipping away from her. While she poured out her love to him in a sequence of long, engaged letters – drowning him with 'points' and solicitations of his feedback – he sent only the odd letter or practical cable. It was for him, he confessed, 'a lousy non-letter writing sweating and unhappy time', and Mead, knowing he was idle and frustrated, feared also – correctly as she later discovered – that he was seeking 'absorbing feminine interest'. There was a poignant moment at the end of July when she was recording a transatlantic panel discussion in the BBC's London studios, and Bateson turned up in the New York studio to listen. They could, perhaps, have snatched a few words after the recording. 'I was suddenly very excited to hear that you were in the studio at the Broadcast after I had given up hope, and I so clumsily said nothing,' wrote Mead afterwards; in a crossing letter, Bateson blamed the authorities: 'I did at least hope that they would allow us a word together and there was no good reason why they should not have except rules and regs.' A classic muddle of intercultural miscommunication, in this case following the predictable Anglo-American character differences – this one, apparently, they could not overcome.[34]

Two brief furloughs from the MOI schedule provided blessed relief and new sources of stimulation. The first was a three-day conference in Oxford on war aims run by the National Peace Council. Here she met

a former international banker, who used to fly from London, to Paris to Brussels, etc. discharging the same kind of business in the different capitals in rapid succession, which gave him the cross cultural sense. He is the nephew of a very famous banker who spent his life combining various sorts of international boards, with a real sense of what that meant. Now, fantastically enough, this man, he looks 30 but must be nearer 40, Erwin Schuller, is working with the National Council for Social Service . . . at least as bright as Geoffrey and has the advantage of always having been a professional, and a responsible professional. He's the only person I have met so far that I can talk to about things that matter intellectually.

Not the most tactful wording to address to Bateson – though she didn't also reveal that Schuller was handsome, sensitive, 'intensely romantic' and in general just the kind of man Mead adored. However, it does not appear that they had a sexual relationship to augment their intellectual one. By coincidence, Schuller was at that very juncture falling in love with a Canadian diplomat, Mary Craig McGeachy, who was more or less Mead's opposite number, posted to Washington by the British Ministry of Economic Warfare to massage Anglo-American relations, particularly among women and voluntary organizations. Many of the key 'points' Mead picked up on her trip were worked out in long letters – and her favoured eight-to-ten-hour face-to-face sessions – with Schuller, and they reappear in the work of McGeachy, whom Mead also met and 'liked very much' when they overlapped in London in October.[35] A few weeks later, she met another kindred spirit at a social-science training school for teachers in Durham. This was Marie (Mitzi) Jahoda, ex-wife of Mead's friend the Columbia sociologist Paul Lazarsfeld, a social scientist herself and by a stroke of luck another Austrian-Jewish émigré like Schuller. Together, they provided a useful cross-cultural check.

I imagine that just as we have found that a picture with two people in it is worth ten pictures with one person in it, so also working with real knowledge on two cultures simultaneously is an enormous economy. Mitzi is a grand person, as good in her way as Erwin is in his, and of course it's great luck to have met two Austrians, both profoundly interested in English culture, both conscious of what observation and understanding of English culture has done to them, and for them.[36]

In early August, Mead was finally put on the road by MOI, beginning an exhausting seven-week lecture tour to all corners of Britain. Her mood continued to be constricted by the tight MOI leash and the unending series of brief, unsatisfying formal visits: she still wasn't getting the deep cultural exposure she expected from fieldwork. Of course, her expectations were heavily biased in certain directions that MOI could not have been expected to recognize. As she wrote to Ruth Benedict on 7 August:

> It is incredibly hard to see cultural regularities when one is heavily confronted with adults as I am here. My principal supply of babies has been got from third class railway carriages when they are not too full to get into. I buy a first class ticket as a guarantee against standing up, then ride third hunting for babies. Adults are really no earthly use.[37]

Then a funny thing happened. As the tour ground on, and as MOI began to respond to her request to stay in more ordinary homes (rather than hotels) and to address larger and more diverse groups (rather than small professional women's groups), she began to wake up to the culture around her – as much to adults, and their earthly affairs, as to children and babies. Getting well away from London helped a lot. She went first to the northeast and the Durham coalfields, touring canteens and clinics and nurseries and council estates, addressing Labour Party groups and Rotary Clubs and branches of the Women's Voluntary Service; then to the big cities of Yorkshire – York, Leeds, Sheffield and Hull – and immediately cross-country to the west – Bristol, Yeovil, the Devon countryside; then the big cities of the northwest – Manchester and Liverpool – a dash back to London, and on to Wales, the Midlands and ending up in early October in Scotland.[38] Rattling around the country in crowded, ramshackle trains, most often with her typewriter in her lap pounding out a letter to Bateson or Schuller with some new 'points', was exhausting but exhilarating. The captive audiences of women and war workers made for some very large turnouts – a thousand aviation workers heard her address the conditions of war workers in the US at a midnight canteen rally at Fairey's in Stockport; nine hundred (admittedly 'for the most part composed of quite young lovers with no place to go') turned up in a Hamilton cinema at short notice to hear her lecture on 'Home Front USA'. What she loved best, though, were the smaller, more intimate gatherings where there was opportunity for give-and-take; she kept a careful note of the questions asked. At the Food Advice Centre in Wrexham she was 'asked to speak for about ten minutes while the pickle was cooking'. The boys of a Birmingham secondary school deluged her with eccentric questions: 'Do American women wear lights in their hats to signal taxis? In America do the bridges move and the cars stand still? Can you get the news on any station any time? Why do you kill people in an electric chair instead of hanging them? Which works better your telephone system or ours? Do people live in skyscrapers?' Her favourite encounter was with the ladies of the East Dulwich Grove Sisterhood, meeting them in their church parlour in that South London suburb where 'a tired, blackclad, middle-aged woman prayed, in a voice of unforgettable sweetness, that "all those who are on holiday may be having a grand time"' – thus far the story as she committed it to print – but also, recorded privately, '"And we do think of the Americans and their Jap war and pray it won't take too long to end for them, pray that something will 'appen to end it sooner."' It was the 'loveliest extempore prayer I have ever heard'.[39]

For she was falling in love with the English, which was, as she put it for Bateson's benefit, 'like falling in love with you all over again'.[40] The English proved much kinder and gentler than she had expected from Gorer's depiction of a miserable, repressed people. Individually they seemed ringed with a 'magic circle of quiet', which allowed them to 'peek out' at others curiously without being self-conscious. Collectively they interacted in the most marvellous ways, in a 'very gentle interaction' involving little direct contact but much indirect care for others. Privately, of course, she had an infant-training explanation for this, at least among the working-class families she observed in her third-class carriages:

> Children are allowed to wriggle – within reason – and simply held firmly by an indifferent, kind arm. The mother does not react as if they were intelligent beings, but holds them rather like puppies or kittens, even letting them bite a little – bite her or another child but never enough to really hurt, and without either pleasure or pain in the proceeding, just quiet sure 'holding on to them'. Under such treatment, a baby becomes very quiet, it can wriggle if it feels the urge, but there is absolutely no reward in wriggling, so mostly it goes to sleep.

This amounted to an application of abstract rules – 'freedom within an impersonally administered narrow range of safety' – as the Mead–Bateson hypotheses had proposed, but in the sweetest way; much more like the Balinese than she had expected, 'very fey', and not at all repressive, with no evident frustration. Rather than insisting on the imposition of authority, the English seemed governed by a 'taboo on power, this insistence that things must be left to grow, to develop', which as a democrat (and nurturer) Mead found immensely appealing. The voluntary organizations that she met with everywhere on her travels, and for which Schuller was a powerful advocate, began to seem like a model from which the Americans could learn. All of this would require some modification of the initial Mead–Bateson hypotheses about the exhibitionism of authority, which in the initial binary and ternary conceptions had been much more paternal, class-sodden and hierarchical. Her ear had been caught by the tone of voice of Mr Gosling, the chairman, at a welfare conference in Birmingham – parental, yes, but not very paternal – rather, gentle but jokily familiar: 'Baaaa. AH, I thought that sheeplike noise would catch your attention, and I must say the cackle you were making was rather like a barn yard – not of course that I mind barnyards, how could I my name being Gosling.' The English were turning out not to be hard like the Germans but soft like the Balinese, and yet still highly moral and effective; more comfortable with the practice of democracy, she speculated, than the Americans, only 'unverbalised and unselfconscious' about it.[41]

Towards the end of September, as her scheduled tour drew to an end, Mead decided to stay for an extra month in London to pull together the threads and to tackle some ambitious propaganda of her own, including broadcasts on topics of her choice that she had negotiated with the BBC and a British edition of *And Keep Your Powder Dry*.[42] She made a happy home in Chelsea with 'Steve' and 'Jolliffe', a lesbian couple – 'Steve' was Betty Cobbold, a former lover of Bateson's (and possibly of Mead's) from their Sepik River days, and 'Jolliffe' was Jolliffe (née Alice) Metcalfe, a writer. They took Mead in to their 'tiny little house . . . which used to rise in the air and curtsey when the rocket gun went off', and, Mead reminisced fondly on her return, 'when there was a bad raid everybody on the street went to stay with the kindest woman, sure that no bombs would find her out. It was rather like going back to just post-college days, only with everyone dreadfully tired out from the war.'[43] 'Steve' in particular was a fund of advice on how to address the English in their own idiom and usefully 'gentled' the new preface Mead was writing for what Penguin would shortly publish as *The American Character*.[44] Mead kept up a busy round of meetings throughout these last weeks in London, cementing her friendships with important contacts – Mary Somerville at the BBC, Letty Harford of the National Council of Social Service, Victor Weybright of the OWI London Outpost – and reaching out to higher-ups, as well – Lady Reading of the Women's Voluntary Service, Lady Cripps, Lord Woolton of the Ministry of Food and, especially, the US ambassador, J.G. Winant, 'a really great man'.[45] The meat-and-potatoes of this final phase of her trip was, however, to hammer out her new formulations about the

English character – and how to relate it to the American – and then to embed it in effective propaganda. She made signal progress on two fronts: a new hypothesis about the national character, based on her admiring observations of the British war effort, from which the Americans might learn; and diffusion of her old hypotheses about the differences between the Americans and the English, aimed at preparing the latter for the rising tide of GIs in the run-up to D-Day.

The new hypothesis entailed, as we have seen, a frank reassessment of the earlier suggestions about English attitudes to authority. Her first clue was about differences in scale. Like so many Americans landing in England, Mead was impressed by how small everything was, but like a good student of pattern she was convinced this impression was the key to a systematic cultural difference. As she wrote to Bateson shortly after arrival:

> I decided after about an hour in London that there was something queer about everything being so small, it wasn't the island, or the size of the population because we'd build larger for one million people. But the point seems to be that your units are infinitely more complex than ours. What goes wrong in understanding is that you point out a lake, which you see as the most intricate and delicate and highly organized pattern, and we see it as a simple blob of blue, and a small blob to boot, and so we say 'You should see Lake Michigan.' . . . When we look at English things we think they are small versions of our big ones, and when you look at our big ones – or rather when English people simply hear a few statistics of size – they feel that our big ones are superior – because they imagine that the complexity of the constituent units is preserved.

Another familiar trope came immediately to mind – England as a garden. It's not that the English couldn't plan, but that the small scale and greater complexity of their environment required a much subtler and more delicate approach: 'the gardener thinks about the colour, texture, the sort of difference which is given by the difference of sizes of the leaf, or the size of the flower, light and shade at different times of the day, with a few clouds calculated in as to whether they might shade the outer most petal of the top most rose.'[46] Thus while Americans tended to think in one dimension and on a single scale, the English thought in a complex hierarchy of dimensions,

> built up from such a large number of intricate, half conscious observations, that there is no possible way of reducing it to the sort of manageable combinations of form and color with which the American gardener

or room decorator traditionally operates . . . The American tendency to over-simplify and so act rapidly, contrasts strongly with the English insistence that no analytical statement ever does justice to the unique, complex quality of the whole. This difference is reflected in the greater interest in England in making an initial model and the American capacity to put such complex models rapidly into mass production.[47]

From this insight she concluded that Bateson's emphasis on the exhibitionism and dominance of authority or even the idea of a ternary structure by which correct relationships were governed was 'an oversimplification of the British refusal to deal in simple hierarchies', as she put it, not to Bateson, but to Schuller. What had been a statement about the assertion of power was now a statement about the diffusion of power.

It seems as if the British child is developed with a need, a sense of incompleteness without the whole of English society, and this expresses itself both in an acceptance and an actual enhancement of own identity by the recognition of all the differences which go to make up England, but also by the tendency to reconstruct a non-hierarchical, mixed function microcosm of English society whenever 'two or three are gathered together'.

The abstract rules were still significant – 'the impersonality of commands and exhortations' – but Mead now saw them less as emanating from a paternal authority and more from an organic sense of wholeness.[48]

This revised sense of social cooperation fitted better with her warm response to the perceived kindness and gentleness of the British people. It also gave a psychological underpinning to her observation of the unique operations of the British voluntary organizations. Schuller supplied the crucial metaphor: that in Britain the State was seen not as the source of authority, but as the 'junior partner', facilitating and enabling but not directing.[49] The 'senior partner' was the abstract code – which she sometimes now thought of as 'the Lord's will', having observed the gentle, diffusive Christianity in which the older voluntary organizations seemed steeped, or as tradition or nature or the feeling for 'home'. That feeling for 'home' brought together professional and volunteer, public and private, State and non-governmental bodies 'in a working team' almost intuitively, without frictions or jealousies, in a way that she found frankly astounding. It was almost more like her ideal microcosm of the world than multicultural America: 'HOME in England is a place into which everyone fits, each with his distinctive and accepted temperament . . . Hence the ease with which Englishmen become a team, fitting together as the

woman said to me "If we don't touch at one place we touch at another."'
Such an attitude cultivated personal qualities that she admired greatly:
'skill and tact', 'the personal touch', a close relationship between teachers
and students. It offered a healthy balance between the individual responsibility that she valued highly in Western, Protestant cultures but also the
sense of collective responsibility that she and Benedict had valued in
'primitive' cultures – what she identified in Britain as an ability to draw
sustenance and pleasure from 'beautiful social achievements'.[50] It was also,
as she saw it, highly democratic. In a summational memorandum on
'Some Significant Aspects of British Social Practice', drafted with Schuller,
she identified as 'the peculiar quality of British social skills': 'its great
ability to train people who work harmoniously in mixed and complementary terms; who not only tolerate divergence and minority atittudes but
cultivate and cherish them; who succeed in building up forms of organisa-
tion in which power is diffused, restrained and muffled, and responsibility
is personal and living.'[51]

These surprisingly democratic qualities helped her to address the role of
the social scientist in a democracy, a subject that had proved so vexing in
America. In Britain, the expert (like the State) was one of a number of
'junior partners', working alongside amateurs and volunteers, and imbued
by 'a salutary humility towards the citizen'. In fact, 'the more articulate,
the more systematic, the more self consciously regulative aspects of life
must be junior to those which by virtue of "character" express the Lord's
will', so that the State was the junior partner of the voluntary societies but
the expert was the junior partner of the State. That entailed, Schuller
admitted, '*prolonged* personal contact and the dangers of too slow a
rhythm'.[52] Mead saw that social science would have to be introduced
slowly into British consciousness, gradually working its way into the
bloodstream, and sold not as a 'quick fix' but rather as an almost biological
feature of social evolution. She now understood why Bateson had been so
frustrated by his failure to make an impact in the autumn of 1939. It
wasn't, she tried to persuade him, that his ideas were alien – on the
contrary, his organismic thinking was quintessentially English – but rather
that, arriving hotfoot off the boat from America, he was taken (and
mistook himself) for an outsider moving too fast, too suddenly:

English thinking is not opposed to what you want to do, really, but
opposed to the insistence of very inferior would-be social scientists on
the need to import whole sale research methods from America or the
continent. But I have a feeling that you have thought of yourself – qua
scientist – as déraciné – far, far more than is true. It's true of Geoffrey.

From here I can see how hopelessly out of key he is; he'll simply have to stay in America, he would do desperate harm over here.[53]

In the summational memorandum, she suggested that America had much to learn from the British model of social service. She used the Citizens Advice Bureaux, set up by Schuller's National Council of Social Service, as the exemplar. These were centrally funded but locally run. Their policies were dictated by local circumstances, determined by a mix of local elected officials and private-sector bodies – just as she had recommended for the American war effort in *And Keep Your Powder Dry*. They were staffed by a mixture of professionals and volunteers, thus keeping the 'experts' in touch with the ordinary citizen and avoiding the dangers of 'excessive professionalisation' encountered in America. The big question was how to graft these valuable qualities on to American 'technical efficiency'. If the American character really was as different from the English as both were from the Balinese, the task might be impossible – but, as we have seen, Mead had begun to doubt whether the English were that different from the Balinese, and here she also downplayed the difference of the Americans. It might be possible to convey the genius of English voluntary organizations to American sensibilities by *demonstrating* it – for example, by role-playing – or by showing how it worked in practical situations, as could be done by reference to the Citizens Advice Bureaux.[54]

The memorandum was written by Mead and Schuller – she was, she told him teasingly, happy to play the role of 'junior partner' and accept any changes he suggested – as an explicitly cross-cultural document, to be shared between British and American readers. Its first outing had a British audience, when the National Council of Social Service convened a large gathering of representatives of voluntary organizations in London to hear Mead speak on 12 October. They were perhaps a little embarrassed to be praised so effusively. (Dame Rachel Crowdy, the doyenne of British welfare workers, writing to thank Mead afterwards, thought it only fair to point out that she was describing an exceptional wartime emergency where amateurs and professionals necessarily mucked in together.)[55] But the real test would come when Mead returned to America: would American audiences accept a dose of English 'common sense', if put to them in their own language?

Mead found the development of this new hypothesis about the quiet, unarticulated practice of democracy and social science by the British – so different from the American, yet so effective in its own way in harnessing expertise to democratic goals – completely absorbing and gripping. It provided the music for her relationship with Schuller, it engaged her intellectual faculties at their highest level, it pointed out a practical road for the pursuits she loved best, it even gave her more opportunities to romance Bateson long distance with her newfound love of all things English (though with doubtful effect). Yet the more humdrum work (for which she had, after all, been engaged by MOI and OWI) of orchestrating Anglo-American relations on the popular level had its own pleasures and attracted a different and much larger audience. While touring Britain in August and September, Mead had sniffed out what were the few underlying preconceptions about Americans among those who came to hear her speak, and also what their anxieties were about the mounting numbers of GIs.

Mead's gentler depiction of the English character made all the more urgent the need to draw the sting of American exhibitionism. This became the centrepiece of her propaganda aimed at the British people. In two broadcasts made for the mass audience of the BBC's Home Service at the end of her trip, she tackled head-on the problem of 'why we Americans "talk big"'. This allowed her to deliver a full-blown popular version of her analysis of the differences between the American and English characters. Hailing from a 'new civilisation', Americans have no absolute standards and so they tend to compare things to each other in a crude way: what is the best, the biggest, the brightest, who is the most successful? As children in the home, they are encouraged to voice these opinions, and in many ways the GI is just an overgrown child, overstating and exaggerating everything. Here Mead had to explain for once not why the English seemed uncomfortably like the Germans (in obeying the paternal voice of authority), but why the Americans did (with their bluster and swagger). Really the Americans were just as moral and respectable as the English, just as opposed to bullying – their loud voices and exhibitionistic speech were simply the culturally specific ways they expressed similar values. The same applied to other nuances of American behaviour that Mead had found, time and time again, irritated their English hosts: the way they stood around on street corners, slouching and chewing gum, leaning up against the walls. These were natural expressions of the different environments in which Americans grew up; learning to accept them could be part of building a peaceful world of many cultures.[56]

The most popular element of Mead's pitch to her mass audience was her analysis of the 'boy meets girl problem', which, she wrote to Bateson at the end of her trip, 'was badly in need of attention' and to which she had devoted much of her energies in her last few weeks in Britain. On her travels she had encountered a good deal of anxiety about the sexual aggressiveness of GIs, especially in those parts of the country that had not seen any yet. That aggressiveness, she explained, was part of the general exhibitionism of American youth – it was happy-go-lucky but not predatory. Boys compete with each other to spin the perfect 'line' in order to 'score'; girls compete with each other to attract the 'line' and spurn it; it's all part of a game, which 'takes a lot of practice' and isn't about love or sex at all. English girls are either unnecessarily alarmed or taken in by it, and offer themselves too wholeheartedly when nothing like as much is expected. The American boys need to learn how to slow down; the English girls need to learn how to deflect American boys who don't. Mead returned time and again to this theme in a host of forums: broadcasts, pamphlets, speeches, journalism (such as 'What Is a Date?' in *Transatlantic*) and even role-playing scenarios.[57] It got her a lot of attention and a good deal of acclaim – typical of the way in which she was able to root her abstractions about national character in scenarios for everyday life that resonated with wide audiences. 'In my own view,' her BBC producer wrote after the first broadcast, 'Margaret Mead achieved more towards real Anglo-American understanding in her ten minutes' talk than most other American speakers put together . . . she certainly possesses a flair for touching the core of the problems of ordinary people.'[58]

Mead's most ambitious efforts to convey a 'culture and personality' understanding of Anglo-American difference to a mass audience in Britain came after her return to America. In a farewell memorandum to Ambassador Winant, written just before her departure, she again pressed the counter-intuitive point that character differences between the Americans and the English were much greater than the superficial simi-larities of their cultures' content implied. A lot of the existing approaches to Anglo-American relations were thus missing the mark, even exacer-bating misunderstandings. One issue was, as she shrewdly noted, that the Americans who knew most about Britain were the more privileged and better-educated, who knew their English literature; the average American lacked this understanding. In contrast, the British who knew most about America were the less privileged and less well-educated, who knew their American movies: they liked the materialism and the can-do mentality; the upper classes did not. Attempts to surmount this dilemma invariably failed. Stressing 'blood ties', for example, was 'in a sense a denial of American democratic tendencies' and was bound to be repudiated by immigrant Americans. Half-hearted acceptance of difference was no better: 'Everytime an Englishman does something he believes wrong or inferior, because "it's the only thing the Americans will accept", he is laying the ground work for a later rejection of Americans as representing his worse self.'[59]

There was no substitute, Mead argued, for the full and honest explica-tion of cultural difference that only an anthropologist could provide. One tool she had for this was the British edition of *And Keep Your Powder Dry*, which appeared early in 1944, with a preface 'from England' written with Steve's help in her little Chelsea home. She was unapologetic about the book's native account of the American character which, she thought, would give the British a more authentic flavour than the sensationalism of their own wartime press – so long as it was understood that it was written *for* Americans, in their language, and that a genuinely cross-cultural product would have to be written differently.[60] But she also wanted to write that genuinely cross-cultural product. This initially took the form of a report back to OWI, worked up into a bilingual version for general circulation – 'The Yank in Britain' – that was published in the main 'Current Affairs' pamphlet series of both the American and the British armies for distribution to the troops.[61]

There had been other such publications before. The most famous was Eric Knight's *Short Guide to Great Britain*, published in 1942 to coincide with the first build-up of American troops in advance of the invasion of North Africa, which has since become a nostalgia item, marketed as 'Instructions for American Servicemen in Britain 1942'. It was mostly a straightforward job of translation: don't say 'bloody', don't criticize the king and queen, learn to handle pounds and pence, get to know cricket and football and the pub. The psychological content was thin but familiar: the British are reserved because they live on a crowded island; they're leisurely, but not backward; Britain is a small country and the British don't care about 'biggest', but it's an old country and they do care about 'oldest'; they're tougher and more democratic than they look. Above all, be polite and don't boast. There was even a glossary at the back. But to Mead's tastes this kind of cultural translation was *too* straightforward. It wasn't the case, she thought, that 'in their major ways of life the British and American people are much alike', still less that 'The best way to get on in Britain is very much the same as the best way to get on in America'.[62] So in 'The Yank in Britain' she was unusually frank both about the distinctive take of the anthropologist and about the counter-intuitive conclusions it could throw up. As the foreword explained: 'Margaret Mead's views on the subject are important and particularly worth discussing because – however new, surprising and fantastic-sounding they may be to some of us – she is a professional student of the American character, where we are amateurs.' The surprise came in that counter-intuitive point, that 'the British and American societies are "systematically" different. An American is not just an Englishman who has a few odd habits; an Englishman is not just an American with a rather different accent and idiom . . . in some respects, the Americans are as systematically different from us as we are from the French or the Russians.' (Presumably the Balinese were *too* exotic a comparator.) Mead then ran through the themes she had rehearsed during her tour: why Americans talk big (and, conversely, why the British seem to be so superior), 'what is a date', the impatience of the American fixer versus the British art of compromise. But she now played up the bigger framing issues, especially the ways in which New and Old World cultures differed: the problems of scale, the different modes of exhibitionism, and the way in which its history gave Old World people a tradition to be deferred to while the New World people trumpeted their own more active role. Above all, there was that insistent message of cultural relativism, that foreigners are *not* like you but with 'a few funny customs': 'Every detail of behaviour, because it is part of a different systematic character, a character developed in a new country settled by peoples from many different societies, a character developed in the machine age without any shadings from a pre-industrial period of society, contrasts with the British character.' Rather than relying on the sentimental assumption that 'the English-speaking peoples of the world are very much alike', it would be better to strive for 'real understanding' of difference. 'If each group accepts the other as different and then really explores the differences it may work better.'[63] That was a moral that Mead hoped to take from Anglo-America to the world.

Although the Army education corps on both sides of the Atlantic liked Mead's closing salvo very much, the diplomats were not so sure. As with the 'breakfast table' broadcast, there was some concern about this odd business of cementing the Anglo-American alliance by highlighting Anglo-American difference. In part, this merely reflected the tight-lipped instincts of the diplomat. Was it a good idea, queried Alan Dudley of the Foreign Office, to joke about the GIs' dating habits among the British troops, 'who are already pretty worried about what the Americans may be doing with their wives and girl friends in their absence'? But there was also a reasonable concern that Mead's method could be unnecessarily exaggerating the Old World/New World divide at a moment of rapid social change in Britain that might actually be narrowing it. Dudley was concerned about the 'implicit assumption in the text that the British love antiques and the Americans aren't interested in them. Myself, I can't see much difference between the two. Indeed, I think I have heard more sorrow expressed by Americans than by British about the bombing of old buildings.' 'We quite agree with what you say,' replied OWI's Victor Weybright, 'about the overwhelming interest of the British people in the future, with a certain disdain of tradition – but it is never wise for an American to express too much of that. In my experience, it generally inspires a defensive attitude toward the old things and old ways.' In fact, he thought that, as 'a trans-atlantic character and writing as an anthropologist', Mead might have been able to do more than most to minimize the cultural differences, had she wished to.

But Margaret was Margaret – and Weybright was a diplomat too. He told her that she had been responsible for the 'most significant job of translation that has been done in the war':

> When I look back at the by-products of your visit, I find them immeasurable in their influence and importance. If you had never made a speech while here, your investment of time and energy would still be good, but your penetrating genius has left its educative effect in every region in the land, and through organizations and groups, including those which you encountered almost casually when on the wing.[64]

What lessons can be taken away from this most extended of Mead's experiments in intercultural communication? The theoretical premises with which she began look feeble if not pernicious today: the very idea of 'national character'; the centrality of infant and child training in forming it; the insignificance of cultural 'contents', and of history, economics and politics (except as registered in family relationships); the tendency to differentiate nations radically on the basis of 'character' alone. Contemporaries not coming from a 'culture and personality' standpoint were much more attentive to differences of class, region and ethnicity, and, since Mead's day, cultural analysts have emphasized other distinctions, especially gender. As we have seen, Mead's own sympathizers were inclined to criticize her reliance on the likes of Gorer and Bateson – public school- and Oxbridge-educated, with childhoods dating back to before the First World War – and the resulting failure of their national-character analysis to register the pace of social change. The English national character that she had hypothesized with Bateson before her visit actually looked more like the older stereotypes of an upper-crust 'John Bull' than it did the stereotypes prevalent in the interwar period, of a timid and gentle petty-bourgeois 'Little Man', which Gorer and Bateson had been too 'déraciné' to notice.

At the same time, our greater appreciation of cultural diversity ought to help us see the other side of the coin too. Mead was right to feel that the ideological imperatives of the wartime alliance caused the diplomats and the more hard-headed propagandists to ignore too blithely the real cultural tensions between the two peoples. She had pointed out accurately the paradox that the Americans who knew about Britain and the British who knew about America liked each other – but for different reasons, representing different slices of the population; everyone else had a problem. Those problems were exacerbated by the unique wartime problems of real cultural contact. By the spring of 1944 there were 1.5 million Americans in Britain, preparing for D-Day; that level of foreign visitation wouldn't be reached again until the advent of mass air tourism in the 1960s. Real human contact did tend to elicit awareness of cultural difference that had been absent before: there was a genuine thirst for explanations of phenomena such as 'the date', boasting, racism and super-patriotism. And Mead had plausible, comprehensible answers that gave both sides permission to 'be themselves'. Her candour about cultural difference established a precedent that allowed, for example, the Army to commission from her brother-in-law Leo Rosten the even riskier *112 Gripes about the French* for distribution to US forces in France in 1945.[65] While Mead's national-character hypotheses may have led her astray in certain respects, her skill as a participant-observer stood her in good stead. Her observations did change her mind, and she shucked off, imperceptibly, some of the grosser generalizations about the English style of paternal authority, instead substituting more sensitive observations of the ways in which authority relations were handled in a wide range of wartime makeshifts. She worked into her analysis of the culture very up-to-the-minute observations of, for example, the newly enhanced role that women volunteers were playing in the war effort – causing one of her local feminist admirers to call her visit 'a land-mark in the women's move-ment in this country'[66] – which did capture an element of social change and build it into an analysis of national character. It helped, here, that Mead was doing fieldwork, and on her own, while Bateson and Gorer were far away, both becoming increasingly engrossed in 'enemy' research, for which their native land was a sideshow.

Granted, what Mead saw as deep-seated national traits we might now see as more superficial acts of 'performance': the culturally specific ways in which British people of certain classes behaved when under pressure, or in the chair of a meeting, or greeting an honoured guest, or, conversely, the ways in which American people of a certain age and sex behaved when thrown into an unfamiliar culture with spending money and time on their hands. Nevertheless, whether these were deep-seated psycho-logical characteristics or simply performances of culturally approved behaviours, Mead was able to recognize them and interpret them in an idiom that both peoples could understand, and which they could apply in performing their casual interactions in the months leading up to D-Day.[67] And she did so with evident love and understanding for both sides, a stance that she adopted deliberately, not only because her job was to improve Anglo-American relations, but also because she saw it as a model for how all nations ought to approach each other in the postwar world.

*   *   *

Oddly, she found the job of cultural translation more difficult after she returned to her own native ground in November – for reasons both personal and cultural. She came back exhilarated by her experiences and ready to apply them to improving her own Anglo-American relations. Bateson reported to his old family friend Nora Barlow that he found Mead 'better in health and energy than I have seen her for years' and 'completely in love with England'. She felt she had been personally altered by her extended exposure to the English. 'Gregory says my manner, especially my platform manner, has become much gentler,' she wrote to Schuller in late December. This ought to have brought her closer to Bateson, but she admitted that they both found her new mood a little disorienting. As she confided to Steve and Jolliffe: 'Gregory has had to learn to get used to a wife who (1) can walk and doesn't insist on riding for a block or so, (2) smokes of her own volition and may even have cigarettes, and (3) knows a lot about England. He finds this confusing but reports that it is also on the whole an improvement.'[68] But Bateson was not really in a state of mind to appreciate this transformation. As Mead found out, he had had 'one abortive and one unsatisfactory affair while I was gone'.[69] He had, it is true, finally made the breakthrough for which he had been yearning since the autumn of 1939, and while Mead was away had begun to work for OSS in Washington on 'morale operations' – black propaganda – in the Far East theatre. This raised the possibility that they could establish a more stable joint household in Washington. Bateson floated the bizarre idea that they should move with Cathy into Gorer's sizeable apartment in Washington. This would mean Mead taking back the 'housekeeping' duties from Mary Frank, which with her busy schedule she might not be able to handle; and in any case, he sensibly concluded, 'I don't see Geoffrey and Cathy combined', not in his jewel-box of an apartment.[70] They did spend a little time at Gorer's, when he was on PWE business in San Francisco, but otherwise Mead had to return to her mad commute between New York and Washington, now with responsibility for running the CIR office in New York as well as her Food Habits office in Washington.[71] Within a few months, Bateson had made the ultimately suicidal decision – suicidal for their marriage, and for his peace of mind – to join the OSS field unit in Ceylon (Sri Lanka) and undertake black propaganda in earnest. He would be gone for over a year and a half. Although Mead again kept up a stream of letters with 'points' and plans for the future, to all intents and purposes personal communications between the couple had broken down.

At the same time the mildly anglicized Mead was finding it difficult to communicate with the Americans about the English. Having worked out how to talk about America in England, she now focused on talking about

England in America – and it wasn't easy. She was beset by 'extreme worry about how to shade every word to the feelings of at least two cultures'.[72] Worse, her higher opinion of the English seems to have triggered in her a lower opinion of the Americans. Their 'total absence of humility' was striking, their 'predetermination either to love or hate – and no intellectual interest in just understanding what it is all about'. What she had once found charming about the 'chip on the shoulder' she now found infuriating: Americans could never admit that they were in a position of strength, they always had to pretend they were the weak ones so they could surprise themselves with success. She was dismayed by the outbursts of unreasoning anti-British feeling with which her attempts at intercultural communication were met, 'a symbol of so many of our own little conflicts', a sign of the deep-seated insecurity that the 'younger brother' of the New World still felt towards its 'big sister' of the Old. She couldn't respect even their pro-British feelings, stemming as they did from snobbery or guilt. But Anglo-American relations was now her supreme specialism and she was determined to work hard on it, lecturing and broadcasting on the subject here, there and everywhere; proselytizing for the British way of voluntary action; and repeatedly calling for more direct contact between the cultures, the only antidote to the yawning gap of values and material standards. 'The major job is actually here,' she wrote to Victor Weybright as D-Day loomed; 'sooner or later I have to write a book on the subject.'[73]

For help with 'points' that might untangle the knots of miscommunication, Mead turned back to her private seminar in Washington. After Bateson's departure she had moved into the 'lovely little house' in Georgetown of Georgiana Stevens, an OSS analyst whose husband, Harley, was one of Bateson's bosses in the Far East (and thus a convenient source of information about him). Her seminar was at its peak – the core group of Gorer, Rhoda Metraux, Claire Holt and Phil Mosely now sometimes reinforced by the magnetic presence of Erwin Schuller, over on United Nations Relief and Rehabilitation Agency (UNRRA) visits – and she put them to work on cracking Anglo-American relations. Gorer and Schuller tended to wrangle – perhaps there was some competition for Mead's attention? – but Mead loved the crackle in the atmosphere.[74]

Gorer did offer one fruitful insight into Anglo-American relations which, typically, he made in challengingly Freudian terms. Mead had hypothesized that, for the English, 'initiation' of a relationship was taboo – similar to, but not quite like, the Balinese, where the taboo was on 'response' – and Gorer provided the complement: that, for the Americans, 'initiation' was OK but 'over-response' was taboo. Gorer then analysed the resulting failure of communication in terms of latent homosexual relations between men: 'one male is always trying to betray another into an aggressive role', the English wanting 'an opening so that I will not have made the opening', the American also wanting an opening 'so I can respond to you'. They saw no immediate solution to this problem except in the presence of a third party – the 'gooseberry', in English argot – 'that institutionalized non-initiatory receptivity and responsive aggression'. (Mead wrote plaintively to Bateson, 'If you were here we could finish that one in an hour.')[75] For public consumption, they put it in terms that still packed a sexual punch but that were more acceptable. Americans were terrified of looking like 'suckers', and so as always they feigned weakness in the presence of unknown strength. The English didn't play this game; they relied instead on the 'rules of good sportsman-ship', which they assumed could be articulated without offence. Thus the American might say to the Englishman today, 'With our bad diplomacy you must be able to take advantage of us always', and the Englishman, rather than seeking to allay the American's fear of being a sucker, would reply, 'Yes, but we don't as often as we could' – 'infuriating to an American,' Mead observed. Here was a practical refinement of the earlier theses about communication differences, now presented not in familial terms but in a language of conventions about strength and weakness – 'it's easier and arouses less antagonism,' Mead confessed in a letter to Bateson – and with real-world applications. The dialogue about diplomacy actu-ally happened, reported in an anglophobe outburst by the isolationist senator Owen Brewster in a magazine article entitled 'Let's Not Be Suckers Again'.[76]

In an attempt to model these miscommunications, Mead staged a role-playing exercise one evening in November 1944. Gorer and a young social psychologist working for the Army Research Branch, Irving Janis, played British and American liaison officers respectively. Mead reported the proceedings in a letter to Bateson:

It was lovely, Geoffrey becoming drier, thinner, more impersonal, the American bursting with personality. The plot was one in which one liaison officer asks the other for a favor and then takes it back having made a deal with the higher ups for something else. G's opening phrase in the second interview, 'I'm afraid I've made rather a fool of both of us', simply heard as 'I've been a fool'. The American wanted the Britisher to 'take his hair down', give him the low down, curse the higher ups or in the reversed position tell about similar jams he'd been in, and make it a matter of identification and personality. The Englishman wants a single word of sympathy, 'I say, tough luck', then the whole thing got through very impersonally, and a word at the end to disassociate their personal relations from this unpleasant business. Furthermore you get a fake 'hair down', like a charge of nepotism, being the usual British polite falsehood which says, 'the real reason behind this is policy and none of your business', so that when the American does let his hair down, the Englishman merely suspects he's telling a polite lie – and so can not make anything of it. I think we may try to make a recording. That would be for teaching, but anyway, it's a grand way of learning more than one ever could by mere interview. The gestures, the way the smoke is blown, etc. all become so revealing.[77]

Mead and Gorer then put their heads together to find formulations that might overcome these cultural differences – not so much on the ordinary GI level as on the higher levels of relations between officials that would be relevant in postwar diplomacy. There were ways to simulate the presence of a 'gooseberry' – to make Americans realize that their own anglophile snobs were pro-British for the wrong reasons, or that the British had their own problems with other Europeans – but that seemed too roundabout, too complicated a way to approach what ought to be a straightforward relationship. How to convey the idea of a genuine *partnership* between the two nations? Again they came up against their own self-inflicted conviction that every concept was inflected differently by radically different characters. To the English, they thought, 'partner' evoked a friendly sporting relationship, a meaning derived from the culture of 'the great public schools', whereas to the Americans it had a more businesslike, middle-class significance. This was a huge difference – between a symmetrical relationship (where the two partners speak as equals, as in a doubles match, egging each other on) and a complementary one (where the two partners are only temporarily allied, edgily wary of each other). Mead recalled how angry she had got with Bateson's friend Claude Guillebaud, when the Americans were struggling at the Battle of Anzio, and 'he said in a voice of deep sympathy, "The Americans are having a lot of trouble aren't they". He was saying, "Hard luck partner". I thought he was saying, "You aren't pulling your weight."'[78]

In the end, Mead was finding that while it was possible to phrase Anglo-American relations to either one audience or the other in an acceptable way, it was – if you accepted the radical difference in character – exceedingly difficult to phrase it acceptably to both at once. The best you could do, possibly, was to raise culture consciousness, to make people *expect* such frictions and to understand them as the pleasure of diversity rather than the necessity of antagonism. As the end of the war came into sight after D-Day, Mead presented her formulations for Anglo-American relations more and more as a model for intercultural relations on a global scale. Ideally the hundreds of thousands of GIs would come back from Europe having learned a little lesson in intercultural relations, 'which will influence American international attitudes for generations to come'.[79] Her job was to drive that lesson home. In January 1945 she began to write a column, 'Learning to Live in One World', distributed by the Common Council for American Unity for publication in dozens of immigrant newspapers in seventeen languages across the country. The foreign-born Americans, she thought, already had the experience of living in the 'nation of nations', an experience that they could teach to the native-born.[80] And she began to write the book that she had promised Weybright – also tentatively titled 'Learning to Live in One World' – in which the lessons learned from her fieldwork in Britain, and applied on her return to America, would come centre stage. If one lesson was that even the Anglo-American relationship was fraught with irreconcilable differences, that was a salutary reminder of the real 'variety of cultures' that would have to be orchestrated in any peaceful postwar order. She had at least learned how to tell each culture about the other, if not in the presence of both together; how to get them to recognize difference, to respect it, and to laugh at it (so long as one was thereby laughing at oneself). 'The types of clarification and types of presentation which will increase understanding between pairs of cultural groups,' she hoped, could then be extended to 'more complicated groupings.'[81]

Mead's transition from war to peace would be remarkably smooth. That was a planned consequence of her strategy to remain independent, to keep her war work relevant for peace, to ensure that the aggression inevitable in wartime not become permanently embedded in the structures created for the postwar order. That was not, though, a strategy available to – or even attractive to – everyone. By the end of 1944, nearly all of her closest associates were involved intimately and messily in psychological warfare against the enemy. Gorer had long been attracted by the manipulation of the German and Japanese psyches and at PWE was now devoted to it full time. Bateson had succumbed, in his loneliness and frustration, to the dark arts of black propaganda, and while Mead was gaily peppering him with 'points' about the English idea of partnership he was preparing to plunge into the jungles of Burma as part of an OSS 'dirty tricks' field unit. Even Ruth Benedict, from the autumn of 1944, was being directed firmly by her superiors at OWI to the analysis of Japanese morale in preparation for the big push into the home islands in 1945. All of Mead's friends had to deal with much trickier ethical issues than ever confronted her among the natives of Great Britain.

What damage did it do to the method – and the practitioner – to manip-ulate and distort rather than to translate and mediate? How could you orchestrate cultural diversity if not all cultures were deemed equally worthy of recognition, and some were stigmatized as diseased and dangerous? These experiences would pose intellectual problems – and leave emotional scars.

Bateson in the East Indies on the last day of war

CHAPTER 4

Culture Cracking for War
II. Enemies (1942–5)

Margaret Mead was right to avoid associating herself too closely with the analysis of the national character of the Allies' enemies, Germany and Japan. Her personal attraction to the idea of national character was as a means of building 'culture consciousness' for a postwar order, through which Americans would learn to understand and to accept many other, different cultures on a basis of equality. Anthropologists could best build up their credibility during the war, she felt, by showing Americans what their own culture looked like, how it differed from other cultures that they thought they knew well (like that of the British), and especially by acclimatizing Americans to the novel deluge of other cultures that they had encountered for the first time in fighting this world war. For these purposes Germany and Japan were worse than useless. Depictions of the German and Japanese character were bound to be tainted by the ideological hostilities that had led to the war in the first place. Building domestic morale to gird Americans against the Germans and Japanese would require an intensification of that hostility, not its mitigation. Worse, the use of culture cracking against enemies would undermine the basic anthropological perspective on cultures as healthy, functional wholes: in wartime, the goal was to find weaknesses in the enemy, not strengths; to sap the enemy's unity, not build it up; in short, to crack the enemy's culture up, not just crack it open.

On the other hand, it was not possible, or even desirable, to resist entirely the temptation to apply the new techniques to enemies as well as neutrals and allies. Mead wanted to win the war. A postwar order based on cultural diversity would not be possible without an Allied victory, and she could hardly deny her own side what she thought to be one of its most powerful weapons. If it was a matter of finding 'clients' for social science, in government and the military, there were many more clients interested in Germany or Japan than in Burma or Romania. The uses of anthropology for 'enemy' work were still greater than they were for communicating with neutrals or allies. In addition to white propaganda, as useful for enemies as for others, there were dangerous but tempting and valuable opportunities for black propaganda aimed at sapping both civilian and military morale. Captured POWs would need management by culturally skilled experts as well as psychological interrogation to further aid propaganda. Then there was the still more enticing (if distant) prospect of postwar reconstruction. Here the opportunities went well beyond the business of orchestrating intercultural communication to the much more interventionist business of rehabilitating enemy cultures for reincorporation into the comity of nations. If it was a matter of selling the uses of 'culture and personality' to a mass market, again there was vastly more public interest in what made the Germans and the Japanese tick – certainly more than what made the Americans and the British tick, which the public must have thought they already understood.

Mead's unsatisfactory compromise was to reserve her own energies and reputation for peace, but to aid and abet behind the scenes those of her intimates who were playing their part in pursuing psychological warfare against the enemy. In that difficult period before the war in the Pacific began, Bateson and, to a limited extent, Gorer were bending their minds to fathoming the Germans in the same terms in which Mead was considering the Anglo-American relationship. By the end of the war, Gorer, Bateson and even Benedict were working full time in psychological warfare against Japan. Their wartime commitments caused Mead – and 'culture and personality' more generally – political and intellectual problems that would trouble her project well into the postwar years.

* * *

Unlike many of the other wartime functions of anthropologists, where the relevant expertise in culturally specific psychology could only be got from them, the study of German and specifically Nazi psychology was already crowded well before anthropologists came to it. Unlike the little-studied cultures in which anthropologists normally trafficked, the German national character had been an object of much curiosity to other Europeans for generations. The contradiction between the dreamy, idealistic people who had seemed to characterize German literature and philosophy at least since the eighteenth century, and the brutal militarism of the Prussians that was thought to have forged the nation since the 1860s, had produced a wealth of commentary on the 'Janus-faced' or 'two-character' nature of Germanness among historians, literary scholars, political scientists and latterly psychologists. 'Zwei Herzen schlagen in meiner Brust' went the allegedly characteristic German saying (from Goethe's *Faust*) – 'two hearts beat in my breast'; or, as Larry Frank once put it, the Germans were split between Beethoven and Bismarck.[1] This picture was further complicated by the views of the average American, who tended to have yet another image of the German: the pious, hard-working, conscientious immigrant who was thought to have made the best kind of American (even better than the English strain).[2]

The rise to power of the Nazis offered one way out of this tangle. The Nazis could be seen as the 'bad' Germans, tyrannizing over the 'good', or as an extreme version of the bad half of the German split character.[3] Either way, it was still possible to find some essential goodness in the Germans, even in the depths of Nazi wickedness. One opinion poll after the outbreak of the European war showed that fully two-thirds of Americans thought that the Germans were basically good people ruled by gangsters.[4] The understanding that something new and special had happened in Germany since 1933 fostered historical, political and socio-logical interpretations, but not anthropological ones. The particular conditions of capitalism and modernity in Depression-era Germany seemed to have created an entirely novel phenomenon, concentrated in particular sections of German society worst hit by those conditions. Attention focused on the lower-middle class. Squeezed between socialism and capitalism, between the working class and the big bourgeoisie, the German lower-middle class seemed terribly frightened and insecure. Given contemporary psephological estimates of the strength of the Nazi vote among the lower-middle classes, it was easy and reasonable to connect the rise of Nazism with a powerful emotional reaction among just this social group. That was certainly the theory most prevalent among the neo-Freudians when Mead first encountered them in the mid-1930s, both Marxists like Erich Fromm and non-Marxists like Harold Lasswell, whose 1933 article on 'The Psychology of Hitlerism' was one of the earliest and most influential statements of this view.[5]

So when Mead and Bateson began to develop their formulations on national character in the years before Pearl Harbor, the German case had already been closely scrutinized, including by some of their own associates, within frameworks quite different from their more holistic anthropological one. Nevertheless, they did try to fit Germany into the same scheme, based on the idea of schismogenesis, that they used to explain dominance and submission behaviours in the British and American family dramas. For much of 1940 and 1941, Bateson considered that his best chance of finding satisfying war work lay in retooling himself as an expert on psychological warfare against the Germans, building on the work he had begun during his brief spell back in Britain. His basic idea was that German culture was saturated to an unusual extent by 'complementary' schismogenesis – especially dominance and submission – without either the 'symmetrical' checks (such as competition between equals) that provided stability in Britain or America, or the reversals of the dominance-submission relationship between older and younger that gave America its peculiar dynamism. Bateson puzzled over how a culture could survive without these checks and balances: should not the dominance of authority become so overbearing as to spin out of control? One possible check, though not a stable one, was that overtly submissive behaviour on the part of the dominated in German culture was not approved any more than it was in Britain or America, although much more submission was in fact required. Instead, in Germany submission was 'masked', portrayed as obedience not to a dominant authority figure but to an impersonal code. (One can see why, when Mead discovered the significance of the impersonal code in Britain in 1943, she was concerned that this might make Britain look too much like Germany.) In this way, submission became a point of honour, 'a sort of heel-clicking exhibitionism which takes the place of overt submissive behavior', hinting at the ways in which remorseless submission might be made psychologically tolerable.[6]

Yet Bateson was dissatisfied with this schema. How could such a society remain stable for long? It was one of the fundamental assumptions of the 'national character' approach that the character structure identified must have been laid down over many generations. After all, the Nazis themselves must have been brought up in pre-Nazi families.[7] One idea that occurred to Bateson and Mead later was that recent changes in German society might have removed some of the essential 'symmetrical' checks: for example, the old tradition of *Wanderschaft* by which German boys escaped for a time the insufferable pressures of their family drama.[8] That and similar ideas would later provide some hope for reconstructing German culture on a healthier basis that was still consistent with their fundamental national-character structure. But the principal difficulty was that Bateson and Mead lacked the rich and detailed sense of the German family drama that they had gained first-hand for its British and American equivalents, a defect they continued to lament as late as 1943 when they were preparing the 'breakfast table' broadcast.[9]

Some resources could be found close at hand. Following the pattern common to all of their early national-character studies, Bateson and Mead interviewed German émigrés and fieldworkers, read novels and journalism, watched films. Bateson devoted quite a lot of time to an analysis of a German propaganda film, *Hitlerjunge Quex*, which seemed to offer insights into the German family drama.[10] Their collaboration with Philip Mosely, later a mainstay of the seminar group in Washington, began with two interviews Bateson and Mead undertook with him at this time. Though best known as a Russianist, Mosely had done fieldwork in

Romania, among the ethnic German community in Transylvania, and although Mead was frustrated by his lack of psychological data – 'Your information is majorly political,' she groused – she was struck by the account he gave of a German community separated from the main body of Germans that had nonetheless retained its distinctive character for eight hundred years.[11]

Their main inspiration, however, came from the émigrés – a fact that, Mead admitted later, might have skewed their findings. The idea for the significance of the impersonal code came from Kurt Lewin, an émigré psychologist at the University of Iowa, whom Mead had first met through Larry Frank at the time of the Hanover conferences.[12] More important were the theoretical perspectives provided by the neo-Freudian émigrés. Erich Fromm's was the best-known. *Escape from Freedom*, published in the US in 1941, was certainly the most widely read psychological account of the Germans in the English-speaking world at the time. Fromm had been fruitfully exchanging ideas with Mead since the Hanover days.[13] Like Gorer, he was particularly impressed by the problem of loneliness in modern capitalist societies – the ways in which capitalism insisted on individuation but gave individuals no way to express themselves through work or love – with the consequence that they took refuge in submitting to authority (the 'escape from freedom'). Germany, Fromm argued, had been peculiarly susceptible to this 'authoritarian character' since at least the time of Luther, and Nazism represented only the most extreme form characteristic of a lower-middle class that had fewest of all opportunities for satisfying love or work. Despite its Marxist and anti-Protestant themes, Fromm's analysis resonated with Americans because it presented the German problem as a subset of modern problems common to all – the anonymity of modern life, the crisis of the Great Depression, the search for individual identity – and it offered hope for the future (for Americans and Germans alike).[14] For Mead's purposes, however, Fromm's vision was both too universalistic and too particularistic. She was not attracted by universal models of 'modernity'. As Benedict pointed out in a review of *Escape from Freedom* in Lasswell's journal *Psychiatry*, 'individualism' was not a discovery of modern societies; some 'primitive' societies had similar problems. But neither did Fromm's class analysis fit with the emerging national-character school: the problem had to lie with Germans, not with Germans of a particular class or rank, and to be played out in family relations unlikely to be fissured neatly on class lines. In taking on the neo-Freudians' psychological analyses, the anthropologists still needed to keep central their own distinctive contributions based on whole cultures.[15]

Better suited to the national-character framework was another neo-Freudian analysis of the German problem, by Erik Erikson, to which

Mead, Bateson and Gorer all contributed and which they ultimately embraced as their own. Erikson's basic modus operandi was very close to their own – he looked to the family drama to illustrate the culturally specific development of the personality – and he was keen to develop an analysis that combined a basic understanding of the German family with factors specific to Nazism that had exaggerated its fundamental weaknesses. For the former, he had his own German childhood to draw on; for the latter, he paid special attention to Nazi propaganda, principally Hitler's *Mein Kampf*, but also transcripts of Nazi speeches with which Mead supplied him. Finally, to connect Nazi propaganda to the German character, he was able to draw on interviews with the first German POWs taken in 1940 and 1941 and interned in Canada.[16]

All of this he put together into an important essay, published in *Psychiatry*, entitled 'Hitler's Imagery and German Youth'. His most important point, modifying Bateson's depiction of paternal dominance in the German family, was that the German father 'lacked true inner authority'. Formed without a national and democratic revolution, the German Reich had never achieved psychic integration and its unity was therefore always fragile and artificial, without 'an integrated meaning on a national scale'. This model of authority was reproduced on the familial scale, where the father's authority was deprived of 'the tenderness and dignity which comes from the participation in an integrating cause', leading to bluster and petty tyranny. The hapless mother was left to bear the brunt. In the father's absence, she nurtured her children and sought to make up for the lack of tenderness on the paternal side, but when the father came home, she had to switch sides and cater to his authoritarian demands. As a result sons came to view their own mothers with ambivalence: as ideal figures but also as betrayers.

In traditional German society there had been ways and means of relieving the psychic pressures established by this family drama – Erikson specifically mentioned the *Wanderschaft* – but in modern conditions healthy adolescent releases had been gradually shut down. The sense of geopolitical encirclement felt by Germans of all ages, much aggravated by defeat in the First World War, raised the pressure higher still. German youth increasingly took refuge in 'mystic-romantic' dreams (associated with the ideal mother), which were not only never realized but, as youth entered adulthood, cruelly crushed by the realities of humdrum daily existence. The frustrations of 'disillusioned, obedient citizenship' they then took out on their own children. So the cycle continued, in deteriorating economic conditions where opportunities for expression (as Fromm had argued) were further restricted. Thus Erikson explained the famous German dualism – a cracked idealism associated with the mother, grim submission associated with the father. This was the situation that Hitler was able to exploit. He offered himself to German youth as 'an adolescent who never gave in', an opportunity for a permanent enjoyment of the aggression and self-realization in the gang that would never have to give way to frustrated submission. Obedience to the gang leader could be portrayed as a kind of freedom, albeit only the kind of freedom enjoyed by a delinquent adolescent. In this way Erikson took on board the 'gangster' portrayal of Hitler and the Nazis without detaching the Nazis from the fundamentals of the German national character.[17]

Mead and Bateson were delighted by this analysis, which fitted all their desiderata: a culturally specific account of the German national character, based on the family drama, which could explain the lineaments of that character and how it was propagated; an account of both strengths and weaknesses that might be useful to government in wartime for propaganda purposes; and an etiology of the Nazi deviation that offered ideas about how it might be reversed to make the Germans safe for the postwar world. Better still, Erikson had an 'in' to the only government client for such an analysis before Pearl Harbor, Donovan's shadow propaganda agency, COI. The man Donovan had chosen to run his Psychological Division, Bob Tryon, had been a colleague of Erikson's at Berkeley. Donovan had even provided a small subsidy to CNM to help with Erikson's expenses for the Canadian POW interviews in 1941. Try as he might, however, Erikson could not make any further headway with Donovan after America entered the war in December 1941. A research plan to study the Canadian POWs more systematically – both for further propaganda hints and to begin to prepare for reconstruction – was aborted once it became clear that America might soon have POWs of its own.[18] A memorandum Erikson prepared, based on his *Psychiatry* paper, but aimed more purposefully at guiding Allied propaganda – seeking to peel off 'mature' Germans from support for Nazi delinquents – was resolutely ignored.[19]

A further memorandum on 'problems of German character structure', put together by Bateson, Mead and Gorer, combined ideas based on schismogenesis with Erikson's account of the German family drama. This memorandum aimed its propaganda points not only at appeals to the 'mature' side of the Germans but also directly at subverting Hitler's appeal to the perpetual adolescent. It might be possible, they thought, to 'turn Hitler from a symbol of adolescent rebellion to a symbol of a father, more powerful and more hateful than the fathers against whom they are now rebelling'.[20] This was too much even for Erikson. 'You know that I love the way in which Margaret and you, in conversation and discussion, open up provocative depths,' he cajoled Bateson, 'there is nobody to whom I would rather listen than to you two (with a bit of whiskey).'

But this memorandum seems not to be the place for provocative formulations. Especially your propaganda suggestions seem to ignore broadcasting reality on both sides of the Atlantic, for the sake of a provocative construct which will antagonize everybody and leave the Germans cold. After all, what we are saying is that Hitler's success is based on a formidable array of traditional forces. You yourself coin . . . the phrase of 'a new synthesis of a very great toughness'. Do you really think that propaganda against this tough synthesis can be based on a mere construct made in U.S.A.? Can one 'turn' Hitler from his deeply rooted symbolic position into another one? In fact, Hitler seems the least assailable part of German reality. Even if it were possible, the point is not to 'turn' his present magic position into an equally magic one which would suit us better, but to help the Germans to see how unnecessary and harmful their whole attitude toward politics and world politics is: and to make them wish to become a part in a *synthesis of even greater toughness*. But I am afraid we are not helping this synthesis by trying to play Goebbels' game in Freudian terms.[21]

Mead admitted that the memorandum would have to be toned down before it went to policymakers. But in fact none of these initiatives had made the slightest impact on the one policymaker to whom Mead thought they had access: Donovan. They were confronting several obstacles at once. First, Donovan already had a variety of psychological theories to hand, ranging from armchair analysis of Hitler's own personality to commentary on the psychological impact of short-term social and economic dislocations from the Harvard sociologists Talcott Parsons and Ted Hartshorne. Then, Mead and Bateson's association with the eccentric Arthur Upham Pope in CNM was doing them no good, since Pope was regarded in Donovan's circles as being 'loaded with dynamite'.[22] But above all, once the war started, Donovan began to lose interest in the psychological theories that had seemed appealing in the abstract before Pearl Harbor. He was not interested in any more theories that might 'explain National Socialism'. Erikson tried in vain to emphasize to Donovan the practical implications of his analysis for propaganda, which was why he was so worried about Mead and Bateson's rather highfalutin memorandum.[23] As Donovan's office split into OSS and OWI, and he took over OSS, his concerns shifted to more practical matters – mapping the terrain on to which his agents would be moving in Europe, providing verifiable information about society and politics, or, at the most psychological, assessing military and civilian morale. The Research and Analysis Branch was kept at arm's length from the propaganda war. Its own analyses of Nazism were more sociological than psychological or anthropological, heavily influenced by Marxism. Its pile of reports was probably of most use for basic logistical details: for instance, the material that went into the civil-affairs handbooks designed to orient occupying armies. When, in 1943, the Psychological Division was dissolved, some of its personnel were dispersed among the new area divisions, but more of them went to OWI, which was further from operational concerns and thus to some extent more open to speculative and theoretical work.[24]

The anthropologists, as we have seen, had more luck with OWI. Leo Rosten got Gorer his post there by the end of 1942 on the strength of his Japanese rather than his German research, and although Rosten had difficulty finding relevant work for Gorer to do, the national-character idea was well established at OWI by the time Benedict arrived to take up the slack in 1943. Again there was no shortage of rival theories of German psychology: among those influential in OWI were the team of Nathan Leites and Paul Kecskemeti, who propounded a more orthodox Freudian interpretation of the German character, and a sociological contingent including Donald McGranahan, Ed Shils and Morris Janowitz.[25] The atmosphere at OWI was less insular than at OSS R&A, and a fruitful batting back and forth of ideas ensued, especially with Leites, whom Gorer (as always stimulated by raw Freudianism) thought 'undoubtedly one of the most brilliant people on the Socio-political scene'.[26] But there was less scope at OWI to do work on Germany, as the agency's purpose was to do white propaganda to friendlies, allies and neutrals, which was why Gorer and Benedict ended up working on Burma, Thailand and Romania. Nor was it easy to do 'research' on the German character during this period, owing to the limited supply of Nazis to study.[27] That would not change until the end of 1943, when the Allied invasion of Italy opened access to large numbers of POWs, and Ted Hartshorne, now working for OWI, began chasing up the Italian peninsula in search of Wehrmacht captives to give psychological clues.[28] In the meantime, Bateson's campaign to get himself accepted as an expert on the German national character had stalled. His frustrations were building. Gorer at least had found a job in OWI, but neither man was content to hang around at the height of the war doing 'research'. Both ended up much nearer the frontlines – Bateson in the very heart of darkness – of the psychological war against the Japanese, where there was more room for novices.

* * *

Japan was always likely to be a more fertile ground for the anthropologists than Germany. Unlike Germany, Japan was little known in America or Britain. There were very few academic specialists with first-hand knowledge of Japan – at one estimate, only about a dozen at the time of Pearl

Harbor – and anthropology by no means took a back seat to history or politics.[29] The one expert who could claim the most expertise on Japanese psychology was in fact an anthropologist, John F. Embree, son of the CIR benefactor Edwin Embree, whose Japanese village ethnography was published as *Suye Mura* in 1939. He was snapped up almost immediately by the OSS Psychological Division.[30]

More broadly, as a racial 'Other', the Japanese were seen by government officials from the beginning as the natural province of anthropologists. This fact created an odd imbalance in the wartime handling of the Japanese. On the one hand, as John Dower has eloquently shown, the Japanese were subjected to a race war by the Allies in a way that the Germans were not. There were few positive stereotypes of the Japanese existing in popular culture and there was no Japanese equivalent of the 'good German'. On the contrary, racist stereotypes could be exploited to stoke American hostility at home and to raise the temperature in battle. The 'treachery' of Pearl Harbor added fuel to this fire. Japanese-Americans living on the West Coast were interned en masse during the first stage of the war and prevented from returning to their homes thereafter.[31] On the other hand, the anthropologists employed to explain the Japanese were nearly all staunch anti-racists. Not only did they see their life's mission as opposing racism, they also saw the anti-fascist war specifically as an opportunity to propagandize against racism. To the extent that they could influence the propaganda war, they thus sought to draw parallels between the Germans and the Japanese on psychological and *not* racial grounds. A mass of contradictions resulted. The most anti-racist elements in American society sometimes collaborated with, even if only in order to mitigate, explicitly racial policies such as internment. They propounded theories of psychological defect that were supposed to resonate with non-racial, anti-fascist tendencies but that could just as easily, of course, be embraced by racists. In short, anthropologists' engagement with the Japanese enemy raised all of the same contradictions involved in their engagement with the German enemy in more acute form. And the opportunities for engagement, and action, were much greater.

* * *

Geoffrey Gorer knew next to nothing about Japan before Pearl Harbor. To the extent that he had been engaged with the war at all in 1940–1, in retreat with his mother at Yale, he had been working on the German problem with the psychiatrist Richard Brickner. Shortly after Pearl Harbor, Donovan's Psychological Division put out a call for advice on interpreting Japanese propaganda and Gorer, probably at Mead's prompting, threw himself into a crash course. 'All that I know could go on the back of a postage stamp and still leave room for a couple of love letters,' he admitted cheerfully.[32] Within a week or two, Psychological Division had found John Embree and thereafter relied on him for its research into Japanese character, but at a summit meeting on 'Anthropologists and the War', organized by Mead, Bateson, Benedict and Eliot Chapple on 27 December 1941, it was decided to go ahead with their own investigation for CNM. Probably because Bateson was already fully engaged with Erikson on Germany, Gorer was pressed to continue with Japan.[33] Drawing on the eclectic range of sources recommended by Bateson and Mead in their preliminary work on the American, English and German characters in 1940–1 – an exhaustive search of the secondary literature, psychological interviews with émigrés, and novels and films where translations were available – Gorer began the first of the 'rapid diagnostic sketches' that he and Benedict would continue in 1943 for the Children's Bureau and OWI.[34]

In contrast to the early work of Mead and Bateson, focusing on the family drama, Gorer's more naked Freudianism – now fortified by his own analysis by Earl Zinn at Yale – took him directly to infantile sexuality. He admitted to Mead that he had become fixated on 'the sex point'. The literature was obliging, providing 'unbelievably complete material on sex'. Within six weeks he was declaring: 'I now know more about Japanese sex life than I do about English or Lepcha – and boy, is it a picture.'[35] He was not wanting for other sources of information and advice. Mead pestered him to think about propaganda implications of the kind she had developed for the Americans, the English and the Germans: how would the Japanese respond to successes or setbacks, victory or defeat? Gorer also consulted John Embree, who was working on his parallel study for OSS, and Douglas Haring, virtually the only other expert on Japanese psychology. Haring was something of a divided personality, a former Baptist missionary with strong moral concerns about the Japanese, who had, however, raised children in Japan, and had studied anthropology with Boas and Benedict after breaking with his church in 1926.[36] Embree and Haring provided helpful comments on a first draft in March, and by April 1942 Gorer had a completed memorandum, 'Japanese Character Structure and Propaganda', which became the first general circular for CIR in the spring of 1942. It would become notorious not only as the most widely circulated of the national-character studies but also as Gorer's first essay in what became known as 'diaperology'.[37]

Gorer began with some covering justifications for the national-character approach, asking the reader to assume that the standardized Japanese is 'a moderately well-off male of the common people living in a city'. He then moved immediately to infant training: 'It is the thesis of this

memorandum that . . . early and severe toilet training is the most important single influence in the formation of the adult Japanese character.' At
birth the Japanese infant is pampered and overfed, creating a strong
mother-son bond further reinforced by a teasing sexuality (at this point
Gorer had to excise his initial claim that 'peasant mothers masturbate
their sons', because his alleged source for this claim, Embree, denied it).[38]
From about four months, however, the infant was subjected to a series of
traumatic reversals aimed at training in bodily control: how to walk carefully so as to avoid damaging the joins between tatami mats; how to sit
upright; above all, how to control the sphincter, taught by means of
'severe and continuous punishment'. The contrast between toleration of
infantile sexuality and strict control over excretion led not to the system
of absolute moral values imposed by the superego, as in Western culture,
but to a system of situational ethics, whereby 'correct' or 'suitable' behaviour was defined entirely by context – and carrying the most terrifying
sanctions in certain contexts. The resulting preoccupation with ritual and
order, which would be considered 'compulsive neurotic' in the West,
could in the Japanese context be seen as compulsive but not neurotic
because it was entirely normal there.

Gorer took for granted that this early and severe toilet training stored
up aggression in the Japanese child, and that a highly ritualized adult
society provided even fewer outlets for venting aggression than in the
West. The one acceptable theatre for male aggression, he argued, was in
the sexual sphere. The infant boy's early experience of sexual indulgence
combined with extreme sex-differentiation from childhood onwards to
divide adult experience sharply in two: on the one hand, men's relations
with other men – 'an ordered pattern in which reward is gained by
compliance and a full knowledge of relative status . . . The male universe
gives assurance and safety, but little indulgence'; and, on the other, men's
relations with women – 'the female world threatens and pleads, but can
always be made to yield if the man is sufficiently strong and persistent in
his aggressions.' Male sexuality was portrayed as almost insatiable, despite
multiple outlets with mothers, maidservants, prostitutes, geishas and
wives. Japanese sexual aggression was to Gorer the key to explaining their
conduct in warfare. Their apparent gentleness in public life exemplified
the appropriate self-control; the 'overwhelming brutality and sadism
of the Japanese at war' represented the sexual release of aggression. When
the Allies declared Manila an 'open city' soon after Pearl Harbor, the
Japanese interpreted this as a feminine appeal to weakness and responded
with untold savagery. The indicated propaganda response was therefore
'the complete abandonment of threats, cajolery and appeals to pity,
which all indicate the female; and adopting instead the calm certainty of

obedience, sanctioned by mockery, which indicates the male'. However, Gorer cautioned, taking the role of the 'self-assured, superior father' in propaganda required the Japanese to accept the speaker as one of them, or at least as judging the Japanese by in-group standards. For this purpose, he recommended, controversially, that no direct attack on Japanese institutions, such as the emperor, and no direct advocacy of Western institutions, such as democracy, be attempted. The result of such actions (as Mead had pointed out to him) might be to stiffen Japanese resistance to the suggestions of an outsider, rather than to play on their recognition of the rebukes of an insider.[39]

It was this quick psychoanalytic sketch of the Japanese that got Gorer his initial access to the corridors of power, or at least to the corridors leading to the corridors of power. One of the advantages of working initially outside of government, under the auspices of CIR, was that Gorer's paper could be circulated widely, both to governmental and non-governmental agencies. Like Erikson's paper, it could also be published, and discussed in other publications. One of the best advertisements it got was provided by Otto Klineberg, a leading social psychologist who had studied with Sapir, Boas and Benedict at Columbia, and who worked alongside Gorer and Benedict at OWI. In a wartime lecture on the new 'science of national character' that was itself widely read, reprinted and recirculated, he provided 'a very friendly good statement', as Mead described it to Bateson, 'good statements of your paper [on morale and national character], my book and Geoffrey's memo, for some reason he missed Erik's'.[40] Another public vehicle for the dissemination of Gorer's theses was a special issue of *Public Opinion Quarterly* devoted to 'the occupation of enemy territory', for which Kurt Lewin wrote the treatment of Germany, and Gorer the treatment of Japan.[41] These entirely public statements – Gorer's original memo, its published version and the article on the occupation of Japan – were then widely taken up by exactly the range of 'consumers' that the CIR mailings intended. Nathan Leites and Otto Klineberg used them as the basis for much of their propaganda analysis at OWI. They formed part of the course material in the Far Eastern sections of the Army Specialized Training Program and the Civil Affairs Training Schools; at the Yale civil-affairs school, Gorer's arguments about the occupation of Japan were presented as the climax of the course. Thus Gorer achieved indirectly the influence on civil-affairs training that Bateson had been unable to achieve directly.[42] So widely known was Gorer's analysis behind the scenes that *Time* magazine did a full-length article on it in the summer of 1944, 'Why Are Japs Japs?', rendering its stark Freudian terms with surprising faithfulness.[43]

Unlike the Greeks, the Japanese were unable to protest against Gorer's 'diaperology', and obviously in some quarters it resonated with racially motivated – as in all quarters it resonated with ideologically motivated – anti-Japanese sentiment. This was certainly what made it more acceptable in the Japanese case than in the case of the Greeks or even the Burmese. Gorer's analysis of the Japanese was actually quite close to the similarly non-racial psychological analyses of the Germans that were equally predominant. His view was indeed that the German and Japanese psychologies were quite similar.[44] His character analysis captured the zeitgeist because it offered something to many different ways of thinking: conventional anti-enemy feeling, including racism in the case of the Japanese, but also the appreciation that a world war required knowledge of hitherto-obscure cultures, and a growing valuation of psychology in wartime as a tool for morale operations, propaganda and military government. And in addressing the Japanese rather than the German character, he was offering something then in short supply.[45]

Some indication of this is given by the degree to which Gorer's psycho-analytic perspectives were taken on even by the few established Japan experts, who had previously been oriented more to the study of social institutions. Douglas Haring's lectures to the Far Eastern Section of the Civil Affairs Training School at Harvard bear close resemblance to Erikson's account of the German family. The Japanese male is portrayed as suffused with neurotic repressed anger at the father, which is then 'a source of sadistic behavior against defenceless inferiors'. Some of Gorer's themes have been incorporated but mildly soft-pedalled. Haring reproduces, fairly closely to the original, the crucial contrast between indulgent feeding and sexual stimulation in early infancy (including maternal masturbation, which Haring unlike Embree recalled from his own time in Japan) and then sudden withdrawal from bodily intimacy, but not the 'diaperological' emphasis on toilet training.[46] Embree's analysis, done originally for the OSS Psychological Division but available publicly through a Smithsonian Institution pamphlet of 1943, tried harder to distance itself from Gorer's analysis. As one might expect, given that both were anthropologists, Embree agreed heartily with Gorer that the differences between the Japanese and the Americans were not based on race (or some other 'mysterious' natural cause) but rather 'a radically different system of child training and cultural values'. In Embree's presentation of culture, however, history, economics and social structure came before psychology, and care was taken not to stigmatize the Japanese psycho-logically. 'Sex is something of great concern to Japanese as to other people,' he remarked pointedly. Yet Embree, who is rightly portrayed as the most genuinely sympathetic to the Japanese of all the Japan experts, and who privately expressed doubts about 'attempts by anthropologists to psychoanalyze societies', reproduced Gorer's fundamental character analysis more directly than did Haring: 'The motherly affection coupled with the severe toilet training and culminating in the sudden loss of attention when the next child is born creates an early sense of insecurity which in turn produces an adult who is never absolutely sure of himself and who through compensation may become almost paranoiac.'[47] Both Haring and Embree also agreed with Gorer's propaganda suggestions, much as the anti-psychoanalytic Burmese experts had disputed his character analysis but still endorsed the propaganda hints that flowed from it. Thus the psychoanalytic flavour of Gorer's national-character writings had, especially in the case of the Japanese, given them a piquancy that made them memorable, without attracting enough practical criticism to discredit their policy implications.[48]

Given how much heat Gorer's similar analyses of the Russians would attract after the war, it is surprising how little criticism the Japanese character study drew in wartime – suggesting again that the racial otherness of the Japanese made it easier for Americans to accept the psychoanalytic critique. One of Mead's closest associates did, however, fire a warning shot that eerily prefigured later objections to Gorer. This was Gardner Murphy, a social psychologist whose rebuke was all the more stinging because he shared all of Mead's fundamental orientations: the need for the world's peoples to understand each other better, the need to displace racism with a grasp of cultural diversity, the usefulness of social science in fulfilling these needs. But he thought Gorer was a very poor social scientist, if he was one at all. Murphy had no objection to the use of psychoanalysis, but he thought it ought to rest on close analytical study of real Japanese, rather than a series of guesses about character structure. The thesis about toilet training was 'a thesis in the sense in which Martin Luther nailed up the 95 theses, rather than scientific manipulation of hypotheses in the open-minded quest for complete data'. Psychoanalytic data needed to be integrated properly with historical, political and economic context, in order to take into account cleavages within Japanese society as well as short-term historical changes. The 'high degree of uniformity and stereotypy in Gorer's report' he thought simply bizarre. And like those analysts of German character who had emphasized the special circumstances of Nazism, he thought the 'insecurity' and 'inferiority' feelings of the Japanese could be largely explained in terms of recent political and economic history. In short:

When used at a distance without deep analysis of individuals and when used without perspective on the entity which is modern Japan, with all its class cleavages, its economic dislocation, its rapid westernization, and most of all, its enormous diversity of eddies and cross-currents, I think it [i.e. Gorer's method] can throw the picture into such extremely bad focus as to do much more harm than good.

At worst, it could do 'extremely serious cultural harm' to the understanding between nations and the prestige of social science in the postwar world.[49]

Mead took this seriously and responded at length. She reproved Murphy for his 'affect', which she thought represented a guild defence of his own expertise against an outsider. As usual, she defended the sketchiness of both Gorer's data and method on the grounds of emergency. But she also defended Gorer's work on scientific grounds. For the first time she made a claim, repeated in postwar reminiscences, that Gorer had 'predicted' that 'declaring Manilla an open city would arouse the Japanese to attack and attack with specific savagery'; in fact, he had not. Manila was declared an open city on 25 December 1941 and was bombed almost immediately, at a time when Gorer was just assembling his materials. Even in private correspondence he made no mention of Manila until 31 December, by which time the Japanese assault was almost over.[50] Murphy was unimpressed, writing to Mead: 'I am very sure you would have predicted the Manila reaction without knowing Gorer's data. I am sure that a knowledge of modern Japanese conduct since 1931 if not earlier would have sufficed, and that knowing about the handling of infants would not have altered the prediction one way or the other.' But he apologized for his intemperate language and thereafter subsided.[51] His was one of the few serious critiques of Gorer's analysis to reach Mead's ears at this time. She would hear a great deal more of this language after 1945.

*   *   *

Social scientists had relatively little practical contribution to make to the war effort in the first few years of fighting. The piling up of reports in the OSS Research and Analysis Branch, and the more freely circulating speculations of OWI's experts, extended the promise of psychological applications to propaganda and occupation, but at a time when the Allies were still on the back foot they had little effective purchase. Nevertheless, their constant airing – including in public – was building up their reputation, and even inflated claims such as Gorer's 'prediction' of the rape of Manila carried some prestige. In 1943 the tide began to turn and many more real opportunities for 'applied social science' arose. The Allied invasion of the Italian peninsula began in September of that year, and the first substantial stock of Axis POWs was acquired, as well as the first substantial stock of foreign nationals to be administered. The American offensive against the easternmost Pacific Islands occupied by the Japanese began in November 1943. In mainland Asia, the Allies set up the South East Asia Command (SEAC) under Lord Louis Mountbatten in August 1943 and began to make their first significant advances against the Japanese in Burma in early 1944.

These advances had multiple implications for the use of social science. The training of soldiers and administrators for service on foreign soil ramped up incredibly. This was the heyday of the Army Specialized Training Program, where intercultural education was carried on (if not quite as Bateson and Mead would have liked it) by anthropologists and others. The higher-level Civil Affairs Training Schools were also at their peak, with Embree teaching the Japan course at Chicago and Haring at Harvard. OSS R&A, and its British equivalent in the Political Warfare Executive (PWE), produced their 'pocket guides' to foreign cultures for ordinary soldiers and more elaborate civil-affairs handbooks for military government. As every minute on foreign territory saved could mean many soldiers' lives saved, the military also took psychological warfare to induce surrender much more seriously. Eisenhower set up an integrated propaganda agency at his Supreme Headquarters Allied Expeditionary Force, the Psychological Warfare Division (PWD-SHAEF), which uniquely combined black and white propaganda, and personnel from both British and American agencies, blending together OSS, OWI and PWE. Mountbatten was not able to put together a similarly integrated department in his Southeast Asia theatre, which meant a proliferation of psychological warfare operations by sometimes ill-coordinated OSS and PWE detachments.[52]

At this stage of the war it is almost impossible to keep track of all of the developments and departments in which social scientists had a hand, or even of the more specialized operations in which 'culture and personality' approaches were applied. A few examples will have to suffice. Gorer and Benedict were, of course, feeding their national-character analyses into OWI's 'basic plans' for white propaganda – mostly non-clandestine radio – in both Europe and Asia. At PWD-SHAEF, the Intelligence Section was thick with social scientists, including Ted Hartshorne, Daniel Lerner, Saul Padover, Ed Shils, Morris Janowitz and Donald McGranahan. A key addition to their number was Henry Dicks. Dicks was a German-speaking psychiatrist who had been assigned by British Military Intelligence early in the war to evaluate Rudolf Hess, the captured Nazi leader, and then from 1942 he began to do psychiatric evaluations of German POWs in Britain. Though completely cut off from the parallel work being carried out in America by Fromm, Erikson, Gorer et al., and more attached to an orthodox psychiatric vocabulary than these neo-Freudians, he still came to remarkably similar conclusions about the German character, including a version of the German family drama resembling Erikson's. He ranged the POWs he examined on a scale of more or less Nazified, arguing that the more Nazified represented an 'exaggerated and concentrated' version of the common German personality type, and characterizing the most Nazi using a barrage of psychiatric epithets:

> likely to be men of markedly pregenital or immature personality struc-
> ture in which libido organisation followed a sado-masochistic pattern,
> based on a repression of the tender tie with the mother and resulting
> typically in a homo-sexual paranoid (extra-punitive) relation to a harsh
> and ambivalently loved and hated father figure, with its attendant
> sadism towards symbols of the displaced bad portion of this figure . . .
> increased secondary ('defensive') narcissism . . . libido splitting vis-à-vis
> female love objects . . . tendencies toward hypochondriacal (internal
> persecutor) and schizoid or hypomanic (guilt denial) features.[53]

While even Gorer distanced himself from such a liberal use of 'abstract terms from psychoanalysis, such as guilt, sadism, masochism, etc.', which he denied had any 'cross-cultural validity', nevertheless when he finally saw the results of Dicks's independent work he called it 'the most outstanding socio-psychological study produced during the war'.[54] (Others later compared it to Gorer's own analysis of the Japanese.)[55] The social scientists at PWD agreed and Dicks provided the 'governing conceptions of PWD Intelligence', the closest they came, Daniel Lerner said, to 'a coherent theory of morale and propaganda'. Working with Ed Shils, Dicks turned his 'F-scale' ('F' standing for fascist or fanatical), by which he had measured the degree of Nazi personality in individual interviews, into a form that could be administered by questionnaire to the much larger numbers of POWs now available to PWD near the frontlines, in order to assess morale and, potentially, as a screening tool for a future denazification programme in an occupied Germany.[56] The quantitative approach proved congenial to the sociologists who were dominant in PWD, because it allowed a breakdown – seen to correspond to social class and status – between more and less Nazi, thus permitting a targeted approach to propaganda which the national-character analysis did not.

In all this frenetic activity, advocates of the national-character analysis found themselves in a peculiar bind. On the one hand, the general atti-tude of the public – and to a great extent that of policymakers – had shifted in their direction. As anger against the Germans hardened, and determination to win the war grew, it was no longer so common to find people making distinctions between Germans and Nazis, or good Germans and bad. Thus generalizations about Germans and Japanese as national cultures flourished. On the other hand, anything like 'understanding' the Germans and Japanese smacked of appeasement. Increasingly a 'hard peace' was demanded. A poll at the end of 1944 found that a third of Americans envisioned the total destruction of both Germany and Japan as nations.[57] What made this dilemma more bewildering to the anthropologists especially was that the demand for a 'hard peace' now came not from old-fashioned conservatives or xenophobes or racists, but from their own former allies on the Left. Though Mead had found it hard to rouse American public opinion to take any interest at all in 'abroad' before Pearl Harbor, midway through the war there was a new spirit of left-wing American nationalism in the air that saw the universal promotion of democracy and social reform as America's duty to the world. As these democratic universalists contemplated the end of the war and the reconstruction of Germany and Japan, they dreamed of bold new programmes that would spread the principles of the New Deal abroad. FDR gave them encouragement with public pronouncements about the 'Four Freedoms'. 'I don't know how interested Americans are going to be in the people of Java,' worried his adviser Harry Hopkins. 'I'm afraid they'll have to be some day, Harry,' Roosevelt responded. 'The world is getting so small that even the people in Java are getting to be our neighbours now.'

But while anthropologists were pleased that Americans were getting interested in the people of Java, they would not be so pleased that Americans saw the Javanese as 'our neighbours now', that is, 'just like us'. And the consequences for the Germans and the Japanese, who had proved so unneighbourly, was that they would have to be *made* 'just like us'. The tension between a New Deal belief in the basic goodness of ordinary people and in the war-wearied belief in the thorough badness of the Germans and Japanese could only be resolved by a top-to-bottom revision of German and Japanese societies. Democratic universalists were cooking up plans to decapitate the elites, introduce democratic institutions and American-style social programmes, in Germany to dismantle militarism and the economic cartels, and in Japan to depose the emperor and break up the *zaibatsu* financial and industrial conglomerates. They were impatient with suggestions that German and Japanese 'difference' had in any way to be respected, or even used for internal reform.[58] The military-political expression of this impatience came at the Casablanca Conference of January 1943, where Roosevelt persuaded a reluctant Churchill to accept 'unconditional surrender' as the Allies' war aim. Henceforward psychological warfare would be limited by a ban on holding out any promise to the vanquished peoples. Especially after D-Day, psychological

141

warfare was expected to stress the impact of 'overwhelming force' rather than focus on any psychological weaknesses that might induce enemy soliders to give up. The message that many propagandists feared would be received by the Germans and the Japanese was that only 'destruction' would be visited upon them.[59]

Cultural relativists thus found themselves opposed by some of their former best friends on the Left, who were now agitating for a democratic universalism. Conversely they found strange allies in the 'old Japan hands' at the State Department, prewar diplomats who had been very cosy with the Japanese court and elites, and who echoed anthropologists' concerns about a wholesale transformation of Japanese society on an American model.[60] There was also a new conservative argument against such trans-formations, on the grounds that it would make the defeated powers ripe for communism, which in certain quarters only strengthened the case on the Left for American-style reform projects. This strange realignment, which would strike a decisive blow against cultural relativism in the Cold War, was already visible in some struggles over psychological warfare in the last years of the hot one. For example, Ruth Benedict got into a tangle with Percy Winner, one of the higher-ups at OWI, a former journalist and an aggressive New Dealer, over a series of memos she wrote in the spring and summer of 1944 on the political values of Europeans. Trying to adopt a relativistic view, she argued that most ordinary Europeans were 'apolitical' and yearned simply to be left alone. 'Our highly moral war aims and the world horizons of our social crusaders' would mean little to them. 'Since this majority is not readily susceptible to our statement of world war aims and to political appeals, it will be necessary to take national habits of thought and action into consideration in order to plan propaganda. This means that national differences are of paramount importance.' Any attempts to reach the apolitical majority would have to play very sensi-tively on nationally specific themes, including 'stepping down some of our claims to idealism in America', and everywhere 'present democracy in the United States as one possible set of arrangements and give due credit to theirs'. Winner was rendered livid by what he saw as a 'shocking and absurd' dismissal of Europeans' passion for liberation and the potential appeal of American interventionism. The last thing the Germans needed or wanted was reticence on the part of America about its power to do good in the world.[61]

The most famous of these struggles between cultural relativism and a mounting democratic universalism was triggered by the violent reaction of Henry Morgenthau, FDR's war secretary, to the civil-affairs handbook for Germany that OSS had prepared for his department in August 1944. Morgenthau was outraged that so much attention was paid to the restoration of order and to rehabilitation, and he demanded more recognition of the Germans as a 'defeated people'. FDR backed him up: the 'whole nation' was to be held responsible for the crimes of the Nazis.[62] The short-term result was the notorious Morgenthau Plan for a virtual dismemberment of the German nation. Although this plan didn't last very long, it left many social scientists with the uneasy feeling that any attempt to establish a sense of German cultural difference – even in the harsh language of psychiatry – would be taken as 'soft' on the Germans. Somehow they had to find a middle way between the 'soft' peace of the appeasers and the 'hard' peace of the democratic universalists, to create a stable and peaceful world that had room for a diversity of cultures. In the latter stages of the war, from the end of 1943, while Gorer, Bateson and Benedict peeled off one by one and devoted themselves to the psychological war against Japan, Mead, whose eyes were always more firmly fixed on the postwar order, found herself enmeshed in just this dilemma.

*   *   *

As we have seen, Mead let Bateson take the lead on Germany before America entered the war, and after Pearl Harbor she devoted herself almost entirely to her more peaceable cultivation of the Anglo-American relationship and the Food Habits work. If she did not share Bateson's and Gorer's sometimes savage enthusiasm for target practice against the enemy, still she did not shrink from the imperative to end the war, and she could often be found behind the scenes egging them on – in truth, having it both ways. Before Pearl Harbor she had been concerned about Americans' disengagement from the world, and had done what she could to align Americans' fundamental motivations with the war effort. In one startling memorandum for CNM before Pearl Harbor, she worried that it would be even harder to engage Americans' hostilities against the Japanese than against the Germans, and toyed with propaganda devices aimed at engaging them, including use of the racist imagery – 'small poisonous animals with fangs or claws or arms' – that, as John Dower has shown, did distinguish anti-Japanese from anti-German propaganda.[63]

That unguarded moment aside, Mead played little role in anti-enemy propaganda and frequently expressed her anxiety about the long-term effects that 'destructive' wartime propaganda might have on preparing the world for peace. When she concerned herself with the Japanese and (more frequently) the German national character, she was focused on the steps that would have to be taken after the war to defuse the aggressiveness that, in the German case, had led to two world wars in her own lifetime. In 1943, as Gorer, Bateson and Benedict became more enmeshed in winning the war, Mead became still more interested in winning the

peace. She and her friends organized two special issues of academic jour-
nals in that year to discuss what Kurt Lewin called 'cultural reconstruction'.[64] They reflected her own three fundamental goals: to repair the
damage of war, to prevent the recurrence of war, and to restore and
protect cultural diversity after the war. American leadership would be
crucial but not 'American imperialism'.[65] Social science could help to
ensure due consideration was given to all peoples by means of 'a coordinated, systematic study of world populations in terms of their personality
dynamics'.[66]

Repairing the damage of war would begin with relief efforts – here
Mead's own newly developed expertise on food habits was invoked –
which had to respect local cultures in order to be effective and to lay the
appropriate foundation for postwar development. International organizations would have to be established – UNRRA was already in formation –
and 'that minimum degree of democracy which is necessary for an
international organization of the type we wish to realize' would have to be
agreed. Internationalism should be organized so as to preserve cultural
diversity, with one exception: 'Intolerance against intolerant cultures.'[67]
That required consideration of the 'special cases' of Germany and Japan,
covered here by Lewin and Gorer. They again urged that 'intolerance
toward intolerance' should only go so far, 'to certain minimum requirements which are probably not too different from the minimum requirements for international peace'. 'Cultural reconstruction' could not be
imposed from without on either Germans or Japanese: not only would this
be ineffective, triggering a counterreaction, but cultures were simply too
highly integrated to be susceptible to that kind of change. At best, one
could, as Gorer put it, 'canalize' German and Japanese characteristics 'in
directions compatible with, instead of antagonistic to, the goals and policies of the peace-loving nations'. Neither Gorer nor Lewin had as yet
many firm proposals towards this end, but the theoretical point provided
Mead with a principled position from which to work. It highlights again
the ways in which anthropologists' understanding of cultural integrity
required them not only to identify but to respect cultural difference, even
in extreme cases such as the Axis powers at the height of the war.[68]

Mead, of course, spent a good deal of 1943 in Britain, but when she
returned to America in the autumn she found herself embroiled in a
controversy over just how far to go in the cultural reconstruction of
Germany after the war. This was the intemperate quarrel that whirled
around the publication of the book by the Columbia psychiatrist Richard
Brickner, *Is Germany Incurable?* Mead and Gorer had had a lot more to do
with this book and its consequences than people realized at the time, or
historians have realized since.[69] Brickner approached Mead in the spring

of 1941 for help with a manuscript he had written, 'Germany Diagnosed', offering his professional diagnosis of the Germans as 'paranoid'. Publishers had rejected it on the grounds that it was too medical and needed a complete rewrite, including a much thicker description of the Germans as a people, in order to be credible. Mead decided to take an interest. One possible motive was to engage Gorer, who was then still at a loose end in New Haven. Reluctantly he agreed to take on the job of teaching Brickner some anthropology and helping him rewrite his manuscript. The inducement was enough money to hire a secretary, and the opportunity to get a short course in German culture and personality, which would stand him in good stead once America entered the war. Working with a journalist, Ladislas Farago, he toiled grumpily for several months to make Brickner's dry psychiatric language come alive. The idea of diagnosing the nation was naturally congenial enough to Gorer, but as a psychiatrist, working on individual patients, Brickner had little familiarity with German culture as lived experience, and little notion of how personality traits were diffused throughout a culture. But even with Farago's help, Gorer had the same problem that Bateson was having before Erikson came on the scene: that is, insufficient contact with real Germans to gain a full understanding of their family drama. With some relief he abandoned the effort after Pearl Harbor when Brickner's money ran out, and Mead anyway directed him to the more pressing question of Japan.[70]

As public interest in the 'cultural reconstruction' of Germany built up in 1943, Brickner's half-edited manuscript eventually became publishable, though it was now an uncomfortable hybrid of anthropological and psychiatric treatments. That mixture was signalled by two introductions: one by Mead, neutrally recommending the book as a contribution to the paramount postwar task 'to organize peoples so that they will not kill'; one by the psychiatrist Edward Strecher, more bullishly denouncing the evils of mass psychosis.[71] Brickner thanked Mead and Farago but not Gorer for helping him bring his work to publication.[72] He first presents the phenomenon of 'paranoia' as a psychiatrist sees it in individual patients – the megalomaniac who takes every opportunity for self-glorification, who believes in destiny but also suffers from a persecution complex. He then argues, relying mostly on Benedict's *Patterns of Culture*, that whole societies can also be described in terms appropriate to the individual personality, taking account of deviants and distribution around the norm. Psychiatrists, he grants, don't really understand why paranoia develops in the individual, and Brickner doesn't seek to explain its development in German culture either. Instead of rich illustrations from German life, he relies on flat descriptions of the rise of militarism and then fascism from the late nineteenth century. Only the final chapter seeks to answer the titular question, arguing against both a hard and a soft peace and in favour of a 'therapeutic approach', even emptier than Lewin's and Gorer's, but apparently involving 'psychiatric therapy for a whole nation'.[73] Analogizing with the only treatment psychiatrists had found for paranoia in individuals – hoping to find a 'clear area' that had remained healthy and could be developed – Brickner concluded hopefully that perhaps 'clear individuals' could still be found from whom a new German nation could also be developed.[74]

Mead had mixed feelings about the whole enterprise. She had no problem with applying epithets, even those quite pejorative in her own culture, to other cultures. As Brickner pointed out in the book, Benedict and Mead had described the Kwakiutl, the Dobu and the Arapesh in terms quite similar to the ones he applied to the Germans.[75] However, she disliked what Gorer had called, in his criticism of Dicks, 'abstract terms from psychoanalysis' that set a single, universal standard of mental health (based on one's own cultural norms) and judged other cultures as pathological by that standard. Even Gorer had insisted that the Japanese should not be considered 'neurotic' on a Western standard.

To an innocent reader the distinction might be hard to see: what was the difference between Benedict's use of the word 'megalomaniac' to describe the Kwakiutl and Brickner's use of the same word to describe the Germans? Yet the difference had tremendous implications, not only for the general view of other cultures, but specifically for the postwar treatment of the Germans. Mead's belief in 'national character' meant that she saw whatever paranoid tendencies the Germans might have as a development of their fundamental character that it would be hard (perhaps impossible) to change. Such characterological terms were meant to differentiate cultures, not to set them up for 'diagnosis' and 'cure'. Cultural relativism made 'cure' inappropriate, and the sticky cohesion of cultures made it almost impossible anyway. These strictures applied to Nazi Germany as much as to the Kwakiutl; Benedict insisted on a minimal diagnosis of psychological problems 'without doing violence to essentially German attitudes'. The most that should be attempted was, as Lewin and Gorer had proposed, to 'canalize' their tendencies into new expressions making for peaceful coexistence. Brickner's idea that there were 'clear individuals' – essentially, 'good' Germans – missed the basic point of their Germanness. So did his belief that one could send sixty thousand psychiatrists to Germany and 'cure' it – a sign of his own grandiose paranoia, Mead thought.[76]

Nevertheless, Mead saw – probably correctly – that Brickner was at least raising her question: that is, what could be done with the German national character after the war to neutralize its danger to the world and bring it along with all the other peoples into a postwar order? Furthermore, the psychiatrists offered a tempting constituency of new allies. Psychiatry was a medical specialty, hitherto little associated with anthropology, and with a higher (and generally favourable) public profile.[77] Its practitioners were mostly hard-headed professional men who frequently lacked broader world views. Some were adepts of orthodox psychoanalysis, but even they might be tempted by neo-Freudian and other culturally conscious alternatives. That had been the goal of Lasswell's journal, *Psychiatry*. Gorer had had considerable success in implanting the idea of culture pattern at the heart of Brickner's book. It was a success that could be built on.

Just as Mead was preparing for her British excursion, the publication of Brickner's book triggered significant interest – and controversy – in the media. The pages of the mass-circulation *Saturday Review* were peppered with commentary on it from May to November. Opinion ranged across the gamut. At one end – the *Review's* own editors leant this way – the multiculturalist Horace Kallen felt that Brickner had too pessimistically associated Nazi ideals with the whole of the German people. The postwar occupation would be able to tap into a huge pool of opposition that had been only temporarily paralysed by fear. The most provocative statement of this 'soft' position was that of Germanophile historian Harry Elmer Barnes, who cast doubt on Mead's credentials to speak about the character of a modern people like the Germans. In the middle, Erich Fromm spoke up for a better understanding of 'national character' than Brickner had provided, more or less as Mead would have done.[78] But at the other end of the spectrum was the worrying massing of New Deal democrats from the Writers' War Board, led by the crime writer Rex Stout. They adopted Brickner's intervention as a tool in their mounting campaign to brand all Germans as Nazis, in order to mobilize Americans to finish off the war and the German nation once and for all. They publicized German atrocities, lobbied the press to stop saying 'Nazi' and use 'German' instead, and in November 1943 sponsored Noël Coward's spoof song on the 'soft' peace, 'Don't Let's Be Beastly to the Germans'. Stout and his allies wrote to the *Saturday Review* in October, accusing Barnes of spouting 'the favorite lines of the propaganda of the enemy with whom we are at war'. The *Review's* editor, Norman Cousins, countered that Stout's alternative seemed to be nothing but 'extermination'. Yet this underestimates the 'hard' peace line. Stout and his comrades could point proudly to their contemporary campaign for racial equality in the USA. They were not bigots, but ideologues. They wanted no compromise with the Germans on the grounds of 'national character', and they had enough faith in American democracy to feel its universal application was the only way to prevent the Third World War. The growing appeal of that democratic universalism was to cause a lot of trouble for Mead after the war was over – for the moment, she may have felt lucky to be *hors de combat* in Britain.[79]

Possibly with this in mind, on her return from England in November, Mead teamed up with Larry Frank to organize a conference with Brickner to publicize their ideas for 'Germany After the War'. For Mead and Frank the goal was 'educative': to get the idea of a 'therapeutic peace' properly in front of the public, clearly distinguished from notions of hard or soft peace, 'retribution or sympathy'. It was also an opportunity to educate the psychiatrists further by introducing them to Erikson's ideas about the German family drama. Brickner had dreams of getting on board all of the principal agencies planning for the German occupation, and busied himself in Washington meeting with a variety of luminaries, cooking up a menu of policies to lay before them. But Mead and Frank were more realistic: it was enough to get the idea of the 'therapeutic peace' on the drawing board. In fact, they saw the very *idea* of a 'therapeutic peace' as a form of therapy, for Americans as much as for Germans, getting both nations beyond the question of 'victors' and 'defeated' – 'We don't want the "guilty Germans" angle,' Mead said – and instead thinking progressively about the future.[80]

Brickner's efforts did secure some limited State Department funding for a brief series of small confidential meetings of psychiatrists and social scientists, to be held in the spring of 1944.[81] Larry Frank took formal control as chair of a joint committee of sponsoring organizations, and he and Mead worked hard to craft just the right cast of characters – advocates of both 'soft' and 'hard' peace had to be avoided. About thirty invitees were lined up, a mixture of psychiatrists and social scientists. Gardner Murphy initially jibbed, declaring himself willing to participate only if the 'therapeutic peace' were applied 'globally', 'to the Russians, to the British, to ourselves, as well as to Germany'. Mead agreed with this position in theory – 'We accept the fact that German culture is different and French is different and Bulgarian is different' – but saw it as a diversion; the problem of avoiding 'defeat and victory' was a 'national' problem, between Germany and America, and had to be dealt with as such. Murphy attended in the end.[82] Close attention was paid to the papers prepared for discussion at the conference: every participant was invited to send a statement for pre-circulation, but the statements that were steered into the centre of the discussion were drafted by Mead and her home team. Frank contributed an introduction on the 'psycho-cultural approach' to be adopted, basically a crash course in 'culture and personality' for the psychiatrists. All political and economic institutions had to be seen as 'different patterns of endeavor and of life careers which the cultural traditions and the social order offer to individuals as designs for living'.[83] Mead provided the main paper on 'regularities in German national character'.[84] It briskly presented Bateson's ideas on dominance and submission, Erikson's on the triple image of the mother (companion to the child, betrayer of the child, suffering in relation to the father), and the resulting 'swing' between rebellion and submission.[85] Erik Erikson, who was unable to make it over from California, issued a warning against drawing up a 'psychiatric master plan'. The analytical tools that he himself had helped to provide – 'a small vocabulary' of terms such as 'ego, libido, character structure, reeducation, neuropsychiatric, etc.' – were clumsy and feeble. In the end, 'only history can change peoples', and it would be better to think modestly and suggest only 'specific, specialized tasks' that United Nations institutions might carry out. In the meantime, he said, 'It will not do to call one nation psychiatric names', and, steering close to Murphy's position, he argued for considering '[t]he problem of Germany's reeducation' as 'neither a *national* nor an *individual* one', but '*understood* as a *European* problem' and '*attacked* as a *regional* one'.[86]

The conference convened on 29–30 April 1944, and then spilled over into specialist meetings on 6 and 20–21 May, before reconvening on 3–4 June. Mead sought to control the agenda by launching immediately into a restatement of her idea of the German national character and posing the question of what specific steps might be taken to stop the swing between rebellion and submission: not to eliminate them, as both 'contain elements of value', but to provide a 'new integration' for them. Again steering between the 'soft' peace – a partial solution, focused on a few bad eggs – and a 'hard' peace – which would seek to 'uproot the traditions' – she emphasized the need to offer the Germans 'an alternative to work toward' compatible with their existing character structure. Despite these best efforts, on the second day a stormy dispute broke out between two psychiatrists essentially espousing the 'hard' and the 'soft' positions. Lawrence Kubie laid down the hard line: before they did anything else, the Allies needed to show their strength, in order to avoid the errors of Versailles. This set off Thomas French in defence of the Germans. Given their recent history, especially in the Weimar period, French argued, they were not wrong to feel 'paranoid' about being surrounded and beset. Coming closer to Mead's position, he continued, 'We have a right to insist they do not threaten us, but no right to reform them.'[87]

That was a bad way to end the first plenary session. Mead tried to hammer out an acceptable overall statement, and found an ally in Talcott Parsons. Parsons was worried by both French and Kubie, but especially by Kubie's 'very dangerous' position that Germany could be 'cured by the imposition of outside force'. Mead reassured him. 'French, you and I, and most of the group, agree that it cannot, and I think this feeling is so strong that no show down need be had.' However, this still left open multiple possibilities. On the one hand, as Erich Fromm and Kurt Lewin had argued, the German character could be 'a difficult, or anti-international, or pathological form of a character structure which is essentially sound, basically, but responsive to unfavorable conditions'. In that case, 'our job is to change the situational factors, expedite industrialization, the emancipation of women, etc.', and wait for the new, healthier integration of the German character to assert itself. But the other possibility was that there was a more deeply rooted and flawed structure which was dangerous 'even though it may be held in abeyance for several hundred years – as in Transylvania'; in which case, 'the job of restructuring the whole social field so that a new orientation will result is far more difficult'. Mead kept remembering Phil Mosely's evidence of '[t]hose Transylvanian Germans sitting there since the Middle Ages . . . feeling themselves encircled by the Roumanians with whom they refused to blend', 'the most disturbing evidence against your argument that German character is more malleable'. Parsons himself was not dogmatic: he understood the arguments in favour of 'a relatively rigid typical German character structure which is in the short run not subject to alteration'. Yet he didn't like the psychiatric language of paranoia, which made a 'cure' seem too improbable, and which in his view as a sociologist underestimated the role of institutions and also of short-term situations in modifying character or at least its expression.[88]

Mead could live with Parsons' sociological optimism. The final statement of the conference after its reassembly in June followed the modus vivendi she and Parsons had reached. The conference agreed that a lasting peace would require 'a gradual and lasting change in the German character . . . which would substitute for a compulsion to dominate the world, the will to cooperate with other nations'. It explicitly repudiated both the 'hard' peace – the destruction of the German nation – and the 'soft' – the 'over-kind and over-forgiving' but delusory search for ' "good" Germans'. An Allied occupation would need to be imposed on the basis of 'unconditional surrender', and major institutional changes set in train, to denazify the military, the economy and the polity, and to free the educational system and the media from Nazi control. But within this new institutional setting the Germans would remain German, and would have to find their own 'new image of themselves', which could not be imposed from on high or from without.[89]

Thus a balance was struck both between drastic short-term ('hard') and ameliorative long-term ('soft') interventions, and between the kind of institutional change Parsons sought and the behavioural change Mead wanted. Special attention should be paid to remodelling the German family, giving women more opportunity for leadership, starting immediately by charging them with relief efforts, and then by expanding their employment opportunities, especially in education. In an appendix, almost certainly drafted by Mead, the question of how far it was legitimate to seek to influence the development of German children in pursuit of a peaceful Germany was left open.[90] Other appendices reprinted Frank's and Mead's initial papers, and a new paper by Parsons arguing for the reciprocal effects of institutional and behavioural change.[91] Finally, the report concluded – in terms taken straight out of *And Keep Your Powder Dry* – that care must be taken to ensure that the solution to the German problem did not create new American problems of cultural imperialism. Here Mead had to balance her desire to engage Americans with her anxieties about democratic universalism. It would be a mistake to stir up 'crusading enthusiasm for democracy everywhere in the world', which after the First World War had led only to disillusionment and reaction. Americans should 'not [be] cocky this time', but rather be 'in a mood to study and find out'. The occupation must 'not mean that we shall be imposing our own particular way of life upon the Germans. It will mean that we shall be helping to build attitudes that are essential to the continuance of a peaceful world.' (On the other hand, Mead also phrased this in engineering terms Americans would find congenial: 'Germany has a system that won't work . . . let's fix it.') Such an attitude would presage a heartening new development, 'the beginning of a genuine concern with the problems of peoples beyond our shores'.[92]

The outcome of the 'Germany After the War' conference was about as positive as Mead could have hoped for. She had completed the job of editing Brickner that Gorer had abandoned – the report was almost wholly the work of Mead, Frank and Parsons. Although the report was at first marked confidential, it circulated freely among various government agencies, and, most significantly, to the experts on the ground in Eisenhower's PWD. As Parsons realized, after D-Day social scientists in America had diminishing opportunities to influence German occupation policy. Most of the civil-affairs training had been done and the trainees were flooding into Europe; power was shifting to the military occupation itself. He fed the report to his friend Ted Hartshorne, who had growing influence in PWD in Europe, especially recommending Mead's sketch of the German national character. Hartshorne embraced it gladly as 'by a good deal the best thing on Germany which has been done by any group, governmental or otherwise', and found that it particularly suited the 'integrated perspective' that PWD was now able to adopt, sociologists working with psychiatrists, the British with the Americans, the military with civilians. Mead and Parsons did not really expect the report to have that much impact – although Hartshorne was in a position to influence policy – but hoped that its effect would be 'educative', showing how much more their own disciplines could achieve in this area than economics or politics, and opening up new spheres for research among captured POWs and eventually among the occupied Germans themselves.[93] Another target of their publicity campaign was Henry Dicks, who got the report from Hartshorne. Dicks, then knee-deep in his psychiatric analysis of POWs for PWD, discovered with delight how closely his own work on the German character among POWs paralleled the theoretical analysis generated in America, and distributed the report widely in the British ranks. By this means, the circle was completed, as news of Dicks's work got back to Gorer. Dicks warmly recommended to his bosses in the British War Office the report's proposals for both short-term and long-term occupation policies, especially Mead's suggestions for improving the status of women. The Americans, he emphasized, needed to be taught that 'mere political and economic adjustments will only scratch the surface' – 'character', not 'ideology', had to be addressed. But the British, he thought, out of traditionalism or social prejudice or 'our national habit of improvisation', were even more likely to adopt a superficial approach to the occupation, and against these temptations the report was an excellent antidote.[94] By the spring of 1945, it proved possible to publish the report in full in a professional psychiatric journal. That generated some good publicity. But by then it was only one note in a vast outpouring of opinion on what to do with Germany – much of which, in the angry but hopeful state of public opinion at the end of the war, chimed with the report's diagnosis of a psychiatric disorder and its recommendation of thoroughgoing re-education.[95]

Mead was right to be cautious about the actual policy impact of the report. As the war ended, events accelerated and the occupation went not at all as any of the experts had predicted. First, Germany was dismembered, not as a result of any conscious policy, but due to the Realpolitik decision taken to divide occupied Germany into British, French, American and Russian Zones: so far, a 'hard' peace – by accident. Then the scope of the problem of denazification proved to be overwhelming. Even the quantifiable 'F-scale', devised by Dicks to spot the most Nazi personalities, proved to be too elaborate and time-consuming. Examinations would never be possible for more than a tiny fraction of the population. In the American and British Zones, a long questionnaire with a simple scoring system, the *Fragebogen*, which owed little to advanced psychological techniques, was used to screen virtually the whole of the adult population for Nazi views. Large numbers of employees in key positions, such as schoolteachers, were swept out of their jobs on this basis. Bureaucratic convenience was at a premium. For similar reasons, the institutional side of Mead and Parsons's institutional-behavioural dialectic was heavily favoured by the British and American authorities. New teachers, new textbooks, new ownership of media outlets were established; behavioural change was left to fend for itself. Only the French adopted a more 'cultural' approach, but their solution was to import French culture, not to attempt to reshape the Germans' own culture.[96]

Most importantly, the timescale of the occupation shrank more suddenly than anyone would have predicted beforehand. The conventional explanation for this shift rests on the Cold War imperatives that were emerging in 1946 and 1947. 'Good' Germans were coming forward to take control of their own economy and polity, offering to defend them as a bulwark against communism. But there was also the practical problem that the Americans and British simply lacked the manpower – and possibly the will – to take direct control of German culture. In the American Zone, the Information Control Division, responsible for the media, was reasonably well staffed, but Education and Religious Affairs were never promoted above branch level. The one man in the branch in a position to steer the occupation in a cultural direction, Ted Hartshorne, who had significant responsibilities for reopening German universities, was killed in a random act of violence mid-mission in August 1946. But already in the first year or so of the occupation there was a tendency to turn away from 're-education' and talk about 'reorientation' only, based on providing a good example to the Germans and trusting that they would follow it.[97] While on the surface this appears close to the approach recommended by Mead and Parsons, it all happened much more quickly than they had anticipated – and for reasons they could not have guessed. For ideological reasons too, American public opinion was very quickly swinging around to a more favourable view of the Germans. By 1949 there were calls for clemency even for convicted Nazi war criminals. Former supporters of the idea of 'national character' began to suggest that German and Japanese 'paranoia' had been, after all, but a 'temporary and accidental' wartime psychosis. 'National character' had either changed more suddenly than Mead could explain, or perhaps it didn't matter as much as she would have liked.[98]

Mead continued to see postwar Germany more as a field for research than as a test case for policy applications. She and Brickner kept together a committee of psychiatric experts after the war's end which communicated with colleagues working in occupied Germany.[99] They had good connections with (and provided some research funds for) the psychiatrists working on top Nazis at the Nuremberg Trials.[100] They were even more closely connected to the two screening centres that were using advanced

psychological methods, Henry Dicks's in the British Zone and David
Levy's in the American. Dicks's German Personnel Research Branch was
an avowedly experimental centre and so laborious that it found it difficult
to get occupation agencies to refer candidates to them. Dicks was keen to
move beyond the mechanical screening process to broader social research
and tried (but failed) to get Gorer to join him in early 1946.[101] But he
could see that the wartime perspectives he had carefully built up were
already breaking down. Whereas he had told Daniel Lerner after the war
that his postwar findings validated the extent of Nazi personality that his
F-scale had predicted – 35 per cent – by the end of 1946 he was writing a
confidential report to the War Office that conceded that 'the experience
of defeat and the disintegration of German society had profoundly modified the average German personality'. This didn't, he maintained, invali-
date the screening process, but it required them 'to pay less attention to
the negative qualities of their subjects and seek rather to find positive
characteristics, to reject more and more the policy of excluding the unfit
in favour of one which would direct the energies of the "greys" into useful
channels'.[102] With this admission Dicks was more or less writing his own
dismissal notice, and he was back on Civvy Street soon thereafter.

David Levy's screening centre in the American Zone was given specific
responsibilities to help Information Control Division purge the media of
identifiable Nazis. Levy, a neo-Freudian psychiatrist who had been a
participant at the 'Germany After the War' conferences, was keener to
prove his practical efficacy than to open new frontiers for research, and
his screening process was more political and less psychological than
Dicks's, but he had two anthropologists on his staff, both students of
Benedict, William Lipkind and David Rodnick; his successor in 1946 was
an acolyte of Mead's and Brickner's, Bert Schaffner.[103] Rodnick and
Schaffner threw themselves into research projects that aimed to test the
wartime theses about the German national character – with mixed results
in the very different atmosphere of the early Cold War. Like Dicks's ambitions, these ventures fell victim to the rapidly changing priorities of the
occupation authority, and by the end of 1946 their screening centre had
shut up shop.[104]

The post-mortems on the German national character belong to the
postwar period, to the early Cold War and its changing priorities. At the
end of the European war, Mead was happy enough to have got a foot in
the psychiatrist's office door, and to have made a statement with the
'Germany After the War' report that fully imported her national-character
perspective into the crowded field of Nazi character analysis. She had
successfully avoided falling into either the 'soft' or the 'hard' camp,
appearing as neither appeaser nor avenger, and charted instead a course

that she thought might take both the Germans and the Americans responsibly into preparations for the postwar world. If she had got that far from the unpromising starting point of Brickner's *Is Germany Incurable?* in 1943, how much more successful might her colleagues be in applying the national-character analysis to the more open field of Japan?

* * *

At a time when Mead was distancing herself from the immediate demands of war, looking ahead to 'after the war', both Gorer and Bateson were anxious to get closer to the war effort. There was a gender dynamic here – a sense of expectation laid upon the man from which the woman was exempted – although in those terms Bateson was a good deal more anxious than Gorer to see real 'action'. Both men certainly wanted to prove the practical efficacy of their scientific knowledge. Gorer had been fortunate to land the OWI job at the end of 1942 on the back of his Japanese memo while Bateson continued to stew in the CIR office. Over the course of 1943, however, he grew impatient with the freewheeling culture cracking, which drew on his strengths but which made only an imponderable contribution to the war effort. He had been hoping for a job in 'propaganda analysis to and from the Far East', but that would have entailed a move to San Francisco where the OWI broadcasts to the Far East originated, and he was reluctant to give up his cushy Washington lifestyle.[105] Then, as the war shifted in 1943, a new opportunity arose. The propaganda campaign against Japan intensified as Mountbatten set up SEAC and prepared to move militarily. The British PWE, which combined responsibility for black and white propaganda, decided to expand its Washington Mission and augment the OWI broadcasts to the Far East across the Pacific. There was a political dimension to this decision too, as the British authorities wanted to keep an eye on OWI, which was suspected of slanting its anti-Japanese propaganda against British imperialism.[106] In mid-1943 Gorer was asked to help run PWE's San Francisco operation but from the Washington Mission's base in the British Embassy. Occasional trips to San Francisco were necessary – this accounted for the absences in 1943–4 during which Mead, Bateson and Cathy occupied his Washington apartment – but most of the work, developing propaganda ideas for the broadcasts and monitoring the scripts as they went out, could be done at a desk in Washington.

The PWE Mission that Gorer joined in Washington was a small but significant unit. Its chief was the queen's brother, David Bowes Lyon. Its principal aim was to coordinate with the American propaganda bodies in Washington, for example, in preparing the civil-affairs handbooks for European occupation, but with special attention to the Far East, where

Britain was supposed to be the senior partner. For this purpose, it had attached to it one of Britain's most distinguished Japanese specialists, Sir George Sansom, who had been serving with the British Foreign Office in Japan on and off since 1904.[107] While the British and the American propaganda shops in the Far East were mutually very suspicious, PWE Washington was pretty well received by its American counterparts, notably for the radio expertise that its BBC veterans brought.[108] The San Francisco operation that Gorer was asked to monitor was very nearly a joint OWI-PWE enterprise. OWI handed over some of its airtime so that PWE could do daily broadcasts in English, Japanese, Cantonese, Mandarin, Burmese and Malay, mostly devoted to news of the progress of the war in both Europe and Asia. Ludicrously, the Japanese broadcasts had to be scripted in San Francisco, teleprinted to Denver – because the people of Japanese ancestry who translated them were still excluded from the West Coast – then teleprinted back to San Francisco for recording and transmission. At the same time, the opportunity was taken to influence the content of OWI broadcasting from San Francisco to the same Asian audiences.[109]

Gorer went out to San Francisco in November 1943 to help set up the shop, and thereafter made repeated visits of inspection, reporting back to Bowes Lyon.[110] His principal responsibility was to exercise quality control over the propaganda broadcasts, to rein in the broadcasters' journalistic instincts and align them instead with the propaganda directives. For most of 1944 and 1945 he wrote weekly reports, in his inimitably tart style, aimed both at his bosses and at the scriptwriters in San Francisco. The first priority was to ensure accuracy and truthfulness – 'a report of news as accurate, sober and unsensational as we can make it' – to maintain the credibility of Britain's white propaganda. At the same time, it was essential to keep the broadcasts lively and substantial, so as to attract listeners. Finally, and here Gorer's special expertise came into play, close attention had to be paid to language to ensure that the correct psychological effect was registered. Gorer particularly deplored 'journalistic clichés', such as 'Hitler's rugged southern defences', that made Allied triumphs over the odds seem impressive but in the process gave a false picture of the enemy's strengths.[111]

Gorer got a mixed reception from his new colleagues in PWE. George Sansom had grumbled on his arrival, 'I've got this young man sicced onto me who's supposed to be an expert on Japan, but all he knows is an article he'd written on the connection between toilet training and imperialism.'[112] But Sansom was now too senior to contribute directly to operations; he had been kicked upstairs to the British Embassy and played no role in the day-to-day affairs of the PWE Mission, leaving Gorer as the

Japan expert on the ground. The objects of Gorer's editorial scorn were, unsurprisingly, also sensitive about the stream of 'astringent' comments he ladled over them. The chief of the San Francisco operation was permitted to edit out the 'less tactful' wording. But in truth Gorer doled out as much praise as criticism. The man responsible for the Malay broadcasts admitted that he found Gorer's editorial contributions 'generous, constructive and helpful'. And Gorer's Washington chiefs backed him up. They endorsed his critique of 'certain lapses from time to time from the standard of dignity and impartiality, which we should aim to maintain', and felt that his editorial control could serve 'a useful purpose, by emphasising the political warfare needs of our output'.[113]

As the war in Asia dragged on, Gorer inevitably got bored, complaining in September 1944, 'The increasingly good war news has meant more and more work and I have become more and more a routine white collar worker. (I don't like it so well.)'[114] But he stuck to his white-collar work. Though his national-character studies made a far greater intellectual impact, the painstaking editorial job he did on Far Eastern propaganda was surely his most practical contribution to winning the war. Even after the Japanese surrender, he kept to his post and continued to monitor the output of broadcasts, 'the unique "Voice of Britain" reaching Japan'.[115] Although the San Francisco operation shut down at the beginning of 1946, he was still in his post at the British Embassy in Washington in February when Dicks tried to lure him into the German Personnel Research Branch. But Gorer was tired and wanted to go home. War service had lost its charm.

*   *   *

Bateson's war service was much more traumatic. By July 1943, when Mead left for England, he had been minding her office for over three years. By that point he was determined to go in at the deep end. While Mead was away, and without much warning, he finally persuaded an American secret-service outfit to take on an unqualified British citizen. OSS, like OWI and PWE, was then ramping up its Far Eastern operations. Because General MacArthur jealously kept OSS out of his Pacific theatre, that meant finding points of entry into Southeast Asia from China and India in Mountbatten's theatre. OSS began to train agents for 'morale operations' – black propaganda near and behind Japanese lines – in New York and Washington in mid-1943. (The New York shop was necessary because the Secret Service had ruled out deployment of people of Japanese descent anywhere near the White House.)[116] As was usual, OSS R&A employed historians, lawyers and political scientists to do background research on the Far East in Washington, but anthropologists were seen as particularly useful for operations in the field: an OSS field detachment was established in Delhi in July 1943 with an anthropologist, David Mandelbaum, providing R&A support there. When another OSS field detachment was set up at Mountbatten's new headquarters in Kandy, Ceylon, in early 1944, OSS took the unusual step of appointing a female anthropologist, Cora Du Bois, as head of R&A there, despite 'the handicap of sex'.[117]

Bateson's initial task was to help train agents in Washington for 'morale operations' in the Far East. He proposed lecturing on 'what is common to the Far East' – for example, the 'special importance of the mother', 'fatalism', 'passivity' – and on what was specific to the Japanese, Chinese, Burmese, Thai and Balinese characters. Pulling out the materials he had prepared in vain for the Army Specialized Training Program, he wanted to show films he and Mead had made in Bali and Japanese propaganda films he had analysed with Gorer, and provide advice on how to extract useful information from native informants. His superiors were dubious about the relevance of some of this material – they thought it too 'theoretical' – and preferred the more familiar political, social and geographical analysis they were used to getting from R&A. Nevertheless, Bateson's and Du Bois's influence ensured that plenty of anthropological expertise was offered up at the Morale Operations (MO) school, including lectures by Mead on 'working relations with Allied personnel, particularly the British', by Lewin on inducing surrender, and by Clare Holt on politics and society in the East Indies. One trainee recalled a special exercise at what was supposed to be the end of the course, when Mead and Bateson arrived with a load of celebratory booze: it turned out to be a test to see how well the trainees held their liquor.[118]

But Bateson didn't want to be the trainer, he wanted to do 'MO' himself. In spring 1944 he followed Du Bois out to Kandy, not as part of her R&A team but as a fully fledged member of MO. At first his bosses didn't think he was suited to MO work in the field.[119] He thus had to content himself with sitting in Kandy, continuing to train agents for the field and thinking up bright ideas for black propaganda. Among his collaborators was another anthropologist, Weston La Barre, who had done some fieldwork on Japanese internees, had prepped for an abortive MO operation in Indochina, and had now been posted to Kandy to help Bateson with 'social and psychological' briefings for the MO agents. La Barre was a red-hot Freudian, and when Bateson introduced him to Gorer's national-character analysis of the Japanese he began to fizz with wicked ideas for destabilizing frontline Japanese soldiers. Exploit Japanese shame about eating, as described by Gorer, by planting faked menus for a Japanese officers' mess behind the lines in Burma to suggest 'decadence and unworthiness of the officers'. Gorer had suggested the Japanese had oral anxieties more generally, so they should spread rumours about rampant tooth decay. Or, something Gorer had missed, play on the acute hypochondria of the ordinary soldier by exaggerating the incidence of beriberi.[120] 'Not at all bad,' reported Bateson of La Barre to Mead, 'but so sloppy in his theoretical framework. Now that we have benefited by Freud, how long will it take us to get rid of the errors of thinking which he introduced?'[121]

During this period, Bateson earned a lot of respect from his OSS colleagues in Kandy (who included, in addition to Cora Du Bois, the future cookery expert Julia Child). Du Bois was glad to have the opportunity to set right the misunderstandings between her, Mead and Bateson that had arisen in the late 1930s when she was uncomfortably associated with Abram Kardiner's rival 'culture and personality' school. Her collaboration with Bateson in Kandy provided, she later recalled, the 'most pleasure and interest' of any of her OSS work. But Bateson was lonely and depressed, and the 'skulduggery' – Du Bois's word – in which he was involved was only further sapping his capacity for healthy emotion. He got some satisfaction out of acting as the 'Father superior' of his Kandy team, but this involved soaking up their own anxieties rather than venting any of his own. On the whole, he kept a poker face. Mead was told that 'puzzled Americans report that he neither smiles nor gripes, but just *is*.' One of his superiors later remembered a disturbing conversation with him in Kandy towards the end of 1944, when Bateson delivered 'a very plausible and well-reasoned opinion, a most cool and scientific one', on a propaganda device that might unleash 'a frenzy of torture and killing' by the Japanese, surprising him with 'his cool, detached consideration of the paranoid fantasy, disguised as a military plan'. Later Bateson said that the only decent contribution he made in Kandy was easing relationships between the Americans and the British in Mountbatten's command, in the Mead fashion. Yet he felt he could not back off from the dirty tricks, he could only dive further in, as if he were in one of his feedback loops, without knowing whether it was ultimately for good or for ill – perhaps both: at this stage he was thinking that even if the enterprise ended in the sacrifice of his own life, it might yet prove a fruitful suicide.[122]

At the end of 1944 he got his wish when his superiors allowed him to join the OSS field unit as head of MO on the frontlines in the Arakan mountains of Burma, where the British 15 Corps was beginning its counteroffensive against the Japanese occupation. There he was able to do something like fieldwork, interviewing locals to get more focused ideas for MO, to sow suspicion of the Japanese and to cultivate friendliness for the Allies among the Arakanese.[123] He was reunited with Jim Mysbergh, a freewheeling agent with whom he had worked in Kandy, who had been pulling off daredevil MO actions behind the lines in Arakan since the summer.[124] Later Bateson entertained his young daughter, Cathy, with stories about the tricks he and Mysbergh had got up to in Burma: cremating a Japanese soldier's corpse in order to produce 'authentic' ashes for some misconceived black-propaganda stunt; trying and failing to dye the Irrawaddy River yellow to fulfil a Burmese prophecy associating that colour with the end of the Japanese occupation.[125]

Again Bateson won praise from his colleagues. The British thought his 'the most useful and most intelligently directed branch' of the whole OSS unit in the Arakan.[126] Again he quickly turned sulky and bored – 'stuck at the moment in a pretty useless dead end' and 'doing all [I] can to get out of it'. Increasingly he fretted about the abuse the methods he was employing would engender in peacetime. 'How in hell are we ever going to get anybody except the bastards to use our stuff?'[127] And yet, again, in order to move on, he moved in deeper. For the rest of the war Bateson's precise movements remain obscure, even after all this time. From his coded letters to Mead, and from information she gleaned through Washington channels, she could only say he was 'in the interior' – a telling phrase in more ways than one – and would not now be home until the war was over.[128] It is possible that he joined 'Gold Dust', a self-contained MO unit operating mobile print and broadcast facilities for black-propaganda purposes to induce Japanese surrender in northern Burma; one of the activities to which he admitted after the war was publishing 'four issues of an underground newspaper behind the Japanese lines in Burma'.[129]

Whatever he was doing, its effects on his own morale were not good.

> Lord – what a waste of human time, emotion, personal relations and everything it all is . . . It's more or less a trap situation – a mood of feeling that there will never be any more ideas ever, synchronized with a shift in status to a branch which really wants the ideas. And I fought for the shift – now I have to justify it . . . So – I am going to stick to this thing for a while longer till I feel that I have justified my new position or that I simply cannot. After that I shall try to head for home as soon as possible.[130]

On the day the atomic bomb was dropped on Hiroshima, he was back at his desk in Kandy, typing away as the news came over the radio. He kept typing, apparently oblivious while the office buzzed around him, until one of his MO colleagues finally blurted out, 'Gregory, what in God's name are you typing?' 'I'm writing about the future of life insurance in the atomic age,' he replied impassively.[131] In the last few weeks of the war he threw the dice again and joined an expedition to rescue some stranded agents in the Batu Islands in the East Indies, and was rewarded with a week in China after the war was over, which almost reignited his appetite for field anthropology.[132] He finally straggled home to New York in October, worn out and damaged. Not only had he failed to make any impact at the policy and planning level, but at the MO level he felt he had done more harm than good to the peoples of Asia. His self-disgust was such that for him the whole enterprise of applied anthropology seemed tarnished beyond redemption – and with it his partnership with Mead.

* * *

Ruth Benedict's war was more like Mead's than Gorer's or Bateson's. She did not have masculine expectations to live up to, nor was she driven by other motives to apply her anthropological techniques to the nitty-gritty of psychological warfare. Like Mead, her concerns were focused on the 'need for cultural understanding' in the postwar world. She moved into 'culture cracking' at OWI relatively late in the war, only after Gorer had left a gap, and devoted herself to mitigating the more negative, Freudian elements in Gorer's analyses and to preparing for postwar cultural relations, especially in laying out the differences between American and European ideas of 'freedom'. Here she came into conflict with the advocates of democratic universalism, her former allies, thanks to her insistence that 'the commonwealth of the postwar world will necessarily be built upon a set of folk commitments which differ from ours'.[133]

How she got from this position before D-Day to working on Japanese morale in the final year of the war involves one of the more bizarre and subsequently excoriated episodes in the wartime history of anthropology. The story begins just after Pearl Harbor, when the American government created a War Relocation Authority (WRA) to handle the mass internment of Americans of Japanese descent. Twenty anthropologists and seven sociologists were employed by WRA, in Washington and in the internment camps, at first to help manage the internees and then to prepare for their relocation outside the camps away from the West Coast. Their number included Weston La Barre, Bateson's OSS colleague, who developed his early theses about the Japanese character while at the Topaz camp in Utah, and John Embree, who did Japanese community analysis for WRA in Washington between his stints at OSS and in civil-affairs training. One camp, at Poston in Arizona, was run not by WRA but by the Bureau of Indian Affairs (BIA), because it was sited on an Indian reservation. The BIA chief, John Collier, who had more experience with anthropology than anyone else in government, decided to turn the entire camp into a piece of applied social science and set up a Bureau of

Sociological Research under a psychiatrist, Alexander Leighton. Leighton and his wife, Dorothea, also a medical doctor, had from early in their career been unusually 'culture conscious' for doctors; they had attended the Linton-Kardiner seminars, had done fieldwork with Clyde Kluckhohn among the Navaho and worked closely with BIA on Indian health care.[134] At Poston, Leighton employed a number of Japanese social scientists, whose role as participant-observers was more than usually ambiguous. While on the whole the anthropologists involved worked to respond to grievances in the camps, to develop self-government and to limit coercion as far as possible, the fundamentally coercive nature of the camps meant that their loyalties were fatally split in a way that made Leighton and Embree deeply uncomfortable at the time and has since made Poston an object lesson in how and why not to do applied anthropology at all.[135]

When WRA shut down the camps in 1943, Leighton was anxious to keep together the Japanese expertise he had accumulated and hoped to persuade the Navy to incorporate his unit as part of its civil-affairs training team for military government. But the Navy was opposed to 'having practical analysis carried out in the field at all analogous to the work at Poston' – it wanted its field commanders to rule supreme, without intrusion from Washington experts – and even more so to allowing Japanese-Americans into their theatre of operations. Hence, in March 1944, Leighton was taken on instead by OWI's deputy director for the Far East, George Taylor, to staff a new unit at OWI, the Foreign Morale Analysis Division (FMAD). At that stage OWI had done little work on Japanese morale. The early work by Gorer and Embree had laid down a basic analysis of the Japanese character but there had as yet been few opportunities for practical applications to enemy propaganda, which had not hitherto been part of OWI's brief. Gorer's propaganda work at OWI had been mostly directed at neutrals and friendlies. Apart from ignorance about the Japanese, there was also a vague feeling that the Japanese soldiers were such automata, practically inhuman, that psychological warfare couldn't work against them.[136] That notion began to change in 1944, as the European war swung decisively in the Allies' favour, PWD took over much of the European work that had been handled by OWI and OSS in Washington, and Washington's attention began to shift to Japan. This led to Gorer's employment by the PWE Washington Mission and also to OWI's adoption of Leighton's team for the new FMAD.

Leighton's experience with anthropologists early in his career and at Poston had left him with a profound respect for the power of cultural analysis. As he built up the FMAD staff in the autumn of 1944, he added to his considerable stock of native-Japanese experts a formidable array of anthropological expertise to create 'a team in which social anthropology, psychobiology, knowledge of Japan and reporting abilities will be combined'.[137] Clyde Kluckhohn came in as Leighton's co-chief. John Embree, who was engaged in civil-affairs training for Japan, joined later. Gorer was, of course, otherwise engaged on the British side. George Taylor later said that he had 'quietly let Gorer go off on his own way' because he didn't believe toilet training could explain very much. Nevertheless, FMAD employed a much more orthodox Freudian, Herman Spitzer, who shared most of Gorer's views but whose 'strict psychoanalytic thinking' explained uncontrolled Japanese aggression by reference to traumatic weaning rather than toilet training.[138]

Ruth Benedict moved over to FMAD from her culture-cracking job at the same time. Her European responsibilities were being phased out, and she had already begun to think about Japan before joining FMAD, exchanging views with her OWI colleague Nathan Leites, who was also called in to FMAD to work with Benedict on special assignments.[139] Benedict and her colleagues at FMAD tackled three main issues, all rather against the grain of mainstream military and political thinking. First, they tried to persuade the military that Japanese fighting morale did have chinks in it after all and that it was worth pursuing psychological warfare against it, to induce apathy and surrender. Second, in anticipation of an invasion of the Japanese home islands, they began to assess Japanese home morale and to consider how psychological warfare might be waged against it too. Third, although here (as with PWD in Europe) they were constrained by the 'unconditional surrender' demand, they shared their views about the peace terms that might be offered to the Japanese, with both the inducement of surrender (among elites as well as the general public) and the 'cultural rehabilitation' of postwar Japan in mind.

In seeking to understand the Japanese character as a basis for both psychological warfare and postwar reconstruction, FMAD found itself enmeshed in exactly the same dilemmas that its fellow social scientists had faced in tackling the German problem. Conservatives and 'old Japan hands' – prewar diplomats at the State Department close to the Japanese court, the elites and the *zaibatsu* – wanted a quick, compromise peace. Their position favouring minimal social changes would be strengthened after the war by fears of stirring up communism in Japan. The military and political leaderships, however, were committed to 'unconditional surrender'. Any use of psychological techniques, except to induce surrender, was considered suspect. Increasingly they were now joined by left-wing democratic universalists, who wanted to bring the New Deal to Japan. They too were suspicious of compromises, especially the idea floated by the 'old Japan hands' that the war could quickly be ended, and Japan stabilized, if it was hinted that the Japanese could retain the emperor. In this complex mesh the anthropologists in FMAD appeared to take an inconsistent position that threatened to alienate everyone. Their belief in the cultural integrity of the Japanese caused them to emphasize a distinctive character to be played on in psychological warfare but also to be respected in any postwar reconstruction. Although they kept their distance from the 'old Japan hands', they did believe that a policy of retention of the emperor would help to end the war more quickly and might even be essential to preserve what was essentially Japanese in any postwar reconstruction. On the other hand, as with Germany, if they did not want a 'hard', vengeful peace, neither did they advocate a 'soft' one that would leave Japanese militarism intact. Hence they advocated what Leighton called 'an intelligent policy rather than a vengeance policy'. The Japanese national character needed to be understood and respected, but also, as Gorer had said, 'canalized' to prevent any recurrence of aggression that might threaten the postwar order.[140]

Some of these crosscurrents were on display in a conference held in New York in December 1944 by the Institute of Pacific Relations (IPR), a left-leaning think-tank. According to Mead, this was the idea of Benedict, Gorer and Ronald Lippitt (who had succeeded Lewin at the OSS training school), conceived as an opportunity to bring together representatives of all the government agencies working on Japanese morale with psychiatrists and anthropologists.[141] Many of the 'Germany After the War' participants reassembled, including Mead, Parsons, Brickner, French and Kubie, as well as all the leading Japanese specialists, including Embree, Haring, Gorer and, from FMAD, Leighton and Benedict. The discussion was not dissimilar to that at the 'Germany After the War' conferences.[142] But Embree in particular was shocked by the casual bandying about of psychiatric terms – 'pathological', 'adolescent', 'neurotic', 'gangsters' – applied to a whole people among whom he had contentedly done fieldwork before the war. His disagreements with Gorer over the balance between psychological and socio-economic factors in explaining Japanese militarism now blew up. In an article in the professional journal *American Anthropologist*, Embree denounced 'so-called scientists' whose writings 'have been largely in the form of "confidential" mimeographed pamphlets and so not subject to scientific criticism', yet 'nonetheless their conclusions are presented to government agencies as the findings and methods of "anthropology"'. 'There is a strong implication that because of our enemy's undesirable character structure and our own desirable virtues in this regard (plus better firearms), we have the moral right to walk in and reform, by force if necessary, the family life, education, and religion of peoples different from ourselves. A curious doctrine for the heirs of Franz Boas.' It was, he fumed, tantamount to racism.[143]

Douglas Haring disputed his account. The composition of the conference was very diverse, he said, and there was no consensus around the use of psychiatric, still less of semi-racist epithets.[144] What Haring did not point out was that he had himself applied the label 'neurotic' to the Japanese at the conference. Reading Karen Horney's description of the 'neurotic personality of our time' as if it were about the Japanese, he said, gave 'the most perfect description of the Japanese that he had ever read' – to which someone (very possibly Embree) had rejoined: 'the same results would be achieved by substituting the word "American".'[145] But Haring was right to say that there was no consensus around the use of psychiatric language. Benedict, for one, was adamantly opposed to the use of a universalistic word such as 'neurotic' to characterize a distinctive and intelligible culture pattern. Just as she had done for Burma, she was in the process of toning down Gorer's excessively psychiatric terms as applied to the Japanese national character, making them more relativistic and in closer harmony with other aspects of Japanese society. Her position on 'reform', like Mead's on Germany, was that a culture pattern could not be reformed by force; that an American occupation ought to adopt the minimal measures necessary to help the Japanese re-establish their own equilibrium.[146]

But she also knew that any argument for understanding the enemy could be taken as a plea for 'sympathy', and America's military and political leaders were not in the mood for anything but unremitting warfare. Embree's denial of a moral right to reform the Japanese sounded suspiciously like the call for a 'soft' peace by the 'old Japan hands'. Democratic universalists in government (and in the IPR, the sponsor of the conference) were scornful about the 'Sunday school approach' that would treat the Japanese – and especially the emperor – with kid gloves. They felt far more strongly than any anthropologist that 'we have the moral right to walk in and reform, by force if necessary ... peoples different from ourselves' – not perhaps their family life or religion, but certainly their educational, economic and political systems. They, too, sometimes compared the anthropological approach to racism: surely the Japanese were not 'different from ourselves' at all, but just like us, eager to throw off militarism and embrace American-style democracy if given the chance? But they tended to be more pessimistic about the Japanese than about the Germans; 'thorough-going – even ruthless' reform might be necessary to make democrats out of them. Between the 'old Japan hands' and democratic universalists, the anthropologists – most of whom shared

Embree's fellow feeling with the Japanese – found it difficult to define a relativist defence of the Japanese people and their culture.[147]

For most of their existence, the social scientists of FMAD felt that they were struggling futilely against two views deeply entrenched in the military and political leadership: that the Japanese were nearly robotic fanatics impervious to psychological warfare; and, not entirely contradictorily, that the Japanese were human beings much like the Americans who would respond best to direct threats to their personal security or, at the most idealistic, to the universal appeal of democracy and human rights. Against these views FMAD strove mightily to show that Japanese morale *could* be broken down, not by attacking their most deeply cherished beliefs head-on, but by exploiting internal divisions and war-weariness. Only towards the end of the war – at the beginning of the summer of 1945 – did they feel they were making some headway, as the Allies prepared for an invasion of the home islands and began for the first time to take seriously propaganda based on genuine breakdowns of housing, health, subsistence and labour, and growing disillusionment with the military clique. Although he took little pleasure in the fact, Leighton noted later that postwar surveys confirmed FMAD's suspicions that Japanese morale had been seriously vulnerable since at least late 1944. But its ultimate failure was registered by the decision to drop the atomic bombs, a decision based on the military leadership's unrealistically high estimate of Japanese fighting morale.[148]

For the FMAD social scientists, as for the social scientists in Eisenhower's PWD, the principal source of frustration was the 'unconditional surrender' demand, which severely limited the scope of their propaganda. As in the German case, they argued that Japanese morale might be fortified by the suspicion that defeat or surrender could be a prelude to their total destruction as a nation. Leighton thought their arguments might have been responsible for some small concessions in the implementation of the propaganda war, grudgingly viewed as compatible with 'unconditional surrender'. But the FMAD social scientists went further, reflecting the greater significance they attached to the culture pattern. They argued explicitly that the Japanese culture pattern ought not to be disrupted but defended, both on pragmatic grounds – that head-on attacks would build morale rather than weaken it – and on principled grounds – that 'the best in her system of ethics is worthy of attention and perpetuation' in the postwar order. For them, the bottom line was defence of the emperor institution. Leighton granted that 'serious damage to a symbol that affects a wide range of Japanese values, ethical ideals and religious beliefs . . . would no doubt speed the end of the war' – precisely the argument of his military and political opponents. But would it be worth it?

[I]n the end the United Nations would lose more than they would gain due to the postwar difficulties of dealing with a country of multiple competing leaders, in a state of economic and moral collapse, and full of civil wars, *ronins* (roving bandits), pretenders to the throne, nests of resistance and underground movements. It is even possible that considerable sympathy and support might arise in other Asiatic nations. At the same time, it can be effectively argued that Japanese morale may be attacked at least equally effectively from many angles other than the imperial institution and that while the emperor is a most important pillar of strength, he is not by any means the only one.

With its eyes firmly on postwar 'cultural reconstruction', FMAD put the case that attacks on the emperor now would

> make progress toward legitimate moral values and goals more difficult. Not only are national ideals kept intact, lofty and inviolate despite the course of ordinary affairs by their identification with the Emperor, but there is a personal identification of the average Japanese with the Emperor and a tendency for many Japanese, by a process of projection, to ascribe to the Emperor their own philosophies or aims . . . we must ask ourselves whether changes in [Japanese culture] should not be those largely dictated from within Japan and ratified in spirit by the Japanese people . . . the alternative may be the serious disruption of acceptable institutions and patterns, and the division and confusion of people who now must cooperate and work together for their food and very survival.

Not only was it futile to try to change from without the Japanese culture pattern – 'the manifold effects of the Japanese family system, the force of sentiments inculcated from early infancy, the symbolism of innumerable festivals, the whole range of poetry, art and drama, and the very structure of the language itself' – but, in fact, Leighton suggested, the desire to do so related principally to America's own culture pattern:

> the emperor has during the war become a symbol to us of the evil enemy we wish to punish and . . . we have far reaching and deep-going attitudes of antipathy to authoritative figures and these attitudes spring from our own cultural patterns of family life, individual independence and history of revolution and pioneering. Valuable as those are to us, they are beside the point in considering the emperor and the Japanese people.[149]

This argument infuriated democratic universalists, for whom the emperor was 'the symbol of what we are fighting against'. J.K. Fairbank, a

Chinese historian who had worked for OSS in China and was now Taylor's deputy in the Far Eastern section of OWI, mocked Leighton's suggestion that 'without compromising . . . our determination to avoid militarism, we could exert considerable influence on the Japanese if we were to tell them that we do not hold the Japanese Emperor responsible for the war . . . This statement to my mind betrays confusion as to what militarism is and why we are fighting it.' It didn't help that those arguing for the same position 'in high places' in the State Department were the 'old Japan hands',

> who crave stability rather than progressive adjustment to modern prob-
> lems, who set store by realpolitik and the preservation of reactionary
> regimes as allies against potential enemies, or who insufficiently appre-
> ciate the economic, social, and ideological causes of Japanese militarism
> [and] are inclined to stress the possible usefulness of the Emperor for
> short term purposes, or the impropriety of meddling in the internal
> affairs of other countries after we have destroyed them.[150]

FMAD's position between the 'soft' and the 'hard' peace shows how diffi-
cult it was to defend the integrity of Japanese culture while trying to defeat the Japanese people in war. Yet that was the position anthropolo-
gists seeking to create a peaceful world out of a war-torn one very broadly felt they had to take. As the war drew to a close, they focused on 'the problem of reeducating the American public in relation to post-war and occupied territory problems' in order to secure that 'intelligent policy' Leighton was advocating.[151]

As with Germany, the social scientists played only minor roles in the actual occupation of Japan. The policy outcome with which they were most closely associated – the decision to retain the emperor in the peace settlement – had been embraced by MacArthur even before FMAD came into existence, on the advice of his wholly amateur 'psychological warfare' specialists who urged him to 'drive a wedge' between the emperor and the people, on the one hand, and the militarists, on the other. For their different reasons, the social scientists and the 'old Japan hands' both endorsed this policy, but neither appears to have had much impact on its devising or adoption. Actual occupation policy was driven by yet another force, a new wave of younger democratic universalists who provided an idealistic element in the occupation that pushed American-style democratization and modernization. Mediating this complex process was the dominating character of General MacArthur, who had a deeply paternal view of the 'tuitionary condition' of the Japanese, 'like a boy of twelve', and took it upon himself to re-educate them according to his own models:

Washington, Lincoln and Jesus Christ. Japanese experts of any kind – whether 'old Japan hands' or social scientists – were unnecessary.[152] The social scientists were hardly surprised by this attitude. Leighton, who spent some time in Japan after the war assessing morale, had been disillusioned by FMAD's failure to make an impact in policy circles and especially by its complete irrelevance in the decision to drop the atomic bombs. Embree was so opposed to democratization by military occupation that he kept deliberately aloof.[153] MacArthur did employ a small sociological research section to monitor Japanese public opinion but it included only very junior personnel. When Clyde Kluckhohn visited Japan in 1947, he proposed a substantial extension of this work. Although MacArthur did not favour his plan, the sociological research division did restart the Western study of Japan on a different basis from that rooted in the wartime experience.[154]

Yet it was Ruth Benedict's work on Japan for FMAD, rooted in that wartime experience, that would make the most enduring contribution to Western understandings of Japan. Hers was a slow-burning influence. Benedict played second fiddle to Leighton and Kluckhohn in the jockeying for influence in the corridors of power during the closing months of war. She provided much of the intellectual back-up for their arguments for the retention of the emperor, but, like Mead's, her eyes were firmly fixed on the postwar. She spent the summer of 1945 preparing a full-length memorandum on Japanese character, aimed explicitly at 'cultural reconstruction'; it wasn't yet completed at the time of the Japanese surrender. When the war ended, she was barred by the military from working either in Germany or in Japan – the former on health grounds, the latter on grounds of sex – so she decided instead to do what she did best, address her Japanese memorandum to the public in the hopes of educating opinion.[155] *The Chrysanthemum and the Sword: Patterns of Japanese Culture* – the subtitle was her working title until the publisher insisted on something more picturesque at the last minute[156] – emerged in autumn 1946.

The book was aimed at stimulating debate about America's (and not only Japan's) place in the postwar world. Its principal argument was for *difference*. The postwar world was going to be a lot harder to bring into being and negotiate than Americans imagined: the Japanese were very different from them, 'the most alien enemy' they had ever faced, and a stable, peaceful world required a recognition of that difference, displacing comforting illusions about 'the brotherhood of man', the essential likeness of all humans. Consonant with this postwar orientation, Benedict's emphasis was not on explaining (still less 'curing') Japanese aggression, but rather on explaining those aspects of Japanese society and culture least familiar to American democrats. Japan's was a hierarchical not an egalitarian society, yet neither did this take the form of 'a simple Occidental authoritarianism', but rather of an intricately interlocking set of mutual responsibilities.[157] The core of the book was devoted to explaining the Japanese concept of *on* – obligation to others – which might be limitless (*gimu*, owed, for example, to one's parents or the emperor) or, more commonly, limited (*giri*, owed to others and to one's own honour), in a complex economy of obligations. Keeping track of *giri* was an onerous business, requiring much stoicism and self-control – inexplicable to Americans with their preference for activity and competition – but, and here Benedict was emphatic, it did not generate the 'frustration' that Americans thought led to aggression. This was a stable pattern – one exemplifying the very high 'synergy' that Benedict had been seeking when she wanted to move beyond relativism – and although it had been harnessed to nationalism, it could just as easily be harnessed to peaceful reconstruction. Its ethics were, as Gorer had suggested, not absolute but relative, reliant not on 'guilt' but on 'shame', on external sanctions rather than internal ones – but for that very reason these ethics could be more easily realigned with a situation that required peace rather than war.[158]

Benedict did devote her penultimate chapter to child training, and some of Gorer's themes are present, though in much modified form. There is still a contrast between the indulgence of the infant and the more severe disciplines imposed on children and young adults, leading to some swinging between wildness and restraint. But the contrast is not as deeply embedded as Gorer's emphasis on severe toilet training suggested. Infant and child training is now seen as better aligned with the adult discipline of *on*, and, unlike the swings to a crass authoritarianism depicted in the German character (which need to be checked to make them safe for others), the impulse to take *on* seriously is seen as a viable and even admirable quality, however different it might be from American instincts.[159] Whereas German reconstruction might require a thoroughgoing reform of family and civic life, Benedict concludes explicitly, the Japanese would benefit from a lighter touch: 'the traditional social order of the nation' ought to be defended, and only those excessive strains that had led latterly to aggression need be treated. It was the Japanese fear of others that had caused an overtightening of self-control and allowed the militarists to get the upper hand. As she had said in her popular book on racism at the beginning of the war, 'Japan has a history of peace and non-aggression that cannot be matched in the Western World', and its recent reputation as 'one of the most aggressively warlike nations of the world' had come about only as a result of conflict with the West.[160] So long as Americans did not try to force the Japanese to be like them, the Japanese might see for themselves that they had nothing to fear, and if they allowed themselves to relax they need no longer pay the very high charge that they had recently levied on themselves.[161]

For a book that was based on an internal OWI memorandum, *The Chrysanthemum and the Sword* was an astonishing success. It sold hundreds of thousands of copies in the US and, more extraordinarily still, millions in Japan. As late as the 1980s, one-third of all Japanese knew something about Benedict or her book.[162] For the Japanese immediately after the war, it served as a starting point for a national debate about the causes of the war, the bases for postwar reconstruction and the nature of the national identity. As the social scientists in MacArthur's research division pointed out, it gave Japanese social science a kickstart that encouraged it to develop its own more empirical critiques of the generalizations that the national-character approach entailed.[163] In their own way Americans have ended up agonizing over it more. Does the book's roots in the wartime quest to destroy Japan render pernicious its persistence since?[164] Undoubtedly it has to be seen as a work of its moment, with all of the weaknesses of the national-character approach we have noted, including its simplistic homogenization of the nation and a thinning-down of national attributes to personality types. But in that moment it distinguished itself sharply from some of its rivals. As she had done inside OWI, Benedict dramatically toned down the psychoanalytic content that had made Gorer's treatments attractive to those seeking a 'hard' peace. She made every effort to portray Japanese culture as, fundamentally, healthy and stable in its own terms. Of course, this meant 'othering' it in relation to American culture, but at the same time she was 'othering' American culture in relation to Japanese.[165] If she referred to Japan as 'a shame culture', she also called America 'a guilt culture', and she refused universalist judgements that preferred 'guilt' to 'shame'.[166] As she wrote to her FMAD colleague Robert Hashima after the Japanese surrender, 'no Western nation has ever shown such dignity and virtue in defeat . . . Now I hope and pray that America will play her part with restraint and dignity too. It will be difficult for many Americans because they are so different.'[167]

While her book was written in the context of the American military occupation, as any book on Japan published in 1946 would have been, her recommendation was for a mild and minimally interventionist occupation, in striking contrast to the much more rigorous occupation her friends were recommending for Germany. In this respect her book resembled John Embree's *The Japanese Nation* (1945), which also argued that 'future social developments' ought to be 'in accord with Japanese history and culture' and urged the Allies to 'withdraw gracefully' as soon as possible. Embree was here reacting against the psychiatric language he had heard at the IPR conference, but then he had used such language himself earlier in the war, and like Benedict was now toning it down in order to prepare for peace.[168] In his own review of Benedict's book, he praised it highly for 'not taking the all too easy step of arguing that the Japanese have such and such culture patterns *therefore* they indulge in aggressive wars', but emphasizing instead the 'many strengths in Japanese culture which may serve as a foundation for a prosperous and peaceful future'.[169] That was, at least, how it looked to the readers most sympathetic to a non-American future for Japan at the time. If it also looked that way to the wider readership, then *The Chrysanthemum and the Sword* has some claim to be one of the most effective ambassadors for cultural relativism published in the twentieth century. Here Benedict took advantage of the anthropological edge that Mead had exploited so effectively before the war, using the colourfulness of ethnography and the relative mysteriousness of lesser-known cultures to reach and persuade audiences beyond the reach of the colder, more analytical varieties of social science. To have achieved that in the immediate wake of war in respect of an 'enemy' was a considerable achievement that even Mead, with her public pronouncements limited to cultivating understanding between allies, could not match.[170]

*　*　*

Subsequent lore has occasionally attributed to Margaret Mead the decisions to retain the emperor and even to drop the atomic bomb – decisions held to have won the war for the Allies, at least in that theatre. One report had it, third-hand, that Mead claimed that she felt most 'truly powerful' when she rang up FDR to tell him not to bomb the Imperial Palace. 'Margaret got on the telephone and asked for FDR, "Mr. President, we've been doing a study . . . we think that the military should not bomb the Imperial Palace. Without the Emperor we've got real problems . . . our anthropological studies prove he's the only figure who can do it . . ." He said, "you're right, thank you for calling."'[171] Conversely, Abram Kardiner maliciously spread the rumour that Benedict and the anthropologists had advised the government that the Japanese would never surrender, thus leading to the dropping of the atomic bombs.[172] Such stories are significant only because they indicate people believed Mead and her associates might indeed have had a direct line to the White House, which they did not. At best, occasionally Mead had the ear of Eleanor Roosevelt, for example in support of the 'Germany After the War' conferences, which Harold Ickes, secretary of the interior, and other notables also backed.[173] Despite her role in FMAD Benedict had little if any influence on the surrender terms offered to the Japanese.[174] It is possible that the top political leaders who made the decision to retain the emperor had never even heard of FMAD.[175]

On the other hand, Mead felt at the end of the war that the goals she had set for herself and for her discipline had been satisfied almost beyond expectations. In this sense, she could rightly claim that she had won the war for anthropology. In 1941 her fear had been that the economic and political experts would make all the running, as they had done after the First World War. By 1945 'applied anthropology' had come of age, and within anthropology the 'culture and personality' approach had been seen to have the greatest relevance. A wide range of government agencies had recognized that the knowledge of cultural difference in which anthropologists specialized was immensely valuable in a true world war. They were used for purposes ranging from the very mundane – briefings on physical and human terrain in out-of-the-way places like New Guinea or Burma – to the most abstract – profiles of 'national character' that might be used to tailor psychological warfare to specific cultures, Western as well as non-Western. In those areas where the anthropologists were almost the only experts in the field, such as propaganda, occupation and relief policies towards peoples in remote places, they had considerable freedom to infiltrate their own views and techniques into what they were doing. In areas where they offered new approaches that were compatible with older ones – adding a psychological or anthropological dimension to economic and political analyses of more familiar Western peoples – their influence was variable, depending on the stakes and the competition. As we have seen, national-character analysis of the Germans was harder to put across than in the case of the Japanese, and both were harder to put across than in the cases of the Dutch or the Romanians. The hard-boiled Harold Lasswell told Arthur Upham Pope that the national-character memoranda were 'the joke of Washington'.[176] But internal evidence suggests that they circulated far and wide, and were embraced – often enthusiastically – by policymakers either when they had no alternative or when the anthropological conclusions coincided with their own. The latter was common enough. As Benedict's boss at FMAD, Alexander Leighton, pithily summed up his position: 'You always get one of two requests: to show that some policy the executive has already decided upon is badly needed; or, to show that some policy the executive is already employing is working well . . . The administrator uses social science the way a drunk uses a lamppost, for support rather than for illumination.'[177]

Such a conclusion would hardly have surprised or shocked Mead. She had generally stayed aloof from 'inside' involvement in policymaking because she didn't wish to sacrifice her independence or to see her ideas twisted into unrecognizable shapes. The experience of people like Leighton only confirmed her suspicion that, as she summed it up after the war, 'you can't advise an adviser'. It was necessary either to get in deeper or to keep more aloof. Mead's own choice during the war was to keep more aloof, and the very bad experience that Bateson had had getting in too deep confirmed her conviction that her own strategy was the right one. Still, she thought, even learning the lessons of the limits to their participation in the war effort had built up a stock of experience, and credibility, for anthropologists that they might turn to good use after the war.[178] She was hardly naïve, as is sometimes suggested, about the personal and ideological consequences of war work. Her critics, writing in a strongly anti-authoritarian (and in fact anti-governmental) mood after the debacle of Vietnam, have generally concluded that any connection to war work damaged both anthropology and the peoples of the world to which it was committed.[179] Mead, working in a different atmosphere after Kristallnacht and Pearl Harbor, strongly disagreed. She thought winning the war important enough that one might reasonably go to almost any lengths. But she was always aware of and concerned about the long-term damage, both to her loved ones and to her own culture, wrought by aggression and manipulation even in a good cause. After the war, she was not shy about warning against the malign consequences, especially of black propaganda.[180] On the whole, however, she trusted her friends and colleagues to make good choices – to know where to draw the line. During the war, she could be very harsh with Gorer, especially when she felt he had failed to do so, though she was also sometimes complicit in his poor choices. But she knew that poor choices came with the territory of war, and she looked eagerly to a change of scene that might provide better choices in peace. With her focus on the postwar order, she was confident that anthropologists could learn to use tools honed in war for peace as well, and that, as she reassured Bateson, they would find ways to reforge those tools 'which will make them unacceptable to the bastards'.[181]

Above all, Mead and Benedict could feel in 1945 that they had succeeded triumphantly in doing what they did best – influencing the climate of opinion from the outside, by writing (without the trammels of secrecy or concerns about policy impact) for the widest possible audiences. *And Keep Your Powder Dry* introduced Americans to the anthropological view that they themselves were 'different', and that their own difference needed to be taken into account when dealing with every other people in the world, including their closest allies. In her journalism, broadcasting and incessant public speaking, Mead had shown how that might work in practice as an ambassador for Anglo-American relations on both sides of the Atlantic. At the end of the war, Mead was sitting down to write a book of prescriptions for a new international order based on cultural difference under the working title 'Learning to Live in One World'. Benedict, too, had kept aloof from policymaking until she joined OWI in mid-1943. Her greatest contribution to the war effort up until that point had also been in the public sphere, her million-selling anti-racist tract *Races of Mankind*, with Gene Weltfish, which had presented the world war, just as Mead had done, as a lesson in how 'people of different races and nationalities have to live together and be part of one community'.[182] Still more significantly, in *The Chrysanthemum and the Sword* she had made a telling case for considering even America's 'most alien enemy' as a future partner in such a world community.

In 1945, when the postwar order that Mead and Benedict had been anticipating before the war began to take shape, Mead's hopes for the contribution of anthropology to the 'orchestation of cultural diversities' were therefore justifiably high. In 1941 she had worried that Americans were too disengaged from the world to mobilize to fight fascism. That worry had proved unfounded. Then during the war she had worried that mobilization against an enemy might so taint Americans' view of other cultures with aggression and overconfidence that their newfound engagement would be unsuited to a peaceful world. That worry, too, she came to feel in the closing weeks of war, as she wrote 'Learning to Live in One World', was at least manageable. The most serious challenge she faced was the growing force of democratic universalism. Here she knew she had not *quite* won the Second World War. For though Americans had successfully mobilized for war, they had done so in a very American way, by identifying too closely with their neighbours, taking an interest not in their difference but in their identity. Mead thought she could work with that. Americans' democratic universalism, their 'passionate desire that others be like ourselves', had to be harnessed as their contribution to the world order as surely as *gimu* and *giri* had to be accepted as the contribution of the Japanese. It 'must be understood and woven into the framework of a United World', or else, she concluded uneasily two days before V-J Day, 'it can easily become a force for evil'.[183] That was the task that Mead set herself as the world moved from hot war to cold.

Benedict

CHAPTER 5

Culture Cracking for Peace
(1945–50)

The techniques and methods of Mead's national-character studies, while honed in wartime, were meant to be 'as useful for peace as for war': that was her mantra both during the war and after it. She had kept her own hands free in wartime precisely, she said, to ensure that her work didn't fall into the hands of the 'bastards', so that it would thus be applicable to the making of a peaceful world rather than to the continuation of hostilities.[1] Subsequent generations have inclined to be sceptical about such claims, to say the least. Among the post-Vietnam generation, it has been more common to argue that social science – including anthropology, and including Mead – had become so entangled with the 'National Security State' during the war that it would have been nearly impossible for them to disengage thereafter, had either side actually wished to do so. And in fact, it is argued, neither side did try to disengage. With the Cold War following so nearly on the heels of the hot war, government was hardly likely to want to dismantle an apparatus of intelligence-gathering and behavioural manipulation that had proved itself in combat against the nation's enemies. For their part, social scientists were eager to establish their credentials as 'policy scientists' and to share some of the funding and power bonanza from which the atomic scientists were already benefiting. A novel super-discipline – 'behavioural science' – was in the making, and anthropology, with its newly acquired psychological techniques and its powerful new claims to knowledge of 'complex, modern societies', was seen to be positioning itself consciously alongside psychology and sociology as an equal partner in this new super-science.[2]

In fact, such claims tell us more about the post-Vietnam generation than about their mid-twentieth-century predecessors. It has been important for the anti-authoritarian identity of the later generation to assert the complicity in authoritarianism of their elders, even where many years later they were repeating critiques that their elders had laid down themselves at the time.[3] The survivors of that older generation, reading the denunciations of the new historiography in the 1980s and 1990s, viewed them with the mixture of puzzled incomprehension and angry defensiveness that those on the 'wrong' side of yawning generation gaps normally show.[4] There is no reason to believe the retrospective testimony of the elders any more than the retrospective polemics of the young, of course. What we can do instead is follow their choices through the rapidly changing years after the hot war ended. Restoring some agency to our protagonists, we can see that their highly variegated wartime experiences led them along different career paths after the war, and their different reactions to the advent of Cold War hostilities further differentiated their understandings of social science's proper relationship to government and the world scene.[5] Anthropologists, in particular, had their long-standing commitments to the 'natives' to take into account, commitments for which a science of behavioural control oriented to American national interests was not an obviously congenial vehicle. Mead, for her part, found it increasingly difficult to retain the respect and leadership of her discipline and at the same time to pursue her mission to implant 'culture consciousness' at the heart of international relations. She had done her best during the war to keep her independence from government and so safeguard her credibility as an anthropologist. Having thus 'kept her powder dry' for peace, her attempts to use it as she hoped for the 'orchestration of cultural diversities' in a new world order would run up against Americans' growing ambitions to remake the world in their own image.

*   *   *

'When the end of the war came, of course everybody was a little tired and anxious to go home,' Mead wrote many years later.[6] For most young or aspirant social scientists, there were no peacetime jobs in military or government service to stay in or go to. OWI was immediately disbanded. OSS's Research and Analysis Branch was cut down to a small fraction of its former size, retained for intelligence purposes by the State Department, with the result that 'intelligence research has been decapitated', as the R&A chief William Langer complained in 1947.[7] Despite furious lobbying efforts by social scientists, led by Talcott Parsons, the government decided to exclude the social sciences from the vastly enhanced package of funding it provided for the 'hard' sciences when the National Science Foundation (NSF) was set up after the war.[8] The Army at first declined to continue its own psychological-warfare research beyond the narrowest operational requirements. The Navy and the Air Force in different ways sought to step into the gap, through the Office of Naval Research (ONR), which contracted outsiders (mostly academics) to do 'basic' social-science research, the Human Resources Research Institute (HRRI), an integral part of the Air Force, and what was initially called 'Project RAND' (for Research AND Development), a think-tank that did research on behalf of the Air Force. But these were at first limited and tentative ventures, which in the case of ONR and HRRI did not survive Congressional scrutiny of 'blue-sky' research (especially by 'long-haired professors') in the early 1950s.[9]

Those few who did stay in government service were not necessarily motivated by a sense of political mission, or, if they did have such a sense, it was not necessarily associated with the as-yet-unannounced Cold War. One of the few anthropologists to remain in peacetime government service was Cora Du Bois. When the war ended she was summoned back to Washington from Kandy to discuss her future, and en route was casually told that her Southeast Asia unit of OSS R&A was being reconstituted as a desk inside the State Department. As a single female scientist, without an academic job to go to, she accepted the reassignment initially for pragmatic reasons. But she went in believing that here was an opportunity to assist in the decolonization of Southeast Asia and to support the new nations in formation there. It was only gradually, she later recalled, that she saw that her wartime freedom of action – unimpeded by the interests of the French, Dutch or British colonial authorities – was becoming oddly constrained by a new Cold War foreign policy 'formed out of reports from Paris and London'. She told her idealistic staff, who included Claire Holt from Mead's wartime seminar, 'Get the hell out of here and back to academic life. You can't stand this, it's destroying you.' Finally she saw that it was destroying her too, and jumped, but not until 1950.[10] As a more established academic, Du Bois could find other jobs to go to, and within a few years became only the second woman to be appointed to a professorship at Harvard. Holt, younger, a single mother and without credentials, had fewer options; she hung on until 1953.[11] A similar story could be told about John Embree, who was highly critical of anthropologists in government for representing the interests of the governors (often colonial or neocolonial) rather than the governed, yet who himself accepted work as a State Department cultural-affairs officer in Southeast Asia in order to help give voice to emerging nationalisms there. When he too saw that his job was becoming merely 'propagandistic', he left to take an academic job in Southeast Asian studies at Yale.[12]

Most social scientists employed in war work went straight back to academic life as soon as the war was over. Their highly diversified experience of the war, characterized, as Abbott and Sparrow have nicely put it, by 'career disruption, heteronomous work for huge and often irrational organizations, erratic mobility in both geographic and social space, and exposure to the peculiar mixture of volunteerism, propaganda and coercion that undergirded the citizen-soldier concept', did not in fact give them much of a common bond.[13] They entered a rapidly expanding academy enjoying the boom years of the GI Bill – membership of the American Anthropological Association (AAA) doubled in size in the three immediate postwar years to over 1,700 – and ascended the career ladder quickly.[14] Some features of this new academic world undoubtedly made the entire community more conservative; it was, proportionately, more male (as the huge influx of new college students was disproportionately male) and, as it grew, it became more self-consciously professionalized and specialized. Efforts were made to emulate the hard sciences in specifying more precisely the data, methods and procedures of each discipline, and, sometimes, in preferring quantitative over qualitative methods.

However, many of these developments made social science less rather than more amenable to policy application. 'Pure' research was often elevated over the merely 'applied', and on narrow career grounds specialization was preferred to interdisciplinary efforts at problem-solving. As Barry Katz, the historian of OSS R&A, has argued, wartime collaborations across disciplinary lines for problem-solving purposes proved difficult to sustain in the altered postwar environment.[15] Young anthropologists who were eager to return to fieldwork in remote parts of the world, and to the founding premises of their discipline, showed little interest in multi-disciplinary behavioural-science laboratories in their home universities. Older, more policy-oriented academics seeking to promote 'behavioural science' thus found it difficult to recruit the younger, more disciplinary academics to their banner.

The attractions of an interdisciplinary, policy-oriented 'behavioural science' were strongest for those 'nervous liberals' who before the war had championed the development of 'objective' methods in social science that offered means of controlling individuals and groups, theoretically available to anyone but naturally more available to the holders of wealth and power. There were certainly plenty of 'nervous liberals' about in the immediate postwar years. The crisis of 1939–41, during which it had proved so difficult to galvanize ordinary Americans to oppose fascism, threatened to repeat itself in the late 1940s when ordinary Americans were expected to confront a new form of totalitarianism. Those social scientists who had had the most intimate experience of Americans' war-fighting capabilities were not heartened by the experience. Notoriously, Samuel Stouffer's wartime work for the Army Research Branch gave him both the tools and the appetite to attempt behavioural control on individuals and small groups. As a result of his wartime research, Stouffer had developed a low opinion of the calibre of the

American soldier and the functioning of the basic units of the armed services. While he was avowedly motivated by a scientific zeal to unlock the secrets of the human mind, his conservative politics – unusual among social scientists – and his keenness to use the tools he had devised made him an enthusiastic client for government and foundations after the war. With a grant from the Carnegie Corporation, he set up a Laboratory of Social Relations at Harvard, and in 1949 he published what is widely seen as the founding text of the new behavioural science, a three-volume compendium of wartime and postwar research called *The American Soldier*.

This work established many of the key concepts of behavioural control: how to select personnel for tasks; how to adjust the individual to the collective (especially to the 'primary groups' that were deemed most significant for individual identity); how to control individuals' perceptions of the world (their 'frames of reference').[16] You didn't have to share Stouffer's conservative politics to rejoice in the sense of power and discovery that such work brought, the feeling that the basic 'science of human relations' was finally being cracked. At a time when government and military agencies were only tentatively sponsoring research of this kind, foundations picked up the slack, attracted by the prospect of big interdisciplinary projects. The Ford Foundation in particular spearheaded the funding of behavioural science in the 1950s, although again always having to battle against academics' insistent disciplinarization.[17]

For this kind of behavioural science hardly went unchallenged. The same debates between 'objectivists' and 'purposivists' that had enlivened social-science research in the 1930s resurfaced after the war. Historians' tendency to view the prewar and postwar periods as distinct subjects obscures substantial continuities here. Older purposivists like Robert Lynd were still critiquing value-free 'social science for hire' – Lynd denounced 'the science of inhuman relations' as a threat to democracy in a widely noticed *New Republic* review of *The American Soldier* in August 1949 – and a rising generation chimed in.[18] The young sociologist Nathan Glazer contributed a regular column on the frontiers of social science ('The Study of Man') to the new liberal magazine *Commentary*, crusading against 'government by manipulation' and calling for the widest possible diffusion of knowledge about social science so that its means and ends would not be monopolized by elites. He recruited his friend Daniel Bell, another young sociologist-journalist, to the same cause, and together they identified a number of targets from both wartime and postwar behavioural research for biting critique: Alexander Leighton's experiments in the Japanese internment camps, industrial-relations experts who 'uncritically adopt industry's own conception of workers as *means* to be manipulated or adjusted to impersonal ends', the 'Germany After the War' conferences,

The American Soldier.[19] So troubling was this wave of 'purposive' critique that a book-length defence of *The American Soldier* was published in 1950, in which Daniel Lerner – whose wartime work for PWD had applied similar techniques to German POWs that Stouffer had applied to American soldiers – denounced the critics for trashing social science altogether.[20]

Most anthropologists hadn't previously been much attracted by 'objectivism'; their loyalties to their 'natives', and the Boasian tendency to use cultural diversity to satirize American norms, made them poor servants of American vested interests, whether corporate, governmental or even academic. On these grounds they were reluctant to work on behalf of one people against another, or for one group within a culture against the interests of the whole. Even the Society for Applied Anthropology (SAA), the professional body most committed to research with 'real-world' applications, adopted an ethics code in 1949 – in an initiative spearheaded, inevitably, by Margaret Mead – that required anthropologists to take into consideration the effects of their applied work on all parts of the culture, a form of self-hobbling that amused objectivists as either naïve or needlessly inhibiting.[21] Similar inhibitions limited anthropologists' willingness to apply themselves too exclusively to the study of their own people: thus their lack of receptiveness to behavioural science with its domestic social-engineering agenda. The point of anthropology had always been to *compare* Americans to other people, not simply to cater to Americans' self-obsessions.[22]

More troubling after the war was a new kind of 'purposiveness', the democratic universalism that had been gathering force in intellectual as well as popular circles towards the end of the war. Where prewar purposivists were more likely to argue that social science needed to help Americans *strive* for democracy at home, postwar purposivists were more likely to argue that social science needed to help Americans *defend* and *spread* freedom and democracy around the world. This reflects the growing confidence in the achievements of American democracy that emerged during the war, on the Left as much as on the Right. One of the effects that studying character 'defects' among the Germans and the Japanese had had on many wartime social scientists was to develop the conviction that American character was not only healthy but 'normal', an archetype for humanity, although there were still plenty of dissidents (such as Erich Fromm) who saw character deformation as a broader problem generated by capitalism or modernity.[23] As the Cold War heated up at the end of the 1940s, this view of American normality gathered further strength: Americans were seen increasingly (by Americans) to represent 'humanity'. This new kind of purposiveness was not actually incompatible with the doubts about Americans harboured by people like Samuel Stouffer, who otherwise sheltered behind scientific objectivity. As Nils Gilman has argued, anxiety and boastfulness were twinned in this period: 'relentless optimism' could be a shibboleth to ward off the spectres of nuclear holocaust, relativism and totalitarianism.[24] Lerner's defence of *The American Soldier* argued that 'the profession has a job to do *for* democratic thought and practice'. For people like Lerner and his collaborator Harold Lasswell, the job of social science was to advocate a certain idea of liberty and democracy aggressively, and everywhere.[25]

Whereas prewar anthropologists had found the old purposiveness nicely compatible with their cultural relativism – awareness of diversity abroad dovetailing neatly with awareness of diversity at home – the new democratic universalism was harder to square with Boasian relativism. While internationalist (itself a sign of anthropologists' success in raising Americans' consciousness of the wider world), it was defined too narrowly to suit American cultural norms. Some anthropologists tried to reconcile American values with other cultures' values by turning away from relativism to search for human universals. Ambitious projects were launched, like the behavioural sciences often espousing quantitative and interdisciplinary methods, to derive universals from an exhaustive survey and comparison of all the world's cultures. At Harvard, Clyde Kluckhohn teamed up with Samuel Stouffer to pursue such a study of world 'values', with funding from the Rockefeller Foundation.[26] At Yale, G.P. Murdock had already begun a similar 'cross-cultural survey' before the war, and during the conflict he had pursued the same ends in a more applied way by compiling and sorting useful cultural information for the government in Latin America and for the Navy in the Pacific, where he also helped to write the civil-affairs manuals for Micronesia. After the war Murdock's survey was reborn with foundation and military funding as the Human Relations Area Files (HRAF) – fodly known as 'the files' – which accumulated a vast stock of ethnographic information, expanding its scope from forty cultures in 1938 to 150 in 1949. 'The files' took in ethnographies that had mostly been compiled as coherent wholes, broke them down into their component parts and coded them for comparative purposes, seeking explicitly to draw out similarity rather than difference. Seventy-five alleged human universals were thereby identified by 1949, though only, as Mead complained, by 'collating bits of disassociated information that have been dissected out of imperfectly defined wholes' – 'instant anthropology like instant coffee'.[27]

Such efforts appealed not only to democratic universalists, keen to demonstrate the general purchase of the American values of freedom and democracy, but also to their Marxist counterparts, who were just as anxious to recruit the less-developed world to universal, evolutionary processes of economic development and political transformation.[28] At Boas's Columbia, for example, a group of young leftist scholars who gathered around a new appointee, Julian Steward (hired when Ralph Linton went to Yale in 1946), took an evolutionary approach of this kind that conflicted with Benedict's persistent cultural relativism. There was undoubtedly a gender dimension to this conflict too, as ambitious young men, fresh from war service, were eager to sink their teeth into a harder, material theory that emphasized political and economic development, while distancing themselves from the softer, seemingly 'feminized' approach of comparing and contrasting cultures and personalities.[29]

Yet relativism was still very much in play, and in certain respects given its own impetus by the aftermath of war. The heightened awareness of national difference, triggered by the war's unprecedented levels of intercultural encounter and conflict, brought a new internationalist flavour to social science in the immediate postwar years. The United Nations spun off an Educational, Scientific and Cultural Organization – UNESCO – in 1946, and UNESCO set up a Social Sciences Division, the principal task of which was to apply the social sciences to the understanding (and ultimately the taming) of conflicts between nations. A project on 'Tensions Affecting International Understanding' was set up in 1948 under the social psychologist Otto Klineberg, who had established his own profile in this field during the war by calling for more extensive research programmes on the subject of 'national character'. The Tensions Project did this and more: its ambitious research agenda began with 'national character' but ranged onwards to the study of national stereotypes, the sources of aggression, anxiety, toleration and compromise, the sources of group identification, the possibilities of transnational and international identities, the impacts of population growth and technological change. There was something for everyone here: behavioural scientists who wanted to focus on techniques of control, advocates of nationalism and of internationalism, those who thought internationalism represented universal human values, but also those who thought it entailed the bringing together of a heterogeneous collection of nationalities in peace. In that respect the Tensions Project reflected a genuine uncertainty prevailing in the late 1940s about what internationalism meant – but also, again, the conviction that social science might shed some light on what it could mean.[30]

Among anthropologists the multilateral rather than supranational version of internationalism remained dominant. This view was certainly evident in the most famous collective statement of the anthropological profession in the immediate postwar years, the AAA's 'Statement on

Human Rights' of 1947. Asked by UNESCO to comment on a proposed Universal Declaration of Human Rights, the AAA's statement, drafted by the militant Boasian Melville Herskovits, opposed a 'universal' declaration 'conceived only in terms of the values prevalent in the countries of Western Europe and America'. The declaration's championing of individual freedom had to take into account, the AAA argued, the different ways in which different cultures defined and achieved their idea of freedom – and therefore it also had to defend the freedom of whole cultures against colonialism and neocolonialism. The AAA's statement was furiously opposed by objectivists, who felt (as with the ethics code) that the profession was once again unnecessarily limiting its relevance to the 'real world'. More damagingly, it was also criticized by purposivists on both the Left and the Right who saw 'human rights' as a crucial element in a postwar settlement righting the wrongs of war and fascism. They pointed out that the Boasians' cultural relativism had not impeded their opposition to Nazism during the war – something of which most Boasians were uneasily aware, just as Mead had been made uneasy by discussion of the 'cultural reconstruction' of Nazi Germany. However, the AAA statement does seem to have reflected the consensus of the profession in the US – the dangers of neocolonialism now seemed greater than the dangers of a resurgent fascism – and it met with a sympathetic reception abroad as well, where it chimed with efforts by a caucus of non-Western nations in UNESCO to broaden the definition of 'human rights'.[31]

Another disciplinary factor conducive to the persistence of cultural relativism was the premium still placed on fieldwork in remote spots – a premium raised, if anything, by the widened horizons tantalizingly opened by the Second World War. While the older generation, Mead included, were sensitive to new funding and political opportunities at home that might flow from their war service, the younger generation, with less to show from war work, were itching to get into the field. The greatest appeal of anthropology remained, as it had to Boas's students before the war, the chance to escape one's own culture and find an alien culture to explore, to explicate and to defend. Mead herself saw the younger generation's choices in these terms, understanding that they had still to undergo the basic training in culture consciousness that could only be acquired by fieldwork. 'For the very young graduate student,' she wrote,

it was his role to get into the field as quickly as possible, to take advantage of the only way we know of to make an anthropologist, before all the primitive people were finally annihilated. The War had demonstrated that such training was useful, and more people so trained were bound to be useful. The needs of science – to rescue the materials which were vanishing even more rapidly thanks to the war – and the needs of citizenship in a hard pressed century coincided perfectly.[32]

After all, there would be no ethnographies for the Human Relations Area Files to plunder if the young anthropologists didn't make their pilgrimages to the field and produce them – as they did, often employing the 'culture and personality' techniques that Mead and Benedict had pioneered with 'primitive' cultures.[33]

This generational tension can be seen in the strange fate of another of G.P. Murdock's postwar projects, the Coordinated Investigation of Micronesian Anthropology (CIMA). As with the Human Relations Area Files, CIMA flowed directly from Murdock's war work for the Navy in the Pacific. The largest collective anthropological project in history, it funded forty-one PhD students to do research in twelve Micronesian island groups in 1947 as part of the US Navy's administration of the region as a United Nations Trust Territory. The hope was that a whole generation of anthropologists would acquire their fieldwork training in a form aligned with American national interests, at once fulfilling objectivist goals, to perfect anthropological tools of behavioural control, and purposivist ones, to bring US-style democracy to the region. CIMA can accordingly serve as Exhibit A for historians seeking to argue that the 'weaponization' of anthropology in the Second World War was smoothly transferred to American purposes in the Cold War.[34]

But CIMA didn't work out the way Murdock had planned. Few of his young anthropologists shared his conservative politics and fewer still shared his desire to govern Micronesia. Mostly they signed up to CIMA because it provided funding for fieldwork in a relatively 'unspoilt' part of the world, and furthermore a part of the world likely soon to be spoilt by Navy administration, thus adding to the urgency of the opportunity. As far as possible, they tried to distance themselves from Navy administration so as to retain their credibility with their subjects, and to complete as quickly as possible their PhD dissertations on traditional topics such as social structure or 'culture and personality' in order to be able to take up academic careers. When the Navy handed over administration to the Interior Department, the latter tried to employ CIMA anthropologists as permanent administrators, but most had left or were seeking to leave for academic jobs. Those who agreed to stay on found themselves betwixt and between: mistrusted as administrators by their bosses, encumbered by their ethics code and professional scruples, and yet marooned from the world of academia. The most enthusiastic among them, Homer Barnett, concluded sadly, 'the truth is that anthropologists and administrators do not, on the whole, get along well together': the anthropologists were too scholarly and too relativist, and when they did choose a side they chose to be 'aligned ... with subject peoples' rather than colonial administrators.[35]

This, then, was the varied scene that faced Margaret Mead as she too emerged, drained and perplexed, from the rigours of war. It was very far from preordained that wartime experiences would set anthropology on a path of serving American national interests. Mead's own goals for the postwar period had been set before the war began – the creation of a new international order based on the recognition of cultural difference, and an enhanced role for anthropology in making such an order function – and she had done her best to protect her goals from the vicissitudes of the war itself. But her own position was delicately poised between competing forces. On the one hand, there were those who sought to force anthropology into a narrower, more instrumental role as a tool for behavioural control, or into the service of a more militant American foreign policy. On the other hand, there remained compelling Boasian scruples about abandoning the cause of the 'natives' to grasp perhaps fruitlessly at the temptations of power. Her own mission required firm engagement with the powers-that-be in order to bring them into a new world order in which all cultures, the traditionally dominant and the traditionally subordinate or marginalized, could participate. She had full confidence in her ability, if necessary single-handedly, to pull the profession behind her.

*   *   *

Mead ended the war as she had begun it – planning for the postwar world. Her slogan was 'Learning to Live in One World', which combined her address to Americans (who had to do the learning) and her conception of the paramount task (the unparalleled confluence of world cultures in the postwar order). This was the title of a series of articles she wrote for the US foreign-language press in the first half of 1945 and published in seventeen languages, reverting to the prewar idea of America as a 'nation of nations' that had modelled intercultural communication domestically and was needed now in order to apply the same models globally. If Americans could learn to address each other as both 'equal' and 'different', then they might be able to address other nations with the same tolerance and respect.[36]

She took the same slogan, 'Learning to Live in One World', as the working title of a book she began to draft after V-E Day, holed up for the summer in the Franks' New Hampshire home, with Bateson apparently vanished without trace in the jungles of Southeast Asia.[37] It was envisioned as a summing-up of everything she had learned in war and how it might be applied in peace: 'how to use anthropological insights in problems of communication – or that painful inverse of communication, psychological warfare – between different kinds of people.' It was to cover her conceptualization of the Americans themselves, her Anglo-American experiments in intercultural communication, similar experiments in the Army Specialized Training Program and her Food Habits work, and developments aimed more explicitly at the postwar world such as the foreign-language press series.[38] The world she envisaged was one in which each culture accepted – or had to accept – that it was only one of many cultures, each 'valid in its own right'. That lesson, she pointed out acerbically, was one that many 'primitive' cultures had had to learn painfully in their encounter with expanding Western cultures, but it was now a lesson the expanding Western cultures had to learn too. It would entail not only 'communication', but a frank acceptance of difference: 'all human values', not only those most readily accepted by one's own culture, had to be accommodated. This did not require any one culture to embrace the values of other cultures, which anthropologists might attempt for themselves, but most cultures could not without endangering their own values. It did, however, require all international relations – including anthropologists' – to be conducted in a spirit of mutually acknowledged difference. For that to work, Americans needed Thai, Balinese and Uruguayan anthropologists to observe Americans and not just the other way around.[39]

From here Mead turned to the nub of the problem: how to take Americans as they are, with their present-day national character, and teach them to 'live in one world'. She was all too aware that the problem presented itself very differently now, in 1945, than it had at the beginning of the war, when Americans had had to be coaxed into global engagement. Having been accused of too much social engineering before 1941, she would now be accused of too little – of accepting Americans as they were.[40] As she saw them, Americans were now fully engaged, willy-nilly, and with their characteristic mixture of idealism and self-sufficiency it would be easy for them to relate to others on the basis of 'cultural imperialism', as missionaries had once done – 'culture-wrecking' as she called it.[41] It is notable that in explaining Americans' characteristic relations to others she tried on the whole to avoid the language of the family drama as unsuited to a popular book about international relations. As an immigrant people, Americans were more than usually sensitive about their 'identity' (Erikson's favoured word which she had now adopted). Having successfully bonded their disparate materials around some common ideals at home, they were becoming increasingly suspicious of outsiders just at the moment when they were encountering more and more of them on the world stage. (This had consequences at home too: Mead contrasted the relative ease with which foreign-born immigrants had been accepted as Americans before the war with the hostility she predicted would ensue after the war towards Jews and Negroes.) Americans were now increasingly suspicious of 'people, who ... aren't interested in modernity in American terms'. Showing their unconscious vulnerabilities, they were inclined to overreact when they detected ingratitude or indifference – 'an alert unwillingness ever to be a sucker', Gorer's point, but shorn of its provocatively Freudian language – hence their 'violent rejection' of the British, the people from whom they got most such signals.[42]

There was no point in ignoring this 'passionate desire that others be like ourselves'; it had to be 'understood and woven into the framework of a United World, or it can easily become a force for evil'. So Mead thought about ways in which it could be harnessed. She acknowledged and admired Americans' idealism – their tendency to 'hitch their wagon to a star', in a phrase of Ralph Waldo Emerson's that became a talisman for her in these years – but she also knew that it had been strained considerably during the war, by international responsibilities that Americans thought they hadn't asked for and for which they weren't being adequately recompensed. On her lecture tours around America after her return from Britain she had learned how resentful Americans were even of their closest ally. Americans seemed to need Britain to be the hated 'Mother Country', 'frozen ... as of about 1812'. In her book draft, Mead took the cheerier view that the experience of wartime collaboration had reframed Britain's status as the 'older sister', getting her at least into the same generation and triggering feelings of gallantry and protectiveness as well as rivalry. But if the process of 'learning to live' with Britain was proving long and wearisome, how much more difficult would it be to learn to live with a new, yet more rivalrous partner, the Soviet Union, the significance of which Mead fully appreciated, not to mention all the other three hundred or so cultures of this 'one world'? It might almost be easier to accept Americans' own self-sufficient formula: 'If everybody would behave just like us, and none of them were younger or bigger, we would have, we believe, a good world, a peaceful world.'[43]

At this point Mead had written herself into August, and so deeply into the complexities of intercultural relations on a global scale that she might never get out. When news came of the dropping of the atomic bombs on Hiroshima and Nagasaki on 6 and 9 August she grasped at this dramatic change of context – almost joyfully ('I feel infinitely peaceful and content,' she wrote to Bateson, who had finally resurfaced in Kandy) – as a possible way out. At first she hoped that the bomb might shock Americans out of their immaturity, 'blast a path' through their resistance, taking on a significance akin to that with which the Star of Bethlehem had been endowed. 'The atomic bomb seems a mercy in so many ways because it may really dramatise for people that a new era has begun,' she wrote to Bateson, in stark contrast to the remorseful language Benedict adopted in her letter to Robert Hashima.[44] In this vein Mead began a new chapter devising a universal language of international cooperation, at its centre a metaphor that Americans could understand: 'the team'. Thinking of nations as teams depersonalized them and thus reduced the emotional burden they carried, while also emphasizing their internal homogeneity and cohesion; it channelled competition from a martial into a more manageable sporting context. And thinking of the world as a league of teams at least provided a transitional language for 'one world' – not 'good enough', but it is 'what we have got to work with, watching the pitfalls, counting our strengths and our weaknesses, looking for every chance to use our potential strengths towards a new pattern'.[45]

But after another week's writing she abandoned this last stab at optimism as well. Though she had the Franks and the Lynds, whose summer house was nearby, to turn things over with, and even conducted some interviews with locals (including the town drunk), she told her publisher that she just didn't know enough, stowed away up there in New Hampshire, about how Americans would react to the dawning of the atomic age.[46] She told herself that this was just a postponement. *Fortune* magazine was doing a survey of American attitudes to the Russians and they had promised to send her a representative sample in September; that would provide fresh grist for her mill.[47] But the truth was that she had reached an impasse that could not be cleared with more data. It was proving more difficult than she had imagined to theorize how Americans might learn to live in one world: even in the best of circumstances, as her Anglo-American perplexities had revealed, intercultural communication was an intellectually and emotionally fraught enterprise, and the American mood in 1945, insecure and ambitious at the same time, did not provide the best of circumstances.

Furthermore, Mead's own circumstances were not propitious either. She knew she had to return to the American Museum of Natural History in the autumn and sort out the accumulated mess of four years of war; she had a daughter to rear with the father nowhere in sight; besides, she was tired and fed up and lonely. She told everyone that she had torn up the manuscript after the dropping of the bomb: 'I didn't of course literally tear it up and it contained a lot of these interim conversations and formulations in which Geoffrey and I had engaged in between 42 and 45,' she later admitted. It remained on her mind and she would make another attempt at writing more or less the same book seven years later, when the international scene had again shifted unpredictably. But, for the moment, she returned to New York in September empty-handed, and empty in spirit too. When Bateson limped home later in the autumn, physically shattered and disillusioned, she had further domestic tasks to perform: finding him temporary work, providing emotional support and seeking to restore the marital communication that both felt had lapsed during the war. For the next year or so she was preoccupied, depressed, intellectually almost *hors de combat*. Fortunately, Ruth Benedict was in better shape to take up the cause of 'learning to live in one world'.[48]

* * *

Benedict came out of the war energized and for the first time in her life focused clearly on public questions; it was almost as if Mead's sense of mission had migrated temporarily into her old friend's conscience.[49] When the war ended she was not eager to return to civilian life. She applied to go to Germany to join the Information Control Division but was turned down on health grounds: she had a weak heart and the authorities had a bias against 'women over 45'. Japan was out of the question as women were barred by 'a blanket rule' from service with the postwar survey on the effects of the bombing to which she applied. 'All my male friends went,' she complained bitterly afterwards, explaining why she had not been able to do the fieldwork among the Japanese that she craved: 'but the American army and the American government insisted that the Japanese would all rape me. I assured them that the Japanese would not, that the Japanese were going to accept Americans and they would accept an American woman . . . it was not my fault that the American army and American government thought a woman would be in danger in Japan after V.J. Day!'[50] 'Why didn't I transvestite when I was young?' she wrote grumpily to Mead at the end of September from Washington, where she was still nominally employed by FMAD.[51] When she was finally released from FMAD at the end of 1945 and returned to Columbia, she was thinking of her next steps very much in Mead's terms. As she wrote to her former FMAD colleague Clyde Kluckhohn, now returned to Harvard:

it's become a really crucial matter whether people can be 'culture conscious' about our co-members in a world organization. It's fatal to all peace when Americans see every evidence of other nations' different cultural assumptions as examples of their moral perfidy. They hardly even look to see how a piece of unfamiliar behavior of France or Russia or China is really an expression of their total cultural experience; they think every point these countries make is something Americans must accept as part of their own beliefs or else throw out of the window. I want to talk about how anthropologists can acquaint themselves with the necessary facts and how we can influence policy makers and the public.[52]

The question was how to combine this mission with her teaching responsibilities at Columbia. The answer she came up with was a research project that would continue the work she had done at OWI on cracking European cultures 'from a distance'. To the Columbia authorities she proposed a seminar in 'contemporary European Cultures' that would combine straight teaching with fieldwork among European immigrant groups in New York. They were dubious – the teaching was fine, but where would the funding for the fieldwork come from? – and so she began to forage for sources of external support. An award of $2,500 from the American Association of University Women allowed her to launch a pilot project immediately for a 'serious study of learned cultural behavior' to improve 'international understanding' and to determine what 'kinds of strength . . . the people of each area could use in a world organized for peace'. But this was only a stopgap: something much more ambitious was brewing.[53]

At a party late in 1946 Benedict sidled up to a circle of friends clustered around Mead and said coyly, 'I know where we can get $100,000 to do a research project.' She was, Mead recalled, 'unaccountably gay and mischievously refused to tell us anything more', although in reality Mead herself had long been in on the secret.[54] The mysterious source, it soon transpired, was the Navy; Benedict's Washington connections had come good. Over the summer officials from ONR had approached her and Erich Fromm to solicit proposals for 'basic research'. ONR was eager to step into the gap left by the reluctance of the federal government to fund social-science research, and it took pains to present itself to researchers as open-minded and strings-free. '"Basic research", in the Navy's quaint definition, is research in which the professor sets the problem,' Benedict wrote to Kluckhohn gleefully, encouraging him to apply too.[55] That the Navy approached Benedict and Fromm early on indicates both some of the prestige that Benedict had acquired at OWI, and also that known 'troublemakers' were not only tolerated but were actively being sought out as part of the Navy's charm offensive. Even the top brass had a rosy view of anthropology in the aftermath of the war. Benedict reported jokingly to Mead:

> When I was taken in to meet the top man, Admiral Boylan, and introduced as an anthropologist, he began right off to tell me about an anthropologist, 'a woman too', who went down to the Pacific long ago and said the Navy did all right in their administration of Samoa . . . So

I named you and said you would be working and helping direct this project. Bread comes back on the waters in devious ways.[56]

In October 1946 Benedict and Fromm were asked to join ONR's new Advisory Panel on Human Relations to dispense part of the $2 million allotted for basic research in social science. Its meetings were 'quite odd', as the Navy granted. One psychologist on the panel recalled that its early meetings had 'an Alice-in-Wonderland aspect ... we resembled nothing so much as a group of belligerent tom-cats arriving in an already crowded neighborhood.' There were big culture gaps not only between the Navy and the social scientists but between different varieties of social scientist, as the panel included freethinkers like Benedict, Fromm and Lewin and much more straitlaced professionals of the behavioural-science type. Benedict got into a wrangle with one ONR official about whether (as the Navy man worried) one could ever fathom the 'oriental mind'. At the same time she and Fromm had to fend off some of the psychologists' scepticism about the very concept of 'national character'. The range of projects considered ran the gamut from Benedict's ambitious 'comparative study of cultures' to microscopic studies of the functioning of individuals and small groups. Fromm may have puzzled some of his more conventional colleagues by proposing as one of the most significant questions to be considered, 'Are the people in the United States happy?'

Above all, the panel was characterized by a nervousness on all sides about the novelty of the task and the potential stakes. The Navy had seen a gap in the market for 'basic research' and wanted to attract academic customers, but it didn't want to look foolish among its rivals and funders in government. The academics were cautious at first – worried about strings, worried about how 'practical' the Navy really expected them to be, worried about making decisions to give money to themselves, but also worried that if they failed to take this opportunity the door might close. The mood was hesitant, experimental. Perhaps, given time, things might coalesce around more deliberate, policy-oriented goals, but at the beginning the parameters were deliberately loose and the disbursement of funds almost giddy, and Benedict was the first to benefit.[57]

Her modest proposal for a seminar on European cultures had now blossomed into a 'training center' for 'Research in Contemporary Cultures' (RCC), initially funded by ONR from spring 1947 for two years at $90,000 a year.[58] Benedict was to get the chance to do properly the 'culture cracking' that she had attempted hurriedly during the war at OWI: to accumulate a wide variety of sources on specific national cultures and attempt to derive the culture pattern from them. Locating the project in New York, that 'laboratory of all nations', would give easy access to immigrant groups from any desired culture. Mead ensured that additional strands of prewar and wartime experience were woven in: the project was meant to be the summation of the whole 'culture and personality' idea. Sapir's original plan in his prewar Yale seminar, to introduce multiple culture patterns among the investigators by importing anthropologists from abroad, was to be implemented with a fellowship scheme. The results of the culture cracking could also be used to train future workers in international relations, and Mead incorporated a scheme for a manual for such purposes, building on the materials gathered for the Army Specialized Training Program. Needless to say, Benedict and Mead also saw the centre as an opportunity to wean a new generation of graduate students off the 'natives' and prepare them for the study of 'contemporary cultures' instead.[59]

The choice of cultures to be studied was Benedict's. Her initial idea to specialize in Europe could expand with the new funds available. On the other hand, as her ambitions broadened, new sensitivities emerged. It was suggested to her that a Navy-funded project aimed at deciphering the culture pattern not only of allies but of potential enemies, such as Russia, or of hotspots, such as China (not yet communist), might be interpreted as an espionage project. So on the strength of her wartime experience she decided to continue to do her research strictly 'at a distance'. That meant using only foreign-born immigrants and cutting the plans for fieldwork abroad and importing foreign scholars.[60] The change did free up more money to bring foreign-born immigrants onto the RCC staff. But it would end up exposing RCC to both methodological and political suspicion. Why pursue 'the study of culture at a distance' when the wartime emergency no longer required it? Why not undertake proper anthropological fieldwork in 'contemporary cultures' unless the true motives were to pursue 'enemy' research from a safe distance? It would also embroil RCC in New York émigré politics in ways that had not been encountered in the limited wartime experiments.

However, the decision was made to base the research in America precisely because Benedict did *not* want to embroil RCC in security issues and 'did not wish this project to be identified merely with war efforts'.[61] The choice of cultures was motivated by a raft of competing considerations. There is no question that Benedict wanted to attract government interest by including Russia in the project, no doubt encouraged in this by Mead, who hoped to dangle the prospect in front of Geoffrey Gorer as a way of luring him back to New York. China was of less immediate political interest, but was correctly seen as a coming world power, with a large immigrant community in New York to work on; and this, too, might have been seen as an inducement to lure back an alienated Gregory Bateson, who had longed in his peaceful moments in Asia to do some honest work on China. In the event Bateson could not be so lured and the China work was taken on by Ruth Bunzel, 'Bunny', one of Mead and Benedict's closest collaborators since their Boas days. The other cultures chosen for the first stage of the project were all European. France was selected as a 'control' for the immigrant-based studies, an important friendly country on which no 'culture and personality' analysis had yet been attempted and where fieldwork could still take place; the anthropologist Claude Lévi-Strauss, cultural attaché at the French Mission in New York, had offered assistance, and Mead's former assistant at Food Habits, Rhoda Metraux, now starting a PhD at Columbia with Benedict, was eager to tackle her husband's native land. Czechoslovakia and Poland were chosen as useful Slavic comparators to Russia, 'a link between East and West', with large immigrant communities at hand; both had figured in Benedict's OWI work, and one of her collaborators there, David Rodnick, was now available to take charge of the Czech part of the project. A spin-off of the Slavic studies, on Eastern European Jewry, was undertaken simply because of the unparalleled opportunities offered by the immigrant community in New York. Plans to extend the project yet further to include Spain, as a comparator to France, and Syria, for wider geographical coverage, never got off the drawing board, however.[62]

Benedict took great pains to design the project's inner workings to make them maximally congenial, socially and intellectually, for her and for the large staff of mostly young people whom she employed. For decades thereafter its veterans spoke lovingly of the special environment she had cultivated. About 120 people in all were involved, including about twenty academics who directed the research and thirty graduate students who did the grunt work and received the 'training'. The remainder were an extraordinary amalgam of visitors, neighbouring academics, émigré social scientists and carefully cultivated 'amateur' experts – 'the aberrant, the unsystemic, the people with work habits too irregular ever to hold regular jobs', as Mead put it – again trying to recreate wartime conditions in peacetime. If the postwar period is supposed to be a crucial moment for quantification and professionalization, RCC certainly wasn't part of it.

The project came together in separate seminars for each culture area and a general seminar, launched in September 1947, in which everyone (including stenographers and visitors) combined to give reports, make comparisons, draw conclusions – and also to quiz Benedict about the meaning of it all. Benedict strove to keep the whole project, and the general seminar especially, flat and non-hierarchical. A typical general seminar would bring together about seventy-five people of all ages, ranks and backgrounds, who would be encouraged to throw in whatever expertise they had, and (given the significance of their multinational backgrounds) to make it personal as well as professional. In the area seminars, 'each seminar takes on the ethos of the culture being studied. For instance, in the Russian seminar twelve people will all talk at once and yet it is possible to follow what is said' – or so Mead claimed. The promiscuousness of the source material – films, novels, folk tales, personal reminscences, psychological tests – cultivated an atmosphere of 'extreme permissiveness', in Mead's words. The psychological content reflected Benedict's more capacious interests rather than the tighter focus on infant training that Gorer had cultivated: child-rearing, parenting and the whole 'family drama' were part of the scheme, but 'friendship' was a major theme as well. Benedict found money for flowers and parties and taxi rides to nurture the spirit of her staff, as well as for the bread-and-butter of stenography and research materials. RCC was to some extent the family that she had never had, with far more women than the usual academic enterprise of the time, and with her partner, Ruth Valentine, as administrator. Some found this atmosphere frustrating – 'Ruth can't tell the difference between research and therapy' was one complaint – but most found it liberating.[63]

While in atmosphere and ethos RCC was very far from the professional 'behavioural science' outfit often hypothesized as the postwar model for social science, it did sit close by operations that fitted that model better – some of which were also funded by ONR – and it could be seen in retrospect as serving American national, political and military interests in its own distinctive way. Younger anthropologists – though significantly not those who were involved in it – sometimes looked back and saw it in that light. Many years later the sociologist David Riesman recalled being rather shocked at hearing Benedict speak casually about 'our people' in a Cold War sense, as in 'how were "our" people doing vis-à-vis those other people, our enemies?'[64] But this sounds like projection backwards in light of later developments with which Benedict was not connected. Both in public and in private at this time Benedict spoke clearly and consistently from an internationalist and intercultural perspective. Her position 'beyond relativity', developed at the beginning of the war, did not move in the direction of 'human values' (still less 'American values') as it did for some others after the war. It was, rather, designed to find ultimate criteria to legitimize other cultures' values under pressure from America: to show, for example, that Japanese culture could provide as much 'synergy' as any Western culture (or more). For her address on election as president of the AAA in December 1947, she chose to speak about anthropology not as a social science but as a discipline with a kinship to the humanities – one that could show us how to live in different ways, much as history and philosophy showed that past ages had lived happily under different values.[65] Like Mead, her principal concern in these postwar years was the old Boasian one of preserving the diversity of the world's cultures and the newer postwar goal of 'orchestrating' them so that their growing interactiveness led neither to homogenization nor conflict – 'one world', yes, but one of many cultures. As she said to an audience at Yale in the spring of 1948: 'Even if we on this planet ever achieve the ideal of "One World", humanity would be the poorer if they were lost in a general and universal character structure. No one culture can maximize all human potentialities ... [there were] different man-made ways of solving the universal human problems of human gregarious living and human morality.'[66]

Despite her Navy funding, Benedict saw herself and her team as independent of US military and governmental thinking. She acknowledged frankly both to her ONR funders and to her RCC staff that everything she did could be used either for peace or for war – but she chose peace. When the Air Force began to canvass for social-scientific projects to fund through its Project RAND think-tank, she complained that too many of its initial ideas were oriented to war rather than peace.[67] Approached by her OWI colleague Nathan Leites in the spring of 1946 to join in a more purposive social-scientific enterprise aimed at confronting Russia with a nuclear deterrent, she rebuffed him gently but firmly: 'When we've conquered Russia, what will we do? Where will atomic coercion have led us? ... however badly I think Russia behaves, I see nothing on the horizon which would force me to think that war was the desirable alternative for it.' Instead, she told Leites, she wanted to show the US government how much cheaper and easier a 'world organization' would be than a plan for nuclear war.[68] Her postwar mission was to make both public and policymakers '"culture conscious" about our co-members in a world organization'; RCC was the result. Including Russia in the project was, of course, one way to attract funds, but it was also a way to show that an intercultural approach had as much relevance to the most crucial areas of international conflict as to relations with small, geopolitically insignificant cultures. For Benedict and Mead, it raised fewer qualms than 'enemy' work in the war because now they could argue for the *same* approach to all nations, without covert or 'black' operations. Indeed, the intercultural approach had to be applied to Americans as well. Benedict and Fromm argued on the ONR Advisory Panel that all of its programmes, including those focused on domestic issues, needed to be evaluated in terms of the different character structures of Americans and other peoples.[69]

In this sense Benedict continued to think of herself as an outsider looking in on American culture. As she wrote in a critical review of American cultural relations in autumn 1947, intercultural programmes under 'nationalistic sponsorship' could never suffice to make a peaceful world; inevitably their goal was to 'further economic and political penetration of another country', and what was needed instead was proper international organization. Until that international organization fully materialized, she saw efforts such as her own as steps in that direction.[70] Such efforts could only have flourished in the internationalist window of opportunity immediately after the war, but they should be read in that context and not in the light of a later Cold War struggle in which, as we will see, projects like RCC did not thrive.

* * *

It was always Benedict's intention to make RCC a collaboration between her and Mead, and, if he was so inclined, to make it a home for Bateson as well. Although Mead pretended to be as much in the dark about the Navy negotiations as everyone else, it's unlikely the others were fooled by this pretence, and once the project was up and running in the spring of 1947 she threw herself into it with enthusiasm and some relief, as providing a rallying point at last both for her spirits and her ambitions. Since Bateson's return in November 1945, she had been much preoccupied by his deepening depression and gradual withdrawal. She tried to chivvy and manage him into new work, but she became convinced that he had transferred his revulsion against his dark deeds in wartime into a revulsion against the whole business of anthropology, and with it their partnership. She thought he associated her with the 'sober course' of professional life, while 'almost anyone with a beautiful face or a lovely voice' offered the chance of a blissful escape into a life of romance and adventure. The crisis came in spring 1947, just when RCC was getting off the ground; his old girlfriend Steve came over for a visit from England and catalysed some kind of break in Bateson's mind. Mead and Bateson had been planning a joint summer trip to England – her last-ditch strategy to re-energize him was to propose that he reconnect with his native land – but after a confrontation Mead got on the boat by herself. Their marriage was over. Bateson took a visiting professorship at Harvard for a year and then at the end of 1948 moved to California, where he spent much of the rest of his life. He had indeed lost interest in anthropology as such and sometimes thought he had almost lost interest in the human race. His future work focused on the processes of communication, considered almost as an engineering problem. 'Perhaps if I had had more intimate contact with your culture cracking projects, I should by now have sounder opinions,' he wrote sarcastically to Mead from San Francisco in 1949.[71]

On the boat to England in July 1947, Mead's thoughts turned inevitably to Geoffrey Gorer. The break with Bateson had come as a relief, she wrote to Benedict; it allowed her finally to plan for the future, and she was 'finding that I could day dream about the possibility of marrying Geoffrey five years from now, say when his mother dies. It doesn't mean, I don't think, that I want to marry Geoffrey, particularly, but simply that I found it an entertainable idea, gave me a sense that life still held tolerable alternatives.'[72] From the beginning of the RCC negotiations her plan had been to lure Gorer over to take charge of the Russian side of things, but he had resisted. His mother's dementia was deteriorating and he was reluctant to commit himself to any long-term projects while she still needed his care. Besides, he seemed to be enjoying life in England for the first time. His wartime service had given him the professional credentials he craved and British customers were available for a variety of projects – a book on the American national character, a BBC series (to which Mead and Benedict contributed), growing contacts with British anthropologists and psychiatrists. But Mead could be very persuasive. Couldn't he just commit to a series of visits? '[I]t ought to be the dream no red tape, adequate resources, all of us together, culture cracking job we have all talked of. I'd bless it if only because it will bring you back again. I miss you very much.' Finally, he broke down, just at the point when Bateson had left and Mead's need was greatest. He could come in autumn 1947 for a spell of three months, possibly, and then return for similar periods thereafter if the set-up seemed right. That was enough for Mead, as she told Benedict from that summer ocean voyage to England, to fill the void Bateson had left both emotionally and intellectually:

if Geoffrey only comes for three months at a time, he can have the study next year, and I can feed him breakfast, and generally, he will be around and a pleasant and stimulating companion. I know well enough that one of my blocks is that I can't conceive of my life not oriented to a man. No number of women and children really mean the same to me, as a way of life. I feel no desire whatsoever, to orient my life around Cathy. I want to leave her free, and I think that would make far too great demands on her . . . after all the big job next year is culture cracking, and that is your and Geoffrey and my shop and not Gregory's primarily. He would of course be a big help, but it isn't his primary metier, and it is Geoffrey's.[73]

Alongside Gorer, Mead found other sources of emotional and intellectual support. She was growing closer to Rhoda Metraux, who had worked as her assistant on the Food Habits committee before moving to OSS and who had now joined the RCC team to work on France, while her husband, Alfred Metraux, took a post as staff anthropologist at the new United Nations headquarters in New York. The French work brought Mead into close association with another social-science couple, Nathan Leites and Martha Wolfenstein. Mead had known Leites a little in the Washington years, when he had worked with Gorer and Benedict on psychological diagnoses of the Germans for OWI.[74] He was a complicated character who would cause Mead more than a little grief in their years of collaboration. In many respects he fitted the mould of the kind of cultivated European-Jewish intellectual whose company she so enjoyed – like Gorer or Erwin Schuller, though shyer – with boundless curiosity and a biting sideline in psychoanalytically flavoured critique. But he was also a classic 'nervous liberal' with growing doubts about Americans' backbone, and like many Americans of Russian-Jewish background he was also increasingly exercised by the Soviet threat.[75] His wife, Martha Wolfenstein, a New York psychologist, was more sympathetic, and shared Mead's interests in children's issues; on many occasions she served as an emollient mediator between Mead and Leites.

After the war Leites had hoped to stay in government service, perhaps working for an OSS successor organization in the Paris Embassy, but had failed to find a place. Mead wrote references for both him and Wolfenstein when they applied for Guggenheim Fellowships, but warned his potential sponsors that his work on psychological warfare was or should be unpublishable – 'it would amount to a "Handbook of Terror", to loosing upon the world recipes for which we have at present no proper antidote' – which can hardly have helped. Leites thus spent a year with Klineberg's UNESCO Tensions Project in Paris, where Mead met up with him when she passed through in the summer of 1947, and she, Gorer, Leites and Wolfenstein together had fun beginning the job of culture-cracking the French, whom Leites knew very well.[76] Mead was delighted, and probably relieved, when Leites and Wolfenstein returned to New York and set to work on a book on the psychological implications of American movies – less sensitive territory, though Leites continued to worry about Americans' tendency to retreat from public life into filmic fantasies, drawing conclusions not unlike Gorer's on Americans' endemic loneliness. Between them, Leites and Wolfenstein became part-time substitutes for Gorer's stimulation when he was absent, contributing to RCC's French and Russian seminars, and in general playing the role of provocateur that Mead needed. And yet, she assured Gorer, 'although Nathan and Martha are very good, still, there is none of that swift movement through uncharted waters' that she and he enjoyed together.[77]

* * *

Within a few years of the end of the war, then, Mead had endured the break-up of her Washington network, of her long wartime spell of collaboration with Gorer and of her partnership with Bateson, and had begun to find her footing in the changed postwar environment. Thanks to Benedict's connections, renewed sense of mission and the high public profile she enjoyed after publication of *The Chrysanthemum and the Sword* in 1946, the business of culture cracking had been more or less smoothly transferred from its complex of wartime uses, for good and for ill, to the mission that Mead had long been anticipating, of orchestrating the world's cultures in new international organizations. It was, as Mead often complained, hard to read the future in these immediate postwar years. But at least up to 1948 the prospects for a balanced and equitable new international order, and one in which anthropology would be deemed both necessary and useful for the establishment of genuine intercultural communication, were reasonably bright.

On the international level, the UN was now set up in New York and UNESCO in Paris. A UN General Assembly resolution of December 1946 pledged to supply 'expert advice' to member nations needing technical support on a wide range of social, economic and cultural topics, and anthropologists were staking their claim as 'all-rounders' in the provision of expertise in culturally relevant forms. Mead had plenty of allies in these circles – Alfred Metraux at UNESCO's Division of Social Science, Otto Klineberg at the Tensions Project and Ashley Montagu at a further, highly controversial commission working on an expert statement on racial problems.[78] Mead had a hand in founding yet another international organization, the World Federation for Mental Health (WFMH) established at an international congress in London in summer 1948. This was a continuation of the work that Mead and Larry Frank had begun with Richard Brickner during the war, to divert psychiatrists away from 'Psychiatric Imperialism' – 'an attempt . . . to impose Western standards of behaviour on cultures whose character patterns stem from different "internalisations"' – and to find instead patterns of 'good human relations' that recognized cultural diversity.[79]

At the national level in the US, there was also, as Elizabeth Borgwardt has argued, a 'multilateralist moment' in the immediate postwar years when Roosevelt's 'One World' ideals still carried a good deal of cachet in the Truman Administration, and it was not yet exclusively a 'One World' in the American image. There were, of course, plenty of democratic universalists about, and also more aggressively imperialist advocates of what the *Time* magazine publisher Henry Luce had dubbed 'the American Century'. But there were countervailing tendencies, notably a modesty and pragmatism about what America could do in the world, that encouraged an effective multilateralism. Just as universalists and relativists had coexisted in wartime agencies, united by a common cause, so they could coexist in peacetime agencies, united against isolationist tendencies.[80] One focus of this common internationalism was support within the US government for UNESCO, which even as tensions between the US and Soviet Union grew was seen by hopeful liberals such as Eleanor Roosevelt and Archibald MacLeish as a point of continued multilateral contact.[81] This position became harder to maintain after the Smith-Mundt Act of 1948 authorized the State Department to undertake its own cultural propaganda in peacetime, signalling a more nationalist understanding of cultural relations of the kind that Benedict had warned against.[82]

Even so, intercultural understandings of international relations that had been developed in wartime remained embedded in the system. The State Department's Foreign Service Institute (FSI), which trained diplomats and other government workers posted abroad, inherited a good supply of these wartime assumptions and techniques. Its staff anthropologist, Edward Kennard, a Boas student who had used Mead's intercultural materials during the war, now turned to RCC for more of the same.[83] The course he devised on 'Understanding Foreign Peoples' was based on the standard 'culture and personality' reading list of Benedict, Mead, Bateson and Kardiner; it took Benedict's analysis of Japan as its core case study, and featured guest lectures from Benedict, Kluckhohn and Cora Du Bois. An experimental approach involved teaching foreign-service officers the 'culture and personality' idea and then asking them to present back their assigned cultures in these terms.[84] FSI remained an unusual centre of intercultural thinking in a State Department being gradually sucked into more polarized Cold War frameworks, right into the frenzied period of the Korean War and McCarthyism after 1950. In the words of the sociologist David Riesman, 'while beginning with [the State Department's] very concrete and even chauvinistic aims', FSI's intercultural training 'has also tended to transcend its military or cold-war origins and to add to the traditional ways in which we as a people have sought to understand who we are and how we compare with and differ from other countries'.[85]

For all these limited incursions into government, anthropologists were always going to find it easier to raise 'culture consciousness' among Americans by more direct forms of address in the public sphere, through their writing and broadcasting and opinionating, as Mead had realized even in wartime. The immediate postwar years again seemed to vindicate this view, as anthropology achieved a peak of public recognition as a source of orientation and advice in a complicated world of proliferating nations, peoples and tongues. Though cultural relativism might be thought to have lost relevance in a postwar world yearning for 'human values', in fact the unprecedented jumble of cultures facing Westerners did create a demand for navigation tools, and the popular understanding in America especially of individual character as a product of distinctive family experiences gave the 'culture and personality' idea an intuitive appeal as a basis for understanding cultural difference.

What anthropologists were able to argue more persuasively after their wartime experiences was that the same kind of 'culture and personality' explanations could now be applied equally to 'primitive' cultures, modern cultures and to American culture itself. The years just after the war saw the publication of many books by anthropologists recounting their wartime experiences. Alexander Leighton published two books, *The Governing of Men* (1945), on the Poston experiment for WRA, and *Human Relations in a Changing World* (1949), reporting on FMAD's work on the Japanese. Two contrasting accounts of the German national character appeared in 1948 based on the occupation, Bert Schaffner's *Father Land: A Study of Authoritarianism in the German Family* and David Rodnick's *Postwar Germans: An Anthropologist's Account*. By far the most influential of these postwar reckonings was, of course, Benedict's own *The Chrysanthemum and the Sword*, published in 1946. And that success triggered an even bigger success – the paperback edition of *Patterns of Culture*.

The paperbacking of *Patterns* was hailed at the time as marking an epoch in the popular reception of anthropology.[86] The idea came from Mead's old friend Victor Weybright. After his wartime work for OWI in London, he was hired by Penguin Books to launch a New York branch of its immensely successful paperback enterprise. Among the first books Weybright published in New York in 1946 was *Patterns of Culture* as a cheap 25-cent Pelican paperback. A year later he spun himself off from Penguin and launched the New American Library, a pioneering experiment in the cheap paperbacking of literary and non-fiction books in the US, which reached new audiences by distributing through drugstores and news-stands. Again *Patterns* was one of his star titles under the hugely popular Mentor non-fiction imprint. (Another was *Coming of Age in Samoa*.) It was in this form that *Patterns* became what David Hollinger has called 'the single book that did the most to define cultural relativism in the mind of the general reader ... one of the most widely read books ever produced by a social scientist in any discipline', selling 800,000 copies in the first ten years of the Mentor paperback.[87] Written in a more cautious vein in the early 1930s, *Patterns* did not make explicit the connection between the study of 'primitive' and modern cultures. That would have been done by Mead's 'Learning to Live in One World', had she finished it, or by a follow-up book planned by Benedict in 1948, based on her wartime work on European cultures, 'a volume on men, women and children whose different habits and values, insofar as they are the outcome of their cultural experiences, can teach us an understanding of ourselves as well as of them, since their customs, however strange to us, are only variant solutions of the same problems which face us.'[88] But Benedict had already made that connection in *The Chrysanthemum and the Sword*, and other books published in this period made it too, such as Clyde Kluckhohn's attempt to reach the audiences of Mead and Benedict, *Mirror for Man: The Relation of Anthropology to Modern Life* (1949).[89] It was in a follow-up article (coyly titled 'Anthropology Comes of Age') that Kluckhohn announced, 'Anthropology has returned from the natives', a slogan that was taken up by friends and enemies alike.[90]

Inevitably, the greatest impact made by the 'culture and personality' idea on the American public was in its treatment of the Americans themselves. Mead's *And Keep Your Powder Dry* was the oft-cited model. Gorer's sudden decision to write a book on the Americans in 1947 resulted from his shrewd perception that an unmissable opportunity had presented itself to update her wartime book for the postwar audience. Written initially for the British market, and based on his wartime experiences of Anglo-American collaboration, Gorer told Benedict that he was approaching the task 'in a very detached way, as though I were describing the Lepchas or the Chinese, making no explicit cross-cultural points at all except purely verbal ones; the theme of the book is the "different-ness" of Americans from any other culture, and only by acknowledging this difference, instead of expecting them to be English, can collaboration be fruitful'. Although he admitted to Mead that he was repeating a good deal of the substance of *And Keep Your Powder Dry*, he argued that, writing for a British audience, he would necessarily have to tackle topics Mead had omitted or soft-pedalled for reasons of tact or tactics – Americans' behaviour in groups, their attitudes to business, above all the excessive dominance of the maternal conscience and resulting oral fixations and panics about homosexuality.[91] Mead was understandably anxious. She knew that Gorer's exposure to American culture was actually pretty limited; she feared his 'detached' tone would put off American readers, having failed herself to find the right tone in which to address Americans; and she wanted him to turn his mind to the Russians instead. But reading through the manuscript, she decided to see only its light-hearted qualities and concluded that the psychologically hazardous material 'was strewn through the book in a sufficiently unconcentrated form so that it would do no harm'.[92]

She was right to be anxious, however. Gorer's book got more attention in America than in Britain, exemplifying the boundless appetite for psychological treatments of culture then prevalent on Mead's side of the Atlantic. It was excerpted racily in *Life* magazine, with cartoons poking fun at American characters, and more soberly in the *New York Times*, before publication in 1948 as *The American People: A Study in National Character*.[93] It was even honoured with a full-length spoof, *Americans in Glasshouses*, by the pseudonymous 'Leslie James', published by small presses on both sides of the Atlantic, gently sending up Gorer's exaggerated psychological distinctions between the Americans and the English: Mead and Gorer decided in the end to treat it as friendly (and funny), and Mead even agreed to write a blurb for the American edition.[94] A similar ambivalence characterized the American reviewers of Gorer's book. Armed with their own cultural stereotypes, many accepted Gorer's persona as the dashing British amateur, half-enjoying, half-resenting his breezy self-assurance and condescension, as they had done with his prewar excursions to Africa and Asia. But as Mead might have predicted, the psychoanalytic imputations against American masculinity rankled. On balance, Gorer just about got away with it. But there was a danger that his British aloofness would be confused with 'the high-toned language and one-way-glass point of view of anthropology', as *Time*'s reviewer put it, doing damage to their common cause.[95] Mead was quietly furious with Gorer for running this risk. After processing the reviews, she concluded that 'one should not present a people with a statement of their conscious *and* unconscious motivations simultaneously . . . this is a challenge to their effective integration which they must and will resent . . . using the culturally approved symbolism, is safer and more protective.' In her own subsequent study of American attitudes to sex-roles – *Male and Female* (1949), Mead's only major book of this period – she drew back sharply both from the psychoanalytic formulations and from the 'high-toned language', and ended up writing a book that was criticized by later generations for too blandly accepting the status quo.[96]

Other contemporary books about the American character inspired by the 'culture and personality' idea managed to strike a better balance between relativizing and reassuring Americans. These were the years, for example, when the émigré neo-Freudians Erik Erikson and Erich Fromm, having introduced themselves to Americans as experts on the German psyche, turned their lens on the Americans themselves. Neither elicited the same hostility as Gorer had done. Erikson's *Childhood and Society* (1950) was his most influential work with the American public. It combined elements of Benedict's *Patterns*, by making explicit comparisons between some 'primitive' cultures (the Sioux and the Yurok, two Native American peoples) and contemporary America, with cross-cultural comparisons of the family dramas of modern cultures, including his wartime work on the Nazi family ideal and postwar work for the RCC project on the Soviet family ideal. Although Erikson also used a very psychoanalytic language, placing emphasis on oral, anal and genital fixations, and cast aspersions on the American 'Mom', he was careful to trace the formation of 'ego identity' across the life span, not placing too much weight upon infancy and, most importantly, giving adult readers a chance to get in on the act by influencing their own character development. In this way, Erikson at the same time gently placed Americans in their cultural context and helped them feel a sense of freedom or agency.[97] Fromm's *Man for Himself* (1947), a follow-up to the wartime success *Escape from Freedom*, took a more sharply critical view of contemporary American society as a psychologically peculiar manifestation of broader problems of capitalist modernity, dominated by the 'marketing character' in which people attempt to sell their personalities to others rather than to live for themselves. Less cross-cultural than Erikson's, Fromm's approach had some of the same appeal to adult readers seeking guides to conduct and self-formation in the rapidly changing conditions of postwar American culture.[98]

Most influential of all in applying 'culture and personality' to Americans' sense of self was a new figure on the social-science scene, David Riesman. Riesman had had a very successful prewar career as a lawyer, but after undergoing analysis with Fromm he found himself interested in the psychological determinants of social behaviour – he used Fromm's term 'social character' – and in 1947 began work on a study of the American character. Attracted to Fromm's humanistic approach, he kept himself aloof from organized social science and shared then-current anxieties about the pretensions of social scientists to dissect and control human relations; in fact, he found Nathan Glazer's columns in *Commentary* on this subject so convincing that he recruited him as a co-worker on his project and ultimately as co-author of the resulting book.[99] *The Lonely Crowd* (1950) written with Glazer and Reuel Denney, gave a historical account of the development of the American 'social character', from the pioneer generations' Puritanical self-reliance – what Riesman called 'inner direction' – to the modern generations' reliance on the opinions of others – 'other direction' (similar to Fromm's 'marketing personality'). Riesman's own position, like Fromm's, was critical. While he thought both 'inner direction' and 'other direction' had served many social functions relevant to the conditions in which Americans had lived, as an ego ideal he felt neither was fully satisfactory, and he posited a universal human goal – 'autonomy' – to which he felt people in all conditions and times could aspire. To his annoyance, it was not this utopian vision of autonomy that seemed to make *The Lonely Crowd* so incredibly popular, at least in the 1950s. It was, rather, the colourful gallery of American 'types', still recognizable today, that he offered – the 'moralizer', the 'inside-dopester', the 'glad-hander', the 'glamorizer' – and the opportunities for self-rating, comparison with others, one-upmanship. In the end, he found, Americans didn't even seem tempted by the vision of autonomy he dangled in front of them, instead priding themselves on escaping 'other direction' (everyone else's problem) by remaining atavistically 'inner-directed'.

Riesman testifies in *The Lonely Crowd* that his interest in 'social character' had come straight out of the 'culture and personality' movement, and not only through Fromm but, as he says in the opening pages of the book, from the writings of Kardiner, Benedict, Mead, Gorer and Horney as well.[100] Mead's wartime accounts of American character formation were a prime influence, and the core idea of *The Lonely Crowd* may have come from Mead's observation about the inability of immigrant Americans to rely on parental codes and their resulting dependence on peer standards instead, with damaging consequences not only for intergenerational relations (the problem of 'cultural lag') but also for ego strength. The young American, Mead wrote in 1940, 'in some degree surrendered his sense of moral autonomy for the comfort of a crowd', the central concern of *The Lonely Crowd*, as Riesman acknowledged.[101] Indeed, his depiction of character formation in both the inner-directed and other-directed family owed a great deal to the 'family drama' as depicted by Mead and Gorer, although he was inclined to place as much emphasis on subsequent phases of the life cycle, and especially on adult socialization through contact with workmates, playmates and the mass media – again stimulated by Mead's observation about the significance of peer standards.[102]

What distinguishes Riesman most clearly from Mead and Erikson, and reveals his greater debt to Fromm, is his relative lack of interest in other cultures' different processes of character formation. Like Fromm, Riesman tended to view American developments as an instance of a broader modernization process, which he tied to increasing population density, though, as Mead pointed out to him, more cross-cultural comparisons might have shown this was too simple. For example, if he had consulted Pacific cultures, 'a real laboratory for your theory', he would have had to account for 'my Manus', strangely resembling Americans but in very different circumstances.[103] But Riesman freely admitted he was only really interested in Americans. Even a chapter on Benedict's *Patterns* was devoted to wondering whether Americans were most like the Kwakiutl, the Dobu or the Zuni. Furthermore, as he confessed to Erikson, he was prejudiced against cultural relativism because he believed in the universal ideal of autonomy. He shared Mead and Benedict's desire to offer Americans choice in their lives, but in place of the rather unreal alternatives posed by other cultures he held that autonomy was the only viable defence for the individual against the 'contemporary "other-roles" offered him on the impoverished shelves of his culture'.[104]

But in his disappointment in American readers' solipsistic uses of his text, Riesman came to see that a dose of cultural relativism might be just what they needed to jolt them out of their complacency. As the Cold War hotted up, and other social scientists began to back off from Mead's cultural relativism, Riesman came closer to it. In the 1950s he would become the principal defender of her brand of 'culture and personality' anthropology outside of her discipline, praising her bravery in continuing to bring other designs for living back from the 'natives' at a time when Americans were otherwise being encouraged to see the world in their image. Anthropology's influence on the universities, he felt, was decidedly beneficent – 'As time goes on,' he told Clyde Kluckhohn, 'I find my students growing considerably less ethnocentric, at least on the surface' – and, thanks to the cheap distribution of books like *Patterns of Culture* and *Coming of Age in Samoa*, its influence was diffusing more widely as well. Looking back from 1961, he attributed to this reaction against 'provinciality' the ability of young people 'to shape their own character by their selection among models and experiences' from around the world, which was what he had sought with his notion of autonomy.[105]

Mead shared Riesman's frustrations with the tendency of Americans, when made 'culture conscious' of themselves, to use this consciousness to become more, rather than less, self-referential. She saw Erikson and Riesman as reinforcing her and Gorer's theses on the American national character – they 'really agree fundamentally it seems to me with you and me, although they don't always seem to know it,' she joked to Gorer – but was concerned when they were taken by Americans to be depictions of 'normality', against which they ought to measure themselves.[106] It was this unpleasant normalizing influence that made her so dead set against the best-publicized social-science survey of them all, Alfred Kinsey's reports on male and female sexual behaviour, published in 1948 and 1953. Kinsey's reduction of all sexual activity to forms of biological 'outlet' seemed to rip sexual behaviour out of its cultural context, not only depriving it of meaning but also presenting it as a universal standard. While Kinsey, much like Riesman, thought that by arraying Americans along a spectrum of numbers and types of 'outlet' he was advertising diversity rather than conformity, his readers seemed impelled to compare themselves against what Sarah Igo has called the norm of 'the averaged American', indulging again that terrible habit of self-rating.[107]

Yet in certain ways Mead herself colluded with this trend towards American self-absorption. Her shift of emphasis between the 1930s and the 1940s, from using cultural diversity to give Americans diverse options for themselves to using cultural diversity to help Americans relate to others, actually had the effect of portraying Americans as more homogeneous than they were. As Mead had discovered in failing to write 'Learning to Live in One World', it was almost impossible to talk about intercultural relations without suppressing the complexities of intracultural relations, and vice versa.[108] She had grappled consciously with this problem during those vexed weeks in the summer of 1945, concluding that eventually she would have to write *two* books – the one she was actually drafting, on intercultural relations, and another on intracultural relations, which would have to wait.[109] In the meantime, she was speaking to Americans as Americans, and her principles of intercultural communication required her to address them in their own familiar idiom, a practice reinforced by Gorer's mishaps with the 'detached' tone. These principles sometimes caused her to portray Americans in an artificially homogeneous and static condition: for example, in *Male and Female*. In this vein, trying to capture Americans' confidence, her more emollient tone of address undoubtedly did have the effect of shoring up Americans' sense that there was *an* American way of doing things against which they could measure themselves, even if unintentionally, much as *The Lonely Crowd* did.[110]

If her postwar efforts had been primarily bent on showing her own culture a flattering mirror, then she might be reasonably accused of cultivating America's postwar self-absorption and, ultimately, its arrogance – its tendency to impose its norms on others. But that was not Mead's purpose; rather, she was trying to show Americans themselves, the better to compare and contrast them with others, so that they would *not* confuse their norms with others'. If she had been able to finish 'Learning to Live in One World', she might have been able to convey the complex task of both accepting diversity at home and relating to others as Americans abroad. Better still, Benedict's mooted book on international relations would likely have cut straight to the point, as Benedict was never invested in a detailed depiction of the American character and kept herself firmly focused on the orchestration of cultural diversity on the global scale.

* * *

The unparalleled public attention given to the 'culture and personality' idea in these years brought with it unparalleled levels of scrutiny, too. In fact, as the public profile of 'culture and personality' rose after the war, it also became the target of increasingly fierce criticism, as a pressure point in the shifting balance of national and international interests at the dawn of the Cold War. The mildest set of criticisms came from those moving from a war to a peace footing who felt that the national distinctions entailed by Mead's approach were no longer appropriate for the new international situation. This was a criticism that could be adopted either by supranationalists, who blamed the war on nationalism and were determined to find and assert 'human values', or by various other types of ideologue – advocates of capitalism or Marxism – who saw their causes as transnational. The former variety of criticism was the hardest for Mead to ignore, because it came from those she was accustomed to view as friends. Otto Klineberg, for example, who had championed the national-character studies in wartime, was now oriented at UNESCO to finding 'the most effective methods of modification in the direction of rationality and moral consensus among men'. National-character research, in this view, must be on the lookout for elements of consensus as much as of difference and, further, where it found difference, its job was to find ways of blurring and bridging it.[111]

Two important surveys of the 'culture and personality' idea after the war took a similar view. While praising the AAA for its stance in favour of cultural relativism, and efforts at intercultural communication – 'A world rigidly pressed into one culture could be held together only by brute force, and that for a short time' – Stuart Chase in *The Proper Study of Mankind* nevertheless argued that the best uses for the culture concept were in finding 'the universals which govern *homo sapiens*, from the deepest jungles to traffic-snarled cities', as any lasting international order must be based on 'the common denominators of human existence'.[112] Most significantly, Clyde Kluckhohn, who had worked so closely with Mead and Benedict on culture cracking during the war, now backed off from the national-character approach with an appeal to 'human values'. His public presentations of anthropology's 'return from the natives' were accordingly couched in friendly, respectful but ambivalent terms. 'We have sometimes confused the right to be different with a demand for the perpetuation of differences,' he confessed, and so he ignored the need for a positive moral code based on 'absolute' or 'intrinsic' values. As he and others pointed out, the rapid adjustment of Germans and Japanese to the postwar order had already belied some of the more pessimistic conclusions about the persistence of their dangerous national characteristics. Yet Kluckhohn also remained attracted to Mead's vision of 'orchestrated heterogeneity', for which his book remained a generally positive adver-tisement, adding his own resonant apophthegm: 'the world must be kept safe for differences.'[113]

Mead was herself aware that the war against fascism had committed her and Benedict to some irreducible 'human values', and she was now more prone to combine her calls for 'the orchestration of cultures' with the recognition that some cultural manifestations were beyond the pale, as a danger to world peace.[114] In the late 1940s, however, as the screws of the Cold War began to tighten, it was not enough to tout 'human values' – social science came under growing pressure to genuflect to *American* values, or at least to set itself unambiguously against communism. Nineteen forty-eight was a bellwether year, in which the 'loss of China' to communism became a rallying cry for a newly energized Right, and although the moderate Democrat Harry Truman narrowly won re-election that year, his enemies scented blood. By 1950, with the rise of Joseph McCarthy and the outbreak of the Korean War, America had descended into an atmosphere of crisis in which 'longhairs' of all kinds were suspect and those unwilling to champion American causes against the Soviet Union were tagged as traitors. In this atmosphere even an 'orchestrated' relativism came under siege. Within the social-science community calls went up for a policy orientation suited to the emergency. This was the point at which Harold Lasswell started in earnest to mobilize his Second World War veterans behind a behavioural science that would serve 'the intelligence needs of policy' and bring about 'a more thorough integration of the goals and methods of public and private action': that is, not only enemy analysis but the manipulation of domestic opinion as well. Veterans of psychological warfare such as Donald McGranahan, Hans Speier and Daniel Lerner now spoke more openly about the need to use social science to align public opinion with the policy requirements of 'national security'.[115] The story they told – readily taken up by post-Vietnam accounts – was of a natural continuity between the techniques devised for mobilization for 'war' and those now available for mobilization in 'crisis'. Daniel Lerner, in particular, was responsible for some devas-tating accounts, published in 1949 and 1951, of the 'Sykewar' against the Germans and the lessons it taught for Cold War purposes. Such stories were more in the nature of recruiting posters than sober accounts of intellectual history.[116]

Mead tried at first to remain aloof from such pressures. She was a (small 'd') democrat and personally hostile to communism, but not inclined to see it as a threat to her personally, to America generally or (on its own) to world peace. There were many leftists and in fact members of the Communist Party in her personal circle and employed at RCC. As she had shown during the New Deal, she was not terribly interested in American domestic politics – another attitude enabled by her tendency to view Americans as a bloc, rather than riven by divisions. Her narrative of what had happened during and since the Second World War was quite different from Lasswell's; techniques once used for war were now to be deployed for peace, not for a new kind of war. She even contributed a chapter on the study of national character to one of his 'policy science' books arguing that 'the exceedingly critical state of the entire world' in fact underscored 'the urgent need to devise better methods of co-operation between national groups and within national groups' – not at all what Lasswell had in mind.[117] At a meeting of the Conference on Science, Philosophy and Religion in 1949, she summarized the past decade as a learning process in which the social sciences had accumulated practical experience but at the same time learned lessons about how to use it responsibly: to avoid covert manipulation, to raise self-consciousness, to think about how one's actions affect others. In a rare explicit reference to the mounting Cold War, she concluded that, while the challenge in war was to ensure that the battle against fascism did not capsize democracy, 'the crucial question of 1950 becomes how to develop a social science which can raise men's level of social insight so that the battle between two idealisms does not destroy men's souls far more effectively than could any battle between good and evil'. Needless to say, 'the battle between two idealisms' was not the orthodox way to describe the Cold War.[118]

Mead could no longer ignore the Cold War – because the Cold War was not ignoring her. At about this time *Commentary* magazine had launched a campaign against her. Though Mead connected the two, this new campaign bore little or no relationship to Glazer's earlier democratic critiques of social science in the same magazine. The manifesto of the new campaign came in the form of a polemical article by Robert Endleman, 'The New Anthropology and its Ambitions', published in September 1949. Endleman was a disgruntled former graduate student of Kluckhohn's, who had done 'culture and personality' fieldwork on Native Americans in Colorado but had been reported by the Bureau of Indian Affairs for misconduct there in the summer of 1948. In his later career he turned sharply against cultural relativism on orthodox Freudian grounds and became a stern critic of cultural-radical movements such as women's and gay liberation.[119] In the *Commentary* article, he combined a critical survey of Mead and Benedict's social-reform efforts before the war with a harsh condemnation of their 'return from the natives'. Their 'political naivety', he wrote, had taken on 'serious political relevance'. Reducing political similarities and differences to similarities and differences in culture dangerously underrated the role of power and ideology in the modern world. Neither Benedict's cultural relativism nor Kluckhohn's watered-down humanism could explain – or treat – the growing divide in the world today. It would be more honest to admit that the universalization of American values could only be achieved by a Pax Americana. Fortunately, he concluded, to date 'the practical political influence of the anthropologists (and a few other politicized branches of social science) has consisted of a somewhat awe-inspiring ability to extract large sums of money from the armed forces and related sources'. But their salience in the public sphere provided a dangerous insight into the illusions Americans wished to retain about the ability of science to solve their political as well as personal problems.[120]

Endleman's attack struck a nerve because it did not confine its critique to the political implications of 'the new anthropology'. It also bore down upon *methodological* criticisms that were more widespread – not limited to its political adversaries, though method and politics could be thoroughly mixed together. As we have seen, social scientists of all stripes were struck by 'science envy' after the success of the nuclear scientists in gaining public attention and money. Even after they failed to gain admission to the National Science Foundation, many social scientists still sought to prove to government that they were capable of the same kind of rigour, attention to system and detail as the hard scientists. In the context of a deepening masculinization of the university, 'rigour', 'discipline' and 'professionalism' could also be read, implicitly or explicitly, as 'manly'. Fringe elements – too amateur, too speculative, too 'feminine' – had to be trimmed. Endleman played deliberately on these themes. Benedict's 'intuitive' approach, he opined, might have sufficed for dealing with remote island peoples in a more innocent time when anthropologists were 'strange ducks', but such 'unabashed impressionism' was hardly suited to the study of complex modern societies for which politics, sociology and economics had already devised appropriate tools.[121] This chimed with a mounting chorus of critiques of the 'impressionism' of the wartime national-character studies that was emerging at the same time in academic forums as well.

The mixture of motives driving this campaign is neatly illustrated in the case of Ralph Linton. Linton's animus against Benedict and Mead, already well established before the war, reached a nearly hysterical peak after the war. On the surface Linton's intellectual trajectory seemed hardly distinguishable from that of Benedict and Mead; many of the rising generation of 'culture and personality' researchers cited Benedict, Mead, Linton and Kardiner equally as inspirations. True, in his prewar seminars with Abram Kardiner, Linton had already tried to set a tone of greater sobriety and caution, which drove Benedict crazy: his idea of 'basic personality structure' was applied primarily to simple, homogeneous cultures, as a logical, functional response to local social and economic conditions rather than as a quasi-aesthetic choice for a particular way of life. During and after the war Linton drifted away from Kardiner and from the 'basic personality' idea. He hated having his ideas confused with Benedict's, he was maddened by the way in which 'culture and personality' was being gaily applied to complex, modern societies, and he resented mightily the way that military and government authorities had swallowed these applications. Contemporary cultures, he argued, must have a multiplicity of personality types, relating to subcategories of occupation or status; furthermore, a true science of culture and personality ought to be able to measure and quantify their distribution by means of personality tests.

These arguments were enforced, however, with a stridency that betrayed deeper, murkier feelings. Linton prided himself on being a 'man's man', a noted raconteur, gourmand and womanizer who worked hard and played hard, and who was successful in the eyes of the world. Both he and Kardiner expressed horror at women such as Benedict, Mead and Du Bois who seemed indifferent to their masculine charms. Benedict was a 'witch', he told anyone who would listen.[122] He worried that her sloppy feminine ways of thinking were degrading the scientific purity of anthropology. Although he had less personal contact with Mead and Gorer than with Benedict, who until his departure in 1946 was his chief senior colleague at Columbia, he thought their intellectual influence was if anything more pernicious. Their depiction of the American family drama infuriated him for its downplaying of the positive influence of men. 'I gather [Mead] thinks Americans are produced by a sort of social parthenogenesis,' he sneered to Kluckhohn, trying to elicit a hostile review of *And Keep Your Powder Dry* for the *American Anthropologist*.[123] Gorer's book on the Americans was still worse. In a review in *Scientific American*, Linton identified Gorer with 'the Margaret Mead-Ruth Benedict school of anthropologists', and warned: 'anyone familiar with their techniques knows that they vary from precise, careful and well-documented studies of child care and adult behavior to a free exercise of feminine intuition unhampered by either facts or frequencies.'[124]

Linton did his best to make anthropology a discipline safe for proper scientists. With a few other senior figures, he masterminded a restructuring of the AAA immediately after the war, in the name of fitting it for federal science funding, but with a wider agenda of excluding amateurs and exercising greater control from the centre. This manoeuvre, only partially successful, had the added bonus of limiting Benedict's term as AAA president, in which post she had succeeded Linton when the reform was already under way, to six months.[125] And he led the methodological crusade against the 'intuitionism' of the national-character studies: he sponsored a critical conference on 'culture and personality' in New York in 1947 and advised on Harold Orlansky's critique of Gorer's infant-training thesis, which was, significantly, kited in a popular article in *Commentary*, 'Destiny in the Nursery', in 1948.[126] On top of all this, he was a highly ideological anti-communist, who as early as the late 1930s had tried to purge 'Reds' from the Columbia department, and who with G.P. Murdock was one of the most dedicated witch-hunters in the discipline after the war. Towards the end of his life – his overeating brought on multiple heart attacks in the eight years before the last one killed him in 1953 – he identified cultural relativism as the principal adversary of 'universal values'.[127]

Some of the same mixture of motives in weaker form can be seen in Clyde Kluckhohn. Kluckhohn had been even closer to Mead and Benedict before and during the war, having a much warmer relationship to the Boasian tradition, and worked happily with them on intercultural training during the war. He tried to be an honest broker between Linton, Mead and Benedict. He did write that review of *And Keep Your Powder Dry*, even borrowing Linton's crack about parthenogenesis, and he shared Linton's concerns about the application of 'culture and personality' ideas to complex, modern societies. But he was also in public generous about Mead and Benedict's contributions, and towards the end of the war he seriously tried to get Mead to join the new interdisciplinary social-science department that he was planning with Parsons at Harvard. (In the event, Harvard's president decided his university was not quite ready for a woman professor.)[128] To all appearances happily married to a fellow anthropologist, Florence Kluckhohn, he did not have Linton's hang-ups about women and was capable of gently chiding Linton about them. After the war he showed signs of wanting to play Mead's role as the public face of the discipline, and that meant both advertising her wares and gently putting her in her place. In many respects he had a very similar view of the task of the public-spirited anthropologist – to educate Americans about the otherness of other cultures, to develop ways for all cultures to meet and cooperate in 'One World' without seeking to impose one cultural ideal on all. But he had a more agonistic view of the possibilities, reflecting a more orthodox Freudian view of the innateness of aggression, but also reflecting his own personal struggle for self-control: he had flirted with professional disaster by developing homosexual relationships while doing fieldwork among the Navaho, carefully noted on his FBI file. His idea of 'One World', therefore, was less about the orchestration of cultures and more about 'collective security' against the ever-present threat of outbreaks of aggression.[129] As with Linton, this wariness about the dangers lurking in the world caused him to draw back from cultural relativism and place more emphasis on 'universal values'. He started to intervene more aggressively than previously in some of the controversies surrounding the national-character studies. Though he tried hard to keep lines of communication open to Mead and Benedict, Mead later summarized the split opening up in anthropology between a more scientistic and a more humanistic world view as one that divided her from both Linton and Kluckhohn.[130]

What made the Endleman attack in *Commentary* most damaging, though, was that it was possible to share the methodological criticisms without tacking on any personal or political implications. Here the postwar move towards disciplinarization and professionalization can be seen at work independent of bigger agendas. Calls for closer scrutiny of the assumptions and speculations of wartime studies resonated with a younger generation eager to make its mark in the more settled and careerist conditions of peacetime. 'Impressionism' and 'intuitionism' were charges that could be made without Linton's sneer. The quick connections made between disciplines in wartime were particularly vulnerable. One of the principal targets of young psychologists after the war was the unscientific claims of psychoanalysis. Orlansky's critique of Freudian studies such as Gorer's made a great impact because it assembled a large body of empirical studies that questioned the hitherto assumed connection between infant training and adult personality. A similar critique, by sociologists Alfred Lindesmith and Anselm Strauss, also criticized the impressionism of Freudian-inspired interpretation, which as enemy analyses such as Gorer's and La Barre's showed could be dangerously manipulated to serve immediate cultural and political biases. Shouldn't the 'natives' have a chance to answer back against these war-inspired characterizations of their cultures? 'We know what happened when the "natives" read the Mead and Gorer material on the United States,' they wisecracked, perhaps a little overconfidently, since Mead's American writing had had a much warmer reception than postwar revisionism might suggest.[131]

Such criticisms need not even be hostile; they might simply be honest calls for empirical testing of rival theories. That was Otto Klineberg's position in setting afoot the UNESCO Tensions Project. At the conference in New York in 1947 instigated by Linton, he pointed out the different diagnoses of the Japanese offered by Benedict and La Barre (from apparently similar methodological starting points), and the different conclusions about the Germans derived from Benedict's holistic 'ethnological' standpoint and McGranahan's statistical social-psychological approach (from different starting points). Did these arise from differences of method, or from differences of bias, or from different samples, or from different questions being asked? Klineberg thought it not unreasonable to ask the different schools to offer at least some testable propositions so that the 'unbiased external observer' could assess them. It was not necessarily a question of choosing one method over another. 'I will be faithless to my occupational identity [i.e. as a psychologist rather than an anthropologist] to the extent of saying that if I had to choose one or the other method, Dr Benedict's would seem to me definitely superior to Dr McGranahan's. But I think there is no need to choose.'[132] Klineberg commissioned a report from the French sociologist Jean Stoetzel on the attitudes of Japanese youth that at the same time praised the holism of Benedict's ethnography and criticized on sociological and historical grounds its failure to capture division and change in Japanese society.[133]

Mead had to some extent laid herself open to these lines of criticism by hitching herself to Gorer's infant-training bandwagon. Benedict's initial idea of pattern and Bateson's version of the family drama based on schismogenesis, both concerned with relationships and the relation of individuals to a whole culture, were not so vulnerable to statistical breakdown or personality testing. They took the view that any individual in a culture was a good sample, as any individual could give an insight into their relationship to the whole. Gorer's theses about infant training, in contrast, made assertions about the origin and prevalence of specific personality types in specific cultures. However much Mead protested that examination of infant training was only one way of looking at a cultural whole – one point of entry into a feedback loop – Gorer had exposed their school to the charge of monocausality, and a cause, too, that psychologists insisted could be tested. At the 1947 conference, more or less his last performance on the 'culture and personality' stage, Bateson distanced himself from the kind of national-character analysis – he instanced La Barre but, tactfully, not Gorer – that applied psychiatric and ideological epithets to whole cultures. He himself had not claimed, as Klineberg alleged, that the Balinese were inured to frustration – rather, that 'frustration' appeared in Balinese culture in different forms incommensurable with its more familiar Western manifestations. He was not against quantifying – 'But what in God's name would he quantify?' Yet Gorer's quasi-psychiatric diagnoses were less abstract and they *were* more vulnerable to quantification.[134]

Most seriously of all for Mead and Benedict's future, disciplinarization and professionalization were inducing disenchantment with the national-character approach in the heart of their own discipline, anthropology. For young anthropologists, the problem was not that 'national character' had deviated too far from the norms of psychology and sociology, with their concerns for universal human drives and social variation, but rather that it had deviated too far from the norms of anthropology – especially that compelling Boasian imperative to escape your culture and go far, far afield. Mead herself could see that the young were anxious 'to get into the field as quickly as possible . . . before all the primitive people were finally annihilated', an even more urgent task than it had been when she left for Samoa a generation earlier.[135] Those who had not been directly involved in war work did not see the attractions of studying the humdrum and non-primitive Czechs or Norwegians, especially if (as was the case in RCC) no fieldwork was involved. Whereas they saw both the intrinsic value of studying vanishing cultures and also the fresh light such studies shed on their own culture, as Mead and Benedict had demonstrated before the war, they saw no such benefit on either score from studying 'contemporary' cultures. One reason why Clyde Kluckhohn's *Mirror for Man* fell flat was that it gave no account at all of the richness and difference of a living 'primitive' culture; 'human values' would simply never have the inspirational value of a lovingly detailed Dobu or Kwakiutl. Riesman's only 'semicomparative' references to 'primitive' cultures in *The Lonely Crowd* had, as Mead pointed out, failed to recruit fully the insights of anthropology to his study of American character. Riesman recognized this himself, and used it to explain eloquently and at length the opposition Mead encountered within her own discipline:

> anthropologists are themselves very ambivalent . . . concerning the partial shift of focus in their profession away from old-style ethnography and towards national-character investigations. They have lost, to some extent, the protection of the British Navy, the protection of social class arrogance for the wandering, uncommitted upper-class archaeologist or ethnographer who must render account to no foundation project, even the protection, not always pleasant, of being a small, powerless tribe, scarcely to be thought of, as economists were once invariably thought of, in connection with large governmental or university undertakings. More important still, it may be, they have lost the implicit ethical armor

of the thorough-going anthropological conviction that we can learn as much from a small power that has no navy, no archives, and only an embryonic old elite as we can learn from big powers that make and consume headlines and psychological warfare ... cultural relativism includes among its non-relativistic assumptions the passionate belief that each power, irrespective of size or ability to threaten or be exploited, counts [as] one: an international democracy of one culture, one vote ... The consequence is that anthropologists at work on the interdisciplinary frontier of Soviet or other big-power national-character studies can be hurt not only by the attacks they meet from the already entrenched but by the fact that they have internalized many values which make them vulnerable to the criticisms of their professional brethren who have gone on working on the Fox or the Navaho, the Ifaluk or the Trukese.[136]

Riesman here points to another source of uneasiness that many young anthropologists felt about Mead's national-character approach: its potential for embroilment in power politics. At the same time that Mead was coming under criticism from the likes of Lasswell and Lerner for her failure to embrace 'national security' considerations, she was coming under criticism from her younger colleagues for embracing them too closely. Those who had not contributed to the war effort had less experience of dealing with the moral and ethical dilemmas such engagement entailed, and had less conviction that anthropology had anything distinctive to offer in this area. Many of the young anthropologists returning from Micronesia at this period, at the end of the CIMA project, felt that their brief brush with 'administration' there had proved how little they could do that was compatible with their professional methods and ethics. As Cold War pressures intensified, even those already committed to Mead's project got nervous. At a summational meeting of their general seminar after the first year of the RCC programme in May 1948, Natalie Joffe voiced a common concern among the young: 'What is the ultimate disposition of this material going to be? There is a definite vague feeling it can be transmuted into potential dynamite if *they* get hold of it.' Mead's frustration comes through clearly in her scattershot reply:

This material is *all* unclassified ... This research is financed by the Office of Naval Research. It was instituted in a discussion when somebody in the Navy suggested using some of the Navy's research money for peace ... This project is totally unrestricted; anything that comes out of this project can be published ... We feel that everything we're learning in this project is as useful for peace as for war. We know more about destructive techniques than about constructive, but are not doing this order of research. Everything we're doing is potentially valuable for peace. It can also be used for war. There are no forms of research relevant only to peace. But every single point we work on in anthropology is at least as relevant for peace as for war.

'If any of you have any doubts about the project,' she concluded gloomily, 'you'd better not work on it.'[137]

* * *

By the time the RCC project had got properly under way, therefore, Mead was at the centre of a vortex of competing pressures – to be more interdisciplinary and less, more politically engaged and less, more applied and less. It was not in her nature to back off, however. She had not slaved through the long years of war to abandon quickly any hopes that 'culture and personality' could be applied to making a peaceful world order. At the moment when Joffe was voicing her anxieties, Mead was realizing her goal of getting Geoffrey Gorer attached to the project in order to develop a new analysis of the Russian national character. In the next year she would throw herself deeper into this most controversial part of the RCC project – the closest one could come at the end of the 1940s to straightforward 'enemy analysis' – and in conjunction with Nathan Leites take on more research on the Soviet Union not only for the Navy but also for the Air Force. There were ethical and professional challenges here, and Mead was willing to face them.

It is likely, given the way the tide was already turning in 1948, that Mead's headlong engagement with the Soviet Union would have got her into deep trouble even under Ruth Benedict's watchful eye. But one of those accidents of history intervened in September 1948 that make all such assertions academic. Benedict had been deeply frustrated by her inability to do fieldwork in Germany or Japan after the war. Presented with an opportunity to view her new subject matter – the Europeans – more directly without a military sex bar to stop her, she had gladly taken up the chance provided by a UNESCO seminar in Czechoslovakia to spend the summer of 1948 in Europe, to see at last those several cultures about which she had been writing 'from a distance' since joining OWI in 1943. But her heart *was* weak and the trip took a lot out of her. Almost immediately after her return, she was hospitalized, and on September 17 she died of heart failure.

Cora Du Bois has left a brief account of the memorial meeting for Benedict held in New York City, where five of her most intimate colleagues, 'each in [their] way her lover', spoke emotionally of her life and work. But her enemies were present too, in the full figure of Ralph Linton, who 'had sat erectly and centrally in one of those small folding chairs ill fitting his bulk that had been set up' in the room. At the reception afterwards in a small Manhattan apartment, he cornered Du Bois, his former colleague, in the kitchen.

'You know as well as I that she was a witch. A devil. We both know enough of the world to know that witches are real! She hated men; look what she did to her students! She destroyed them by feeding on them. She tried to kill me too – But I've won out – She's dead but I'm still alive.' He put a plump but shapely hand on his fleshy chest – alluding to what we both knew was his precarious vitality after three heart attacks. The high pink of his face darkened; the wattled chins shook . . . The strain of our love against his hatred broke through between us in that small kitchen.

He insisted on accompanying Du Bois home in a taxi, and on the crosstown journey made a clumsy play for her that he must have known was grossly misplaced. Later he would show his graduate students a Tanala charm bag which, he said, he had used to kill Ruth Benedict.[138]

For Du Bois, telling this story was a way of telling of her own love for Benedict, as well as of Linton's hatred. Benedict's death did not at first weaken, but rather crystallized a stylistic, intellectual and political division within the profession, of which Benedict and Linton represented opposite poles. It left to Mead the job not only of being herself – more than a full-time job in itself – but of 'being Ruth' too, taking over the management of RCC and trying to think herself into Benedict's values and life tasks as Benedict had seemed to think herself into Mead's while she was recuperating at the end of the war.[139] It was a daunting prospect, and not one she was happy to face alone. She was again putting pressure on Gorer to give himself fully to the Russian part of the project. 'I am alright. I am sleeping and maintaining a moderate degree of tension only. This is not a call for help,' she wrote him a few months after Benedict's death.[140] But it was – and as he responded, their joint effort to crack the Russians would have decisive consequences for the whole business of applying 'culture and personality' to problems of international relations.

Gorer in 1947

CHAPTER 6

Swaddling the Russians
(1947–51)

Even had she wanted to, Mead could not have avoided tackling the Russians in the immediate postwar years. Just as with the Germans and the Japanese during the war, after the war the Russians were the foreign people about whom Americans most needed and wanted to know. If anthropology were to demonstrate its usefulness to international relations, it had to show that it could say something cultural about the Russians that other analyses – based on communist ideology or 'totalitarianism' or some other framework – could not. But just as with the Germans and the Japanese during the war, tackling the Russians after the war brought with it great dangers. Work on peoples whom Americans considered 'enemies' imperilled the whole enterprise of cultural relativism, as Gorer and La Barre's analyses of the Japanese demonstrated. These dangers were likely to be exacerbated by the covert methods and propagandistic goals of the chief 'customers' for such analysis in government and the military. Worries about these dangers had kept Mead aloof from 'enemy analysis' in the Second World War. But she could not remain aloof forever. The late 1940s were uncertain years. America was at least not yet at war; it was still possible to address the Russians in other than 'enemy' terms. Mead's heedlessness about politics caused her to view the mounting Great Power conflict sometimes as an almost personal irritation. When the Korean War broke out in 1950, she expressed great annoyance at the inconvenience and hoped that it would soon blow over. As a result she could and did get drawn further in, incrementally, to American psychological-warfare planning. Her own personal disorientation, with the loss of Benedict and Bateson, did not help. Yet as she drew closer to the unfamiliar territory of war-fighting and black propaganda, little voices inside her – and louder voices around her – called out warnings. Where was she taking anthropology? Would the anthropologists follow? And the 'natives' were calling her back too.

* * *

The intellectual world of 'Sovietology' was just as crowded in the postwar years as the study of Nazism had been at the outbreak of war. Anthropologists had no special claim to knowledge in this field such as they had had about Japan in 1941.[1] In a 1958 survey of Sovietology, Daniel Bell joked that there were at least 'ten theories in search of reality' – the 'culture and personality' (or 'psycho-cultural') approach, which he put first on his list, was just one among many.[2] As David Engerman has since shown, prewar American attitudes to Russia had been highly coloured by old-fashioned views about the 'Slavic soul', overlaid in the 1930s as Soviet Russia began to challenge for world power with compatible views of the Soviet leadership as 'Great Russian' nationalists, fanatical power-seekers who were alternately insecure about, and jealous of, the West. These older ideas needed rapid updating after the war. A Soviet Union that had defeated the industrial and military might of Nazi Germany, and that now possessed the atomic bomb, had to be understood more as a 'modern' than as a backward nation.[3]

The historians, economists and sociologists who returned to academia from service in OSS R&A's USSR Division – a staff of sixty, the core of existing Soviet expertise at the end of the war – were determined to provide this updated analysis. The Division's head, the historian Geroid Robinson, moved a large part of his R&A staff to a new Russian Institute at Columbia, with funding from the Rockefeller Foundation; among his early hires was Mead's friend Phil Mosely, who had ended the war as a Soviet expert in the State Department. Another batch of R&A grads moved to Harvard, where a Russian Research Center (RRC) was established with Carnegie funding, under the unlikely leadership of a non-expert, none other than Clyde Kluckhohn. Between them, Columbia and Harvard pumped out about three-quarters of the hundreds of Soviet experts generated by the American academic system in the first postwar decade.[4]

Columbia's Russian Institute struck no distinctive intellectual pose. It provided basic facilities for the study of the Soviet Union: language training, archives, publication series, scholarly exchanges.[5] But at Carnegie's instigation, Harvard's RRC adopted a more idiosyncratic line of attack. One of the purposes of siting Carnegie's centre at Harvard was to take advantage of Talcott Parsons's interdisciplinary Department of Social Relations, where Parsons was laying the groundwork for 'modernization theory' – a theory that explained the evolution and convergence of all 'modern' societies around a set of behavioural norms and forms of social organization dictated by the needs of a complex, dynamic and highly differentiated industrial society. Such a theory required bringing together sociologists, economists, political scientists and anthropologists, just as Parsons was seeking to do at Harvard. It seemed the perfect setting for a new approach to the study of Russia that would fully appreciate the modernization of that country set afoot by the Bolshevik Revolution, Stalinism and the war.[6]

Parsons's view of modernization as an evolutionary process dictated by social and economic development still left room for different paths to modernity, allowing for considerable cultural variation among modern societies. That was why he and Mead had been able to collaborate amicably on the 'Germany After the War' conferences, where they agreed that Germany's difference from other modern societies could not be easily re-engineered from without. Admittedly, after the war Parsons's followers adopted a more normative modernization perspective which saw something like American cultural and social norms as vital for modern development. But at the time of RRC's founding both Parsons and his funders still had a more open mind about the scope for cultural difference among modern nations. It was with this awareness of difference in mind that Carnegie suggested an unlikely candidate to direct the new centre, Clyde Kluckhohn.[7]

As Carnegie's John Gardner put it:

> A year ago one of our better known business leaders told this writer that the Russian people would never put up with their present regime, and he then went on to ascribe to the Russian people a series of characteristics which were as American as apple pie. It will never be entirely possible to understand Russia and the Russians unless we achieve a less ethnocentric view of their attitudes toward such matters as authority, hierarchy, and suppression of individual freedom.[8]

Thus the 'psycho-cultural' element of RRC's research programme was intended to provide a relativist dimension to study of the Soviet Union. On the other hand, the trend in Parsons's thinking towards those elements that all 'modern' societies had in common encouraged the view that the Soviet system would ultimately have to adapt to the needs of a modern society for more individual freedom and mobility.[9] Kluckhohn, who was moderating his own relativism in the name of 'human values', was open to this perspective. And such a position also coincided nicely with the dominant doctrine in US policy towards the Soviet Union under the Truman Administration, that is, 'containment' – a degree of acceptance of Soviet power within its existing frontiers, a willingness to 'wait it out' and hope for internal changes conducive to a lessening of tensions.[10]

Kluckhohn's background in 'culture and personality' therefore played only a limited role in RRC's programme of research. Its principal use of the 'psycho-cultural' approach was in the Refugee Interview Project, funded by the Air Force's HRRI and run by the young sociologist Alex Inkeles, which employed the interview and testing techniques developed in wartime on POWs to try to draw out the behavioural characteristics of ordinary Russians. Like Benedict and Mead's RCC, it used displaced persons (refugees both in Europe and in the US), in this case to try to guess at how ordinary Russians viewed and responded to the communist regime. Inkeles and his field director, the social psychologist Raymond Bauer, were enthusiastic about the 'psycho-cultural' approach to which Kluckhohn had introduced them. Of Russian-Jewish background himself, Inkeles thought he could use it to find out exactly how far the 'traditional' Russian personality type had in fact been affected by efforts to make a 'New Soviet Man' more suited to a modern, communist state. Thus he blended the anthropological starting point of cultural relativism with Parsons's more dynamic view of the modernization process, in which social and economic institutions might be shown to be remodelling individual character.[11]

Although Gardner may have expected Kluckhohn to emphasize the Russians' cultural difference, in fact most of RRC's work focused conventionally on issues of law, politics, international relations and, especially, economics, consistent with the emerging modernization perspective.[12] One reason for Kluckhohn's shyness about a cultural approach to the Soviet Union was the rapid shift after RRC was set up in 1948 towards a more aggressive foreign-policy stance vis-à-vis the Soviet Union, away from containment towards a higher-pressure policy, what Scott Lucas has called 'containment plus', and in some quarters towards a more 'liberationist' perspective, advocating increased US support for freedom movements among the 'captive peoples'.[13] Along with this policy shift came a new framework for viewing the Russians: totalitarianism. Ironically, this began as a psycho-cultural approach; indeed, more closely allied to a relativist 'culture and personality' analysis than to a universalistic behavioural science. Since the 1930s Erich Fromm and other neo-Freudian émigrés of the so-called 'Frankfurt School' had been blaming the rise of the 'authoritarian character' on the forces of capitalism and modernity. The individual, crushed by the pressures of mass society, had sought to 'escape from freedom' by embracing submission to leaders. That had seemed to many a persuasive analysis of the rise of Hitler and, although Fromm with his Marxist origins didn't stress this connection, of the rise of Stalin too. Part of Fromm's appeal to Americans was that he had applied the same analysis to them as well, standing as the advocate of the individual against the anonymity and conformity of mass society. Some of his former Frankfurt

School associates tried to put these arguments on a more scientific basis with a huge research project, *The Authoritarian Personality*, the first fruits of which were published in 1950 – a kind of left-wing counterpart to the *American Soldier* project. The emergence of McCarthyism at about the same time gave ammunition to those left-leaning intellectuals who wanted to see 'authoritarianism' as an American as much as a Russian problem.[14]

But the wind was blowing very much in the opposite direction. Americans were being encouraged now to look on the Russians as a special case. From this point of view the concept of 'totalitarianism' served a useful purpose. Although it had originated as a way of discriminating extreme versions of authoritarianism, rooted in the behavioural problems of mass society, 'totalitarianism' could shift emphasis to the mechanisms of control from above, and away from the susceptibilities of the people.[15] Wartime scruples about lumping together the enemy (Hitler) and an ally (Stalin) no longer applied, and the Soviet system could now be singled out as a unique, and uniquely bad, phenomenon. Blame rested on a power-mad elite, a ruthless ideology, institutions of terror and control, and not on the people. In the most optimistic versions, the Russian people could be transformed into innocent victims – very far from the 'authoritarian personalities' of the bad Germans. As we have seen, this view of other people as 'just like us', awaiting and needing American-style democracy, was increasingly prevalent on the Left as well as on the Right. This view of the Cold War as almost entirely an ideological and political struggle against totalitarian rule cast doubt on all previous analyses of the Soviet Union. It rejected traditional views of the 'Slavic soul', and any other psycho-cultural analysis that implicated the Russian people, but it also suspected the newer currents of social and economic analysis – those that viewed the Soviet Union as a type of modern society, with its distinctive features but at least in the short term essentially stable – of being soft on communism.[16]

Although in the immediate postwar years none of these rival analyses clearly had the upper hand, they all posed problems for the application of Mead's 'national character' approach to the Soviet Union. As she had found in the wartime cases of Germany and Japan, she had to be careful to distance her 'culture and personality' approach from old-fashioned 'national character' analysis based on race or ancient prejudice. At the same time, she now had to defend her own 'national character' analysis from the charge that it was too static and had failed to take into account the modernizing zeal of the Soviet system. Most pressingly, she had to defend it against a democratic universalism that saw the Russians as human beings suffering under tyranny rather than as in any relativist way significantly 'other'. Her brand of Sovietology was in danger of appearing 'softer on communism' than any of its competitors – not a pleasant position to be in at any time, least of all as the Korean War and McCarthyism loomed.

* * *

Into this minefield Mead strayed with a surprisingly clumsy tread. Part of the problem was that she had not previously paid much attention to Russia. She seems only to have awakened suddenly to the Russians' significance in the spring of 1945, when she, Gorer and Benedict began to toss around some ideas about the Russian family drama: what were their characteristic attitudes to strength, weakness and authority that might help them to predict their future relations with other powers?[17] Later that year, as she struggled with 'Learning to Live in One World', she began to see that Britain was 'out of the running' as a force to be reckoned with in the postwar world, and she started to accumulate material on Russia instead.[18] But in her distressed and distracted state after Bateson's return, she did not have the heart for this new enterprise and increasingly pinned her hopes on Gorer taking it up. Only in autumn 1947 was he free and willing to come over to New York for a spell and turn his mind to the subject.[19] A revivified Mead now prepared to plunge into the Russians full time. She proposed to Benedict that while Gorer tackled the Russian national character she and Nathan Leites would work his findings into a model for intercultural communication between America and the Soviet Union. For this purpose, she prepared a separate proposal for the Air Force's new think-tank, RAND, and with the aid of her ever-helpful brother-in-law Leo Rosten, now a consultant to the RAND Social Sciences Division, she secured a new tranche of funding – which would also pay Gorer and Erik Erikson as consultants – for a project, 'Studies in Soviet Culture' (SSC), to begin in 1948 in parallel with the RCC work.[20]

When Gorer arrived in autumn 1947, he tore into the Russians with a vengeance. As the nominal leader of the RCC Russian study group, he had at his disposal about a dozen fellow researchers, most of them with Russian or Russian-Jewish backgrounds, and over three hundred interviews with Russian émigrés accumulated by RCC, as well as a heap of documentary material ranging from films to novels to press reports.[21] But if he consulted this great reservoir of expertise, he did so very quickly, for he had developed his hypothesis on the Russian national character 'in the form in which he expects to publish it' within a few months, by the beginning of 1948.[22] Very much as he had done with the Japanese in the months after Pearl Harbor, he zeroed in immediately on the infant-training side of the family drama as a quick fix. His earlier chats with Mead and Benedict had had a more promiscuous character, jumping around aspects of the family drama including infant and child training, maternal and paternal ideals, attitudes to time and strength, self and others.[23] Now he discovered a new key to unlock the Russian psyche, effective in the very first months of life: swaddling.

Although there was a substantial anthropological literature on the practice of swaddling – the tight binding of infants to a cradle or board, and thence to the mother – Gorer claimed to have hardly known of the existence of swaddling until at a meeting of the RCC study group Mead asked one of their Russian members, 'were you swaddled?', at which point he decided that this was the decisive clue he needed. Subsequently, he claimed to be able to 'tell at a glance, and with practically no errors, if a Russian had been swaddled as a child'.[24] Gorer took what he thought he already knew about Russian infant care – that babies were fed at the breast generously, though without emotional warmth, and subjected to easy and late toilet training – and combined this with the new and contradictory insight that the same babies were also tightly swaddled for at least their first nine months, being released sporadically only for their generous feeding. Given this bizarre combination of indulgence and denial, the infant found swaddling 'extremely painful and frustrating' and 'responded to [it] with intense and destructive rage', including 'fantasies of biting and destroying', at the same time fearing that if it indulged its fantasies it was at risk of being bitten and destroyed itself. Because the swaddled infant was unable to explore its own body, neither did it have a strong sense of self, and the routine, unemotional way in which it was fed did not encourage it to develop bonds to its parents.

Key features of the Russian character could be read directly off this unusually intense form of infant training. Infant rage and fear bred a kind of guilt unlike the guilt found in other Western cultures, which developed at a later stage through the superego or conscience: Russian guilt was more primitive, inchoate, formless, a 'fear of dark forces' and the omnipresence of sin rather than a more developed moral code, an atavism further encouraged by the mysticism of the Orthodox Church. After infancy, once unswaddled, the child never developed the more complex moral relationship with adults characteristic of other family dramas. Instead, with its uncertain sense of self it sought to immerse itself in an undifferentiated collectivity. Fear and guilt continued to predominate in a diffuse way, encouraging depression and passivity, and there was no way of dispelling these feelings, apart from indulging in occasional bouts of destructive rage, or in emotional, confessional outbursts of sympathy for fellow victims, 'pouring out the soul'. The adult Russian yearned above all to rediscover those blissful moments of infancy when it was temporarily unswaddled and fed, thus a search for 'maximum total gratifications' such as 'orgiastic feasts, prolonged drinking bouts, high frequency of copulation', melting into the undifferentiated mass of fellow Russians typical of the village community. Activity was unusual but, when indulged, it had to be taken to 'the limits of one's strength', in violence or in gratification. Thus the typical Russian oscillates between extremes of frustration and satisfaction: 'At one moment they are lonely, filled with rage, constricted by the swaddling; the next moment their limbs are free, they are held in warm and strong arms and given the bountiful breast.'[25]

Gorer acknowledged that the Soviet regime had striven to create a 'New Soviet Man', characterized by more discipline and self-denial on Western lines, but he did not think it had made much headway. He maintained adamantly that since 1917 most Russians had still been swaddled and their character had formed accordingly. Rather, he viewed the Soviet elite and its associated intelligentsia as perpetuating an older pre-Soviet differentiation between leaders and masses, a differentiation that was itself part of the traditional Russian character. At least since the Middle Ages, he argued, Russians had looked to an 'all-wise and all-knowing' Leader as a matter of 'psychological necessity', their very sanity requiring 'at least one figure completely uncontaminated by the all-pervading suspicion and fear'. Gaining such authority required a degree of self-discipline and activity unusual among Russians, but equally *submitting* to such authority reinforced among the vast majority their traditional preferences for passivity and depression. The sharp differentiation between elite and masses was written into the Russian constitution, as it were. Russians needed and expected firm, authoritative, impersonal leadership, 'derivative of the fact that the earliest constraining "authority" – the swaddling – is not part of the self, and is not personified'.

From this relationship between elite and masses Gorer extracted a set of maxims about how the West might cope with the Soviet Union. For policy purposes Gorer granted that there was no point in trying to take account of the mass of the people: only the elite mattered. But because the elite dealt with the outside world as it dealt with its own people, applying firm pressure to the limit of their strength, but no further, so it should be countered with the same firm pressure, but without pressing too hard. Ideological arguments were 'a complete waste of time and energy'. Only 'firmness, strength, consistency' mattered: 'If Russia is faced with *permanent* strength, firmness, and consistency there would appear to be no reason why a tolerable and durable *modus vivendi* should not be maintained indefinitely.' In short, 'containment' once again.[26]

A number of features of this argument evoke Gorer's earlier argument about Japanese toilet training. Although he claimed not to be exaggerating infant training at the expense of other influences across the life cycle, he repeated his practice in the Japanese analysis not only of beginning with infant training but more or less stopping there as well, at least in making causative arguments; he had paid no attention to Benedict's more balanced presentation in *The Chrysanthemum and the Sword*. He acknowledged the possibility that other lines of analysis 'might well have reached the same results by a different route', but not that they might have led to different results.[27] Again ignoring Benedict's alternative model, he gave little if any consideration to the ways in which historical change, social and political structures, economics or any other factors might have altered or modified the character supplied by infant training.

Gorer did introduce some novel features, reflecting new (and, as they proved, unfortunate) influences on his own thinking. He had become enamoured of the work of the British psychoanalyst Melanie Klein, which emphasized the long-term effects of the relationship between mothers and infants. Klein was unusual in discussing the aggressive as well as the nurturing side of mother-baby relations: in her view, babies were driven among other motivations by greed and anxiety, and waged almost a war against the maternal breast. Gorer's own long-standing conviction that loneliness and aggression were the endemic human problems found sustenance here. The irony is that Gorer presented Klein's revision of Freud as another step away from Freud's universalistic neglect of culture. Others, including Mead, worried that replacing one universal mechanism (Freud's Oedipus complex) with another one (infantile aggression), coming even earlier in life, had the opposite effect, making societies seem all the same and all doomed, beset by something very much like 'original sin'.[28]

Certainly Gorer's depiction of the Russians was very fatalistic, and very static. Unlike other family dramas studied earlier, the Russians' submission to authority was almost primal, not subject to development in later stages of the life cycle as were dominance-submission relationships based on child-parent interactions. In Bateson's terms, the Russians' most important relationships were symmetrical, not complementary, and thus not subject to the feedback loops and balancing acts that made American or British (or even German) relationships so dynamic.[29] Given the extraordinary upheavals in Russia since the Revolution of 1917, Gorer's argument – superficially (as he admitted)[30] so much like the old-fashioned view of the Russian 'soul' – felt like a deliberate provocation to other social scientists alert to the impact of modernization. The circularity of his approach – a certain kind of leader needs a certain kind of follower, and vice versa – blurred the distinction hopelessly between elite and masses that other psycho-cultural analysts such as Inkeles and Bauer were trying to build up. It was not at all clear why in Gorer's schema the elite shared some psychological features with the masses (the need to exert their strength to the limit, for example, or the tendency to outbursts of violent rage) but not others (a taste for order and self-discipline, or a belief in inequality). And if the elite was that different from the people, and only the elite counted, why attend to the swaddled masses at all?[31]

*   *   *

Gorer got his first intimation of the likely reaction to his swaddling hypotheses when he gave them their first public outing at the inaugural seminar of Harvard's RRC in January 1948. Although the discussion was polite enough, the Harvard audience was privately scornful and dismissive – more than that, offended. The assembled experts on history, economics, law, official ideology, politics and social structures all felt they were being told their fields counted for nothing. According to Gorer, little had changed in the Russian character since 1917 and still less could be done from outside to change it. Worse still, many of the audience were of Russian or Russian-Jewish extraction. However much Gorer might differentiate the intelligentsia from the peasantry, these Russian intellectuals were horrified to have paraded before them yet again the age-old depiction of the Russians as sunk in squalor, depravity, depression and despair, all because of a swaddling practice that none of them recognized from their own experience, and on the sole authority of an amateur English gentleman lacking in scientific credentials and with almost no direct experience of Russians himself. Afterwards the historian Michael Karpovich circulated the story that Gorer had seemed surprised to discover that Stalin was not himself a Russian at all but a Georgian, such was the depth of his ignorance.[32]

Surprisingly, Gorer seems to have got little direct criticism of this kind from within his own Russian study group at the RCC project. The preponderance there of social psychologists and anthropologists, primed to detect and value cultural difference, and the absence of economists and political scientists, provides a partial explanation. But the RCC study group was also salted with Russian émigrés who were made uneasy by Gorer's disparaging language and cavalier approach. Ina Telberg, a comrade of Bateson and Du Bois from OSS R&A, complained to her former OSS boss C.B. Fahs that Gorer had 'grossly misrepresented' the extent of his research and come to conclusions that the rest of the study group did not share; she considered him 'a very valuable person because of his brilliant insights but believes him very weak on scholarship', noted Fahs.[33] Yet criticism at the group itself was muted; it seemed to function more as a freewheeling discussion forum, in which thoughts and ideas were thrown out liberally and in an off-the-cuff manner without any attempt at synthesis or consensus. Gorer's presentation of his hypotheses to the RCC general seminar in February 1948 got a similarly non-judgemental reception.[34] Inside the project, awareness that Mead had brought Gorer over personally to run the Russian study group certainly encouraged his colleagues to indulge him, and Benedict too in the final months of her life seemed to be endorsing his approach. Unusually it was she who raised Gorer's swaddling hypotheses at a discussion in April 1948, defending RCC's emphasis on 'the ways in which children are brought up to carry on in their turn their parents' manner of life', although without drawing many specific conclusions from the different swaddling and diapering practices that she described.[35]

At such early presentations outside the project, criticism started to get sharper. The folklorist Ernest Simmons, who admired Benedict, nevertheless spoke to their Columbia colleagues 'very disparagingly of her whole research project as one that attributes all culture to toilet-training or other childhood practices'.[36] The historian Karl Wittfogel and his wife, Esther Goldfrank, an anthropologist, who ran the Chinese History Project at Columbia, were more harshly critical. It was at Benedict's April 1948 presentation that Wittfogel is said to have coined the scornful term 'diaperology' to stigmatize what he now took to be the RCC approach.[37] At this stage, criticism focused on evidence and method, not on politics – Telberg was said to be pro-, Wittfogel viscerally anti-Soviet – and seems to have derived largely from the Russians' shock at the sudden irruption of Gorer's 'diaperology' into their territory. Unlike the situation in wartime, where the Japanese and the Burmese were unable to speak for themselves, the Russians – pro- and anti-communist – were out in force.[38]

Undaunted, Gorer returned to England in early 1948 and proceeded to write up his findings for publication with the nimbleness and speed that Mead so admired but that often got him into trouble. Having produced a completed draft by April, Gorer submitted it to the *American Slavic and East European Review*, a journal published by Columbia's own Russian Institute as part of its programme of infrastructural support for the new field. There it ought to have met with a friendly reception, smoothed by Phil Mosely, although the journal's editor was the folklorist Ernest Simmons who had declared himself a sceptic. Simmons sent it out for peer review to a sociologist, an anthropologist and two historians, one of whom was probably the hostile Michael Karpovich. Normally their response would have been fatal – two were strongly against publication (one called the whole thing 'utterly fantastic'), one was hesitant, only one supportive – but Simmons, probably prodded by Mosely, generously agreed to publish on the grounds that his journal had 'an obligation to bring before its readers ... an article such as this which involves new evidence, scholarly techniques, and methodology'. Somewhat humiliatingly, however, Simmons demanded a preface – which Mead wrote under her own name – justifying the peculiar techniques of 'field anthropology and clinical intensive psychiatry' as applicable to a complex modern culture.[39]

Although Gorer at first felt, with unusual modesty, that his material was too thin to make a book, when he found himself back in London penned in with his mother he changed his mind. He devised an ingenious solution. Having discussed his ideas with a British psychoanalyst friend, John Rickman, who had worked as a doctor in Russia during the First World War, he hit on the idea of combining his *American Slavic and East European Review* article with a set of sketches Rickman had written about Russian characters based on those Great War experiences. The two halves of the book would be published side by side without comment, the juxtaposition intended to reinforce the impression of an unchanging Russian national character. Somewhat reluctantly, Rickman fell in with this plan, and the book – *The People of Great Russia* – appeared under both their names in October 1949. Apart from an appendix on the 'swaddling hypotheses', which was explanatory but fairly unapologetic, the book made few concessions or responses to the major criticisms already raised.[40] The 'swaddling hypotheses' were thus complete; the 'swaddling controversy' was about to begin.

* * *

The swaddling controversy must be firmly set in the precise historical context in which it erupted, at the end of the 1940s. It came at a moment when Mead's whole 'national character' approach was coming under severe scrutiny, intellectually, professionally and politically. During 1948, while Gorer was preparing his hypotheses for publication, his book on the Americans was inspiring a certain amount of bemusement about his methods. *Commentary*'s attack on anthropology's new pretensions was written in the summer of 1949 before the swaddling hypotheses were published, and therefore its criticism of diaperology was based mostly on Gorer's Japanese hypotheses.[41] A sharper political attack was also being generated by retrospective critiques of national-character analyses of the Germans. The simultaneous publication of Schaffner's *Father Land* and

Rodnick's *Postwar Germans*, which both argued vigorously for the salience of the German national character but came to apparently opposite conclusions about its true nature, exposed the weaknesses in their common approach; it didn't help that both authors were RCC employees. But more significantly, at a time when for Cold War reasons self-government was being quickly handed back to the Germans in the British and American Zones, Americans were suddenly ill-disposed to old arguments about a deficient German 'national character' – democracy, it seemed, could cure all ills.[42] Only the continuing prestige of Benedict's *The Chrysanthemum and the Sword*, and the slower pace of democratization in Japan, protected that flank. But the Cold War lurch towards extolling the power of 'freedom' over all other considerations was already undermining the 'national character' school, even before Gorer ventured on to the sensitive territory of Russia.

The first and most intense attack came from very close to home. The RRC Russian study group was a mixed bag, ranging from militant anti-communists such as Nathan Leites to alleged Soviet sympathizers such as Ina Telberg. But above all it was rooted in New York and its politically and intellectually engaged émigré Russian community, composed of successive waves of dissident leftists – socialist-Zionist, Menshevik, Trotskyist – all passionately committed to the democratic and socialist potential of the Russians and equally passionately anti-Stalinist. As time passed, these émigrés' messianic identifications shifted to their adopted country: that is, they became more passionate about the democratic mission of the United States than they were about their home country, and they formed one source of inspiration for Reagan-era neoconservatism. But at this early stage their primary identification was still with the democratic potential of the Russian masses. This put them squarely in the camp of those left-wing democratic universalists whose position Benedict and Mead had found so personally troubling in wartime. In the early Cold War, they were among the principal architects of new theories of totalitarianism aimed at further distinguishing the captive peoples behind the Iron Curtain from their tyrannical masters.

The chief organ of these dissident left-wing Russians in New York was the magazine *The New Leader*, a strongly pro-New Deal and anti-communist weekly, and its chief Russian specialist was the Menshevik émigré David Dallin. A couple of members of the RCC study group were closely connected to Dallin. The anthropologist Mark Zborowski, a Trotskyist refugee from Stalinism, had been introduced to the Dallins in Paris (where they had been based before the war) by Trotsky's son in 1935. The linguist Elsa Bernaut had been married to Ignace Reiss, an NKVD (secret police) agent who emigrated to the West after Stalin's show trials and who had been assassinated in Switzerland by the NKVD in 1937; the Dallins had taken her into their Paris circle too. The Dallins, Zborowski and Bernaut all moved to New York when the war broke out and Zborowski rented an apartment in the same building as the Dallins in upper Manhattan. Bernaut and Zborowski eventually found work with Benedict's RCC and Dallin's son Alexander, who did some of the interviewing for the Harvard refugee project, started a PhD at Columbia with Phil Mosely. Some indication of the incestuousness but also the complexity of this group is given by the fact – which only came out in 1955 – that Zborowski too had been an NKVD agent before the war and may have been the source of information that led to the assassination of Bernaut's husband. At the time of RCC, however, they lived and worked together closely, united by their Russian-Jewish backgrounds, by their left-wing politics and by an abiding hatred of Stalinism.[43]

From all of these sources – he was also close to Wittfogel and Goldfrank – Dallin heard about Gorer's swaddling hypotheses earlier than most, and to say they infuriated him would be putting it far too mildly.[44] As soon as Gorer's article was published in October 1949, Dallin went on the attack in the *New Leader*. While accepting the importance of cultural difference for international relations, Dallin thought cultural difference a peculiarly wrong-headed way of understanding totalitarian states. If you assume that 'there is no distinction between people and government', that 'in its political behavior every nation is guided by a set of relatively stable traits acquired in early childhood, and that its members cannot help but follow habits and customs peculiar to their nation', then neither military conquest nor internal revolution will ever change a 'bellicose, or totalitarian, or aggressive' nation such as Nazi Germany or Stalinist Russia. 'Containment' would never be enough; only a war of extermination would do. Needling Mead and Gorer in a way he knew would be effective, Dallin pointed out how similar this creed was to Nazi racism, 'although this time it is not "blood" that predetermines a people's character, as the Nazi philosophy taught, but methods of rearing children'. Adding insult to injury, he also trotted out Wittfogel's 'diaperology' sneer and the Harvard story, which he got from Karpovich, that Gorer didn't even know that Stalin was a Georgian. In contrast, Dallin's own belief – that the problem was communism, not the Russians – offered much more hope for the Russians, and much wider scope for US government policy, to foment movements for liberty and democracy of which the captive peoples were surely capable. The only justification that Dallin could find for 'the highly placed officials who sponsor and pay for' such 'quackery' 'is that they themselves do not understand its meaning and its implications'; he had assigned himself the personal mission of enlightening them.[45]

The news that the US Navy was backing a theory that seemed to condemn the Russian people either to eternal slavery or to extermination immediately struck a nerve. A prominent anti-communist crusader, Anthony Marcus – also a Russian émigré and a former New Dealer – fired off a protest to the president of Columbia University (who happened at the time to be Dwight D. Eisenhower) against the 'shocking and idiotic conclusions' of 'a *British* ignoramus', inexplicably in the pay of the US military. 'It will cost us billions of dollars,' Marcus alleged, 'it will delay the liquidation of the Soviet tyranny by decades.' Such exaggerated charges were perhaps easily parried, but Marcus proved prescient when he added in a follow-up letter to Mead, 'your report is most injurious to the cause of helping the Russian people rise against their tyrants. They will now be told by their oppressors that the people of America want to destroy the Russian people.'[46] That was just what happened. Having been given a propaganda opening by Dallin, within a few months the Soviet organ *Red Fleet* chimed in with its own ridicule of Gorer's 'anti-Soviet' pseudo-science, which it portrayed as 'a rank-and-file voice from the sinister ensemble of the instigators of a new war'.[47] Attacks on both Mead and Gorer as 'slanderers in diapers' followed in the newspaper *Izvestia*.[48] This suited Dallin, who in another *New Leader* diatribe lumped Gorer in with others who were 'spreading the false and harmful notion that the Russian people have no understanding of democracy and, hence, are lost to the free world', and thus were lazily unable to discriminate between being 'anti-Communist, anti-Soviet and anti-Russian'. At the same time the *New Leader* ran a spoof by Boris Shub, purporting to be a Soviet report blaming American neuroses on commercial diaper services.[49]

Mead at first tried to ignore these gibes. Gorer was back in Britain and she was busy with her own Soviet research for RAND. Besides, Elsa Bernaut had pleaded with her to stay out of what might turn out to be just an internal brouhaha among the émigré community.[50] But the *New Leader* was now bringing out the big guns. Its next salvo came from a leading anti-communist campaigner, Bertram Wolfe, chief ideological adviser to the State Department's broadcasting services to captive peoples in Eastern Europe. Wolfe resurrected *Commentary*'s earlier charges about the dangerous amateurism of applied anthropology in international relations: 'in less time than you can unswaddle a baby or change its diapers, they can tell MacArthur how to administer Japan, Truman how to deal with Russia, and McCloy how to handle all the problems of German thought and institutions'. Moving away from Dallin's overblown association of

Gorer with a policy of racial extermination, Wolfe in fact made a sharper political critique by linking him to the policy of containment, now increasingly discredited as the Korean War took off. Anti-communist militants such as Dallin and Shub pressed harder for an ideological campaign to liberate the captive peoples, a policy aimed at inspiring Democrats as well as Republicans to take a more positive interest in freedom and democracy behind the Iron Curtain. For their purposes Gorer's swaddling hypotheses were a wonderful foil, highlighting the immorality of abandoning the captive peoples to slavery, much as democratic universalists during the Second World War had scorned anthropologists' hesitancy about 'imposing' democracy on the captive peoples of Nazi-dominated Europe.[51]

Belatedly, Mead organized a response. Gorer was allowed to write a bland rebuttal to Wolfe in the pages of the New Leader, weakly complaining that he had been misrepresented, and Phil Mosely contributed a review of Dallin's book praising its characterization of the Soviet Union but defending Gorer too as offering an 'experimental' new approach that might yet yield fruit.[52] By then the controversy had spilled out much further than the pages of the New Leader, however. In this new phase of the Cold War, with McCarthyism as well as Korea afoot, containment-era policies were being viewed as soft on communism; anything short of a 'liberation' policy on behalf of the captive peoples fell under suspicion. Gorer's swaddling hypotheses became an easy target for critics of containment. The ridicule heaped upon them was not completely unmerited, but neither was it proportionate, except in the context of the altered political environment. The ideological polarization of the Cold War was finally reaching the point where culturally relativist understandings of national difference were not only becoming unacceptable, but almost literally unspeakable.

Although Mead's Navy paymasters were surprisingly relaxed about the swaddling hypotheses,[53] RAND was not at all happy about them. Unlike ONR, whose bosses knew little about social science, RAND was actually run by social scientists, the hard-headed, behavioural-control variety that wanted verifiable, preferably quantitative results with clear-cut policy implications. They were thus also more closely attuned than some other sponsors to the shifting winds inside the policy elite and, as in this case, were more than willing to trim their sails to suit their masters. Hans Speier, an OSS veteran and a keen advocate of Lasswell's policy science, was the director of RAND's Social Science Division and he was not going to accept any nonsense about the Russian national character. His own view was that all Soviet power lay with the elite and that only an internal crisis within that elite would cause the Soviet system to crumble.[54] As he saw it, he was paying Mead for a study of *Soviet* culture, supposed to give insights into the behaviour of the elite, and Russian 'diaperology' was not only irrelevant and impressionistic but suggested a dangerous 'swaddling' of Soviet power. Mead was coming to the end of her first year of the RAND project with Leites at the time that the controversy broke, and she was suddenly confronted with a panicked instruction from Speier: 'you either omit or keep to a minimum a presentation and discussion of the stimulating hypothesis on the importance of swaddling for the development of the Russian national character, which you developed in cooperation with Geoffrey Gorer.' Loose hypothesizing about the Russian national character may have been tolerated by the Navy, but 'your work under the RAND contract was oriented toward a more specific, political, problem'.[55] '[W]hile the Navy is apparently becoming what might be called, "pro-baby" or at least "pro-babies as clues", Speier, as the social science director of the SSC project has gone into a terrific "non-baby" spin,' Mead moaned to Gorer. RAND was asking her to censor precisely those elements that she felt added the extra anthropological content – paying attention to psychological characteristics peculiar to Russian culture – to what might otherwise be a conventional analysis of Soviet power politics. It made her wonder – perhaps for the first time – if it was all worth it. 'RAND does not purchase me as a scientist, except to the extent that they leave me free,' she wrote to Leites. 'I merely cannot write without using my own framework.'[56]

If the opprobrium attracted by Gorer's swaddling hypotheses was beginning to limit Mead's political efficacy, more significantly for the long term it was also beginning to limit her efficacy as an anthropologist. At this specific moment at the end of the 1940s, the application of anthropology to international relations was under attack from all manner of universalists, asserting the essential unity of humanity, both for internationalist and Cold War purposes. If any mud stuck to Mead, their most prominent public representative, then it might also stick to anthropologists as a group, tarnishing the reputation they had carefully built up since the 1920s as experts on the 'natives'. As Alistair Cooke had warned in a review of Gorer's book on the Americans; 'Mr. Gorer's "preliminary survey" fills you with piercing doubts about the whole anthropological method. For Mr. Gorer is a disciple of Malinowski and a colleague of Margaret Mead. It makes you wonder if it's true what they say about the Trobriand Islanders.'[57] Or the other way around, as a friendly critic put it to Mead: 'I fear that only pure kindness and the obviousness of our discipline's successes amongst "primitives" saves us from being branded the fools we are.'[58]

Quite apart from her enemies – she was lucky that Ralph Linton was on his last legs – her friends in the profession began to take steps to defend their discipline against the damage they feared the swaddling controversy might be doing to it. The *American Slavic and East European Review* published a powerful critique of the original Gorer article by an anthropologist, Irving Goldman, who had formerly had warm relations with Mead but who now attacked both the overly simple connection alleged between infant training and adult personality, and the connection between personality and culture. The implicit claims that infant training determined adult personality and that adult personality captured everything that was worth knowing about a culture would not only unnecessarily alienate other disciplines – history, economics, politics – but also gave a narrowly sectarian idea of what anthropology was all about. He was motivated, Goldman told Clyde Kluckhohn, by the sense that 'it will do anthropology no good at all if social scientists were to regard Gorer's abuse of history as the "anthropological approach"'. Kluckhohn himself defended Mead in print, but only moderately; he supported Goldman in private.[59]

Mead realized what was at stake, though she was not in a very good state to mount a counterattack. To another former ally, who had criticized her for something else entirely, she revealed how thin-skinned she was feeling, and also how grandiose her self-perception had become:

> These attacks on the work we are doing at present, these continuous misrepresentations and misstatements are going to do harm, and harm of a subtle and serious kind, not a gross kind, but harm that in the end may mean that whereas in World War II, many millions of lives were saved through a proper handling of the Japanese, the same thing may be made impossible.[60]

Though Mead was furious at what she saw as a series of betrayals, she presented them to Gorer as a 'challenge', an opportunity 'to invent a way in which what we have to say gets through at least part of the resistances which are offered to it'.[61] But of course it was she, not he, who was doing most of the work. She began to scurry around the professional meetings, taking on all-comers, waggling her finger at the young ones: 'Now, you know that's not what Geoffrey meant!' All this did, of course, was to weld Mead and Gorer ever more closely together in the younger generation's mind – and make them wonder in embarrassment what was going on.[62] What *was* going on? Why had Mead hitched herself so closely to Gorer's wagon, in such a damaging way at such a critical time?

* * *

The obvious answer is that, after the loss of Bateson and Benedict, she needed him. There are cruder and more refined versions of this explanation. Ina Telberg, the disgruntled Russian study-group member, put it this way: 'Margaret always had to have someone to mother and . . . since Gregory Bateson had left her she had adopted Geoffrey.' Mead had said as much to Benedict herself when she admitted that 'one of my blocks is that I can't conceive of my life not oriented to a man'.[63] Her relationship with Gorer at this point – alternately egging him on to some of his more outré conclusions and then drawing back from the consequences – is not dissimilar to the relationship they struck up in Washington during Bateson's wartime absence. Then, however, she had had Benedict's salutary judiciousness to check her. From the end of 1948, she lacked that backstop. Benedict's sudden death had shaken her badly and left her feeling more needy still. Since the summer of 1947, when the final break with Bateson had come, she had confessed to Benedict that she had been daydreaming about marriage to Gorer; now the daydreams became more serious. After Benedict's death she continued to press Gorer to spend more time in New York on RCC and SSC business, and she began to spend more time in Europe, on brief business trips and in the summers. Life was easier there now, and Gorer more relaxed; he had bought a beautiful country house in Sussex with plenty of room for guests and a garden to cultivate. On one of her trips, in November 1949, she broached the topic of marriage with Gorer and he gave her 'permission to daydream', leaving marriage at least 'half hoped, or half planned'. 'My dear,' she wrote on her return, 'you have made me extraordinarily happy – I feel still as if I were glowing.' On another trip Mead took along Cathy, now entering adolescence, and asked her how she would feel if she married Gorer and they moved as a family to England.[64] Had his mother finally died at this juncture, she later reflected, she might indeed have taken the plunge.[65]

But then she began to have second thoughts. Extended exposure to him reminded her of their differences, perhaps irreconcilable. She did not find him physically attractive (though that wasn't decisive for someone so easily enamoured of a fine mind). More problematically his greater reticence was making talk about intimate matters too difficult. As their relations began to deteriorate over the course of 1950 – when her firefighting on his behalf over the swaddling controversy was at its most intense – her frustration at the damage the controversy was doing to her professional reputation must also have played a role.[66] At the end of 1950, at a particularly difficult moment in the controversy, they had some tetchy exchanges concerning Gorer's contributions to the RCC project, in which she allowed herself to voice some of her own long-repressed criticisms of Gorer's professional behaviour, citing in particular:

the excessive slimness of everything you have published since Himalayan Village, and the fact that nothing is documented, even when it could be, and that you shift your lines of comparison without specifically stating that you do it . . . We may very well stand to lose all we have gained, unless we can really make clear that this is a method, with strong, clear theoretical roots, that the use of 'the whole personality' or the 'whole culture' is methodologically sound.[67]

By then Gorer was backing off too. He was losing interest in the Russians; he was not much interested in meeting Mead's criticisms of his work for the project. Above all, after years of coy skittishness about tackling his real obsession, the loneliness of the English people, he had just been made an offer he couldn't refuse by the publisher of a popular daily newspaper: a large budget and a pool of tens of thousands of ordinary newspaper readers for a systematic study of the English national character.[68] Here was a chance to assert his independence from Mead on a subject that she had made her own, and on which, of course, he had always thought himself the real expert. By the end of 1951, the prospect of marriage, or some other kind of intimate relationship, was over. They remained close friends, and frequent travelling companions, for the rest of their lives, but the intensity was lost and hereafter their professional lives also diverged.

* * *

It is, however, really too simple, and unfair, to hinge Mead's defences of the swaddling hypotheses solely on her personal dependence upon Gorer. Just as importantly, she had already committed herself – and the RCC project, and to a great extent the whole line of research on 'national character' – to addressing the question of US-Soviet relations. Though she tried to couch her analysis in terms less controversial than Gorer's swaddling hypotheses, it was hard to separate the two in the public mind. The mud thrown at swaddling stuck to her too, and she could not easily repudiate Gorer, for personal reasons but also for professional reasons, without casting doubt on the whole anthropological enterprise of intercultural relations. Still, she tried to distinguish between Gorer's work on the 'Great Russian' character and her own on the Soviet elite. The SSC project she was running for RAND was based on Benedict's work in FMAD in trying to connect 'patterns of conduct' in a foreign culture to their leaders' 'political behavior', to shed light on internal Soviet politics but also on US-Soviet political communication.[69] It was, therefore, a more explicitly 'applied' project than the more 'blue-sky' research of

RCC, which was why it was suited to the more 'applied' brief of RAND. Understanding Soviet (as opposed to Russian) attitudes to authority would serve the dual purpose of exploring how the traditional Russian character enunciated by Gorer was affected by Soviet power, in the elite's attempt to create a 'New Soviet Man', and also of exploring how the Soviet elite's attitudes and American attitudes were likely to interact – RAND's interest, but also a classic exposition of Mead's approach to intercultural communication.[70]

The emphasis of SSC allowed Mead to work closely with Nathan Leites, otherwise a difficult combination. Leites was very interested in the 'psycho-cultural' approach but not very interested in the Russian masses. Both his anti-communist politics and his high-powered intellectual elitism attracted him more to Lasswell's policy science and RAND's security-oriented research programme. Shortly after the SSC project began he left RCC and joined the RAND staff, leaving him little time to participate even as a visitor in the Russian study group.[71] Although his relationship with Mead was combustible, he remained a valuable conduit to the more policy-oriented types such as Lasswell and Speier. It was Leites, for example, who helped Mead negotiate with RAND an exceptional clause in their contract that all SSC materials would be unclassified, something that Mead insisted upon – 'in order to conduct this work within the conventional scientific canons,' she explained, 'this specification of non-classification is essential' – but that conflicted with RAND's own contract with the Air Force.[72]

As Gorer's swaddling hypotheses emerged in 1949, however, the complementarity of these projects was imperilled, and with it the delicate relationship between Mead and Leites. With her more holistic, anthropological view of culture, Mead simply would not admit any fundamental contradictions between the attitudes of the Russian masses and the attitudes of the Soviet elite; any differences could be encompassed within schismogenic patterns such as 'dominance-submission'. As the political dangers of this position became clear in 1949, RAND went into its 'terrific "non-baby" spin': it wanted any report to stick strictly to the mentality of the Soviet elite, separate from the RCC speculations on the Russian national character, where 'empirical evidence' seemed to Speier 'quite scanty'.[73] Mead replied furiously to Speier. She had always considered the two projects to be inextricable. 'I find no criteria for discriminating between say, an hypothesis about the concept authority, and an hypothesis about the body imagery involved in verbal and artistic comment on restraint. I don't know how to regard "The Opposition" [i.e. a political concept] as empirical, and a photograph of a row of swaddled infants as non-empirical.' Leites used psychoanalytic terms like 'guilt' or 'identification', she pointed out, as applied to the elite; why shouldn't they be applied to ordinary people as well? In her view, such terms only acquired meaning if they were integrated into an analysis of the culture as a whole. Furthermore, as she told Leites, she did not know how to write in any other way:

> If I write this integration and sign it, I am going to write it in the empirical terms which I use, and not someone else's. Furthermore, I am not going to put up with guilt being allowed to pass as 'empirical' and 'swaddling' as non-empirical ... If they insist on a more descriptive piece, I will write it, but not sign it, as a piece of routine work with which I have no desire to be personally identified ... Your and my framework will of course fit together perfectly and I think that Hans [Speier] should be made to face the relationship between them, squarely.

She was, she was making it clear, not available for hire – either RAND published Mead the anthropologist or they did not publish Mead at all.[74]

Unfortunately Leites did not see it this way. He did not share Mead's holistic view of culture and he was not interested in being used as a complement to, or balance for, Gorer's hypotheses. He was, furthermore, now firmly in RAND's camp. He refused point-blank to submit anything to RAND that violated Speier's stipulations. A full-blown row broke out between him and Mead. Her fury was mingled with petulance, as she had been hoping to lure Leites (and his paymasters) into some limited accept-ance of a national-character analysis, almost unawares, and now the jig was up.[75] Mead and Leites initially attempted to strike a compromise whereby they would write together a flat, descriptive, uncontroversial report on the project for RAND, which he would approve, in which (as she fumed to herself) 'there will be a rigorous avoidance of any reference to the fact that Russian adults have ever been children, have central nervous systems, or bodies, except as the concept body may be relevant to such categories as mastery of skills, or disposal of corpses'. The quid pro quo was that she would then be free to write a book for publication drawing on their material in any terms of her own that she chose. Even this compromise proved unworkable; such were their relations that they could not agree on what constituted a flat description. Mead finally agreed to write the uncontroversial RAND report herself, and she and Leites would then each write their own separate books. 'It's not an optimum solution,' she wrote to Gorer, but 'it disposes once and for all of any possibility of having to write and publish anything with Nathan –

what I was looking on with absolute horror.' 'I am so furious with Nathan and I can't even enjoy burning him in effigy in phantasy.'[76]

Leites did very well out of this agreement. The book he wrote for RAND based on the Soviet research, *The Operational Code of the Politburo* (1950), was an outstanding success as a policy document, and even caught the public's attention thanks to puffing by Leo Rosten. A short, pithy pamphlet based entirely on the writings of Lenin and Stalin, Leites's *Operational Code* gave a sketch of the psychology of the Soviet elite that only indirectly took into account the putative Russian national character, portraying Communist Party ideology as a *reaction* to Russian moodiness and spontaneity, which it was seeking to control. The result was a Soviet elite that was highly rationalistic, determinedly active, methodical and focused on long-term goals. The policy implication of his analysis was therefore different from that suggested by Gorer – not firm pressure but 'extreme pressure' was called for. Although short-term accommodations were possible, long-term coexistence was not. 'Containment' had to give way to something more like 'containment plus' or 'liberation'.[77] In its own way Leites's was as thin and static a depiction of the Soviets as Gorer's of the Russians. It did not satisfy many professional Russian experts, nor did it capture the imagination of the public.[78] But it was grabbed at eagerly by policymakers during the Korean War as 'a handbook of Communist political strategy', as Rosten dubbed it, and it was relied upon extensively in the Korean armistice negotiations as engineered by Leites's RAND colleague Herbert Goldhamer.[79]

Mead did much less well out of their agreement. It took her a long time to hammer out the report in a form that satisfied both her and RAND. After all that effort, it seemed a shame to go over the same material again, and so the book that she published, *Soviet Attitudes toward Authority* – which did not appear until 1951 – did not depart much from the original report, and it appeared in a RAND series.[80] Although she claimed that it incorporated the RCC approach as well, and asserted that the Soviet personality was only 'a particular variant of the traditional Great Russian character', she did not bring the swaddling hypotheses – or infant training of any kind – into the book any more than she had in the report. Like Leites, she treated the Soviet elite as a distinct class with its own ethos – 'a kind of delayed Protestantism', as Erik Erikson had described it – although one that derived from its schismogenic relationship to the masses.[81] Thus the picture of the whole culture was obscured, precisely as she had feared, by an emphasis on Communist Party ideology – 'the Party Line'. Any insight Mead hoped to glean on the subject of intercultural communication between the US and the Soviet Union was couched lopsidedly in terms of a relationship not between two cultures but between a culture and an ideology.[82] Policy prescriptions she eschewed almost entirely.[83]

As a result the book puzzled its reviewers. What had happened to the swaddling hypotheses? What indeed was anthropological about Mead's approach?[84] To one reader it appeared to be 'hardly more than an indifferently organized content analysis'.[85] Alex Inkeles of the Harvard RRC thought that Mead's new focus on the psychology of the Soviet elite rather than the masses meant that her project was almost indistinguishable from his. There was indeed a growing convergence between the two; they shared personnel, though not data, and Inkeles even performed a little espionage to get hold of Mead's files that might be relevant to the book he was writing with Kluckhohn and Bauer.[86] When the findings of the Harvard project finally emerged, they did endorse some limited national-character differences between Americans and Russians, but they laid more emphasis on the modernizing aspirations of the Soviet elite, which on the whole they thought were successful in accommodating Russians to the new regime.[87] David Riesman, always in this period eager to salvage as much as he could from Mead's method, praised her book for the very fact that it left vague the extent to which the Russian people were integrated into the system, one way or the other. What remained was a picture of 'Soviet officialdom as, not "just like us", but as understandably different', which Riesman preferred to Hannah Arendt's vision of totalitarianism as a completely inhuman system. '[T]he relatively undestroyed humanity of major elements in the Soviet population is for me the most encouraging conclusion of the Mead book,' Riesman summed up, a reading that says more about Riesman's optimism than about Mead's outlook.[88]

The main RCC project was now threatened with eclipse by its Soviet offshoot. As early as February 1949 Mead had told the RCC general seminar that Benedict's plan had always been to fold it into the Columbia anthropology department after a few years; after her death, that was no longer possible, and so the project was to be run down. The Navy renewed funding for the 1949–50 academic year, but at a reduced level, principally to fund a writing-up phase for the Jewish, Chinese and Polish groups.[89] One of the more enduring products of this final phase was Mark Zborowski and Elizabeth Herzog's *Life Is with People: The Jewish Little-Town in Eastern Europe* (1952), which remained in print for over half a century and was one of the inspirations for the musical *Fiddler on the Roof*. The principal fruit of the Jewish study group, it resolved the group's doubts about the diversity and instability of the Jewish experience in a familiar way, by identifying the Eastern European shtetl as the true 'Jewish community' and thus the source of the Jewish character – much to the annoyance of subsequent generations of Jewish scholars.[90]

However, Mead's own attention remained fixed on the Soviet Union. While running down RCC, she had a longer-term plan for continuing her Soviet work with the considerable pool of Russian expertise that she had assembled in New York. Her idea was to refine further her statements about Soviet attitudes, match them up with comparable statements about American attitudes, and then run some experiments – of the kind that the behavioural-science community was always pressing on her – to see how American-Soviet communications might actually work (and be improved) under controlled conditions. In this way she hoped to combine more of a policy orientation that would attract attention from the authorities with her long-standing goals of improving intercultural communication. Rather against the odds, she was still hopeful that she might be able to collaborate with Leites in this extended project, as well as with old members of the Russian study group like Phil Mosely, Elsa Bernaut and Mark Zborowski.[91] The new emphasis on intercultural communication allowed her to shelve the arguments over national character and to revive older ideas based on schismogenesis in the same terms as she had treated the Anglo-American relationship,

> using the categories of symmetrical, complementary and reciprocal relationships, and also the ways in which ego, libidinal and super-ego segments of assumed Bolshevik character are reflected, counter-reflected, etc. in their image of the US. I am also using a background of interpersonal relationships with their various overtones of exhibitionism, spectatorship, types of rivalry, types of superordination, subordination, etc. For example, not only do we tend to cast the Soviet Union as a symmetrical vis-à-vis, an other team, but we are always in danger of slipping into a younger brother role – as an alternative to being a moralizing older sibling, reflecting mother's voice, etc.[92]

The second-year report for RAND, submitted in the autumn of 1950, presented a fully developed theory about US-Soviet communication. Mead thought the Soviet elite, anxious about its control over its own people, 'over-identified' with the US elite, attributing to it the kind of control it would like to exert itself; this overidentification was said to be the psychological source of Soviet demonizing of, for example, Wall Street's power. But she was just as, if not more, interested in American attitudes to the Soviets. Adapting her earlier conclusions about the Anglo-American relationship, she argued that American identification with the Soviets was less anxious and more 'symmetrical', a friendly rivalry with a power seen to be similar to oneself. Thus Americans adopted a jokier tone towards rivals: 'The United States handling of a rival group that is as strong as itself is to cast the other group as the "other team", and the other team is seen as in the same league, in the same class, as very much like the self, to be treated with a mild, often almost affectionate, razzing.' Here she was more or less consciously injecting herself into the feverish debates of 1950 around Korea and McCarthyism, aiming herself squarely against campaigns demonizing the Soviet Union. Not only would such a policy reinforce the Soviets' own overidentification, it would also represent a fatal deviation from the normal American response, 'a weakening of our moral strength':

> Such attempts are likely to be accompanied by attacks on parts of our population – on hyphenated Americans in World War I, on the Nisei in World War II ... Any similar attempt to deal with the Soviet Union as a wholly evil rival is likely to involve repudiation of parts of the American people so as to leave a *wholly* good, *wholly* American residue, although which part will be repudiated will depend upon whether the black image of the Soviet Union is based upon the accusation that the Soviet Union is representative of 'old European tyranny', or consists of Asiatics, or of mixed breeds, or of backward and uncivilized people. Whatever vilification images might be chosen, the attempt would boomerang in the United States, in attacks on parts of the United States population, and increased possibilities of our national behavior approximating more closely those Soviet practices which we most deplore – concentration camps, political police, surveillances, etc.

Her alternative, as it had been in 'Learning to Live in One World', was 'making instead statements that ally the United States with *all* the rest of the world ... in a common enterprise that can be identified with progress for mankind'; her only concession to the dark shift in the political atmosphere was to instance the UN's Korea intervention as such a common enterprise.[93]

Whereas in 'Learning to Live in One World' Mead had realistically assessed the problems of Anglo-American communication and prescribed the 'other team' line as a psychologically opportune alternative, she was now presenting – with extraordinary optimism – the 'other team' line as the *normal* way in which Americans viewed the Soviet Union. This rosy picture was largely based on editorial cartoons in US daily newspapers – thus the jokiness she found. Furthermore, the whole approach assumed that American policymakers *wanted* better 'intercultural communication' with the Soviets, a fading prospect in 1950. It failed to convince either Mosely or Leites. Mosely thought she should emphasize the point about Soviet overidentification: it would give some useful and practical hints to the psychological-warfare boys, although even Mosely assumed cheerfully that propagandists would want to lessen Soviet hostility rather than aggravate it. Leites didn't assume that at all. He was quite happy with her proposal for a propaganda line that associated the US with the rest of the world, 'Only I think it can be combined with the treatment of the Soviet Union as "wholly evil"', which in his view it was, and he didn't worry either that it would boomerang on to the American self-image, or care much about whether it would irritate the Soviets.[94] For similar reasons, RAND wasn't much interested in this line of attack either: it was, after all, getting its advice on such questions from Leites. At this stage it terminated its relationship with Mead. The parting was not amicable. Mead retained the right to withdraw her name from any association with the research if she didn't like the use RAND made of it; RAND retained the right to make any use of it that it chose. It appears to have disappeared into the bowels of the secret state, never to resurface.[95]

But Mead wouldn't give up. By the end of the RAND project, in autumn 1950, the Korean War was in full flow and customers for insights into communist psychology were abundant; psychological warfare, which had been on the retreat in the late 1940s, was now coming back into fashion across all of the services. Although Mead's self-appointed task was to pull together with Rhoda Metraux a 'manual' summing up the lessons of the RCC project on 'the study of culture at a distance', she spent a lot of time beating the bushes, looking for what was now tantamount to war work. Rather like Bateson in the final stages of the Second World War, she seemed to be falling into a divided mental state that was doing great damage to her personally and professionally. She was flirting with commitments that threatened to violate her most cherished ethical principles: to work for peace not for war, to work like a good scientist only for the public, to consider all sides of an intercultural communication equally as a good anthropologist should. In the autumn of 1950 she signed a new contract with Capt. Caleb Laning of the Naval Research Laboratory for a project exploring 'military vulnerability inherent to the Russian culture'. The idea was to seek 'clues of Russian methods of getting rapid decisions at high command level in combat' based on a scrutiny of Red Army manuals as well as classified material supplied by the Navy; her self-justification was that Laning might fund her proposed simulations in US-Soviet communications. Far from insisting on a completely unclassified project, as had been her practice in the past, Mead was now furious when Laning tried to block her access to classified material.[96] At the same time, she accepted a commission for RCC from the interservice Research and Development Board to provide briefings on the national character of Americans, Poles, Jews and Chinese for a Working Group on Human Behavior under Conditions of Military Service. Although Mead wrote an introductory memorandum on the Americans for this study that displayed all of her and Gorer's neo-Freudian hypotheses in full fig – it began, 'American character structure is based upon an oral optimistic infancy', and went on in a similar vein for many pages – the actual report assembled by Rhoda Metraux from the various RCC study groups was much more restrained and pitched carefully at practical military considerations. In this it resembled far more than anything else for which Mead was responsible the behavioural-control agenda of Stouffer's *American Soldier* study, from which Metraux quoted liberally.[97]

So tempting was this new rush of potential customers during the Korean War that in 1951 Mead went back to ONR for yet a further extension of the original contract. In wartime conditions ONR had so much money for research that it was finding it difficult to give it away; the additional appropriations were approved almost on the nod, and RCC won a final lease of life until 1952 under the new title of Studies in Contemporary Cultures (SCC), with Rhoda Metraux as research director.[98] SCC came in three parts: an attempt to reconcile the divergent Schaffner and Rodnick studies of postwar Germans that had caused Mead so much irritation; a final effort to run experimental simulations of US-Soviet communications, using MIT students and Russian displaced persons as the lab rats;[99] and an extension of the RCC Chinese study group under Ruth Bunzel to consider the relationship of Chinese communist ideology to Chinese national character, much as Mead had attempted for the Soviet Union with the RAND study. Incredibly Mead was still trying with this last effort to combine the militantly anti-communist Leites with a bunch of fellow travellers; this mix was even more combustible than its predecessors. Leites was no more prepared to consider the 'Chineseness' of the Chinese communists than he was to consider the 'Russianness' of the Soviets and he refused point-blank to talk to people who had an 'open mind'

> as to how much China and how much bolshevism there is in the top
> level of the Chinese party. I am quite aware of the fact first that I don't
> know the answer, and second that I have a prejudice that there is a great
> deal of bolshevism there – a somewhat irrational prejudice as I don't

know the facts really, although I feel that I have been able to predict major events since 1945 quite well on the basis of my assumption.

'I find it very hard at this point in history,' he confessed, 'to work together with people on Stalinism, in the Soviet Union or elsewhere, who do not have a vivid sense of this being a major enemy', and he flounced out of Mead's project once and for all.[100]

Almost nothing came out of this final phase of the 'national character' research.[101] The problem was that the anthropologists were now hardly contributing anything distinctive. Their customers in government and the military were no longer interested in 'national character', preferring as Leites did studies that zeroed in on communist ideology alone – better suited to propaganda work and better suited to the rising tide of liberationism, which saw the peoples of the communist bloc not as participants in their own culture but as slaves to ideological zealots. And by taking on these propaganda tasks, aimed at bolstering US fighting morale, undermining Chinese and Russian combatants, and disrupting Soviet communications, Mead, too, was in danger of losing not only the disciplinary but also the ethical and political stance that had inspired her and Benedict to launch the RCC project in the first place.

Mead was not unaware of these contradictions. She strove to reconcile them: for example, by persisting in mixing rabid anti-communists like Leites with area experts whom Leites considered communists. She clung to the illusion – as, during the Korean War, it certainly was – that work on US-Soviet communications was a contribution to US-Soviet understanding, and that work on the 'Chineseness' and the 'Russianness' of the Chinese and Soviet Communist Parties was improving understanding of cultural difference on a global scale.[102] At an anthropologists' gathering in April 1951, Mead defended her Russian work as representing '[t]he anthropologists' stance', neither pretending to be objective (the view from 'Mars'), nor representing one's 'own culture at war or competing with the world', but rather acknowledging one's 'own culture *in* the world as a whole, in humble acknowledgement of the need for cooperation to build a useful, culturally based world anthropology'.[103]

But her paymasters were less and less interested in 'understanding', her reports had fewer and fewer customers, and the anthropologists were drifting away too. She was feeling terribly isolated. Not only had she lost Bateson and Benedict, but her relationship with Gorer was rapidly fading. Her standing in the anthropological profession had been imperilled by the swaddling controversy. Increasingly she was reliant on Rhoda

Metraux's presence as amanuensis and go-between, but the younger woman, who tended to see her role as chief zealot in Mead's camp, could never provide the same frank advice or criticism that Mead had got from Benedict.

Even without those checks from outside, however, Mead could see that the RCC's distinctive anthropological mission was dwindling into insignificance. If she had really been a keen Cold Warrior, she would at this point have thrown herself into the arms of the psychological-warfare establishment once and for all. That, however, would have meant abandoning her role as an anthropologist, and giving up the disciplinary leadership she had sedulously cultivated for decades. Instead, her Boasian instincts kicked in: she yearned for that escape back to the 'natives' that had always provided for Boasians their distinctive relativizing mission. At the end of 1950 and the beginning of 1951, when the pressures upon her reached a peak, she began to daydream about a return to the field, 'my own kind of work' (which international relations, she recognized, was not), though she could think of all manner of obstacles: the 'emergency situation' at home and abroad, the Korean War, her responsibilities to Cathy.[104] In the summer of 1951 she essayed a scouting expedition to Australia, and this decided her that

> it was time for those of us who had given up our major task – studying primitive peoples as a way of throwing light on the processes of human society – for wartime work on problems of morale, communication among allies, and psychological warfare against totalitarian forces, to go back to our laboratories in the jungles, on the small islands, around the arctic fringes of the world.[105]

Yet international relations would not release her. In the autumn of 1951 she was still trying to get Gorer to come to New York, but he was now fully committed to the easy life in Sussex and his new flow of data on the English national character.[106] Her frustrations were very near the surface. At an anthropological meeting in New York in June 1952, when she came (as she so often did in this period) under fierce criticism for subordinating anthropology to public policy, she retorted angrily, 'Your statement that out of some kind of fervor people dropped other things and went into national character is true, and almost all of us who have devoted our time to it in the last ten years would much rather have done something else.'[107] Her position was very finely balanced, 'poised in the air' as she put it to Gorer, between further engagement and withdrawal, again strikingly like Bateson's state in 1945, though without the pressures of jungle warfare to blame. The international situation was both an opportunity – demanding anthropologists' input – and an obstacle – standing between them and their 'major task'. In the last year or two before her actual 'return to the natives', Mead was still searching restlessly and irritably for ways to serve both masters at once.[108]

Mead and Paliau

CHAPTER 7

Return to the Natives
(1947–53)

During her peak years of engagement with 'modern' cultures in the 1940s, Mead had not turned her back on the so-called 'primitive' cultures on which she had founded her reputation. Both *And Keep Your Powder Dry* at the beginning of the war and the uncompleted 'Learning to Live in One World' at the end of the war aimed to engage Americans' imagination with a new vision of 'one world' of many cultures, each 'valid in its own right', without regard to size or power. After the war, her continuing concern with Great Power politics was motivated in no small part by her awareness that the fate of smaller and more vulnerable cultures lay in the Great Powers' hands. In her mind international organizations were the places where great and small might just be placed on some rough level of equality. Nevertheless, as Riesman had pointed out, younger anthropologists resented her over privileging of the Great Powers in this period, and her circle's dalliance with international relations made them 'vulnerable to the criticisms of their professional brethren who have gone on working on the Fox or the Navaho, the Ifaluk or the Trukese'.[1]

This vulnerability became acute as the political winds shifted against internationalism in the late 1940s, and Mead began to contemplate a return to the field for the first time since she had sailed from New Guinea in 1939. It is not surprising, then, that her last stab at parlaying her wartime influence into a role in postwar international relations came in the field of what would later be known as 'international development'. If politicians were reluctant to acknowledge anthropologists' expertise in relations between modern cultures, surely they still needed their expertise in relations between modern and 'primitive' ones. It was only after this final play also ended in political failure that Mead made her literal return to the natives, embarking on a restudy of the Manus of New Guinea in the summer of 1953. That decision to leave the political playing field coincided with the end of the New Deal era, and an end to a brief-lived period of American internationalism, with the advent of a Republican administration in the White House. It also marked the effective end of her high hopes that anthropology might play a constructive role in the 'orchestration of cultural diversities' in a new world order.

*   *   *

Mead's engagement with the less developed world was the acid test for cultural pluralism – for the protection of cultural difference – in the postwar years. Cultural differences between modern cultures in the end were more difficult to sell to a wider public, since modernity was seen as giving them a high degree of common interest; cultural difference could be treated as icing on the cake, acknowledgement of which might ease communication but had little wider import. Where Mead claimed more significance for cultural difference between modern cultures, as in the case of the swaddling controversy, she had been rudely slapped down. The defence of cultural difference in the less-developed world was closer to anthropology's *raison d'être*. The discovery of cultural relativity had been anthropology's foundational achievement, and its protection was the heart and soul of the Boasian creed. In the postwar years it was now threatened by powerful globalizing forces unleashed by the world war. Both the democratic and the communist versions of universalism had a powerful appeal: the motor of economic growth promised to relieve the world's peoples of famine and disease, and to level them up politically so that they could take their place at the world's bargaining tables. This appeal was not limited to developed-world internationalists; it spread like wildfire in these years among the new elites of the less-developed world as well. In these conditions, it was not clear what place there was for anthropology's insistence upon cultural relativism. It could be seen as a sentimental impediment, denying the world's peoples what they most wanted for themselves. Or could it be made compatible with 'development'? That fundamental question has bedevilled accounts of 'development' for half a century; it was first formulated, though, of course, not resolved, by anthropologists like Mead who worked through the first great enthusiasm for 'modernization' in the immediate postwar years.[2]

Right after the war, Mead was more concerned with the theoretical question of whether Americans could learn to respect the peoples of the world than with practical questions relating to those peoples. Her determination to understand and to engage Americans lent her something of their self-absorption; her research in intercultural communication, with Benedict, focused almost exclusively on relations between the US and other modern nations. But she had not stopped thinking about the rest of the world, and in the immediate postwar years Mead made a series of appearances at UNESCO events, where she made an honest attempt to survey the international scene with both realism and vision. The prospects for a war-ravaged world were indeed grim, and yet hopeful. If even Europe required a helping hand for relief and rehabilitation, then how much more desperate was the situation across Asia and the Pacific, the parts of the world Mead knew best? And the problems were not only those of relief and rehabilitation. If the peoples of Asia and Africa were to meet the Great Powers on anything like a basis of equality, then they needed not only to be fed and housed, but to be mobilized as *nations*, that is, entities credentialled and qualified to sit around the table of the UN and other international organizations with the achieved nations of the developed world in order to speak for themselves. Furthermore, whereas at the beginning of the war Mead had had to coax Americans on to the world scene from a position of self-perceived weakness, at the end of the war she had to persuade them to deal fairly with the world from a position of self-perceived strength – not to treat the world as inferiors, as the missionaries had done, but rather as brothers.[3]

Her frankest and fullest statement to this effect came in a report she wrote in 1947 for a preparatory commission for UNESCO. In this she envisaged two polarized alternatives: on the one hand, a global uniculture, scientific and democratic but globally homogeneous, at worst completely Westernized, at best integrating Chinese and Indian elements; on the other hand, the pure Boasian ideal of a world of nearly infinite diversity, which would preserve 'the cultures of the Samoan, the Banyankole, the Greenland Eskimo, the Kaingang of Brazil, the inhabitants of the Isle of Man'. Realistically, she thought, they were more likely to get the uniculture than the culture of maximum diversity, especially given the universalistic mood of the Americans. In that event, some effort ought to be exerted on behalf of the happier, Orientalized version of the uniculture, but in the meantime *every* culture ought to be given the benefit of the doubt and the chance to make its contribution to the whole. For that to happen, the first priority was to stabilize the 'proletarianized' millions who had no effective culture at all, 'torn from their cultural moorings by the unsystematic, sporadic and uncontrolled contact with parts of the higher cultures'. (She must have had New Guinea in mind here – Manus had been overwhelmed by the invasion of as many as a million foreign troops during the Pacific War.) They needed not to be integrated with the world but reintegrated with themselves – 're-construction rather than instruction, therapy rather than the acquisition of knowledge'. Thus reconstructed, they might be able to contribute a newly flexible, change-oriented mentality to the world much as the Americans, 'deculturalized' by immigration, had done in the past. Then, second, the 'intact' cultures of the developing world such as Indonesia needed to be given maximum possible access to the resources of the modern world, in a way that preserved their own distinctive ways of learning and employing knowledge, much as Japan had done before the war, though learning from Japan's unhappy experience. Finally, the West had to adapt its own cultures so as to make room for others – the message of 'Learning to Live in One World'.[4]

The obvious place for these programmes was the UN and its offshoots, that is, UNESCO and the many specialist organizations devoted to problems of food, health, labour and culture. These multilateral organizations, rather than bilateral deals such as the Marshall Plan (which only cultivated American paternalism), were Mead's preferred instrument, seen as 'one member of a group of brothers asking help from their own group'[5] – and, not uncoincidentally, the instrument preferred by the peoples of the non-Western world represented at the UN. The demand for the fruits of economic growth, after all, came most loudly from the poorer peoples of the world, and had been firmly embedded in the UN Charter as a commitment to 'higher standards of living, full employment, and conditions of economic and social progress and development'.[6] The obvious tool to achieve these goals was what the UN called 'technical assistance' (TA), that is, 'expert advice' provided 'to Member Nations who desire this assistance' via multilateral bodies.

In its later incarnation as 'development aid', TA has had a very bad press from historians. The idea current in the 1940s – among recipients as well as donors of TA – that something 'technical' could be abstracted from power relations and conveyed innocently, separate from the donor's agenda, seems naïve in the light of later history. The whole idea of 'development' assumes an agreed goal towards which all peoples were supposed to develop, and in the 1950s a powerful current within social science – dominated by economists, political scientists and sociologists – advanced a 'modernization theory' that prescribed very precisely not only the goal (democracy, individualism, capitalism) but the road to be taken towards it. Furthermore, the mere offer of aid in Cold War conditions was likely to become an instrument of US or Soviet foreign and military policy rather than a neutral exchange between equals. Modernization theory certainly aimed to direct peoples along a path that suited American policy, much as Soviet theorists re-engineered Marxist theory to direct peoples along a path that suited their own regime.[7]

Looking backward from Vietnam, TA seems merely to be the first stage in this inexorable absorption of the less-developed world into global politics and economics. But looking forward from 1945 provides a different perspective – one in which anthropologists involved in technical assistance started from a different point, and going forward learned some of the pitfalls for themselves.[8] It is true that anthropologists, Mead especially, tended to be rather naïvely enthusiastic, and often quite paternalistic, about the value of nutrition and health, wishing not only to bestow these benefits but to persuade their clients to *want* them. But, then, they were unusual Westerners in having had to confront the immediate human consequences of starvation and epidemic disease. And they were surely not naïve in thinking that nutrition and health were vital prerequisites if non-Western peoples were to participate as equals in world organizations. Nor were they content to see only these basic material needs satisfied: equal participation required that the peoples of the world be given access to more constructive tools as well, notably literacy. 'In past years,' Mead wrote, 'education of dependent peoples was for the purpose of their successful exploitation by more advanced economies. It is now recognized that the dependent and under-developed peoples will have to be given education in literacy so that they can participate in the larger world-community.' This was an argument that harked explicitly back to Mead's advocacy of 'education for choice' in the America of the 1930s.[9]

The UNESCO 'Fundamental Education' programme that resulted from Mead's 1947 report, directed by Rhoda Metraux's husband, Alfred, was solicited by twenty-seven member nations in its first five years, proof to Alfred Metraux at least that it was a tool for empowerment rather than exploitation.[10] Literacy was only the beginning, a starting point without which member nations could not benefit from (or contribute to) TA. As the Fundamental Education programme recognized, member nations also needed to be acknowledged as nations – free from the imperial designs of the great powers, and with the power to accept, reject and modify TA proposals. Above all, anthropologists recognized from the beginning – it was, after all, their stock-in-trade – that TA could only be successfully delivered in forms that suited, respected and ideally strengthened indigenous cultural patterns. This was particularly true of TA that was aimed not only to relieve poverty and disease but also to promote economic growth, which tended to disrupt the existing value systems of less-developed cultures. 'Higher standards of living – industrialization – will inevitably destroy such values and thus tend toward the impoverishment of the human race,' Alfred Metraux wrote in a summary of the anthropological contribution to TA. 'The choice lies not between guns and butter but between butter and certain forms of art, certain religious or philosophical traditions.' Where indigenous peoples asked for TA, whether for relief or for economic growth, it was the job of anthropologists to help them minimize the cost to their own cultures, a reversal of the priorities being established in modernization theory by the economists. 'Economists and technicians ... become imbued with an alarming self-confidence,' Metraux observed. 'They seldom have any inkling of the relationship that exists between the various institutions of a group and fail to realize that its culture cannot be altered piecemeal.' It was up to anthropologists to advocate for the integrity of that culture. On the other hand, as Nils Gilman has put it, the anthropological commitment to cultural holism was 'Janus-faced': it did not want cultures to be altered 'piecemeal' or by accident, but it also saw that cultures embracing economic growth might want or need to be altered wholesale and by their own design. As Metraux also argued, nations wanting full participation and economic growth would need

> the development of qualities to fit men to live in the modern world, such as personal judgment and initiative, freedom from fear and super-stition, sympathy and understanding for different points of view ... spiritual and moral development, belief in ethical ideals, and the habit of acting upon them, with the duty to examine traditional standards of behavior and to modify them to suit new conditions.

It remained to be seen how or whether these tensions could be squared. How could a culture embrace participation and growth and remain itself? Could there be, as Metraux urged, a 'successful synthesis between tradi-tional forces and ideas and the modern progressive movement'?[11] That was something that would be learned only in practice.

*   *   *

Preoccupied as she was by Europe and Russia, and with little time or energy to give to the wider international scene, Mead was still anxious to find a place in the UN set-up from which she could get a handle on the burgeoning TA industry. UNESCO was highly various and sprawling and, especially when her resources were limited, Mead was never sure that she would be able to impress her particular vision upon it. She was happy with the work that Metraux was doing on Fundamental Education – once the programme was launched, he went off to Haiti to pilot a direct application – but less so with the woolly internationalism of the UNESCO Tensions Project that Otto Klineberg ran, which seemed to want to ignore or tran-scend cultural difference rather than build upon it.[12] A better potential vehicle was the World Federation for Mental Health, which she and Larry Frank had helped to set up in 1948 as a continuation of their wartime work with Brickner and the psychiatrists. While the wartime work had been impeded by the need to deal with the culture of an enemy, in the postwar world it seemed possible to redefine 'mental health' in a non-normative, culturally diverse way, and to develop a psychiatric arm of the TA movement that could both provide mental-health services to TA clients and more generally educate TA providers in the techniques of intercultural communication.[13]

The problem was that as late as 1949 there was as yet very little TA on offer – it remained mostly a pipe dream of idealists and the budding UN bureaucracy. The first years of the UN were dominated by political wrangles between the US and the Soviets, during which non-aligned states tried and failed to wring economic concessions from the developed world. One by one the Soviet bloc states withdrew from many of the specialist organizations, UNESCO included. Meanwhile TA remained a good idea saluted by all but observed by few. The earliest plans placed the onus of responsibility on recipient states, which had meagre resources and no support systems. Initiatives from the centre responded to emergencies only: for example, mass treatment of tuberculosis, cholera and malaria.[14]

All of this was changed in January 1949 from an unlikely source, powerful but hazardous. On 20 January, launching his second term, President Harry Truman made as the last of the four main planks of his inaugural address – Point IV – the launch of 'a bold new program for making the benefits of our scientific advances and industrial progress available for the improvement and growth of underdeveloped areas'. Point IV had something for everyone. For isolationist Republicans, there was the prospect of new avenues of investment for American private enterprise. For patriotic Americans, there was a paean of praise to American pre-eminence in science and industry. For humanitarians, there was the promise to provide immediate relief for hunger, disease and poverty. For modernizers, there was the commitment to economic growth. For democratic universalists, there was a commitment to 'democratic fair-dealing'. For the Left, there was a repudiation of 'imperialism' and 'exploitation for foreign profit', and an acknowledgement of other people's own aspirations. And for all internationalists, there was a commitment to 'a cooperative enterprise in which all nations work together through the United Nations'.[15]

This clever mixture reflected Truman's political situation. In the first years of his presidency he had confined his proposals for foreign aid principally to Europe. As the Cold War heated up, he looked to build on Marshall Aid's success with 'a kind of democratic manifesto' aimed at the entire world. At the same time, he was also conscious of the dangers of stirring up anti-imperialism and specified in composing his plans that 'foreign developments are being done in the interests of those countries', and only at the initiative of recipient nations. Aware of the potential for political gains overseas, he was nevertheless insistent that political calculations be kept out of the plans as far as possible. As Melvyn Leffler has suggested, after his triumph in the 1948 elections he was more optimistic about the beneficent effects of economic growth, with or without an anti-communist agenda.[16]

This formula proved a success with a wide range of interests. Congress appropriated $24.2 million for a Technical Cooperation Administration (TCA) in September 1950; in 1951 the appropriation soared to $140 million. At the same time, Truman proposed channelling further funds through UN agencies, and over Republican opposition the US pledged $12 million of a total of $20 million from fifty-four countries to the UN's Expanded Program of Technical Assistance (EPTA), itself a direct consequence of the 1949 inaugural address. As Sergei Shenin has shown, Point IV was thus responsible both for the US's and for the UN's TA experiments in the early 1950s, which worked complementarily; the UN's programme, while much smaller, reached out to many more countries (nearly a hundred by 1953 compared to thirty-five for TCA), including those like Indonesia, Burma, Bolivia and Syria which due to political sensitivities would not accept US aid.[17]

While small in comparison to the scale of Marshall Aid – on which more than $2 billion in total was spent – the Point IV programmes turned TA almost overnight from an ideal into a reality. These programmes, operating through both US and UN authorities, were so diverse and loosely coordinated that they offered scope for people of nearly all ideological stripes. As David Lumsdaine has argued, they unleashed forces for TA in UN circles that had long predated (and many of which had little connection to) America's Cold War plans; in this sense, the Cold War did not create TA, but it did provide the 'swing vote' that made US funding for it possible in 1949. Most aid that resulted from Point IV went to places that the US had not prioritized for its own political purposes. And Point IV stimulated further initiatives in TA – for both humanitarian and development purposes – in labour and religious circles, and among the developing nations themselves.[18]

For anthropologists, and social science in general, this open-endedness portended both opportunity and danger. On the surface the tremendous opportunities opened up by Point IV gave at last a point of direct entry into postwar international politics for anthropologists interested and expert in the less-developed world. However, by blurring the boundaries between multilateral UN programmes and bilateral US programmes, Point IV also had the potential to draw anthropologists who were either uninterested in or overtly hostile to America's interests overseas into compromising situations. This had been the experience of those CIMA anthropologists who had gone to Micronesia as fieldworkers and were just at this very moment straggling home, disillusioned by the Interior Department's efforts to turn them into American administrators – an experience very much on anthropologists' minds as they came to consider Point IV.[19] Mead should have been more alert to these political dangers than she was, especially given the outpouring of enthusiasm for Point IV among her democratic-universalist antagonists. The *New Leader*, for example, hailed it only semi-ironically as 'a kind of technically fortified and democratic Shangri-la', promising 'an era of green pastures and green (peasant) internationals, of purring dynamos and purring pressure groups, a chaste international marriage of science and politics', which was at the same time 'thoroughly self-interested, being one of the best ways available to us for checking communist aggression in under-developed countries, and thereby preventing war'.[20]

However, thanks in large part to the *New Leader*'s abuse of her on other fronts, Mead was ripe for the temptation to join Point IV in 1950. RCC was winding down and her commitments to Europe were thus coming to an end. The debacle of the swaddling controversy had reached its height and was putting her off the Russians too; even her relationship with Gorer was starting to unravel. She was increasingly aware of the need to reconnect with the anthropological profession and its historic commitments to the 'natives'. Although her instinct was to return to the field, the outbreak of the Korean War stymied that prospect for the time being and a proxy engagement with the non-Western world via the UN looked very appealing.[21] She envisaged, correctly, a sudden demand for TA specialists who would need training both in devising TA schemes that respected cultural difference and in communicating interculturally between donors and recipients. How could she provide them?

Quickly she devised a two-track solution, one bearing on the US and the other on the UN programme. On the American side she already had connections to the State Department's FSI, where the Boasians Edward Kennard and Cora Du Bois had been training diplomats in intercultural techniques since 1947. Kennard, Du Bois and a handful of other anthropologists in government were keenly aware of the opportunities for disseminating 'cultural relativism' through Point IV, but equally alive to the 'very real danger of having [their] objective investigative functions warped by the administrative outlook and desires'.[22] This group soon reached out to the Society for Applied Anthropology (SAA), of which Mead was then president, with a view to getting it oriented to Point IV work and to help recruit anthropologists directly for it. Mead was delighted. Within a few months she had set up an SAA committee on Point IV, which she chaired, and began bombarding the authorities with advice and encouragement. Seeking to help Truman with his Congressional critics, she also got the AAA to endorse Point IV with a letter pointing out its democratic credentials against totalitarianism and at the same time endorsing Truman's insistence 'that Point IV is no naïve attempt to remake the world in our own image' but that 'a basic minimum of health, education, and productivity is the prerequisite for a decent world'. In December 1950 a conference of social scientists assembled in Washington to give advice on Point IV issued a sobering warning about the variety of approaches possible. There were plenty of social scientists, notably economists, keen to undertake a dramatic experiment in 'social engineering' that might produce 'a positive pro-United States orientation', but there were also others operating on a different model, putting the culture first.

> On the one hand, it was said that it was necessary to make large changes in an antiquated social structure by striking at its key points, or as it was expressed, 'hitting the solar plexus of the *Gestalt*'. On the other hand, various cautions were urged against the uprooting of fundamental elements of a culture lest more loss than gain should ensue.

There was, therefore, a jockeying for position between different varieties of social scientist, between those dedicated to modernization at any cost and those equally concerned with cultural integrity. The anthropologists were not necessarily at a disadvantage to the economists at this stage. The SAA had already persuaded Point IV to put a senior anthropologist in charge of the social-science aspects of the programme at policymaking level, and the job was offered to Cora Du Bois, despite her recent resignation from the State Department on political grounds. When she declined, having had her fill of government, it was decided to go ahead more slowly with junior appointments, but in the meantime to place an anthropologist at FSI to train Point IV workers in techniques of intercultural communication before they went into the field. The person selected was Ned Hall.[23]

Hall's appointment brings out neatly the messy political situation in which anthropologists going into government service at this juncture found themselves. Hall was a Columbia-trained anthropologist with a long history in applied anthropology, reaching right back to its origins in the Bureau of Indian Affairs in the 1930s and including a spell in Micronesia before the CIMA anthropologists arrived. At the time of Point IV's launch he was teaching at Bennington College, where he had become an acolyte of Erich Fromm and David Riesman. He was both a very patriotic American and a fierce advocate of cultural relativism, and a critic of both the Navy and the CIMA anthropologists for what he saw as their blundering interventions.[24] From this point of view he was perfect for the FSI job, able to communicate with his superiors in the State Department and at the same time to collaborate with anthropologists who were sharply critical of American foreign policy, such as Cora Du Bois, who had just quit the State Department in despair at its policy in Southeast Asia.

Hall found the existing state of FSI's training programmes fairly rudimentary, focused mostly on languages, with the odd lecture on 'understanding foreign peoples' by Kennard or Du Bois. He set about building an integrated four-week training programme for Point IV workers which amounted to America's first official 'two-way interpretation' of culture contact. For this purpose he imported wholesale Ruth Benedict's 'culture and personality' approach to understanding other cultures, supplied with reams of material from RCC by Rhoda Metraux, and called in friends as reinforcement: Du Bois, in a freelance capacity, and her former deputy Claire Holt, still employed at the State Department and now posted to FSI as regional specialist on Southeast Asia; Rhoda Metraux, standing in for Mead herself; it was also planned to bring in John Embree until his sudden death in a car crash.

Most distinctive was Hall's insistence with his American trainees that they had to be culture conscious of themselves as well as of their clients: intercultural training had always to be 'two-way'. As Embree had found in training civil-affairs officers for the Navy during the war, young Americans were initially rather discomfited by this approach – perhaps not reassured by the parallel suggested, that psychoanalysts needed to be psychoanalysed themselves first. To overcome their resistance, Hall began his pioneering studies of the subliminal behaviours that marked out cultures as surely as did language or overt personality traits – matters of tone, gesture, time and space – in order to persuade his trainees how profoundly acculturated their own behaviours were. More unsettling was the trainees' cynical view that Point IV could only be a trick to wean the poor of the world away from communism. Hall, Kennard and Du Bois found themselves defending Truman against the trainees, trying to get across the message that Point IV marked a new era in international relations. In place of 'enforced programs based on European philosophies, degree of economic development, and good intentions', Point IV was basically about 'cooperation and sharing'. This required a rude culture change for diplomatic personnel who, Hall recalled later, 'frequently misunderstood and actively resisted' his line on Point IV and clung to their conventional 'Realpolitik', 'twist their arm, gun to the head' approach.[25] This tension, which reflected the balance of interests represented in Point IV and which probably felt creative at the time, was precarious: it was not clear how long the State Department would tolerate these relativists in their midst.

* * *

With this potential avenue into the American Point IV programme opening up, Mead turned her energies to the UN's TA programmes. She and Larry Frank devised the idea of an all-purpose manual on intercultural relations that could be used by TA personnel from all countries to implement TA programmes 'with proper regard for the existing culture and with as little violence as possible to the folkways of the group concerned', and also to assess 'the changes in living habits resulting from technological development' instigated by these programmes. By the time the UN had funded its new TA programme in mid-1950 she had already secured a commission from UNESCO to write their manual on 'Technological Change and Mental Health'. It would absorb much of her energies over the next year, just at the time when Gorer's withdrawal, the winding-up of RCC and the whole swaddling fiasco made it seem crucial to salvage something valuable from her fading hopes for a new world order.[26]

In fact, the UNESCO manual project provided Mead with one of her few happy experiences in these gloomy years. It marked a return to the conditions she had enjoyed in wartime, where she retained freedom of action, was able to surround herself with congenial characters, and could keep aloof from the skulduggery endemic to the wartime agencies and the postwar State Department. The operation ran out of the Mead-Frank townhouse in Greenwich Village. It was masterminded by a small team composed of Mead, Frank and two of Mead's closest wartime collaborators, Dorothy Lee and Claire Holt; additional assistance was provided by John Embree (before his untimely death), Eliot Chapple, Cora Du Bois and a new acquaintance, Elizabeth Hoyt. Mead was even able to call on the services of Philomena Guillebaud, her wartime ward, now relocated to New York to pursue a degree at Columbia's Russian Institute, to do double-duty as secretary to the manual project and child minder for Cathy.

The thinking and writing that went into the UNESCO manual was highly imaginative for the time, owing largely to the input of Holt and Hoyt and to the freedom that Mead and Frank gave them to think deeply about the implications of 'development'. A warm and engaging Eastern European Jewish émigré whom Mead and Bateson had befriended in Bali, where she was studying dance, Holt had joined Cora Du Bois's OSS R&A unit in 1944, played a full part in Mead's wartime seminar group in Washington and then transferred with Du Bois to the State Department in 1945. Like Du Bois, she had been sadly disillusioned by the latter's 'obsessive preoccupation with communism and anti-communism, which', she wrote in an unpublished paper, as 'the yardstick in practically all foreign affairs, poisons even such great occasions as when Americans, true to their great traditions, could reassert unconditionally their faith in the principles of liberty'. But Holt had no academic credentials to fall back on and, as a single mother, could not as easily abandon her job in the State Department as could Du Bois; she took consolation in providing some of the intercultural training at FSI and jumped at the chance Mead offered to take leave from the State Department and work full time on the UNESCO manual.[27] Hoyt only came to Mead's attention, providentially, at the point at which the manual project was being dreamed up. Hitherto she had been far out of Mead's orbit – trained as an economist, teaching at Iowa State – but she had always been a highly unusual economist, interested in the cross-cultural and psychological dimensions of economic behaviour. After the war she had organized an ambitious field study of the cultural impact of the United Fruit Company on the village of Tiquisate in Guatemala. This brought her into closer contact with anthropologists just at the time when Point IV was being launched. Passing through New York early in 1950, Hoyt spoke about her experiences in Guatemala to a meeting of anthropologists organized by Mead at the Mead-Frank house, and Mead immediately took the opportunity to recruit her as a long-distance adviser to the UNESCO manual.[28]

The core group – Mead, Frank, Lee and Holt – came quickly to a realistic assessment of the complexities of their task. They understood that expertise on culture was only being called for because the economists and technicians were encountering 'resistance' to social and economic change. It was expected, therefore, that they would come up with cultural changes that would reduce 'resistance'. Mead was not unsympathetic to this goal, as she thought the peoples of the world did need higher minimum standards of health, nutrition and education, and probably considerable economic growth, if they were to participate as anything like equals in a new world order. On the other hand, with her belief in cultural holism and integrity, she was not sympathetic to the view that changes in supposed economic 'fundamentals' could or should drive change – a view that, she pointed out, was held in common by capitalist and communist modernizers. Cultural holism held that other aspects of life were in their own way equally important: ideas about community, family, culture, religion, indigenous ideas of rights and freedoms. Change could not be driven by economics alone, nor was economic change the only desirable goal. Non-Western religions, in particular, represented a bundle of values that Westerners had trouble recognizing; Mead complained that the psychiatrists in WFMH tended to see 'mental health' as 'a religion that would replace other religions': '[they] really want to secularize life and [they] really want to destroy all these other systems as wrong and bad and old.' How, then, to reconcile economic development and cultural integrity?[29]

In their discussions, the group considered a range of challenges to cultural integrity posed by economic development that have since been claimed by a later generation as their own discoveries. First, they held that the approach to economic development being advocated by the 'technicians' was itself culture-bound, a reflection of the Western, and particularly American, appetite for 'bigger and better' that was not necessarily shared by other cultures – not by many Asian cultures, nor even by the Greeks, as Holt and Lee pointed out.[30] Mead learned to prick the idea of 'underdeveloped' countries by referring in this period to the 'overdeveloped' West, a usage that became common only much later.[31] It was necessary to proceed slowly and cautiously; not to assume from the start, for example, that recipients wanted anything except basic relief.[32] Holt, in particular, worried about the indiscriminate application of TA programmes to cultures that did not have the 'felt needs' to which TA was supposed to cater; she was thinking of Asian cultures, Hindu and Buddhist, that cultivated 'detachment' and were hostile to 'desire'. In these areas, 'one of the functions of technical assistance is to help governments and their peoples first to feel the need and then to fill it!' In place of this circular logic, she urged that TA be 'unequivocally placed within the limits of the immediately lacking and immediately feasible', eschewing the 'uncautious stimulation of "felt needs"' and sticking at first to programmes 'easily imaginable in terms of local customs'.[33]

Second, the group showed an awareness – here they owed much to Hoyt's work in Guatemala – that capitalist development had a tendency to create its own 'wants' and 'needs', to develop a runaway logic of its own that could wreak havoc with cultural integrity. At Tiquisate, Hoyt had witnessed the effect of high wages on what she called 'want development': new products had to be developed in order to soak up wages in a non-wage economy, and the new products – alcohol, cigarettes, sweetened foods, prostitution – tended to offer immediate gratifications that bore no relation to other sources of satisfaction in the culture. At the same time the new capitalist economy also introduced 'values of display and emulation' to stimulate consumption further in ways that often conflicted with existing patterns. The result was a progressive disequilibrating of the culture where the new satisfactions grew uncontrollably and the old satisfactions shrivelled away. Hoyt thought that these conclusions applied around the world, and Holt, fresh from her experiences of neocolonialism in the State Department, agreed: 'one of the dangers lies in the creation of new wants of the sort that makes American wheels go round.'[34] This kind of critique of 'want development' was very unusual for the time; it is usually associated with work over a decade later, when more radical critiques of 'development' were brewing.[35]

Again, the group was conscious of the American tendency to normalize these 'new wants' and to see them, not as an artificial construct of capitalist development, but as the 'the new "democratic" way of life'. Hoyt pointed out that this way of life was not being democratically chosen or governed by those it affected: 'it is in no sense their community and they have very little chance of becoming a part of it.' Calling it 'democracy' was just not good enough:

> we need to do much more than to preach the virtues of democracy and of private-enterprise capitalism in our centers of foreign employment. The ideology of private-enterprise capitalism, which has a very considerable social value for most of us, is quite uncomprehended by peons, fellaheen and coolies when they first give up their own social system to work under it. We ourselves can plainly see various goals to which private-enterprise capitalism has led and is leading; but for these humble and ideologically inexperienced workers under it private-enterprise capitalism is only a vast power with no points of contact with the social aspect of their lives.[36]

Third, the group also understood that demands for 'development' from intellectuals and elites in the less-developed world couldn't simply be taken as 'democratic' demands either, making the application of TA problematic even under UN programmes that responded to recipient requests. Mead's experience with the debates over the SAA ethics code, which had sensitized her to the need to consult the desires and interests of all parties in a complex social system, and Du Bois's and Holt's experiences with international development, had raised their consciousness of elites' own interests in 'development', often in the face of other people's needs and wishes. As Mead pointed out, the TA world tended to assume that 'democracy' operated everywhere, 'a straight New-Deal ethic with no cross-cultural allowance, and dangerous, too'. In fact, her group realized that in many less-developed countries a Westernized elite 'insist on identifying themselves with the worst elements of our own technicians', out of a 'touchy eagerness to prove themselves' to the West rather than out of a sense of connection to their own culture, which they might well have lost.[37]

How, then, to find out what the people of a culture really needed and wanted? The only solution, the group felt, was to insist on a full-fledged 'social diagnosis' of the needs and wants of the whole of the culture, as the ethics code had suggested. Mead was still using the language of 'equilibrium' that she had picked up from Chapple and the industrial anthropologists, but after the ethics-code debate she recognized better that a range of economic interests was represented in any given equilibrium. It could not be taken for granted that development would preserve or improve that equilibrium: for example, it might 'lead to strengthening exploiting classes'.[38] It was not enough therefore that recipient governments request the aid, as TA programmes required. All parties, down to the local community, had to participate in social planning. Returning to her own New Deal roots, to 'education for choice', Mead concluded:

> The only thing you can do is to involve the people of the country sufficiently in the plan in enough places, in enough ways, working on it, putting it into effect at a local level, at a county level, so that a lot of these difficulties get ironed out. But any suggestion that what we are talking about here of cultural integration, can be made by a plan at the top, is absolutely hopeless. We don't know enough, and no machine that can be made at MIT is going to know enough to take the factors into account at present. The only way you can do it is with the human beings.

Or, in Larry Frank's similar formulation:

> I like to say we have had a planned society, but it wasn't planned by government officials. It was planned by the unseen hand of tradition in people, and today what we have to do is to help them to clarify and reinstate those aspirations and beliefs whereby they can have an orderly society not by authority but by their own way of life.

Their group understood that such a 'social diagnosis' would involve delicate internal questions about land ownership, taxation and social programmes (as the Marxists tended to argue, which, Larry Frank quipped, did not make it wrong); it was not possible, or desirable, for the UN and its agencies to meddle in such questions. On the other hand, it was not the UN's role either to come in and arm elites with expertise to be used against their own peoples. The hope was that, once recipient nations solicited UN TA, the application of social-science expertise would stimulate the extension of 'social planning' at all levels from the UN to the member governments and all the way down to the grass roots, ideally (here a typical Mead-Bateson touch) with 'provision for "feed-back" from an area where any new activity is introduced'.[39]

All of these perspectives were embedded in the UNESCO manual as actually written – mostly by Mead, Holt and Lee[40] – although not as barefacedly as in the group's internal discussions. The significance of cultural integrity was, however, put at the centre of the enterprise, both by titling the manual *Cultural Patterns and Technical Change* – the language of 'mental health' was cut back severely – and by the controversial decision to devote the first half of the manual to depictions of whole cultures, in the manner of *Patterns of Culture*. In its universalist way UNESCO preferred a more cross-cultural approach, stressing commonalities rather than differences between peoples, but Mead lobbied hard for the intercultural approach on which her entire career had been founded and, with support from Alfred Metraux, won the point.[41] The cultures chosen offered a range of reactions, some more negative and some more positive, to 'development'. Burma, written up by Dorothy Lee, gave a very negative view of the impact of British colonialism. Burmese individualism, Lee concluded, had actually been undermined by the decay of 'the inherited unity of a way of life' at family and village level. A similar account was given of the Tiv people of Nigeria under British rule: no wonder the British put pressure on UNESCO to tone the manual down. Greece, also written up by Lee, was an example of a recipient culture that accepted aid under tight conditions, 'when it is their right within a structured relationship'. Finally, the people of Palau in Micronesia represented a happier category of cultures 'which have adapted to the modern world and offer to the individual members means for working out personal adjustments to contemporary life within a traditional framework'.[42]

It was indeed the 'whole cultures' approach that drew the most comment after the manual's publication in 1953 and that may have accounted for its enduring influence. Those who already accepted the importance of cultural integrity were glad to have it acknowledged and defended in this unusual context, normally dominated by the economists; the more gung-ho modernizers, for their part, thought the warnings about cultural integrity would be a disincentive to development.[43] Certainly no one thought at the time that the UNESCO manual was just propaganda for Cold War development.[44] It did exactly the opposite of what 'behavioural science' and modernization theory were supposed to do: instead of disaggregating cultures and identifying 'key points' or 'fundamentals' that could act as triggers for systemic change, the manual insisted on the coherence of cultures and the dangers of forced or unbalanced change.

It could be argued that the 'whole cultures' approach was just a more insidious and devastating way of promoting capitalist development. Modernization theory had its own version of the 'whole cultures' argument, which was that there were necessary psychological and cultural concomitants to economic development without which it could not proceed. But Mead's anthropological holism was not like that. She explicitly rejected the idea that change could or should be driven by economic development, with other aspects adjusted to it. She talked instead of a mutual approach, a need to make development adjust to existing psychological and cultural (and especially religious) forms as much as vice versa. For Mead was of two

minds about 'development'. She worried about anthropologists' sentimen-
talizing hunger and disease and primitive simplicity, she thought less-
developed peoples often did want 'development', and she thought they
would need to learn at least some of the West's tricks to take their place at
the global table. But she did not see 'development' in teleological terms, as
did proponents of an American-style universalism or more evolutionary-
minded anthropologists. Mead's 'whole cultures' approach put greater
emphasis on cultural integrity, and on the need to equip all cultures with
the tools to cope with modernity as much on their own terms as possible.
Many peoples, she saw, were now being faced willy-nilly with the bewildering choices that had faced newly modern Americans in her youth. Now
as then, what such people needed was 'education for choice' in order to
manage, and not simply succumb to, the challenges of modernity. 'Now we
know that it is possible to rear human beings who can nest in the gale,'
she wrote.[45] The tough-minded confrontation between these two sets of
ideals – development and cultural integrity – which characterized the
working and the writing of the manual project produced insights into the
ironies of development that would not be fully realized until the next
generation, which naturally thought it had discovered them for itself.

Mead's manual was not unique. Alexander Leighton at Cornell
produced another – based on his own wartime experiences and his
students' postwar experiences with 'applied anthropology' in the American
Southwest, India, Peru and Thailand – with similar cautions about social
engineering and the need to protect global cultural diversity.[46] Yet
another was prepared by an AAA committee chaired by Conrad Arensberg
to support FSI's intercultural training for Point IV workers, which also
emphasized cultural relativism, with FSI's characteristic insistence on
Americans understanding their own cultural distinctiveness.[47] They are
all evidence of a 'relativist moment' in the early history of TA, when Cold
War imperatives had not yet bitten deep, modernization theory was not
yet triumphant and anthropologists were still relatively free – even in
demand – to offer a more plural understanding of development.[48] But
Mead's UNESCO manual further testifies to the continued importance of
cultural relativism in her own thinking at a time when she is usually
thought to have drifted into a more universalist position; and to her
continuing search for independence from American interests and policy
at a time when she is usually thought to have become a prisoner of 'policy
science'. Unlike the other manuals, this one too had the imprimatur of a
global celebrity which gave it a currency that manuals for develop-
ment-aid workers can rarely dream of, including a puff in the *New York
Times* and a mass-market paperback edition published by Mead's old pal
Victor Weybright under the New American Library imprint in 1955. As

so often, Mead's greatest impact came in the public sphere, among readers and searchers rather than among spooks and wirepullers.[49]

*   *   *

The UNESCO manual project provided, on a smaller scale, the same sense of independent community and warm-hearted idealism that the RCC project had over a longer period. But, just as in the dying days of RCC, Mead had also sought more compromised relationships with RAND and with various military clients during the Korean War, so during the manual project she was simultaneously pursuing a relationship with the State Department on very different terms than she had concluded with UNESCO. This seeking to serve both masters – anthropology and the State, the UN and the US – that characterizes this phase of Mead's career makes her 'true' intentions, her 'real' beliefs, particularly hard to fathom. It arose from her stubborn disbelief in what the CIMA veterans (and, indeed, earlier veterans of operations such as WRA or the civil-affairs training schools) had mostly concluded, that anthropology and 'adminis-tration' simply were not compatible, especially not in a period when the intercultural standpoint of anthropology was increasingly at odds with America's aggressive Cold War universalism. Right up until she left for the field in 1953, Mead continued to hope, against the odds and against the evidence, that gaining a foothold inside the political establishment was better than nothing.

In this final phase, her hopes were paradoxically invested in the State Department – at precisely the time when she was closest to Claire Holt, who was trying desperately to get out of the State Department – and her partner-in-crime was Eliot Chapple, the industrial anthropologist whose partiality to the bosses she had never entirely trusted. Mead's initiative to get SAA involved with training Point IV workers in intercultural tech-niques had also led to a contract between it and the International Moving Picture Division of the State Department, concluded in early 1951, to advise on the production of Point IV propaganda films.[50] This Film Planning Project, directed by Chapple but with much editorial input from Mead, aimed to provide briefing reports on the cultures concerned that highlighted potential problems in intercultural communication. The goals were similar to those of the UNESCO manual – delivering TA without disrupting indigenous culture and social structure, involving local communities in TA by expressing it in terms they could understand and embrace – but the context was much closer to American interests.

The targets were all on the 'crucial periphery' of the emerging Cold War: Iran, Iraq, Greece, Turkey, Southeast Asia, the Philippines. The State Department's initial ideas for the films were about the projection of

America and its values rather than about benefits to recipient countries: 'Films about America which will make America intelligible to and liked by members of other countries', 'concepts' films promoting American values, 'anti-communist quickies'. Of course, Mead tried to tutor her State Department clients in two-way relations:

> *The only goal* which can be overtly stated as a US goal, is to help the people of a country realise their goals, of better food, better ways of life, survival for the newborn, care for the new mother, dignity for the common man, better use of land, more shoes, etc. *But* it must not appear that the US is giving planes, or shoes, or food for babies, because this introduces uncomfortable images of past colonization, dependency and gratitude, but instead the people want the babies to live, have always wanted the babies to live, or the plants to grow better, and the US is sending a few special people, and the national government of the country is sending more special people, to help the people of a given area, realise their ambitions.[51]

Some of the SAA reports to the State Department pursued this line of argument, drawing on the anthropologists' TA manuals. But as they got closer to the frontline of the Cold War, their tenor changed menacingly. Point IV was portrayed as a partnership between the US government and developing-world elites struggling to gain control of their own peoples. 'Nationalism' was encouraged, not to acknowledge national and regional differences as Du Bois and Holt had argued unsuccessfully inside the State Department, but to strengthen developing-world governments for geopolitical purposes.

> It is to the interest of the United States and the United Nations to help these countries become independent and strong rather than to have them become satellites of the Soviet power. Consequently, throughout the whole area, the emphasis must be upon those things which symbolize the unification of the country rather than glorify and, hence, foster its break-up into dissident national elements.[52]

A series of field reports on Indonesia again placed as much emphasis on recruiting village support for Indonesian national-government goals as it did (though it also did this) on the need to respect the integrity of local cultural patterns in promoting TA.[53]

It is hard to tell how much or what kind of influence Mead exerted over these reports. Her attitudes to the SAA project were highly contradictory. Both in private and in public, she could be very critical of Chapple, who shared her desire to bring anthropology into government but not her commitment to cultural pluralism. In a public debate at the height of her collaboration with Chapple, she charged him with ignoring power rela-tions within the systems his applied anthropology addressed. Chapple was quite breezy about working for big business or developing-world govern-ments. Mead pressed him: surely it was his responsibility under the terms of the SAA ethics code to take the whole social system into account, and 'to point out what the human consequences would be of the alternate sets of action'? 'Oh, sure,' Chapple replied expansively, he wouldn't be a very good consultant if he didn't; but neither did he think that unions or local villagers had the broad views or the resources to take advantage of his services, and he didn't feel responsible for any of the consequences:

> The changes are going to take place, anyway; I mean, we at least in the foreseeable future are not in the position of making the ultimate decisions as to whether you put a mine in a particular area or build a whole series of plantations. However, we can say what the consequences of doing it will be. Whether or not somebody takes our advice is something else.[54]

This insouciance set Mead's teeth on edge. She had always felt that above all else the anthropologist advising government had to take personal responsibility for the advice. On the other hand, she had a high opinion of her own ability to make the right moral judgements in these morally ambiguous cases, and she tended to project that confidence on to other anthropologists. As she summed up this period much later:

> although individual anthropologists may work for pay within projects of this sort, sheer professionalism in the invocation of scientific input into national policy should be confined to bureaucrats and administrators . . . There is a need for an element of ethical commitment that goes beyond professionalism; this is essential for the enlistment of the anthropolog-ical community, even when local studies of nutrition, reproductive techniques, and cultural practices leading to soil erosion are concerned.[55]

Thus her suspicion of Chapple's – and the State Department's – partisanship did not impede her in the closing years of the Truman Administration from seeking to deepen the SAA's involvement in the government's TA programmes. Although she preferred multilateral (UN) programmes to bilateral (US) programmes, she was not so particular as to spurn the latter. Neither was she very particular either about how deeply implicated anthropologists got in such programmes. In this headlong period she tended to ignore the boundary between anthropologists as advisers and as administrators that others, especially after the Micronesian experience, were more careful to maintain. Thus, while championing truly multilateral, intercultural approaches at UNESCO and FSI, she also sought with Chapple to extend the SAA's contacts with government, in 1952 contracting for further area briefings for the new Mutual Security Agency (MSA) to assist American penetration into Burma, Indochina, Indonesia, Malaya, the Philippines and Taiwan, and seeking to recruit anthropologists directly to the Point IV field staffs as Assistant Program Officers in the Middle East and Africa.[56]

However, it did not prove possible for her to maintain these contradictory positions – serving both masters, the UN and the US, cultural relativism and American imperialism – for very long. She knew that her deepening commitments to government were losing her the trust of her profession, especially among the young. If she needed evidence, it came plainly in the pathetic trickle of applications for the 'seven good jobs in technical assistance begging for anthropologists' that she had arranged in Point IV. On the other hand, she also knew that the government's patience with her and her kind was flagging. In retrospect she realized that the Korean War really had proved the turning point, away from the genuinely multilateral world for which she had been hoping, though she had kept plugging away through 1951 and 1952.[57] Cora Du Bois had already pulled her troops out of the State Department. In 1951 Truman had only been able to secure renewal of Point IV by subordinating it to MSA, with its blunter military and business agenda. This made it harder for people like Ned Hall at FSI to sell Point IV as a genuinely intercultural programme: it was rapidly losing its distinctive identity.[58] But the *coup de grâce* came with the fall of the Democrats in the election of 1952. Eisenhower's mistrust of longhairs and his preference for military men and businessmen led to a further reorientation of foreign-aid programmes towards US military and business interests, which made intercultural education (it was thought) superfluous. The relative latitude given internationalists in the Truman Adminstration now collapsed, and McCarthyite suspicions of 'outsiders' with knowledge of the non-Western world were unleashed. Even FSI guest speakers had to be put through a gruelling security clearance, conditions, complained Claire Holt, that 'transcend the limits of decency and sanity', and that finally triggered her resignation in December 1953. Then the call came from on high, Ned Hall remembered: 'clean out the anthropologists.' He was interrogated by security goons and fired.[59] Although some people who happened to be trained as anthropologists remained on Point IV field staffs, their role as anthropologists in policy formation and programme development came to an end.[60]

How dire the situation was is indicated by the fact that even the usually pragmatic Eliot Chapple unleashed a scathing indictment of what he called 'the liquidation of Point IV' in the SAA's journal in the autumn of 1953. Subordination to security needs had been bad enough.

> The activities of MSA had the dramatic quality and the political appeal of a direct attack against communism. It was building plants to manufacture war materials as well as channeling such materials to our allies. This program contrasted greatly with one whose primary concern was to help the poor peoples in the under-developed areas of the world help themselves . . . MSA operated on the simple principle that in return for its cooperation it expected military assistance and political allegiance in the struggle against communism. However justified this conception might be, it was clearly far removed from the philosophy of Point Four which did not require people to choose sides.

But the final straw for Chapple had come with the Republicans' philistine repudiation of the expertise that anthropologists had to offer.

> In the name of business efficiency, the top planning staff and many of the operating heads in the various regions have been fired – people with years of painfully-acquired experience in this type of activity – and are being replaced by retired businessmen and by retired military officers . . . It is not enough to sit on the sidelines and say 'A fool and his money are soon parted.' The difficulty is that as citizens, as well as scientists, we cannot avoid feeling a sense of direct responsibility for the conduct of our government, particularly where its relationships to other countries of the world are concerned.[61]

Mead, too, had felt strongly that sense of responsibility. At this point she finally joined the other refugees and more or less abandoned her efforts of the past fourteen years to bring anthropology to government. In the summer of 1953, as Chapple was composing his broadside, she decamped to New Guinea, truly returning to her 'natives'.

* * *

Mead had been contemplating a return to the field since the autumn of 1950, as RCC began to wind down and the swaddling debacle showed her which way the wind was blowing. The Korean War gave her pause: it would make fieldwork difficult, and it also showed that international relations were still so critical that her presence was needed closer to the centres of power. Furthermore, she knew it would be a few years until she was ready to leave her eleven-year-old daughter for an extended period. But she also knew that her credibility as an anthropologist was dwindling, and that to restore it she needed 'to get back to my own kind of work again'. Her frustrations came out at the same international conference where she had lashed out at Chapple for his bias towards the powerful. She wanted the audience to know that she had abandoned the natives only reluctantly, her hand forced by the international situation:

> we are in a very unstable world situation in every respect today ... information organized nationally appears to be useful; but if somebody would guarantee that everything would stay nice and comfortable and no research would be needed for the next twenty-five years, I would not touch national character for the next twenty-five years, because I think it is more important to go back to New Guinea.[62]

Why New Guinea? At first she had been undecided between attempting a new study – an Australian aboriginal culture, for example – or tackling a restudy in New Guinea.[63] A lecture tour to Australia with Cathy in autumn 1951 had clarified the situation. But it was not Australia that captured her attention – it was the Manus, the people whom she had studied with Reo Fortune for *Growing Up in New Guinea*. Word came to her in Australia of extraordinary changes among the Manus, triggered by the upheavals brought on by the Second World War and particularly by the one million American troops who used the Admiralty Islands as a staging base for operations against the Japanese. Her Australian informants told her that, far from being completely disordered by this unprecedented incursion from the outside world, the Manus had organized themselves in a series of dramatic movements: first, 'The Noise', a movement combining Christian revivalism and a 'cargo cult', a mass destruction of indigenous goods and a fetishization of imported Western products; second, a political movement led by a man from the nearby island of Baluan named Paliau, calling for something like representative democracy for all the peoples of the Admiralty Islands. Paliau's struggle was finely poised at the time when Mead heard about it in Australia. This seemed an opportunity too great to be missed, and from this point on Mead's energies were focused on organizing a return to the Manus.[64]

Before she left – before putting behind her fourteen years of hard labour on international relations that seemed to have ended badly – Mead tried to work out her frustrations in the best way she knew how: by writing a book. This was one last effort to rally Americans behind a responsible engagement with the wider world, 'a sort of Latter Day *And Keep Your Powder Dry*', just as the abortive 'Learning to Live in One World' had been a few years earlier.[65] This 'Latter Day Book' was entitled, tentatively, 'Stars for Our Wagons: An Anthropological Study of America in the 1950s', after her favourite Emerson characterization of the idealistic Americans, always seeking to hitch their wagon to a star. The themes are familiar from previous efforts: how to engage Americans' interest in the world for the good of all, to play on their strengths but dodge their weaknesses, to develop an ethic that would commit but not overcommit American power, 'stated in terms of *responsibility*'. She was aware that America had moved on considerably from 1942; the issue was not whether America would commit, but how. How would Americans react 'in the most new and uncongenial position of having responsibility greater than our power, power greater than we wish, and dependence upon what happens at other centers over which we have no power whatsoever'? Here the anthropological tools of cultural relativism were as urgently needed as ever. Americans needed to be culture conscious of themselves, and of their differences from others. The peoples of Germany, Russia, India, China and Japan are *not* 'just like us'. There was a lesson here for internationalists, but also for Cold Warriors: 'those who feel a genuine surge of fellow feeling for the human beings who all over the world are being tyrannized, liquidated, degraded, beaten and shot and starved to death . . . are compromised by a demand that those who sympathize should be just like themselves, made in the image of Americans so that Americans may fitly give their lives in their behalf.' Neither internationalism nor liberation could be achieved without a due estimate of the cultural patterns that make all the people of the world so deeply and nearly indelibly what they are.[66]

There is an elegiac tone to the fragments of the manuscript that Mead completed. It was framed autobiographically: 'Why I am writing this book before returning to the field.' 'The anthropologist, trained in the primitive laboratory, ready for return to that laboratory to test out each new and promising hypothesis, is specially fitted to keep more alternatives open, to keep us from freezing our future sooner than we must.' She hoped that while she was gone the Americans would not lose their own open-mindedness about international relations, which she had stayed at home for more than a decade in order to shore up. The book was a kind of babysitter, to be left behind to keep her own people on the right course while she left to explore the lives of others. But she could not be in two places at once, even in this figurative way. A bout of ill-health caused the book to falter in late 1952, and she never returned to it. Once she had recovered in the new year, she had to prepare for departure. In June 1953 she returned to the field for the first time since 1939.[67]

*   *   *

It is a little artificial to end an account of Mead's engagement with inter-national relations with her departure for Manus. As the babysitter book suggests, she did not intend this spell of fieldwork to mark the end of this chapter in her life. What had attracted her in the stories she had heard about the Manus in Australia was that they seemed to be weathering the 'gale' of modernity well, in a way that suited them but that would also please the Americans. The story that she then came to tell about the Manus was 'a parable', aimed not at unsettling Americans (as her prewar ethnographies had aimed to do) but at reassuring them, that others could adapt to the modern world in ways that Americans approved and yet preserve 'their sense of identity and dignity'.[68] She had always found the Manus to be like Americans in their almost Protestant sense of striving and conscience, 'acting as if they were catching subways right on the equator, and dying of hypertension or something very like it at forty'. Although she had not liked this very much in 1928, it was a useful quality in 1953.[69] The Manus had proved to be good Protestants too in facing up to the pressures of 'development' and embracing them as their own. Mead did get caught up in the romance of modernization here, hymning rapid adaptation to changing conditions over the virtues of cultural integrity in terms that she had just been criticizing in the UNESCO manual. There she had defended 'whole cultures'; now she felt that 'whole cultures' were unaffordable luxuries in the face of poverty, disease and the imminent disfranchisement of millions of people in the non-Western world. The Manus, at least, were using their 'whole culture' to choose modernity and thus to enfranchise themselves.[70] Never mind that the young couple that she had brought along with her to help with the fieldwork, Ted and Lenora Schwartz, didn't see the story at all that way. It was the story Americans needed to hear.[71]

Though Mead did not intend the field trip to the Manus to spell the end of her adventures in international relations, in practice it did. The world she had wanted to build, a world in which Americans could be persuaded to engage with myriad other cultures in some kind of rough equality, had been receding even from the most hopeful field of vision since the late 1940s, and Mead could not allow herself to pretend other-wise long after her return from the Pacific at the end of 1953. The mani-festo for self-determined modernization that she produced from her fieldwork, *New Lives for Old: Cultural Transformation – Manus, 1928–1953*, failed to capture the imaginations either of anthropologists or of Mead's mass-market audience. The anthropologists did not want a parable for Americans, and the mass market did not need one. Many Americans already believed that other people were 'just like us', and Mead's account of how they had become that way by their own methods lacked the excitement of the more bracing 'others' she had offered before the war. Mead would never again attempt to appeal to this audience with the literary type of first-person ethnography that had made her reputation.[72]

Nor was she able to rebuild her political connections. Those professional associates who had shared her commitment to government work under Truman had all dispersed to academia or the private sector. Cora Du Bois had joined the Harvard faculty in 1954; after his purge from FSI, Ned Hall set up a private-sector consultancy, Overseas Training and Research Inc., and became a bestselling author of works on intercultural communication; Claire Holt, despite her lack of academic credentials, got a Rockefeller grant in June 1955 to do Indonesian research for Cornell University, and became a mainstay of Cornell's celebrated (and radical) East Asian Studies programme.[73] After the dissolution of the RCC team, without an academic base and without Benedict to connect her to Columbia, Mead had no students with whom to rebuild either – she had only her general reputation as the most famous anthropologist in America, and that she had imperilled by pushing her adventures in US foreign policy further than most of the young would go.

Although many social scientists, especially economists and political scientists, took up modernization theory in this period as a new way to inject their expertise into international relations – and influential Democrats around John F. Kennedy proved receptive – Mead, in common with most anthropologists, did not do so. Her brief love affair with modernization, intimately connected to her field experiences among the Manus people in 1953, faded away quickly, as she saw that fundamental principles of anthropological relativism and cultural integrity were incompatible with modernization theory. Instead, in the late 1950s she began to forge for herself a new, more diffuse kind of authority. Rather than seeking to lead anthropologists into government – now, she saw, an impossible task – she worked to develop the role in which she had always had most success, that of an all-purpose cultural commentator, a moral muse, an advice columnist to the nation and the world. As Nancy Lutkehaus has observed, she began to coin her famous 'Meadisms', oracular aphorisms on the whole gamut of cultural issues ranging from race and sex to the generation gap and nuclear war, retailed through a barrage of women's-magazine columns, radio and TV appearances, and testimony before Congress.

In this final phase of her career, lasting until her death in 1979, she gave up the attempt to keep her credibility with both academic anthropology and with the highest circles of government: she did without either, and became instead 'mother (later, grandmother) to the world'. The overreaching of the immediate postwar period was forgotten outside narrow disciplinary circles. Mead once again became one of the best-known women, and one of the most celebrated social scientists, anywhere in the world; but her ambitious attempt to bring anthropology to international relations had ended in failure. As one of the few anthropologists remaining in government put it, while Mead's name and reputation were 'familiar to most Western diplomats', her field had become 'more of an after-coffee outlet for intellectual curiosity than a serious source of concepts for foreign affairs problems or for helpful approaches to the psychological dimension of public diplomacy'.[74]

* * *

Did Margaret Mead, then, lose the Cold War? She thought so. In a series of retrospectives, she compared unfavourably and bitterly the peak of influence that she felt she had won for anthropology at the end of the Second World War with the gradual throttling of that enterprise by the early 1950s. From the sunnier uplands of the mid-1960s, she looked back on the 'dismal' 1950s, full of 'apprehension and apathy'.[75] At different times she blamed different culprits. Although she knew on some level that it had been 'the Joseph McCarthy era and the Korean War' that had put paid to her ambitions, 'when everybody inside the government who could have used the new material or insights that anthropologists could have produced went home or got fired', she could not stop herself from blaming everyone else as well – everyone who lacked her vision and her gumption to stick it out. 'By 1952, there was no one in the government to ask for information of the sort anthropologists would have provided or to use it if it had been provided.' But, she added: 'Even if the government did ask us, we were not sure we were going to tell them what we knew.'[76]

Anthropologists had not only been chased out of government, she felt, they had also scampered away of their own accord. She contrasted the full-blown internationalism of her own Second World War generation with the self-centred apathy of the young. As early as 1955 she complained about a 'new isolationism'. After a brief period from 1945 when Americans had shown signs of 'becoming integrated into the world', they were now becoming obsessed with their own 'identity', that newfangled word that Erik Erikson had helped to popularize.[77] It was bad enough that young Americans in general had become such navel-gazers, but for young anthropologists it meant abandoning the peoples that Boas had taught her needed them the most. They had been bribed by the new treats available in the burgeoning academic world of the baby-boom era: 'A great many young men and women wrote their dissertations, their three short papers, did a few reviews, presented a paper or so, and went on to a tenured appointment with very little opportunity to show their mettle.' Even fieldwork went out of fashion: it was too messy, too time-consuming. The young preferred the mind games of Claude Lévi-Strauss's structuralism – which involved making pretty patterns from field data gathered by other people on rituals and symbols and kin relationships – to the laborious business of gathering field data themselves.[78]

Mead's frustrations – and her indomitable self-belief – prevented her from admitting what in some lucid moments at the end of her life she appreciated (and which other anthropologists knew well), which was that the Cold War had simply squeezed out what enthusiasm had remained in America for cultural relativism.[79] She had been more willing than most to serve the two masters – the pluralist and internationalist vision of 'orchestrated cultural diversities' on the one hand, US foreign policy on the other – but in the end she, like most anthropologists, was unwilling to subordinate the former completely to the latter, and had to accept (if not always to admit) defeat. Unsurprisingly, she had not been able to direct American energies in the world along lines compatible with cultural pluralism, to get Americans to 'hitch their wagon to the star' of a cooperative world of equals that she had tried to sketch in her abortive books of 1945 and 1952. Instead, American foreign policy in the 1950s became ever more robustly universalist on an American model, as Eisenhower at least paid lip service to an ideological war for the 'liberation' of captive peoples under communism, and Cold War military and political imperatives increasingly drove aid to the developing world – 'a bribe, to keep the peoples of other countries on our side against communism', as Mead mourned in January 1955, like 'setting up school lunch programs, not to feed children but to dispose of surplus agricultural products'.[80]

What made matters worse is that the liberal opposition to Eisenhower's utilitarian foreign policy had also shed the remnants of its New Deal pluralism and committed itself to varieties of democratic universalism. Among social scientists, this democratic universalism increasingly took the form of modernization theory, which posited a single path to modernity on an American model and plotted out the policy moves necessary to help other countries follow it. Modernization theory attracted a liberal following, both among intellectuals and among Democratic politicians, because it counterposed a humanitarian concern for mass hunger and poverty in the 'underdeveloped' world to Eisenhower's apparently more self-interested concern with American business and military interests. To employ Mead's analogy, it was in favour of setting up school-lunch programmes to feed children *and* to bribe them against communism. For this reason it could be seen as a more effective and insidious way of promoting American interests around the world.[81]

Although the modernization project was centred on a set of economic universals – an apparently inevitable evolution towards 'industrial society' with its characteristic urban and factory institutions – there was plenty of room for other social sciences to join in to show how specific social, cultural and psychological behaviours would, or could, be made to accompany changes in economic organization.[82] But as in the case of Sovietology, and again in social-scientific discussions of TA, there was a crucial divide between those behavioural scientists who wished to align society and culture with economic modernization, and those who upheld cultural difference for its own sake, either as a wholesome barrier to modernization or as a vector for different paths to modernity than that laid down by the American model. It is no coincidence that one of the principal intellectual architects of modernization theory in the 1950s and 1960s was Alex Inkeles, who in the early 1950s had advanced a 'psycho-cultural' analysis of the Russians that suggested they were on the road to modernization, against Mead and Gorer's analysis which he felt greatly exaggerated the Russians' cultural and psychological difference. Now, at the other end of the decade, he was making much stronger statements about the ability of modernization *everywhere* to override cultural difference: 'the same situational pressures, the same framework for living, will be experienced as similar and will generate the same or similar response by people from different countries . . . its force is sufficently great to assert itself clearly despite the countervailing influence of personal idiosyncracy [*sic*] and traditional cultural ways of thinking and feeling.'[83]

Such statements were a deliberate provocation to Inkeles's old relativist adversaries who had upheld the 'countervailing influence' of 'traditional cultural ways of thinking and feeling'. To be sure, anthropologists were not immune to the appeal of universalism themselves. It was impossible to speak about 'the brotherhood of man', as anthropologists had traditionally done in order to argue against racial distinction, without making some bottom-line appeal to humanity. Mead adopted this language also to encourage Americans to reach out to the world, as it was a language for which she thought they had a special affinity. Christina Klein, describing Cold War Americans' encounters with Asia through middlebrow sources such as the musicals *South Pacific* and *The King and I*, calls this 'pluralistic universalism', 'differences among the world's peoples as evidence of cultural variety within a larger human sameness'.[84] Like Mead, many anthropologists further acknowledged their historical tendency to romanticize 'traditional cultural ways of thinking and feeling', and regretted this where it impeded efforts (including by the peoples themselves) to address poverty and disease. There was undoubtedly a renewed interest in this period in large-scale processes of change, as the 'simple, homogeneous' cultures in which the early Boasians had specialized were broken up by a wide variety of forces linked to 'modernization'.[85]

None of this, however, made anthropologists convert en masse to a single (still less an American) road to modernization, as was more evident in other social-science disciplines. To equate the 'pluralistic universalism' of Cold War modernization with the Boasian project, as Klein does, is to collapse some of the distinctions that were most important to contemporaries. 'I do not know why,' Ruth Benedict had written in *The Chrysanthemum and the Sword*, 'believing in the brotherhood of man should mean that one cannot say that the Japanese have their own version of the conduct of life and that Americans have theirs.'[86] The thrust of Mead's UNESCO manual, as with other anthropological contributions to TA of the period, was to try to combine cultural integrity with economic development, for example, by charting *different* paths to modernity. For her, UN programmes were 'more compatible with the practice of the brotherhood of man' than US programmes like Point IV precisely because 'we who wish to help and they who need help meet in an equality of interest and dignity' rather than in an unequal relationship.[87]

There was something almost in the DNA of anthropology that made this so: the long-established Boasian sense of loyalty to 'their' peoples, but also the impulse that Mead and Benedict had pioneered to show cultural diversity to Americans for their own good as well as the good of others. This was particularly true of the 'culture and personality' school that Mead and Benedict had established, which showed that 'culture' was highly various and resistant to engineering by modernization or other non-cultural forces, because so deeply embedded by infant and child training, education and socialization processes across the life cycle. But it was also true of anthropology more generally. The whole history of the discipline, as Cora Du Bois put it in 1967, was 'less inclined to be time and culture bound' and 'rarely deterministic', in contrast to the 'ethnocentric' and 'discipline-bound' economists and sociologists. Thus anthropology in her view 'should bring to bear on modernization in the contemporary world a more nearly culture-free, relaxed and perceptive comprehension of the world of rapid change in which we live than is now generally entertained by many scholars, policy makers and practitioners'.[88] These primary loyalties made anthropology peculiarly uncongenial to the US government's policy goals, as the few government officials charged with recruiting social-science expertise in the 1950s and 1960s repeatedly regretted.[89]

Anthropology boomed in the 1950s and 1960s, along with universities generally and the social sciences in particular. As late as 1947–8 only twenty-four PhDs in anthropology were granted anywhere in the United States; the equivalent figure in 1974–5 was 445.[90] It thus did become more 'academic', as Mead fretted. But this had highly various intellectual and political effects. Whereas in Mead's youth there were only a handful of mentors such as Boas and Lowie, and only a handful of competing schools, for the rising generation there were many centres, many supervisors and a much wider world in which to work. Cora Du Bois, on her return to academia in 1954, was surprised to find how far 'specialized fragmentation' had already gone.[91] There were, as we have noted, new interests in very abstract processes, as in Lévi-Strauss's structuralism, and in long-term processes of change, as in the neo-evolutionary tendencies. There were a few flirtations with modernization theory, and also some freelance (and normally covert) work for government in the field, but also experiments in 'action anthropology', in which anthropologists, also in the field, sought to defend indigenous peoples against the forces of modernization – a trend that Mead welcomed, though she still felt it a paltry substitute for influence in the upper echelons.[92]

More broadly, there was also a new scepticism about 'culture' as a thing or a coherent whole, as Mead and Benedict had seen it. This scepticism would have been engendered anyway by a growing awareness of the pace of change. But Mead could not see that her own adventures in 'national character' had profoundly deepened that scepticism. Her overreaching – going beyond hypotheses about intercultural relations, based on ideas about how relationships were formed within cultures, to grandiose ideas about 'national character', seeking to apply techniques honed on small, homogeneous cultures to large, complex ones – brought discredit on the techniques themselves. What Alistair Cooke had said of Gorer on the Americans ('It makes you wonder if it's true what they say about the Trobriand Islanders')' the critic Bernard de Voto also said of Mead on the Americans: 'The more anthropologists write about the United States, the less we believe what they say about Samoa.'[93] Such reservations resonated widely. 'Diaperology' sent up warning signals across the 1950s in both the corridors of power and the groves of academe. There is a general consensus now that Mead's 'return from the natives' to the complex, modern cultures put an end to the 'culture and personality' tradition even as applied to simple, homogeneous ones. There remained only a very marginal strain of 'psychological anthropology'.[94] But this did not, as Mead alleged, put young anthropologists off the 'natives', or off fieldwork; it only encouraged a modest, perhaps humbler, approach. Instead of studying 'whole cultures', young fieldworkers made more particularistic studies, often rediscovering older anthropological interests such as kinship or ritual. They also developed a more conceptually sophisticated idea of 'culture', not as something solid and palpable, easily conveyed from one generation to the other (or from informants to observers), but rather as something more fluid, changeable, requiring constant reconstruction and reinterpretation. This may have made anthropology less 'political' – less useful for mediating between cultures, or conveying knowledge of one culture to another – but it also made it intellectually more respectable.[95]

Epilogue
To Vietnam, Iraq, Afghanistan

If Margaret Mead did lose the Cold War – if her own attempts to influence international relations were brought to an end by the Cold War, and
in fact her imbroglio with the Cold War lost her influence in the wider
anthropological community – why then have so many of the post-
Vietnam accounts of her and her discipline's history asserted the opposite?
Why has Mead got a reputation as a Cold Warrior, and why are anthropologists today so keen to assert their discipline's complicity with American
imperial interests in the postwar decades? The answer is, of course, that
after the depoliticization of the 1950s anthropology experienced a repo-
liticization in the 1960s, on a quite different basis. This made even recent
history look very different. A sudden revulsion was felt, especially as
American involvement in Vietnam escalated, against America's global
impact. Now *any* complicity with such involvements began to look
suspect.[1] The modern research university itself appeared to be an integral
part of America's imperial ambitions, fuelling them with linguistic skills
and area expertise once considered neutral. In this analysis, the very existence of area-studies and language programmes on a huge scale had armed
the American military and political establishment with capabilities for
more global adventures. This now seemed to implicate anyone doing
social-scientific research outside US borders, whatever the nature of their
activity or politics.[2] Suspicion was rife that people involved in the study
of sensitive areas – which included all of Latin America, Africa and Asia,
precisely the places where anthropologists traditionally worked – were
also colluding with more explicitly political projects such as 'counterinsurgency' techniques, that is, culturally informed military and propaganda
work, whether they were or not.[3] When American military involvement
in Southeast Asia escalated over the course of the 1960s, these sensitivities rose to a furious pitch, and even the most innocent ethnographic
activity seemed liable to horrific misuse. As Mead herself noted with
alarm, 'a publication of routine socio-cultural data about identified village
communities . . . might be used for the annihilation by bombing or other
forms of warfare of whole communities'.[4]

Anthropologists' anxieties about their complicity in war waged by 'their' government against 'their' peoples broke out into the open in the mid-1960s after government again resumed active attempts to recruit their expertise. Kennedy's administration was not so averse to 'longhairs' in government as had been Eisenhower's. 'Counterinsurgency' strategies to fight communism, which combined traditional military techniques and development aid with 'local knowledge' to stabilize client states and undermine 'insurgency', were back in vogue. Egged on by modernization theorists, who thought developing countries needed special protection against communism before they 'took off' into Western-style economic growth, the Kennedy administration reached out to social scientists to help them with counterinsurgency programmes in sensitive areas such as Latin America and Southeast Asia. Although the US military remained resistant to techniques that threatened their own traditional areas of expertise, the development agency AID and the Defense Department's research wing ARPA were both interested in programmes that combined military and economic assistance to client states, and by the mid-1960s Defense was spending about $5 million a year on mostly contracted-out social-science research in support of such programmes.[5]

As the Defense Department's special assistant for counterinsurgency found, anthropologists would prove to be 'the first, the loudest, and the harshest against their colleagues undertaking work for government agencies having operational concerns overseas'.[6] Two incandescent public controversies in this period proved this to be so. The first was the exposure in 1965 of Project Camelot, an Army project cooked up in 1963 to predict the effects of social change, principally in Latin America, and to develop counterinsurgency techniques to deal with them. The project was mostly the work of sociologists and psychologists, though a few anthropologists also participated, one of whom, Hugo Nutini, was responsible for the project's collapse when he was found to be lying about its Army links to Chilean scholars. A huge outcry broke out across the social sciences about the ethics and politics of such a venture, but it was only the AAA that took the opportunity to question 'the very foundation of the bond between behavioral science and government'. Concerned not only about ethics but also about the practical effects of clandestine operations in impeding fieldwork, it launched a special commission of enquiry and concluded with a series of resolutions in 1967 condemning 'both involvement in clandestine intelligence activities and the use of the name of anthropology, or the title of anthropologist, as a cover for intelligence activities'. An ethics committee was set up and discussions began about the AAA following the SAA in adopting an ethics code. In the Department of Defense view, these resolutions 'effectively prevented most anthropologists from participating in work for the DOD'.[7]

A year later some research files kept by an anthropologist, Michael Moerman, were stolen and papers leaked to the AAA ethics committee revealing what 'seemed to be plans for counterinsurgency activities in Thailand'. Another outcry, another special commission of enquiry, this one headed by Mead herself. Desperate to keep the profession united, her report condemned the war, acknowledged the new ethical challenges posed by government determination to channel ethnographic work into 'counterinsurgency', and exonerated Moerman and other anthropologists associated with the Thai projects, who had all denied supporting counter-insurgency efforts. The problem, she concluded, referring back to her own earlier work for intercultural relations which had been sold to government as 'intercultural communications' or 'mental health', was the stealthy repurposing of intercultural work for counterinsurgency uses by govern-ment, 'a pervasive corruption of the life of the scholarly community in its relations with the government' that had led to uses of anthropological data that anthropologists themselves could not condone. But the report also criticised the ethics committee for 'hastily, unfairly, and unwisely' using the purloined documents to make public condemnations. In a feverish midnight debate at the ensuing AAA convention in November 1971, Mead's recommendations were overwhelmingly rejected. Many people had concerns about the theft, but these were greatly outweighed by concerns about any imputation of complicity in counterinsurgency, however remote. Instead of accepting Mead's report, the AAA in 1971 formally adopted an ethics code modelled on the one that Mead had helped to draft for the SAA in 1949, asserting the paramount responsi-bility of anthropologists to 'those they study', taking into account 'the social and cultural pluralism of host societies', the need to consider 'the foreseeable repercussions' of their research and incorporating the ban on 'clandestine and secret research'.[8]

In these debates, Mead's wartime work on national character began to be seen as the beginning of the slippery slope that led to counterinsur-gency in Southeast Asia, even though Mead had first grappled with the implications of this kind of engagement through the ethics code and then, like most anthropologists, had got off the slope in the 1950s. This reinter-pretation intensified greatly after her death in 1979. Her reputation was badly hit in any case by a quite separate controversy, kicked off by a right-wing physical anthropologist from Australia named Derek Freeman, who in some vividly publicized exposés accused her of systematically distorting her evidence from Samoa to support a Boasian fantasy of free love in the South Seas. Authority figures of all kinds were being knocked off their perch anyway in this period. But Mead got it from both ends of the political spectrum, as right-wing critics of her interwar progressivism were joined by left-wing critics of her postwar collusion with US imperialism. From the 1980s right up to the present moment, a steady stream of 'revisionist' histories of anthropology's involvement in the Cold War has made a direct and close connection between Mead's work in the 1940s and counterinsurgency in the 1960s. Mead, it seemed, had not only lost the Cold War, but she had lost the Vietnam War too.[9]

Mead's wartime experiments still cast their shadow. In recent years US military intervention in Iraq and Afghanistan has led to renewed attempts to recruit area specialists, including inevitably anthropologists, to inform counterinsurgency campaigns. The AAA has again publicly repudiated these efforts to enlist the name of anthropology behind counterinsurgency. Mead's precedents have again been cited as instructive, although this time not by the opponents of counterinsurgency – who seem to have backed off somewhat, accepting the limits to anthropological involvement in the Cold War[10] – but by its advocates. Citing the Second World War work of Mead, Benedict and Gorer among others, a few lonely voices advocating for anthropology inside the military have spoken wistfully of a 'tradition of military-academic cooperation' that has lapsed and needs urgently to be revived.[11]

None of these analysts, looking backwards from the present moment – neither those who regret Mead's experiments in international relations in the 1940s and see them as unfortunate precedents for the Cold War uses of social science, nor those who celebrate Mead's experiments and regret that they had so few Cold War successors – adequately appreciates the difficulty of the tasks that Mead took on, going forward from the 1930s. She was working not in a post-Vietnam world, at a period when the US was arguably taking too much interest in other people's business, but in a prewar world where it was arguably taking too little interest. Her goal was to bring to bear on the relations between a world of nations the insights she had gleaned from her understanding of 'simple, homogeneous' cultures in the Pacific. She had to persuade Americans to take enough interest in the world even to recognize the value of anthropological expertise. Along with many others of an internationalist bent, she also had to work to persuade Americans to join an initially unpopular war against fascism. She then had to persuade wartime officials to hire anthropologists for tasks relevant to their expertise.

Under pressure of the emergency but also of her own ambitions for her discipline, she tried to develop anthropological ideas about complex, modern cultures of which she and other anthropologists knew little – not only American and English cultures, where she had a head start, but also the Germans and the Japanese. In doing this, she argued that anthropologists knew something that economists, sociologists and political scientists did not, which led her to underrate the contributions those disciplines could make to her own analyses. She had to grapple with the ethical challenges raised by psychological warfare and by developing techniques the 'bastards' could use in causes less worthy than the Second World War. If she was an architect of the SAA, she was also an architect of the SAA's ethics code, which served as a model for the AAA's Vietnam-era code. When the war was over, she sought to widen her remit to cover all of the world's cultures, hoping that the 'orchestration of cultural diversities' would form the basis for a new international order. She discovered long before the 1960s the social and cultural problems that what she called 'overdevelopment' brought to the allegedly underdeveloped world, and tried to work out ways that TA could be conveyed without violating the cultural integrity or political equality of recipient peoples. She tried to persuade her younger colleagues to stay in the game of applied anthropology when all they really wanted to do was to get back into the field or win tenure. She wrestled with the challenges of working for government within the terms of the ethics code and of her own personal ethics, at a time when the early Cold War was putting severe pressure on the internationalism for which she hoped. As she felt the opportunities for the 'orchestration of cultural diversities' around the world slipping away around 1950, she made mistakes – intellectual ones, as in the swaddling controversy, and ethical ones, in brief flirtations with secret work or psychological-warfare work that violated her own principles. Ultimately, after 1953, she found her prewar hopes for a role for anthropologists in international relations, as honest brokers between cultures, to be unrealizable – Cold War governments didn't want honest brokers, and anthropologists didn't believe they could play that role – and, bitterly, she abandoned the attempt.

The lessons she learned from that hard work have not, however, gone unregarded. The tests of anthropological method and principle that Mead underwent, and the intellectual and ethical principles developed to meet them by the post-Vietnam generations, have served them as guides. But Mead's 1940s experiences may hold a promise as well. It is no part of this book to argue for anthropological engagement with US military and foreign policy in the twenty-first century: I, too, am a member of the post-Vietnam generation and if I were an anthropologist I would be joining those who warn against professional betrayals of informants and professional engrossment of academia by government. As a historian, however, I know that the world will continue to change, and that in future it may not only be a self-interested American government that needs anthropologists' help in addressing relations between the peoples of the world. Any future attempt at 'learning to live in one world' on a genuine basis of equality and diversity will benefit from anthropologists' participation, and, in thinking about whether and how to contribute to that endeavour, anthropologists – and the rest of us – will benefit from pondering the lessons Margaret Mead learned in those turbulent mid-twentieth-century years.

Notes

Introduction: Return from the Natives

1. Handler, 'Boasian Anthropology and the Critique of American Culture', esp. 267.
2. See Hollinger, 'Cultural Relativism', 709.
3. 'Margaret Mead Today: Mother to the World', *Time*, 21 Mar. 1969; 'Grandmother to the World', *New York Times*, 16 Nov. 1978.
4. Lutkehaus, *Margaret Mead*, 211.
5. Endleman, 'The New Anthropology', 286, coined the phrase in 1949; it was taken up elsewhere, for which see below, pp. 212–19.
6. For some examples of these direct connections, see Price, *Anthropological Intelligence*, xiii, 264–6, 281; Price, 'Cold War Anthropology', 390–3, 396; Nader, 'The Phantom Factor'; Fabian, *Time and the Other*, 46–9; di Leonardo, *Exotics at Home*, 196–8, 224; Hegeman, *Patterns for America*, 159, 167–9; Engerman, *Modernization*, 273–6; Ferguson, 'Anthropology and its Evil Twin', 160–1; Lemov, *World as Laboratory*, 190, 218–19, 245–6.
7. On Mead, there is still no better biography than Jane Howard, *Margaret Mead: A Life* (1984); on Benedict (with or without Mead), we now have, in chronological order, Modell, *Ruth Benedict* (1983), Caffrey, *Ruth Benedict* (1989), Lapsley, *Mead and Benedict* (1999), Banner, *Intertwined Lives* (2003), Young, *Ruth Benedict* (2005).

Chapter 1 From the South Seas

1. Jean Houston, 'The Mind of Margaret Mead', 10–11: Mead Papers, Q18.
2. Metraux (ed.), *Margaret Mead*, 170.
3. Mead to Martha Ramsay Mead, 20 May 1926: Caffrey and Francis (eds), *Selected Letters*, 15–16.
4. Jean Houston, 'The Mind of Margaret Mead', 34: Mead Papers, Q18.
5. Bateson, *With a Daughter's Eye*, 85–90.
6. Gary, *Nervous Liberals*, esp. 2–7; Bannister, *Sociology and Scientism*, 4–9; Graebner, *Engineering of Consent*, 8–10; Ross, *Origins of American Social Science*, esp. 305–19; Purcell, *Crisis of Democratic Theory*, 16–37 (more sensitive to diversity); Jordan, *Machine-Age Ideology*, 4, 6, 24; Lemov, *World as Laboratory*, 4–7, 34–45.
7. Jean Houston, 'The Mind of Margaret Mead', 10–11: Mead Papers, Q18; Mead to Benedict, 30 Aug. 1924: Mead, *Anthropologist at Work*, 285.
8. Banner, *Intertwined Lives*, 173–4.
9. See the excellent discussion in Igo, *Averaged American*, esp. 39–42, 65–6; also Smith, *Social Science in the Crucible*, 133–8.
10. Mead to Daniel Lerner, 3 Jun. 1951: Mead Papers, C24; see also Bannister, *Sociology and Scientism*, 171–9; Caffrey, *Ruth Benedict*, 119–20; Gilkeson, *Anthropologists and the Rediscovery of America*, 39–42.
11. Lemov, *World as Laboratory*, 7.
12. Smith, *Politics and the Sciences of Culture*, 109–10.
13. See, for example, di Leonardo, *Exotics at Home*.
14. This argument is made effectively by Liss, 'Patterns of Strangeness'.
15. Patterson, *Social History*, 53–62.
16. See the discussions in Mead, *Anthropologist at Work*, 11–13; Caffrey, *Ruth Benedict*, 120–8; Kuper, *Culture*, 60–6.

17. Darnell, *And Along Came Boas*, 274–90, 294–6, and *Invisible Genealogies*, 44, sees these developments as natural extensions of Boas's own teaching, though she also emphasizes the students' frustration with Boas's 'extremely specialized' teaching.

18. Mead, *Anthropologist at Work*, 203–5; Gilkeson, *Anthropologists and the Rediscovery of America*, 35–9.

19. Caffrey, *Ruth Benedict*, 270.

20. Interview with Cora Du Bois by Lawrence C. Kelly, 9 Apr. 1978 (2nd, corrected, draft), 6: Du Bois Papers, Box 11; Patterson, *Social History*, 64–5.

21. Mead, *Anthropologist at Work*, xvii–xviii.

22. Ibid., xviii.

23. On the differences as well as the similarities between Mead and Benedict's idea of 'culture and personality', and Sapir's, see Darnell, 'Personality and Culture', and LeVine, 'Culture and Personality Studies'. Banner, *Intertwined Lives*, ch. 7, gives a full account of the personal and intellectual relations between Sapir, Benedict and Mead at this time.

24. Lapsley, *Mead and Benedict*, 191–3.

25. Jean Houston, 'The Mind of Margaret Mead', 435–6: Mead Papers, Q18.

26. See also Handler, 'Vigorous Male and Aspiring Female', for a slightly different (but complementary) analysis of the gender differences entailed here.

27. Sapir, 'Culture, Genuine and Spurious', esp. 312–14, 318–19, 324–5, 330.

28. Benedict to Mead, 16 Oct. 1932: Mead, *Anthropologist at Work*, 325.

29. Caffrey, *Ruth Benedict*, 169.

30. Mead to Benedict, 30 Aug. 1924: Mead, *Anthropologist at Work*, 285; and see also ibid., 4–7.

31. Modell, *Ruth Benedict*, 109–11, 118.

32. See e.g. Boas's foreword to Mead, *Coming of Age*, xiv–xv.

33. Mead, *Anthropologist at Work*, 13–14.

34. Mead, *Coming of Age*, 1–5.

35. Mead, *Blackberry Winter*, 127–32.

36. Mead, *Coming of Age*, 196–200.

37. For the classic example of the right-wing critique, see Freeman, *Margaret Mead and Samoa*; for the left-wing critique, see di Leonardo, *Exotics at Home*, esp. 164–83.

38. Mead to Daniel Lerner, 3 Jun. 1951: Mead Papers, C24; Lutkehaus, *Margaret Mead*, 86–7.

39. Mead, *Coming of Age*, esp. 200–23, 246–8.

40. See Lutkehaus, *Margaret Mead*, 86–94, 102–3, 127–8, for a thoughtful analysis of the reception of *Coming of Age*.

41. A.L. Kroeber, review of *Growing Up in New Guinea*, *American Anthropologist* 33 (1931), 248–50; this review of Mead's second book looked back to the first as well in order to generalize about her method.

42. Mead, *Blackberry Winter*, 292–3. You don't have to take such statements completely at face value to see nevertheless that the kind of 'laboratory' envisaged here is not *just like* the kind sought by 'a classic Progressive social engineer': cf. di Leonardo, *Exotics at Home*, 170–2.

43. The book was also published immediately in Britain, and interestingly – given Mead's future interest in intercultural communication – revised so that the analogies with 'our' culture were made with British rather than American references.

44. Mead to Daniel Lerner, 3 Jun. 1951: Mead Papers, C24.

45. Mead, *Growing Up in New Guinea*, 6–7, 160–6.

46. Mead, *From the South Seas*, xiii.

47. Mead, *Growing Up in New Guinea*, 202–3.

48. Ibid., 3–5, 175–6, 196–7.

49. Ibid., 205, 209.

50. Howard, *Margaret Mead*, 137–8.

51. Mead, *Letters from the Field,*, 108; Mead, *Sex and Temperament*, 253–9.

52. Mead, *From the South Seas*, xix–xxi; Mead, *Blackberry Winter*, 198–9, 205–6.

53. Mead, *Sex and Temperament*, 165.

54. Ibid., 290–309.

55. Mead to Benedict, 31 Jul. 1932: Mead Papers, S3.

56. Benedict, *Patterns of Culture*, 12–16, 46–50, 223–4. For excellent discussions of the genesis and orientations of *Patterns*, see Banner, *Intertwined Lives*, ch. 10, and Modell, 'Benedict's Concept of Patterns Revisited'.

57. See Kardiner and Preble, *They Studied Man*, 211, 244–5, for Kardiner's criticisms.
58. See below, p. 19.
59. Benedict, *Patterns of Culture*, 52–3, 78–9.
60. Ibid., 228–9.
61. Ibid., 17, 53–5, 229–30.
62. Ibid., 251–76.
63. This was the version Fortune gave to his brother Barter, but Fortune told Bateson's biographer David Lipset that he had sent his copy straight back to Benedict. Jane Howard interview with Barter Fortune, 17 Mar. 1981: Jane Howard Papers, Box 38; Lipset, *Bateson*, 137. Howard herself chose to believe the gentler version: Howard, *Margaret Mead*, 164.
64. Bateson, *Naven*, 2. Although Radcliffe-Brown was one of the mentors against which Bateson was chafing here, in fact Radcliffe-Brown had been sympathetically prodding Benedict to improve her own conception of 'ethos' at the same time. See Mead to Benedict, 13 Aug. 1931; Benedict to Mead, 19 Aug. 1931: Mead Papers, S3; and cf. *Naven*, 26–30.
65. On the 'squares', see Banner, *Intertwined Lives*, ch. 11, and the very insightful analyses of Sullivan, 'A Four-Fold Humanity' and 'Of Feys and Culture-Planners'. For Mead's awareness of the difference between the 'squares' and Benedict's patterns, Mead to Bateson, 4 Oct. 1935: Mead Papers, R2.
66. On New Deal employment of anthropologists, see Patterson, *Social History of Anthropology*, 80–6.
67. On this theme, see Gleason, *Speaking of Diversity*, 156–67; Wall, *Inventing the 'American Way'*, 65–72.
68. Cf. Graebner, *Engineering of Consent*, 189; Bannister, *Sociology and Scientism*, 222–4, 236–7; Gary, *Nervous Liberals*, 26–9; Jordan, *Machine-Age Ideology*, esp. 78, 176–8, 225–31; Purcell, *Crisis of Democratic Theory*, esp. 191–5, gives a more complex picture, while still emphasizing the 'objectivist' position.
69. Smith, *Social Science in the Crucible*, draws attention to the 'purposive' counterattack against 'objectivity' with special attention to Robert Lynd; and cf. Mead's own statement of 'purposiveness' in *Growing Up in New Guinea*, 167.
70. On the Murphys, and the connected work of Gordon Allport, see Pandora, *Rebels within the Ranks*.
71. See Stears, *Demanding Democracy*, chs 2–3, for a more nuanced understanding of the democratic dilemmas of 'purposive' expertise, to which I am much indebted.
72. Mead, *Anthropologist at Work*, 347–9.
73. Benedict, *Patterns*, 271–2, 278.
74. Modell, *Ruth Benedict*, 204–8; Modell, 'Patterns Revisited', 225–8. Cf. Hegeman, *Patterns for America*, 97–103, who more or less accepts this diagnosis, but in my view understates the significance of Benedict teaching about *others* as well as about Americans: thus she is endorsing cultural relativism between cultures but not ethical relativism within her own culture.
75. For the influence of the 'culture and personality' work of Sapir and Benedict on other social scientists, see e.g. Smith, *Social Science in the Crucible*, 34–6, 154–6; Pandora, *Rebels within the Ranks*, 100–5; and on the broader influences of Boasian cultural anthropology, Ross, 'Changing Contours of the Social Sciences', 223, 228; Handler, 'Boasian Anthropology', 267–9; Gleason, *Speaking of Identity*, 156–9; Purcell, *Crisis of Democratic Theory*, 65–72.
76. Mead to Benedict, 20 Jul. 1931; Mead to Frank, 21 Jul. 1931: Mead Papers, S3, R8.
77. Bryson, *Socializing the Young*, 11–13; Lemov, *World as Laboratory*, 61; Herman, *Romance of American Psychology*, 35–6, 122–3; Graebner, *Engineering of Consent*, 130–5; Cross, 'Designs for Living', 797–9, 891–3. There is a tendency in these works to suggest that the undemocratic tendencies implicit in this kind of expertise *deepened* in the 1930s, and a real reluctance to see any possibility of democratic amelioration: see Bryson, *Socializing the Young*, 100–11; Lemov, *World as Laboratory*, 67, 73–4; but cf. Jordan, *Machine-Age Ideology*, 208, 266–75, and Brick, *Transcending Capitalism*, ch. 3.
78. Frank, 'Social Problems' (1925), in *Society as the Patient*, 20.
79. Frank, 'Society as the Patient' (1936), in ibid., 1, 6, 7–8.
80. Helen Lynd, Interview #909, 80: Oral History Research Office, Columbia University.

81. Although there is little sign of the 'machine process' or similar in his writings of the 1930s, see Frank, 'Mental Security' (1937) and 'The Reorientation of Education' (1939) for essays that have a more normative tone and clearly put the expert above the people, in *Society as the Patient*, 226–38, 239–52.

82. 'Cultural Coercion and Individual Distortion' (1939), in ibid., 166–92; 'Dilemma of Leadership' (1939), in ibid., quotes at 319, 322; see also 'Freedom for the Personality' (1940), in ibid., 197, 205–6, and 'The Cost of Competition' (1940), esp. 31–4, where he explicitly condemns 'the rules of the legal-economic game' for coercively suppressing individuality and talks about the creative and democratic possibilities of culture in terms heavily influenced by Benedict; and see also Fromm, *Escape from Freedom*, 61, on his debt to Frank.

83. See, for example, Cottrell and Gallagher, 'Important Developments', 121–2, for a very different understanding of the phrase 'society as the patient'.

84. Mead and Bateson to C.H. Waddington, 29 Mar. 1938: Mead Papers, O2.

85. Frank, 'Social Problems' (1925), in *Society as the Patient*, 15, 19–20.

86. Darnell, *Sapir*, 332–44; Darnell, 'Personality and Culture', 167–71; Bryson, *Socializing the Young*, 167–72; Gilkeson, *Anthropologists and the Rediscovery of America*, 123–5. For Frank's own diagnosis of its failure, see Frank to Mead, 'Re Yale Seminar on Personality & Culture', n.d. (1957?): Mead Papers, B5; and see also Benedict to Mead, 4, 10 Mar. 1933: Mead Papers, B1.

87. Bryson, *Socializing the Young*, 172–5; Houston, 'The Mind of Margaret Mead', 468–9: Mead Papers, Q18.

88. Little has been written about 'neo-Freudianism' as a movement, but see an important early statement, Birnbach, *Neo-Freudian Social Philosophy*, and, more recently, McLaughlin, 'Neo-Freudianism as a Case Study', and Gitre, 'The Great Escape'. Orthodox Freudians are inclined, of course, to marginalize these 'heretics' in their own accounts, but Hale, *Rise and Crisis of Psychoanalysis*, provides a balanced view, esp. 50–3, 124–40, 173–8, 232–42, and see also Zaretsky, *Secrets of the Soul*, esp. 231–7, 250–1.

89. Abram Kardiner, Interview #590, 171–3: Oral History Research Office, Columbia University.

90. Darnell, 'Personality and Culture', 163–71; Mead, 'Retrospects and Prospects', 123–9; Friedman, *Identity's Architect*, 134–62; Sullivan, 'A Four-Fold Humanity', esp. 198–202.

91. Graebner, *Engineering of Consent*, 129–39; Bryson, *Socializing the Young*, 100–19, 149–58; but cf. Selig, *Americans All*, for a different perspective.

92. See, for example, the discussion of Harold Lasswell in Smith, *Social Science in the Crucible*, 223–45, and Birnbach, *Neo-Freudian Social Philosophy*, ch. 7.

93. This remained true in *Sex and Temperament*, ch. 18, which argued that sexual 'deviance' in American society had much to do with the overprescriptiveness of sex norms.

94. Mead, *Blackberry Winter*, 183; Lapsley, *Margaret Mead and Ruth Benedict*, 274.

95. Smith, *Social Science in the Crucible*, 233, makes the distinction between those like Lasswell who sometimes seemed more interested in adjusting the individual to society, and those like Dewey and Lynd who wanted society to change; see also Banner, *Intertwined Lives*, 296–9, 309. But those who wanted society to adapt can just as easily be charged with counterrevolutionary social engineering: see Bryson, *Socializing the Young*, 110–11, 152–5, 161–5. After all these academic critiques it is almost impossible to imagine what *would* be a democratic form of social science.

96. And in fact some of those who did worry about American 'authoritarianism' attributed it to capitalism along more or less Marxist lines – notably Erich Fromm, notwithstanding Mead's euphemistic labelling of him as 'Weberian': Mead, 'Retrospects and Prospects', 131–2.

97. 'Minutes of Meeting, Commission on Secondary School Curriculum', 11–12 May 1935; 'General Criticism', n.d. [late 1935]: Mead Papers, E107. These critiques came out of Mead's work with the Progressive Education Association's Commission on the Secondary School Curriculum, alongside Helen Lynd and Carolyn Zachry among others. The final report did incorporate some of Mead's recommendations on acknowledging diversity and cultivating 'education for choice' – Thayer, Zachry and Kotinsky, *Reorganizing Secondary Education*, e.g. 13–16, 163–74, 333–5, 348–9 – but Mead did not feel it had properly taken on board her critique. Mead to V.T. Thayer, 10 May 1939; Thayer to Mead, 15 May 1939: Mead Papers, E108.

98. Mead, 'An Anthropologist Looks at America', Progressive Education Association, Philadelphia, 21 Feb. 1941: Mead Papers, E108.
99. See e.g. Zachry's embrace of Mead's argument that culture consciousness represented the minimum level of 'adjustment' to the culture necessary 'in order to be able to participate in satisfying ways and to be able perhaps to change it': Zachry, 'Contributions of Psychoanalysis', 98. Mead did acknowledge a place for 'a large amount of stereotyped automatic social responsibility', something she probably got from Bateson (see below, pp. 59–60), but only to free more psychic energy for individual choice. Mead, 'Report to the Committee on the Social Studies of the Commission on the Secondary School Curriculum', 26 Oct. 1935: Mead Papers, E107.
100. A tendency in Hegeman, *Patterns for America*; Molloy, *On Creating a Usable Culture*; and Gilkeson, *Anthropologists and the Rediscovery of America*.
101. Mead, *Sex and Temperament*, 310–22; and see also Mead, 'On the Institutionalized Role of Women', challenging Dollard's culturally specific assumption that the dominance of women in the family was by definition a maladjustment.
102. Mead, *Sex and Temperament*, ix.
103. Caffrey, *Ruth Benedict*, 248–53; Banner, *Intertwined Lives*, 342.
104. This was a project that began in 1935, funded by the National Research Council at Sapir's urging, and that involved Fromm and Horney as well: see Benedict Papers, Box 20/7; Darnell, 'Personality and Culture', 174–7.
105. Mead (ed.), *Cooperation and Competition*, esp. v–ix, 1–14, 509–11.
106. Mead to Bateson, 4 Oct. 1935; Bateson to Mead, n.d. [c. Oct. 1935]; Mead to Bateson, 9–10 Jan. 1936; Mead to Benedict, 14–20 Oct. 1938: Mead Papers, R2, R3, S1, B1.
107. Gregory Bateson, 'Psychology and War: Tendencies of Early Man', *The Times*, 13 Dec. 1934; see also Grafton Elliot-Smith, 'Psychology and War: Primitive Man', *The Times*, 20 Dec. 1934, and Gilbert Murray to Bateson, 15 Dec. 1934: Mead Papers, O1.
108. Bateson, *Naven*, 2–3, 29–34, 118–19 and, on the debt he owed to Mead and Fortune, 258, 265–6.
109. Ibid., 25–6, 32–3, 109–17.
110. Ibid., 171–8.
111. For some later criticisms of Bateson on the 'naven', suggesting that he read the 'naven' through his belief in the significance of relational contexts rather than vice versa, see Gewertz, *Sepik River Societies*, 222–32, and Houseman and Severi, *Naven*, esp. 16–24.
112. Bateson, *Naven*, 119–22.
113. Ibid., 178–95; in this section Bateson considers individual (psychiatric) as well as social and political malfunctionings of schismogenesis, which formed the basis for his later work on the 'double-bind' diagnosis of schizophrenia.
114. Bateson, 'Culture Contact and Schismogenesis', 70–2; Bateson, *Naven*, 196.
115. Bateson, *Naven*, 266.
116. Bateson to Mead, 4 Sep. [1935], n.d. [Oct. 1935], referring to the bombing of Adowa, n.d. [Oct. 1935], referring to Justin Blanco White and Lloyd George, n.d. [Dec. 1936], before Christmas, and n.d. [Dec. 1936], after Christmas: Mead Papers, R3. Amber Blanco White – the original of the heroine of H.G. Wells's *Ann Veronica* – was a leading feminist, writer and educator, the mother of Bateson's friend Justin Blanco White (about to marry one of his closest friends, the biologist C.H. Waddington).
117. Bateson to Mead, n.d. [Oct. 1935], referring to the bombing of Adowa: Mead Papers, R3.
118. Mead to Gorer, 25 Jan. 1938: Gorer Papers, Box 91; Mead to Bateson, 14 Dec. 1935: Mead Papers, S1; Gorer, *Himalayan Village*, 29–31; Lipset, *Bateson*, 82, 84.
119. What follows draws on the analysis developed in Mandler, 'Being His Own Rabbit', which also adduces further material on Gorer's psychological and anthropological thinking.
120. Gorer, *Bali and Angkor*, 56–7.
121. Gorer, *Nobody Talks Politics*, 215; Gorer, *Bali and Angkor*, 101; Mead to Gorer, 15 Jul. 1942 (photocopy): Jane Howard Papers, Box 37.
122. Gorer, 'Notes on the Way', 752.
123. Gorer, *Hot Strip Tease*, 20–4.
124. Gorer, *Bali and Angkor*, 104; Gorer to Mead, 27 Jan. 1939; Mead to Bateson, 9–10 Jan. 1936: Mead Papers, B5, S1; see also Gorer, *Himalayan Village*, 448–9; Gorer, *Exploring English Character*, 292.

125. Gorer, *Bali and Angkor*, 52; Mead to Gorer, 20 Aug. 1936; Gorer to Mead, 5 Sep. 1936; Mead to Gorer, 1 Oct. 1936; Gorer to Mead, 16 Oct. 1936: Mead Papers, B5; see further Mandler, 'Being His Own Rabbit'.

126. Gorer, *Nobody Talks Politics*, 218.

127. Mead to Daniel Lerner, 6 Jul. 1951: Mead Papers, C24.

128. Mead to Benedict, 30 Jan. 1937, 22 Nov. 1938: Mead Papers, S4, B1. Part of Mead's diagnosis here was that Gorer was very self-conscious about his outsider status as a 'deviant' and as a Jew, and that this encouraged 'opinionatedness and exhibitionism'.

129. Mead to Bateson, 3, 9–10 Jan. 1936; Mead to Gorer, 31 May 1936; Mead to Daniel Lerner, 6 Jul. 1951: Mead Papers, S1, N5, C24. Among other indications, Mead's sign-off in her letters to Gorer shifted from 'yours' on 31 December to 'lovingly' on 15 January – for her, a telling choice.

130. Mead to John Dollard, 23 Sep. 1936; Mead to Gorer, 4 Dec. 1936, 4 Apr. 1937: Mead Papers, N5; Mead to Gorer, 1 Oct. 1936; Gorer to Mead, 16 Oct. 1936: Mead Papers, B5.

131. Gorer, *Hot Strip Tease*, 3–5.

132. Mead to Gorer, 15 Jan. 1936: Gorer Papers, Box 91; Gorer to Mead, 7 Jan. 1936, n.d. [mid-Jan.? 1936]: Mead Papers, R8, B5.

133. Benedict to Mead, 26 Mar. 1936; Gorer to Mead, 23 Apr. [1936]; Mead to Gorer, n.d. [late 1951/early 1952]: Mead Papers, S5, B5, S6. See also Banner, *Intertwined Lives*, 344–5, for a slightly different interpretation of their relationship.

134. For debates among social scientists over the domestic implications of 'totalitarianism', see Alpers, *Dictators, Democracy*, esp. 60–156, and Purcell, *Crisis of Democratic Theory*, 181–212.

135. Mead, *Anthropologist at Work*, 347–9; Caffrey, *Ruth Benedict*, 286–93; Modell, *Ruth Benedict*, 247–53.

136. Young, *Ruth Benedict*, esp. 78–81.

137. Benedict to Mead, 7 Apr. 1939: Mead Papers, B1.

138. Mead to Benedict, 5 Apr. 1939: Mead Papers, B1.

139. Kardiner had begun the seminar at the New York Psychoanalytic Institute before Linton's arrival, in conjunction with Cora Du Bois; Linton took over from Du Bois when he came to New York (during a period when Du Bois was doing fieldwork in Indonesia), and brought it to the Columbia department.

140. Cottrell and Gallagher, 'Important Developments', 118, 120–1, 132; Honigmann, 'Personal Approach', 306–11; Barnouw, 'An Interpretation', 66; Hall and Lindzey, 'Psychoanalytic Theory', 171; Cole, *Ruth Landes*, 187–8.

141. Though in fact Du Bois mistrusted Kardiner, and got him to convey the funds via Benedict to Columbia so that she would not be dependent upon him. Interview with Cora Du Bois by Lawrence C. Kelly, 9 Apr. 1978 (2nd, corrected, draft), 12: Du Bois Papers, Box 11.

142. It is certainly not true, as Kardiner felt, that Mead and Benedict's growing interest in parent-child relations was learned from Kardiner: it was clearly rooted in the Hanover seminar and Mead's close relations with other neo-Freudians such as Dollard, Erikson and Fromm. Cf. Manson, *Psychodynamics of Culture*, 85–7; and see the exchange between Mead and Kardiner in *Science*, 25 Dec. 1959, 1728, 1732.

143. For Kardiner's very jaundiced views of nearly everyone (including Linton), see Abram Kardiner, Interview #590, 281–303: Oral History Research Office, Columbia University.

144. Benedict to Mead, 7 Apr. 1939: Mead Papers, B1.

145. Lemov, *World as Laboratory*, 108–43; see also Darnell, 'Personality and Culture', 167–74; but cf. Bryson, *Socializing the Young*, 138–40, 155–8, making no distinction between the Dollard and Mead approaches. For Mead's protests against the 'frustration-aggression' hypotheses, see Mead to Dollard, 23 Aug. 1937; Dollard to Mead, 8 Oct. 1937: Mead Papers, N5.

146. Gorer to Mead, 14 Feb., 29 May, 20 Aug. 1936: Mead Papers, B5; Gorer to Benedict, 16 Jun. 1936: Benedict Papers, Box 28; Mead to Dollard, 26 Jul. 1936: Mead Papers, B1.

147. Mead, 'Notes for Geoffrey Gorer', n.d. [Jan. 1936]; Mead to Benedict, 3 Apr., 28 Sep. 1938; Mead to Gorer, 5 Apr. 1939: Mead Papers, B5, B1, B7; Mead, review of Gorer, *Himalayan Village*, *Oceania* 9 (1938–9), 351–3.

148. Mead to Gorer, 4 Dec. 1936: Mead Papers, B5.

149. Mead to Gorer, 4 Apr., 12 Oct. 1937; Mead to Dollard, 20 Jan. (1939): Mead Papers, N5.

150. Gorer to Mead, 17 Feb. 1937: Mead Papers, B5.
151. Mead to Gorer, 16 Aug. 1937: Mead Papers, N5; Gorer to Eric Blair, 17 Aug. 1937: Orwell Papers, Letters to Orwell I; Gorer to Mead, 18 Nov. 1938: Gorer Papers, Box 91.
152. Gorer to Mead, 20 Oct. (1937): Mead Papers, R8.
153. Gorer, *Himalayan Village*, 431–51.
154. Mead to Benedict, 14–20 Oct. 1938; Mead to Gorer, 17, 20 Oct. 1938; Gorer to Mead, 27 Jan. 1939: Mead Papers, B1, R8, B5; Mead to Gorer, 16–17 Jan. 1939: Gorer Papers, Box 91; see further Mead, review of Gorer, *Himalayan Village*, Oceania 9 (1938–9), 351–3.
155. Mead to Dollard, 3 Dec. 1937; Dollard to Mead and Bateson, 10 Jan. 1938: Mead Papers, N5. In *Himalayan Village*, 29–31, Gorer had expressed his debt to *three* 'inspiring teachers', that is, Mead, Benedict and Dollard.
156. Gorer to Mead, 24 Jun. (1938): Mead Papers, B5 (misfiled as 1936); Mead to Gorer, 6 Aug. 1938: Mead Papers, R8;
157. Gorer to Mead, 24 Jun. (1938); Gorer to Mead, 27 Aug. (1938); Benedict to Mead, 28 Aug. 1938: Mead Papers, B5, B1; Gorer to Mead, 18 Nov. 1938: Gorer Papers, Box 91.
158. Mead to Gorer, 20 Oct. 1938: Mead Papers, B5.
159. Mead, *Letters from the Field*, 183 (21 Jun. 1936).
160. Mead to Boas, 29 Mar. 1938, in ibid., 227; see also Mead to Jeanette Mirsky, 7 Apr. 1937: Mead Papers, N5.
161. Mead to Helen Lynd, 6 Feb. 1937; Mead to Gorer, 6 Aug. 1938: Mead Papers, N5, R6.
162. Mead to Dollard, 23 Sep. 1936; Mead to Helen Lynd, 6 Feb. 1937; Mead to Erich Fromm, 28 Mar. 1937: Mead Papers, N5. 'Fey' was another term from the language of the squares, its sense close to the word's colloquial meaning.
163. Mead to Gorer, 1 Oct. 1936; Gorer to Mead, 16 Oct. 1936; Mead to Gorer, 17, 20 Oct. 1938: Mead Papers, B5, R8. Sex again came into the equation: Gorer had had a higher estimate of the Balinese because he saw their artistic creativity as a good use of psychic energy, whereas Mead deplored their relegation of love and sex.
164. Sullivan, 'Of Feys and Culture Planners'; see also Yans-McLaughlin, 'Science, Democracy, and Ethics', 198. Cf. Newman, 'Coming of Age', 53, which connects Mead's analysis to 'the racist formulations of evolutionary anthropology'; Graebner, *Engineering of Consent*, 130–5, 189; Lemov, *World as Laboratory*, 133–43. Mead herself made the point – against Gorer – that aggression didn't seem to be the crucial factor in determining whether a 'primitive' culture could successfully resist Western cultural imperialism, as witness the independent but non-aggressive Balinese: Mead, review of Gorer, *Himalayan Village*, Oceania 9 (1938–9), 351–3; and see further Bateson, 'Frustration-Aggression Hypothesis'.
165. Mead, *From the South Seas*, xxiii–xxxi.
166. Benedict to Mead, 15 Nov. 1938: Mead Papers, B1; see also the helpful comments by Pandora, *Rebels within the Ranks*, 159–61.
167. Bateson to E.J. Lindgren, 16 May 1937: Mead Papers, O1.
168. Mead to Benedict, 11 Jan. [1938]: Mead Papers, B1.
169. Young, *Ruth Benedict*, 83–4.

Chapter 2 Culture Cracking for War: I. Allies

1. Mead to Daniel Lerner, 6 Jul. 1951; Mead, *Blackberry Winter*, 249; Bateson to E.J. Lindgren, 27 Apr. 1940: Mead Papers, C24, O2.
2. For his early thinking on zygogenesis, see Bateson to Benedict, 23 Nov. 1937; for its application in wartime, Bateson to Mead, 27 Oct. 1939, and esp. Bateson to Mead, 17 Nov. 1939: Mead Papers, S1, R3.
3. Bateson to E.A. Benians, 20 Sep. 1939: Mead Papers, O2. See also 'Extract from a Letter from Gregory Bateson to F.C. Bartlett', 31 Dec. 1939: Mead Papers, F3, for 'clean' propaganda suggestions aimed at neutralizing the Germans' assumed preference for complementary relationships.
4. Bateson to Mead, 30 Sep. 1939: Mead Papers, O2; Bateson's impression is confirmed by McLaine, *Ministry of Morale*, 142. Bateson's overtures to MOI were made through the Cambridge psychologists F.C. Bartlett and J.T. MacCurdy, who were acting as expert advisers to MOI.
5. McLaine, *Ministry of Morale*, 217, 232.

6. Tom Harrisson to Gorer, n.d.: Gorer Papers, Box 85; Gorer to Mead, 6 Sep. 1938: Mead Papers, B5. Nick Hubble suggests that Bateson's *Naven* had been an early (though 'diminishing') influence on M-O: *Mass Observation*, 60–1, 130.
7. Bateson to Mead, 15 Oct. 1939: Mead Papers, S1.
8. Mead, *Blackberry Winter*, 252–4. It does not appear as if Bateson had made a firm decision to return until early January, however.
9. Bateson to Mead, [3] Jan. 1940; Bateson to Lloyd Free, 4 Mar. 1940: Mead Papers, S1, R3.
10. Gorer told Mead that 'they are encouraging everyone – I don't know how that is qualified – to stay who can – can meaning financially and whose immigration is in order, I fancy', suggesting that there might, indeed, have been a financial difference between Gorer's and Bateson's positions. Mead to Bateson, 8 Sep. 1939; Mead to Priscilla Rosten, 30 Sep. 1939: Mead Papers, S1, A19.
11. For the Hollywood study, see Rockefeller Foundation Archives, RG 1.1, Series 200R, Box 200, Folder 2400, Box 201, Folder 2402, and for the Communications Seminar, Boxes 223–4; and Gary, *Nervous Liberals*, ch. 3, Buxton, 'Marshall and the Humanities', and John Marshall, Interview #1013, 323–9: Oral History Research Office, Columbia University.
12. Mead to Bateson, 30 Sep. 1939: Mead Papers, S1.
13. Gorer to Mead, 27 Jan. 1939, 14 Sep. 1940: Mead Papers, B5, R8.
14. Mead to Daniel Lerner, 6 Jul. 1951: Mead Papers, C24.
15. Gorer to E.C. Olsen, 30 Oct., 15 Dec. 1941; Olsen to Gorer, 26 Aug. 1942, packed with innuendo about their 'suspicious' allegiances and 'inclinations': Gorer Papers, Box 96. On Olsen, see Lehmann, 'Erling C. Olsen'.
16. Mead to Bateson, 30 Oct. 1939: Mead Papers, R3.
17. Purcell, *Crisis of Democratic Theory*, 181–95, 200–12; Stears, *Demanding Democracy*, ch. 4; and see also Kleinman, *A World of Hope*, 131–40.
18. Purcell, *Crisis of Democratic Theory*, 218–22.
19. Gary, *Nervous Liberals*, 91–9. Lynd's view of Gorer was that he was just an opportunist trying to get more money for 'a nice movie research program'. Robert Lynd to John Marshall, 23 Aug., 9 Dec. 1939: Rockefeller Foundation Archives, RG 1.1, Series 200R, Box 223, Folder 2672.
20. 'Research in Mass Communication', Jul. 1940, and 'Needed Research in Communication', n.d.: Rockefeller Foundation Archives, RG 1.1, Series 200R, Box 224, Folder 2677; Gary, *Nervous Liberals*, 105.
21. The phrase 'beyond relativity' comes from an unpublished manuscript of 1942, 'Ideologies in the Light of Comparative Data', in Mead (ed.), *Anthropologist at Work*, 384–5.
22. On this phase in Benedict's life, see Modell, *Ruth Benedict*, 247–66; Caffrey, *Ruth Benedict*, 309–18; and esp. Young, *Ruth Benedict*, 78–84, 92–8.
23. Margaret Mead, review of Geoffrey Gorer, *Himalayan Village*, *Oceania* 9 (1938–9), 351–3; Mead to Gorer, 5 Apr. 1939; Mead to Bateson, 30 Oct. 1939: Mead Papers, B7, R3; Benedict, 'Synergy', 328, 332; Mead, 'The Arts in Bali', 346–7; Bateson, 'Frustration-Aggression Hypothesis'; Mead, 'Not Head-Hunters, Nor Appeasers, But Men', *New York Times Magazine*, 30 Nov. 1941, pp. 3, 29.
24. The manuscripts of five of the six lectures have been rediscovered and analysed by Young, *Ruth Benedict*; Benedict published one lecture in the *Atlantic Monthly* in 1942, and some notes for the series were published in 1970 with an introduction by Mead as Benedict, 'Synergy'.
25. Benedict, 'Synergy', 325–30; Benedict, 'Ideologies in the Light of Comparative Data', 'Primitive Freedom', esp. 395–6, in Mead (ed.), *Anthropologist at Work*, 384–5; Benedict, *Race and Racism*, 162–3.
26. Benedict, *Race and Racism*, 163.
27. Ruth Benedict, review of Erich Fromm, *Escape from Freedom*, *Psychiatry* 5 (1942), 111–13. Mead was still arguing for 'education for choice' in 1941; 'An Anthropologist Looks at America', Progressive Education Association, Philadelphia, 21 Feb. 1941: Mead Papers, E108.
28. Mead to Daniel Lerner, 6 Jul. 1951: Mead Papers, C24.
29. Sproule, *Propaganda and Democracy*, 131, 168–70, 180–2; Finison, 'Psychological Insurgency', 30; Allport and Veltfort, 'Social Psychology and the Civilian War Effort', 166–7; Mead to

Frank, 14 Oct. 1940; Memorandum, 'Society for Study of Personality and Culture', 25 Nov. 1940: Mead Papers, E126; Gerhardt, 'Parsons and the War Effort'.

30. Lipset, *Bateson*, 161–2, 166.
31. 'Minutes of the Meeting of the Sub-Committee on American Social Structure of the Morale Committee', 23 May 1941: Parsons Papers, HUGFP 42.42, Box 1; Parsons to Hartshorne, 29 Aug. 1941: Parsons Papers, HUGFP 15.2, Box 3.
32. Bateson to Horace Kallen, 4 Jun. 1940: Mead Papers, O2.
33. Bateson, 'Morale and National Character', 76–9; Bateson and Mead, 'Principles of Morale Building', 216.
34. Information from Philomena Guillebaud.
35. Lipset, *Bateson*, 162–3; Bateson, *With a Daughter's Eye*, 22.
36. In fact, their first major formulation of 'national character' did not appear until 1942, Bateson's essay 'Morale and National Character'; see Mead and Metraux (eds), *Study of Culture*, 407. But Mead was using the term at the end of 1940. 'Memorandum upon the Need for Exploring Existing European Character Structure', 21 Dec. 1940: Mead Papers, M4.
37. Mead, 'Comparative Study of Culture', 61–3, 68–9, comment by Kluckhohn, 72.
38. Gardner Murphy to Bateson, 5 May 1942; Murphy to Mead, 6 May 1942: Mead Papers, M36; see further below, pp. 137–8.
39. Mead, 'Anthropological Contributions', 148; Mead, 'National Character and the Science of Anthropology', 19; Mead, commentary on Fisher, 'Role of Anthropology in International Relations', 14. These were *post facto* responses to the critique made long after the war. But see also Mead to Gardner Murphy, 1 May 1942: Mead Papers, M36; Bateson, 'Human Dignity', 251.
40. Bateson, 'Morale and National Character', 80.
41. Bateson, 'Morale and National Character', 80–4, 90; Bateson and Mead, 'Principles of Morale Building', 216–17; Friedman, *Identity's Architect*, 165–71; Bateson to Claude Guillebaud, 20 Oct. 1941–18 Mar. 1942: Mead Papers, O2.
42. Mead, 'Social Change and Cultural Surrogates', 102–9, credited to Fromm, 107; see also Bateson, 'Cultural Determinants of Personality', 727–8.
43. Mead, 'Comparative Study of Culture', 61–3, and comment by Bateson, 93–7; Bateson to Claude Guillebaud, 20 Oct. 1941–18 Mar. 1942: Mead Papers, O2; see also Mead, 'On Methods of Implementing a National Morale Program'. See above, p. 297, for Mead's comments on automatism in 1935.
44. Bateson and Mead, 'Principles of Morale Building', 214–15; cf. Yans-McLaughlin, 'Science, Democracy and Ethics', 198.
45. Mead, 'Comparative Study of Culture', 66–9, comment by Bateson, 85–6; see also Bateson to Nora Barlow, 10 May 1941: Mead Papers, O2.
46. Mead to Lloyd Warner, 22 Jun. 1941; Mead to Eliot Chapple, 19 Feb. 1944: Mead Papers, E118; Mead to Erwin Schuller, 21 Dec. 1943: Mead Papers, C10; cf. Price, *Anthropological Intelligence*, 29–30. For a taste of Chapple's rhetoric, see Chapple, 'Anthropological Engineering'. For some of Chapple's jaundiced views on Mead, see Jane Howard interview with Eliot Chapple, 12 Dec. 1979: Jane Howard Papers, Box 38, and Mabee, 'Margaret Mead and Behavioral Scientists'.
47. Bateson to Nora Barlow, 10 May 1941; Mead, 'Major Facts about the Plan', n.d. [May 1941]; scraps of correspondence for this period between Mead and Chapple: Mead Papers, O2, A19, F2. For a more pessimistic view, see Jane Howard interview with Gregory Bateson, n.d.; for a more optimistic view, Jane Howard interview with Eliot Chapple, 12 Dec. 1979: Jane Howard Papers, Box 38.
48. Arthur Upham Pope to Talcott Parsons, 3 Jun., 28 Nov. 1941: Parsons Papers, HUGFP 15.2, Box 3; Pope to Gorer, 16 Feb. 1942: Gorer Papers, Box 28; Robert Lynd to James B. Baxter, COI, 27 Aug. 1941: National Archives (US), RG226/57A-D, Box 1. For Erikson's early work on the psychology of Nazism, see Friedman, *Identity's Architect*, 166–71, and below, ch. 4. Under Hartshorne's and Parsons's influence, COI was also considering at this stage 'national character' studies of both enemies and allies on similar terms to Mead and Bateson's. Talcott Parsons to Edward Hartshorne, 26 Dec. 1941: Parsons Papers, HUGFP 15.2, Box 27.

49. Edward Hartshorne to Talcott Parsons, 26 Aug. 1941; Parsons to Hartshorne, 29 Aug. 1941: Parsons Papers, HUGFP 15.2, Box 3. The head of the Psychological Division, R.C. Tryon, was resistant to psychoanalytic approaches. Parsons to Hartshorne, 26 Dec. 1941. For an indication of the Psychological Division's early thinking about morale questions, see Psychological Division, COI, 'Morale Determination', 19 Nov. 1941: Parsons Papers, HUGFP 15.2, Box 27. The agenda was similar to Bateson's – levels of aggression, reactions to success and failure, leadership, collective and individual integration – but the psycho-analytic content was lighter and less specific. For the more sociological orientation of the Psychological Division's early work on foreign propaganda, see Psychology Division, 'Social and Psychological Analysis of a Nation: A Working Outline', 2 Jan. 1942: National Archives (US), RG226/57A-D, Box 1.

50. See e.g. Benedict, 'The Natural History of War', and 'Primitive Freedom', in Mead (ed.), *Anthropologist at Work*. The Kaingang were a Brazilian people then being studied by Benedict's student Jules Henry. The Chukchee (or Chukchi) were a Siberian people, discussed in a classic anthropological work by Boas's contemporary Waldemar Bogoras.

51. See the related argument made by Bateson, 'Human Dignity', 251.

52. Mead to Bateson, 2 Oct. 1939; Bateson to Mead, 15 Oct. 1939; Mead to Bateson, 6 Nov., 28 Dec. 1939; Lawrence K. Frank, 'Cultural Approach to European Peace', Feb. 1940; Bateson, 'Comparative Study of European Cultures', 21 Feb. 1940: Mead Papers, S1, F2.

53. 'Memorandum upon the Need for Exploring Existing European Character Structure', 21 Dec. 1940: Mead Papers, M4.

54. 'Memorandum on the Inclusion of Culture and Personality Insights in the Post War Planning', Oct. 1941; 'Memorandum on Utilizing Data on Character and Culture for National and International Problems', 20 Oct. 1941: Mead Papers, M4.

55. Frank, 'World Order and Cultural Diversity' (1942), in *Society as the Patient*, 391–2, 395. This article was published in *Free World* in June 1942 and circulated by the new Council: Mead Papers, B5. For notice of it, see e.g. Louise Rosenblatt to Mead, 22 Jul. 1942: Mead Papers, F6; Riemer, 'Individual and National Psychology', 259–60; Leighton, *Governing of Men*, 249–50.

56. Edwin Embree to Lawrence K. Frank, 23 Oct., 5 Nov. 1941: Mead Papers, M1.

57. Initially it was called the Council on Human Relations, which Embree thought sounded more innocuous, but Mead preferred the 'intercultural' idea and the new name was phased in over 1942; it was then renamed the Institute for Intercultural Studies in 1944; it remained Mead's vehicle for a range of public activities until her death, and was then continued by Mary Catherine Bateson until 2009 as a means of preserving the memory of her parents and their work.

58. See, for example, Rose, *Governing the Soul*, 16–52; Buck, 'Adjusting to Military Life'; Simpson, *Science of Coercion*, 22–50; Herman, *Romance of American Psychology*, e.g. 9–12, 22–5, 77–9, 124–7; Hollinger, 'Science as a Weapon'; Lemov, *World as Laboratory*, e.g. 245–6; Parmar, 'Engineering Consent'; Abbott and Sparrow, 'Hot War, Cold War'. For 'militarization' in particular, see Sherry, *In the Shadow of War*, esp. 35–7, 88–90; for 'weap-onization', see Price, *Anthropological Intelligence*, 89–90, 272, 278.

59. See Schneider and Handler, *Schneider on Schneider*, 19, 34, 61, and his wartime letters to Gorer, esp. 7 Oct. 1942: Gorer Papers, Box 99.

60. Abbott and Sparrow, 'Hot War, Cold War', 291–3.

61. Coon, *North Africa Story*, 4–5, 10–12.

62. Lemov, *World as Laboratory*, 158–61, 170–80. For Benedict and Mead's horror at Murdock's displacement of Sapir, see Benedict to Mead, 18 Mar. 1938, 19 Feb. 1939: Mead Papers, B1.

63. Abbott and Sparrow, 'Hot War, Cold War', 287–8. In total, they find that 36 per cent of all sociology PhDs did some kind of military or government service in the war; many of the rest would have remained in universities, though not unconnected to war work. Cf. Lemov's unfootnoted assertion that 'Almost 90 percent of American social scientists worked in some capacity for the government and military during the war'. See *World as Laboratory*, 245, and Rose, *Governing the Soul*, 36–9, for a more slippery overstatement.

64. 'Wallace Starts to Educate Aides', *New York Times*, 27 Feb. 1938, p. 12. Benedict's prewar association with Henry Wallace (secretary of agriculture, later vice-president) and M.L. Wilson (his under-secretary, a great enthusiast for anthropology) provided Mead with her

most potent wartime connections. On this fascinating episode, see Kirkendall, *Social Scientists*, 183–92.

65. Abbott and Sparrow, 'Hot War, Cold War', 286–90, 294–5, 301; Buck, 'Adjusting to Military Life'; Herman, *Romance of American Psychology*, 67–76; Sproule, *Propaganda and Democracy*, 195–207.
66. Price, *Anthropological Intelligence* is by far the most thorough account we have: see esp. 25–7; Price, 'Bateson and the OSS', 379; Partridge and Eddy, 'Development of Applied Anthropology', 26–33.
67. Technically, PWE was a liaison group linking the 'white' propaganda outfit, the Ministry of Information, and the 'black' outfit, the Special Operations Executive (SOE).
68. Katz, *Foreign Intelligence*, xii–xiv, 4–24. Katz's superb account focuses on the European theatre, whereas the anthropologists were concentrated in the Asian theatre.
69. Hawkins and Pettee, 'OWI', 24.
70. Winkler, *Politics of Propaganda*, esp. 36–7, 64–71, 73–6, 104–29.
71. Price, *Anthropological Intelligence*, 78–84.
72. Katz, *Foreign Intelligence*, 154.
73. Embree, 'American Military Government', 212–13.
74. Ibid., 213–14; Useem, 'Social Reconstruction in Micronesia'.
75. M.L. Wilson, Dept. of Agriculture, to Benedict, 6 Nov. 1940; Carl E. Guthe, 'History of the Committee on Food Habits', in *Bulletin of the National Research Council* 108 (Oct. 1943), 9–19: Mead Papers, F6; Banner, *Intertwined Lives*, 415–16, makes the link between Benedict and Mead.
76. Mead, 'Anthropological Contributions', 140; Mead to Edwin Embree, 22 Nov. 1943: Mead Papers, M1. Mead later traced the breakdown of their relationship to the death of Bateson's mother in the spring of 1941, 'his subsequent withdrawal from me and election that I go to Washington in Jan. 42'. Mead to Erik Erikson, n.d. [spring 1947]: Mead Papers, R8.
77. Mead, 'Anthropological Contributions', 140; Mead, commentary on Fisher, 'Role of Anthropology in International Relations', 13; Mabee, 'Mead and Behavioral Scientists', 11n5; Jane Howard, interview with Eliot Chapple, 12 Dec. 1979: Jane Howard Papers, Box 38.
78. Mead, 'Anthropological Contributions', 140, 153; Mead, commentary on Fisher, 'Role of Anthropology in International Relations', 13; Jane Howard, notes of a seminar by Philleo Nash and Rhoda Metraux, 21–2 Mar. 1980; Jane Howard, interview with Gregory Bateson: Jane Howard Papers, Box 38; Mead to Daniel Lerner, 6 Jul. 1951: Mead Papers, C24; Mead to Molly Harrower Erickson, 5 Jul. 1944: Benedict Papers, Box 12/6.
79. Mead, commentary on Fisher, 'Role of Anthropology in International Relations', 13.
80. Mead to Daniel Lerner, 6 Jul. 1951; Jean Houston, 'The Mind of Margaret Mead', 435–6; Mead to Mabel Brown Ellis, YWCA, 18 May 1943: Mead Papers, C24, Q18, M39; Mead, 'Anthropological Contributions', 163; Mead to Gorer, 15 Jul. 1942 (photocopy): Jane Howard Papers, Box 37.
81. Mead, 'Facilitating Anglo-American Relationships', n.d., 11–12: Mead Papers, E155.
82. Mead to Gorer, 15 Jul. 1942 (photocopy): Jane Howard Papers, Box 37.
83. The relationship can be followed from spring 1941 in Mead Papers, M31, M29.
84. Gorer to Peter Gorer, 19 Sep. 1941: Gorer Papers, Box 84.
85. Gorer to Erling Olsen, 15 Dec. 1941; Gorer to Peter Gorer, 23 Dec. 1941; Arthur Upham Pope to Gorer, 8, 16 Jan. 1942; Mead to Gorer, 9 Jan. 1942: Gorer Papers, Boxes 96, 84, 28; Robert Tryon to James B. Baxter, 6, 16, 21, 29 Jan. 1942: National Archives (US), COI Psychological Division, RG226/57A-D, Box 1; Gorer, 'Japanese Character Structure and Propaganda', 1st ed. (Mar. 1942), 2nd ed. (Apr. 1942): Gorer Papers, Box 28.
86. Mead, 'Facilitating Anglo-American Relationships', n.d., prefatory note; Mead, 'Learning to Live in One World', 1945, 6–8: Mead Papers, E155, I28; Mead and Metraux (eds), *Study of Culture*, 34–5.
87. Memorandum, Gregory Bateson, 22 Apr. 1942: Mead Papers, M3, and see M2. Gorer also began work on China for CIR in this period. Bateson to Ralph Linton, 27 Oct. 1942; Gorer to 'Miss Steinberg', 9 Dec. 1942: Mead Papers, M28.
88. Gorer to Peter Gorer, 27 Mar. 1942; Leonard Doob to Gorer, 1 May 1942; Gorer to Reuben Katz, Board of Economic Warfare, 26 May 1942: Gorer Papers, Box 84, 28.

89. Gorer to Peter Gorer, 28 Aug., 8 Nov. 1942: Gorer Papers, Box 84; Gorer to Mead, 22 Jul., 2 Sep. 1942; Mead to Jane Belo, 8 Jan. 1944: Mead Papers, B5, B1. Gorer, however, was not able to divest himself of his mother until summer 1943.
90. Gorer to Peter Gorer, 8 Jan. 1943: Gorer Papers, Box 84.
91. Gorer to William Whitney, OWI, 'Interview with Sgt. Sedgwick; Propaganda Techniques and the Hitler Jugend', 7 Jan. 1943: Mead Papers, M29.
92. Gorer and T. Cole to William Whitney, OWI, 2 Jan. 1943; Leo Rosten to John R. Fleming, 7 Jan. 1943; Leo Rosten to Gorer, 21 Jan. 1943; Gorer to Leo Rosten, 22, 26 Jan. 1943: National Archives (US), Correspondence of OWI Deputy Director Rosten, RG208/75; Gorer to Lt Martin Herz, 'German Popular Psychology and its Implications for Propaganda Policy', 9 Feb. 1943: Benedict Papers, Box 16/12; Gorer to Maj. C.A.H. Thomson, Central Intelligence Panel, OWI, 'Prisoner Questionnaires', 24 Feb. 1943: National Archives (US), OWI Director of Overseas Operations, Outpost Cables and Reports, RG208/362, Box 131; Gorer to Leo Rosten, 'Similarity between Germany and Japan', 19 Apr. 1943: National Archives (US), OWI Bureau of Overseas Intelligence Central Files, RG208/366, Box 223.
93. Gorer to Benedict, 13 Apr. 1943: Benedict Papers, Box 28.
94. Lawrence K. Frank to Mead, n.d. [Mar. 1943]; Mead, 'Children's Bureau Report', 24 Mar. 1943: Mead Papers, M26.
95. Mead, commentary on Fisher, 'Role of Anthropology in International Relations', 16. Sereno was a political scientist at OWI who later worked alongside Ruth Benedict.
96. Geoffrey Gorer and Dorothy Demetrocopolou Lee, 'The Greek Community and the Greek Child from the Viewpoint of Relief and Rehabilitation', n.d. [Apr. 1943]: National Archives (US), OWI Bureau of Overseas Intelligence Central Files, RG208/366, Box 223.
97. The term was already current about now, mid-1943. Although Mead once said it was Bateson's term, he associated it with Mead and Gorer and – rather bitterly – with their own estrangement. Ai-li Chin (Mrs Robert Chin) to Benedict, 24 May 1943; Mead to Molly Harrower Erickson, 5 Jul. 1944: Benedict Papers, Boxes 112/10, 12/6; Lipset, *Bateson*, 184; Mead to Benedict, 14 Jul. 1947: Mead Papers, R7; information from Mary Catherine Bateson.
98. Dorothy Lee to Mead, 21 Apr. 1943; Lee to Bateson, 8 May, 2 Jul. 1943: Mead Papers, C10, M34, O2.
99. Katherine Bain to Mead, 14 May 1943; Bain to Dorothy Lee, 1 Jul. 1943: Mead Papers, M26. A revised version of the report was widely circulated by CIR, including to Greeks. Gorer to Rose Kolmetz, 22 May 1943; Lee to Kolmetz, 11 Jun. 1943: Mead Papers, M34.
100. Gorer to Benedict, 28 Apr. 1943: Benedict Papers, Box 28.
101. 'Interview with Captain Christian, 21 Apr. 1943'; 'Burma. Notes from OSS Material (Courtesy of Dave Mandelbaum)', n.d.; Mead, 'Burma – Interpretation', 19 Apr. 1943: Gorer Papers, Box 29. For Christian's own views – more sociological – see Lt Col. J.L. Christian, Memorandum, 12 Dec. 1944: National Archives (US), OSS Field Station Files (Kandy), RG226/154, Boxes 73, 74; also Christian, *Modern Burma*, 14–18, 317–18.
102. Gorer, 'Burmese Personality', OWI, Bureau of Research and Analysis, 13 Jul. 1943. There are copies scattered about the OWI files, e.g. National Archives (US), OWI Bureau of Overseas Intelligence Central Files, RG208/366, Box 223.
103. Gorer, 'Burmese Personality', with annotations by 'J.R.A.': National Archives (US), OWI Bureau of Overseas Intelligence, Informational Files on Asia, RG208/370, Box 375.
104. OWI Bureau of Overseas Intelligence, 'Background for a Basic Plan for Burma', 13 Sep. 1943; Overseas Planning Committee, Political Warfare (Japan) Committee, 'Plan of Political Warfare for Burma: Policy Plan', 2 Jan. 1944, approved by Chiefs of Staff: National Archives (US), OWI BOI Informational Files on Asia 1942–6, RG208/370, Box 375. The 'Background' paper was 'based in large part, but not exclusively, on an extended study of the Burmese prepared by Geoffrey Gorer'; it was collated after his departure from OWI by Ruth Benedict, for which see below, p. 79.
105. See e.g. the copy of Gorer, 'Burmese Personality', in National Archives (US), OSS Field Station Files (Kandy), RG226/184, Box 74, lightly but less critically annotated by someone interested in the psychological points – very possibly Bateson or Cora Du Bois; for Weston La Barre's use of Gorer, see below, pp. 158–9; and see also Hanks, 'Quest for Individual Autonomy', 285–6.

106. John Chamberlain, 'Books of the Times', *New York Times*, 19 Dec. 1935; Katherine Woods, 'The Strange Worlds of Bali and Angkor', *New York Times Book Review*, 9 Aug. 1936.
107. Jane Howard, interview with Leo Rosten, 13 Jul. 1981: Jane Howard Papers, Box 39. But cf. 'Philleo Nash Comments', 28 Oct. 1983, Box 73.
108. Jane Howard, interview with Anne Fremantle, 6 Apr. 1979: Jane Howard Papers, Box 38. Fremantle claimed to have entertained Gorer and the cab driver as a couple on many occasions, so the rumour carries some additional credibility.
109. Jane Howard, interview with Philleo and Edith Nash, 27–8 Oct. 1979: Jane Howard Papers, Box 38.
110. See, for example, Clyde Kluckhohn to Bateson, 4 Feb. 1943; A.L. Kroeber to Mead and Bateson, 25 May 1943: Mead Papers, M2; Nathan Leites to Benedict, 9 Mar. 1944: Benedict Papers, Box 112/9; and further below, on the Japanese memorandum, pp. 135–7.
111. Ai-li Chin (Mrs Robert Chin) to Benedict, 24 May 1943: Benedict Papers, Box 112/10.
112. Caffrey, *Ruth Benedict*, 297–300; Denning, *Cultural Front*, 419–20.
113. Benedict, 'A Note on Dutch Behavior', n.d. [1943]; Mead to Bateson, 5 Jan. [1943?]; Mead to Liesje Geleerd, 24 May 1943: Mead Papers, M38, R3, E49; Gorer to Benedict, 28 Apr. 1943: Benedict Papers, Box 28.
114. Modell, *Ruth Benedict*, 269, 271–2, says that Benedict had already moved to Washington by December 1942. I can't find any evidence of this myself, and she certainly didn't start to work for OWI until Gorer left. Patricia Woodward to Mead, 14 Jul. 1943: Mead Papers, F6.
115. Mead to Mabel Brown Ellis, YWCA, 18 May 1943: Mead Papers, M39.
116. Jane Howard, interview with Leo Rosten, 13 Jul. 1981: Jane Howard Papers, Box 39; Benedict to Dr Karl A. Menninger, 28 May 1943: Benedict Papers, Box 112/9.
117. Benedict to Dr Margaret Brenman, Menninger Clinic, 28 May 1943; Benedict to John Murra, 18 May 1943: Benedict Papers, Boxes 112/9, 11/5. Brenman was to become a close associate of Erik Erikson.
118. Price, *Anthropological Intelligence*, 80–3, places a good deal of emphasis on the papers generated by this CIR initiative; but it didn't come to much. Bateson wrote sadly to Mead in July 1943, 'No response from the universities to our offers and no response from the army except continued politeness – "Very valuable work – and we wish you every success".' Bateson to Mead, 29 Jul. [1943]; also Charles S. Hyneman, Office of the Provost Marshal General, to Bateson, 27 May 1943: Mead Papers, R3, M34.
119. Benedict to Bateson, 5 Mar. 1943: Mead Papers, M25.
120. 'Position Description', n.d.; 'Memo to Mr. Katz from Ruth Benedict', n.d. [annotated 2 Jul. 1943]: Benedict Papers, Box 112/9, 112/3.
121. Modell, *Ruth Benedict*, 270.
122. In July 1943 Benedict and Rodnick comprised the Basic Analysis section, with another five full-timers doing regional and interregional work: Benedict Papers, Box 112/9.
123. Lucien Warner to Benedict, 17 Nov. 1943; Benedict to Lucien Warner, 21 Dec. 1943; Nathan Leites to Ruth Benedict, 21 Dec. 1943; Benedict to Nathan Leites, 28 Dec. 1943; Leonard Doob to Benedict et al., 10 Jan. 1944; Samuel T. Williamson to Benedict, 1 Feb. 1944; Nathan Leites to Benedict, 9 Mar. 1944: Benedict Papers, Box 11/10, 11, Box 12/1, 2. See also van Ginkel, 'Typically Dutch'.
124. Benedict to Erik Erikson, 7 Mar. 1944: Benedict Papers, Box 112/10.
125. Mead to Daniel Lerner, 6 Jul. 1951: Mead Papers, C24.
126. Mead, *And Keep Your Powder Dry*, 19.
127. Ibid., 39–40.
128. On wartime concerns about 'momism', see Zaretsky, *Secrets of the Soul*, 250–1; Michel, 'Danger on the Home Front', 112–13.
129. Alpers, *Dictators, Democracy*, ch. 6; Sherry, *In the Shadow of War*, 57, 68; Gilliam and Foerstel, 'Mead's Contradictory Legacy', 125–6.
130. Mead, 'Not Head-Hunters, Nor Appeasers, But Men', *New York Times Magazine*, 30 Nov. 1941, pp. 3, 29.
131. Mead, *And Keep Your Powder Dry*, 96–7.
132. Ibid., 95–6, 99–100; Mead to Bateson, 15 Aug. 1945; Mead to Daniel Lerner, 6 Jul. 1951: Mead Papers, R3, C24; Mead, 'Case History', 146.

133. Mead, *And Keep Your Powder Dry*, 123, 130–8.
134. Ibid., 106–9, 115–22.
135. Ibid., 5–7. Helen Lynd apparently thought that Mead was not being straight but rather 'manipulative' in her form of address, although it wasn't clear (even to Mead) exactly why she thought this; Mead to Helen M. Lynd, 2 Apr. 1946: Mead Papers, C15.
136. Stears, *Demanding Democracy*, 136–8, including *And Keep Your Powder Dry* in the analysis.
137. See Gordan (ed.), *Mead: Bibliography*, 77–85.
138. Mead to Eleanor Roosevelt, 21 Jan. 1943; A. Perry Osborn to Mead, 30 Mar. 1943; Mead to Bateson, 7 Apr. 1944: Mead Papers, C10, R3.
139. Lutkehaus, *Margaret Mead*, 211–15; Howard, *Margaret Mead*, 228–9.
140. Fern Marja, 'Anthropology Is Such Fun', *New York Post*, 17 May 1944.
141. See the wide range of reviews in Mead Papers, 120–1. For some discussions of the influence of the book, see Handler, 'Boasian Anthropology', 261–7; Gleason, *Speaking of Diversity*, 167–71; Wall, *Inventing the 'American Way'*, 91–4; Yans-McLaughlin, 'Science, Democracy and Ethics', 204–12; Gilkeson, *Anthropologists and the Rediscovery of America*, 144–53.
142. Mead emphasizes the differences between her and Gorer's modes of address in Mead to Daniel Lerner, 6 Jul. 1951: Mead Papers, C24.
143. Mead, 'Facilitating Anglo-American Relationships', n.d.: Mead Papers, E155; Mead, 'Application of Anthropological Techinques'; Mead, 'Case History'.

Chapter 3 Among the Natives of Great Britain

1. 'Memorandum on the Inclusion of Culture and Personality Insights in the Post War Planning', Oct. 1941: Mead Papers, M4.
2. Howard, *Margaret Mead*, 235–6.
3. Mead, 'Facilitating Anglo-American Relationships', n.d., 2–3: Mead Papers, E155.
4. Ibid., 11–12.
5. Mead, *And Keep Your Powder Dry*, xxxviii (from the preface to the British edition, written in October 1943 at the end of her tour). See also Mead, 'A Case History' – this version of the story, which first appeared in a volume edited by Lyman Bryson in 1948, was itself based on a 1947 lecture, for which see Mead, 'Application of Anthropological Techniques'. About the same time she started to draft a more detailed account – 'Facilitating Anglo-American Relationships: A Case Study in the Application of Anthropological Methods to Understanding between Peoples' – as an Institute for Intercultural Studies handbook; it is undated but internal evidence suggests 1946 or 1947. The same case study was meant to play a prominent role in the 'postwar' book that Mead half-wrote in the summer of 1945, 'Learning to Live in One World', for which see below, pp. 187–90, and Mead and Metraux (eds), *Study of Culture*, 407–28. Mead, 'End-Linkage', provides her own retrospective account.
6. Mead, 'Facilitating Anglo-American Relationships', n.d., 3–4: Mead Papers, E155.
7. Ibid., 4.
8. Bateson, *Naven*, 119–21.
9. Mead to Bateson, 9 Nov. 1935: Mead Papers, R2; Lipset, *Bateson*, 150.
10. Lipset, *Bateson*, 162.
11. Ibid., 168.
12. Bateson, 'Morale and National Character', 86–9; Bateson, 'Some Subsidiary Approaches', 80; Bateson to Conrad Waddington, 20 Oct. 1941–18 Mar. 1942; Mead, 'Facilitating Anglo-American Relationships', n.d., 13–14: Mead Papers, O2, E155.
13. Mead to Mary Fisher, Vassar College, 16 Mar. 1942: Mead Papers, M3.
14. Mead, 'Facilitating Anglo-American Relationships', n.d., 13–14, 17: Mead Papers, E155; Bateson, 'Morale and National Character', 81–2; Bateson and Mead, 'Principles of Morale Building', 218–20; Bateson, 'Human Dignity', 249. The clue to the 'ternary' structure Mead said came from Bateson's old friend Amber (Reeves) Blanco White: see her *The New Propaganda*.
15. Mead, 'Facilitating Anglo-American Relationships', n.d., 13–14: Mead Papers, E155; Mead, *And Keep Your Powder Dry*, 89–100; Bateson, 'Morale and National Character', 84; Bateson, 'Some Systematic Approaches', 78–9; Bateson and Mead, 'Principles of Morale Building', 216–17.

16. Mandler, 'Being His Own Rabbit', 206–7.
17. Bateson, 'Morale and National Character', 76.
18. Orwell, 'Lion and the Unicorn', 75–6.
19. Eric Blair to Gorer, n.d. [May? 1936]: Orwell Archive, Letters from Orwell I.
20. Mead to T.S. Matthews, executive editor, *Time*, 21 Jan. 1943; T.S. Matthews to Jeffrey Mark, 20 Feb. 1943; Mead, Bateson and Gorer, 'Formulations of the English about Themselves (For Discussion Feb. 1, 1943)': Mead Papers, M24.
21. Dyer and Mead, 'It's Human Nature'; Mead, *And Keep Your Powder Dry*, 97–8; Mead, 'Facilitating Anglo-American Relationships', n.d., 19–23: Mead Papers, E155. The full script was published in the journal *Education* in 1944; it was later revised, naturally toning down the anti-Germanism, and rebroadcast in 1946.
22. [Mead, Bateson and Gorer], 'Schematic Background for a Series of Radio Programs on Anglo-American Similarities and Differences', n.d. [Apr. 1943]; Mead to Davidson Taylor, CBS, 19 Apr. 1943: Gorer Papers, Box 30; John Salt, BBC, to Mead, 2 Apr. 1943; Taylor to Mead, 2 Apr. 1943: Mead Papers, M24.
23. Davidson Taylor, CBS, to Mead, 14 May 1943: Mead Papers, C9. Bateson did, however, record a broadcast along the same lines for the Mutual Broadcasting System, 'Science for the Seven Million: An Anthropologist Looks at America and Britain in the Light of Bali and New Guinea', 21 Apr. 1943: Mead Papers, O14.
24. Lt Cmdr Herbert Agar to Robert Sherwood, director of Overseas Operations, OWI, 30 Nov. 1942; 'Chapter VII. Outposts': National Archives (US), OWI, Outpost Records 1942–6, RG 208/6J, Box 3, Draft Historical Reports, RG 208/6H, Box 3; Winkler, *Politics of Propaganda*, 125–6; Reynolds, *Rich Relations*, 179–81; Brewer, *To Win the Peace*, 107–16.
25. Howell, 'Writers' War Board', esp. 810–11.
26. Margaret Leech to Geoffrey Crowther, 27 Apr. 1943: National Archives (US), OWI, Records of Office of Communications Control, Letters and Reports from Outposts, RG 208/387, Box 704.
27. Kuhn/Williams (OWI) to Eliot/Agar (OWI British Division), 1 May 1943; Eliot/Agar to Kuhn/Williams, 5 May 1943: National Archives (US), OWI, Records of Office of Communications Control, Classified and Clear Operational Cables, RG 208/380, Box 88; 'Ten OWI Speakers Will Tour England', *New York Times*, 30 Sep. 1943, p. 19.
28. Or so she said years later. Mead to Erik Erikson, n.d. [1946–7]: Mead Papers, R8.
29. Mead to Victor Weybright, OWI, 20 Aug. 1943; Mead to Margaret Owen, 27 Aug. 1943; Mead to Weybright, 8 Oct. 1943: Mead Papers, E154.
30. Mead Papers, E156.
31. Mead, 'Memorandum on the Sort of Things Which I Should Like to See', 8 Jul. 1943: Mead Papers, E154.
32. See the correspondence between Mead and Owen, Jul.–Aug., and Mead to Victor Weybright, 8 Oct. 1943: Mead Papers, E154.
33. Mead to Bateson, 18 Jul. 1943; Mead to Jane Belo, 8 Jan. 1944: Mead Papers, R3, B1.
34. Mead to Bateson, 26 Jul., 5–12 Aug. 1943; Bateson to Mead, 29 Jul. 1943; Mead to Erik Erikson, n.d. [1946–7]: Mead Papers, R3, R8.
35. Kinnear, *Woman of the World*, 111–15, 122–3, 131–46; Mead to 'Steve' [Betty Cobbold], 29 Jan. 1945: Mead Papers, C12.
36. Mead to Bateson, 26 Jul., 1 Sep. 1943; Mead to Erwin Schuller, 17 Aug. 1943: Mead Papers, R3, R10.
37. Mead to Benedict, 7 Aug. 1943: Mead Papers, S4.
38. The itinerary can be pieced together by means of the papers preserved in Mead Papers, E154–5, and also 'Speaking Engagements of Miss Margaret Mead during July, 1943', and similar for October and November: National Archives (US), Records of OWI Office of Communications Control, Letters and Reports from Outposts, RG 208/387, Box 705.
39. Mead, 'Notes on Questions Asked after Address'; cf. Mead to Bateson, 5–12 Aug. 1943: Mead Papers, E155, R3; and the published version in Mead, *And Keep Your Powder Dry*, xxxiv (from the preface to the 1944 British edition). Fairey's huge Stockport factory is my best guess at what appears in the papers as 'Fairlie's' in Manchester.
40. Mead to Bateson, 1 Sep. 1943: Mead Papers, R3.
41. Mead to Bateson, 18 Jul., 5–12 Aug. 1943; Mead to M.L. Wilson, 6 Aug. 1943: Mead Papers, R3, F6.

42. Mead to Victor Weybright, OWI, 20 Sep. 1943: Mead Papers, E154; Margaret Bucknall to George Barnes, 11 Aug. 1943; Mead to Bucknall, 20 Sep. 1943: BBC Written Archives Centre, RCONT1, Dr Margaret Mead, Talks, File 1: 1943–62.

43. Mead to Jane Belo, 8 Jan. 1944: Mead Papers, B1. 'Steve' and 'Jolliffe' are very slippery and hard to pin down. See the brave attempt of Banner, *Intertwined Lives*, 322, 325–6, 337–40, and cf. Caffrey and Francis (eds), *To Cherish the Life of the World*, 72–3, 91–2, 396 n17. 'Steve' (so-called by Mead and Bateson in private but often 'Betty' in public) seems to have been born Mildred Denton Stephenson, and was briefly married to Sterling Neville Cobbold in the early 1930s; my thanks to Anthony Cobbold of the Cobbold Family History Trust for this information. She seems to have preferred 'Betty Cobbold' at the time of Mead's visit. She is Mrs Mildred D. Cobbold in official correspondence with the immigration authorities when she visited Mead in 1947: Mead Papers, C16. 'Jolliffe Metcalfe' is listed as the pseudonym for Alice Metcalfe in bibliographic records of her writings in the early 1930s. She committed suicide about a year after Mead's visit. Mead to Bateson, 25 Feb. 1945: Mead Papers, R3.

44. Mead to Bateson, 13 Sep. 1943; Mead to 'Steve and Jolliffe', 10 Dec. 1943: Mead Papers, R3, E155. Mead thanks Betty Cobbold and Jolliffe Metcalfe for their hospitality in 'Facilitating Anglo-American Relationships', n.d., 2–3: Mead Papers, E155.

45. Mead to Bateson, 24–7 Oct. 1943: Mead Papers, O2; 'Itinerary of Dr. Margaret Mead for the Month of October 1943', and same for November 1943: National Archives (US), Records of OWI Office of Communications Control, Letters and Reports from Outposts, RG 208/387, Box 705; Metraux (ed.), *Margaret Mead*, 253; Mead to Gorer, 1 Jan. 1974: Gorer Papers, Box 93.

46. Mead to Bateson, 5 Jul. 1943; Mead to Benedict, 7 Aug. 1943: Mead Papers, R3, S4; Mead, 'A GI View of Britain', 18.

47. Mead, 'Facilitating Anglo-American Relationships', n.d., 27–9: Mead Papers, E155.

48. Mead to Erwin Schuller, 25 Aug. 1943: Mead Papers, R10.

49. Mead to Bateson, 26 Jul. 1943: Mead Papers, R3.

50. Mead to Benedict, 7 Aug. 1943; Mead to Bateson, 17 Aug., 1 Sep. 1943; Mead, 'Some Significant Aspects of British Social Practice' (Oct. 1943): Mead Papers, S4, R3, E154.

51. Mead, 'Some Significant Aspects of British Social Practice', (Oct. 1943), 25 Oct. 1943: Mead Papers, E154, E155. For the genesis of this memorandum, see Erwin Schuller to Mead, 30 Jul., 28 Aug. 1943; Mead to Erwin Schuller, 17, 25 Aug. 1943; for the drafting, Mead to Erwin Schuller, 13, 24, 25 Sep., 3 Oct. 1943; Erwin Schuller to Mead, 16, 29 Sep., 4 Oct. 1943: Mead Papers, R10.

52. Mead to Bateson, 17 Aug. 1943; Erwin Schuller to Mead, 16 Sep. 1943; Mead, 'Some Significant Aspects of British Social Practice' (Oct. 1943): Mead Papers, R3, R10, E154.

53. Mead to M.L. Wilson, 6 Aug. 1943; Mead to Bateson, 1, 13 Sep. 1943: Mead Papers, F6, R3.

54. Mead, 'Some Significant Aspects of British Social Practice' (Oct. 1943): Mead Papers, E154.

55. Rachel Crowdy to Mead, 14 Oct. 1943: Mead Papers, E155.

56. Adaptations of the scripts of the two broadcasts were published in the *Listener*: 'The Americans – Are They Human?', broadcast 10 Oct. 1943, appeared as 'Why We Americans "Talk Big"', 28 Oct. 1943; 'The Americans – Can You Tell One from Another?', broadcast 14 Nov. 1943, appeared as 'Can You Tell One American from Another?', 2 Dec. 1943.

57. Mead to Bateson, 24–7 Oct. 1943: Mead Papers, O2; Mead, 'Why We Americans "Talk Big"'; Mead, *And Keep Your Powder Dry*, xxxvii–viii; OWI Memorandum (Secret), 'Why American Soldiers Are the Way They Are': National Archives (UK), FO371/38623; Mead, 'The Yank in Britain'; Mead, *American Troops and the British Community*; Mead, 'What Is a Date?'; Mead, 'A GI View of Britain'.

58. Margaret Bucknall to George Barnes, 2 Nov. 1943: BBC Written Archives Centre, RCONT1, Dr Margaret Mead, Talks, File 1: 1943–62; Kluckhohn, *Mirror for Man*, 165; Reynolds, *Rich Relations*, 265; Juliet Gardiner, 'Guys and Dolls', *Guardian*, 11–12 Jan. 1992, 'Weekend Guardian', 4–6; Brewer, *To Win the Peace*, 113–14.

59. Mead to Ambassador Winant, 17 Oct. 1943: Mead Papers, E155; similar in Mead to Benedict, 7 Aug. 1943: Mead Papers, S4, and Mead to Margaret Bucknall, 20 Sep. 1943: BBC Written Archives Centre, RCONT1, Dr Margaret Mead, Talks, File 1: 1943–62.

60. Mead, *And Keep Your Powder Dry*, xxxvi–xxxviii.
61. OWI Memorandum (Secret), 'Why American Soldiers Are the Way They Are': National Archives (UK), FO371/38623; 'The Yank in Britain' appeared as no. 64 in the Army Bureau of Current Affairs pamphlet series, 11 Mar. 1944. She had used as her model a previous ABCA pamphlet, 'Woman after the War', by Phyllis Bentley. Mead to Victor Weybright, 15 Jan. 1944: Mead Papers, I26. The Americans reprinted it in the 'Army Talks' series published by the European Theater of Operations, United States Army (ETOUSA), 15 Mar. 1944. See Victor Weybright to Alan Dudley, 4 Feb. 1944; A. Malcolm to Alan Dudley, 11 Feb. 1943; Alan Dudley, Note, 23 Feb. 1944: National Archives (UK), FO371/38623.
62. [Eric Knight], *Short Guide*, 2, 10. The British had their counterpart, 'Notes for Guidance of United Kingdom Officials Visiting the United States', obviously with a narrower readership: see Brewer, *To Win the Peace*, 112–13.
63. Mead, 'Yank in Britain', 2–3, 15–16; Mead, *American Troops and the British Community*, 4–5. Knight had made the same point about the virtues of acknowledging difference – *Short Guide*, 2 – but downplayed what he saw as 'minor' differences in national characteristics; as Reynolds, *Rich Relations*, 175, notes, 'current affairs' pamphlets before Mead's had also argued that 'Americans and English think alike'.
64. Note, Alan Dudley, 23 Feb. 1944; Alan Dudley to Victor Weybright, 1 Mar. 1944; Weybright to Dudley, 2 Mar. 1944: National Archives (UK), FO371/38623; Weybright to Mead, 24 Apr. 1944; Mead to Bateson, 13 Nov. 1944: Mead Papers, E155, R3.
65. *112 Gripes*, published anonymously by the US Army Information and Orientation Branch; Kluckhohn, *Mirror for Man*, 165. See also Knox, 'GI Gripes on France'.
66. Caroline Haslett, president, British Federation of Business and Professional Women, to Mead, 13 Sep. 1943: Mead Papers, E154.
67. In addition to the extensive distribution of Mead's leaflets by the US and British Armies, the Women's Voluntary Service applied them to their own work and to the 'Welcome Clubs' designed to smooth relations between GIs and the native population. Lady Reading to Mead, 24 May 1944; Elsa Dunbar, WVS, to Mead, 26 Jul. 1944: Mead Papers, M28.
68. Bateson to Nora Barlow, 11 Feb. 1944; Mead to Erwin Schuller, 21 Dec. 1943; Mead to 'Steve and Jolliffe', 10 Dec. 1943: Mead Papers, C10, E155.
69. Mead to Erik Erikson, n.d. [1946–7]: Mead Papers, O8, R8.
70. Bateson to Mead, 29 Jul. [1943]; Mead to Bateson, 5–12, 17 Aug., 13 Sep. 1943: Mead Papers, R3.
71. Mead to Erwin Schuller, 21 Dec. 1943; Mead to Jane Belo, 8 Jan. 1944: Mead Papers, C10, B1.
72. Mead to Bateson, 7 Apr. 1944: Mead Papers, R3.
73. Mead to Erwin Schuller, 21 Dec. 1943; Bateson to Nora Barlow, 11 Feb. 1944; Mead to Letty Harford, 19 Feb. 1944; Mead to Victor Weybright, 5 Apr. 1944; Mead to Jolliffe Metcalfe, 30 Jan. 1945: Mead Papers, C10, Q12, E155, C12; Mead, 'As Johnny Thinks of Home'; Mead, 'A GI View of Britain'; Mead, 'Ferment in British Education'.
74. Mead to Bateson, 7 Apr., 7 May, 7 Jun., 14 Jun. 1944; Mead to 'Steve', 29 Jan. 1945: Mead Papers, R3, C12.
75. 'Formulation of Triangular Relationship to Reconcile Anglo-American Incompatabilities [*sic*]', 5 May [1944], and subsequent notes; Mead to Bateson, 20 May 1944: Mead Papers, M25, R3.
76. Mead to Daniel Lerner, 6 Jul. 1951; Mead to Bateson, 12–16 Jan., 7 Feb. 1945: Mead Papers, C24, R3; Mead, 'A Case History', 156–7. Brewster's article appeared in the *American Magazine* for January 1945.
77. Mead to Bateson, 13 Nov., 26 Dec. 1944; Mead to Gorer and Rhoda Metraux, 'Experimental Socio-Drama on Anglo-American Relationships on Difficulty about "Taking your Hair Down"', 19 Nov. 1944: Mead Papers, R3, M24. Also present were Marjorie Janis and Nathan Leites. Bateson thought the British had their own idea of 'taking down your hair' – 'losing your temper with the resulting release of tensions'. Bateson to Mead, 4 Feb. 1945: Mead Papers, R3.
78. Mead to Victor Weybright, 5 Apr. 1944; Mead to Bateson, 27 Sep. 1944: Mead Papers, E155, R3; Mead, 'A Case Study', 158; Mead, 'Anthropological Contributions', 149; Mead, 'National Character', 650.

79. Mead, 'A GI View of Britain', 18, 34.
80. Mead, 'Learning to Live in One World', FLIS Press Releases, Common Council for American Unity, 3 Jan. 1945: Mead Papers, I29.
81. Mead, 'A Case History', 159–60.

Chapter 4 Culture Cracking for War: II. Enemies

1. Frank, 'The Historian as Therapist' (1944), in *Society as the Patient*, 306; for a contemporary citation of 'zwei Herzen', see 'F.I.S. Basic Propaganda Plan for Germany', Secret, 4 Mar. 1942: National Archives (UK), FO898/108.
2. Moore, *Know Your Enemy*, 21; Nicholls, 'German "National Character"', 27–9.
3. Alpers, *Dictators, Democracy*, 87–92, 99, 102–4.
4. Moore, *Know Your Enemy*, 76.
5. Lasswell, 'Psychology of Hitlerism', esp. 374–5; see further Hoffman, 'Psychoanalytic Interpretations of Hitler'.
6. Bateson to F.C. Bartlett, 31 Dec. 1939: Mead Papers, F3; Bateson, 'Morale and National Character', 84, 88; Bateson and Mead, 'Principles of Morale Building', 216–17; Bateson and Mead, 'Preliminary Memorandum on Problems of German Character Structure', Oct. 1942: Mead Papers, M31.
7. 'Memorandum upon the Need for Exploring Existing European Character Structure', 21 Dec. 1940: Mead Papers, M4.
8. Erikson, 'Hitler's Imagery', 478–9; Dicks, 'Personality Traits', 137–9; Kecskemeti and Leites, 'Some Psychological Hypotheses' (1947), 177–8.
9. See above, ch. 3.
10. Bateson, 'Cultural and Thematic Analysis'.
11. Mead and Bateson, 'Interviews with Dr. Philip Mosely', 24 Nov. 1941, 12 Jan. 1942; Mead, 'Notes for R. Brickner on the Relationship between Individual Psychology and Culture', n.d. [c. Aug. 1941]: Mead Papers, M28, M31, and see further German interviews in M33; Mead, 'Introduction', to Byrnes (ed.), *Communal Families*, xviii–xx.
12. Mead to Bateson, 3 Jan. 1936; Bateson to Kurt Lewin, 6 Nov. 1940; Mead, 'Facilitating Anglo-American Relationships', n.d., 17: Mead Papers, S1, O2, E155; also Bateson, 'Morale and National Character', 74. I do not discuss here Mead's interest in Lewin's Gestalt and 'topological' theories.
13. Mead, 'Retrospects and Prospect', 131–2; Mead, 'Anthropological Contributions', 138; Mead to Daniel Lerner, 6 Jul. 1951: Mead Papers, C24; Fromm, *Escape from Freedom*, 61, 156.
14. See, for example, the insightful conclusions of Alpers, *Dictators, Democracy*, 103–12; also Samelson, 'Authoritarianism from Berlin to Berkeley', 195–8; McLaughlin, 'Why Do Schools of Thought Fail?', 122–6; Gitre, 'The Great Escape', 17–20. The success of *Escape from Freedom* among wartime Americans still remains slightly mysterious, and worthy of further consideration.
15. Ruth Benedict, review of Erich Fromm, *Escape from Freedom*, *Psychiatry* 5 (1942), 111–13; and see Mead to Louis Finkelstein, 28 Dec. 1943: Mead Papers, E59. But see also Fromm, 'Problems of German Characterology', closer to Mead's position.
16. On the genesis of Erikson's analysis, see Friedman, *Identity's Architect*, 166–9; Hoffman, 'Erikson on Hitler'.
17. Erikson, 'Hitler's Imagery and German Youth', esp. 478–80, 490–3.
18. Bateson to Col. William J. Donovan, COI, 5 Feb. 1942; E.H. Erikson, 'Notes on the "Canadian Project"', Committee for National Morale, n.d. [Apr. 1942]; Mead to Erikson, 4 Apr. 1942: Mead Papers, M32.
19. Erik H. Erikson, 'Comments on Anti-Nazi Propaganda', CIR, n.d. [1942]: Mead Papers, M32. On Erikson's memoranda for Donovan, see Hoffman, 'Erikson on Hitler', 72–3; Hoffman, 'American Psychologists and Wartime Research', 266, goes further to suggest that Donovan was instigating these memoranda, which seems an overstatement.
20. Bateson and Mead, 'Preliminary Memorandum on Problems of German Character Structure', Oct. 1942: Mead Papers, M31. There is also a copy in Gorer Papers, Box 30.
21. Erik Erikson to Mead, n.d. (two letters); Mead to Erikson, 3 Nov. 1942: Mead Papers, M31.

22. Hoffman, 'American Psychologists and Wartime Research', 267–8; Gerhardt, 'Parsons and the War Effort', esp. 262–5, 268–70. Parsons's memorandum for COI, 'Some Aspects of German Social Structure and National Psychology', can be found in Parsons Papers, HUGFP 42.42, Box 1. Cf. Leo Rosten to Mead, 21 Nov. 1941: Mead Papers, A19.

23. Erik Erikson to Col. William J. Donovan, COI, 15 Apr. 1942: Mead Papers, M32.

24. Katz, *Foreign Intelligence*, 14–19, 22, 33–41; Hoffman, 'American Psychologists and Wartime Research', 265–6.

25. Kecskemeti and Leites, 'Some Psychological Hypotheses'; McGranahan and Janowitz, 'Studies of German Youth'. McGranahan had been in OSS Psychological Division, then OWI, but was later reunited with former OSS colleagues when the Psychological Warfare Division of Eisenhower's European command (PWD-SHAEF) was set up in 1944; see further below, pp. 139–40.

26. *Remembering Nathan Leites*, 15; Gorer to Peter Gorer, 8 Jan. 1943: Gorer Papers, Box 84.

27. Erikson was still in pursuit of POWs in early 1943. Confidential Memorandum, E.H. Erikson to CIR, Feb. 1943: Mead Papers, M32.

28. E.Y. Hartshorne to Talcott Parsons, 18 Dec. 1943: Parsons Papers, HUG(FP) 15.2, Box 12.

29. Minear, 'American Japanists of the 1940s', 558.

30. Pelzel, 'John Fee Embree', provides a contemporary assessment.

31. Dower, *War without Mercy*, 8–11, 34, 79–82, 89–91.

32. Gorer to Erling C. Olsen, 15 Dec. 1941; Gorer to Peter Gorer, 23 Dec. 1941: Gorer Papers, Boxes 96, 84.

33. Mead to Gorer, 23 Dec. 1941, 9 Jan. 1942: Mead Papers, M36; A.U. Pope to Gorer, 16 Jan. 1942: Gorer Papers, Box 28. Psychological Division held its own summit meeting at exactly the same time, where the contribution of anthropologists was more sociological.

34. Gorer to Mead, 22 Feb. 1942: Mead Papers, M36.

35. Gorer to Mead, 31 Dec. 1941, 22 Feb. 1942: Mead Papers, M36.

36. See the correspondence with Mead, Embree and Haring for early 1942 in Gorer Papers, Box 28. On Haring, see Minear, 'Wartime Studies of Japanese National Character', 45–9.

37. Gorer, 'Japanese Character Structure and Propaganda', Committee on National Morale and Council on Human Relations (as the CIR was as yet named), Apr. 1942. This circulated in several forms, the '2nd edition' of Apr. 1942 (incorporating the critiques of Embree and Haring) being the more-or-less final version that Gorer continued to circulate through the 1950s: see the copy in Gorer Papers, Box 28. Another version was published as Gorer, 'Themes in Japanese Culture', in 1943.

38. On the other hand, Haring confirmed it. John Embree, 'Corrections and Comments on Japanese Character Study', n.d. [2 Apr. 1942]; 'Comment by Douglas G. Haring', 5 Apr. 1942: Gorer Papers, Box 28. Gorer omitted the headline claim about toilet training as 'the most important single influence' in the published version.

39. Gorer, 'Japanese Character Structure'; Mead to Gorer, 24 Feb. 1942: Mead Papers, M36.

40. Mead to Bateson, 7 Apr. 1944: Mead Papers, R3. See Klineberg, 'Science of National Character', in *Journal of Social Psychology*, and reprinted in *American Scientist*; see also Mead, 'National Character and the Science of Anthropology', 17.

41. Lewin, 'Special Case of Germany'; Gorer, 'Special Case of Japan'.

42. Nathan Leites to Ruth Benedict, 21 Dec. 1943; Benedict to Leites, 28 Dec. 1943: Benedict Papers, Box 11; Clyde Kluckhohn to Gorer, 22 Apr. 1943, 20 Mar. 1944; Kluckhohn to Hadley Cantril, 13 Mar. 1944: Kluckhohn Papers, HUG 4490.3, Boxes 1, 2; Williams, 'From Charlottesville to Tokyo', 420–1.

43. *Time*, 7 Aug. 1944, p. 66. Dower, *War without Mercy*, 124–8, considers Gorer's the 'single most influential academic analysis' of the Japanese psyche.

44. Gorer to Leo C. Rosen, 'Similarity between Germany and Japan', 19 Apr. 1943: National Archives (US), OWI Bureau of Overseas Intelligence Central Files, 1941–5, RG208/366, Box 223.

45. Cf. Dower, *War without Mercy*, 119–24, 129–30, and Kent, 'Ruth Benedict and her Wartime Studies', 34–6.

46. D.G. Haring, 'Individual Development in Japanese Family and School', School for Overseas Administration, Harvard University, Civil Affairs Training School – Far Eastern Area, 2 Nov. 1944: National Archives (US), OWI, Bureau of Overseas Intelligence Central Files, Informational File on Asia 1942–6, RG208/370, Box 39. For more on

Haring's views on maternal masturbation and toilet training, see 'Comment by Douglas G. Haring', 5 Apr. 1942: Gorer Papers, Box 28. Embree was responsible for the equivalent Far Eastern Section of the Civil Affairs Training School at Chicago between 1943 and 1945.

47. Embree, *The Japanese*, esp. 22–3, 37–8; John Embree to Clyde Kluckhohn, 31 Oct. 1944: Kluckhohn Papers, HUG 4490.3, Box 2. Cf. Embree's prewar treatment of early childhood, *Suye Mura*, 183–5, which draws none of these psychological conclusions. By omitting from his consideration Embree's views in 1942–3, Minear in my view underestimates the overlap of his position with Gorer's: 'Wartime Studies of Japanese National Character', 49–54. This changed later: see below, pp. 164–5.

48. John Embree to Gorer, 2 Apr. 1942; 'Comment by Douglas G. Haring', 5 Apr. 1942: Gorer Papers, Box 28.

49. Mead to Gardner Murphy, 1 May 1942; Murphy to Mead, 6 May 1942: Mead Papers, M36.

50. Gorer to Mead, 31 Dec. 1941: Mead Papers, M36; Gorer, 'Japanese Character Structure', 14–18: Gorer Papers, Box 28. For the postwar claim, see Mead, 'National Character', 660.

51. Mead to Gardner Murphy, 1 May 1942; Murphy to Bateson, 5 May 1942; Gardner Murphy to Mead, 6 May 1942: Mead Papers, M36.

52. PWD-SHAEF had by far the largest psychological-warfare capability of any wartime operation: Daugherty and Janowitz (eds), *Psychological Warfare Casebook*, 134–5. Mountbatten kept OWI out of his theatre because he mistrusted it ideologically, fearing its democratic propaganda would carry anti-colonial messages. Cruickshank, *SOE in the Far East*, 223.

53. Dicks, 'German Personality Traits and National Socialist Ideology', in Lerner (ed.), *Propaganda in War and Crisis*, 102–4, 160–1. This version, published after the war, reflects exposure to the work of Brickner, Erikson, Fromm, Kecskemeti and Leites; cf. Lt Col. H.V. Dicks, 'The Psychological Foundations of the Wehrmacht', Directorate of Army Psychiatry, Research Memorandum 11/02/9A, Feb. 1944: Gorer Papers, Box 32. On Dicks and the Hess analysis, see Pick, *Pursuit of the Nazi Mind*.

54. Gorer to Lt Col. G.R. Hargreaves, War Office, 27 Apr. 1945: Gorer Papers, Box 32.

55. Lerner (ed.), *Propaganda in War and Crisis*, 54.

56. Lerner, *Psychological Warfare*, 44, 62n9, 93n9, 121–4.

57. Moore, *Know Your Enemy*, 165–8, 212–15; Dower, *War without Mercy*, 53–4; Lerner, *Psychological Warfare*, 345; Balfour, *Propaganda in War*, 318–20.

58. Borgwardt, *A New Deal for the World*, esp. 21, 73–5, 133–5; Schonberger, *Aftermath of War*, 90–8.

59. Balfour, *Propaganda in War*, 313–20; Doob, 'Utilization of Social Scientists', 658; Winkler, *Politics of Propaganda*, 131–4.

60. Mayo, 'American Wartime Planning', 26–43; Dower, *Embracing Defeat*, 214–20.

61. Benedict, 'German Defeatism at the Beginning of the Fifth Winter of War', 15 Dec. 1943, 'The Need for Escapist P.W. in Western Europe', 5 May 1944; Percy Winner to Leonard W. Doob, 6 May 1944: Mead Papers, M33; Benedict, 'A Note on Long Range Communications Planning for Europe', n.d. [Jul. 1944], 'Target-Oriented Propaganda for European Nations during the Liberation Period and after Germany Collapses', 24 Jul. 1944, 'The Apolitical Majority in Western Europe in Long-Range Propaganda', n.d. [Jul. 1944], 'The Depoliticized Majority in Western Europe as a Target Area during the Medium-Range Period', 17 Jul. 1944: Benedict Papers, Box 112. On Winner's anti-fascist political strategy, see Winkler, *Politics of Propaganda*, 99–100, 113–15, 125; Soley, *Radio Warfare*, 84, 92–3.

62. Moore, *Know Your Enemy*, 295–301; Katz, *Research and Analysis*, 34–5, 77–9; Winks, *Cloak and Gown*, 94–5. Cohen, *Remaking Japan*, 16–43; and Mayo, 'American Wartime Planning', 26–7, suggest that Japanese policy was not so contested in part because the civil-affairs handbooks for Japan spelled out a more detailed programme of intervention.

63. 'Basic Difficulties to Be Overcome or Guarded Against', Morale Committee, Japan, 8 Nov. 1941: Mead Papers, M35. Internal evidence suggests Mead's authorship.

64. 'Psychological Considerations in Making the Peace', a special issue of *Journal of Abnormal and Social Psychology* (Apr. 1943), and 'The Occupation of Enemy Territory', a special issue of *Public Opinion Quarterly* (winter 1943–4).

65. Lewin, 'Cultural Reconstruction', esp. 171.

66. Murphy, 'Psychology in the Making of Peace', 133, but also repeating his critique of Gorer's 'diaperology'.

67. Lewin, 'Cultural Reconstruction', 168, 171–2; Mead, 'Food and Feeding'.

68. Lewin, 'Special Case of Germany', 556–8; Gorer, 'Special Case of Japan', 573.
69. See e.g. Moore, *Know Your Enemy*, 217–32; Alpers, *Dictators, Democracy*, 211–13, but cf. n54; Herman, *Romance of American Psychology*, 35; Gerhardt, 'Hidden Agenda of Recovery', 309–10; Pick, *Pursuit of the Nazi Mind*, 104–5.
70. Mead to Richard Brickner, 5 Jul., 30 Aug. 1941; Mead, 'Notes for R. Brickner on the Relationship between Individual Psychology and Culture', n.d.; Gorer to Brickner, 10 Sep. 1941; Mead to Gorer, 18 Nov., 23 Dec. 1941: Mead Papers, M31, 29, 36; Gorer to E.C. Olsen, 30 Oct. 1941: Gorer Papers, Box 96.
71. Mead, 'Introduction', to Brickner, *Is Germany Incurable?*, 7–8.
72. Gorer is acknowledged only more allusively: ibid., 21–3.
73. Ibid., 297–307.
74. Ibid., 100–2, 301–7.
75. Ibid., 127–39.
76. Mead to Gorer, 23 Dec. 1941; Benedict, 'Comment on Statement on Regularities in German National Character' (29 Apr. 1944); Mead to Bateson, 17 Jun. 1945: Mead Papers, M36, M31, R3. Thus it is not correct to identify Mead with Brickner's more normative psychiatric desire to 'cure' the Germans; cf. Herman, *Romance of American Psychology*, 35–6; Hegeman, *Patterns for America*, 163–4; Alpers, *Dictators, Democracy*, 211–13; Gitre, 'The Great Escape', 17–18.
77. Mead thought the 'medical' approach would go down better than anthropology, psychology, even 'education' – all 'lousy fronts' in comparison. 'Notes of a Discussion at 72 Perry Street, New York', 19 Dec. 1943: Mead Papers, M29.
78. H.M. Kallen, *Saturday Review*, 29 May 1943, 4–6; H.E. Barnes, *Saturday Review*, 18 Sep. 1943, 13–14, 9 Oct. 1943, 13–14; Erich Fromm, *Saturday Review*, 29 May 1943, 10; and see Fromm, 'Problems of German Characterology', very much in Mead's terms.
79. Rex Stout (with Cecil Brown, H.S. Commager, Carl van Doren, Clifton Fadiman, W.L. Shirer), *Saturday Review*, 2 Oct. 1943, 17; Norman Cousins, 'Editor's Note', *Saturday Review*, 2 Oct. 1943, 17–18. On the Writers' War Board campaigns, see Howell, 'Writers' War Board', esp. 803–7. On Stout and the 'hard' peace more generally, see Casey, 'The Campaign to Sell a Harsh Peace'.
80. 'Report of Meeting', 21 Nov. 1943; Mead to Richard Brickner, 7 Dec. 1943; 'Notes of a Discussion at 72 Perry Street', 19 Dec. 1943: Mead Papers, M31, 29.
81. On the Brickner conferences, see Gerhardt, 'Hidden Agenda of Recovery', 312–19, 'American Sociology and German Re-education', 47–53, and *Talcott Parsons*, 110–20. Gerhardt exaggerates Brickner's significance, the success of his efforts to gain official attention and the impact the conferences had on later policy. Her strength is in her discussion of Parsons's role and thought, which does give a more nuanced account of the Brickner conferences than those cited above, n. 76; and see Moore, *Know Your Enemy*, 230–2, on 'disagreements among the authors'.
82. Gardner Murphy to Richard Brickner, 1 Dec. 1943; 'Notes of a Discussion at 72 Perry Street', 19 Dec. 1943: Mead Papers, M29, M31.
83. 'Germany After the War', 385. All quotes are taken from the proceedings published in 1945, but they are virtually identical to the mimeographed version, 'Report of a Conference'. Copies of the Frank and Mead papers can also be found in Parsons Papers, HUGFP 15.2, Box 11.
84. Benedict, 'Comment on "Statement on Regularities in German National Character"', n.d.; Mead, 'Corrections to Draft on German National Character', 17 Apr. 1944; Mead, 'Final Revisions of German National Character', 23 Apr. 1944: Mead Papers, M31, M32.
85. 'Germany After the War', esp. 389–94.
86. Erik Erikson, 'Letter from California': Parsons Papers, HUGFP 15.2, Box 11.
87. 'Conference on Germany After the War. First Day', 29 Apr. 1944, 'Second Day', 30 Apr. 1944: Mead Papers, M31.
88. Parsons to Lawrence K. Frank, n.d. [early May 1944]; Frank to Parsons, 9 May 1944; Mead to Parsons, 12 May 1944; Parsons to Mead, 19 May 1944: Parsons Papers, HUGFP 15.2, Box 11.
89. 'Germany After the War', 431–9.
90. Ibid., 410–18 (Appendix 7 in the original report).

91. Ibid., 382–6, 386–95, 397–404 (Appendices 2, 3 and 5 in the original report). Parsons published his paper in its full original form in *Psychiatry* in 1945. See the discussion by Gerhardt, *Parsons*, 113–18.
92. 'Germany After the War', 439, 424–31 (Appendices 9 and 10 in the original report).
93. E.Y. Hartshorne to Talcott Parsons, 11 Apr. 1944; Parsons to Hartshorne, 19 Jul. 1944; Hartshorne to Parsons, 27 Mar. 1945: Parsons Papers, HUG(FP) 15.2, Box 12.
94. E.Y. Hartshorne to Talcott Parsons, 10 Apr. 1945: Parsons Papers, HUG(FP) 15.2, Box 12; Gorer to Lt Col. G.R. Hargreaves, 27 Apr. 1945: Gorer Papers, Box 32. Included in this same box in the Gorer Papers are Dicks's four key wartime memoranda, one of which was 'Germany After the War: A Résumé with Commentary', Directory of Army Psychiatry, Research Memorandum 45/03/13, Feb. 1945. Dicks's conclusion about the British inclination to take a superficial approach conflicts with later scholars' view – based more on British colonial than foreign policy – that 'brainwashing whole nations', or at least their elites, came naturally to the British. Pronay, 'To Stamp Out the Whole Tradition', 2, 8–12; Torriani, 'Nazis into Germans', 139–41. See also Balfour, 'Britain's Policy of "Re-education"', 141–2.
95. 'Scientists Outline Plan for Germany', *New York Times*, 27 Apr. 1945; '2 Doctors Urge Psyching All Germans to Nip Nation's Mania', *Daily News*, 22 May 1945; '2-Generation Psychiatric Cure for Germany Urged', *Daily News*, 23 May 1945; 'Prescription for Germany', *Time*, 14 May 1945, 77; for an early criticism, Glazer, 'Study of Man'.
96. Balfour, *Four-Power Control*, 171–7, 182–5; Torriani, 'Nazis into Germans', esp. 99–112, 121, 139–41, 185–7, 253 (but cf. 259); Schwartz, *America's Germany*, 31–2, 38–9; cf. Gerhardt, 'Hidden Agenda of Recovery', 319–24, and 'American Sociology and German Re-education', 52–7, which I think significantly exaggerate the real impact of the psychiatric approach in the occupation.
97. See Tent, *Mission on the Rhine*, on Education and Religious Affairs, esp. 48, 53, 61, 123–4, 254–7; and see also Tent, 'Hartshorne and German Universities'.
98. Nicholls, 'German "National Character"', 37–8; Schwartz, *America's Germany*, 157–68. For reassessments of 'national character' after the war by wartime propaganda experts, see Taylor, *Richer by Asia*, 362–6; Balfour, *Four-Power Control*, 51–2, and below, n. 102, for Dicks's views.
99. Richard Brickner, 'Conference on Germany After the War', 23 Mar. 1945; Mead, 'Research on German Character Structure and its Implications for the Post War World', n.d.: Mead Papers, M31.
100. 'Partial Minutes of the Meeting of the Executive Committee of the Conference on Germany after the War Relating to Post Trial Plans', 22 Oct. 1945; 'Conference with Dr. Ewen Cameron on December 14th and 15th, 1945, on Day of his Return from Nuremberg'; Lt G.M. Gilbert to Mead, 5 Feb., 11 Mar. 1945; Mead to Gilbert, 26 Feb. 1946; Bert Schaffner to Brickner and Mead, 11 Feb. 1946; Mead to Schaffner, 28 Feb. 1946: Mead Papers, M31.
101. H.V. Dicks to Gorer, 29 Jan. 1946; Wing Cmdr O.E. Oeser to Gorer, 17 Jan., 4 Feb. 1946; Gorer to Dicks, 6 Feb. 1946: Gorer Papers, Box 32. Gorer did make two visits to the British Zone in 1946 as a special consultant: Gorer, 'British Zone'.
102. Lerner, *Psychological Warfare*, 158nn18, 21; 'The German Personnel Research Branch: A Brief Historical Sketch and Summary of Findings', 31 Dec. 1946: Gorer Papers, Box 32. For Dicks's later comments on how changing circumstances aborted his 1942–6 studies, see Dicks, 'Personality Traits and National Socialist Ideology', 153; Dicks, 'The Psychological Approach to the German Character', Conference on Some Aspects of the German Problem, Royal Institute for International Affairs, 22 Sep. 1947: Mead Papers, M33.
103. Levy, *New Fields of Psychiatry*, 105–19; Bert Schaffner to Richard Brickner and Mead, 11 Feb. 1946; Mead to Schaffner, 28 Feb. 1946: Mead Papers, M31.
104. Schaffner, *Father Land* (with preface by Mead and foreword by Levy); Rodnick, *Post War Germans*; and see below, pp. 234–5.
105. Gorer to Mead, 2 Sep. (1942): Mead Papers, B5.
106. Thorne, *Allies of a Kind*, 162, 454, 591; Donnison, *British Military Administration*, 323–7; Cruickshank, *SOE in the Far East*, 222–3; Aldrich, *Intelligence and the War against Japan*, 177–8. While a great deal has been written about OWI and OSS broadcasting, there is almost nothing on PWE in this area.

107. Garnett, *Secret History of PWE*, 135–7. For the PWE Washington Mission's work, mostly its liaison with OSS, see National Archives (UK), FO898/108.

108. See the reports of missions to New York by Leonard Miall and Mark Abrams in 1942–3: National Archives (UK), FO898/105; D.M. MacDougall to F.G. Healey, Washington, n.d.: National Archives (UK), FO898/279.

109. R. Leonard Miall to Rosemary O'Neill, PID London, 31 Dec. 1943: National Archives (UK), FO898/279.

110. David Bowes Lyon to D.M. MacDougall, 28 Nov. 1943: National Archives (UK), FO898/279.

111. Some of Gorer's weekly reports can be found in National Archives (UK), FO898/285. Sometimes they go out under other names, but it is clear from *obiter dicta* that he was usually the author. (For example, when he was ill for a time in March 1945 there was no report.) See esp. Washington Office to San Francisco Office, 10 Mar. 1945, and 41st, 47th, 49th and 50th reports. In the final stages of the war, OWI allowed OSS to use some of its facilities (including in San Francisco) to broadcast black propaganda direct to the Japanese home islands, but I have seen no evidence that Gorer and the PWE operation had any hand in this: Soley, *Radio Warfare*, 185–8; McIntosh, *Sisterhood of Spies*, 68.

112. Jane Howard interview with Anne Fremantle, 6 Apr. 1979: Jane Howard Papers, Box 38.

113. F.S. Tomlinson to Washington Office, 5 Apr. 1945; Colin Macdonald to F.S. Tomlinson, 10 Apr. 1945; T.G.M. Harman, 'Discussions with Mr. Tomlinson, Washington, D.C., 17–18 May 1945'; A.C. Baker, 'Memorandum on the Malay Language Section', 28 May 1945: National Archives (UK), FO898/285.

114. Gorer to John Marshall, 9 Sep. 1944: Rockefeller Foundation Archives, RG 2, Series 401, Box 273, Folder 1870.

115. Gorer to T.G.M. Harman, 13 Sep. 1945; Colin Macdonald to Washington Office, 21 Sep. 1945; T.G.M. Harman to Colin Macdonald, 7 Nov. 1945: National Archives (UK), FO898/285.

116. Soley, *Radio Warfare*, 158–61, 167–8, 184–5; McIntosh, *Sisterhood of Spies*, 67–8, 245–9.

117. The quote is from an undated memorandum in the OSS Field Station Files (Kandy), National Archives (US), RG226/154, Box 125. A similar phrase is used by W.L. Langer in a letter to Col. Donovan of Dec. 1944, cited by Katz, *Foreign Intelligence*, 26.

118. Bateson to Maj. Harley Stevens, 'MO-FE School', 21 Feb. 1944; P.H. Hiss to Stevens, 'MO-FE School – Discussion of Bateson's Recommendations', 24 Feb. 1944; Hiss to Stevens, 4 Mar. 1944: Mead Papers, O5; McIntosh, *Sisterhood of Spies*, 67; Foster, *Unamerican Lady*, 106–10.

119. Carleton F. Scofield, Acting Chief, MO/SEAC, to Lt Charles Fenn, OSS SU Detachment #101, 9 May 1944: National Archives (US), OSS Field Station Files (Kandy), RG226/154, Box 119.

120. Lt Weston La Barre to Gregory Bateson (via Cora Du Bois), 'Some Suggestions for Japanese MO', 11 Sep. 1944; La Barre to Dr R.S. Lyman and Lucien Hanks, 22 Nov. 1944: National Archives (US), OSS Field Station Files (Kandy), RG226/154, Boxes 93, 74. Although La Barre developed his own theses about the Japanese character while working at the internment camp in 1943, it is not therefore true that La Barre was 'unfamiliar with Gorer's pioneer analysis' when he prepared his paper on the subject for publication in *Psychiatry* in 1945, which, as Dower points out, *War without Mercy*, 136, would have been 'a surprising oversight given the wide impact of that earlier study in professional circles'. On La Barre, see further Suzuki, 'Retrospective Analysis', 33–41; Price, *Anthropological Intelligence*, 155–6; Spector, 'Allied Intelligence and Indochina', 25–7.

121. Bateson to Mead, 4 Oct. 1944: Mead Papers, R3.

122. Interview with Cora Du Bois, 20 Aug. 1981: Walzer, 'Oral History'; Jane Howard interview with Bateson, n.d.: Jane Howard Papers, Box 38; Bateson to Mead, 1 Jun., 4 Oct., 8 Oct. 1944, 29 Jul. 1945; Mead to 'Steve' [Cobbold], 29 Jan. 1945; Mead to Nora Barlow, 7 Feb. 1945 (misfiled as 1944): Mead Papers, R3, C12, C10; Taylor, *Richer by Asia*, 299–304; Foster, *Unamerican Lady*, 133–5; Bateson, *With a Daughter's Eye*, 227, 240, 247–8; Price, 'Bateson and the OSS', 381–2; Lipset, *Bateson*, 175.

123. Lipset, *Bateson*, 175; 'O.S.S. Mission, Arakan', n.d. [Dec. 1944]: National Archives (UK), HS1/307; Bateson and Lt Lawrence S. Riggs to Cora Du Bois, 'Ethnological and Psychological Notes on the Arakanese', 27 Jan. 1945; Bateson and Riggs, 'Suggestions for

MO in the Arakan', 27 Jan. 1945; Bateson to Du Bois, 'Attitudes of Ethnic Groups in the Arakan', 31 Jan. 1945; Bateson to Du Bois, 'Politics and Government in the Arakan', 2 Feb. 1945: National Archives (US), OSS Field Station Files (Kandy), RG226/154, Box 74.

124. Carleton F. Scofield, acting chief, MO/SEAC, to Lt Charles Fenn, OSS SU Detachment #101, 9 May 1944; C.B. Fahs to Dr W.L. Langer and Ed Martin, 'R&A at 101', 19 Dec. 1944: National Archives (US), OSS Field Station Files (Kandy), RG226/154, Box 119; HQ Force 1936 to Adv. HQ Force 1936, 'Combined Operations and General Relations with Other Clandestine Organizations', 6 Sep. 1944: National Archives (UK), HS1/307; Jane Howard interview with J.A. Hamilton, n.d.: Howard Papers, Box 38.

125. Bateson, *With a Daughter's Eye*, 42; Price, *Anthropological Intelligence*, 240–1. The stories differ slightly.

126. 'O.S.S. Mission, Arakan', n.d. [Dec. 1944]: National Archives (UK), HS1/307.

127. Bateson to Mead, 5 Mar. 1945: Mead Papers, R3. But cf. Bateson to Mead, 1 Oct. 1945, which spoke of a week he spent in China after the war as 'the best week I have had since Jan–Feb when I was up in Burma'.

128. Mead to Bateson, 23 May, 30 Jun. 1945; Mead to Nora Barlow, 8 Jul. 1945: Mead Papers, R3, C12.

129. Brockman (ed.), *About Bateson*, 9. On 'Gold Dust', see National Archives (US), OSS Field Station Files (Kandy), RG226/154, Box 119, and the further documents from the National Archives available at http://www.icdc.com/~paulwolf/oss/osscbi.htm. The 'Gold Dust' unit was activated in Washington in mid-1944, where they consulted Kurt Lewin and the MO-FE files that Bateson had helped to assemble; they began operations in northern Burma, near the Chinese border, in January 1945. Bateson, with OSS Mission Arakan in western Burma, was certainly not part of this unit before March, but he may have joined it then.

130. Bateson to Mead, 27 Apr., 14, 29 Jul. 1945: Mead Papers, R3. The 'shift' may refer to his original move from R&A to MO, or to his reassignment from MO back to R&A in the last phase of the war, although evidently he continued to run MO operations. Bateson's 'War Department Strategic Services Unit Questionnaire' in Mead Papers, R3, shows that he transferred to R&A in Mar. 1945.

131. Bateson to Mead, 7–9 Sep., 10 Sep. 1945, 1 Oct. 1945; Bateson to A.R. Radcliffe-Brown, 21 Aug. 1946: Mead Papers, R3, O3.

132. Foster, *Unamerican Lady*, 135–6.

133. Benedict, 'Recognition of Cultural Diversities', 101, 106–7.

134. Griffin, 'Dorothea Cross Leighton', 232–3.

135. For critiques of the Poston experiment, see Lemov, *World as Laboratory*, 177–8; Herman, *Romance of American Psychology*, 26–9; Mabee, 'Margaret Mead and Behavioral Scientists', 6–7; and most fully in Hirabyashi, *Politics of Fieldwork*, esp. 43–53; Suzuki, 'Anthropologists in the Wartime Camps', esp. 23–7; and Price, *Anthropological Intelligence*, ch. 7. For Leighton's own account, *Governing of Men*, 371–97; see also Leighton's comment on Kluckhohn, 'Anthropological Research and World Peace', 158–63. For Embree's auto-critique, see Embree, 'Applied Anthropology', and Embree, 'Anthropology and the War', 489–90, 494–5.

136. Leighton, *Human Relations in a Changing World*, 46–8; Dower, *War without Mercy*, 136–7; for Leighton's Navy plan, see A.H. Leighton, FMAD, to George E. Taylor, OWI, 20 Mar. 1945: National Archives (US), OWI/FMAD, RG208/378, Box 443.

137. A.H. Leighton to Vice Adm. R.T. McIntire, Surgeon General, US Navy, 'Monthly Report', 10 Oct. 1944: National Archives (US), OWI/FMAD, RG208/378, Box 443. Leighton was technically a Navy medical officer, seconded to OWI. See also Leighton, *Governing of Men*, 249–51, on the influence of the Poston experience and writings by Larry Frank and John Embree.

138. Price, *Anthropological Intelligence*, 171–3; Spitzer, 'Psychoanalytic Approaches', 136–7, 150–2; see also Herman M. Spitzer, 'Considerations on Psychological Warfare Directed against Japan', 9 Dec. 1944: National Archives (US), OWI/FMAD, RG208/378, Box 443.

139. Daily Log, 7 Dec. 1944: National Archives (US), OWI/FMAD, RG208/378, Box 443.

140. Daily Log, 16–21 Apr. 1945: National Archives (US), OWI/FMAD, RG208/378, Box 443.

141. Mead to Daniel Lerner, 6 Jul. 1951: Mead Papers, C24. The agenda was set by a group gathered at FMAD that included Mead, Benedict, Gorer, Lippitt, Leites, Lewin, Rhoda Metraux, Clare Holt, Leighton and Kluckhohn. Daily Log, 'Work of the Day – Cdr. Leighton', 1 Dec. 1944: National Archives (US), OWI/FMAD, RG208/378, Box 443.
142. See 'Provisional Analytical Summary of IPR Conference on Japanese Character Structure', 16–17 Dec. 1944: Mead Papers, M36, based on Mead's own notes. Kluckhohn was not able to attend. Talcott Parsons to Clyde Kluckhohn, 12 Dec. 1944: Kluckhohn Papers, HUG 4490.3, Box 2.
143. Embree, 'Applied Anthropology', 636; also Embree, 'A Note on Ethnocentrism', 430.
144. Haring, 'Re: Ethnocentric Anthropologists', 135–6.
145. 'Provisional Analytical Summary of IPR Conference on Japanese Character Structure', 16–17 Dec. 1944, 19: Mead Papers, M36. It is very much not the case that Haring had 'the last word': Gilkeson, *Anthropologists and the Rediscovery of America*, 137–9.
146. Benedict, 'What Shall Be Done about the Emperor?', n.d.: Mead Papers, M35; another copy in Benedict Papers, Box 13/5.
147. See the shrewd judgement of Dower, *Embracing Peace*, 218–24; also Mayo, 'American Wartime Planning', 30–6; Cohen, *Remaking Japan*, 16–20, 32–6; Schonberger, *Aftermath of War*, 90–1, 94–8. As Cohen points out, Philip Mosely helped to advance an intermediate policy at the State Department that favoured 'the "other Japan" of the poor and oppressed common people', which might have brought together the cultural relativists and the democratic universalists, but his was 'one of the smallest, most junior, and least prestigious units in the Department'.
148. Leighton, *Human Relations in a Changing World*, 48–84, 117–27; see also Bernstein, 'Seizing the Contested Terrain', and 'Understanding the Atomic Bomb', for other considerations.
149. Clyde Kluckhohn to Harold M. Vinacke, 'Annex on Treatment of Japanese Emperor', 19 Nov. 1944; A.H. Leighton to Vinacke, 21 Nov. 1944; Leighton to William Doerflinger, 15 Feb. 1945; Morris E. Opler to Leighton, 15 Jun. 1945; Leighton to George E. Taylor, OWI deputy director, 'The Japanese Emperor', 13 Jul. 1945; 'The Japanese Emperor', FMAD Report No. 27, 31 Oct. 1945: National Archives (US), OWI/FMAD, RG208/378, Box 443.
150. John K. Fairbank, OWI, to George E. Taylor, 'The Japanese Emperor (Reference Leighton Memo of July 13)', 16 Jul. 1945: National Archives (US), OWI/FMAD, RG208/378, Box 443; see also Ninkovich, *Diplomacy of Ideas*, 57–60.
151. Daily Log, 16–21, 23–8 Apr. 1945: National Archives (US), OWI/FMAD, RG208/378, Box 443.
152. Dower, *Embracing Defeat*, 220–4, 280–6, 550–7; Dower, *War without Mercy*, 338n4.
153. Leighton, *Human Relations in a Changing World*, 15, 126–8; Pelzel, 'Embree', 221.
154. Bennett and Ishino, 'History of the Public Opinion and Sociological Research Division'; Oppenheim, 'Locations of Korean and Cold War Anthropology', 233–5.
155. Benedict to Mead, 20 Sep. 1945: Mead Papers, Q11.
156. Mead to Benedict, 17 Sep. 1945; Benedict to Mead, 25 Jul. 1946: Mead Papers, S4, Q11; Benedict to Ferris Greenslet, 22 Oct. 1945, 23 Apr. 1946; Greenslet to Benedict, 26 Oct., 16 Nov. 1945, 9 May, 7 Jun. 1946: Benedict Papers, Box 13/8.
157. Benedict, *Chrysanthemum and the Sword*, 1, 13–16, 47.
158. Ibid., 98–175, esp. 146, 172–3, differentiating 'giri' from 'aggression'.
159. Ibid., 257–96, esp. 258–9 on toilet training and 290–1 on dualism; and see Kent, 'Benedict's Original Wartime Study', 92–3.
160. Benedict, *Race and Racism*, 10–11.
161. Benedict, *Chrysanthemum and the Sword*, 297–301, 314–15.
162. On the Japanese reception, see Kent, 'Japanese Perceptions', 182–4.
163. Bennett and Nagai, 'Reactions to American Anthropology'; Kent, 'Japanese Perceptions', 186–90.
164. For critical accounts, see Minear, 'American Japanists of the 1940s', 559–61; Yoneyama, 'Habits of Knowing Cultural Differences'; for more positive accounts, Kent, 'Benedict and her Wartime Studies', 36–9; Kent, 'Misconceived Configurations'; Modell, 'Wall of Shame'.

165. I cannot agree that Benedict was 'largely disaffected' from Japan or that her argument rested on 'the romanticization of America through otherizing Japan': Minear, 'American Japanists of the 1940s', 559–61; Yoneyama, 'Habits of Knowing Cultural Differences', 71–2; Lummis, 'Ruth Benedict's Obituary', 126–8.

166. Benedict, *Chrysanthemum and the Sword*, 220–5; cf. Young, *Ruth Benedict* 182–3; Kent, 'Benedict and her Wartime Studies', 39; Brick, *Transcending Capitalism*, 176–7; and esp. Modell, 'Wall of Shame', a very sensitive reading.

167. Benedict to Robert Hashima, 15 Aug. 1945: quoted in Hashima's memoir, translated in Suzuki, 'Ruth Benedict', 62; see further Suzuki, 'Overlooked Aspects', 224–5; see also Benedict's review of John Hersey's *Hiroshima* in *Nation*, 7 Dec. 1946, 656–8.

168. Embree, *Japanese Nation*, 260–2; but cf. Embree, *Japanese*, 21–3, 37–8. Minear, 'American Japanists of the 1940s', and 'Wartime Studies of Japanese National Character', lumps together Benedict, Gorer and La Barre, to set up Embree as a 'good' critic of Benedict. Cf. Suzuki, 'Retrospective Analysis', 45n84.

169. John F. Embree, review of *The Chrysanthemum and the Sword*, *Far Eastern Survey*, 15 Jan. 1947, 11. Embree also reviewed the book for the *American Sociological Review* 12 (1947), 245–6, where he took the opportunity again to criticize some of Gorer's generalizations but repeated his high praise for Benedict and for the pacific implications of her analysis.

170. For Mead's own slightly jealous recognition of this, see Mead, *Anthropologist at Work*, 428.

171. Jane Howard interview with Bob Schwartz, 18 Jul. 1979, with Bob Suggs, 23 Jul. 1979, and cf. Howard annotation on Bob Suggs to Jane Howard, 9 Jul. 1979: Howard Papers, Box 38.

172. Abram Kardiner, Interview #590, 423: Oral History Research Office, Columbia University.

173. 'Notes of a Discussion at 72 Perry Street', 19 Dec. 1943; Harold L. Ickes to Richard Brickner, 28 Dec. 1943; Eleanor Roosevelt to Richard Brickner, 17 Jan. 1944: Mead Papers, M29, M31; and see Yans-McLaughlin, 'Science, Democracy and Ethics', 195–7.

174. For Mead's own claims, see Partridge and Eddy, 'Development of Applied Anthropology', 29; 'Social Duty Laid on Anthropology', *New York Times*, 14 Apr. 1951, p. 14; Mead, 'Study of National Character', 93–4; and esp. Mead, 'Political Applications', 443. Cf. Mabee, 'Margaret Mead and Behavioral Scientists', 8–9, 11; Hendry, 'Chrysanthemum Continues to Flower', 118; Kent, 'Ruth Benedict and her Wartime Studies', 41.

175. Leighton, *Human Relations in a Changing World*, 118–21; Dower, *War without Mercy*, 136–9; Dower, *Embracing Peace*, 218–24; Price, *Anthropological Intelligence*, 183–94.

176. Yans-McLaughlin, 'Science, Democracy and Ethics', 196–7.

177. The first part of this quotation is Leighton citing someone else's experience (probably Samuel Stouffer's), the second is in his own words: Leighton, *Human Relations in a Changing World*, 127–8; cf. Doob, 'Utilization of Social Scientists', Mandelbaum, 'On the Study of National Character', 179–80.

178. Mead's use of this phrase, 'you can't advise an adviser', shifts between advocating less and more intervention: cf. Mead, 'Anthropological Contributions', 154; Mead, 'Changing Styles of Anthropological Work', 41; Mead, comment on Fisher, 'Role of Anthropology', 13–18.

179. Price, *Anthropological Intelligence*, xiii, 266–7, 270–1, claims not to be criticizing the choices of those who did war work, but the lesson he consistently draws is that it is always better to stay outside; see also his letter in *American Anthropologist* 18 (2002), 22, which proclaims the highest responsibility of the anthropologist as to 'protect those who share their lives with us when political winds shift against them', but cannot imagine that service in the Second World War might have aimed to do precisely that.

180. Mead, draft letter of recommendation for Nathan Leites, n.d. [Nov. 1945]; Mead to Daniel Lerner, 6 Jul. 1951: Mead Papers, C13, C24; Mead, 'Anthropological Contributions', 153; Mead, 'Comparative Study of Cultures' (1950), and Gorer's note minimizing the potential harm, 93–103; Mead, 'Political Applications', 443–4.

181. Mead to Bateson, 26 Dec. 1944: Mead Papers, R3.

182. Benedict and Weltfish, *Races of Mankind*, 2.

183. Mead, 'Learning to Live in One World' drafts, 'Perhaps Chapter IV making present IV V', 13 Aug. 1945, 6: Mead Papers, I28.

Chapter 5 Culture Cracking for Peace

1. Cf. e.g. Mead to Bateson, 26 Dec. 1944, and Mead at 18th general seminar, Research in Contemporary Cultures, 26 May 1948: Mead Papers, R3, G14.
2. See e.g. Simpson, *Science of Coercion*, 95–105; Simpson (ed.), *Universities and Empire*, xii–xiii, xxviii–xxix; Kuklick, *Blind Oracles*, 11–14; Herman, *Romance of American Psychology*, 124–7, 137–47; Gilliam and Foerstel, 'Mead's Contradictory Legacy', 128; Nader, 'Phantom Factor', 107, 136; Price, 'Cold War Anthropology', 391–8, 413; Price, *Anthropological Intelligence*, xiii–xiv, 264–77; Lemov, *World as Laboratory*, 190, 245–8.
3. Thus also repeated claims that such views remain 'heretical' and 'undiscussed' today, although they have become virtually hegemonic in the historiography of social science: e.g. Simpson, *Science of Coercion*, 116–17; Price, *Anthropological Intelligence*, 278; David Price, letter to *American Anthropologist* 18 (2002), 22; Wax (ed.), *Anthropology at the Dawn of the Cold War*, 2–3.
4. See e.g. Lippitt, 'Small Group and Participatory Democracy', 155–6; Lewis, 'Misrepresentation of Anthropology'; Lewis, 'Anthropology, Cold War and Intellectual History', 108–9; Stocking, '"Do Good, Young Man"', 255; Black, 'Psychological Anthropology and its Discontents', 246.
5. For an endorsement of such an approach, see Stocking, '"Do Good, Young Man"', 254.
6. Mead, comment on Fisher, 'Role of Anthropology', 14.
7. Glander, *Origins of Mass Communications Research*, 62–3.
8. Gerhardt, 'Parsons and the War Effort', 279–82; Haney, *Americanization of Social Science*, 27–38.
9. Lyons, *Uneasy Partnership*, 136–45; Geiger, *Research and Relevant Knowledge*, 23–5; Robin, *Making of the Cold War Enemy*, 43–53; Kuklick, *Blind Oracles*, 22–52.
10. Interview with Cora Du Bois by Lawrence C. Kelly, 9 Apr. 1978 (2nd, corrected, draft): Du Bois Papers, Box 11; Interview with Cora Du Bois by Judith B. Walzer, 20 Aug. 1981: Walzer, 'Oral History'; see also Price, *Threatening Anthropology*, 294–7.
11. Burton, 'Life and Ethnography of Claire Holt', 153–69. I am grateful to Sarah Bekker and Evelyn Colbert for further suggestions about Du Bois's and Holt's career choices.
12. Embree, 'American Military Government'; Embree, 'Applied Anthropology'; Embree, 'Micronesia'; Embree, 'Anthropology and the War', esp. 494–5; Embree, 'Some Problems of an American Cultural Officer'; Embree, 'A Note on Ethnocentrism'.
13. Abbott and Sparrow, 'Hot War, Cold War', 291–3.
14. Patterson, *Social History of Anthropology*, 107.
15. Katz, *Foreign Intelligence*, 197–8.
16. Herman, *Romance of American Psychology*, 67–76; Abbott and Sparrow, 'Hot War, Cold War', 301–10; Sproule, *Propaganda and Democracy*, 301–5; Buck, 'Adjusting to Military Life', 211–28; Robin, *Making of the Cold War Enemy*, 19–25. On the career networks spawned by Stouffer's Research Branch, see Clausen, 'Research on the American Soldier'.
17. Lagemann, *Politics of Knowledge*, 153–4, 164–5; Robin, *Making of the Cold War Enemy*, 28–9, 34–6; Geiger, *Research and Relevant Knowledge*, 97–105.
18. Lynd, 'Science of Inhuman Relations'. A very elderly John Dewey also weighed in again: Dewey, 'Liberating the Social Scientist'.
19. Glazer, 'Study of Man' (Nov. 1945); Glazer, 'Government by Manipulation'; Bell, 'Adjusting Men to Machines'; see also Glazer, 'From Socialism to Sociology', 198–200; Brick, *Daniel Bell*, 136–41, an excellent account which surprisingly says nothing about Bell's relationship to Glazer.
20. Lerner, '*The American Soldier* and the Public', esp. 237–41, 244–6.
21. 'Report of the Committee on Ethics.' For a criticism of the ethics code from a 'practical' anthropologist, see Barnett, *Anthropology in Administration*, 182–7; for a criticism by a post-Vietnam historian of anthropology, see Price, *Anthropological Intelligence*, 274–7, though cf. ibid., xvi, critical when the ethics code *isn't* applied.
22. Cf. Hegeman, *Patterns for America*, 164–5; Gilkeson, *Anthropologists and the Rediscovery of America*, 177–8.
23. For differences of this kind, see debates over the 'authoritarian personality', discussed below, pp. 226–7.
24. Gilman, *Mandarins of the Future*, x.

25. Lerner, 'The American Soldier and the Public', 244–5; Lasswell, 'Policy Sciences', 10–12; Lasswell, 'Propaganda and Mass Insecurity', 23–9. Lasswell and Lerner were together responsible for a series of books on the 'policy sciences', funded by Carnegie. For further discussion of Lasswell's position at this time, see Birnbach, Neo-Freudian Social Philosophy, ch. 7; Robin, Making of the Cold War Enemy, 64–9.

26. Powers, 'Harvard Study of Values', 20–2; Gilkeson, Anthropologists and the Rediscovery of America, ch. 4.

27. A critical account of HRAF can be found in Lemov, World as Laboratory, 149–68. For the seventy-five universals, see Kluckhohn, Mirror for Man, 27–9. For Mead's views, see Mead and Metraux (eds), Study of Culture, 53n; Mead to Kenneth L. Little, 11 May 1951: Mead Papers, C24; Wilcken, Claude Lévi-Strauss, 349n32.

28. Harris, Rise of Anthropological Theory, 452–62.

29. On this conflict, see Young, Ruth Benedict, 87–8, 160–2; Pinkoski, 'American Colonialism', 66–7; Peace, 'Mundial Upheaval Society', 146–53; see also a significant exchange in the American Anthropologist in 1947–8 between the young leftist Elgin Williams and Benedict's student Virginia Heyer Young (then writing as Virginia Heyer): Williams, 'Anthropology for the Common Man'; Heyer, 'Reply to Elgin Williams'; also Gregg and Williams, 'Dismal Science'. Di Leonardo, Exotics at Home, 225–6, cites Williams's critique but not Young's defence.

30. The Tensions Project can be followed through the UNESCO International Social Science Bulletin from 1949; see e.g. Klineberg, 'UNESCO Project'.

31. The statement by the AAA's Executive Board was issued on 24 June 1947 and published in American Anthropologist: 'Statement on Human Rights'; for contemporary criticisms, see Steward, 'Comments'; Barnett, 'On Science and Human Rights'; Redfield, Primitive World, 147–9; also Barnett, Anthropology in Administration, 61. For the wider context, see Morsink, Universal Declaration, esp. ix–xiii, 131–3; Renteln, International Human Rights, 64–9, 83–7; Engle, 'From Skepticism to Embrace', 536–47.

32. From an unpublished book draft, 'LDB Introduction', 6 Oct. 1952: Mead Papers, 156. I discuss this 'Latter Day Book' further below, pp. 278–9.

33. For some reflections on this mood in the 1940s, before a more 'positivist' mood set in, see Honigmann, 'Personal Approach', 302–8; Spiro, 'Culture and Human Nature', 337–46; Caffrey, Ruth Benedict, 327–37.

34. For discussions of CIMA along these lines, see Lemov, World as Laboratory, 170–87; Bashkow, 'Dynamics of Rapport'; Alcalay, 'United States Anthropologist in Micronesia'. For alternative views, emphasizing the failure of Murdock's programme, see Campbell, 'A Chance to Build a New Order'; Kiste and Falgout, 'Anthropology and Micronesia'; Petersen, 'Politics in Postwar Micronesia'; Falgout, 'Americans in Paradise'; Mandler, 'Deconstructing "Cold War Anthropology"'.

35. Barnett, Anthropology in Administration, 49–85; see also Beals, Politics of Social Research, 56–7. Unsurprisingly, Barnett had also been one of the objectors to the AAA statement on human rights. See also Redfield, Primitive World, 145–6.

36. See e.g. Foreign Language Information Service press releases, 'Learning to Live in One World', 3 Jan. 1945; 'Wider Loyalties Needed', 16 Feb. 1945; 'Talking About Other Groups', 5 Mar. 1945: Mead Papers, I29. A similar mission informed the summer school she ran at Wellesley College in 1944.

37. Mead prepared a rough outline of the book in late spring, discussed it with Rhoda Metraux and Ruth Benedict, and began to write in earnest in New Hampshire in early July. 'Tentative Outline of New American Book', 3 May 1945; 'Second Tentative Outline of New American Book', n.d. [Jun. 1945]: Mead Papers, 128. The surviving drafts begin on 3 July.

38. Mead, 'Learning to Live in One World', drafts, 'Ch. III': Mead Papers, I28.

39. Ibid., ch. 2.

40. See below, p. 209.

41. Mead, 'Human Differences and World Order', 43–4.

42. Mead, 'Learning to Live in One World', drafts, 'Perhaps Chapter IV making present IV V', 13 Aug. 1945, 'VIIc. (Question 3)', 22 Aug. 1945, 'Appraising our international potential for any specific country', n.d.: Mead Papers, I28. And see Mead's explication to Bateson, 15 Aug. 1945: Mead Papers, R3.

43. Mead, 'Learning to Live in One World', drafts, 'Perhaps Chapter IV making present IV V', 13 Aug. 1945; 'Ch. IV'; 'Ch. V, 9 Jul. 1945, 'Second attempt'; 'Appraising our international potential for any specific country'; 'Question One: How does Britain figure in our sense of national identity?': Mead Papers, I28.
44. Mead to Bateson, 10, 15 Aug. 1945: Mead Papers, R3.
45. Mead, 'Learning to Live in One World', drafts, 'Probably Part I also V or VI', 20 Aug. 1945: Mead Papers, I28.
46. Mead to Thayer Hobson, William Morrow & Co., 24 Aug. 1945; 'Atomic Bomb Interviews', 11–12 Aug. 1945; 'Key Reactions to the Atomic Bomb', 11 Aug. 1945: Mead Papers, I28.
47. Robert Williams, Roper Organization, to Mead, 2 Oct. 1945; Mead to Rhoda Metraux, 21 Mar. 1946: Mead Papers, I29, M39. See below, ch. 6, for her work on these questionnaires with Gorer.
48. Mead to Melville Jacobs, 27 Aug. 1945; Mead to Benedict, 'Proposed Plan for International Relations Book', 11 Sep. 1945; Mead to Daniel Lerner, 6 Jul. 1951: Mead Papers, E4, I28, C24.
49. Mead, *Anthropologist at Work*, 432–4, comments on this 'reversal of the roles'.
50. Benedict, in discussion, in Sargent and Smith (eds), *Culture and Personality*, 139.
51. Benedict to Mead, n.d. [Sep. 1945], n.d. [Sep. 1945], 20 Sep. 1945; Mead to Benedict, 17 Sep. 1945: Mead Papers, B1, Q11, S4.
52. Benedict to Clyde Kluckhohn, 16 May 1946: Benedict Papers, Box 14/4. The occasion was a meeting of the SAA and a session organized by Alex Leighton on 'Cultural Differences: Asset or Liability in World Relations', to which Benedict was trying to recruit Kluckhohn.
53. Benedict to Duncan Strong, 14 Nov. 1945; Benedict to Frank Tannenbaum, 14 Nov. 1945; Benedict to Kurt Lewin, 19 Dec. 1945; Benedict to Kathryn McHale, AAUW, 30 Apr. 1948: Benedict Papers, Boxes 13, 59; Benedict, 'Study of Cultural Patterns', 279; Mead, *Anthropologist at Work*, 430–2.
54. Jean Howard, notes of a seminar on RCC with Rhoda Metraux, 21–2 Mar. 1980: Howard Papers, Box 38; Mead, *Anthropologist at Work*, 432–4; Benedict to Mead, 26 Jun. 1946: Mead Papers, G2.
55. Benedict to Capt. Robert Conrad, ONR, 17 Jun. 1946 (misfiled as 1949); Benedict to Mead, 26 Jun. 1946: Mead Papers, G4, G2; Benedict to Clyde Kluckhohn, 19 Aug. 1946: Kluckhohn Papers, HUG 4490.3, Box 1.
56. Benedict to Mead, 26 Jun. 1946: Mead Papers, G2.
57. Transcripts of the early meetings of the ONR Advisory Panel on Human Relations, 3–4 Oct., 6–7 Dec. 1946; 'Statement Prepared by the Advisory Panel on Human Relations of the ONR', 7 Dec. 1946: Mead Papers, G8; Darley, 'Five Years of Social Science Research', esp. 5 (and see also 13–15 on the 'objectivity' question). John Darley, a psychologist specializing in personnel selection, was something of a bête noire of Benedict's. Benedict to Mead, 26 Jun. 1946: Mead Papers, G2.
58. The Human Relations panel's budget was $250,000 in the first year and $500,000 in the second.
59. The evolution of the proposal can be traced in Benedict Papers, Box 59 and Mead Papers, G8.
60. Benedict to J.W. Macmillan, ONR, 16, 22 Oct. 1946; Macmillan to Benedict, 13 Jan. 1947 (misdated 1946); ONR Advisory Panel on Human Relations, 3–4 Oct. 1946: Mead Papers, G8.
61. Minutes of Seminar Meeting, RRC, Harvard University, 7 Jan. 1949: Mead Papers, G87. LeVine, 'Culture and Personality Studies', 813–15, and Gilliam and Foerstel, 'Margaret Mead's Contradictory Legacy', 143–4, more or less invert Benedict's reasoning.
62. Benedict to Gorer, 21 Oct. 1946; Mead to Gorer, 12 Nov. 1946, 19 Oct. 1961: Mead Papers, O38, B5, B6; Benedict at RCC, 1st general seminar, 18 Sep. 1947, and at 18th general seminar, 26 May 1948: Mead Papers, G13, G14; Mead, 'Research in Contemporary Cultures', 107–13.
63. Mead, *Anthropologist at Work*, 432–7; Mead and Metraux (eds), *Study of Culture*, 96; Minutes of Seminar Meeting, RRC, Harvard University, 7 Jan. 1949: Mead Papers, G87; Jane Howard, notes of a seminar on RCC with Rhoda Metraux, 21–2 Mar. 1980; Jane Howard, interviews with Asen Balikci, Leila Lee, Ruth Landman: Howard Papers, Box 38; and see Young, *Ruth Benedict*, ch. 5, by one of Benedict's graduate students on the project.

64. David Riesman to Laurence Veysey, 6 Jan. 1975: Riesman Papers, HUG(FP) 99.16, Box 40.
65. Benedict, 'Anthropology and the Humanities' (1948), in Mead, *Anthropologist at Work*, 459–70.
66. Young, *Ruth Benedict*, 29–30.
67. ONR Advisory Panel on Human Relations, 3–4 Oct. 1946; RCC, 18th general seminar, 26 May 1948; Abraham Kaplan, Project RAND, to Benedict, 1 Oct. 1947: Mead Papers, G8, G14, G76. Benedict's presence at the first RAND social-science conference, which David Price finds so sinister, was clearly aimed at moderating its war-fighting orientation: Price, 'Subtle Means', 377–8.
68. Benedict to Nathan Leites, 30 Mar. 1946: Benedict Papers, Box 14.
69. Benedict and Fromm, 'Recommendations to the Office of Naval Research', n.d. [early 1948]: Mead Papers, G8.
70. Benedict, 'A Slender Reed'; Embree, 'Some Problems of an American Cultural Officer', 156.
71. Mead to Luther Cressman, 7 Jan. 1973 (photocopy): Jane Howard Papers, Box 48; Mead to Erik Erikson, 27 Apr. 1947: Mead Papers, R8; Mead to Caroline Tennant Kelly, 13 Jul. 1947: Caffrey and Francis (eds), *To Cherish the Life*, 113–17; Lipset, *Bateson*, 175–83.
72. Mead to Benedict, 14 Jul. 1947: Mead Papers, R7.
73. Ibid.
74. On Leites's wartime work with Lasswell, see Sproule, *Propaganda and Democracy*, 193–6; Hoffman, 'American Psychologists and Wartime Research', 269–70. For some general impressions, see RAND, *Remembering Nathan Leites*, esp. 55, 63–6, 71, 82.
75. For Leites's anxieties about the weakening will of democratic society, see e.g. Kris and Leites, 'Trends in Twentieth-Century Propaganda'; and see Kuklick, *Blind Oracles*, 32–6, and esp. Robin, *Making of the Cold War Enemy*, 131–43, which nicely captures Leites's blend of elitism and 'psychoculture'.
76. Nathan Leites to Clyde Kluckhohn, 10 Nov. 1945: Kluckhohn Papers, HUG 4490.3, Box 3; Mead, draft letter, Nov. 1945; Gorer to Benedict, 9 Aug. 1947: Mead Papers, B5, C13.
77. Mead to Gorer, 9 Dec. 1948: Mead Papers, B6.
78. On the statements on race, see Shipman, *Evolution of Racism*, 156–70; Brattain, 'Race, Racism, and Antiracism'.
79. Calder, 'Sanity Fair'; 'The World Federation for Mental Health'.
80. Borgwardt, *A New Deal for the World*, esp. 15, 73–82, 250–1; cf. Fousek, *To Lead the Free World*, esp. 8–15, 103–21, 187–8, more pessimistic about the chances of 'One World' thinking.
81. Ninkovich, *Diplomacy of Ideas*, 87–106.
82. Ibid., 126–36; Hixson, *Parting the Curtain*, 11–13; Simpson, *Science of Coercion*, 64; Caute, *Dancer Defects*, 24. Fousek, *To Lead the Free World*, 130, dates the changed orientation earlier, to the enunciation of the Truman Doctrine in 1947.
83. Kennard's requests for CIR materials in Mead Papers, R3; Hall, *Anthropology of Everyday Life*, 200–2; Kennard, 'Anthropology in the Foreign Service Institute'.
84. Kennard's assistant was a Parsons-trained sociologist, Frank Hopkins. Frank S. Hopkins to Benedict, 23 Oct. 1947: Benedict Papers, Box 15; Cora Du Bois, FSI correspondence, 1946–7, draft lectures, 1946–7: Du Bois Papers, Box 31, 67; William P. Maddox, State Department, to Du Bois, 17 Jan. 1947: National Archives (US), State Department Central Decimal File, 1945–9, RG 59, 111.745/1–1747.
85. Riesman, 'Study of National Character', 602–3.
86. Williams, 'Anthropology for the Common Man', 84; Riesman, 'Changes in Leisure Attitudes', 142.
87. Hollinger, 'Cultural Relativism', 714; Gleason, *Speaking of Diversity*, 156–7; Mead, 1959 preface to Benedict, *Patterns*, xi.
88. Mead to Grayson Kirk, 21 Oct. 1948 (quoting Benedict's original proposal to Kirk): Mead Papers, G3.
89. Chase and Kluckhohn tried to moderate the relativist message of cultural anthropology in the name of 'human values'; at the same time, they did publicize explicitly the value of anthropology for building 'One World'. See esp. Chase, *Proper Study*, 60–8, 275–84; Kluckhohn, *Mirror for Man*, 25–49, 241–62.

90. Kluckhohn, 'Anthropology Comes of Age', 241.
91. Gorer to Benedict, 28 Dec. 1946; Gorer to Mead, 28 Dec. 1946: Mead Papers, O38, B5.
92. Mead to Gorer, 12 Mar. 1947; Mead to Daniel Lerner, 6 Jul. 1951: Mead Papers, B6, C24.
93. *Life*, 18 Aug. 1947, pp. 94–112 (with letters to the editor, 25 Aug. 1947, pp. 9–15); *New York Times*, 22 Feb. 1948, 30 May 1948.
94. Familiar themes sent up include infant aggression, the rituals of dating, the standardization demanded by immigrants, maternal dominance, women's clubs (one of Gorer's pet subjects) and loneliness: 'James', *Americans in Glasshouses*, 17, 19–21, 51–4, 56–60, 64, 68, 118–19. I have been unable to work out the identity of 'Leslie James' and would welcome elucidation. Gorer's speculations included Alistair Cooke (unlikely) and 'two American graduate students (one of each sex)' at the LSE. Gorer to Mead, 7 Oct., 28 Dec. 1950, 10 Aug. 1951; Mead to Gorer, 19 Dec. 1950; Mead to Ralph Shikes, Henry Schuman Inc., 22 Jan. 1951: Mead Papers, R8, B6, C22.
95. *Time*, 29 Mar. 1948, 42; see also Duncan Aikman in the *Saturday Review*, 27 Mar. 1948, 10–11, Alfred Kazin in the *New Yorker*, 20 Mar. 1948, and John Chamberlain in the *New York Times*, 21 Mar. 1948. For John Marshall's assessment of the book's reception, interview with Gorer, 15 Mar. 1949; Marshall to Robert Silvey, 13 Jun. 1949; Silvey to Marshall, 16 Jun. 1949: Rockefeller Foundation Archives, RG 2, Series 401, Box 458, Folder 3077.
96. Mead to Jules Henry, 14 Dec. 1950; Mead to Daniel Lerner, 6 Jul. 1951: Mead Papers, C22, C24; Mead, *Male and Female*, 451–2. For the most influential critique from the next generation, see Friedan, *Feminine Mystique*, 108–11; for a recent reassessment, Tarrant, *When Sex Became Gender*, 75–90.
97. Erikson, *Childhood and Society*, esp. chs 8–10; see also Freedman, *Identity's Architect*, 176–89, 237–41; Gleason, 'Identifying Identity', 923–8.
98. Fromm, *Man for Himself*; see also McLaughlin, 'Critical Theory Meets America'.
99. David Riesman, Interview #632, 2–16: Columbia University, Oral History Research Office.
100. Riesman, *Lonely Crowd*, xxxiv–xxxv (from the preface to the 1961 ed.), 4.
101. Mead, 'Social Change and Cultural Surrogates', 107–8; cf. Riesman, *Lonely Crowd*, 41n.
102. Riesman, *Lonely Crowd*, 41, 49; Riesman to Mead, 12 Jul. 1948: Mead Papers, C19; Riesman with Glazer, 'The Lonely Crowd: A Reconsideration', 434–5. On Riesman's interest in Gorer's *The Americans*, see Harold Lasswell to Gorer, 13 Apr. 1948: Gorer Papers, Box 87; on Riesman's interest in Erikson, see David Riesman to Erik Erikson, 11 Mar. 1948: Riesman Papers, HUG(FP) 99.12, Box 8, and see also Brick, *Transcending Capitalism*, 173–8; on Riesman's relationship with Mead (she and Rhoda Metraux both read the manuscript for him in autumn 1949), see David Riesman to Mead, 12 Jul. 1948; Rhoda Metraux to Mead, 10 Oct. 1949: Mead Papers, C19, C21; Mead to David Riesman, 19 Oct. 1949: Riesman Papers, HUG(FP) 99.16, Box 41.
103. Mead to David Riesman, 19 Oct. 1949, 21 Jan. 1952: Riesman Papers, HUG(FP) 99.12, Box 31.
104. David Riesman to Erik Erikson, 11 Mar. 1948: Riesman Papers, HUG(FP) 99.12, Box 8.
105. David Riesman to Alex Morin, 24 Mar. 1953; Riesman to Clyde Kluckhohn, 1 Dec. 1953: Riesman Papers, HUG(FP) 99.8, Box 31, HUG(FP) 99.12, Box 25; Riesman, *Lonely Crowd*, lxx. For Riesman's defences of Mead in the 1950s, see below, pp. 218–19.
106. Mead to Gorer, 3 Jan. 1951 (misdated 1950): Gorer Papers, Box 91.
107. Mead, 'An Anthropologist Looks at the Report', esp. 281–3; Gorer, 'Justification by Numbers', 168–70; Igo, *Averaged American*, 217–28, 239–80.
108. She criticized Riesman for employing only a 'semicomparative inclusion of other cultures' in *The Lonely Crowd* which suppressed the complexities of intercultural relations: Mead, 'National Character and the Science of Anthropology', 24–6.
109. Mead, 'Learning to Live in One World', drafts, ch. 3, 8–9; 'Proposed Plan for International Relations Book', 11 Sep. 1945 (accepting that material on 'internal cleavages' will 'probably never be used'); see also the file, 'Is There an American Type?', n.d. [c. Jan.–Feb. 1945]: Mead Papers, I28.
110. Mead and Metraux (eds), *Study of Culture*, 24. Cf. Wall, *Inventing the 'American Way'*, 89–93, 165–8, 280; Janiewski and Banner (eds), *Reading Benedict/Reading Mead*, xiii.

111. See, for instance, UNESCO, Social Sciences Section, 'Preliminary Outline of Project on Tensions Affecting International Understanding', 12 May 1947: Benedict Papers, Box 112, importantly with Benedict's critical annotations.

112. Chase, *Proper Study of Mankind*, 60, 275–80.

113. Kluckhohn, *Mirror for Man*, 48, 243–62.

114. Mead, 'Comparative Study of Cultures', 91–3.

115. Lasswell, 'Policy Orientation', 3–4; Lasswell, 'Propaganda and Mass Insecurity', esp. 23–33; Lasswell, 'Policy and the Intelligence Function', 60; Lerner, 'Effective Propaganda', 348–50; Speier, 'Psychological Warfare Reconsidered', 482–9; Kris and Leites, 'Trends in Twentieth-Century Propaganda'. For this line of argument, see Simpson, *Science of Coercion*, 44–6.

116. Lerner, *Psychological Warfare*; Lerner (ed.), *Propaganda in War and Crisis*; and see the full narrative, linking back to prewar experiments in social control such as Beardsley Ruml's, in Lasswell, 'Policy Orientation', 5–7.

117. Mead, 'Study of National Character', 94–5.

118. Mead, 'Comparative Study of Cultures', 93–103. Gorer, who was present, thought Mead was overconcerned about the anti-democratic potential of the uses of social science: ibid., 93–5n.

119. See the file of correspondence in Kluckhohn Papers, HUG 4490.5, Box 8; Endleman, *Psyche and Society*.

120. Endleman, 'The New Anthropology'; see also Berger, 'Understanding National Character', 385–6.

121. Endleman, 'The New Anthropology', 286–8.

122. Linton and Wagley, *Linton*, 49–50; Kluckhohn, 'Ralph Linton', 243–5; Gillin, 'Ralph Linton', 278; Young, *Ruth Benedict*, 155–6; Cora Du Bois, 'Notes from the Field: Colleagues', annotated 'Ralph Linton', n.d.: Du Bois Papers, Box 11. I am also grateful for a reminiscence of Linton in this period from Mel Spiro.

123. Ralph Linton to Clyde Kluckhohn, 7 Dec. 1942: Kluckhohn Papers, HUG 4490.3, Box 3.

124. Ralph Linton, review of Geoffrey Gorer, *The American People*, *Scientific American*, May 1948, 58–9.

125. Patterson, *Social History of Anthropology*, 105–6; Caffrey, *Ruth Benedict*, 331–3. For Mead's critique, see Mead to Carl Guthe, 6 Oct. 1945: Mead Papers, E4.

126. Sargent and Smith (eds), *Culture and Personality*, vi; Orlansky, 'Infant Care and Personality', acknowledging Linton's advice; Orlansky, 'Destiny in the Nursery'; Linton, 'Concept of National Character', 142.

127. Benedict to Mead, 7 Apr. 1939: Mead Papers, B1; Price, 'Cold War Anthropology', 412.

128. Florence and Clyde Kluckhohn, review of Margaret Mead, *And Keep Your Powder Dry*, *American Anthropologist*, n.s., 45 (1943), 622–4; Mead to Clyde Kluckhohn, 10 Dec. 1943; Kluckhohn to Mead, 28 Dec. 1943, 31 Oct. [1944] (misfiled as 1947); Mead to Bateson, 10 Sep., 4 Nov. 1944; Talcott Parsons to Mead, 1 Nov. 1944: Mead Papers, C10, C16, R3.

129. Of course, Mead was jealous of Kluckhohn as well as vice versa. For Kluckhohn's postwar views, see *Mirror for Man*, 187–8 (on universal values), 192–206 (on impulse control) and 206–8, 235–8, 243–6 (on international implications).

130. Mead, 'Retrospects and Prospects', 134–6.

131. Orlansky, 'Infant Care and Personality'; Lindesmith and Strauss, 'A Critique of Culture-Personality Writings'; and see Inkeles and Levinson, 'National Character', for the best-known critique.

132. Klineberg, 'Recent Studies of National Character'; see also Klineberg, 'Historical Perspectives', 40–2, 52–3; and Farber, 'Problem of National Character'.

133. Stoetzel, *Without the Chrysanthemum*, esp. 16–18, 50–63, 193–9.

134. Sargent and Smith (eds), *Culture and Personality*, 140–1.

135. 'LDB Introduction', 6 Oct. 1952: Mead Papers, I56.

136. Riesman, 'Comments on Dr. Kluckhohn's Paper', 68–9; see also Barnett, *Anthropology in Administration*, 56–61, for a similar verdict from a much less sympathetic position.

137. RCC, 18th general seminar, 26 May 1948: Mead Papers, G14.

138. Cora Du Bois, 'Notes from the Field: Colleagues', annotated 'Ralph Linton', n.d.: Du Bois Papers, Box 11; Caffrey, *Ruth Benedict*, 278. Even on a casual meeting with Linton, who was not his supervisor, Mel Spiro too was gleefully shown the fatal charm bag.

139. Mead to Gorer, 14 Jan. 1952: Gorer Papers, Box 91.

140. Mead to Gorer, 9 Dec. 1948: Mead Papers, B6.

Chapter 6 Swaddling the Russians

1. Engerman, *Know Your Enemy*, 1, points out that there were only twenty-five Soviet experts in US government employ in 1946, but there were only about a dozen Japanese experts *anywhere* in the US in 1941.
2. Bell, 'Ten Theories', esp. 315–19.
3. Engerman, *Modernization from the Other Shore*, 245–66; Bell, 'Ten Theories', 325–6; Katz, *Foreign Intelligence*, 137–57.
4. Katz, *Foreign Intelligence*, 160–4; Engerman, *Know Your Enemy*, 71; Engerman, 'Cold War's Organization Man'.
5. Engerman, *Know Your Enemy*, 25–40.
6. Gilman, *Mandarins of the Future*, 79–88.
7. Price, 'Cold War Anthropology', 402–3, following Diamond, *Compromised Campus*, 58, 296–7n9, speculates that Kluckhohn was blackmailed into taking the RRC job on the basis of FBI knowledge of his homosexual relationships.
8. John Gardner, 'Russian Studies', 14 Jul. 1947: Kluckhohn Papers, HUG 4490.7, Box 3.
9. Gerhardt, *Talcott Parsons*, 175–7.
10. Gaddis, *Strategies of Containment*, esp. 26–8, 32–6, 106; Engerman, *Modernization from the Other Shore*, 257–71; cf. Fousek, *To Lead the Free World*, 6–11, 42–5, 103–21; Lucas, *Freedom's War*, 55–68; Hixson, *Parting the Curtain*, xiv, 12.
11. Alex Inkeles, Interview #1419, 2 Jan. 1985: Oral History Research Office, Columbia University; Inkeles, 'Clyde Kluckhohn's Contribution'; Engerman, *Know Your Enemy*, 44–7.
12. This conclusion can be gleaned from the chronological order of RRC's publications in its first decade; and see Kluckhohn, 'Russian Research at Harvard', 267.
13. Lucas, *Freedom's War*, 63.
14. Adorno et al., *Authoritarian Personality*; see also Samelson, 'Authoritarianism from Berlin to Berkeley'.
15. Alpers, *Dictators, Democracy*, 139–56.
16. Ibid., 244–9, 274–90; Katz, *Foreign Intelligence*, 162; McClay, *The Masterless*, 209–25; Haney, *Americanization of Social Science*, 92–109; Cotkin, *Existential America*, 64–7; Gilman, *Mandarins of the Future*, 49–53; Gleason, *Totalitarianism*, 72–7.
17. Mead and Gorer, 'Unorganized Transcript of Notes of Original Conversation', 21 Apr. 1945; Benedict and Mead, 'On Russia', n.d. [c. 29 Apr. 1945]: Mead Papers, M39.
18. Mead, *And Keep Your Powder Dry*, 167–8 (from the 1965 preface). See above, pp. 189–90.
19. See above, pp. 198–9.
20. Benedict to Joseph Goldsen, 27 Apr. 1948; Mead to Benedict, 27 Apr. 1948; [Mead and Rosten], 'Current Soviet Conduct Models and Deviations', 27 Apr. 1948: Mead Papers, G76.
21. Gorer and Rickman, *People of Great Russia*, 7–8, 10–11.
22. RCC, 10th general seminar, 5 Feb. 1948: Mead Papers, G13. Ina Telberg complained at the time that he had in fact consulted only fifty of the RCC's Russian interviews, and had misinterpreted her own interview research. C.B. Fahs, interview with Ina Telberg, 11 Feb. 1948: Rockefeller Foundation Archives, RG 2, Series 401, Box 420, Folder 2832.
23. In addition to their April 1945 exchanges, transcribed for Gorer's use in autumn 1947, see also Gorer to Mead, 30 Apr. 1946; Mead, 'Points', 1 Aug. 1946, 18 Sep. 1946: Mead Papers, M39.
24. Mead to Gorer, 14 Nov. 1950; Gorer to Mead, 20 Nov. 1950: Mead Papers, B6, S6; Gorer and Rickman, *People of Great Russia*, 143–4.
25. Gorer and Rickman, *People of Great Russia*, 74–7, 88–106, 112.
26. Ibid., 114–19, 129–31.
27. Ibid., 16–17, 136–8.
28. For an early disagreement between Gorer and Mead about Klein along these lines, see Gorer to Mead, 27 Jan. 1939, Mead to Gorer, 5 Apr. 1939: Mead Papers, B5, B7; on original sin, see Mead to Benedict, 28 Sep. 1938: Mead Papers, B1, and Riley, *War in the Nursery*, 74–6, a good summary of Klein's thinking in this area; on Gorer's application of Klein to the Russians, see RCC, 17th general seminar, 20 May 1948; RRC, Minutes of Seminar Meeting, 7 Jan. 1949: Mead Papers, G14, G87; Gorer and Rickman, *People of Great Russia*, 90, 147–9; Gorer, 'Internal Monsters'.

29. Gorer and Rickman, *People of Great Russia*, 130; Mead, 'Study of National Character', 99.

30. Gorer, 'Some Aspects', 160.

31. Gorer and Rickman, *People of Great Russia*, 129, makes a particularly problematic distribution of traits common or specific to elite and people.

32. 'Notes on a Talk by Dr. Geoffrey Gorer on "Some Aspects of Russian Psychology"', 9 Jan. 1948; Mead to Clyde Kluckhohn, 13 Dec. 1949: Mead Papers, G87, G12; Mead to Gorer, 15 May 1952: Gorer Papers, Box 91; Engerman, *Know Your Enemy*, 47. By January 1949, when Mead herself visited RRC to talk about Gorer's hypotheses, the criticism was more voluble, though Kluckhohn and Bauer sought to keep peace between the two groups. Minutes of Seminar Meeting, RRC, Harvard University, 7 Jan. 1949: Mead Papers, G87.

33. Fahs's own view of the Gorer theses, when he heard them at an RCC seminar in early February, was that they were 'stimulating, intriguing, and perhaps even half right', but that the 'depth psychology' was applied with unsettling overconfidence. C.B. Fahs, 'Meeting of Dr. Ruth Benedict's Seminar at the Viking Fund on Foreign Cultures', 5 Feb. 1948; C.B. Fahs, interview with Ina Telberg, 11 Feb. 1948: Rockefeller Foundation Archives, RG 2, Series 401, Box 420, Folder 2832.

34. RCC, 10th general seminar, 5 Feb. 1948: Mead Papers, G13.

35. Benedict, 'Child Rearing', 342–8, with Mead's commentary, 349–50.

36. Mead to Philip Mosely, 19 Jul. 1948: Mead Papers, G12.

37. Goldfrank, 'Another View', 6–7. Goldfrank had been a student of Boas's with an interest in culture and personality, but whose work emphasized personality formation across the life cycle rather than in infancy; she also held professional grudges against both Mead and Benedict. See Lindesmith and Strauss, 'Critique of Culture-Personality', 595–6; Kluckhohn, 'Culture and Behavior', 949; Caffrey, *Ruth Benedict*, 228.

38. Peake, 'OSS and Venona', 22. On Wittfogel and Goldfrank's anti-communist informing, including RCC, see Price, 'Materialism's Free Pass', 42–3, 45–9.

39. Mead to Benedict, 15 Jul. 1948; Mead to Philip Mosely, 19 Jul. 1948; Ernest J. Simmons to Mead, 1 Nov. 1948, 10 Jan. 1949: Mead Papers, G12. Karpovich was a member of the *American Slavic and East European Review*'s editorial board, as well as of Harvard's RRC; he had been Mosely's PhD supervisor at Harvard before the war.

40. Gorer to Jean Parker, 4 Aug. 1948; John Rickman to Gorer, 15 Dec. 1948: Gorer Papers, Boxes 102, 98; Gorer and Rickman, *People of Great Russia*, 24, 136–50.

41. Endleman, 'The New Anthropology', 288 and cf. 291: 'It is most unlikely that Gorer's speculations on Russian character will be more useful than his speculations on the Japanese.'

42. Erwin H. Ackerknecht, review of Rodnick, *Quarterly Review of Biology* 23 (1948), 405; Howard Becker, review of Rodnick, *Annals of the American Academy of Political and Social Science* 264 (1949), 137–8; Harold D. Lasswell, review of Rodnick, *Public Opinion Quarterly* 12 (1948), 505–6; Everett C. Hughes, review of Rodnick and Schaffner, *American Journal of Sociology* 55 (1949), 101–2; de Sola Pool, 'Who Gets Power', 129, but cf. 132; Endleman, 'The New Anthropology', 287.

43. On Dallin and the New York émigré community, see Liebich, *From the Other Shore*, esp. 228, 406n14, on Zborowski and the Dallins; on the *New Leader*, Wilford, 'Playing the CIA's Tune?'; on the Zborowski case, 'Scope of Soviet Activity in the United States: Hearing before the Subcommittee to Investigate the Administration of the Internal Security Act and Other Internal Security Laws', 84th Congress, 2nd Session, 29 Feb. and 2 Mar. 1956: Mead Papers, M18.

44. Goldfrank, 'Another View', 7–11; Jane Howard, interview with Esther Goldfrank, 14 Aug. 1980: Jane Howard Papers, Box 38.

45. Dallin, 'Exterminate the Russians?'

46. J. Anthony Marcus to Gen. D.D. Eisenhower, 30 Oct. 1949; Mead to Dr J. Enrique Zenetti, associate provost, 8 Nov. 1949; J. Anthony Marcus to Mead, 30 Nov. 1949; Mead to J. Anthony Marcus, 7 Dec. 1949: Mead Papers, G3, G76.

47. M. Petrov, 'The Filthy Concoction of Mr Gorer', *Red Fleet*, 14 May 1950, translated by the British Foreign Office and sent to Gorer in J.H.A. Watson, Foreign Office, to Gorer, 12 Jun. 1950: Gorer Papers, Box 83.

48. 'Reds Angry over Diapers', *New York Times*, 20 Feb. 1952, 9.

49. Dallin, 'The New Anti-Russians'; Shub, 'Soviets Expose American Baby'.

50. Mead to Gorer, 5 Dec. 1949, 17 Jan. 1950: Mead Papers, R8, S1.
51. Wolfe, 'Swaddled Soul'; Berger, 'Understanding National Character', 384–6; Dallin, *New Soviet Empire*, 50–66.
52. Gorer, 'Swaddling and the Russians'; Wolfe, 'Swaddling and the Russians'; Mosely, 'A Pro-Russian, Anti-Soviet Policy'; Mead to S.M. Levitas, *New Leader*, 9 Feb. 1951: Mead Papers, G76.
53. J.W. Macmillan, ONR, to Mead, 3 Feb. 1949, 28 Feb. 1949, 7 Jul. 1949; Mead to Macmillan, 26 Aug. 1949; Gorer to Macmillan, 19 Sep. 1949: Mead Papers, G3, G4.
54. Speier, 'Psychological Warfare Reconsidered', 472–7; on RAND, see Kuklick, *Blind Oracles*, 22–36.
55. Hans Speier to Mead, 27 Jul. 1949: Mead Papers, G76.
56. Mead to Gorer, 27 Aug. 1949; Mead to Nathan Leites, 29 Jul. 1949: Mead Papers, B6, G76.
57. Howard, *Margaret Mead*, 277.
58. John Golden to Mead, 23 Oct. 1951: Mead Papers, I54; see Golden's review of Gorer and Rickman, *People of Great Russia*, in *American Anthropologist* 54 (1952), 415–16.
59. Goldman, 'Psychiatric Interpretation', esp. 157–9; Irving Goldman to Clyde Kluckhohn, 13 Nov. 1950: Kluckhohn Papers, HUG 4490.5, Box 10; Mead to Gorer, 6 Nov. 1950; Mead to Goldman, 18 Oct. 1950: Mead Papers, B6, C21.
60. Mead to Jules Henry, 14 Dec. 1950: Mead Papers, C22.
61. Mead to Gorer, 9 Dec. 1950: Gorer Papers, Box 91.
62. See Mead's report on the American Association for the Advancement of Science meetings in December 1950, in Mead to Gorer, 3 Jan. 1951 (misdated 1950): Gorer Papers, Box 91; Mead, 'Outline for Paper to Be Given at Ethnological Society Meeting April 13, 1951': Mead Papers, E46; Rhoda Metraux's report on American Ethnological Society meeting, Sep. 1951; Metraux to Mead, 10 Jan. 1952 (misdated 1951): Metraux Papers, Box 3. I am also grateful to Audrey Spiro for a reminiscence dating from around 1952.
63. C.B. Fahs, interview with Ina Telberg, 13 Feb. 1948: Rockefeller Foundation Archives, RG 2, Series 401, Box 420, Folder 2832; Mead to Benedict, 14 Jul. 1947: Mead Papers, R7.
64. Mead to Gorer, 20 Nov. 1949: Gorer Papers, Box 91; Mead to Gorer, n.d. [1951–2]: Mead Papers, S6; information from Mary Catherine Bateson.
65. Mead to Rhoda Metraux, 10 Jan. 1954: Caffrey and Francis (eds), *To Cherish the Life*, 183.
66. Mead to Gorer, 20 Jul. 1950, n.d. [1951–2]: Mead Papers, R8, S6; information from Mary Catherine Bateson.
67. Mead to Gorer, 19 Dec. 1950: Gorer Papers, Box 91. This coincides exactly with her wounded exchanges with Goldman and Henry.
68. Gorer to Mead, 28 Dec. 1950: Gorer Papers, Box 91; Gorer to Mead, 18 Aug., 18 Sep., 4 Oct. 1951; Mead to Gorer, 27 Sep. 1951: Mead Papers, I62, B6. See further Mandler, 'Being His Own Rabbit'.
69. Benedict to Joseph Goldsen, 27 Apr. 1948; Mead to Benedict, 27 Apr. 1948: Mead Papers, G76.
70. 'Current Soviet Conduct Models and Deviations', 27 Apr. 1948 (the proposal that went to RAND under Benedict's name, but was drafted by Mead and Rosten); J.W. Macmillan, ONR, to Benedict, 11 Jun. 1948: Mead Papers, G76.
71. Leites, 'Psycho-Cultural Hypotheses'; Speier, 'Nathan Leites', 63–4; and see also Kuklick, *Blind Oracles*, 32–3, 46–7; Robin, *Making of the Cold War Enemy*, 131–4; and Engerman, *Modernization from the Other Shore*, 274–5, 285 (but failing to distinguish between Leites, Mead and Gorer).
72. F.L.W. Richardson to J.S. King, 23 Sep. 1948; Mead to J.S. King, 25 Sep. 1948; Nathan Leites to Mead, 30 Sep. 1948; Mead to King, 15 Oct. 1948; King to Mead, 18 Nov. 1948: Mead Papers, G76, G92.
73. Hans Speier to Mead, 27 Jul. 1949; Mead to Gorer, 27 Aug. 1949: Mead Papers, G77, B6.
74. Mead to Hans Speier, 29 Jul. 1949; Mead to Nathan Leites, 29 Jul. 1949: Mead Papers, G77, G76.
75. For instance, she had been fomenting an alliance between Gorer and Elsa Bernaut inside RCC as 'a subversive plot vis-à-vis Nathan'. She also claimed to have taken on the RAND project only as 'an emergency measure' after Benedict's death: Mead to Gorer, 16 Jul. 1949, 17 Jan. 1950; Mead to Hans Speier, 29 Jul. 1949: Mead Papers, G12, S1, G77; Mead, *Soviet*

Attitudes, 171; Minutes of Seminar Meeting, RRC, Harvard University, 7 Jan. 1949: Mead Papers, G87.

76. Mead to Hans Speier, n.d. (not sent); Nathan Leites to Mead, 8 Aug. 1949; Mead to Speier, 12 Aug. 1949; N. Leites and M. Mead, 'Some Soviet Attitudes towards Authority', n.d. [Oct. 1949]: Mead Papers, G76–8; Mead to Gorer, 20 Nov., 5 Dec. 1949: Gorer Papers, Box 91.

77. Leites, *Operational Code*, esp. 20–30; Rosten, 'How the Politburo Thinks'; Leo Rosten to Clyde Kluckhohn, 1 Oct. 1951: Kluckhohn Papers, HUG 4490.5, Box 22.

78. George, 'Nathan, My Teacher', 3–4; Bell, 'Ten Theories', 329–37.

79. Kuklick, *Blind Oracles*, 32–3, 46–7; Robin, *Making of the Cold War Enemy*, 134–43, a fascinating case study.

80. An early version of the report, dated 15 December 1949, is in Mead Papers, G78, but the final version was not submitted until April 1950. 'Current Soviet Conduct Models and Deviations: A Pilot Study in Soviet Attitudes toward Authority', 1 Apr. 1950, lightly annotated with edits for the published version; Mead to Joseph Goldsen, 21, 28 May 1951: Mead Papers, G79, I54.

81. Mead, *Soviet Attitudes*, 171–7, 190–4. See also Erikson's analysis of the Soviet 'family drama' in *Childhood and Society*, ch. 10.

82. *Mead, Soviet Attitudes*, 178–86, 196–219.

83. Ibid., 277–9, weak and inconclusive. Price, *Threatening Anthropology*, 257, describes its 'crude personality and culture generalizations' as 'closely aligned with the American government's anti-Soviet stance', but there are remarkably few 'personality and culture generalizations' in the text. It is anti-Soviet without being anti-Russian, and poorly aligned with the government's aggressive stance of 1951. Conversely, however, Mead can hardly be given much credit for avoiding a causal infant-training argument in this work; cf. Young, *Ruth Benedict*, 111.

84. e.g. Harry Schwartz, 'The Model's Name Is Stalin', *New York Times*, 7 Oct. 1951, p. 227; Alex Inkeles, review of Margaret Mead, *Soviet Attitudes toward Authority*, *World Politics* 16 (1951), 893–4; Klein, 'Groping for World Order'.

85. Hennessy, 'Psycho-Cultural Studies', 40–2.

86. Hans Speier to Alex Inkeles, 19 Apr. 1950; Mead to Speier, 26 May 1950; Alex Inkeles to Mead, 5 Sep., 3 Oct. 1950; Mead to Inkeles, 30 Nov. 1950: Mead Papers, G76–7. Among links between the two projects were Herb Dinerstein, who worked on both, and Gorer's old collaborator Henry Dicks, who tried to mediate between them.

87. Bauer, Inkeles and Kluckhohn, *How the Soviet System Works*, esp. 131–50, 192–7, 226–9. Cf. Dicks, 'Observations', esp. 122, 137–41, 147–59; Kluckhohn, 'Recent Studies', 214–26, 233–8.

88. Riesman, 'A Grammar of Soviet Motives'; see also Riesman's comment in Friedrich (ed.), *Totalitarianism*, 377–8, on the compatibility of the geopolitical and psychocultural schools.

89. RCC, Minutes of 28th general seminar, 17 Feb. 1949: Mead, 'Important Notice to All Members of Columbia University RCC', 19 Sep. 1949: Mead Papers, G14, G3.

90. Zipperstein, 'Underground Man'.

91. Mead, 'Progress Report on Studies in Soviet Culture', 16 Feb. 1949; Mead to Alex Bavelas, 16 Mar. 1949; Mead to Hans Speier, 1 Apr. 1949; Speier to Mead, 18 May 1949; 'Proposal for a Continuation of the Project Entitled Studies in Soviet Culture, 1949–1950', n.d.: Mead Papers, G76–8.

92. Mead to Joseph Goldsen, RAND, 3 Aug. 1950: Mead Papers, G77.

93. Mead, 'The Postwar Soviet Image of the United States', 30 Sep. 1950, 160–8: Mead Papers, G79.

94. Philip E. Mosely to Mead, 24 Aug. 1950; Nathan Leites to Mead, 15 Sep. 1950: Mead Papers, G80.

95. Mead to Joseph M. Goldsen, RAND, 31 Oct. 1950; Goldsen to Mead, 13 Nov. 1950; Mead to Nathan Leites, 12 Mar. 1951: Mead Papers, G77, C24.

96. Capt. Caleb B. Laning to Mead, 15 Sep., 3, 26 Oct., 24 Nov. 1950, 18 May 1951; Mead to Laning, 26 Sep. 1950, 22 May 1951; Leo Haimson to Mead, 26 Sep. 1951: Mead Papers, G4, C24. The report, 'The Ideal of "Conscious Activity" – Some Aspects of Decision Making and Communications in Soviet Theory and Practice', was based on research by Francis Rawdon Smith and Leopold Haimson (an RCC Russian study group veteran) and submitted to the Navy in September 1951; a copy is in Mead Papers, G63.

97. Capt. P.E. McDowell to Mead, 19 Sep. 1950; Mead to Capt. McDowell, 17 Oct., 11 Dec. 1950; Mead, 'Tentative Outline of National Character for Working Group on Human Relations [sic]', 19 Dec. 1950; Mead, Memorandum for the Working Group, 28 Jan. 1951; RCC, 'A Report on National Character', Feb. 1951: Mead Papers, G4, G11, G12.

98. Howard Page, ONR, to Mead, 6 Dec. 1950; Mead to Page, 15 Mar. 1951: Mead Papers, G71.

99. Studies in Contemporary Cultures, Minutes, 1 May 1951; Mead to Alex Bavelas, Memorandum, 3 Aug. 1951: Mead Papers, G70, G76.

100. RCC, 'Communism and Chinese Culture: A Research Proposal', 6 Feb. 1951; Mead to Howard Page, ONR, 5 Feb. 1951; Page to Mead, 5 Mar. 1951; Mead to Nathan Leites, 12, 14 Mar. 1951; Leites to Mead, 13, 15 Mar. 1951; Leites to Mead, memorandum, n.d.: Mead Papers, G62, C24. Leites took Elsa Bernaut with him and they subsequently published jointly authored reports for RAND on Soviet affairs, using a totalitarianism model.

101. On the German research, see Rhoda Metraux and Nelly Schargo Hoyt, 'German National Character: A Study of German Self-Images', 1953; Mead, Final Report, Studies in Contemporary Cultures-B, to chief of Naval Research, 20 May 1953: Mead Papers, G71; on the US-Soviet communications work, Mead (ed.), *Studies in Soviet Communication*, an in-house MIT publication; on the Chinese project, John Weakland and Ruth Bunzel, 'An Anthropological Approach to Chinese Communism', Apr. 1952; Celine M. Ganel, Office of Intelligence Research, State Department, to Mead, 6 Oct. 1952: Mead Papers, G62, C28.

102. See below, pp. 275-6.

103. Mead, 'Outline for Paper to Be Given at Ethnological Society Meeting April 13, 1951': Mead Papers, E46.

104. Mead to A.P. Elkin, University of Sydney, 19 Oct. 1950; Mead to Raymond Firth, 5 Mar. 1951; Mead to Noel and Muss Porter, 17 Jul. 1951: Mead Papers, C21, C23, C25.

105. Mead, *New Lives for Old*, 11.

106. Gorer to Mead, 18 Sep., 4 Oct. 1951; Mead to Gorer, 27 Sep. 1951: Mead Papers, B6.

107. Tax et al. (eds), *Appraisal of Anthropology*, 136; Mead to Gorer, 3 Jan. 1951 (misdated 1950): Gorer Papers, Box 91.

108. Mead to Gorer, 2 Jun. 1951: Mead Papers, B6.

Chapter 7 Return to the Natives

1. Riesman, 'Comments on Dr. Kluckhohn's Paper', 68-9.

2. During the war, Mead had been more sceptical of 'development', but when she found that even the greatest defenders of cultural integrity were swinging around 'to fight for bath tubs on Pacific islands – one of the places where they are rather less needed than others', she began to see that anthropologists would have to work within the development paradigm. 'Margaret Mead's Comments at the Annual Dinner Forum of East Indies Institute', 18 Mar. 1944: Mead Papers, E64.

3. Mead, 'The American Character in its Relation to International Understanding', UNESCO Summer Seminar on International Understanding, 31 Jul. 1947; speech to the Pacific Regional Conference on UNESCO, 15 May 1948: Mead Papers, E145.

4. Mead, 'A Report to the Preparatory Commission for Unesco on Some Problems of World Educational Planning', n.d. [Oct. 1947]: Mead Papers, E145. Cf. the published version, UNESCO, 'Fundamental Education and Cultural Values', and Mead, 'Applied Anthropology, 1955', 103-7.

5. Mead, 'Christian Faith and Technical Assistance'.

6. Cited in Mead (ed.), *Cultural Patterns*, 303-6.

7. For an influential critique of 'development' along these lines, see Escobar, *Encountering Development*; on modernization theory, see esp. Gilman, *Mandarins of the Future*; for an unusual critique that takes into account both US and Soviet modernization programmes, see Westad, *Global Cold War*.

8. For critiques of anthropologists' involvement in modernization programmes, see Ferguson, 'Anthropology and its Evil Twin'; Gilman, 'Involution and Modernization'; Latham, 'Modernization'; Nader, 'Phantom Factor'; more ambivalent views in Cooper and Packard, 'Introduction', 2-5, 14-15; Stocking (ed.), *Colonial Situations*, 3-5; Clifford, *Predicament of Culture*, 78-80.

9. Mead (ed.), *Cultural Patterns*, 254–5.
10. Metraux, 'Applied Anthropology', 882–3.
11. Ibid., 882, 884–5; Gilman, 'Involution and Modernization', 3.
12. See above, p. 184.
13. 'World Federation for Mental Health'; Thomson, *Psychological Subjects*, 239–41; see also 'Outline by Dr. Mead', 11 Jan. 1948; Ben Morris to Mead, 17 Aug. 1948: Mead Papers, M32, F50.
14. Staples, *Birth of Development*, 78–94, 132–50; Amrith, *Decolonizing International Health*, 75–83.
15. *Inaugural Addresses*, vol. 2, 112–13.
16. Shenin, *United States and the Third World*, 5–20; Packenham, *Liberal America and the Third World*, 35–49; Leffler, *Preponderance of Power*, 267, 291.
17. Shenin, *United States and the Third World*, 35, 41–2, 64, 67, 144–55; Paterson, *Meeting the Communist Threat*, 151–6.
18. Lumsdaine, *Moral Vision in International Politics*, 27, 32–7, 45–7, 55–60, 90–1, 222–38.
19. Hall, 'Military Government'; Gladwin, 'Civil Administration on Truk'; Hall, 'A Reply'; Hsin-Pao, 'Guideposts for the Point 4 Program'; Hall, *Anthropology of Everyday Life*, 167–8; Macgregor, 'Anthropology in Government'.
20. Rorty, 'Point Four Begins at Home'.
21. Mead to A.P. Elkin, University of Sydney, 19 Oct. 1950: Mead Papers, C21.
22. Gordon R. Willey, 'Anthropology and the Point 4 Program', 22 Sep. 1949; Gordon R. Willey to Rowena Rommel, 22 Sep. 1949: ISA Records, Box 1.
23. Mead to John Provinse, 21 Dec. 1949; Gordon Macgregor to Mead, 8 Mar. 1950; Gordon R. Willey to Mead, 27 Apr., 29 Jun., 13 Jul. 1950; Mead and Willey to C.M. Waynick, 7 Jul. 1950; AAA to C.M. Waynick, n.d. (draft only); Edward Kennard to Gordon Willey, 14 Sep. 1950; Kennard to Mead, 14 Sep. 1950; SAA, Executive Committee Minutes, 21 Oct. 1950; 'First Conference on Social Science Problems of Point Four', Washington, 2 Dec. 1950: Mead Papers, E120, C22, E125; Samuel P. Hayes to Cora Du Bois, 27 Oct. 1950: National Archives (US), RG59, State Department Central Decimal File, 1950–4, 840.00TA.
24. Hall, *Anthropology of Everyday Life*, 158–62, 181–2, 192; Edward T. Hall to Mead, 10 Jan. 1951: Mead Papers, C24; Hall to David Riesman, 11 Jan. 1951: Riesman Papers, HUG(FP) 99.16, Box 41.
25. Hall, *Anthropology of Everyday Life*, 200–4; Leeds-Hurwitz, 'Foreign Service Institute', 262–70; Rogers et al., 'Edward T. Hall', 8; transcripts of orientation and evaluation sessions led by Cora Du Bois and Edward Kennard, 5–7 Mar. 1952: Macgregor Papers, Box 3; Claire Holt, 'Statement of Background, Reasons, Purposes and Plan of Travel-and-Study Project in South and Southeast Asia', n.d. [1951]; Claire Holt, 'Culture-Contact Mediation in American-Southeast Asian Relations', paper presented to 4th Annual Meeting of Far Eastern Association, 1–3 Apr. 1952, Boston: Mead Papers, B9.
26. The genesis of this project can be traced in Mead Papers, E51–2; WFMH to Social Sciences Department, UNESCO, 'Technological Change and Mental Health', n.d. [1950], written by Frank and Mead; Mead to Lawrence K. Frank, 4 Aug. 1950; Frank to Elizabeth Hoyt, 16 Oct. 1950: Mead Papers, I59.
27. Burton, 'Life of Claire Holt', esp. 153–62; Claire Holt to Mead, 1 Feb. 1950; Lawrence K. Frank to Elizabeth Hoyt, 16 Oct. 1950: Mead Papers, I59. I am grateful to Sarah Bekker for further information about Claire Holt and her association with Cora Du Bois in this period.
28. Hoyt deserves closer study. See Hoyt, 'Tiquisate', and for her encounter with Mead, Elizabeth Hoyt to Mead, 20 Jan., 1 Mar., 8 Apr. 1950, Mead to Hoyt, 14 Feb. 1950: Mead Papers, C22, I59.
29. Transcript of meeting, 31 Oct. 1950, 2–4, 11; transcript of meeting, 24 Nov. 1950, 13–19, 21–6: Mead Papers, I60.
30. Transcript of meeting, 31 Oct. 1950, 11; Claire Holt, 'Notes Relating to "Mental Health Implications of Technological Change"', 10 Oct. 1950: Mead Papers, I60; cf. Mead (ed.), *Cultural Patterns*, 89, 238–52.
31. Mead on 'U.N. Album', United Nations Radio, 10 Sep. 1952: Mead Papers, F53; Mead, 'Technological Change and Child Development', 181; Mead (ed.), *Cultural Patterns*, 299–300.

32. Claire Holt to Cora Du Bois, 12 Nov. 1950; transcript of meeting, 24 Nov. 1950, 21–6: Mead Papers, B9, I60.
33. Claire Holt, 'Notes Relating to "Mental Health Implications of Technological Change"', 10 Oct. 1950; transcript of meeting, 31 Oct. 1950, 11; transcript of meeting, 24 Nov. 1950, 26–7: Mead Papers, I60; cf. the manual, Mead (ed.), *Cultural Patterns*, 238–46.
34. Hoyt, 'Want Development'; Hoyt, 'Tiquisate'; Elizabeth Hoyt, 'New Worlds to Conquer: The Socio-Cultural Problem of Point IV', n.d. [Feb.? 1950]; transcript of meeting, 24 Nov. 1950, 13–17; Claire Holt to Cora Du Bois, 12 Nov. 1950: Mead Papers, C22, I60, B9; cf. the manual, Mead (ed.), *Cultural Patterns*, 18–20.
35. Cohen and Dannhaeuser, 'Development in Practice and Theory', xv. Compare Hoyt's analysis to the later and more celebrated study of another Guatemalan community by Manning Nash, which does not mention Hoyt once, and took a comparatively benign view of the cultural impact of high wages: Nash, *Machine Age Maya*, esp. 44–5, 47, 54, 63.
36. Elizabeth Hoyt, 'New Worlds to Conquer: The Socio-Cultural Problem of Point IV', n.d. [Feb.? 1950]: Mead Papers, I60.
37. Transcript of meeting, 31 Oct. 1950, 4–5; cf. Mead (ed.), *Cultural Patterns*, 292.
38. Mead to Dorothy Lee, 28 Feb. 1952; Mead, 'Aspects of the Impact of Large-Scale American Operations in Other Countries', 3 Mar. 1952: Mead Papers, C27, E120.
39. Transcript of meeting, 24 Nov. 1950, 13–17; Claire Holt to Cora Du Bois, 12 Nov. 1950: Mead Papers, B9; cf. Mead (ed.), *Cultural Patterns*, 17–20, 276–9, 291–303.
40. Mead to I.E. Lord, 3 Jun. 1952: Mead Papers, I60. Lee seems to have drafted the 'whole culture' portions, Mead and Holt the cross-cultural and contextual material.
41. Mead to Alfred Metraux, 28 Jan. 1952; Mead to Thomas Gladwin, 9 May 1955: Mead Papers, C27, E121.
42. Mead (ed.), *Cultural Patterns*, 53–63, 122–6, 150; Claire Holt to Mead, 15 Feb. 1953: Mead Papers, B9. A final case study discussed Hispanic people in New Mexico. Mead later told Thomas Gladwin that she thought the Burmese case study was *too* negative, burdened by anthropologists' guilt about colonialism, but she may have been telling Gladwin what he wanted to hear. Mead to Thomas Gladwin, 9 May 1955: Mead Papers, E121.
43. For the former group, see reviews in *American Anthropologist* 58 (1956), 190–1, *American Political Science Review* 48 (1954), 854–6, *Journal of Farm Economics* 36 (1954), 555–6; for the latter, see reviews in *Annals of the American Academy of Political and Social Science* 294 (1954), 199, *Population Studies* 8 (1954), 193–4. More problematic were reviews by anthropologists committed to administration, who felt Mead had been too negative: see the reviews by Tom Lupton, *Man* 54 (1954), 143, and Thomas Gladwin, *American Anthropologist* 57 (1955), 177–9.
44. As it is characterized by di Leonardo, *Exotics at Home*, 231–2; see also Cross, 'Design for Living', 797–9.
45. Mead, 'Technological Change and Child Development', 184–5; cf. Redfield, *Primitive World*, 157–60.
46. Spicer (ed.), *Human Problems*, esp. Leighton's foreword.
47. For a draft text, 'Intercultural Transfer of Techniques: A Manual of Applied Social Science for Point IV Technicians and Administrators Overseas', 1951, and papers related to its drafting, see Macgregor Papers, Box 1. Arensberg subsequently adapted it as *Introducing Social Change: A Manual for Americans Overseas* (1964).
48. See e.g. the early years of Bert Hoselitz's journal *Economic Development and Cultural Change* (from 1952), discussed in Singer, 'Work of Bert Hoselitz', 2, 5, 8–9; and Herskovitz, 'Motivation and Culture-Pattern'.
49. 'UNESCO Book Maps Foreign Cultures; Margaret Mead Heads Group of Scholars Compiling It for Technicians Going Abroad', *New York Times*, 2 Apr. 1952, p. 31.
50. SAA, Executive Committee Minutes, 12 Dec. 1950, 9 Jan. 1951; Elizabeth Purcell to SAA EC, 7 Mar. 1951: Mead Papers, E120.
51. Mead to Eliot Chapple, 'IMP USDS Project', 2 Nov. 1950; Mead, 'Notes for TA Memos', 26–7 Apr. 1951: Mead Papers, E122, E123.
52. 'General Report No. 1: Cultural Background', 9 May 1951, 'General Report No. 2: Sources of Stress', 9 May 1951; general reports 3 and 4 covered intercultural communication more broadly and possible TA themes: Macgregor Papers, Box 2.

53. See the four reports on Indonesia, 3–9 Aug. 1951: Macgregor Papers, Box 2. The SAA also produced a series of reports on Germany with a rather different orientation, pursuing Mead and Frank's older concerns about the fostering of democracy 'in German terms'. See e.g. Film Planning Project, SAA, to IMP Division, Dept. of State, 'Germany, Report No. 6, The Problems of Centralization', 1952: Mead Papers, E122.
54. 'Anthropology Today', 16 Jun. 1952, 59–69, and Mead's summational comments at 89: Mead Papers, E163; cf. Tax et al. (eds), *Appraisal of Anthropology*, 178–88. A similar criticism was voiced by Julian Steward.
55. Mead, 'Anthropological Contributions', 154.
56. Gordon Macgregor to Eliot Chapple, 13 Feb. 1952; *Applied Anthropology Newsletter* 11 (21 Feb. 1952); SAA, Executive Committee Minutes, 4 Apr., 22 Jun. 1952: Mead Papers, E120; Macgregor, 'Anthropology in Government', 424; Kennard and Macgregor, 'Applied Anthropology in Government', 838–9. Macgregor was an applied anthropologist, another veteran of Micronesia, who was employed by Point IV in 1951 as the deputy to the administrator for Middle East programmes, though not, Kennard noted sadly, in the position recommended by the SAA, 'namely an anthropologist on the Administrator's staff so that the professional approach to cross-cultural processes might permeate the thinking of the entire staff'. Edward Kennard to Gordon Willey, 15 Oct. 1951: ISA Records, Box 1.
57. Mead in 1975, commentary on Fisher, 'Role of Anthropology in International Relations', 14–15.
58. See Macgregor's apologetic comments in FSI, Evaluation, 7 Mar. 1952: Macgregor Papers, Box 3; also Paterson, *Meeting the Communist Threat*, 154.
59. Burton, 'Life of Claire Holt', 165–9; Hall, *Anthropology of Everyday Life*, 250–1; Edward T. Hall to Mead, 1 Mar. 1954: Mead Papers, C30.
60. Macgregor, 'Anthropology in Government', 424–6.
61. Editorial, 'The Liquidation of Point Four', *Human Organization* 12:3 (fall 1953), 2–3.
62. Tax et al. (eds), *Appraisal of Anthropology*, 136.
63. Mead to A.P. Elkin, University of Sydney, 19 Oct. 1950; Mead to Raymond Firth, 5 Mar. 1951; Mead to Gorer, 7 Jun. 1951; Mead to Noel and Muss Porter, 17 Jul. 1951: Mead Papers, C21, C23, B6, C25.
64. Howard, *Margaret Mead*, 295–7; Mead's account of 'what happened' to the Manus between 1946 and 1953 can be found in Mead, *New Lives for Old*, ch. 9.
65. Mead to Jim Mysbergh, 3 Oct. 1952: Caffrey and Francis (eds), *To Cherish the Life*, 224.
66. See esp. 'Second Draft of Table of Contents', 7 Oct. 1952, 'LDB Introduction 1952', 2–20 Oct. 1952, and 'Tentative Chapter II, Anthropological Approach', 22 Oct.–5 Nov. 1952: Mead Papers, I56.
67. Note, 21 Oct. 1952; 'Tentative Introduction', 7 Oct. 1952; David Riesman to Mead, 31 Dec. 1952: Mead Papers, I56, C27.
68. Bateson, *With a Daughter's Eye*, 185; Caffrey, 'Parable of Manus', 142.
69. Mead, 'Social Change and Cultural Surrogates', 107; Mead, *And Keep Your Powder Dry*, 80–2, 126; Mead to David Riesman, 19 Oct. 1949, 21 Jan. 1952: Riesman Papers, HUG(FP) 99.12, Boxes 3, 31.
70. Cf. Bateson, *With a Daughter's Eye*, 185–91, Lutkehaus, *Margaret Mead*, 181–9, Caffrey, 'Parable of Manus', with Janiewski and Banner (eds), *Reading Benedict/Reading Mead*, xiii, and Newman, 'Coming of Age', 53, 60–1.
71. Mead, *Letters from the Field*, 276; Mead, *New Lives for Old*, esp. 438–58; but cf. Mead, 'Applied Anthropology, 1955', 103–8; Schwartz, 'Where Is the Culture?', esp. 419–22; Ted Schwartz, 'TS comments on MM Ch. 17', 20 Mar. 1955, esp. p. 5: Mead Papers, I82; Foerstel, 'Margaret Mead' (by the former Lenora Schwartz).
72. For the brutal reaction of the profession, see Rodney Needham, *American Anthropologist* 59 (1957), 562–4 ('her worst book'), and Murray Groves, *Man* 57 (Apr. 1957), 62 ('slovenly', 'irresponsible').
73. Leeds-Hurwitz, 'Foreign Service Institute', 276n20, 277n23, gives the employment details of FSI anthropologists; on Overseas Training and Research, see correspondence from Wilton Dillon to Mead: Mead Papers, B3; on Holt, see Burton, 'Life of Claire Holt', 171–5.
74. Lutkehaus, *Margaret Mead*, 216–23; Dillon, 'Margaret Mead and Government', 326–7; Fisher, *Public Diplomacy*, 14–16; 'Margaret Mead Today: Mother to the World', *Time*,

21 Mar. 1969; David Dempsey, 'The Mead and Her Message', *New York Times*, 26 Apr. 1970; 'Grandmother to the World', *New York Times*, 16 Nov. 1978.

75. Mead, *And Keep Your Powder Dry*, xxxii (from the 1965 preface); Maday (ed.), *Anthropology and Society*, 14; Mead, 'Anthropological Contributions', 147–8.

76. Mead, commentary on Fisher, 'Role of Anthropology in International Relations', 14–15.

77. Mead, 'New Isolationism', esp. 380–2; see also Mead, *And Keep Your Powder Dry*, 170–2 (from a new chapter added in 1965).

78. Mead, 'Retrospects and Prospects', 144–5; Mead, 'Changing Styles', 41–2; Maday (ed.), *Anthropology and Society*, 15; Mead, *Blackberry Winter*, 293–6. Interestingly, Ralph Nader agreed with this diagnosis of Mead's – Nader, 'Anthropology in Law and Civic Action', 31–3 – although his sister Laura Nader, 'Phantom Factor', did not.

79. Mead, 'Anthropological Contributions', 147–8, 154.

80. Mead, 'Christian Faith and Technical Assistance'.

81. Gilman, *Mandarins of the Future*, 38–40, 69–71, 174–81.

82. See e.g. the relationship of some psychologists to modernization theory, as discussed in Herman, *Romance of American Psychology*, 137–51, and the role of Parsonian sociologists, as discussed in Gilman, *Mandarins of the Future*, 79–107.

83. Inkeles, 'Industrial Man', 2.

84. Klein, *Cold War Orientalism*, 79–80.

85. Harris, *Rise of Anthropological Theory*, 449–62.

86. Benedict, *Chrysanthemum and the Sword*, 14.

87. Mead, 'Christian Faith and Technical Assistance'.

88. Cora Du Bois, 'An Anthropologist Looks At Modernization', Cooper Lecture, Swarthmore College, 7 Apr. 1967: Du Bois Papers, Box 74.

89. Barnett, *Anthropology in Administration*, 48–85; Fisher, 'Role of Anthropology in International Relations', 3; Fisher, *Public Diplomacy*, 14–16; Deitchman, *Best-Laid Schemes*, 379–81.

90. Partridge and Eddy, 'Development of Applied Anthropology', 35. The judgements in this paper are based heavily on Mead's own, in print and as conveyed to the authors, and should be treated with caution.

91. Du Bois, 'Some Anthropological Hindsights', 3.

92. Mead, 'Changing Styles', 41–4; Stocking, 'Sol Tax', esp. 192–5, 250–3; Partridge and Eddy, 'Development of Applied Anthropology', 35–8; Cohen and Dannhaeuser, 'Development in Practice and Theory', xv–xviii.

93. Howard, *Margaret Mead*, 277; Geertz, *Local Knowledge*, 9.

94. Spindler (ed.), *Making of Psychological Anthropology*, 7–9; Bock, *Continuities in Psychological Anthropology*, 131–6; LeVine, 'Culture and Personality Studies', 805, 813–15.

95. Nearly the entire literature on the history of anthropology in the 1950s and 1960s could be adduced here; but see Spindler and Spindler, 'Anthropologists View American Culture', esp. 49–52; Bock, *Continuities in Psychological Anthropology*, esp. 190–204; and the very influential work of Clifford Geertz, esp. 'Ethos, World View, and the Analysis of Sacred Symbols' (1957), laying out his 'prototheory' of a symbolic understanding of culture, and the full-blown analyses in 'The Impact of the Concept of Culture on the Concept of Man', 'Religion as a Cultural System' and 'Person, Time and Conduct in Bali: An Essay in Cultural Analysis' (all 1966), collected in Geertz, *Interpretation of Cultures*.

Epilogue: To Vietnam, Iraq, Afghanistan

1. Beals, *Politics of Social Research*, 16–18, 56–7; Lyons, *Uneasy Partnership*, 174–7; Engerman, 'Social Science in the Cold War', 400.

2. Price, *Anthropological Intelligence*, 88–9; Escobar, *Encountering Development*, 36–7; Ross, 'Cold Warriors Without Weapons'; Gupta and Ferguson, 'Discipline and Practice', 9–10, but cf. the much more modest claim at 11. Cf. Anderson, *Spectre of Comparisons*, 9–11, 18–19, Wallerstein, 'Cold War Area Studies', 218–26.

3. Price, *Anthropological Intelligence*, 115–16, 242–3; Shannon, *World Made Safe*, 15–16; Ohmann, 'England and the Cold War', 75; Nader, 'The Phantom Factor', 123–7; Hegeman, *Patterns for America*, 165. These are all claims based on analogy or connection with the Second World War work, and lack much specificity with regard to Vietnam-era work. Cf.

Wakin, *Anthropology Goes to War*, which gives a detailed account of counterinsurgency-related research.

4. From the report of the 1971 Mead Committee, repr. as Appendix G in Wakin, *Anthropology Goes to War*, 290; see also Mead, 'Anthropological Contributions', 147–8.

5. Beals, *Politics of Social Research*, 100–46; McClintock, *Instruments of Statecraft*, 166–72; Deitchman, *Best-Laid Schemes*, 26–70; Wakin, *Anthropology Goes to War*, 16–29. On military resistance, see McClintock, *Instruments of Statecraft*, esp. 207–11, 217; Blaufarb, *Counterinsurgency Era*, 78. On the contributions of modernization theory, see also Milne, *America's Rasputin*, 87–9, 114–15; Latham, *Modernization as Ideology*, ch. 5. Among Nathan Leites's final contributions to social science was his own 'rational choice' analysis of counterinsurgency: Robin, *Making of the Cold War Enemy*, 193–8.

6. Deitchman, *Best-Laid Schemes*, 204; Beals, *Politics of Social Research*, 57.

7. Herman, *Romance of American Psychology*, ch. 6, quote at 163; Deitchman, *Best-Laid Schemes*, chs 9–15, and esp. 266–77; Beals, *Politics of Social Research*, came out of the AAA Ethics Committee and reports on the activities of most of those anthropologists involved in overseas research in the mid-1960s, but cf. Robert Hancock's afterword to Wax (ed.), *Anthropology at the Dawn of the Cold War*, 168–9, for a darker view.

8. Wakin, *Anthropology Goes to War*, ch. 6, and Appendix G for the Mead Committee report, esp. 289–90, 293; the 1971 'Principles of Professional Responsibility' are reprinted as Appendix E.

9. Freeman's opening salvo, *Margaret Mead and Samoa*, appeared in 1983.

10. Network of Concerned Anthropologists, *Counter-Counterinsurgency Manual*, 7, 47, 161.

11. McFate, 'Anthropology and Counterinsurgency', 29–34; McFate, 'Understanding Adversary Culture', 47–8; Packer, 'Knowing Your Enemy', 65; Nagl, *Learning to Eat Soup*, 40–51, 93, 126–8, regrets the failure of the US military to deploy 'psywar' techniques, as confirmed by the principal non-military source, McClintock, *Instruments of Statecraft*, esp. 35–46, 161–2, 181–7, 214–17, 245–6.

Bibliography

Manuscript Sources

BBC Written Archives Centre: BBC Written Archives Centre, Caversham Park

Benedict Papers: Ruth Fulton Benedict Papers, Vassar College

Du Bois Papers: Cora Du Bois Papers, Tozzer Library, Harvard University

Gorer Papers: Geoffrey Gorer Papers, Special Collections, University of Sussex

ISA Records: Institute of Social Anthropology Records, National Anthropological Archives, Smithsonian Institution, Suitland MD

Jane Howard Papers: Jane Howard Papers, Rare Book and Manuscript Library, Columbia University

Kluckhohn Papers: Clyde Kluckhohn Papers, Harvard University Archives

Macgregor Papers: Gordon Macgregor Papers, National Anthropological Archives, Smithsonian Institution, Suitland MD

Mead Papers: Margaret Mead Papers, Library of Congress, Washington DC

National Archives (UK): National Archives, Kew, London
    FO371, Foreign Office – General Correspondence
    FO898, Political Warfare Executive (PWE)
    HS1, Special Operations Executive (SOE), Far East

National Archives (US): National Archives, College Park MD
    RG59, State Department Central Decimal File
    RG208, Office of War Information (OWI)
    RG226, Office of Strategic Services (OSS)

Oral History Research Office, Rare Book and Manuscript Library, Columbia University
    Alex Inkeles, Interview #1419
    Abram Kardiner, Interview #590
    Otto Klineberg, Interview #1465
    Helen Lynd, Interview #909
    John Marshall, Interview #1013
    David Riesman, Interview #632

Orwell Papers: Orwell Archive, Special Collections, University College London

Parsons Papers: Talcott Parsons Papers, Harvard University Archives

Riesman Papers: David Riesman Papers, Harvard University Archives

Rockefeller Foundation Archives: Rockefeller Foundation Archives, Rockefeller Archive Center, Sleepy Hollow NY

Walzer, 'Oral History': Judith B. Walzer, 'An Oral History of the Tenured Women in the Faculty of Arts and Sciences at Harvard University, 1981', unpublished manuscript, Schlesinger Library, Radcliffe Institute, Harvard University

Printed Sources

Abbott, Andrew and James T. Sparrow, 'Hot War, Cold War: The Structures of Sociological Action, 1940–1955', in Craig Calhoun (ed.), *Sociology in America* (Chicago, 2007), 281–313

Adorno, T.W. et al., *The Authoritarian Personality* (New York, 1950)

Bibliography

Alcalay, Glenn, 'The United States Anthropologist in Micronesia: Toward a Counter-Hegemonic Study of Sapiens', in Foerstel and Gilliam (eds), *Confronting the Margaret Mead Legacy*, 173–203

Aldrich, Richard J., *Intelligence and the War against Japan: Britain, America and the Politics of Secret Service* (Cambridge, 2000)

Allport, G.W. and H.R. Veltfort, 'Social Psychology and the Civilian War Effort', *Journal of Social Psychology* 16 (1943), 165–233

Alpers, Benjamin L., *Dictators, Democracy, and American Public Culture: Envisioning the Totalitarian Enemy, 1920s–1950s* (Chapel Hill NC, 2003)

Amrith, Sunil S., *Decolonizing International Health: India and Southeast Asia, 1930–65* (Basingstoke, 2006)

Anderson, Benedict, *The Spectre of Comparisons: Nationalism, Southeast Asia and the World* (London, 1998)

Balfour, Michael, 'In Retrospect: Britain's Policy of "Re-Education"', in Nicholas Pronay and Keith Wilson (eds), *The Political Re-Education of Germany and Her Allies* (London, 1985), 139–50

Balfour, Michael, *Propaganda in War 1939–1945: Organisations, Policies and Publics in Britain and Germany* (London, 1979)

Balfour, Michael and John Mair, *Four-Power Control in Germany and Austria 1945–1946* (Oxford, 1956)

Banner, Lois W., *Intertwined Lives: Margaret Mead, Ruth Benedict, and Their Circle* (New York, 2003)

Bannister, Robert C., *Sociology and Scientism: The American Quest for Objectivity, 1880–1940* (Chapel Hill NC, 1987)

Barnett, H.G., *Anthropology in Administration* (Evanston IL, 1956)

Barnett, H.G., 'On Science and Human Rights', *American Anthropologist*, n.s., 50 (1948), 352–5

Barnouw, Victor, 'An Interpretation of Wisconsin Ojibwa Culture and Personality: A Review', in Spindler (ed.), *Making of Psychological Anthropology*, 64–86

Bashkow, Ira, 'The Dynamics of Rapport in a Colonial Situation: David Schneider's Fieldwork on the Islands of Yap', in Stocking (ed.), *Colonial Situations*, 170–242

Bateson, Gregory, 'Cultural and Thematic Analysis of Fictional Films', *Transactions of the New York Academy of Sciences*, 2nd ser., 5 (1942–3), 72–8

Bateson, Gregory, 'Culture Contact and Schismogenesis' (1935), in *Steps to an Ecology of Mind* (Chicago, 1972), 61–72

Bateson, Gregory, 'The Frustration-Aggression Hypothesis and Culture', *Psychological Review* 48 (1941), 350–5

Bateson, Gregory, 'Human Dignity and the Varieties of Civilization', in *Science Philosophy and Religion: Third Symposium* (New York, 1943), 245–55

Bateson, Gregory, 'Morale and National Character', in Goodwin Watson (ed.), *Civilian Morale: Second Year Book of the Society for the Psychological Study of Social Issues* (Boston, 1942), 71–91

Bateson, Gregory, *Naven* (Cambridge, 1936)

Bateson, Gregory, 'Some Systematic Approaches to the Study of Culture and Personality', *Character and Personality* 11 (1942–3), 76–82

Bateson, Gregory and Margaret Mead, 'Principles of Morale Building', *Journal of Educational Sociology* 15 (1941), 206–20

Bateson, Mary Catherine, *With a Daughter's Eye: A Memoir of Margaret Mead and Gregory Bateson*, 1994 repr. ed. (New York, 1984)

Bauer, Raymond A., Alex Inkeles and Clyde Kluckhohn, *How the Soviet System Works* (Cambridge MA, 1956)

Beals, Ralph L., *Politics of Social Research: An Inquiry into the Ethics and Responsibilities of Social Scientists* (Chicago, 1969)

Bell, Daniel, 'Adjusting Men to Machines: Social Scientists Explore the World of the Factory', *Commentary*, Jan. 1947, 79–88

Bell, Daniel, 'Ten Theories in Search of Reality: The Prediction of Soviet Behavior' (1958), in Daniel Bell, *The End of Ideology: On the Exhaustion of Political Ideas in the Fifties*, rev. ed. (New York, 1962), 315–53

Bibliography

Benedict, Ruth, 'Child Rearing in Certain European Countries', *American Journal of Orthopsychiatry* 19 (1949), 342–50

Benedict, Ruth, *The Chrysanthemum and the Sword: Patterns of Japanese Culture*, 1st ed. 1946 (Boston, 2005)

Benedict, Ruth, *Patterns of Culture*, 1st ed. 1934 (Boston, 1989)

Benedict, Ruth, *Race and Racism* (London, 1942)

Benedict, Ruth, 'Recognition of Cultural Diversities in the Postwar World', *Annals of the American Academy of Political and Social Science* 228 (1943), 101–7

Benedict, Ruth, 'A Slender Reed', *The Nation*, 13 Sep. 1947, 260

Benedict, Ruth, 'The Study of Cultural Patterns in European Nations', *Transactions of the New York Academy of Sciences*, 2nd ser., 8 (1946), 274–9

Benedict, Ruth, 'Synergy: Some Notes of Ruth Benedict', ed. Abraham H. Maslow and John J. Honigmann, *American Anthropologist*, n.s., 72 (1970), 320–33

Benedict, Ruth and Gene Weltfish, *The Races of Mankind* (New York, 1943)

Bennett, John W. and Iwao Ishino, 'A History of the Public Opinion and Sociological Research Division, SCAP', 1st pub. as *Paternalism and the Japanese Economy: Anthropological Studies of Oyabun-Kobun* (Minneapolis MN, 1963), ch. 1, http://library.osu.edu/projects/bennett-in-japan/3a_docs.html

Bennett, John W. and Michio Nagai, 'Echoes: Reactions to American Anthropology: The Japanese Critique of the Methodology of Benedict's "Chrysanthemum and the Sword"', *American Anthropologist*, n.s., 55 (1953), 404–11

Berger, Morroe, '"Understanding National Character" – and War', *Commentary*, Apr. 1951, 375–86

Bernstein, Barton J., 'Seizing the Contested Terrain of Early Nuclear History: Stimson, Conant, and Their Allies Explain the Decision to Use the Nuclear Bomb', *Diplomatic History* 17 (1993), 35–72

Bernstein, Barton J., 'Understanding the Atomic Bomb and the Japanese Surrender: Missed Opportunities, Little-Known Near Disasters, and Modern Memory', *Diplomatic History* 19 (1995), 227–73

Birnbach, Martin, *Neo-Freudian Social Philosophy* (Stanford CA, 1962)

Black, Peter W., 'Psychological Anthropology and Its Discontents: Science and Rhetoric in Postwar Micronesia', in Kiste and Marshall (eds), *American Anthropology in Micronesia*, 225–53

Blanco White, Amber, *The New Propaganda* (London, 1939)

Blaufarb, Douglas S., *The Counterinsurgency Era: U.S. Doctrine and Performance, 1950 to the Present* (New York, 1977)

Bock, Philip K., *Continuities in Psychological Anthropology: A Historical Introduction* (San Francisco, 1980)

Borgwardt, Elizabeth, *A New Deal for the World: America's Vision for Human Rights* (Cambridge MA, 2005)

Brattain, Michelle, 'Race, Racism, and Antiracism: UNESCO and the Politics of Presenting Science to the Postwar Public', *American Historical Review* 112 (2007), 1386–1413

Brewer, Susan A., *To Win the Peace: British Propaganda in the United States during World War II* (Ithaca NY, 1997)

Brick, Howard, *Daniel Bell and the Decline of Intellectual Radicalism: Social Theory and Political Reconciliation in the 1940s* (Madison WI, 1986)

Brick, Howard, *Transcending Capitalism: Visions of a New Society in Modern American Thought* (Ithaca NY, 2006)

Brickner, Richard M., *Is Germany Incurable?* (Philadelphia, 1943)

Brockman, John (ed.), *About Bateson* (London, 1977)

Bryson, Dennis Raymond, *Socializing the Young: The Role of Foundations, 1923–1941* (Westport CT, 2002)

Buck, Peter, 'Adjusting to Military Life: The Social Sciences Go to War, 1941–1950', in Merritt Roe Smith (ed.), *Military Enterprise and Technological Change: Perspectives on the American Experience* (Cambridge MA, 1985), 203–52

Burton, Deena Elise, '"Sitting at the Feet of Gurus": The Life and Ethnography of Claire Holt', PhD dissertation, New York University, 2000

Bibliography

Buxton, William J., 'John Marshall and the Humanities in Europe: Shifting Patterns of Rockefeller Foundation Support', *Minerva* 41 (2003), 133–53

Caffrey, Margaret M., 'The Parable of Manus: Utopian Change, American Influence, and the Worth of Women', in Janiewski and Banner (eds), *Reading Benedict/Reading Mead*, 141–52

Caffrey, Margaret M., *Ruth Benedict: Stranger in This Land* (Austin TX, 1989)

Caffrey, Margaret M. and Patricia A. Francis (eds), *To Cherish the Life of the World: Selected Letters of Margaret Mead* (New York, 2006)

Calder, Ritchie, 'Sanity Fair', *New Statesman*, 21 Aug. 1948, 148

Campbell, I.C., '"A Chance to Build a New Social Order Well": Anthropology and American Colonial Government in Micronesia in Comparative Perspective', *Journal of Colonialism and Colonial History* 3 (2002), n.p.

Casey, Steven, 'The Campaign to Sell a Harsh Peace for Germany to the American Public, 1944–1948', *History* 90 (2005), 62–92

Caute, David, *The Dancer Defects: The Struggle for Cultural Supremacy during the Cold War* (Oxford, 2003)

Chapple, Eliot D., 'Anthropological Engineering: Its Use to Administrators', *Applied Anthropology* 2:2 (Jan.–Mar. 1943), 23–32

Chase, Stuart, *The Proper Study of Mankind: An Inquiry into the Science of Human Relations* (New York, 1948)

Chomsky, Noam et al., *The Cold War and the University: Toward an Intellectual History of the Postwar Years* (New York, 1997)

Christian, John Leroy, *Modern Burma: A Survey of Political and Economic Development* (Berkeley, 1942)

Clausen, John A., 'Research on the American Soldier as a Career Contingency', *Social Psychology Quarterly* 47 (1984), 207–13

Clifford, James, *The Predicament of Culture: Twentieth-Century Ethnography, Literature, and Art* (Cambridge MA, 1988)

Cohen, Jeffrey H. and Norbert Dannhaeuser, 'Introduction: Development in Practice and Theory – A Positive Role for Anthropology', in Jeffrey H. Cohen and Norbert Dannhaeuser (eds), *Economic Development: An Anthropological Approach* (Walnut Creek CA, 2002), xi–xxxi

Cohen, Theodore, *Remaking Japan: The American Occupation as New Deal*, ed. Herbert Passin (New York, 1987)

Cole, Sally, *Ruth Landes: A Life in Anthropology* (Lincoln NE, 2003)

Coon, Carleton, *A North Africa Story: The Anthropologist as OSS Agent 1941–1943* (Ipswich MA, 1980)

Cooper, Frederick and Randall Packard, 'Introduction', in Frederick Cooper and Randall Packard (eds), *International Development and the Social Sciences: Essays on the History and Politics of Knowledge* (Berkeley, 1997), 1–41

Cotkin, George, *Existential America* (Baltimore, 2003)

Cottrell, Leonard S., Jr. and Ruth Gallagher, 'Important Developments in American Social Psychology during the Past Decade', *Sociometry* 4 (1941), 107–39

Cross, Stephen J., 'Designs for Living: Lawrence K. Frank and the Progressive Legacy in American Social Science', PhD dissertation, Johns Hopkins University, 1994

Cruickshank, Charles, *SOE in the Far East* (Oxford, 1983)

Dallin, David J., 'Exterminate the Russians?', *New Leader*, 29 Oct. 1949, 2

Dallin, David J., 'The New Anti-Russians', *New Leader*, 27 May 1950, 9–10

Dallin, David J., *The New Soviet Empire* (London, 1951)

Darley, John G., 'Five Years of Social Science Research: Retrospect and Prospect', in Harold Guetzkow (ed.), *Groups, Leadership and Men: Research in Human Relations* (Pittsburgh, 1951), 3–15

Darnell, Regna, *And Along Came Boas: Continuity and Revolution in Americanist Anthropology* (Amsterdam and Philadelphia, 1998)

Darnell, Regna, *Edward Sapir: Linguist, Anthropologist, Humanist* (Lincoln NE, 1990)

Darnell, Regna, *Invisible Genealogies: A History of Americanist Anthropology* (Lincoln NE, 2001)

Darnell, Regna, 'Personality and Culture: The Fate of the Sapirian Alternative', in Stocking (ed.), *Malinowski, Rivers, Benedict*, 156–83

Bibliography

Daugherty, William E. with Morris Janowitz (eds), *A Psychological Warfare Casebook* (Baltimore, 1958)

de Sola Pool, Ithiel, 'Who Gets Power and Why', *World Politics* 2 (1949), 120–34

Deitchman, Seymour J., *The Best-Laid Schemes: A Tale of Social Research and Bureaucracy* (Cambridge MA, 1976)

Denning, Michael, *The Cultural Front: The Laboring of American Culture in the Twentieth Century* (London, 1997)

Dewey, John, 'Liberating the Social Scientist', *Commentary*, Oct. 1947, 378–85

di Leonardo, Micaela, *Exotics at Home: Anthropologies, Others, American Modernity* (Chicago, 1998)

Diamond, Sigmund, *Compromised Campus: The Collaboration of Universities with the Intelligence Community, 1945–1955* (Oxford, 1992)

Dicks, Henry V., 'Observations on Contemporary Russian Behaviour', *Human Relations* 5 (1952), 111–75

Dicks, Henry V., 'Personality Traits and National Socialist Ideology: A War-time Study of German Prisoners of War', *Human Relations* 3 (1950), 111–54

Dillon, Wilton S., 'Margaret Mead and Government', *American Anthropologist*, n.s., 82 (1980), 318–39

Donnison, F.S.V., *British Military Administration in the Far East 1943–46* (London, 1956)

Doob, Leonard W., 'The Utilization of Social Scientists in the Overseas Branch of the Office of War Information', *American Political Science Review* 41 (1947), 649–67

Dower, John W., *Embracing Defeat: Japan in the Aftermath of World War II* (New York, 1999)

Dower, John W., *War without Mercy: Race and Power in the Pacific War* (New York, 1986)

Du Bois, Cora, 'Some Anthropological Hindsights', *Annual Review of Anthropology* 9 (1980), 1–13

Dyer, A. Murray and Margaret Mead, 'It's Human Nature', *Education* 65 (1944), 228–38

Embree, John F., 'American Military Government', in Meyer Fortes (ed.), *Social Structure: Studies Presented to A.R. Radcliffe-Brown* (Oxford, 1949), 207–25

Embree, John F., 'Anthropology and the War', *American Association of University Professors Bulletin* 32 (1946), 485–95

Embree, John F., 'Applied Anthropology and Its Relationship to Anthropology', *American Anthropologist*, n.s., 47 (1945), 635–7

Embree, John F., *The Japanese* (Washington DC, 1943)

Embree, John F., *The Japanese Nation: A Social Survey* (New York, 1945)

Embree, John F., 'Micronesia: The Navy and Democracy', *Far Eastern Survey*, 5 Jun. 1946, 161–4

Embree, John F. 'A Note on Ethnocentrism in Anthropology', *American Anthropologist*, n.s., 52 (1950), 430–2

Embree, John F., 'Some Problems of an American Cultural Officer in Asia', *American Anthropologist*, n.s., 51 (1949), 155–8

Embree, John F., *Suye Mura: A Japanese Village* (Chicago, 1939)

Endleman, Robert, 'The New Anthropology and Its Ambitions', *Commentary*, Sep. 1949, 284–91

Endleman, Robert, *Psyche and Society: Explorations in Psychoanalytic Sociology* (New York, 1981)

Engerman, David C., 'The Cold War's Organization Man: How Philip Mosely Helped Soviet Studies Moderate American Policy', *Humanities* 30 (Sep.–Oct. 2009), n.p.

Engerman, David C., *Know Your Enemy: The Rise and Fall of America's Soviet Experts* (Oxford, 2009)

Engerman, David C., *Modernization from the Other Shore: American Intellectuals and the Romance of Russian Development* (Cambridge, MA, 2003)

Engerman, David C., 'Social Science in the Cold War', *Isis* 101 (2010), 393–400

Engle, Karen, 'From Skepticism to Embrace: Human Rights and the American Anthropological Association from 1947–1999', *Human Rights Quarterly* 23 (2001), 536–59

Erikson, Erik H., *Childhood and Society* (New York, 1950)

Erikson, Erik H., 'Hitler's Imagery and German Youth', *Psychiatry* 5 (1942), 475–93

Escobar, Arturo, *Encountering Development: The Making and Unmaking of the Third World* (Princeton, 1995)

Fabian, Johannes, *Time and the Other: How Anthropology Makes its Object* (New York, 1983)

Bibliography

Falgout, Suzanne, 'Americans in Paradise: Anthropologists, Custom, and Democracy in Postwar Micronesia', *Ethnology* 34 (1995), 99–111

Farber, Maurice L., 'The Problem of National Character: A Methodological Analysis', *Journal of Psychology* 30 (1950), 307–16

Ferguson, James, 'Anthropology and its Evil Twin: "Development" in the Constitution of a Discipline', in Frederick Cooper and Randall Packard (eds), *International Development and the Social Sciences: Essays on the History and Politics of Knowledge* (Berkeley, 1997), 150–75

Finison, Lorenz J., 'The Psychological Insurgency, 1936–1945', *Journal of Social Issues* 42 (1986), 21–33

Fisher, Glen H., *Public Diplomacy and the Behavioral Sciences* (Bloomington IN, 1972)

Fisher, Glen H., 'The Role of Anthropology in International Relations', in Bela C. Maday (ed.), *Anthropology and Society* (Washington DC, 1975), 1–12

Foerstel, Lenora, 'Margaret Mead from a Cultural-Historical Perspective', in Foerstel and Gilliam (eds), *Confronting the Margaret Mead Legacy*, 55–73

Foerstel, Lenora and Angela Gilliam (eds), *Confronting the Margaret Mead Legacy: Scholarship, Empire, and the South Pacific* (Philadelphia, 1992)

Foster, Jane, *An Unamerican Lady* (London, 1980)

Fousek, John, *To Lead the Free World: American Nationalism and the Cultural Roots of the Cold War* (Chapel Hill NC, 2000)

Frank, Lawrence K., *Society as the Patient: Essays on Culture and Personality* (New Brunswick NJ, 1948)

Freeman, Derek, *Margaret Mead and Samoa: The Making and Unmaking of an Anthropological Myth* (Harmondsworth, 1984)

Friedan, Betty, *The Feminine Mystique*, 1st ed. 1963 (London, 2010)

Friedman, Lawrence J., *Identity's Architect: A Biography of Erik H. Erikson* (London, 1999)

Friedrich, Carl J. (ed.), *Totalitarianism* (Cambridge MA, 1954)

Fromm, Erich, *Escape from Freedom*, 1st ed. 1941 (New York, 1994)

Fromm, Erich, *Man for Himself: An Inquiry into the Psychology of Ethics* (New York, 1947)

Fromm, Erich, 'On the Problems of German Characterology', *Transactions of the New York Academy of Sciences*, 2nd ser., 5 (1942–3), 79–83

Gaddis, John Lewis, *Strategies of Containment: A Critical Appraisal of American National Security Policy during the Cold War*, rev. ed. (Oxford, 2005)

Garnett, David, *The Secret History of PWE: The Political Warfare Executive 1939–1945* (London, 2002)

Gary, Brett, *The Nervous Liberals: Propaganda Anxieties from World War I to the Cold War* (New York, 1999)

Geertz, Clifford, *The Interpretation of Cultures* (New York, 1973)

Geertz, Clifford, *Local Knowledge: Further Essays in Interpretive Anthropology* (New York, 1983)

Geiger, Roger L., *Research and Relevant Knowledge: American Research Universities since World War II* (New York, 1993)

George, Alexander L., 'Nathan, My Teacher', in RAND Corporation, *Remembering Nathan Leites: An Appreciation* (Santa Monica CA, 1988), 1–5

Gerhardt, Uta, 'A Hidden Agenda of Recovery: The Psychiatric Conceptualization of Re-Education for Germany in the United States during World War II', *German History* 14 (1996), 297–324

Gerhardt, Uta, 'A World from Brave to New: Talcott Parsons and the War Effort at Harvard University', *Journal of the History of the Behavioral Sciences* 35 (1999), 257–89

Gerhardt, Uta, 'American Sociology and German Re-education after World War II', in Geoffrey J. Giles (ed.), *Stunde Null: The End and the Beginning Fifty Years Ago* (Washington DC, 1997), 39–58

Gerhardt, Uta, *Talcott Parsons: An Intellectual Biography* (Cambridge, 2002)

'Germany After the War – Round Table – 1945', *American Journal of Orthopsychiatry* 15 (1945), 381–441

Gewertz, Deborah B., *Sepik River Societies: A Historical Ethnography of the Chambri and their Neighbors* (New Haven CT, 1983)

Gilkeson, John S., *Anthropologists and the Rediscovery of America, 1886–1965* (Cambridge, 2010)

Gilliam, Angela and Lenora Foerstel, 'Margaret Mead's Contradictory Legacy', in Foerstel and Gilliam (eds), *Confronting the Margaret Mead Legacy*, 101–56

Bibliography

Gillin, John, 'Ralph Linton (1893–1953)', American Anthropologist, n.s., 56 (1954), 274–81

Gilman, Nils, 'Involution and Modernization: The Case of Clifford Geertz', in Jeffrey H. Cohen and Norbert Dannhaeuser (eds), Economic Development: An Anthropological Approach (Walnut Creek CA, 2002), 3–22

Gilman, Nils, Mandarins of the Future: Modernization Theory in Cold War America (Baltimore, 2003)

Gitre, Edward J.K., 'The Great Escape: World War II, Neo-Freudianism, and the Origins of U.S. Psychocultural Analysis', Journal of the History of the Behavioral Sciences 46 (2010), 1–26

Gladwin, Thomas, 'Civil Administration on Truk: A Rejoinder', Human Organization 9:4 (winter 1950), 15–23

Glander, Timothy, Origins of Mass Communications Research during the American Cold War: Educational Effects and Contemporary Implications (Mahwah NJ, 2000)

Glazer, Nathan, 'The Anthropological Revolution', The Nation, 15 Jun. 1946, 722

Glazer, Nathan, 'From Socialism to Sociology', in Bennett M. Berger (ed.), Authors of their Own Lives: Intellectual Autobiographies by Twenty American Sociologists (Berkeley, 1990), 190–209

Glazer, Nathan, 'Government by Manipulation', Commentary, Jul. 1946, 81–6

Glazer, Nathan, 'The Study of Man', Commentary, Nov. 1945, 84–7

Gleason, Abbott, Totalitarianism: The Inner History of the Cold War (New York, 1995)

Gleason, Philip, 'Identifying Identity: A Semantic History', Journal of American History 69 (1983), 910–31

Gleason, Philip, Speaking of Diversity: Language and Ethnicity in Twentieth-Century America (Baltimore, 1992)

Goldfrank, Esther S., 'Another View: Margaret and Me', Ethnohistory 30 (1983), 1–14

Goldman, Irving, 'Psychiatric Interpretation of Russian History: A Reply to Geoffrey Gorer', American Slavic and East European Review 9 (1950), 151–61

Gordan, Joan, Margaret Mead: The Complete Bibliography 1925–1975 (The Hague, 1976)

Gorer, Geoffrey, Bali and Angkor, or Looking at Life and Death (London, 1936)

Gorer, Geoffrey, 'The British Zone of Germany', Fortnightly Review, n.s., 160 (1946), 380–7

Gorer, Geoffrey, Exploring English Character (London, 1955)

Gorer, Geoffrey, Himalayan Village (London, 1938)

Gorer, Geoffrey, Hot Strip Tease and Other Notes on American Culture (London, 1937)

Gorer, Geoffrey, 'Internal Monsters', New Statesman, 5 Feb. 1949, 132–3

Gorer, Geoffrey, 'Justification by Numbers: A Commentary on the Kinsey Report' (1948), in The Danger of Equality and Other Essays (New York, 1966), 165–83

Gorer, Geoffrey, Nobody Talks Politics (London, 1936)

Gorer, Geoffrey, 'Notes on the Way', Time and Tide, 23 May 1936, 752–4

Gorer, Geoffrey, 'Some Aspects of the Psychology of the People of Great Russia', American Slavic and East European Review 8 (1949), 155–66

Gorer, Geoffrey, 'The Special Case of Japan', Public Opinion Quarterly 7 (1943), 567–82

Gorer, Geoffrey, 'Swaddling and the Russians', New Leader, 21 May 1951, 19–20

Gorer, Geoffrey, 'Themes in Japanese Culture', Transactions of the New York Academy of Sciences, 2nd ser., 5 (1942–3), 106–24

Gorer, Geoffrey and John Rickman, The People of Great Russia (1949), in Margaret Mead, Geoffrey Gorer and John Rickman, Russian Culture (New York, 2001), 1–159

Graebner, William, The Engineering of Consent: Democracy and Authority in Twentieth-Century America (Madison WI, 1987)

Gregg, Dorothy and Elgin Williams, 'The Dismal Science of Functionalism', American Anthropologist, n.s., 50 (1948), 594–611

Griffen, Joyce, 'Dorothea Cross Leighton', in Ute Gacs et al. (eds), Women Anthropologists: Selected Biographies (Urbana IL, 1989), 231–7

Gupta, Akhil and James Ferguson, 'Discipline and Practice: "The Field" as Site, Method, and Location in Anthropology', in Akhil Gupta and James Ferguson (eds), Anthropological Locations: Boundaries and Grounds of a Field Science (Berkeley, 1997), 1–46

Hale, Nathan G., Jr., The Rise and Crisis of Psychoanalysis in the United States: Freud and the Americans, 1917–1985 (New York, 1995)

Hall, Calvin S. and Gardner Lindzey, 'Psychoanalytic Theory and its Applications in the Social Sciences', in Gardner Lindzey (ed.), Handbook of Social Psychology (Cambridge MA, 1954), 143–80

Bibliography

Hall, Edward T., Jr., *An Anthropology of Everyday Life: An Autobiography* (New York, 1992)

Hall, Edward T., Jr., 'Military Government on Truk', *Human Organization* 9:2 (summer 1950), 25–30

Hall, Edward T., Jr., 'A Reply', *Human Organization* 9:4 (winter 1950), 24

Handler, Richard, 'Boasian Anthropology and the Critique of American Culture', *American Quarterly* 42 (1990), 252–73

Handler, Richard, 'Vigorous Male and Aspiring Female: Poetry, Personality, and Culture in Edward Sapir and Ruth Benedict', in Stocking (ed.), *Malinowski, Rivers, Benedict*, 127–55

Haney, David Paul, *The Americanization of Social Science: Intellectuals and Public Responsibility in the Postwar United States* (Philadelphia, 2008)

Hanks, L.M., Jr., 'The Quest for Individual Autonomy in Burmese Personality', *Psychiatry* 62 (1949), 285–300

Haring, Douglas G., 'Re: Ethnocentric Anthropologists', *American Anthropologist*, n.s., 53 (1951), 135–7

Harris, Marvin, *The Rise of Anthropological Theory: A History of Theories of Culture* (London, 1969)

Hawkins, Lester G., Jr. and George S. Pettee, 'OWI – Organization and Problems', *Public Opinion Quarterly* 7 (1943), 15–33

Hegeman, Susan, *Patterns for America: Modernism and the Concept of Culture* (Princeton, 1999)

Hendry, Joy, 'The Chrysanthemum Continues to Flower', in Jeremy MacClancy and Chris McDonaugh (eds), *Popularizing Anthropology* (London, 1996), 106–21

Hennessy, Bernard C., 'Psycho-Cultural Studies of National Character: Relevances for International Relations', *Background* 6 (1962), 27–49

Herman, Ellen, *The Romance of American Psychology: Political Culture in the Age of Experts* (Berkeley, 1995)

Herskovitz, M.J., 'Motivation and Culture-Pattern in Technological Change', *UNESCO International Social Science Bulletin* 6 (1954), 388–400

Heyer, Virginia, 'In Reply to Elgin Williams', *American Anthropologist*, n.s., 50 (1948), 163–6

Hirabayashi, Lane Ryo, *The Politics of Fieldwork: Research in an American Concentration Camp* (Tucson AZ, 1999)

Hixson, Walter L., *Parting the Curtain: Propaganda, Culture, and the Cold War, 1945–1961* (Basingstoke, 1997)

Hoffman, Louise E., 'American Psychologists and Wartime Research on Germany, 1941–1945', *American Psychologist* 47 (1992), 264–73

Hoffman, Louise E., 'Erikson on Hitler: The Origins of "Hitler's Imagery and German Youth"', *Psychohistory Review* 22 (1993–4), 69–86

Hoffman, Louise E., 'Psychoanalytic Interpretations of Adolf Hitler and Nazism, 1933–1945: A Prelude to Psychohistory', *Psychohistory Review* 11 (1982), 68–87

Hollinger, David A., 'Cultural Relativism', in Theodore M. Porter and Dorothy Ross (eds), *The Cambridge History of Science, Vol. 7: The Modern Social Sciences* (Cambridge, 2003), 708–20

Hollinger, David A., 'Science as a Weapon in Kulturkaempfe in the United States during and after World War II', *Isis* 86 (1995), 440–54

Honigmann, John J., 'The Personal Approach in Culture and Personality Research', in Spindler (ed.), *Making of Psychological Anthropology*, 302–29

Houseman, Michael and Carlo Severi, *Naven or the Other Self: A Relational Approach to Ritual Action* (Leiden, 1998)

Howard, Jane, *Margaret Mead: A Life* (New York, 1984)

Howell, Thomas, 'The Writers' War Board: U.S. Domestic Propaganda in World War II', *The Historian* 59 (1997), 795–813

Hoyt, Elizabeth E., 'Tiquisate: A Call for a Science of Human Affairs', *Scientific Monthly* 72 (1951), 114–19

Hoyt, Elizabeth E., 'Want Development in Underdeveloped Areas', *Journal of Political Economy* 59 (1951), 194–202

Hubble, Nick, *Mass Observation and Everyday Life: Culture, History, Theory* (Basingstoke, 2010)

Igo, Sarah E., *The Averaged American: Surveys, Citizens, and the Making of a Mass Public* (Cambridge MA, 2007)

Inaugural Addresses of the Presidents of the United States, Vol. 2, rev. ed. (Carlisle MA, 2009)

Bibliography

Inkeles, Alex, 'Clyde Kluckhohn's Contribution to Studies of Russia and the Soviet Union', in Walter W. Taylor, John L. Fischer and Evon Z. Vogt (eds), *Culture and Life: Essays in Memory of Clyde Kluckhohn* (Carbondale IL, 1973), 58–70

Inkeles, Alex, 'Industrial Man: The Relation of Status to Experience, Perception, and Value', *American Journal of Sociology* 66 (1960), 1–31

Inkeles, Alex and Daniel J. Levinson, 'National Character: The Study of Modal Personality and Sociocultural Systems', in Gardner Lindzey (ed.), *Handbook of Social Psychology* (Cambridge MA, 1954), 977–1020

'James, Leslie', *Americans in Glasshouses* (London, 1950)

Janiewski, Dolores and Lois W. Banner (eds), *Reading Benedict/Reading Mead: Feminism, Race, and Imperial Visions* (Baltimore, 2004)

Jordan, John M., *Machine-Age Ideology: Social Engineering for American Liberalism, 1911–1939* (Chapel Hill NC, 1994)

Kardiner, Abram and Edward Preble, *They Studied Man* (London, 1962)

Katz, Barry M., *Foreign Intelligence: Research and Analysis in the Office of Strategic Services* (Cambridge MA, 1989)

Kecskemeti, Paul and Nathan Leites, 'Some Psychological Hypotheses on Nazi Germany', *Journal of Social Psychology* 26 (1947), 141–83, 27 (1948), 91–117, 241–70, 28 (1948), 141–64

Kennard, Edward A., 'Anthropology in the Foreign Service Institute', *American Anthropologist*, n.s., 51 (1949), 154–5

Kennard, Edward A. and Gordon Macgregor, 'Applied Anthropology in Government: United States', in A.L. Kroeber (ed.), *Anthropology Today: An Encyclopedic Inventory* (Chicago, 1953), 832–40

Kent, Pauline, 'Japanese Perceptions of *The Chrysanthemum and the Sword*', *Dialectical Anthropology* 24 (1999), 181–92

Kent, Pauline, 'Misconceived Configurations of Ruth Benedict', *Japan Review* 7 (1996), 33–60

Kent, Pauline, 'Ruth Benedict and her Wartime Studies: Primary Materials and References', Ministry of Education, Grants-in-Aid for Scientific Research Report, No. 07710166 (Kyoto, 1996)

Kent, Pauline, 'Ruth Benedict's Original Wartime Study of the Japanese', *International Journal of Japanese Sociology* 3 (1994), 81–97

Kinnear, Mary, *Woman of the World: Mary McGeachy and International Cooperation* (Toronto, 2004)

Kirkendall, Richard S., *Social Scientists and Farm Politics in the Age of Roosevelt* (Columbia MO, 1966)

Kiste, Robert C. and Mac Marshall (eds), *American Anthropology in Micronesia: An Assessment* (Honolulu, 1999)

Kiste, Robert C. and Suzanne Falgout, 'Anthropology and Micronesia: The Context', in Kiste and Marshall (eds), *American Anthropology in Micronesia*, 11–51

Klein, Alexander, 'Groping for World Order', *Antioch Review* 12 (1952), 247–53

Klein, Christina, *Cold War Orientalism: Asia in the Middlebrow Imagination, 1945–1961* (Berkeley, 2003)

Kleinman, Mark L., *A World of Hope, A World of Fear: Henry A. Wallace, Reinhold Niebuhr and American Liberalism* (Columbus OH, 2000)

Klineberg, Otto, 'Historical Perspectives: Cross-Cultural Psychology before 1960', in Harry C. Triandis and William Wilson Lambert (eds), *Handbook of Cross-Cultural Psychology, Vol. 1: Perspectives* (Boston, 1980), 31–67

Klineberg, Otto, 'Otto Klineberg', in Gardner Lindzey (ed.), *A History of Psychology in Autobiography, Vol. 6* (Englewood Cliffs NJ, 1974), 163–82

Klineberg, Otto, 'Recent Studies of National Character', in S. Stansfeld Sargent and Marian W. Smith (eds), *Culture and Personality* (New York, 1949), 127–38

Klineberg, Otto, 'A Science of National Character', *Journal of Social Psychology* 19 (1944), 147–62

Klineberg, Otto, 'The UNESCO Project on International Tensions: A Challenge to the Sciences of Man', *UNESCO International Social Science Bulletin* 1 (1949), 11–21

Kluckhohn, Clyde, 'Anthropological Research and World Peace', in *Approaches to World Peace. Science, Philosophy and Religion: Fourth Symposium* (New York, 1944), 143–66

Bibliography

Kluckhohn, Clyde, 'Anthropology Comes of Age', *American Scholar* 19 (1949–50), 241–56

Kluckhohn, Clyde, *Mirror for Man: The Relation of Anthropology to Modern Life* (London, 1950)

Kluckhohn, Clyde, 'Ralph Linton, 1893–1953', in National Academy of Sciences, *Biographical Memoirs* (1958), 236–53

Kluckhohn, Clyde, 'Recent Studies of the "National Character" of Great Russians', in Richard Kluckhohn (ed.), *Culture and Behavior: Collected Essays of Clyde Kluckhohn* (New York, 1962), 210–43

Kluckhohn, Clyde, 'Russian Research at Harvard', *World Politics* 1 (1948–9), 266–71

Kluckhohn, Clyde and Henry A. Murray (eds), *Personality in Nature, Society and Culture* (New York, 1948)

[Knight, Eric], *A Short Guide to Great Britain* (Washington DC, 1942)

Knox, Edward C., '"Not Our Kind of People" – GI Gripes on France in 1945', *Contemporary French and Francophone Studies* 8 (2004), 405–14

Kris, Ernst and Nathan Leites, 'Trends in Twentieth Century Propaganda' (1947), in Daniel Lerner (ed.), *Propaganda in War and Crisis* (New York, 1951), 39–52

Kuklick, Bruce, *Blind Oracles: Intellectuals and War from Kennan to Kissinger* (Princeton, 2006)

Kuper, Adam, *Culture: The Anthropologists' Account* (Cambridge MA, 1999)

Lagemann, Ellen Condliffe, *The Politics of Knowledge: The Carnegie Corporation, Philanthropy, and Public Policy* (Chicago, 1989)

Lapsley, Hilary, *Margaret Mead and Ruth Benedict: The Kinship of Women* (Amherst MA, 1999)

Lasswell, Harold D., 'Policy and the Intelligence Function' (1942), in Lerner (ed.), *Propaganda in War and Crisis*, 55–68

Lasswell, Harold D., 'The Policy Orientation', in Daniel Lerner and Harold D. Lasswell (eds), *The Policy Sciences: Recent Developments in Scope and Method* (Stanford CA, 1951)

Lasswell, Harold D., 'Propaganda and Mass Insecurity', in Alfred H. Stanton and Stewart E. Perry (eds), *Personality and Political Crisis* (Glencoe IL, 1951), 15–43

Lasswell, Harold D., 'The Psychology of Hitlerism', *Political Quarterly* 4 (1933), 373–84

Latham, Michael E., 'Introduction: Modernization, International History, and the Cold War World', in David C. Engerman et al. (eds), *Staging Growth: Modernization, Development, and the Global Cold War* (Amherst MA, 2003), 1–22

Latham, Michael E., *Modernization as Ideology: American Social Science and 'Nation Building' in the Kennedy Era* (Chapel Hill NC, 2000)

Leeds-Hurwitz, Wendy, 'Notes in the History of Intercultural Communication: The Foreign Service Institute and the Mandate for Intercultural Training', *Quarterly Journal of Speech* 76 (1990), 262–81

Leffler, Melvyn P., *A Preponderance of Power: National Security, the Truman Administration, and the Cold War* (Stanford CA, 1992)

Lehmann, Karl, 'Erling C. Olsen', *College Art Journal* 4 (1945), 107–8

Leighton, Alexander H., *The Governing of Men: General Principles and Recommendations Based on Experience at a Japanese Relocation Camp* (Princeton, 1945)

Leighton, Alexander H., *Human Relations in a Changing World: Observations on the Use of the Social Sciences* (New York, 1949)

Leites, Nathan, *The Operational Code of the Politburo* (New York, 1951)

Leites, Nathan, 'Psycho-Cultural Hypotheses about Political Acts', *World Politics* 1 (1948), 102–19

Lemov, Rebecca, *World as Laboratory: Experiments with Mice, Mazes, and Men* (New York, 2005)

Lerner, Daniel, 'The American Soldier and the Public', in Robert K. Merton and Paul F. Lazarsfeld (eds), *Continuities in Social Research: Studies in the Scope and Method of 'The American Soldier'* (Glencoe IL, 1950), 212–51

Lerner, Daniel, 'Effective Propaganda: Conditions and Evaluation', in Lerner (ed.), *Propaganda in War and Crisis*, 344–54

Lerner, Daniel (ed.), *Propaganda in War and Crisis* (New York, 1951)

Lerner, Daniel, *Psychological Warfare Against Nazi Germany: The Sykewar Campaign, D-Day to VE-Day*, 1st ed. 1949 (Cambridge MA, 1971)

LeVine, Robert A., 'Culture and Personality Studies, 1918–1960: Myth and History', *Journal of Personality* 69 (2001), 803–18

Levy, David M., *New Fields of Psychiatry* (New York, 1947)

Bibliography

Lewin, Kurt, 'Cultural Reconstruction', *Journal of Abnormal and Social Psychology* 38 (1943), 166–73

Lewin, Kurt, 'The Special Case of Germany', *Public Opinion Quarterly* 7 (1943), 555–66

Lewis, Herbert S., 'Anthropology, the Cold War, and Intellectual History', *Histories of Anthropologies Annual* 1 (2005), 99–113

Lewis, Herbert S., 'The Misrepresentation of Anthropology and its Consequences', *American Anthropologist*, n.s., 100 (1998), 716–31

Liebich, Andre, *From the Other Shore: Russian Social Democracy after 1921* (Cambridge MA, 1997)

Lindesmith, Alfred R. and Anselm L. Strauss, 'A Critique of Culture-Personality Writings', *American Sociological Review* 15 (1950), 587–600

Linton, Adelin and Charles Wagley, *Ralph Linton* (New York, 1971)

Linton, Ralph, 'The Concept of National Character', in Alfred H. Stanton and Stewart E. Perry (eds), *Personality and Political Crisis* (Glencoe IL, 1951), 133–42

Lippitt, Ronald, 'The Small Group and Participatory Democracy: Comment on Graebner', *Journal of Social Issues* 42 (1986), 155–6

Lipset, David, *Gregory Bateson: The Legacy of a Scientist* (Englewood Cliffs NJ, 1980)

Liss, Julia E., 'Patterns of Strangeness: Franz Boas, Modernism, and the Origins of Anthropology', in Elazar Barkan and Ronald Bush (eds), *Prehistories of the Future: The Primitivist Project and the Culture of Modernism* (Stanford CA, 1995), 114–30

Lucas, Scott, *Freedom's War: The US Crusade Against the Soviet Union, 1945–56* (Manchester, 1999)

Lummis, Douglas, 'Ruth Benedict's Obituary for Japanese Culture', in Janiewski and Banner (eds), *Reading Benedict/Reading Mead*, 126–40

Lumsdaine, David Halloran, *Moral Vision in International Politics: The Foreign Aid Regime, 1949–1989* (Princeton, 1993)

Lutkehaus, Nancy C., *Margaret Mead: The Making of an American Icon* (Princeton, 2008)

Lynd, Robert S., 'The Science of Inhuman Relations', *New Republic*, 29 Aug. 1949, 22–5

Lyons, Gene M., *The Uneasy Partnership: Social Science and the Federal Government in the 20th Century* (New York, 1969)

Mabee, Carleton, 'Margaret Mead and Behavioral Scientists in World War II: Problems in Responsibility, Truth, and Effectiveness', *Journal of the History of the Behavioral Sciences* 23 (1987), 3–13

McClay, Wilfred M., *The Masterless: Self and Society in Modern America* (Chapel Hill NC, 1994)

McClintock, Michael, *Instruments of Statecraft: U.S. Guerrilla Warfare, Counterinsurgency, and Counterterrorism, 1940–1990* (New York, 1992)

McFate, Montgomery, 'Anthropology and Counterinsurgency: The Strange Story of their Curious Relationship', *Military Review* (Mar.–Apr. 2005), 24–38

McFate, Montgomery, 'The Military Utility of Understanding Adversary Culture', *Joint Force Quarterly* 38 (Jul. 2005), 42–8

McGranahan, Maj. Donald V. and Lt Morris Janowitz, 'Studies of German Youth', *Journal of Abnormal and Social Psychology* 41 (1946), 3–14

Macgregor, Gordon, 'Anthropology in Government: United States', *Yearbook of Anthropology* (1955), 421–33

McIntosh, Elizabeth P., *Sisterhood of Spies: The Women of the OSS* (New York, 1999)

McLaine, Ian, *Ministry of Morale: Home Front Morale and the Ministry of Information in World War II* (London, 1979)

McLaughlin, Neil, 'Critical Theory Meets America: Riesman, Fromm, and *The Lonely Crowd*', *American Sociologist* 2 (2001), 5–26

McLaughlin, Neil G., 'Why Do Schools of Thought Fail? Neo-Freudianism as a Case Study in the Sociology of Knowledge', *Journal of the History of the Behavioral Sciences* 34 (1998), 113–34

Mandelbaum, David G., 'On the Study of National Character', *American Anthropologist*, n.s., 55 (1953), 174–87

Mandler, Peter, 'Being His Own Rabbit: Geoffrey Gorer and English Culture', in C.V.J. Griffiths, James J. Nott and William Whyte (eds), *Cultures, Classes, and Politics: Essays on British History for Ross McKibbin* (Oxford, 2011), 192–208

Bibliography

Mandler, Peter, 'Deconstructing "Cold War Anthropology"', in Joel Isaac and Duncan Bell (eds), *Uncertain Empire: American History and the Idea of the Cold War* (New York, 2012)

Mandler, Peter, 'Margaret Mead Amongst the Natives of Great Britain', *Past and Present* 204 (2009), 195–233

Mandler, Peter, 'One World, Many Cultures: Margaret Mead and the Limits to Cold War Anthropology', *History Workshop Journal* 68 (2009), 149–72

Manson, William C., *The Psychodynamics of Culture: Abram Kardiner and Neo-Freudian Anthropology* (Westport CT, 1988)

Mayo, Marlene J., 'American Wartime Planning for Occupied Japan: The Role of the Experts', in Robert Wolfe (ed.), *Americans as Proconsuls: United States Military Government in Germany and Japan, 1944–1952* (Carbondale IL, 1984), 3–51

Mead, Margaret, *The American Troops and the British Community: An Examination of the Relationship between the American Troops and the British* (London, 1944)

Mead, Margaret, *And Keep Your Powder Dry*, 1st ed. 1942 (New York, 2000)

Mead, Margaret, 'Anthropological Contributions to National Policies during and Immediately after World War II', in Walter Goldschmidt (ed.), *The Uses of Anthropology* (Washington DC, 1979), 145–57

Mead, Margaret, *An Anthropologist at Work: Writings of Ruth Benedict* (London, 1959)

Mead, Margaret, 'An Anthropologist Looks at the Report' (1948), in *Studying Contemporary Western Society: Method and Theory*, ed. William O. Beeman (New York, 2004), 278–87

Mead, Margaret, 'Applied Anthropology, 1955', in Anthropological Society of Washington, *Some Uses of Anthropology: Theoretical and Applied* (Washington DC, 1956), 94–108

Mead, Margaret, 'The Application of Anthropological Techniques to Cross-National Communication', *Transactions of the New York Academy of Sciences*, 2nd ser., 9 (1946–7), 133–51

Mead, Margaret, 'The Arts in Bali', *Yale Review* 30 (1940–1), 335–47

Mead, Margaret, 'As Johnny Thinks of Home . . . He Learns Little in England', *Social Action*, 15 Mar. 1944, 7–13

Mead, Margaret, *Blackberry Winter: My Earlier Years* (New York, 1972)

Mead, Margaret, 'A Case History in Cross-National Communications' (1948), in *Studying Contemporary Western Society: Method and Theory*, ed. William O. Beeman (New York, 2004), 144–61

Mead, Margaret, 'Changing Styles of Anthropological Work' (1973), in *Studying Contemporary Western Society: Method and Theory*, ed. William O. Beeman (New York, 2004), 40–73

Mead, Margaret, 'Christian Faith and Technical Assistance', *Christianity and Crisis*, 10 Jan. 1955, 179–82

Mead, Margaret, *Coming of Age in Samoa: A Psychological Study of Primitive Youth for Western Civilisation* (London, 1929)

Mead, Margaret, 'The Comparative Study of Culture and the Purposive Cultivation of Democratic Values', in *Science, Philosophy and Religion: Second Symposium* (New York, 1942), 56–97

Mead, Margaret, 'The Comparative Study of Cultures and the Purposive Cultivation of Democratic Values, 1941–1949', in Lyman Bryson, Louis Finkelstein and R.M. MacIver (eds), *Perspectives on a Troubled Decade: Science, Philosophy, and Religion, 1939–1949. 10th Symposium* (New York, 1950), 87–108

Mead, Margaret, 'End-Linkage: A Tool for Cross-Cultural Analysis', in John Brockman (ed.), *About Bateson* (London, 1977), 169–231

Mead, Margaret, 'Ferment in British Education: Some Impressions of Educational Thinking in England', *Journal of the American Association of University Women* 37 (1944), 131–3

Mead, Margaret, 'Food and Feeding in Occupied Territory', *Public Opinion Quarterly* 7 (1943), 618–28

Mead, Margaret, *From the South Seas: Studies of Adolescence and Sex in Primitive Societies* (New York, 1939)

Mead, Margaret, 'A GI View of Britain', *New York Times Magazine*, 19 Mar. 1944, 18–19, 34

Mead, Margaret, *Growing Up in New Guinea* (London, 1931)

Mead, Margaret, 'Human Differences and World Order', in Frederick Ernest Johnson (ed.), *World Order: Its Intellectual and Cultural Foundation* (New York, 1945), 40–51

Bibliography

Mead, Margaret, 'Introduction', in Robert F. Byrnes (ed.), *Communal Families in the Balkans: The Zadruga. Essays by Philip E. Mosely and Essays in his Honor* (Notre Dame IN, 1976), xvii–xxvii

Mead, Margaret, *Letters from the Field, 1925–1975*, 1st ed. 1977 (New York, 2001)

Mead, Margaret, *Male and Female: A Study of the Sexes in a Changing World* (New York, 1949)

Mead, Margaret, 'National Character', in A.L. Kroeber (ed.), *Anthropology Today: An Encyclopedic Inventory* (Chicago, 1953), 642–67

Mead, Margaret, 'National Character and the Science of Anthropology', in Seymour Martin Lipset and Leo Lowenthal (eds), *Culture and Social Character: The Work of David Riesman Reviewed* (New York, 1961), 15–26

Mead, Margaret, 'The New Isolationism', *American Scholar* 24 (1954–5), 378–82

Mead, Margaret, *New Lives for Old: Cultural Transformation – Manus, 1928–1953* (London, 1956)

Mead, Margaret, 'On the Institutionalized Role of Women and Character Formation', *Zeitschrift für Sozialforschung* 5 (1936), 69–74

Mead, Margaret, 'On Methods of Implementing a National Morale Program', *Applied Anthropology* 1:1 (Oct.–Dec. 1941), 20–4

Mead, Margaret, 'Political Applications of Studies of Culture at a Distance', in Margaret Mead and Rhoda Metraux (eds), *The Study of Culture at a Distance*, 1st ed. 1953 (New York, 2000), 441–4

Mead, Margaret, 'Research in Contemporary Cultures', in Harold Guetzkow (ed.), *Groups, Leadership and Men: Research in Human Relations* (Pittsburgh, 1951), 106–18

Mead, Margaret, 'Retrospects and Prospects', in Anthropological Society of Washington, *Anthropology and Human Behavior* (Washington DC, 1962), 115–49

Mead, Margaret, *Sex and Temperament in Three Primitive Societies* (London, 1935)

Mead, Margaret, 'Social Change and Cultural Surrogates', *Journal of Educational Sociology* 14 (1940–1), 92–109

Mead, Margaret, *Soviet Attitudes toward Authority* (1951), in Margaret Mead, Geoffrey Gorer and John Rickman, *Russian Culture* (New York, 2001), 161–319

Mead, Margaret, 'The Study of National Character' (1951), in *Studying Contemporary Western Society: Method and Theory*, ed. William O. Beeman (New York, 2004), 87–109

Mead, Margaret, 'Technological Change and Child Development', in Kenneth Soddy (ed.), *Mental Health and Infant Development* (London, 1955), 180–5

Mead, Margaret, 'What Is a Date?', *Transatlantic*, Jun. 1944, 54–60

Mead, Margaret, 'Why We Americans "Talk Big"', *The Listener*, 28 Oct. 1943, 494

Mead, Margaret, 'The Yank in Britain', *Current Affairs* 64 (11 Mar. 1944)

Mead, Margaret (ed.), *Cooperation and Competition among Primitive Peoples* (New York, 1937)

Mead, Margaret (ed.), *Cultural Patterns and Technical Change* (New York, 1955)

Mead, Margaret (ed.), *Studies in Soviet Communication*, 2 vols (Cambridge MA, 1952)

Mead, Margaret and Rhoda Metraux (eds), *The Study of Culture at a Distance*, 1st ed. 1953 (New York, 2000)

Metraux, Alfred, 'Applied Anthropology in Government: United Nations', in A.L. Kroeber (ed.), *Anthropology Today: An Encyclopedic Inventory* (Chicago, 1953), 880–94

Metraux, Alfred, 'UNESCO and Anthropology', *American Anthropologist*, n.s., 53 (1951), 294–300

Metraux, Rhoda (ed.), *Margaret Mead: Some Personal Views* (New York, 1979)

Michel, Sonya, 'Danger on the Home Front: Motherhood, Sexuality, and Disabled Veterans in American Postwar Films', *Journal of the History of Sexuality* 3 (1992), 109–28

Milne, David, *America's Rasputin: Walt Rostow and the Vietnam War* (New York, 2008)

Minear, Richard H., 'Cross-Cultural Perception and World War II: American Japanists of the 1940s and their Images of Japan', *International Studies Quarterly* 24 (1980), 555–80

Minear, Richard H., 'The Wartime Studies of Japanese National Character', *The Japan Interpreter* 13 (1980), 36–59

Modell, Judith S., '"It Is Besides a Pleasant English Word": Ruth Benedict's Concept of Patterns Revisited', in Janiewski and Banner (eds), *Reading Benedict/Reading Mead*, 205–28

Modell, Judith Schachter, *Ruth Benedict: Patterns of a Life* (Philadelphia, 1983)

Modell, Judith S., 'The Wall of Shame: Ruth Benedict's Accomplishment in the Chrysanthemum and the Sword', *Dialectical Anthropology* 24 (1999), 193–215

Bibliography

Molloy, Maureen A., *On Creating a Usable Culture: Margaret Mead and the Emergence of American Cosmopolitanism* (Honolulu, 2008)

Moore, Michaela Hoenicke, *Know Your Enemy: The American Debate on Nazism, 1933–1945* (New York, 2010)

Morsink, Johannes, *The Universal Declaration of Human Rights: Origins, Drafting, and Intent* (Philadelphia, 1999)

Mosely, Philip E., 'A Pro-Russian, Anti-Stalin Policy', *New Leader*, 21 May 1951, 22–3

Murphy, Gardner, 'Psychology in the Making of Peace', *Journal of Abnormal and Social Psychology* 38 (1943), 132–40

Nader, Laura, 'The Phantom Factor: Impact of the Cold War on Anthropology', in Chomsky et al., *The Cold War and the University*, 107–46

Nader, Ralph, 'Anthropology in Law and Civic Action', in Bela C. Maday (ed.), *Anthropology and Society* (Washington DC, 1975), 31–40

Nagl, John A., *Learning to Eat Soup with a Knife: Counterinsurgency Lessons from Malaya and Vietnam* (Chicago, 2005)

Nash, Manning, *Machine Age Maya: The Industrialization of a Guatemalan Community* (Chicago, 1958)

Network of Concerned Anthropologists, *The Counter-Counterinsurgency Manual* (Chicago, 2009)

Newman, Louise M., 'Coming of Age, But Not in Samoa: Reflections on Margaret Mead's Legacy for Western Liberal Feminism', in Janiewski and Banner (eds), *Reading Benedict/ Reading Mead*, 51–69

Nicholls, Anthony J., 'The German "National Character" in British Perspective', in Ulrike Jordan (ed.), *Conditions of Surrender: Britons and Germans Witness the End of the War* (London, 1997), 26–39

Ninkovich, Frank, *The Diplomacy of Ideas: U.S. Foreign Policy and Cultural Relations, 1938–1950* (Cambridge, 1981)

Ohmann, Richard, 'English and the Cold War', in Chomsky et al., *The Cold War and the University*, 73–105

Oppenheim, Robert, 'On the Locations of Korean War and Cold War Anthropology', *Histories of Anthropology Annual* 4 (2008), 220–59

Orlansky, Harold, 'Destiny in the Nursery', *Commentary*, Jun. 1948, 563–9

Orlansky, Harold, 'Infant Care and Personality', *Psychological Bulletin* 46 (1949), 1–48

Orwell, George, 'The Lion and the Unicorn: Socialism and the English Genius', in *The Collected Essays, Journalism and Letters, Vol. 2: My Country Right or Left, 1940–1943*, ed. Sonia Orwell and Ian Angus (London, 1968), 74–134

Packenham, Robert A., *Liberal America and the Third World: Political Development Ideas in Foreign Aid and Social Science* (Princeton, 1973)

Packer, George, 'Knowing the Enemy', *New Yorker*, 18 Dec. 2006, 60–9

Pandora, Katherine, *Rebels within the Ranks: Psychologists' Critique of Scientific Authority and Democratic Realities in New Deal America* (Cambridge, 1997)

Parmar, Inderjeet, 'Engineering Consent: The Carnegie Endowment for International Peace and the Mobilization of American Public Opinion, 1939–1945', *Review of International Studies* 26 (2000), 35–48

Partridge, William L. and Elizabeth M. Eddy, 'The Development of Applied Anthropology in America', in Elizabeth M. Eddy and William L. Partridge (eds), *Applied Anthropology in America* (New York, 1978), 3–45

Paterson, Thomas G., *Meeting the Communist Threat: Truman to Reagan* (Oxford, 1988)

Patterson, Thomas C., *A Social History of Anthropology in the United States* (Oxford and New York, 2001)

Peace, William, 'Columbia University and the Mundial Upheaval Society: A Study in Academic Networking', in Wax (ed.), *Anthropology at the Dawn of the Cold War*, 143–65

Peake, Hayden B., 'OSS and the Venona Decrypts', *Intelligence and National Security* 12 (1997), 14–34

Pelzel, John, 'John Fee Embree, 1908–1950', *Far Eastern Quarterly* 11 (1952), 219–25

Petersen, Glenn, 'Politics in Postwar Micronesia', in Kiste and Marshall (eds), *American Anthropology in Micronesia*, 145–95

Pick, Daniel, *The Pursuit of the Nazi Mind: Hitler, Hess and the Analysts* (Oxford, 2012)

Bibliography

Pinkoski, Marc, 'American Colonialism at the Dawn of the Cold War', in Wax (ed.), *Anthropology at the Dawn of the Cold War*, 62–88

Powers, Willow Roberts, 'The Harvard Study of Values: Mirror for Postwar Anthropology', *Journal of the History of the Behavioral Sciences* 36 (2000), 15–29

Price, David H., *Anthropological Intelligence: The Deployment and Neglect of American Anthropology in the Second World War* (Durham NC, 2008)

Price, David H., 'Cold War Anthropology: Collaborators and Victims of the National Security State', *Identities* 4 (1997–8), 389–430

Price, David H., 'Gregory Bateson and the OSS: World War II and Bateson's Assessment of Applied Anthropology', *Human Organization* 57 (1998), 379–84

Price, David H., 'Materialism's Free Pass: Karl Wittfogel, McCarthyism, and the "Bureaucratization of Guilt"', in Wax (ed.), *Anthropology at the Dawn of the Cold War*, 37–61

Price, David H., 'Subtle Means and Enticing Carrots: The Impact of Funding on American Cold War Anthropology', *Critique of Anthropology* 23 (2003), 373–401

Price, David H., *Threatening Anthropology: McCarthyism and the FBI's Surveillance of Activist Anthropologists* (Durham NC, 2004)

Pronay, Nicholas, 'Introduction: "To Stamp Out the Whole Tradition. . ."', in Nicholas Pronay and Keith Wilson (eds), *The Political Re-education of Germany and her Allies* (London, 1985), 1–36

Purcell, Edward A., Jr., *The Crisis of Democratic Theory: Scientific Naturalism and the Problem of Value* (Lexington KY, 1973)

RAND Corporation, *Remembering Nathan Leites: An Appreciation* (Santa Monica CA, 1988)

Redfield, Robert, *The Primitive World and Its Transformations* (Ithaca NY, 1953)

Renteln, Alison Dundes, *International Human Rights: Universalism versus Relativism* (Newbury Park CA, 1990)

'Report of the Committee on Ethics', *Human Organization* 8:2 (spring 1949), 20–1

Reynolds, David, *Rich Relations: The American Occupation of Britain, 1942–1945* (New York, 1995)

Riemer, Svend, 'Individual and National Psychology: A Problem in the Army Area Study', *Social Forces* 22 (1944), 256–61

Riesman, David, 'Comments on Dr Kluckhohn's Paper', *Human Development Bulletin*, 6th Annual Symposium (1955), 39–61, 67–72

Riesman, David, 'A Grammar of Soviet Motives', *Partisan Review*, Mar.–Apr. 1952, 242–6

Riesman, David, 'Some Observations on Changes in Leisure Attitudes' (1952), in *Selected Essays from Individualism Reconsidered* (Garden City NY, 1955), 126–47

Riesman, David, 'The Study of National Character: Some Observations on the American Case' (1958), in *Abundance for What? and Other Essays* (Garden City NY, 1964), 584–603

Riesman, David with Nathan Glazer, 'The Lonely Crowd: A Reconsideration in 1960', in Seymour Martin Lipset and Leo Lowenthal (eds), *Culture and Social Character: The Work of David Riesman Reviewed* (New York, 1961), 419–58

Riesman, David with Nathan Glazer and Reuel Denney, *The Lonely Crowd: A Study of the Changing American Character*, 1st ed. 1950 (New Haven, 2001)

Riley, Denise, *War in the Nursery: Theories of the Child and Mother* (London, 1983)

Robin, Ron, *The Making of the Cold War Enemy: Culture and Politics in the Military-Intellectual Complex* (Princeton, 2001)

Rodnick, David, *Postwar Germans: An Anthropologist's Account* (New Haven, 1948)

Rogers, Everett M. et al., 'Edward T. Hall and the History of Intercultural Communication: The United States and Japan', *Keio Communication Review* 24 (2002), 3–26

Rorty, James, 'Point Four Begins at Home', *New Leader*, 24 Sep. 1949, 7

Rose, Nikolas, *Governing the Soul: The Shaping of the Private Self*, 1st ed. 1989 (London, 1991)

Ross, Dorothy, 'Changing Contours of the Social Science Disciplines', in Theodore M. Porter and Dorothy Ross (eds), *The Cambridge History of Science, Vol. 7: The Modern Social Sciences* (Cambridge, 2003), 205–37

Ross, Dorothy, *The Origins of American Social Science* (Cambridge, 1991)

Ross, Eric B., 'Cold Warriors Without Weapons', *Identities* 4 (1997–8), 475–506

[Rosten, Leo], *112 Gripes about the French* (Paris, 1945)

Rosten, Leo, 'How the Politburo Thinks', *Look*, 13 Mar. 1951, 31–5

Samelson, Franz, 'Authoritarianism from Berlin to Berkeley: On Social Psychology and History', *Journal of Social Issues* 42 (1986), 191–208

Sapir, Edward, 'Culture, Genuine and Spurious', in *Selected Writings in Language, Culture, and Personality*, ed. David G. Mandelbaum (Berkeley CA, 1985), 308–31

Sargent, S. Stansfeld and Marian W. Smith (eds), *Culture and Personality* (New York, 1949)

Schaffner, Bertram, *Father Land: A Study of Authoritarianism in the German Family* (New York, 1948)

Schneider, David and Richard Handler, *Schneider on Schneider: The Conversion of the Jews and Other Anthropological Stories* (Durham NC, 1995)

Schonberger, Howard B., *Aftermath of War: Americans and the Remaking of Japan, 1945–1952* (Kent OH, 1989)

Schwartz, Theodore, 'Where Is the Culture? Personality as the Distributive Locus of Culture', in Spindler (ed.), *Making of Psychological Anthropology*, 419–41

Schwartz, Thomas Alan, *America's Germany: John J. McCloy and the Federal Republic of Germany* (Cambridge MA, 1991)

Selig, Diana, *Americans All: The Cultural Gifts Movement* (Cambridge MA, 2008)

Shannon, Christopher, *A World Made Safe for Differences: Cold War Intellectuals and the Politics of Identity* (Lanham MD, 2001)

Shenin, Sergei Y., *The United States and the Third World: The Origins of Postwar Relations and the Point Four Program* (Huntington NY, 2000)

Sherry, Michael S., *In the Shadow of War: The United States since the 1930s* (New Haven, 1995)

Shipman, Pat, *The Evolution of Racism: Human Differences and the Use and Abuse of Science* (New York, 1994)

Shub, Boris, 'Soviets Expose American Baby', *New Leader*, 17 Jun. 1950, 11–12

Simpson, Christopher, *Science of Coercion: Communication Research and Psychological Warfare 1945–1960* (Oxford, 1994)

Simpson, Christopher (ed.), *Universities and Empire: Money and Politics in the Social Sciences during the Cold War* (New York, 1998)

Singer, H.W., 'Reflections of Sociological Aspects of Economic Growth Based on the Work of Bert Hoselitz', in Manning Nash (ed.), *Essays on Economic Development and Cultural Change* (Chicago, 1977), 1–15

Smith, Mark C., *Social Science in the Crucible: The American Debate over Objectivity and Purpose, 1918–1941* (Durham NC, 1994)

Smith, Woodruff, *Politics and the Sciences of Culture in Germany, 1840–1920* (New York, 1991)

Soley, Lawrence C., *Radio Warfare: OSS and CIA Subversive Propaganda* (New York, 1989)

Spector, Ronald, 'Allied Intelligence and Indochina, 1943–1945', *Pacific Historical Review* 51 (1982), 23–50

Speier, Hans, 'Nathan Leites: An Uncompromising Intellect', in RAND Corporation, *Remembering Nathan Leites: An Appreciation* (Santa Monica CA, 1988), 63–6

Speier, Hans, 'Psychological Warfare Reconsidered', in Lerner (ed.), *Propaganda in War and Crisis*, 463–92

Spicer, Edward H., *Human Problems in Technological Change*, 1st ed. 1952 (New York, 1965)

Spindler, George D. (ed.), *The Making of Psychological Anthropology* (Berkeley, 1978)

Spindler, George D. and Louise Spindler, 'Anthropologists View American Culture', *Annual Review of Anthropology* 12 (1983), 49–78

Spiro, Melford E., 'Culture and Human Nature', in Spindler (ed.), *Making of Psychological Anthropology*, 331–60

Spitzer, Hermann M., 'Psychoanalytic Approaches to the Japanese Character', *Psychoanalysis and the Social Sciences* 1 (1947), 131–56

Sproule, J. Michael, *Propaganda and Democracy: The American Experience of Media and Mass Persuasion* (Cambridge, 1997)

Staples, Amy L.S., *The Birth of Development: How the World Bank, Food and Agriculture Organization, and World Health Organization Changed the World, 1945–1965* (Kent OH, 2006)

'Statement on Human Rights', *American Anthropologist*, n.s., 49 (1947), 539–43

Stears, Marc, *Demanding Democracy: American Radicals in Search of a New Politics* (Princeton, 2010)

Steward, Julian H., 'Comments on the Statement of Human Rights', *American Anthropologist*, n.s., 50 (1948), 351–2

Bibliography

Stocking, George W., Jr. (ed.), *Colonial Situations: Essays on the Contextualization of Ethnographic Knowledge* (Madison WI, 1991)

Stocking, George W., Jr., '"Do Good, Young Man": Sol Tax and the World Mission of Liberal Democratic Anthropology', in Richard Handler (ed.), *Excluded Ancestors, Inventible Traditions: Essays toward a More Inclusive History of Anthropology* (Madison WI, 2000), 171–264

Stocking, George W., Jr. (ed.), *Malinowski, Rivers, Benedict and Others: Essays on Culture and Personality* (Madison WI, 1986)

Stoetzel, Jean, *Without the Chrysanthemum and the Sword: A Study of the Attitudes of Youth in Post-War Japan* (London, 1955)

Sullivan, Gerald, 'A Four-Fold Humanity: Margaret Mead and Psychological Types', *Journal of the History of the Behavioral Sciences* 40 (2004), 183–206

Sullivan, Gerald, 'Of Feys and Culture Planners: Margaret Mead and Purposive Activity as Value', in Janiewski and Banner (eds), *Reading Benedict/Reading Mead*, 100–14

Suzuki, Peter T., 'Anthropologists in the Wartime Camps for Japanese Americans: A Documentary Study', *Dialectical Anthropology* 6 (1981–2), 23–60

Suzuki, Peter T., 'Overlooked Aspects of the Chrysanthemum and the Sword', *Dialectical Anthropology* 24 (1999), 217–32

Suzuki, Peter T., 'A Retrospective Analysis of a Wartime "National Character" Study', *Dialectical Anthropology* 5 (1980–1), 33–55

Suzuki, Peter T., 'Ruth Benedict, Robert Hashima, and "The Chrysanthemum and the Sword"', *Research: Contributions to Interdisciplinary Anthropology* 3 (1985), 55–69

Tarrant, Shira, *When Sex Became Gender* (New York, 2006)

Tax, Sol et al. (eds), *An Appraisal of Anthropology Today* (Chicago, 1953)

Taylor, Edmond, *Richer by Asia*, 1st ed. 1947 (London, 1948)

Tent, James F., 'Edward Y. Hartshorne and the Reopening of German Universities, 1945–1946: His Personal Account', *Paedagogica Historica* 33 (1997), 183–200

Tent, James F., *Mission on the Rhine: Reeducation and Denazification in American-Occupied Germany* (Chicago, 1982)

Thayer, V.T., Caroline B. Zachry, Ruth Kotinsky et al., *Reorganizing Secondary Education* (New York, 1939)

Thomson, Mathew, *Psychological Subjects: Identity, Culture and Health in Twentieth-Century Britain* (Oxford, 2006)

Thorne, Christopher, *Allies of a Kind: The United States, Britain and the War against Japan, 1941–1945*, 1st ed. 1978 (Oxford, 1979)

Torriani, Riccarda, 'Nazis into Germans: Re-education and Democratisation in the British and French Occupation Zones, 1945–1949', PhD dissertation, University of Cambridge, 2005

UNESCO, *Fundamental Education: Common Ground for All Peoples* (Paris, 1947)

Useem, John, 'Social Reconstruction in Micronesia', *Far Eastern Survey*, 30 Jan. 1946, 21–3

van Ginkel, Rob, 'Typically Dutch: Ruth Benedict on the National Character of Netherlanders', *Netherlands Journal of Social Sciences* 28 (1992), 50–71

Wakin, Eric, *Anthropology Goes to War: Professional Ethics and Counterinsurgency in Thailand* (Madison WI, 1992)

Wall, Wendy L., *Inventing the 'American Way': The Politics of Consensus from the New Deal to the Civil Rights Movement* (Oxford, 2008)

Wallerstein, Immanuel, 'The Unintended Consequences of Cold War Area Studies', in Chomsky et al., *The Cold War and the University*, 195–231

Wax, Dustin M. (ed.), *Anthropology at the Dawn of the Cold War: The Influence of Foundations, McCarthyism, and the CIA* (London, 2008)

Westad, Odd Arne, *The Global Cold War* (Cambridge, 2005)

Wilcken, Patrick, *Claude Lévi-Strauss: The Poet in the Laboratory* (London, 2010)

Wilford, Hugh, 'Playing the CIA's Tune? The *New Leader* and the Cultural Cold War', *Diplomatic History* 27 (2003), 15–34

Williams, Elgin, 'Anthropology for the Common Man', *American Anthropologist*, n.s., 49 (1947), 84–90

Williams, Justin, Sr., 'From Charlottesville to Tokyo: Military Government Training and Democratic Reforms in Occupied Japan', *Pacific Historical Review* 51 (1982), 407–22

Bibliography

Winkler, Allan M., *The Politics of Propaganda: The Office of War Information 1942–1945* (New Haven, 1978)

Winks, Robin W., *Cloak and Gown: Scholars in the Secret War, 1939–1961* (New York, 1987)

Wolfe, Bertram D., 'The Swaddled Soul of the Great Russians', *New Leader*, 29 Jan. 1951, 15–18

Wolfe, Bertram D., 'Swaddling and the Russians', *New Leader*, 21 May 1951, 20

'The World Federation for Mental Health', *UNESCO International Social Science Bulletin* 2 (1950), 71–5

Yans-McLaughlin, Virginia, 'Science, Democracy, and Ethics: Mobilizing Culture and Personality for World War II', in Stocking (ed.), *Malinowski, Rivers, Benedict*, 184–217

Yoneyama, Lisa, 'Habits of Knowing Cultural Differences: Chrysanthemum and the Sword in the U.S. Liberal Multiculturalism', *Topoi* 18 (1999), 71–80

Young, Virginia Heyer, *Ruth Benedict: Beyond Relativity, Beyond Pattern* (Lincoln NE, 2005)

Zachry, Caroline B., 'Contributions of Psychoanalysis to the Education of the Adolescent', *Psychoanalytic Quarterly* 8 (1939), 98–107

Zaretsky, Eli, *Secrets of the Soul: A Social and Cultural History of Psychoanalysis* (New York, 2004)

Zipperstein, Steven J., 'Underground Man: The Curious Case of Mark Zborowski and the Writing of a Modern Jewish Classic', *Jewish Review of Books*, summer 2010, 38–42

Acknowledgements

For me, too, the journey out has been a journey home. I was raised in the 1960s by two social scientists, in an American university community thronged with social scientists, and although I became a British historian who wrote on 'very English' topics I must have retained the imprint of this childhood training. For, while writing a book about the English national character, I became curious about why, just at the time that the idea of national character was fading from the common vocabulary, a group of very intelligent and sensitive anthropologists were trying in vain to re-establish it on some kind of scientific basis. This book is my answer. It has taken me back – not to my parents' generation (rather, the one before theirs), nor to their subject (which is psychology) – but at least to contiguous terrain, and so my first debt is to them, for their early intellectual and cultural influence (along with a lot more), and also for a continuously helpful and absorbing stream of reminiscence, analysis, second-hand books and third-hand anecdote. My childhood experiences also brought me many supportive friendships with other social scientists, the most important of which for the present book was with Audrey and Mel Spiro, who provided more of that vitalizing supply of even more first-hand experiences. Everyone who knew her misses Audrey and values her warm, sceptical intelligence all the more now that she is gone, leaving Mel as, nearly, the oldest living inhabitant; his intellectual generosity has made him my most trusted and valued informant. I have tried to make good use of this material while retaining an awareness of its provenance: for the journey out is never just a journey home, but rather it should equip one with a critical distance on things familiar that lends appreciation of the diversity of subject positions.

Learning a new field, almost from scratch, required me to draw liberally on the kindness of many colleagues. My Americanist friends have been especially welcoming. Pride of place must go to Joel Isaac, who gave me the short course on the history of American social science and has ensured for years now that I keep as up-to-date as possible on a burgeoning literature; these have been busy and preoccupying years for him, and I will always be grateful for all the time and attention he has given a needy colleague. Andrew Preston performed similar services in guiding me through the murky channels of the Cold War. David Reynolds started me out with his own prescient remarks on Margaret Mead among the natives of Great Britain. Tony Badger helped with funding for a conference on the new international history. John Forrester and Deborah Thom provided help with the even murkier history of psychoanalysis. So did Daniel Pick at Birkbeck, whose work on psychoanalysis in the Second World War has thrown up a number of significant parallels. Susan Pedersen, Glenda Sluga and Helen McCarthy taught me a lot about the new histories of internationalism. The two Duncans, Bell and Kelly, kept me au fait with other social sciences. Gary Gerstle and Liz Lunbeck gave me valuable encouragement at the outset. Everyone who works on the history of anthropology owes a debt to George Stocking, Henrika Kuklick and David Price.

A number of opportunities to air these ideas at seminars and conferences gave me plentiful feedback not only from historians, but also from curious anthropologists. I am grateful to audiences at the Institute of Historical Research in London, the University of Warwick, the Centre for Intellectual History at Sussex, Columbia University (three times!), Birkbeck College, the University of Surrey, St John's College, Oxford, Imperial College, the Anthropology Department at the London School of Economics, St John's College, Cambridge, the Department of the History and Philosophy of Science at Cambridge (twice), the University of Bologna, the North American Conference on British Studies in Denver, and two further audiences in Cambridge. More regular feedback – and an impressive stock of insights and newly excavated primary sources – came from classes of Cambridge undergraduates who took my special subject, 'Margaret Mead and the Public Face of Social Science', over three years. Really vital feedback at the end came thanks to Robert Baldock at Yale University Press, who procured three very thoughtful and highly professional referees' reports, from Daniel Pick and David Milne (who have subsequently identified themselves) and a third who remains anonymous but to whom I am just as grateful. Also at Yale Candida Brazil and Robert Shore have worked hard to put a final polish on the text and its presentation, and Matt Broughton devised an ingenious cover design.

In carrying out the research, I received invaluable assistance from a number of informants. I would want to single out Mary Catherine Bateson, who has assuredly had to talk about her mother and father far too often, but was still very willing to do so with me; I hope it helped that I introduced a less orthodox subject, Geoffrey Gorer, as well. Philomena Guillebaud, Lotte Bailyn, Sarah Bekker and Evelyn Colbert patiently answered my questions about events fifty or even seventy years ago. Pauline Kent generously supplied copies of her scholarship not widely available outside Japan. After two books largely written from libraries, it was a pleasure to get back into the archives, and here I had a lot of help from archivists, especially the staffs in the Manuscript Division of the Library of Congress, the Rare Book and Manuscript Library at Columbia, the National Archives of both the UK and the US, the Archives and Special Collections at Vassar, the Special Collections at Sussex, the University Archives at Harvard, and from Gregory Finnegan of the Tozzer Library at Harvard. Michael Riesman kindly granted me access to the papers of his father David Riesman. Crucial support for overseas research expenses was provided by two small grants from the British Academy. A research-leave grant from the Arts and Humanities Research Council provided me with the time to write up my findings.

Finally, I have to mention the two friends who kept closest tabs on the project from start to finish, and who helped me to believe in it: Deborah Cohen (who read the whole manuscript, minutely and forensically) and Mark Mazower (the best kind of friend, the sceptical kind).

Photograph Credits

On pages xvi, 44, 86, 122, 176 and 254: Library of Congress, by permission of the Institute for Intercultural Studies.
On page 222: Special Collections, University of Sussex, by permission of Getty Images.

Index

Abbott, Andrew 64, 179
adolescence 11, 38, 128–9, 164
Admiralty Islands 13–15
  see also Manus; New Guinea
Afghanistan xiv, 290
African-Americans 20, 38, 80, 87, 189
Agency for International Development (AID) 288
aggression 33–4, 38, 40, 47, 74, 110–11, 118, 129, 163, 169–70, 174, 184, 216, 229–31
  and war 52–3, 81–2, 134, 143, 172, 175
Air Force (U.S.) 178–9, 197, 220, 226, 228, 243
  see also RAND
Allport, Gordon 295n70
American Anthropological Association (AAA) 61, 65, 180, 184–5, 196, 210, 215, 263, 272, 288–9, 290, 291
American Association of University Women 192
American Defense 54, 61
American Museum of Natural History 27, 54, 63, 68, 190
The American Soldier 181–3, 227, 250
Andrus, J. Russell 75
Anglo-American relations xi, xv, 56, 70, 85, 87–8, 90–1, 94–100, 102, 106, 109–20, 123–4, 143, 159, 174, 188, 189, 190, 247, 248
anthropology
  applied 60, 162, 173–4, 186–7, 259–60, 262–5, 273, 276, 282–3, 288–92
    see also Mead, and applied anthropology; Society for Applied Anthropology and ethics 182, 185, 186, 262–3, 269–70, 273, 275, 288–9, 291
    see also Mead, and professional ethics
  functionalist 6, 17, 19, 29, 214
  and modernization theory 224–5, 281, 284–5
  physical 5–6

and politics 22, 31, 210, 213, 215, 218–20, 273, 276, 281–2, 285–6
  see also Mead, and politics
  psychological 286
  'return from the natives' 204, 218–19, 252
  and war 65–8, 123–4, 164–5, 173, 177–8, 186, 197, 219–20, 223
    see also Mead, and war
  and women xiii, 6–7, 184, 213–14
    see also social science
Arapesh 16, 28, 146
area studies 179, 281, 287
Arendt, Hannah 246
Arensberg, Conrad 272
Army (US) 67, 77, 112–13, 115, 178, 288
  Army Specialized Training Program 67, 78, 99, 135, 139, 158, 188, 194
  Research Branch 65, 69, 118, 180–1
atomic bomb 160, 166, 169, 172, 189–90
Auden, Wystan Hugh 34, 89
Australia 252, 278, 289
authoritarian character 127, 226–7

Bain, Katherine 73
Bali xi, xv, 28, 32, 34, 35, 41–2, 56, 88, 91, 94, 99, 104, 105, 109, 117, 158, 217–18, 266
Banyankole (Uganda) 257
Barlow, Alan 31
Barlow, Nora 32, 116
Barnard College 2, 17, 37
  see also Columbia University
Barnes, Harry Elmer 147
Barnett, Homer 186–7
Bartlett, Frederic Charles 299n4
Bateson, Gregory xv, 18–20, 23, 28–32, 41–3, 46–9, 54–61, 63, 71, 73, 80, 86, 89–98, 99, 105, 125–6, 128–31, 133, 149, 155, 195, 198–9, 202, 217–18, 266, 270
  in OSS 66, 69, 75, 116, 120, 122, 157–61, 232, 252
  see also schismogenesis

Bateson, Mary Catherine 43, 44, 49, 56, 86, 88, 90, 99, 116, 155, 160, 190, 199, 241, 252, 266, 278, 302n57

Bateson, William 31

Bauer, Raymond 226, 232, 246

behavioural science 177, 180–2, 184, 196, 211, 213, 226–7, 238, 243, 247, 250, 271, 272, 284, 288
see also social engineering

Bell, Daniel 181, 224

Benedict, Ruth xiv–xv, 7–10, 17–19, 22, 28, 34, 35, 36, 37, 39, 43, 50, 51–3, 68, 72, 127, 133, 135, 154, 174–5, 176, 190, 191–8, 199, 213–15, 217, 220–1, 241, 290
in OWI 66, 69, 77–9, 120, 131, 139, 142, 161–72, 175, 192, 193, 195, 200, 220, 242
and RCC 193–8, 202, 218, 233, 246, 256, 265
works
Patterns of Culture, 17–19, 22–3, 57, 145–6, 203–4, 206–8, 271
The Races of Mankind, 77, 175
The Chrysanthemum and the Sword 169–72, 175, 201, 203, 204, 231, 235, 285

Benians, E.A. 47

Bennington College 264

Berkeley, University of California at 6, 7, 37, 129

Bernaut, Elsa 235–6, 247, 327n75, 329n100

Blanco White, Amber 32, 297n116, 306n14

Blanco White, Justin 297n116

Boas, Franz 4–11, 13, 14, 22, 36, 41, 51–2, 61, 77, 133, 135, 165, 202, 282, 285

Bogoras, Waldemar 302n50

Bolivia 262

Borgwardt, Elizabeth 201

Bowes Lyon, David 155

Brazil 257

Brenman, Margaret 305n117

Brewster, Owen 118

Brickner, Richard 70, 132, 144–8, 151, 153, 155, 164, 201, 260

Britain 152, 179, 271
Bateson and 28–9, 43, 46–9, 55, 108, 159
Mead and 43, 87–119, 199, 228, 241, 294n43
see also Anglo-American relations

British Broadcasting Corporation (BBC) 98, 101, 105, 110, 111, 156, 199

Bryn Mawr College 52

Buddhism 74, 268

Bunzel, Ruth 11, 17, 195

Bureau of Indian Affairs 21, 161–2, 212, 264
see also Native Americans

Burke, Edmund 89

Burma 68, 75, 79, 120, 139, 156, 159–60, 173, 262, 276
see also national character, Burmese

Cambridge, University of 29, 32

Carnegie Corporation 181, 224–5

Ceylon (Sri Lanka) 116, 158, 160–1, 189

Chapple, Eliot 60–1, 133, 266, 269, 273–5, 278

Chase, Stuart 210

Charterhouse 32, 92

Chesterfield, 4th earl of 89

Chiang Kai-shek, Madame xii

Chicago, University of 1, 6, 7, 8, 67, 139

Child, Julia 159

child-rearing 14–15, 16, 26, 41, 50, 56, 59, 62, 71, 72–3, 74, 78, 80, 94, 100, 103, 114, 133–4, 136–8, 151, 163, 167, 170, 196, 214–17, 229–34, 236–40, 243–4, 245, 285
see also 'diaperology'; family relationships; swaddling

Children's Bureau 72–3, 77, 133

Chile 288

China xi, 79, 156, 161, 194–5, 204, 211, 233, 257, 279
see also national character, Chinese

Christian, John Leroy 74

Churchill, Winston 141

Citizens Advice Bureau 109

civil affairs 67, 76, 131, 135, 136, 139, 142, 151, 155, 161, 162, 163, 183, 265, 273

class 94, 97, 105, 114, 119, 125, 127, 140

Cobbold, Betty ('Steve') 105, 112, 116, 198, 308n43

Cold War xiii, 177–8, 196, 198, 202, 211, 212, 235, 238, 239, 252, 258, 261–2, 271, 273–4, 279, 282–3, 287, 290, 291

Collier, John 21, 161

Columbia Broadcasting System (CBS) 96–8

Columbia University 2, 4–7, 15, 22, 36–7, 67, 102, 135, 144, 184, 191, 192, 195, 214–15, 233, 237, 246, 264, 281, 298n139
Chinese History Project 233
Russian Institute 224, 233, 236, 266
see also Research in Contemporary Cultures

Commentary 181, 206, 212–13, 215, 216, 234, 237

Committee for National Morale (CNM) 54–5, 60–1, 71, 129, 133, 143

Committee on Food Habits 68–9, 80, 100, 116, 143, 144, 188, 195, 200

Common Council for American Unity 120

Index

communism 36, 37, 51, 55, 84, 142, 153, 211, 212, 215, 223, 226–8, 233, 235–8, 243, 245, 247, 250–1, 256, 263, 266, 267, 274, 277, 283, 288

Conference on Science, Philosophy and Religion 51, 57, 59–60, 212

containment 225–6, 230, 236, 238, 245

Cooke, Alistair 239, 286, 323n94

Coon, Carleton 64

Coordinated Investigation of Micronesian Anthropology (CIMA) 186–7, 219, 262, 264, 273, 276

see also Micronesia

Coordinator of Information (COI) 61, 64, 65, 66, 71, 129

Cornell University 272, 281

Council on Human Relations see Council on Intercultural Relations

Council on Intercultural Relations (CIR) 63, 68–9, 71, 72, 73, 78, 87, 99, 116, 132, 133, 135, 155, 157

counterinsurgency 287–9, 290

Cousins, Norman 147

Coward, Noël 147

Cressman, Luther 2, 8, 14

Crèvecoeur, J. Hector St John de 80

Cripps, Isobel, Lady 105

Cromwell, Oliver 80

Crowdy, Rachel 109

cultural cohesion 6, 9, 13, 15–20, 26, 29, 31, 39, 53, 56–8, 94–5, 149–50, 164, 167, 244, 259–60, 264, 267–72, 274, 280, 281, 285, 291

cultural diversity xi, 5, 7, 11, 12, 20–1, 42, 53, 57, 63, 70, 85, 123, 137, 141, 144, 175, 178, 182, 197, 209–10, 256–8, 272, 275, 283–5, 289, 291–2

cultural lag 3–4, 22, 23, 24, 42, 45, 81, 207

cultural relativism xiii–xiv, 22, 25, 36, 40, 45, 52, 61, 62–3, 68, 113, 142–3, 146, 172, 183–5, 196, 202–3, 208, 211, 212, 215, 216, 219, 223, 225, 226, 238, 252, 256, 263, 264, 265, 272, 276, 279, 281, 283–4, 295n74

culture

'at a distance' 71, 194

'cracking' 73, 80, 161, 193, 199

and equilibrium 60, 269–70

pattern 16–20, 29–31, 41, 56–7, 78, 147, 165–6, 196, 217, 294n23

see also cultural cohesion; national character

and personality 8–9, 17, 20, 24–5, 27, 36–7, 38, 186, 193, 202–3, 208, 210, 214–17, 225–6, 240, 242, 265, 285–6

primitive vs modern 9–10, 11, 13, 14, 15, 18, 41, 45–6, 52, 186, 188, 206, 214, 218–19, 239, 255–7, 272, 279, 290–1

see also anthropology; intercultural relations

culture and personality see anthropology

Curie, Eve xii

Czechoslovakia 195, 220

Dallin, Alexander 236

Dallin, David 235–8

Darley, John 321n57

Darwin, Charles 32

De Pauw University 2

de Voto, Bernard 286

decolonization 179, 185, 271, 274

democratic universalism 141–3, 147–8, 151, 161, 163–8, 171, 175, 178, 182, 183, 201–2, 213, 227–8, 235–9, 256–7, 261, 263, 269, 273, 279, 283

Denmark 40

Denney, Reuel 206

Department of Agriculture (US) 65, 68

Department of Commerce (US) 75

Department of Defense (US) 288–9

Department of the Interior (US) 186, 262

Department of State (US) 69, 142, 148, 168, 178–9, 202, 224, 237, 264–5, 266–7, 275–6

International Moving Picture Division 273–4

see also Foreign Service Institute (FSI)

Department of War see Army (US)

development 255, 258, 266, 267–72, 284–5

Dewey, John 21, 22, 51, 296n95

'diaperology' 133, 136, 156, 163, 214–15, 233–4, 236–7, 239, 286

see also child-rearing; swaddling

Dicks, Henry 139–40, 146, 152, 154, 157, 328n86

Dinerstein, Herbert 328n86

Dobu 17, 22, 146, 208, 218

Dollard, John 24, 25–6, 28, 38, 40, 50, 52, 81, 297n101, 298n142

Donovan, William 61, 64, 65, 129, 130, 132

Doob, Leonard 77, 79

Dorsey, George 12

Dower, John 132, 143

Du Bois, Cora 37, 50, 158–9, 179, 202, 214, 220–1, 232, 263–5, 266, 274, 276, 281, 285, 286, 298n139

Dudley, Alan 113

Dyer, A. Murray 96, 98

East Indies see Indonesia

economics xi, xiv, 31, 62, 218, 224, 226, 231, 232, 240, 258, 259–60, 264, 267, 271, 281, 284, 285, 291

education

for choice 12, 27, 270, 272

in occupied Germany 153

progressive 1, 14–15, 24–7, 60, 63, 296n97
  and technical assistance 259, 264
Eisenhower, Dwight David 139, 151, 166,
  237, 255, 276, 283, 288
Eliot, Thomas Stearns 89
Embree, Edwin 62–3, 71, 132
Embree, John Fee 71, 132, 133, 136–7, 139,
  161, 162, 163, 164–5, 169, 171–2,
  179, 265, 266
Emerson, Ralph Waldo 189, 279
Endleman, Robert 212–13
Engerman, David 224
Erikson, Erik 25–6, 58, 61, 71, 79, 81, 99,
  127–30, 133, 135, 136, 139–40,
  148–9, 188, 205–6, 208, 228, 245,
  282, 298n142, 328n81
Eskimo (Inuit) 4–6, 257
ethical relativism 22, 36, 45, 85, 295n74
eugenics 5
Evans-Pritchard, Edward Evans 13
evolution 5, 10, 40, 272, 286

Fahs, Charles Burton 232–3
Fairbank, John King 167–8
family relationships 56, 58, 62, 71, 80–1, 85,
  90–4, 96–7, 107, 125–6, 128–9,
  133–7, 140, 145, 148–51, 167, 170,
  188, 196, 203, 204–7, 214, 217, 228,
  229, 247, 297n101, 328n81
  see also adolescence; child-rearing
Farago, Ladislas 145
feedback 29, 270
  see also schismogenesis
feminism 212
Fiddler on the Roof 246
First World War x–xi, 6, 18, 37, 54, 151, 234
Foerstel, Lenora see under Schwartz, Lenora
Ford Foundation 181
Foreign Morale Analysis Division see Office
  of War Information
Foreign Office (UK) 32, 47, 113, 156
Foreign Service Institute (US) 202, 263–5,
  272, 276, 281
Fortune 190
Fortune, Reo 14–19, 29, 278
France 153, 179, 195
Frank, Lawrence K. 23–5, 43, 54, 60, 62, 63,
  80, 124–5, 127, 148, 187, 190, 201,
  260, 266–70
Frank, Mary 43, 54, 68, 80, 99, 116, 187, 190
Freeman, Derek 289
French, Thomas 149, 164
Freud, Sigmund 10, 25, 33, 40, 59, 80, 231
  see also neo-Freudians; psychoanalysis
Fromm, Erich 25–6, 28, 37, 58, 80, 125, 127,
  128, 139–40, 147, 150, 182, 192–3,
  197, 205–7, 226, 264, 296n96,
  297n104, 298n142

Gardner, John 225
Geertz, Clifford 333n95
gender roles 16, 19, 27–8, 81, 85, 151, 152,
  204–5, 214, 297n101
  'squares' 19, 20, 29, 32, 34–5, 37, 38, 52
  see also family relationships
General Education Board 24
Germany xi, 25, 140–1, 279
  occupation of 142–55, 157, 164–5, 171,
  172, 181, 185, 191, 225, 235, 237
Gilman, Nils 183, 260
Gladwin, Thomas 331n42
Glazer, Nathan 181, 206, 212
Goebbels, Joseph 130
Goethe, Johann Wolfgang von 124
Goldfrank, Esther 233, 236
Goldman, Irving 240
Gorer, Geoffrey xv, 32–5, 37–9, 47, 48,
  49–50, 51, 52, 64, 92, 94, 97, 104,
  117–19, 128–30, 132–8, 139–40,
  144–6, 154, 158–9, 164, 165, 170,
  171, 189, 196, 207, 208, 214, 216–18,
  222, 223, 245, 252, 290
  in OWI 66, 69, 71–7, 78, 79, 100, 131,
    133, 139, 155, 162, 163, 200
  in PWE 66, 76, 116, 120, 155–7, 162
  and RCC 194, 199–201, 220, 232–3
  and swaddling 229–34, 236–40, 241,
    243–4, 263, 266
  works
    Africa Dances 34
    Hot Strip Tease, 38–9, 49
    Himalayan Village 39–40, 242
    The American People 199, 204–5, 214,
      239, 286
    The People of Great Russia 234
Gorer, Peter 71, 72
Gorer, Rachel 49–50, 72, 76, 132, 199, 234,
  304n89
Greece 273
  see also national character, Greek
Guatemala 267, 268, 331n35
Guillebaud, Claude 54, 119
Guillebaud, Claudia 54, 56, 87, 90
Guillebaud, Philomena 54, 56, 87,
  90, 266

Haddon, Alfred Cort 13
Haimson, Leonard 328
Haiti 260
Hall, Edward T., Jr. 264, 276, 281
Hall, G. Stanley 11
Handler, Richard x
Harford, Letty 105
Haring, Douglas 133, 136–7, 139, 164–5
Harrisson, Tom 28, 42, 48
Hartshorne, Edward 54, 61, 130, 131, 139,
  151–3, 301n48

Index

Harvard University 7, 54, 57, 61, 64, 66, 67, 130, 136, 139, 179, 183, 191, 198, 281
    Department of Social Relations 181, 215, 224–5
    Russian Research Center 224–6, 232, 236, 246
Hashima, Robert 171, 190
Herskovits, Melville 185
Herzog, Elizabeth 246
Hess, Rudolf 139
Heyer, Virginia 320n29
Hinduism 268
Hiroshima 160, 189
history 66, 231, 232, 233, 240
Hitler, Adolf 36, 51, 55, 70, 128–30, 226–7
Hitlerjunge Quex 71, 126
Hollinger, David 203
Hollywood 49, 66, 76, 111, 200
Holt, Claire 69, 117, 158, 179, 265, 266–71, 274, 276, 281
homosexuality 7, 8, 17, 33, 34, 37, 50, 118, 140, 204–5, 213, 214, 216, 325n7
Hopkins, Frank 322n84
Hopkins, Harry 141
Horney, Karen 25–6, 28, 165, 207, 297n104
Hoselitz, Bert 331n48
Hoyt, Elizabeth 266–7, 268
Human Relations Area Files (HRAF) 183, 186
    see also Institute of Human Relations
Human Resources Research Institute (HRRI) 178–9, 226
human rights 184–5

Iatmul 18, 30, 42
Ickes, Harold 172
identity 188, 206, 282
Igo, Sarah 209
immigrants xiii, 3, 5–6, 7, 20, 80–1, 87, 120, 125, 189, 192, 194, 195, 207, 248, 257
In Which We Serve 97
India 158, 257, 268, 272, 279
Indians *see* Bureau of Indian Affairs; Native Americans
Indochina 79, 158, 264, 273, 276
    see also Vietnam War
Indonesia 122, 158, 161, 257, 262, 265, 273, 274, 276, 281
infants *see* child-rearing
Inkeles, Alex 226, 232, 246, 284
Institute for Intercultural Studies *see* Council on Intercultural Relations
Institute for Propaganda Analysis 54
Institute of Human Relations 38, 50
Institute of Pacific Relations 164–5, 172

intercultural relations 46–7, 58, 61–3, 67–8, 76–8, 82–3, 85, 87–8, 90–2, 96, 114, 120, 124, 139, 161, 172, 178, 187–92, 196–7, 201–4, 209–12, 215–16, 228, 242–51, 255–7, 261, 263–74, 276, 278–80, 283, 294n43
    see also Anglo-American relations
internationalism 183–5, 198, 201–2, 210, 239, 255, 261, 279, 282, 290
Iowa, University of 127
Iowa State University 267
Iran 273
Iraq xiv, 273, 290
Ireland 20, 94
Isle of Man 257
Italy 20, 138

Jahoda, Marie 102
'James, Leslie' 205, 323n94
Janis, Irving 118
Janis, Marjorie 309n77
Janowitz, Morris 131, 139
Japan xi, 68, 120, 141–2, 156, 202, 257, 279
    emperor 135, 141, 163–70, 172–3
    Japanese in the US 65, 132, 156, 157, 181
        see also War Relocation Authority
    occupation of 144, 162–72, 191, 237
    see also national character, Japanese
Java 141
Jews xiii, 7, 20, 33, 102, 189, 195, 200, 226, 228, 232, 235–6, 246–7, 250, 266, 298n128
Joffe, Natalie 69, 219
'Jolliffe' *see under* Metcalfe
Julius Rosenwald Fund 62

Kaingang (Brazil) 257
Kallen, Horace 55, 147
Kardiner, Abram 17, 25–6, 37, 38, 159, 162, 172, 202, 207, 214
Karpovich, Michael 232, 233, 236
Katz, Barry 180
Kecskemeti, Paul 131
Kennard, Edward 202, 263–4
Kennedy, John Fitzgerald 281, 288
Kent, Sherman 66
The King and I 284
Kinsey, Alfred 208–9
Klein, Christina 284–5
Klein, Melanie 231
Klineberg, Otto 135, 184, 200, 201, 210, 217, 260
Kluckhohn, Clyde 57, 162–3, 169, 183, 191, 192, 204, 208, 210–11, 212, 213, 214, 215–16, 224–6, 240, 246
Kluckhohn, Florence 215
Knight, Eric 112

Index

Korean War 202, 211, 223, 228, 238, 245, 248, 249–50, 263, 276, 277, 282
Kroeber, Alfred 6, 7, 13
Kubie, Lawrence 149, 164
Kwakiutl 17, 22, 28, 146, 208, 218

La Barre, Weston 158–9, 161, 216, 217, 223, 315n120
Labour Party 103
Langer, William 66, 178
Laning, Capt. Caleb 249–50
Lasswell, Harold 125, 127, 147, 173, 183, 211–12, 219, 238, 243
Laura Spelman Rockefeller Memorial 23–4
law 226, 232
Lawrence, David Herbert 33
Lazarsfeld, Paul 102
League of Nations 18
Lee, Dorothy 72–3, 266–71
Leffler, Melvyn 261–2
Lehman Commission 77
Leighton, Alexander 162–3, 166–9, 173, 181, 203, 272
Leighton, Dorothea 162
Leites, Nathan 131, 135, 163, 197, 200–1, 220, 228, 235, 239, 243–5, 247, 249–51, 309n77, 334n5
Lenin, Vladimir Ilich 245
Lepcha 39–40, 41, 47, 133, 204
Lerner, Daniel 139, 140, 154, 182, 183, 211, 219
Lévi-Strauss, Claude 195, 283, 286
Levy, David 154
Lewin, Kurt 58, 92, 127, 135, 144, 146, 150, 158, 164, 193, 310n12, 316n129
Life 205
Lindesmith, Alfred 216
Linton, Ralph 36–7, 38, 162, 184, 213–15, 217, 221, 240
Lipkind, William 154
Lippitt, Ronald 164
Lloyd George, David 32
The Lonely Crowd see under Riesman
Lowie, Robert 6, 7, 285
Luce, Henry 83, 84, 202
Lumsdaine, David 262
Luther, Martin 127
Lutkehaus, Nancy 281
Lynd, Helen 3, 21, 23, 24, 54, 190, 296n97, 306n135
Lynd, Robert 3, 21, 23, 25, 51, 54, 61, 83, 181, 190, 296n95

MacArthur, Douglas 157, 168–9, 171, 237
Macaulay, Thomas Babington 89
McCarthyism 202, 227, 228, 238, 248, 276, 282
McCloy, John 237

MacCurdy, John T. 299n4
McGeachy, Mary Craig 102
McGranahan, Donald 131, 139, 211, 217, 311n25
Macgregor, Gordon 332n56
MacLeish, Archibald 202
Madge, Charles 48
Malaya 68, 156, 157, 276
Malinowski, Bronislaw 239
Mandelbaum, David 74, 158
Manila 134, 138
Manus 14, 28, 207–8, 255, 257, 277–8, 280, 281
Marcus, Anthony 237
Marshall, John 49–50
Marshall Plan 258, 261, 262
Marxism 31, 33, 40, 125, 127, 131, 183–4, 210, 226, 235, 296n96
Mass-Observation 28, 42, 48–9
Massachusetts Institute of Technology (MIT) 250, 270
Maxwell, Elsa 84
Mead, Edward Sherwood 1
Mead, Emily Fogg 1
Mead, Margaret
    and applied anthropology 60, 161, 173–4, 197, 242–3, 263, 273–7, 282
    life
        early life 1–2, 89
        marriage to Luther Cressman 2, 8, 14
        and Franz Boas 6–7
        marriage to Reo Fortune 14–19
        at American Museum of Natural History, 27, 54, 63, 68
        in Washington 68–9, 116–17, 158, 174–5
        in Britain 101–15
        and RCC 194, 196, 198, 219–20, 228–9, 241, 242–3, 245, 246–7, 249–50, 263, 273, 281
        career xii–xiii
        death 11, 289
    and national character 71–4, 77, 87, 114, 146, 153, 208, 217–19, 227, 242, 247, 250–2, 278, 286, 289
    and politics 22, 35–6, 212, 219–20, 248, 252, 255, 263, 273, 275–6, 281, 282
    and professional ethics 69–70, 83, 174, 182, 197, 243, 249–51, 269–70, 273, 275–6, 287, 289, 291
    and David Riesman 207–8, 218–19, 255
    relationships
        with Gregory Bateson xv, 18–20, 28, 32, 34–5, 56, 68–9, 80–2, 87, 89–90, 99–102, 104, 106, 107, 110, 114, 116, 117, 118, 120, 125–6, 129–30, 155, 161, 174, 187, 189–91, 195, 198–9, 201, 223, 228, 241

Index

with Ruth Benedict xiv, 7–10, 19, 77,
    87, 103, 220–1, 223, 228, 241, 281
with Betty Cobbold ('Steve') 105
with Geoffrey Gorer xv, 34–5, 38–9, 70,
    76, 81, 85, 87, 88, 90, 102, 108–9,
    114, 116, 117, 129–30, 138, 174, 190,
    194, 199–201, 204–5, 208, 209,
    220–1, 228–9, 233–4, 237–42,
    263, 266
with Edward Sapir 8–11, 69
and religion 1–2, 35, 70, 80–1, 107, 108,
    267, 271, 280
reputation xiii, 84–5, 239–40, 280–2, 286,
    287, 289–92
and sex 35, 50, 208–9, 214, 241,
    299n163
and status of anthropology xi, 174, 185–6,
    203, 239–40, 252–3, 255, 263, 281–3,
    285–6, 290–2
and technical assistance 260, 263–4,
    266–77, 285, 291
and war 77, 81–3, 85, 143–4, 154–5,
    173–4, 223
works
    Coming of Age in Samoa, xii, 12–13, 23,
        27, 203, 208
    Growing Up in New Guinea, xii
        14, 278
    Sex and Temperament in Three Primitive
        Societies 19, 28, 34
    Cooperation and Competition among
        Primitive Peoples 28, 57
    From the South Seas 42
    And Keep Your Powder Dry 80–5, 87–8,
        90, 93, 96, 99, 105, 111–12, 151, 174,
        204, 214, 215, 255, 278, 286
    'Learning to Live in One World', 120,
        174–5, 187–90, 204, 209, 248, 255,
        258, 278–9
    Male and Female 205
    Soviet Attitudes toward Authority 245–6
    Cultural Patterns and Technical Change
        266–73
    'Stars for Our Wagons', 278–9
    New Lives for Old 280–1
Mead, Martha Ramsey 1, 88
Metcalfe, Alice ('Jolliffe') 105, 116,
    308n43
Metraux, Alfred 200, 201, 259–60, 271
Metraux, Rhoda 69, 91, 100, 117, 195, 200,
    249–50, 259, 265
Michigan, University of 67
Micronesia 64, 68, 183, 186–7, 219, 255,
    262, 264, 271
    see also Coordinated Investigation of
        Micronesian Anthropology
Middletown 3
Mills, John 97

Ministry of Economic Warfare 102
Ministry of Food 105
Ministry of Information 47–8, 88,
    99–103, 110
Modell, Judith 23
modernization xiii, 168, 207, 231, 246, 256,
    260, 261, 264, 267, 271, 280
    theory 224–7, 258, 272, 281, 283–5, 286
Moerman, Michael 289
Montagu, Ashley 201
Morgenthau, Henry 142–3
Morrow, William 12
Mosely, Philip 69, 117, 126–7, 150, 224,
    233–4, 236, 238, 247, 249, 317n147,
    326n39
Motley, John Lathrop 89
Mountbatten, Lord Louis 139, 155, 157, 158,
    159, 312n52
Mundugumor 16, 18, 28
Murdock, George Peter 64, 183, 186, 215
Murphy, Gardner 21, 54, 57, 137–8, 148
Murphy, Lois 21, 54
Mussolini, Benito 32, 36
Mutual Security Agency (MSA) 276–7
Mysbergh, Jim 159–60

Nader, Laura 333n78
Nader, Ralph 333n78
Nagasaki 189
Nash, Manning 331n35
Nash, Philleo 76
national character xii, 18, 24, 56–8, 61–3,
    94–5, 126, 131, 137, 147, 171, 173,
    193, 210, 213, 217–19, 234–5, 243–4,
    250–1, 286, 289
    American 58, 80–5, 88, 89, 96–8, 110–11,
        165, 167, 175, 182, 188–9, 204–8,
        216, 218, 246, 250
    Burmese 74–5, 79, 100, 131, 136, 137,
        158, 233, 271
    Chinese 79, 96, 158, 246, 250–1,
        303n87
    Czech 195, 218
    Dutch 77, 79, 173
    English 58, 88, 89–98, 104–8, 110–11,
        242, 252
    French 112, 115, 195, 200
    German 58, 70–1, 91, 93, 96–7, 99, 105,
        110, 123–31, 136, 140–1, 143–54,
        173, 203, 206, 217, 234–5, 250
        see also Nazism, psychology of
    Greek 72–4, 77, 100, 136, 268, 271
    Japanese 71, 100, 123–4, 132–8, 140, 143,
        158–9, 161, 162, 164–7, 169–72, 173,
        202, 217, 231, 233, 234
    Norwegian 77, 79, 218
    Polish 195, 246, 250
    Romanian 79, 131, 173

Russian 112, 137, 196, 199, 204, 206, 220,
  221, 228–34, 236–40, 243–7, 250–1,
  284
Thai 79, 131, 158
  see also culture, pattern; Mead, and
  national character
National Council of Social Service 102,
  105, 109
National Peace Council 102
National Research Council 68
National Science Foundation 178, 213
nationalism xii–xiii, 31, 179, 184, 210, 274
  American 141
  Japanese 170
  Russian 224
Native Americans 4, 7, 11, 15, 17, 21,
  80, 162, 206, 212, 216, 219,
  255, 272
  see also Bureau of Indian Affairs
Navy (US) 67–8, 162, 178, 183, 186, 192,
  194, 197, 219, 220, 237, 238–9, 246,
  264, 265
  Naval Research Laboratory 249–50
  see also Office of Naval Research
Nazism 20, 22, 25–6, 50, 60, 71, 141, 143,
  147, 152, 153, 224, 236
  psychology of 61, 70–1, 72, 124–7, 140,
  154, 226
  see also national character, German
Negroes see African-Americans
neoconservatism 235
neo-Freudians 25–6, 28, 29, 37, 54, 56, 125,
  127–9, 140, 147, 154, 205–6,
  226, 250
  see also under Erikson; Fromm; Horney;
  Kardiner
Netherlands 179
  see also national character, Dutch
New American Library 203, 272
New Deal 20, 23, 25, 27, 28, 65, 83, 141,
  142, 147, 163, 212, 235, 237, 255,
  269–70, 283
New Guinea xi, 13, 15–17, 29, 35, 40–1, 42,
  173, 257, 277
  see also Admiralty Islands; Arapesh;
  Iatmul; Manus; Mundugumor;
  Tchambuli
New Leader 235–8, 263
New Mexico 331n42
Nietzsche, Friedrich 18
Nigeria 271
Nuremberg Trials 153
Nutini, Hugo 288

Office of Naval Research (ONR) 178–9,
  192–3, 197, 219, 238–9, 250
Office of Strategic Services (OSS) 65–6,
  67, 69, 74, 75, 88, 117, 130,

  132, 133, 136, 139, 161, 162, 164,
  168, 238
  Morale Operations (MO) 116, 157–61
  Research & Analysis (R&A) 66, 67,
  130–1, 138–9, 157–8, 178–9, 180,
  224, 232, 266
  see also Bateson, Gregory
Office of War Information (OWI) 65–7,
  71–7, 88, 96, 98–100, 110, 112,
  130–1, 135, 138, 139, 156, 168, 178,
  200
  Bureau of Overseas Intelligence 72
  Foreign Morale Analysis Division
  (FMAD) 162–9, 172–3, 191, 203
  London Outpost 98–9, 105, 113
  Overseas Branch 66–7, 98
  see also Benedict, Ruth; Gorer, Geoffrey
Ogburn, William Fielding 3–4
Olsen, Erling 50
Orlansky, Harold 215, 216
Orwell, George 95
overdevelopment 268, 291
Overseas Training and Research Inc. 281
Owen, Margaret 101

Padover, Saul 139
Palau 271
Paliau 254, 278
Parsons, Talcott 54, 55, 130, 149–51, 164,
  178, 215, 224–5, 226, 301n48,
  322n84
Penguin Books 99, 105, 203
Pennsylvania, University of 1
personality see culture and personality
Peru 272
Philippines 273
  see also Manila
Point IV 261–5, 272, 273, 274, 275–7, 285
Poland 195
  see also national character, Polish
policy science see behavioural science
political science 224–6, 232, 258,
  281, 291
Political Warfare Executive 88, 139
  Washington Mission 155–7, 162
  see also Gorer, Geoffrey
Pope, Arthur Upham 54, 61, 130, 173
Project Camelot 288
propaganda 32, 47, 58, 59, 61, 65–7, 69–70,
  76, 79–80, 82–3, 85, 88, 93, 94, 98,
  99, 116, 120, 123–4, 129–31, 134–6,
  138–9, 143, 155–60, 162–3, 173, 174,
  223, 249
  see also Office of Strategic Services; Office
  of War Information; Political Warfare
  Executive
psychiatry 62, 70, 144–50, 154, 164–5, 201,
  217–18, 260–1, 267

Index

Psychiatry 127, 129, 147
psychoanalysis 8, 25–6, 35, 38, 40, 43, 50, 52,
    58–9, 61, 73, 75–6, 81, 85, 94, 117–18,
    130, 131, 133, 135, 137, 139–40, 147,
    149, 158–9, 161, 171, 189, 205–6, 212,
    216, 231, 234, 244, 265
    see also neo-Freudians
psychological warfare 70, 74–5, 120, 125,
    136, 139, 141–2, 161, 162, 163, 173,
    177, 188, 233, 249–50, 252, 291
    see also propaganda
Psychological Warfare Division *see* Supreme
    Headquarters Allied Expeditionary
    Force
psychology 2, 10–11, 15, 25, 62, 135, 137,
    177, 193, 217–18, 232, 288
Public Affairs Committee 77

race xii, 5, 22, 36, 77, 84, 96, 132, 136, 137,
    143, 147, 170, 227, 236, 248, 284
Radcliffe-Brown, Alfred Reginald 15, 18,
    295n64
RAND 178–9, 197, 237–9, 242–9, 273
Reading, Stella, Lady 105
Reagan, Ronald 235
Reiss, Ignace 235–6
relativism *see* cultural relativism; ethical
    relativism
Research & Analysis Branch *see* Office of
    Strategic Services
Research and Development Board 250
Research in Contemporary Cultures (RCC)
    193–8, 202, 206, 212, 218–21, 226,
    232–3, 235–6, 241, 242–3, 245,
    246–7, 249–50
    see also Benedict, Ruth; Gorer, Geoffrey;
    Mead, Margaret; Studies in
    Contemporary Cultures; Studies in
    Soviet Culture
Rickman, John 234
Riesman, David 81, 196, 202, 206–9,
    218–19, 255, 264
Rivers, William Halse Rivers 89
Robinson, Geroid 224
Rockefeller Foundation 24–6, 49–50, 51, 62,
    76, 183, 224
    see also Laura Spelman Rockefeller
    Memorial
Rodnick, David 79, 154, 195, 203, 235, 250
Romania 127, 150
    see also national character, Romanian
Roosevelt, Eleanor xii, 84, 172, 202
Roosevelt, Franklin Delano 20, 141, 142–3,
    172, 201
Rosten, Leo 49, 66–7, 72, 76, 77, 115, 131,
    228–9, 245
Rosten, Priscilla Mead 49
Ruml, Beardsley 23–4, 324n115

Russian Institute *see* Columbia University
Russian Research Center *see* Harvard
    University

Sade, Marquis de 33
St John's College, Cambridge 30, 47
Samoa 11–13, 28, 192, 257, 286
Sansom, Sir George 156
Sapir, Edward 6, 8–11, 24, 25, 26, 38, 64, 69,
    135, 194
Schaffner, Bertram 154, 203, 234, 250
schismogenesis 30–2, 46–7, 49, 53, 55–6,
    90–3, 96, 107, 125–6, 129, 149, 217,
    231, 243, 245, 247
schizophrenia 297n113
Schneider, David 64
Schopenhauer, Arthur 89
Schuller, Erwin 102, 105, 108, 109, 116, 117
Schwartz, Lenora 280
Schwartz, Ted 280
Scotland 91, 94
Sereno, Renzo 72
Second World War
    in Asia 139, 155–61, 166
    in Europe 43, 46, 131, 138–9, 151–2, 162
    in the Pacific 63, 183, 257
    postwar planning 62–3, 77, 82, 88, 99,
        115, 120, 123–4, 141–55, 163, 168,
        174–5, 177–8, 187–90, 225
    prisoners of war 128, 129, 131, 138,
        139–40, 152, 182
    unconditional surrender 141–2, 150,
        163, 166
Shenin, Sergei 262
Sherwood, Robert 66–7, 98
Shils, Edward 131, 139, 140
Shub, Boris 237–8
Simmons, Ernest 233–4
Sitwell, Edith 76
Smith, Francis Rawdon 328n96
Smith-Mundt Act 202
Smithsonian Institution 136
social engineering xi, 4, 13, 15, 21, 22–3,
    26–7, 36, 42, 51, 53, 58–60, 62,
    83, 180–3, 187, 188, 206, 272,
    294n42
    see also behavioural science; social science,
    and democracy
social science 2–4
    and democracy 21, 23–4, 27, 36, 42, 48,
        51, 55, 60, 83, 85, 108–9, 144,
        180–3
        see also social engineering
    and propaganda 54, 173
    and war 50–1, 63–8, 138–9, 143, 169, 173,
        177–8, 211
Social Science Research Council 37
socialism 6, 235

Society for Applied Anthropology (SAA)
  60, 182, 263–4, 269, 273–5, 277,
  288, 289
Society for the Study of Personality and
  Culture 54
sociology xiv, 1, 2, 25, 54, 62, 64–5, 80,
  130–1, 140, 150, 169, 171, 177, 196,
  202, 217–18, 224–5, 258, 285,
  288, 291
Somerville, Mary 105
South East Asia Command (SEAC) 139,
  155, 159
South Pacific 284
Soviet Union xi, 15, 27, 36, 66, 67, 189,
  190, 194, 197, 200, 202, 219, 223–53,
  258, 261, 274, 279, 284
  see also Cold War; communism; national
  character, Russian
Spain 195
Sparrow, James T. 64, 179
Speier, Hans 211, 238–9, 243–4
Spengler, Oswald 18
Spitzer, Herman 163
Spock, Benjamin 43
'squares' *see* gender roles
Stalin, Joseph 36, 51, 225, 226–7, 232, 235,
  236, 245, 251
Stanford University 67
Stears, Marc 84
'Steve' *see* Cobbold
Stevens, Georgiana 117
Stevens, Harley 117
Steward, Julian 184, 332n54
Stoetzel, Jean 217
Stouffer, Samuel 65, 69, 180–1, 183, 250
Stout, Rex 147
Strauss, Anselm 216
Strecher, Edward 145
Studies in Contemporary Cultures (SCC)
  250–1
Studies in Soviet Culture (SSC) 228, 239,
  241, 242–9
Sullivan, Harry Stack 25–6
Supreme Headquarters Allied Expeditionary
  Force (SHAEF)
  Psychological Warfare Division
  (PWD-SHAEF) 139–40, 151–2,
  166, 182
swaddling 73, 229–34, 236–40, 241, 243–4,
  245–6, 263, 266, 277, 291
Sydney, University of 15
Syria 195, 262

Taylor, Davidson 98
Taylor, George 162–3, 168
Tchambuli (Chambri) 16, 18, 28
technical assistance (TA) 258–77, 284,
  285, 291

see also education, and technical
  assistance; Mead, and technical
  assistance; Point IV; United Nations;
  United Nations Educational,
  Scientific and Cultural Organization,
  and technical assistance
Technical Cooperation Administration
  (TCA) 262
Telberg, Ina 232–3, 235, 241, 325n22
Tensions Affecting International
  Understanding 184, 200, 201,
  217, 260
Thailand 68, 79, 272, 289
  see also national character, Thai
Time 96, 97, 135, 202
Tiquisate (Guatemala) 267, 268
Tiv (Nigeria) 271
Tocqueville, Alexis de 80
toilet training *see* child-rearing; 'diaperology';
  swaddling
totalitarianism 180, 223, 226–7, 235, 252,
  263, 329n100
Transatlantic 99, 111
Transylvania 150
Trobriand Islands 239, 286
Trotskyism 235
Truman, Harry S 201, 211, 225, 237, 261–2,
  263–4, 265, 275–6
Tryon, Robert 129, 302n49
Turkey 273
Tylor, Edward Burnett 89

Uganda 257
United Fruit Company 267
United Nations 186, 201, 248
  technical assistance programmes 258,
  260–1, 262, 263, 266, 269–70, 274,
  275, 285
United Nations Educational, Scientific and
  Cultural Organization (UNESCO)
  184, 185, 200, 202, 210, 217, 220,
  256–61
  Social Science Division 184,
  200, 201
  and technical assistance 266–73, 285
United Nations Relief and Rehabilitation
  Agency (UNRRA) 117, 144

Valentine, Ruth 52, 196
Vassar College 7, 72, 91
Veblen, Thorstein 89
Vietnam War xiii–xiv, 174, 177–8, 258,
  287, 290
Virginia, University of 67

Waddington, Conrad 297n116
Wales 91, 94
Wallace, Henry 65

War Office (UK) 152, 154
War Relocation Authority 65, 161–2, 181, 203, 273
Warner, Lloyd 80
Wellesley College 320n36
Weltfish, Gene 77, 175
Weybright, Victor 98, 105, 113–14, 117, 120, 203, 272
Whitney, William 72
Winant, John Gilbert 99, 105, 111
Winner, Percy 142
Wittfogel, Karl 233, 236
Wolfe, Bertram 237–8
Wolfenstein, Martha 200–1
Women's Voluntary Service 103, 105

Woolton, 1st earl of 105
World Federation for Mental Health (WFMH) 201, 260–1, 267
Writers' War Board 99, 147

Yale University 6, 24, 38, 40, 50, 64, 66, 132, 133, 135, 179, 183, 184, 194, 197
see also Institute of Human Relations

Zachry, Caroline 26–7, 296n97
Zborowski, Mark 235–6, 246
Zinn, Earl 38, 40, 133
Zionism 235
Zuni 17, 18, 22, 28, 208